ROUTLEDGE LIBRARY EDITIONS:
SOVIET POLITICS

Volume 11

THE ROAD TO
INTERVENTION

THE ROAD TO INTERVENTION

March–November 1918

MICHAEL KETTLE

Routledge
Taylor & Francis Group

LONDON AND NEW YORK

First published in 1988 by Routledge

This edition first published in 2024
by Routledge
4 Park Square, Milton Park, Abingdon, Oxon OX14 4RN

and by Routledge
605 Third Avenue, New York, NY 10158

Routledge is an imprint of the Taylor & Francis Group, an informa business

British Library Cataloguing in Publication Data
A catalogue record for this book is available from the British Library

ISBN: 978-1-032-67165-9 (Set)
ISBN: 978-1-032-67617-3 (Volume 11) (hbk)
ISBN: 978-1-032-67619-7 (Volume 11) (pbk)
ISBN: 978-1-032-67618-0 (Volume 11) (ebk)

DOI: 10.4324/9781032676180

Publisher's Note
The publisher has gone to great lengths to ensure the quality of this reprint but points out that some imperfections in the original copies may be apparent.

Disclaimer
The publisher has made every effort to trace copyright holders and would welcome correspondence from those they have been unable to trace.

FINLAND

•Murmansk

•Archangel

R   U   S

Ural Mountains

Perm•   •Ekaterinburg

Petrograd   Vologda
Vyatka
Penza
Moscow•   Samara•   •Chelyabinsk
•Omst   Omsk•

Esthonia
Latvia
Lithuania

•Berlin   POLAND   •Kiev

•Vienna   Carpathians   Odessa•   •Novocherkassk

Azov Sea   Caucasus Mountains   Caspian Sea   Tashkent•

Black Sea   •Krasnovodsk

Constantinople   Ashkhabad
TURKEY   •   Merv•
                                                    •Kushk
Kasr-i-shirin•   •Kermanshah   Meshed•
                                                    AFGHANISTAN
Baghdad•   PERSIA

N

0   1000 miles

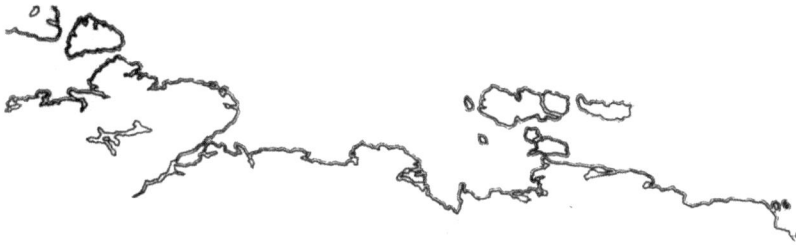

S   I   A

Amur Line

Lake Baikal

Trans-Siberian
Railway

Irkutsk

Karymskaya

MANCHURIA

Khabarovsk

Chinese Eastern
Railway

Harbin

Vladivostok

Altay Mountains

MONGOLIA

Peking

Tokyo

J A P A N

CHINA

INDIA

RUSSIA AND THE ALLIES 1917–1920
VOLUME TWO

THE ROAD TO INTERVENTION
March - November 1918

Michael Kettle

ROUTLEDGE
London and New York

First published in 1988 by
Routledge
a division of Routledge, Chapman and Hall
11 New Fetter Lane, London EC4P 4EE

Published in the USA by
Routledge
a division of Routledge, Chapman and Hall, Inc.
29 West 35th Street, New York NY 10001

British Library Cataloguing in Publication Data

Kettle, Michael
The road to intervention.—— (Russia and
the Allies 1917-1920;v.2).
1. World War, 1914-1918——Diplomatic
history   2. Soviet Union——Foreign
relations——1917
I. Title   II. Series
940.3′22   D621.S6
ISBN 0-415-00371-7

Library of Congress Cataloging in Publication Data
ISBN 0-415--00371-7

Typeset by Leaper & Gard Ltd, Bristol, England
Printed and bound in Great Britain by Mackays of Chatham PLC, Chatham, Kent

In memory
of my nephew
RUPERT GAVIN KETTLE
(1951-1986)

'The evacuation of all Russian territory and such a settlement of all questions affecting Russia as will secure the best and freest cooperation of the other nations of the world in obtaining for her an unhampered and unembarrassed opportunity for the independent determination of her own political development and national policy and assure her of a sincere welcome into the society of free nations under institutions of her own choosing; and, more than a welcome, assistance also of every kind that she may need and may herself desire.

The treatment accorded Russia by her sister nations in the months to come will be the acid test of their good will, of their comprehension of her needs as distinguished from their own interests, and of their intelligent and unselfish sympathy.'

The Sixth of President Wilson's Fourteen Points, in his address to Congress, 8th January 1918.

Contents

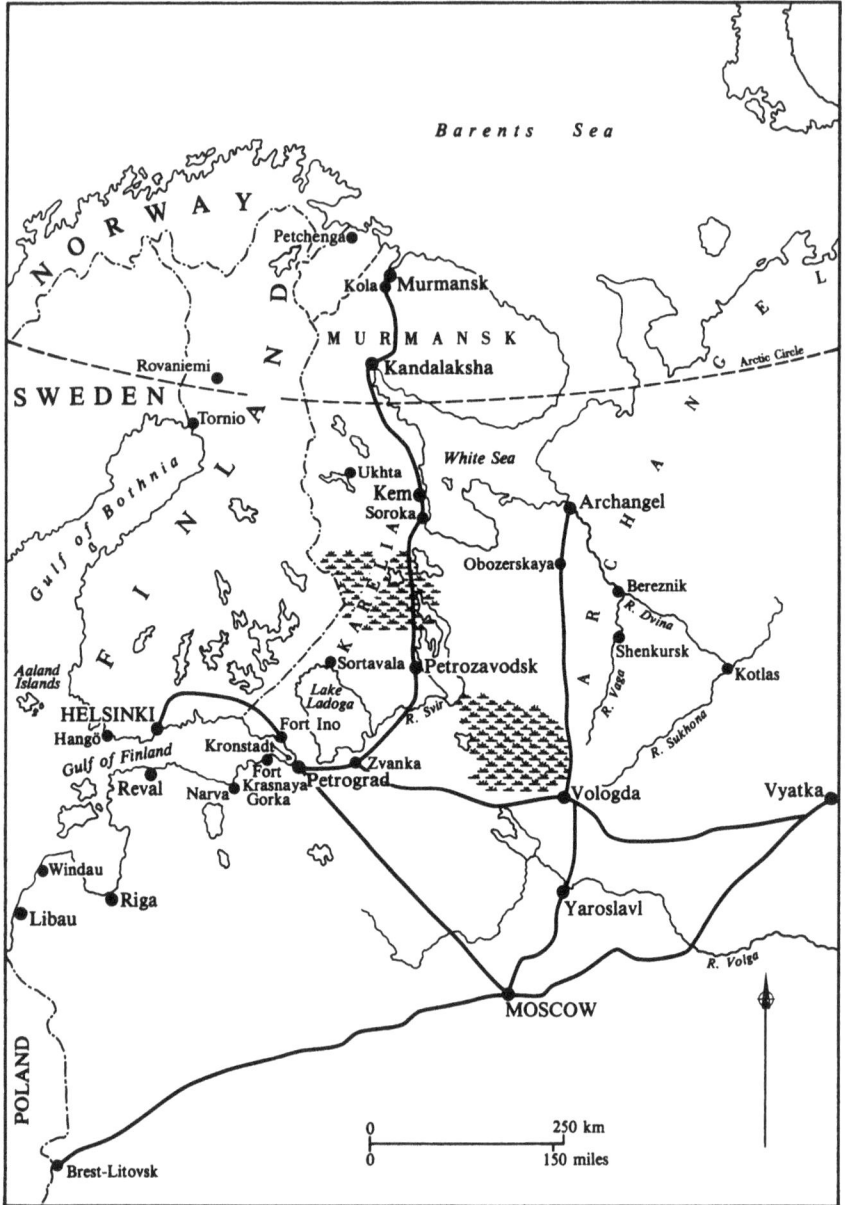

Barents Sea

NORWAY

Petchenga

Kola Murmansk

MURMANSK

Rovaniemi

Kandalaksha

Arctic Circle

SWEDEN

Tornio

White Sea

Ukhta

Kem

Soroka

Archangel

Gulf of Bothnia

Obozerskaya

Bereznik

R. Dvina

Shenkursk

R. Vaga

Kotlas

FINLAND

Sortavala

Petrozavodsk

Aaland
Islands

Lake
Ladoga

R. Svir

HELSINKI

Hangö

Fort Ino

Kronstadt

Zvanka

Vologda

R. Sukhona

Vyatka

Gulf of Finland

Reval

Narva

Fort
Krasnaya
Gorka

Petrograd

Windau

Riga

Libau

Yaroslavl

R. Volga

POLAND

MOSCOW

0   250 km
0   150 miles

Brest-Litovsk

List of Illustrations

The maps of Russia on the inner front and back cover, and the map of South Russia first appeared in Volume One, 'The Allies and the Russian Collapse' and are reprinted by kind permission of André Deutsch.

Southern Russia and the Ukraine

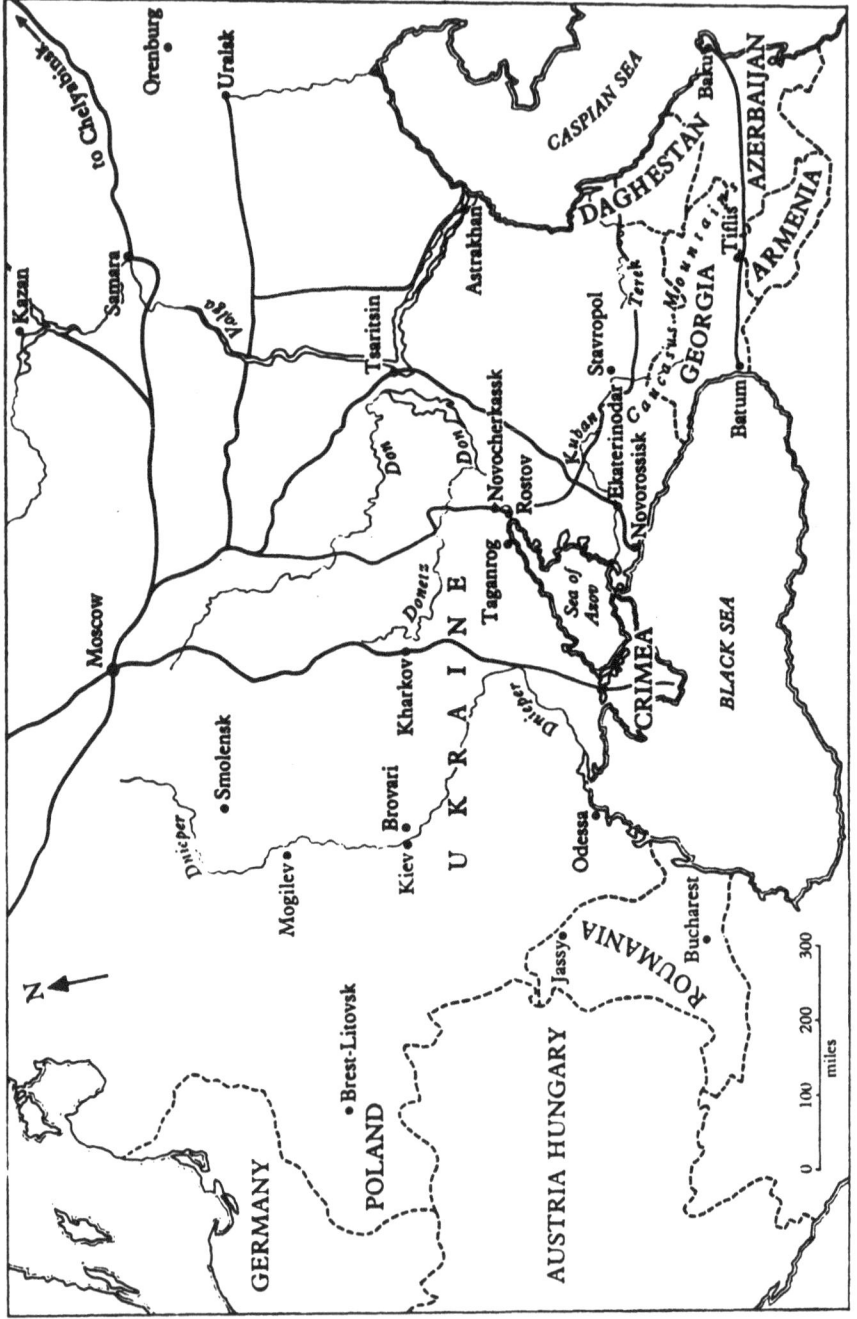

GERMANY

POLAND
• Brest-Litovsk

AUSTRIA HUNGARY

ROUMANIA
Jassy •
Bucharest •

Mogilev •
Kiev •
Brovari •
Smolensk •

Moscow •

Dnieper

UKRAINE

Dnieper

Odessa •

CRIMEA

BLACK SEA

Kharkov •
Donetz

Taganrog
Sea of Azov

Rostov
Novocherkassk

Don

Don

Tsaritsin

Volga

Samara

Kazan •

Orenburg •

Uralsk •

to Chelyabinsk

Astrakhan

CASPIAN SEA

Novorossisk
Ekaterinodar •
Kuban
Stavropol •
Terek

Caucasus Mountains

Baku •

DAGHESTAN

AZERBAIJAN

ARMENIA

GEORGIA
Tiflis

Batum •

N

miles
0   100   200   300

Preface

In my author's note in the first volume in this series ('The Allies and the Russian Collapse: March 1917-March 1918'), which was published in 1981, I stated that this second volume was also ready for the press; and I naturally hoped it would follow the first into print fairly shortly. Publishing problems have prevented that, entailing a delay of seven years. But the remaining three volumes, taking the story down to Denikin's forced evacuation of the Black Sea port of Novorossisk in early spring 1920, when the British finally washed their hands of the White Russian cause, are now entirely completed; and it is hoped that they will now follow this second volume at yearly intervals.

This second volume was largely edited by my former editor Piers Burnett, and completed by Sarah-Jane Evans, my present editor, who has also given me valuable advice with my publishing problems. To both I express my cordial thanks.

A.J.P. Taylor, at an earlier period, also advised me over this volume, and has kindly allowed me to use a small number of documents from the Lloyd George and Davidson Papers, now in the House of Lords.

Professor Norman Stone has given me sound advice more recently, when, in the loneliness of the study, things looked very bleak; and it seemed doubtful whether this volume, or indeed any further volumes, would ever see the light of day.

Next, I would like to thank my new publisher David Croom for acting so swiftly when the manuscript of this second volume did finally reach his hands.

Finally, publication has been assisted by the Crompton Bequest, the Oppenheim-John Downes Memorial Trust and the Twenty-Seven Foundation. To these benefactors, I am extremely grateful.

Though seven years have passed since the first volume appeared, and the second leads straight off where the first ended (i.e. at the Treaty of Brest-Litovsk), and characters already in the text are not re-introduced, the reader can, in my view, safely embark on this second volume without too much pre-knowledge. There is only one thing he or she must bear firmly in mind. By now, the British Government (unknown to its other allies, with the possible exception of the suspicious French), has acquired a major stake in the Russian economy through the secret purchase of a controlling interest in all the major Russian banks, which were huge financial conglomerates — and were still, despite official Bolshevik suppression, in clandestine existence. In particular, they controlled the crucial Russian and Siberian grain trades. Thus, if the Bolsheviks could now be ousted by military intervention, Britain would have virtual control of the entire economy in the new White Russia.

The purchase of these Russian banks (as described in the first volume) was accomplished, in great secrecy, between the Bolshevik revolution and the Brest Treaty by two senior British officers of the old British Supply Mission, who were still in Petrograd — Major-General Poole and Colonel Terence Keyes. The reader should not suppose for one moment that these two officers were acting on their own sweet will, or carrying out some covert operation on behalf of M.I.6. They were acting on the express instructions of the War Cabinet in London. This purchase was made, by means of funds provided by the British Treasury, through the intermediary of the great Polish financier in Petrograd, Karol Jaroszynski, who — unlike most of the panic-stricken Russian bankers of this period — was pro-British. The Siberian Bank, however (which controlled most of the Siberian economy), was purchased direct by Colonel Keyes from the Managing Director, Denisov (who has now left Russia). At the opening of this second volume, General Poole and Colonel Keyes are just back in England to report on what they have achieved; while Jaroszynski himself, and various minor agents in the transaction — Hugh Leech, Vladimir Poliakov, Teddy Lessing and Major Macalpine (a former Treasury official) — remain behind in Petrograd.

1

Siberia and the Russian Fleets

After the Treaty of Brest–Litovsk, the Allies were battling against time. Unless they could hold out in France against the German army, reinforced with troops transferred from the eastern front, until the American troops arrived, and defeat Germany before Bolshevik propaganda undermined their war-weary troops, they would lose the war. As the Germans pushed effortlessly into the Baltic, the Ukraine and southern Russia, the British had to take desperate measures to prevent the Germans seizing either Russian and Siberian raw materials, minerals and grain, or Allied supplies in northern Russia and at Vladivostok — and the various Russian fleets; for the British were desperate to prevent Russian warships falling into German hands.

But the War Cabinet only had a week to consider their new predicament before the great German attack was launched on the western front. Early on March 21, a tremendous German artillery barrage opened up on the Arras–St Quentin sector of the British front on the Somme, held by the Fifth Army. This was the 'Michael' attack: the first blow in the great German effort to split the Allied armies and drive the British back to the Channel ports before American troops could intervene to redress the balance. Ludendorf planned three more attacks to consolidate this; two more on the British front — 'St George 1' on the Lys sector, north of the Somme, and 'St George 2' on the Ypres sector — and one on the French front — 'Blucher' in Champagne — to draw off the Allied reserves in order to protect Paris. All this was preparatory to launching his final blow against the British in Flanders.

The 'Michael' attack routed the Fifth Army and caused severe casualties. Britain was in a desperate position. Germany, she knew, had been immensely strengthened by the transfer of 35 divisions from the Russian front to France. But the extreme gravity of the situation was not immediately realized in London. 'The Boches started their big attack this morning,' wrote the CIGS [Chief of the Imperial General Staff] in his diary for the 21st.

1

'Two hours intense artillery, and then infantry attack on an 85 kilometre front ... This is a big affair. We seem to have fallen back on all this line from our outpost line to our battle position ... We ought to kill them all off ...'.[1]

Would the Germans also occupy Petrograd? After the Treaty of Brest–Litovsk (while the British and other Allied embassies installed themselves at Vologda), the British supply mission remained in Petrograd to try to prevent German seizure of Russian minerals and grain, and the Allies' supplies at both Archangel and Vladivostok; and, it was hoped, they could exercise control over the Russian and Siberian grain trade, which had been secured through the Jaroszynski bank deals. With General Poole on his way back to London, his mission was being run by Major Macalpine, assisted by Vladimir Poliakov and Teddy Lessing (who cloaked themselves under the code-names 'Polly' and 'Teddy Bear'). None of them pursued identical policies, but all were violently opposed to Bruce Lockhart's belief that, if Japanese intervention in Siberia could be avoided, the Bolsheviks must renew war against Germany.[2]

On March 15, Macalpine contacted Poole and Colonel Keyes in London: if the Germans were effectively to occupy Petrograd, the supply mission must adopt a neutral attitude over the 'financial interests' (i.e. the bank deals) until Poole could return. But action could be taken through the various branches of the Siberian Bank in the Far East; in fact, the Vladivostok branch might be used as a base to take them under British control. 'All undesirable influences may be prevented in this way'. On the same day, a British officer wired from Archangel that the local espionage section reported the arrival on the 5th of a special commission sent by Lenin, with unlimited powers, which had obtained the support of the local Bolshevik sailors; its aim was to 'dominate by intimidation; their chief object is to despatch by rail until opening [of the Dvina river], and then upstream by every available barge; my private opinion is that the Commission is German inspired'. It was felt that Germans had also been sent to the port to destroy shipping; if this was true, they would probably also try to get at the munition stores to obtain explosives. (This telegram, however, did not reach London until the 21st.) Some supplies, particularly minerals, could still be kept out of German hands by direct purchase. On the following day (the 16th) Macalpine reported to London that Hugh Leech had recently been offered a considerable quantity of platinum at a high price, and had been 'asked to negotiate a reduction'.

On the 17th, Macalpine wired more dramatic news: 'Today it [has been] announced that German civil control of Petrograd will begin tomorrow. In a few days military control may be expected to follow ... We intend to retreat to Vologda.' Poliakov, however, assured Colonel Keyes on the same day that he had already started work as British financial adviser to the supply mission, and would continue his work when it left Petrograd, so as to prepare for the repurchase of all the required materials. The Dutch minister and the British chaplain were forming a committee to relieve the distress of those British left behind in Petrograd. 'I and my friends will advance the funds'. Poliakov ended sharply: 'Message from a Teddy Bear — Have Lockhart warned immediately if there is any suspicion of Benckendorff'.[2] (This refers to Lessing's plain concern at Lockhart's growing intimacy with the young Countess Marie von Benckendorff, whose husband had been Second Secretary at the Russian Embassy in Berlin prior to joining the Russian army. Lessing was perhaps concerned that because of his pre-war German connections, the Germans might use him as an intermediary with the Bolsheviks. The young Countess, later the Countess Budberg, appears as 'Moura' in Lockhart's *Memoirs of a British Agent*.) On the 18th, Macalpine wired with further bad news: 'Today I hear that we have practically lost the chance of securing the services here of Professor Ipatiev [the Russian chemical expert, who was to advise on which chemicals must be kept out of German hands] Can anything still be done?'

All these communications crossed with a wire from Balfour on the 18th to the British consul at Archangel stating that two ships, with food and supplies on board for the Archangel locality, were about to sail, accompanied by an armed ice breaker. The consul was to announce that if the local people wanted the food — and they certainly did — they must give the Allied stores and supplies at Archangel back to the British, rather than let the Bolsheviks transport them into the interior. This was indeed a forlorn hope — to imagine that unarmed and half-starved Russians would care to argue with, let alone attack, heavily armed Bolshevik troops; but this was the decision forced on the Russia Committee by Lord Robert Cecil on February 20.[3]

However, the chance of consolidating British financial control in Siberia, by taking over the various branches of the Siberian bank through the Vladivostok branch, then seemed to fade. Denisov had not received the first payment under his contract with Colonel Keyes, which was more than a month overdue. Poliakov wired in agitation to Poole and Keyes on the 20th: 'The idea that a contract should not be kept, which is easily traceable to the British government and acknowledged by the embassy in writing, is inadmissible.' He asked for immediate action to prevent not only enormous damage to British reputation but also heavy fines. 'The situation is all the more delicate because Embassy has left, taking shares and transfers with [it], and since the contract has been passed by Keyes to a third person [i.e. Jaroszynski]', explained Poliakov, concluding pointedly, 'I will continue assuring the parties interested that British obligations are never consciously broken until otherwise instructed.'[4]

On the morning of March 21, the Russia Committee took due note of Macalpine's wire from Petrograd that German civil control of the Russian capital would begin on the 18th and that military control would follow; but they were opposed to authorising Lockhart to approach Trotsky about Allied action at Archangel.[5]

This was the background to a discussion on Japanese intervention when Lloyd George and Balfour met the French and Italian Prime Ministers and Foreign Ministers at a special Allied conference in London on March 15. By the Treaty of Brest–Litovsk, the War Cabinet had at least broached the idea. On January 24, it will be recalled, they had decided 'to do all in their power' to open up communications between Vladivostok and south-eastern Russia along the Siberian railway to bring support to the Don Cossacks and volunteer army; and to urge Japan to undertake military control of the railway from Vladivostok to Chelyabinsk. This idea was rejected by the American Government on February 13. On the 25th, with the Don Cossacks and volunteer army out of the issue, and Russian withdrawal from the war imminent, the War Cabinet now decided that they 'viewed with favour' the idea of Japanese intervention in Siberia up to Chelyabinsk, so as to deny to the Germans both the Siberian railway and its grain and produce (which the British claimed to have bought through the Russian bank deals). It was suggested that Japan act as Allied manda-tory. In early March, as President Wilson gave a tentative, verbal approval to the British proposal, the Murmansk Soviet, with Trotsky's approval, agreed with British officers to cooperate in defending the Murmansk area from German incursion. The War Cabinet, hearing of the approval of both Washington and Petrograd, thereupon agreed to small-scale British inter-vention in North Russia — and 130 Royal Marines landed at Murmansk on March 6.

However, as President Wilson drew back from involvement in Siberia, Bruce Lockhart raised the idea of obtaining a Bolshevik invitation for Britain and America to help defend both Archangel and Vladivostok, a project — designed to offset the danger of Japanese intervention — already half in practice. At this point came the Brest–Litovsk treaty, by which Russia left the war. The War Cabinet already harboured doubts about Japan: obviously, she would not go far enough into Siberia to defeat German designs. Japan, in fact, could only be trusted to guard the Vladi-vostok stores. In Washington, President Wilson was considering the despatch of an American civil commission, to be attached to any Japanese force that intervened — provided that the Bolsheviks agreed. Thus, by mid-March, the idea of an Allied intervention was already coming to depend on a Bolshevik invitation, and to be limited to guarding Russia's northern and far-eastern ports (Murmansk and Vladivostok) against German attack.

Although the British were already ashore at Murmansk with Bolshevik approval, they were not considered — whatever General Poole might like to foresee, or Lenin and Trotsky to say — to be seeking Russian territory in the North. Everyone knew that Japan, although she would not move without

4

American consent, did want Russian territory in the Far East. This was the crux of the problem of Siberian intervention.

At the Allied conference on March 15, Balfour briefly outlined the background to the situation. After initial antipathy, President Wilson had become slightly more favourable to the plan, but was 'now rather opposed to intervention', stated Balfour. Indeed, the bulk of the information received in the Foreign Office suggested that Japanese intervention would tend to throw Russia into the arms of Germany. 'We could discount some of this evidence, but not all.' Balfour personally felt that the American government had not quite decided on their attitude; they saw the difficulties, 'but they might be induced to assent to intervention if strongly pressed'. Ought we not to do all we could to induce the State Department to undertake the 'considerable gamble' involved in intervention?

The French Foreign Minister, M. Pichon, agreed with Balfour; President Wilson's assent was essential. If he had strong objections, Pichon would prefer not to risk large-scale intervention. The Italian Prime Minister, Sig. Orlando, said simply that Japanese intervention was desirable. Balfour read out a wire received that afternoon from Lockhart, recounting a conversation with Trotsky, who was 'most violently' opposed to it. Pichon retaliated that they were not going to intervene to help the Bolsheviks: 'The fact was we were doing it in our own interests, and these were necessarily rather opposed to the Bolsheviks.' Trotsky had already put most of Russia at Germany's mercy. The question was whether Russia as a whole would be antagonised; Pichon felt that it would not. Many Russians, he was told, desired intervention in their own interests, and there was no need to trouble themselves too much about Trotsky's views. Pichon strongly urged that pressure be exerted on President Wilson to acquiesce in Japanese intervention. Balfour replied that the wire received from Lockhart that afternoon contained strong evidence that by allowing intervention, 'we should drive the whole of the Russian bourgeoisie into the arms of Germany'.[6] Pichon said that the French government had information from a good many different sources: 'Either we must do nothing, or we must accept intervention, which would probably take place later, whether we wished it or not.' It should be explained to the American government that there was really no choice. Germany did not like the idea of Japanese intervention. In fact, it was the only means of preventing German penetration into Asia.

Balfour did not think the dilemma as conclusive as Pichon made out: 'There was a good deal of evidence to show that, although the Russians could not resist, German penetration would be very slow. There was no immediate fear that Germany would satisfy her needs from Siberia, nor penetrate into the country.' Thus there would be time to persuade Russia that Japanese assistance could save her. It would be 'worth anything' to obtain a Russian invitation to the Japanese to intervene. Trotsky talked 'a great deal of wild nonsense, and displayed great ignorance, and declared that he would resist. We, however, knew that he was incapable of doing so. When it had been brought home to him, or to his successor in office, that Russia was getting weaker every day, it was possible that he might become more malleable and more willing to invite the Allies to give assistance. Hence, he [Balfour] was inclined to suggest a period of waiting, provided that it would not lead to the Germanization of Russia ... But if by delay we should be handing over everything to Germany, he agreed that we must make a decision now between what he styled as the 'gambler's throw', urged by M. Pichon, or losing everything.' Pichon reiterated that 'there was not a day to be lost'; he considered it 'hopeless to wait for Russia to ask for our help. They had not asked for our assistance to save European Russia, and they would not ask it to save Siberian Russia; nations reduced to this condition did not do so.'

Lloyd George pointed out that the Japanese were making all preparations for intervention, 'so that we were not really losing time by a slight delay'. But Clemenceau supported Pichon: 'Events were stronger than our will. Russia was rapidly falling to pieces; we had endeavoured to secure successive points of resistance in Finland, the Ukraine, the Don Cossacks, etc., but all these had collapsed. The country was decomposing. Regarded from a historical point of view, it was probable that some day Russia would revive; perhaps under a Tsarist government, which seemed to be most suited to Russian institutions ... This was not a moment for discussion, but for action. We should ask America what she would do if Japan wanted to act. Then, if President Wilson refused, each government would have taken its own responsibility.' He himself did not quite understand President Wilson's point of view. The President was fighting with us, but 'wished to preserve his own separate political point of view; he wanted to have a free hand for his policy in Europe and in Asia. In Europe this did not matter, although in some shades of policy perhaps he was not very closely informed.' Clemenceau added that he himself had 'complete confidence in President Wilson's good intentions and international morality' (perhaps recollecting that the first secretary of the American embassy in Paris was present). 'In Asia', he continued, 'it was a different thing. There was no time to waste — not a day. Otherwise we might be too late.' He urged Balfour to draft a despatch for the President. 'As to the idea that Russia could be induced to ask for intervention, he did not even want it mentioned. The Russians were at present devoid of patriotism.'

Balfour tried to pour oil on these troubled waters. Everyone was basically in agreement, he claimed, but a good deal of delay was inevitable. Lloyd George then pointed out that if they were to make an approach to Japan, 'two points must be made quite clear': first, that Japan must not stop at the point which suited her in Siberia, but must go to that point which suited the Allies; and second, they must treat Japan as an ally, and not ask for all sorts of guarantees; in fact, they must not treat Japan as though she belonged to an inferior race. He thought this point ought to be put to President Wilson: 'If the Japanese were not to be trusted completely, they ought not to be asked at all.' The conference thereupon asked Balfour to prepare a draft joint despatch to President Wilson, urging Japanese intervention in Siberia.

General Jan Smuts, on whom Lloyd George particularly relied, violently objected to this further plea for Japanese intervention, which undoubtedly he saw as a major extension of the world conflict. 'I saw with deep regret that Wilson is to be pressed to agree to Japanese action in Siberia', wrote Smuts to Lloyd George on the 15th. He hoped a further telegram would be sent, explaining to the President that we only wished to act in agreement with him, or not at all, as Germany would certainly use this 'Japanese business' to drive a wedge between America and the British Empire. 'I view the whole matter with the gravest misgivings.' France was in a panic, thinking only of Alsace–Lorraine. We had to think of public opinion all over the British Empire, 'and of our vast interests in Asia. ... I profoundly distrust Japan.' She seemed to be coming to terms with Germany, which would make her presence in Siberia, at their invitation, catastrophic. It would also deeply disturb democratic opinion in England, which still sympathized with the Russian Revolution, despite Bolshevik enormities. If a combination of German and Japanese pressure reinstalled reaction in Russia, 'progressive opinion will hold the present British government responsible for these developments, while the Russian people will turn their hatred from Germany on to us'. Japan would not go beyond Lake Baikal, where the tunnels and bridges were already down; and unless they went right through to Chelyabinsk, their intervention would have no military or other advantage to the Allies. 'I am sorry to trouble you, but we are taking a fateful decision', wrote Smuts.

Lloyd George deliberately ignored him. On the next afternoon, he brought before the Allied conference a forthright paper by General Knox, now the War Office's main adviser on Russian affairs, entitled *The Delay in the East*, which had the full support of the CIGS. This paper stated that Japanese intervention was essential and that two persons were immediately responsible for its delay: Bruce Lockhart and Colonel Raymond Robins, the unofficial American agent to the Bolshevik government. It was in fact an outright attack on Lockhart, and demanded his recall. Lloyd George pointed out that General Knox was strongly anti-Bolshevik, but had given us 'very valuable' information about Russia all through the war 'and had constantly proved correct'. Knox asserted that Japanese intervention 'was the last chance of the Allies in Russia; otherwise the blockade would be broken, and Germany would get wheat and oil and great quantities of manganese'. Knox also advised, on the recommendation of Captain Proctor, former British military representative at Archangel, that we should send 5,000 troops to Archangel, where there were a million tons of Allied

7

supplies, including large quantities of manganese. In a note attached to Knox's paper, Proctor had suggested, however, the despatch of a joint force of 15,000 troops to Archangel (a) to prevent the Allied supplies falling into enemy hands, (b)'to give the Japanese a lead for action at Vladivostok, and (c) to form a rallying-point for Russian elements that were still prepared to fight'. (On February 9, Proctor had urged upon the Russia Committee the seizure of Archangel, with a view to preventing the imminent German seizure of both Archangel and Petrograd — masterminded, Proctor claimed, by Trotsky. It is reasonable to deduce that Proctor hoped to spur Lloyd George on to organize a march on Petrograd from Archangel.)

Balfour underlined the difficulty of taking action at Archangel because of the ice. When the ice melted, he was told, great blocks of it came down the Dvina river, obstructing navigation for some time. (In fact, Archangel is not open for shipping until mid-May.) This was a question for the Supreme War Council at Versailles. Lloyd George agreed; Knox, he remarked, 'amid many pessimistic things, said one cheerful thing, namely, that if we had miscalculated in regard to Russia, the enemy had done the same, and last autumn had left many divisions (in Russia) which he might have sent to the Italian front'. Pichon pointed out that Knox's proposal was similar to one made by the French ambassador from Petrograd. Balfour added that for some time the Foreign Office had been 'a good deal concerned' about the Allies' supplies at Archangel. It had thus been arranged for the Allies (in fact the British) to send certain goods to Archangel, which it was hoped could be bartered or exchanged for these supplies. Hankey was accordingly instructed to ask the permanent military representatives at Versailles to consider the desirability of sending a military expedition to Archangel to safeguard the Allied supplies, and prevent them falling into enemy hands.

The Allied Conference then considered Balfour's draft despatch to the American government on Siberian intervention. It stated that the danger of German penetration into Russia was 'both great and imminent'. Russia had no power of resistance left. 'Her sole protection is to be found in the vast distances which the invader must traverse before obtaining complete military occupation of her empire. Unfortunately, however, complete military occupation is quite unnecessary. What Germany desires is that Russia should be impotent during the war, subservient after it, and in the meanwhile should supply food and raw material to the central powers. All this can be effectually accomplished in the present helpless condition of the country, without transferring great bodies of troops from West to East.'

The Allied Conference thought there was no remedy possible 'except through Allied intervention. Since Russia cannot help herself, she must be helped by her friends'. There were only two approaches to Russia; the North Russian ports or the Siberian seaboard. Siberia was perhaps the most important, and certainly the most accessible to the 'available forces' of the

Allied powers (i.e. Japan) which could do much more in Siberia than France, Italy, Britain and America combined could do in North Russia. It was recognized, however, that there were 'weighty objections' to Japanese action in Siberia. 'If this be so, it is doubtless due in the main to the fear that Japan would treat Russia in the East as Germany is treating her in the West.' However, 'no such suspicion can be entertained by those associated with Japan in the present war', President Wilson was informed. If she did now intervene, it would be as a friend of Russia, and as Allied mandatory. 'Her object would not be to copy the Germans, but to resist them', the president was assured — though on what authority is unclear. But it would be useless even to approach Japan, unless America actively supported this policy. The Allied Conference approved this wire, and it was sent to the British ambassador in Washington.[6]

On March 18, the Prime Minister informed the War Cabinet of all this, and showed them Knox's paper. They did not respond — though word of this personal attack duly reached Lockhart in Moscow, who courageously replied with an equally blistering attack on Knox for his 'complete misunderstanding' of the Russian situation ever since the Revolution.[7] From now on, Lockhart could rely on the unwavering hostility of the War Office.

The Japanese government, meanwhile, had decided on its Siberian policy. On March 17, it was agreed to reply formally to Balfour's *démarche* of the 9th, which had of course been vitiated by President Wilson's sudden *volte-face*, that Japan could definitely not intervene in Siberia without American moral and material support. On the 19th, the British ambassador in Tokyo sent a wire informing London that the Japanese Foreign Minister requested replies from the British government to two questions before he could say whether Japan could intervene as Allied mandatory:

1. If Japan agreed to act as Allied mandatory, could she count on American moral and material support, in spite of the present American attitude?
2. Did the British government require a declaration from Japan that she would advance to Chelyabinsk or Omsk, as an absolute condition for a Japanese expedition to Siberia?

The Japanese Foreign Minister, added the ambassador, was perplexed by President Wilson's recent friendly message to Russia, which had just made peace with Germany; nor could he understand why even France (let alone Britain) had a political agent accredited to the Bolsheviks and wanted Japan to have one too.[8]

President Wilson discussed Allied intervention at length with the British ambassador in Washington, Lord Reading, on March 19. The President admitted, reported the ambassador that evening to the Foreign Office, that

9

if Germany could carry out her eastern policy unhindered by the Allies, she could indeed concentrate on the western front; but he considered that the Russians themselves would object to German domination, that they would be difficult to manage, and would eventually rise against Germany; and that events were tending towards the consolidation of the Bolshevik elements against the Germans. He agreed that if the Japanese were to intervene, the safest course would be for them to act with the assent or mandate of the Allies and America; but he dissented from the suggestion that an important reason for this was the Russian people's trust in America, which, he stated, hung by a very slender thread: as the Bolsheviks considered that the American administration existed solely for the benefit of capitalists. The President assured Reading that he was very conscious of the perplexities of the situation, and was ready to take the risks, provided he was convinced that the venture had a fair prospect of a successful result; but his main difficulty was that he could not see how Japanese intervention would so seriously affect Germany as to secure the withdrawal of German troops from the western front. He was not convinced that any military advantage would be gained. The distances were great, the railways broken up, there were difficulties with rolling stock; and, further, he did not see how the Japanese forces available to enter Siberia could be so spread out as to guard effectively the whole Siberian railway. General Tasker Bliss, the American military representative on the Supreme War Council, had expressed very serious doubts about the military aspects of the question. At some later stage, however, the President added, Germany might begin to overrun Siberia, and the situation would then need reconsideration. He also added that American opinion was unfavourable to Japanese intervention. When Reading asked for his alternative suggestion, the President said that a decision must be reached on the western front.[9]

On March 19, Wiseman also wired from New York, giving the main points of a recent report by Admiral Knight, the American naval commander at Vladivostok. Intervention in Siberia, stated the admiral, was unnecessary; but should it become so, it must be by joint Allied action, since nothing could shake Russia's belief that Japan wanted to seize a large part of Siberia. But the admiral recognized that, after her Tsing-tao experience, Japan intended to act alone. (The admiral also stated, and this it seems was not included in Wiseman's wire, that at present there was no danger of any munitions stored at Vladivostok reaching the Germans, though some might be destroyed.) There was some German influence in the port, Admiral Knight admitted, which sometimes received Bolshevik support and sometimes not, but stories of a local army of German prisoners (which the British War Office always liked to believe) were untrue; and statements in the Japanese press that German forces might appear in Siberia or on the Pacific coast were preposterous.

Two days later, on the 21st, the Japanese ambassador in London gave the Foreign Office a copy of the Japanese reply to President Wilson's note of March 5, which — after the presidential lapse of March 1, approving Japanese intervention — maintained again that nothing but harm could come of it. The Japanese Foreign Minister replied that they were willing to help the Allies in every way, but must be assured of Allied agreement before intervention. The Siberian situation, however, it was hinted, might become so intolerable that Japan might have to take independent, self-protectory action. In this case, Japan hoped for friendly American support; but even with this, Japan could not move beyond the Amur river basin: this was an absolute condition for any Japanese expedition to Siberia. This reply, Wiseman wired from New York, the President considered satisfactory.[10]

At the War Cabinet at noon — as news of the great German attack began to arrive — the Allied stores at Vladivostok were discussed. The captain of *Suffolk* had reported that the Bolshevik artillery inspector at Khabarovsk, north of Vladivostok on the Amur river, had given orders for 45,000 rounds of 3″ shells to be sent up. A strong Allied protest had been made, but the captain wished to know whether or not to use force to prevent the removal of this ammunition. The War Cabinet's discussion centred on the Allies' right to interfere with the disposal of stores 'which, even if not paid for, had in fact passed into the hands of the previous Russian government, and, from them, to their *de facto* successors, and ... the probable destination of the ammunition'. It was agreed that the ammunition was almost certainly to be used for the forcible propagation of Bolshevism in eastern Siberia, and 'against moderate elements, such as Captain Semenov [sic], whom we ourselves were arming and paying'. It was decided that the Admiralty should inform the captain that the stores should not be removed and instruct him to consult with the Allied commanders how this could best be done.[11]

The War Cabinet then discussed Japanese intervention in Siberia, in the light of the Allied prime ministers' message to President Wilson, and the Japanese Foreign Minister's recent enquiry to Balfour about whether Japan could count on American support, and whether the British government required an explicit declaration that Japan would go as far as Chelyabinsk, or at least to Omsk. The Cabinet concluded that intervention would be of little use unless it could deny to the Germans the 'very large' resources of western Siberia. The case for intervention was, in fact, that there were large supplies actually available at that moment in western Siberia, which might be of 'very great importance' to Germany, if, as all the evidence seemed to show, she was unlikely to get enough food from the Ukraine and European Russia in the next few months to relieve her food shortage. It was also stressed that if western Siberia were left open to German penetration, Turkestan would be completely uncovered and British efforts to prevent a German advance eastward through Persia would be largely frustrated. It was also thought possible that Japanese intervention would have a considerable moral effect upon German and Austrian public opinion; doubts about the wisdom of the peace terms extorted from Russia would be reinforced by the realisation that these had roused against them the whole country, whose military resources they probably exaggerated, and would involve them in an interminable series of new operations in the East. (The 'country' referred to here is presumably Russia.)

The CIGS stated that there were really two problems, Europe and Siberia. 'There was no question of getting Japanese troops to Moscow, nor, on the other hand, one of German regulars being able to get to Vladivostok, or of interfering with Japanese operations in Siberia.' But if the Germans once secured control of Siberia, their influence would extend south into Turkestan, 'and our whole position in India would be imperilled'.[11] The problem was part of the same problem as the danger to Persia: 'It was a question of pulling Siberia out of the wreck, in order to save India.'

But these, it was contended, were arguments of despair, involving the abandonment of European Russia to the Germans and denying any possibility of the Bolsheviks putting up any effective resistance to the Germans, 'in spite of their recent declarations that they meant to renew the war with all their might'. Japanese intervention, it was urged, would not only alienate the Bolsheviks, but make 'all the elements of law and order' in European Russia go over to the Germans. 'It was admitted that the real question was whether there was any prospect of the Bolsheviks really making good their intentions of renewing the contest.' The War Cabinet then considered Lockhart's recent telegrams in this connection, and a speech by Trotsky in which he advocated drastic discipline in the Red Army, and abolishing the election of officers.

It was argued that Trotsky's action was mainly aimed at trying to prevent Japanese intervention. Bolshevik success had, throughout, lain in the fact that they were ambitious for peace at any price, and, 'although it was true that the anti-Bolshevik forces which we had previously attempted to organise for the defence of Russia against Germany had failed us, there was nothing to show that the Bolsheviks were either able or determined to renew the war with Germany'. The CIGS added that it was 'fantastic' to imagine that Trotsky, or anyone else in Russia, could put up a fight against the Germans. General Smuts agreed in so far as meeting a great German army was concerned; but if the revolution had any real spirit in it — and there was no evidence to support this — it might, if seriously bent on resistance, cause great embarassment to the Germans. (And this was, after all, an area in which Smuts spoke with some authority.) At this point, it was suggested that it would be worth the War Cabinet's while to hear the views of General Poole, who was due back in England on the 22nd.

The War Cabinet next considered the queries raised by the Japanese

Foreign Minister. It was thought impossible to assure Japan that she could count on American moral and material support, unless such an assurance — at any rate of benevolent neutrality towards intervention — had first been secured from President Wilson. It was stressed that although Japanese penetration of Siberia might initially prove easy, there would later be 'formidable difficulties', with which Japan could only cope if she could rely on American money and supplies. The only thing to do was to renew efforts to persuade President Wilson of the need for intervention, draw his attention to the latest information, and convince him that a situation was rapidly arising which, as he had suggested in his latest interview with Lord Reading, might make him modify his previous attitude. As such efforts would simply be carrying out the policy already agreed with the Allies on March 15, there was no further need to consult them. Balfour was requested to take action on these lines. The Japanese Foreign Minister himself had already answered his second query: if the British government made it an absolute condition for Japan to advance as far as Chelyabinsk or Omsk, if she did intervene in Siberia; and in his note of the 21st, he had stated that it was an absolute condition for any Japanese expedition that she should not go beyond the Amur basin. The Cabinet therefore did not discuss the point. By dividing England and America, Japan had, in fact, effectively ruled intervention out of court for the moment.

On the 22nd, the War Cabinet were told that a satisfactory reply had been received from the Bolshevik artillery inspector at Khabarovsk; no Allied munitions would be removed from Vladivostok for the moment.

The CIGS was still puzzled by the German attack in France: 'The Boches are pushing on in an awkward way', he wrote that day. 'I don't understand why we are giving ground so quickly, nor how the Boches got through our battle zone apparently so easily. Our casualties yesterday are estimated at 30,000 ... and we have no reserves beyond 50,000 men on which to draw.'[12]

The Treaty of Brest–Litovsk required the Bolshevik government to demobilize both the Russian army and navy. Georgi Chicherin now became Commissar for Foreign Affairs; Trotsky, the new Commissar for War, began feverishly to organize a new Red Army. Hitherto, the Bolsheviks had entirely relied on three small forces: the Red Guards (made up of soldiers, sailors and factory workers) whose revolutionary zeal already far outran their military capabilities; four Latvian regiments, which had remained a cohesive group on the dissolution of the Tsarist army, and who could not return to German-occupied Latvia and, having been bought by Bolshevik bribes, were an unwilling but efficient 'Praetorian Guard'; and lastly, a few thousand Chinese coolies, who had been building the Murmansk railway line, and would cut anyone's throat in return for food. (A few Chinese coolies and Latvians had even helped to storm the Winter

Palace.) To supplement this motley, and mainly foreign, force, the Bolsheviks had been appealing for volunteers from the vast numbers of German and Austro-Hungarian prisoners since early December. On January 21, Counsellor Lindley first reported as a fact that the Bolsheviks were actually organizing and arming large groups of prisoners, especially in eastern Siberia, where most of the prisoners were located. This was a gross exaggeration; but by March, similar and even more exaggerated reports reached London, where they were readily believed — corroborating tales of Bolshevik–German collusion.[13] In fact, the German High Command were outraged at the very thought of their prisoners being enlisted in a Bolshevik army; both the Allies and Germany strongly protested, for their separate reasons, to the Bolsheviks. Such protests were brushed aside — Trotsky needed whatever troops he could lay hands on. By March, however, appeals to defend the revolution were being steadily answered by those enemy prisoners technically released under the Brest–Litovsk treaty, especially Hungarians; the Czechs, who had initially fought alongside the Red Guards in the Ukraine, refused to fight. (But out of an estimated 800,000 enemy prisoners in Russia and Siberia, the Bolsheviks only succeeded in arming some 15,000, of whom 5,000 were in Turkestan.) Trotsky, the grand revolutionary, was only following age-old Russian precedent in recruiting foreign troops; it had long been Russian practice under the Tsars. But to counter Allied fears that the Bolsheviks were enlisting prisoners on a vast scale, Trotsky agreed to a British and an American officer (Captains Hicks and Webster) setting out for Siberia in mid-March to make personal investigations on the spot.

Simultaneously, Trotsky appointed Admiral Altfater (who had been a member of the Bolshevik peace delegation at Brest-Litovsk) as Commander-in-Chief of the new Red Fleet, while Captain Behrens became the Naval Chief of Staff, with Fedor Raskolnikov as Chief Naval Commissar. But the Bolsheviks viewed the Red Fleet, especially the Baltic Fleet, with mistrust. It was a natural, strong, self-contained national entity, which owed allegiance to Russia, not to any particular Russian government, and strongly resented its forced self-destruction under the Brest–Litovsk treaty. It had played a big part in putting the Bolsheviks into power; and might just as easily overthrow them with either British or German support. Lenin and Trotsky, who had decided to play the British off against the Germans to gain a desperately needed breathing space, knew this full well. From any point of view, the Russian navy was now a liability to the Bolsheviks.

The Admiralty were especially anxious about the Russian Baltic Fleet, which consisted of 5 battleships, 9 cruisers, 70 destroyers and 26 submarines. (These figures were given to the War Cabinet by the Admiralty on May 11, but they undoubtedly include old ships, ships temporarily out of commission, and partly-built vessels.) The British Grand Fleet was somewhat short of destroyers; and if these 70 Russian destroyers were to be added to the German High Sea Fleet, the situation would become 'very serious', the First Lord warned the War Cabinet.

Baltic Fleet sailors had played a prominent part in the revolutionary violence of 1917 in Petrograd; for the Baltic Fleet was iced in at Helsinki, across the Gulf of Finland, when the riots first broke out in March, and the discontented sailors on shore leave in Petrograd, with little to do, eagerly participated. Violence soon spread among the sailors and dock-workers at the naval base of Kronstadt in Petrograd Bay. A mob rushed on board the cruiser *Aurora*, lying in the Neva, and shot her captain. Trouble ensued among the battleships at Helsinki (known as the 'convict' ships of the Baltic Fleet because of their reputation for harsh discipline); several officers were killed. Mutiny followed on some destroyers and mine-sweepers; more officers were killed, including the Commander-in-Chief, who was replaced by his irresolute second in command. The ships' crews then organized committees, whose delegates formed the 'Centrobalt', which elected a sailor called Dybenko (an old Bolshevik party member), as Chief Commissar. Continual disputes raged between the officers and the Centrobalt. In July, the officers warned Kerensky that there would be a complete collapse, unless a more resolute commander were appointed. Accordingly, Admiral Verderevsky took over. When the Bolshevik rising took place in mid-July, the provisional government asked him to send some trustworthy destroyers up the Neva to overawe the dissidents. The destroyers were despatched but in the ensuing turmoil, Verderevsky was replaced as commander by Admiral Razvozov, the destroyer commander. Nothing much happened for the rest of the summer and the ships and crews rotted away; and when the provisional government did not meet their pay demands, they openly looted their ships. But it was known to the Admiralty in London that discipline remained much better in the destroyers and submarines than in the battleships.[14]

On November 7, the Winter Palace was stormed and the cruiser *Aurora* appeared to fire a few blank rounds; the Bolshevik revolution had become a fact. In London, the Admiralty received information that the Bolsheviks intended to hand the Baltic Fleet over to the Germans. On the 23rd, the War Cabinet directed the Admiralty to arrange for British submarines in the Baltic to be destroyed, and for Russian naval officers faithful to the Allied cause to be encouraged to man the Russian destroyers and, with the support of British naval forces in the North Sea, to escape from the Baltic. All other warships in the Baltic Fleet were also to be destroyed. No expense was to be spared. ('The very serious political consequences were not overlooked', comments Hankey, who states in his diary that the third part of this War Cabinet directive was in fact more specific: the loyal Russian officers were 'to be induced to blow up the four Russian dreadnoughts'.[14])

15

On December 5, the First Lord informed the War Cabinet that the moment had come for the destruction of the British submarines. But on the following day, the First Sea Lord stated that a wire had just come from Buchanan, suggesting the advisability of an agreement with the Bolshevik government not to negotiate with the Germans over any Russian warships, and if necessary to disable them for the duration of the war, so that they could not be used against the Allies. But the War Cabinet turned this proposal down; in the present confused situation, it was decided that it was impossible to negotiate, though it was agreed that the British submarines should be handed over to the Bolsheviks. On the 7th, this decision was reversed; the Deputy First Sea Lord informed the War Cabinet that instructions had now been issued that the British submarines were to be destroyed.[15]

In Petrograd, the Bolsheviks abolished the post of Commander-in-Chief and gave full power to the Supreme Naval Board and the Centrobalt. At this, Admiral Razvozov called together his senior officers and sent a warning to the Centrobalt that unless the decision were reversed, all the officers would resign. Two envoys were sent to the officers; the sailors, they said, were agitating strongly against the officers. This attempt at intimidation failed. The officers were summoned to a meeting in Marinsky Square, and there their previous day's resolve collapsed through indecision. Admiral Razvozov was replaced by Commissar Ismailev, an 'insolent and stupid' sailor, according to a former Russian naval officer. More and more sailors began to desert and the officers' morale sank lower and lower. Nothing more for the moment could be done to implement the War Cabinet's decision of November 23.[16]

In southern Russia, there were some 5 old and 2 modern battleships, 5 light cruisers, 17 destroyers and 4 submarines in the Black Sea Fleet at the time of the Bolshevik revolution. The area had suffered similar disorders, mutinies and murders, and on January 11, the War Cabinet were informed that 52 Russian naval officers, including an admiral, had been murdered at the naval base of Sebastopol in the Crimea. On January 15, Lord Robert Cecil asked the Russia Committee to consider sabotage in the Black Sea. The DMI said that since a previous discussion about sabotaging warships, a report had been received which indicated that it was desirable to destroy as many ships as possible in the Black Sea. It was agreed that the DMI should discuss the matter with the DID (Director of the Intelligence Department, Admiral Hall, who was to become Director of Naval Intelligence in 1918). On the 25th, the DMI told the Russia Committee that the DID had agreed that both warships and merchant vessels in the Black Sea must be sabotaged.[17]

At their next meeting on the 28th, the Russia Committee held a discussion on both the Baltic and Black Sea Fleets. The DID pointed out that the Baltic Fleet would be ice-bound until April. Cecil feared that the Germans might buy the Fleet off before then. The DID remarked that if the Germans wished, they could seize the Fleet as soon as it was ice-free, 'and no amount of subsidising on our part could alter that fact'. Cecil asked if he had any suggestions about the Black Sea Fleet. The DID replied that he had informed Commander Le Page, the assistant British naval attaché in Petrograd, that there were 150 merchant ships in the Black Sea and that it was vital that they should not fall into German hands in a seaworthy condition. He had also asked for a report on the Black Sea Fleet itself. 'Commander Le Page would read between the lines, but the DID had been unable to be more precise in view of the fears that were entertained with regard to the safety of cypher communications through Russia', state the minutes. On January 29, the Russia Committee had to consider a wire sent on the 22nd by General de Candolle, the British liaison officer with the Don Cossacks, about the possibility of handing Russian merchant ships in the Black Sea over to Roumania, and of helping General Kornilov, the volunteer army's commander, to obtain control of the Black Sea Fleet. It was agreed to reply that General de Candolle could take 'any steps' to assist Kornilov, and could support the first proposal (which more closely concerned the French), but de Candolle should realise — cut off as he was — that Romania was practically at war with the Bolsheviks. Both proposals, of course, foundered.

On February 14, Captain Francis Cromie, the British naval attaché then at Helsinki with the Baltic Fleet, wired that the Bolshevik government had suddenly announced the demobilization of all the Russian fleets, and published a decree that there was to be a new Red Fleet, on a voluntary basis. 'This decision has been taken very quickly', he added. On February 19, the First Sea Lord informed the War Cabinet that Cromie had wired again on the 18th that Commissar Ismailev had been ordered to remove all stores from Reval and Helsinki to prevent their seizure by the Germans, but that many of the warships had refused to recognize him. All bluejackets, who had joined the Red Guards and were now fighting on the Don and Ukraine fronts, had been recalled to the Baltic Fleet.[18] The War Cabinet asked the First Sea Lord what could be done to restore the balance of power if the Germans seized both the Baltic and Black Sea Fleets. He replied that the Americans were ready to help; but the Admiralty felt that even if the Germans did seize the Russian warships, it would be impossible to man them, as they would not have the necessary personnel. This was a sanguine view.

But feelings in the ramshackle Baltic Fleet at Helsinki were now swinging away from the Bolsheviks. In mid-January, civil war broke out in Finland, when Finnish communists tried to seize power and some Finnish troops (which had been trained in Germany, and were German-equipped) had moved against them. The Centrobalt decided to support their Finnish comrades both with men and money, but the Russian sailors were reluctant to join in and hardly any volunteered. Late in February, rumours spread that the Finnish communists would be defeated and German troops were to land. At this news, the ships' crews began to agitate. By now, the Centrobalt had been abolished. Late in January, the Supreme Naval Board had appointed several commissars to run the Baltic Fleet, thus flouting the electoral principle. This caused further unrest. At the instigation of the crews of the better-disciplined destroyer division, meetings were held which openly called for the reinstatement of Admiral Razvozov as commander. On March 9, Cromie wired from Helsinki: 'Battleships have been ordered to Kronstadt, but crews wish to go by train.[19] After several interviews I have succeeded in getting (?order) issued to prepare ships for destruction, but definite action cannot be relied upon', he warned. One icebreaker had deserted, leaving only two to hack a passage through the thick winter ice for the Baltic Fleet to return to Kronstadt.

As more and more (increasingly exaggerated) rumours spread of the imminent approach of White Finn and German forces, the Russian sailors at Helsinki became more and more agitated and began to loot their ships before making off back to Petrograd in groups. The officers and crews of the better-disciplined destroyer division finally convoked a general assembly of all the ships' committees, which the resurrected Centrobalt and Captain Cromie attended. On March 12, 4 battleships and 3 cruisers left Helsinki for Kronstadt with the 2 remaining icebreakers, and it was unanimously decided to ask Admiral Razvozov to resume his post as Commander-in-Chief. As all cyphers and wireless codes had fallen into German hands when they seized Reval, and communications with Petrograd were now very uncertain, Admiral Razvozov agreed, but 'only for the time necessary, to meet the present situation caused by German advance in Finland, and on condition that Smolny (i.e. the Bolshevik government) give him absolute power', wired Cromie, who had been present on board the Russian flagship when the new Commander-in-Chief explained his policy. 'All ships to be got ready for immediate destruction, which is not to be effected without his personal orders. . . . Commander-in-Chief refuses idea of blocking entrance or sinking ships in [Helsinki] harbour, as likely to offend Finns, who will undoubtedly demand enormous sums for damage to harbour. . . . British submarines ready for destruction', added Cromie. In Petrograd, the Bolsheviks were very disturbed at this unexpected turn of events and sent the tough Naval Commissar Raskolnikov to Helsinki to remove Razvozov. In London, the War Cabinet were briefly informed on the 13th of the plans which the Admiralty now had in mind 'for depriving the Germans of any effective use of Russian warships'. But these plans, which the Cabinet minutes do not divulge, would take a little while to put into operation.[19]

In the Far East, there were a few Russian warships, and a considerable number of Russian merchant ships and steamers, mostly based at Vladivostok, where there was also a vast amount of Allied war-material. On December 24, the Russian training cruiser *Orel*, with naval cadets on board, put into Hong Kong; she was followed six days later by two Russian destroyers. The captain of *Orel* told the British admiral in Hong Kong that it was impossible for him to return to Vladivostok, where his cadets would certainly be murdered, and he proposed to hand his ships over to the British government. He suggested that *Orel* should continue as a training ship, but those officers and men who wished to do so should be allowed to return to Vladivostok. On January 31, the First Sea Lord informed the War Cabinet that he proposed to instruct the British admiral in Hong Kong that he could not take over command of the Russian warships, but should tell the captain of *Orel* that if he wished, the ships could be paid off and remain in Hong Kong with a care and maintenance party. In this case, those officers and men who wanted to return to Russia might be sent to Vladivostok at the first opportunity. The War Cabinet approved, and the ships remained in Hong Kong. This disposed of some of the Russian warships — and also increased the turbulent throng of mutinous Russian soldiers and sailors at Vladivostok, which, by early March, was the only major Siberian town not under Bolshevik control.[20]

On March 7, the Admiralty suddenly directed that all Dutch vessels at Vladivostok were to be detained. On the 9th, they directed that two Russian steamers at Vladivostok, and two more at Hong Kong, were to be seized. This was hotly resented; they were warned that local opinion was 'undoubtedly antagonistic' to the seizure of further Russian ships. Nevertheless, they directed that all Russian steamers were to be seized not only in the Far East, but in North American and European ports as well. On March 14, the Admiralty explained that they had information, 'which appears reliable', that in mid-January the German Naval Staff were trying to persuade some Bolshevik commissars in Petrograd to send three German submarines from the Baltic down the Siberian railway to Vladivostok, where three German agents had been seen trying to get control of Russian steamers and workshops at the port for the purpose of forwarding agents and material to carry out sabotage in Japan, America and British colonies in the Far East; and that one Kudriashov had been sent to finance these agents, but had been waylaid and robbed.[21]

This Admiralty message should be compared with 'Sisson Documents' no. 22, no. 9 and no. 23; this seems to show that the Admiralty had been fooled by these elaborate forgeries. No. 22, dated January 10, and allegedly from the German Admiralty to the Bolshevik government, requests that several Russian steamers at Vladivostok be made available to three German agents there for the despatch of agitators and saboteurs to America, Japan and British far-eastern colonies. If no Russian ships were available, it would be 'necessary to charter ships sailing under a foreign flag'. No. 9, dated

January 12 and allegedly from the Imperial Bank in Berlin to Trotsky, agrees to the issue of 5 million roubles from German General Staff funds to the assistant Bolshevik naval commissar, Kudriashov, to go to Vladivostok to see one Panov (the former mayor of Vladivostok and a leading Russian newspaper editor in the Far East), and two of the German agents mentioned above, and three more, with whom 'it would be necessary to think out a plan for carrying out the Japanese and American war materials from Vladivostok to the West'. If this was not possible, they must be destroyed. Also, Chinese agents should be financed to 'carry on an agitation against Japan'. No. 23, dated January 14, allegedly from the German admiralty to the Bolshevik government, requests that three German submarines be sent (in pieces) down the Siberian railway to Vladivostok, on the 'conclusion of peace between Russia and Germany'.[22]

Professor Kennan points out that Anton Ossendowski, the presumed manufacturer of these documents, had for some nine years been carrying on a campaign of blackmail and denunciation in the Suvorin newspapers against a Siberian general merchant firm, Kunst and Albers (originally founded by Germans, and presently run by the former German consul in Vladivostok, now a naturalized Russian), who had employed most of these alleged 'German agents' (three of whom had in fact left Vladivostok long before 1918). During the Russo–Japanese war, Ossendowski had been in the Far East, where he had been arrested and imprisoned by the Russian authorities for his part in organizing a strike; and there were doubtless people in Siberia with whom he wished to settle old scores, some perhaps connected with Kunst and Albers. During his long vendetta, he had used the firm's German connection as a convenient smoke-screen — and had actually been paid to attack them by a rival Siberian firm as well. In 1918, after manufacturing the carefully forged documents 'proving' that the Bolshevik leaders were paid German agents, and distributing them to Allied agents in Petrograd, he was contemplating fleeing to the Far East, where the Allies were supposed to be about to land; for, having denounced his personal enemies there to the Allies as German agents in advance (Panov may well have known something discreditable about his Siberian past as well), he would have amply protected himself on arrival in the Far East.[23] These three documents, though naïvely written, contain some truth, like the other 'Sisson Documents' (Admiral Knight, the American naval commander at Vladivostok, reported to the Navy Department at Washington in mid-March that he knew that Kudriashov had been sent to Vladivostok to arrange for the removal or destruction of the Allied stores, but had been caught by Ataman Semenov, and had his money taken.) They would also, of course, hasten Allied, and especially Japanese, intervention and indeed appear to have had their intended effect at the Admiralty in London.[24]

The great German attack of March 21 also forced the War Cabinet to give further consideration to the Russian Baltic and Black Sea Fleets. Captain Cromie wired on the 21st that he had 'asked Commander-in-Chief [Admiral Altfater of the Red Fleet] for immediate destruction of Black Sea and Baltic Fleets. He and Commissar Blokhin have consented to do their utmost regarding Black Sea, but they do not consider time yet arrived for Baltic Fleet, though they admit it is no longer any use except for Germans.... People's Commissar [i.e. Trotsky] has been asked to issue immediate orders for destruction in Black Sea ... No sign of German advance [on Petrograd], but Reds are failing ...'.[25]

This seemed satisfactory as regards the Black Sea Fleet — but in southern Russia, Allied officers were now taking independent action. On March 21, the Allied military attachés in Roumania decided, as soon as they heard of the big German attack in France, to carry out widespread sabotage in southern Russia and the Ukraine.[26] But that night, the British minister at Jassy wired the Foreign Office to enquire whether, since Russia was now a 'professedly neutral country', they had authority for 'getting into touch with the anarchists and supporting their work' with 'large sums of money', as the Allied officers evidently intended. It seems that it was not clear at the Foreign Office whether this specifically referred to the Black Sea Fleet or not. On the 21st, the Deputy First Sea Lord told the War Cabinet, when asked what steps the Admiralty were taking to prevent German seizure of the Black Sea Fleet, that the Allied Naval Council had considered the matter, but had decided not to take immediate action, since the Germans would find great difficulty in manning the ships. The Germans, he stated, had captured a few small naval vessels at Odessa, but most of the Black Sea Fleet was at Sebastopol. The Cabinet evidently found this as unsatisfactory an answer as they had on February 19.

On March 22, Balfour (who now had the British minister's wire from Roumania) asked what information the Admiralty had about the Black Sea Fleet. His attention was drawn to a further wire from Helsinki stating that the Russian Admiralty had instructed the commanders of both the Baltic and Black Sea Fleets to destroy their warships. (This wire has not been traced in the Admiralty records.) The Cabinet were told, presumably by the First Sea Lord, that there was 'apparently no reason why the Bolsheviks should give up or destroy any ships in the Black Sea, and the War Cabinet felt that the attitude which would be taken by the Bolsheviks as regards these Fleets would be a test as to the sincerity of the Bolsheviks' announced intentions'. It was agreed that Balfour should wire Lockhart in this sense, and ask him for such information about the Black Sea and Baltic Fleets as the Admiralty might think desirable, and that the First Sea Lord should make his wishes known to Balfour. The Foreign Secretary duly wired to Lockhart and asked him what Bolshevik policy was towards the two fleets. We wished to see the Baltic Fleet destroyed, but considered that the Black Sea Fleet should be able to command the Black Sea, if properly handled. Lockhart was to advise if he saw any chance of such a policy being carried out.[27]

But the Foreign and War offices, no doubt with the Admiralty's approval, took out an 'insurance policy' on the Black Sea Fleet, though the War Cabinet were never informed. On the 25th, the DMI, to whom the Foreign Office had referred the wire from the British minister in Roumania, replied that 'any opportunity' should be taken for sabotage in southern Russia. That night, therefore, the Foreign Office authorised the British minister to 'adopt the method suggested' by the Allied military attachés. Since the Germans were closely watching the British embassy in Roumania, General Ballard, the British military attaché, secretly contacted Colonel J. W. Boyle, and asked him to arrange to sabotage the Black Sea Fleet, to destroy ammunition dumps, railways and workshops, and to organize strikes in the Ukraine; and, to ensure secrecy, he gave Boyle no money, but several signed blank cheques on Ballard's own personal account (with Holt's Bank in Pall Mall) which Boyle was to fill in for the agreed sums.[28]

This was a tall order, but Boyle, though now well into middle-age, was a resourceful man; an Irish Canadian, who had sailed before the mast, he had been a fireman in the Chicago fire brigade, the American amateur heavyweight boxing champion, and had later made a fortune in the Klondike gold rush. During the war, he had been sent out to Russia and Roumania by Walter Long, the Colonial secretary, with the backing of the Russian military attaché in London, to assist in the reorganization of the Russian and Roumanian railways. He became a close friend of Queen Marie of Roumania, who awarded him various Roumanian orders for his varied activities in the Allied cause (which he allegedly wore even when in his pyjamas). But his unorthodox methods made him more than a little suspect to the official British community in Russia, though they certainly appreciated the results obtained. 'Is it possible to trust him not to push personal interests?' wired General Barter from Russian GHQ on September 1, 1917, to the CIGS. 'Russian authorities, although they appreciate his abilities and experience, view him with some suspicion.' The CIGS replied that Boyle had been sent out without reference to the War Office and his presence in Russia was not officially recognized. On October 25, General Poole, writing to Colonel Byrne in London, said, 'The Boyle case is getting worse. . . . The real truth as I see it is (1) Boyle is really a thruster and gets things done, but (2) he is also a "bagman" and presses the sale of his own wares, and (3) he gains great kudos with the Russians by promising them that he will get them anything they want.' In his reply on November 7 (the day of the Bolshevik coup), Byrne described Boyle as an 'infernal nuisance'.[29]

Early in December, Boyle and Captain George Hill (a young British agent working for MI6) had offered their services to the Bolsheviks to disentangle the railway chaos near Moscow in order to bring food to Petrograd. Lenin gave them full powers and, by drastic methods, the chaos was resolved in two days and food supplies were soon on their way to both Petrograd and Kiev. In mid-December, when Trotsky began to vent his anger at Allied anti-Bolshevik activities in Roumania, and even threatened invasion, Hill and Boyle somehow managed to take the Roumanian gold reserve and the crown jewels, which had been kept in the Kremlin since the fall of Bucharest, back to Roumania. Ballard, the military attaché, now felt that Boyle's previous contacts with the Bolsheviks would lull German suspicions.[30]

Boyle therefore went down to Sebastopol and contacted various groups of Bolshevik sailors, who agreed to take the Black Sea Fleet to a Russian port further east when the Germans approached the Crimea, stay there as long as possible, then put to sea again and scuttle the ships, the full value of which they demanded as prize money. Boyle flatly refused, and finally induced them to value the ships at £200 per ton, and to accept 10% for ships sunk, 5% for ships damaged, and to take General Ballard's cheques in payment; he was, Boyle explained, the British military attaché, and his cheques were trustworthy. The Black Sea sailors accepted. For military and industrial sabotage and strikes, Boyle contacted various groups of engineers and mechanics, which he had formed in November 1917 when on railway work in southern Russia, and told them to sabotage railways and mines, destroy ammunition dumps, damage machinery and 'lose' parts. He also agreed to keep them paid when out of work.

In Petrograd, Cromie was already making his own arrangements about the Baltic Fleet, irrespective of whatever Trotsky might decide. (On the 20th, Cromie's assistant wired from Petrograd: 'Have obtained order for collecting quantities of explosives previously requested by Captain C. from Naval General Staff.') But on the 22nd, Cromie wired again: 'Captain Behrens [Russian Naval Chief-of-Staff] interviewed March 21 considers surrender of [Baltic] Fleet would not be agreed to, but while admitting that Fleet is useless, he will not order destruction. Commander-in-Chief [Admiral Razvozov, who had just been elected by the ships' committees], who received his full power on 19th was arrested on 20th at instigation of his old enemies Raskolnikov and Ismailev. Verderevsky [former commander, Baltic Fleet] has refused position but offers to criticize any plan that may be laid before him or discuss question with anyone after four p.m.', added Cromie in exasperation.[31]

At Helsinki, where an assault by the White Finns and the landing of German troops was now expected, there were thus yet further changes of command in the Baltic Fleet. Commissar Blokhin was appointed to take charge, while operational control passed to Captain A. M. Chastny, a former destroyer commander, who had been the senior officer on Admiral Razvozov's staff. In Moscow, Trotsky told Lockhart that the Baltic Fleet would be withdrawn to Kronstadt, but destroyed if necessary. But at

Helsinki, Chastny told Cromie that any attempt by the officers to prepare the ships for destruction would meet with opposition from the counter-revolutionaries, who naturally wished the ships to remain intact. Chastny, in fact, took no notice of the contradictory orders from Moscow — first telling him to abandon the ships, then to bring them away — nor of the demands of the British, who wanted them destroyed immediately. With feverish haste, he prepared all the ships for the extremely hazardous passage back to Kronstadt through the thick ice, with only one icebreaker. As many of the sailors had deserted, fresh crews had hurriedly to be taken on, most of whom were Finns. Chastny reported on several occasions to Trotsky that he suspected that many of them were under White Finnish or German influence. No notice was taken of these warnings. As he stood on the ice in Helsinki harbour, Chastny remarked to another Russian naval officer: 'The Bolsheviks are German agents; they are going to try to hand over the Baltic Fleet to the enemy, so that they can use it against the Allies. Something is going to happen, however, which will stop them ... The Baltic Fleet made the Bolshevik revolution possible, the Baltic Fleet will also bring the Bolshevik power to an end.'[31]

2

Allied Intervention: Bolshevik invitation or British ultimatum?

Gradually the full impact of the huge German attack struck home in London. 'An anxious day', wrote Sir Henry Wilson on the 23rd. 'The Fifth Army seems to be beaten, and has fallen back behind the Somme.... I was about five hours with Lloyd George ...'. Then on March 24: 'At 1.30 I heard the Boches had taken Sailly–Sailliselle. This shows the tremendous danger of this colossal attack. At 5 o'c[lock] a telephone message to say Combles and Péronne had fallen, and our troops were retreating to the Ancre. I telephoned at once to Lloyd George at Walton to come up. At 5.30 Foch telephoned asking me what I thought of the situation, and we are of one mind that someone must catch holld, or we shall be beaten.... At 7 o'c[lock] meeting at Downing Street of Lloyd George, Bonar Law, Smuts and me. There is no mistaking the gravity of the situation.... A moving day. We are very near a crash. Lloyd George has on the whole been buoyant; Bonar Law most depressing. Smuts talked much academic nonsense. Winston a real gun in a crisis ...'.

On the 26th, the CIGS was at Doullens, where the historic decision was finally taken — after four years of war — to unify the Allied command. 'After discussion, in which I [Wilson] fell out with Pétain for contemplating a retreat', he writes, 'Milner put up proposal for Foch to coordinate, and, all agreeing, Clemenceau and Milner signed the document.... Got back to Victoria at a quarter to eleven. Milner, Winston and I to 10 Downing Street, and we told Lloyd George and Bonar Law and Hankey result of our labours and, as I summed it up for Lloyd George, "the chances are now slightly in favour of us".'[1]

As the Germans advanced into Russia, the scene was rapidly changing in Moscow, the capital of (officially neutral) Bolshevik Russia, and the pendulum was now swinging against the British. From late March, there was wild speculation in Russian industrial shares on the German bourse as Russian shareholders, who had sold out to the Allies before the Brest-Litovsk treaty, 'repurchased' the shares (many of which had never been delivered) and resold them to German banks, whose agents, helped by the depreciation in the exchange, quickly obtained controlling interests in Russian oil companies, railways, factories, granaries and real estate. German firms, closed since the beginning of the war, began to re-open.[2] Only German citizens, it was claimed, would receive compensation for nationalization.

German agents also attempted to gain control of some of the Russian banks, purchased by the British government through Jaroszynski and Colonel Keyes; and some of the pro-British Russian financiers were now defecting. 'Germans are working to get Russian Bank [for] Foreign Trade into their hands', wired the British ambassador in Stockholm early in April. At present, a large majority of the shares of this bank were safely owned by Jaroszynski. 'Deutsche Bank have large holdings and are buying up shares. As a foreign concern they cannot however at present exercise a vote on board. Deutsche Bank's holdings are therefore being transferred to Davidov who will act for German interests.'

Denisov, the former managing director of the Siberian Bank, was not however to be bought. He told the British ambassador in Oslo that he had had an offer for the shares from the Nya Bank in Stockholm, whom he thought was representing a number of German banks, including the Deutsche Bank and the Mendelssohn Bank. The sum involved amounted to over 100,000,000 roubles.[2]

On March 23, General Poole had arrived back in London with proposals for future British policy in Russia, which he had drafted out while on board ship, together with his idea of the organization needed to carry them out, which, Colonel Byrne told him on the 25th, were 'sound and acceptable'.

Allied policy in Russia during the last six months, Poole wrote, had resulted in a 'complete diplomatic triumph' for Germany, who had now acquired control of all the western districts of European Russia without military opposition. 'Owing to the manner in which Germany has developed her diplomatic policy since the first Revolution, her military forces are now welcomed everywhere in Russia, except by the few hooligans and anarchists, as "saviours" rather than as "conquerors".' The evacuation of Petrograd by the Allied embassies had removed the last anti-German influence. 'Various reports have been made on the futility of bolstering up Russian political movements, such as the French policy in the Ukraine and the Alexeiev movement in the Don. All these were doomed to failure from the outset, as outside force must be brought in to make any Russian soldier (officer or man) fight against Bolshevism and anarchism — which are now practically the same thing — or still more against the Germans.' Past British policy could only be described as 'disastrous'.[3]

While Japan took care of the Far East, Poole continued, British and French forces must reassert Allied influence through Archangel and

Murmansk. Only small forces would be needed. 'The Bolshevik troops are thoroughly undisciplined and disorganised and are quite unfit to oppose any small body of regular troops.' These Allied troops would be welcomed by most people, 'and a local militia or police force could be formed', he wrote. 'Various proposals have been put forward for the formation of a volunteer army from the so-called patriotic Russians, but personally I have no faith whatever in any of these proposals without an outside force behind them.' The local militia or police must be under direct Allied military control, 'and there need be no false sentiment expressed that such a policy would incite animosity amongst the Russians. They know now only too well their entire lack of organizing capacity.' But there must be joint Allied action, which must be publicized throughout Russia, based on restoration of the constituent assembly; local institutions as under the provisional government; revised discipline for the Russian army, and the establishment of a federal Russia. 'Such a programme is essential and must be widely published to prevent the obvious propaganda, instigated by German agents, against the Allies that they are merely coming in to annex parts of Russia for themselves.' This would safeguard the Allied stores at the Russian ports, guarantee the repayment of the Russian foreign debt, and protect Allied business concerns in Russia.

Allied troops should advance down to Petrozavodsk and Vologda and link up with the Siberian railway, to transfer food from Siberia to northern Russia. 'It is very doubtful if any opposition whatsoever would be encountered. The German forces may possibly enter and police Petrograd to break up the headquarters and centre of Bolshevism, but it is unlikely that they will penetrate further north or east.'

At present, there was no means of exercising Allied influence in central or southern Russia. But a political and commercial organization must be started at Tiflis to cooperate with the 'central organization' of Russia, 'which should accompany the Allied Force through the Northern Ports'.[3] Another such organization should accompany the Allied force coming in through Vladivostok. 'When order is restored, the controlling factor on the whole future of Russia must be 'Finance' from outside, and consequently it is of the greatest importance to establish the necessary commercial organizations which must be ready to act at once when the opportunity to do so arrives. Unless some such policy as that outlined above is adopted and energetically carried out, Germany will be in the field first and alone and G[rea]t Britian will be again 'Too Late' to collect a fair share of the best of the commercial undertakings which will be open for development. Further, the execution of such a policy will be very effective during the duration of the war in checking the withdrawal of supplies from Russia to Germany and Austria.'

Poole attached a note on the British official organization that would be needed in Russia, stressing that diplomatic agreements must be based on

27

commercial considerations. 'The Russian nation is completely disorganized and bankrupt and will for some time be involved in open or semi-open civil and political quarrels.' It would be dominated in future either by Germany or by the Allies. 'This [latter] proposition is earnestly desired by all true Russians, and if properly executed would lead to the general reconstitution of Russia for the benefit of the Russians.' It would entail the introduction of capital and personnel 'to instil European methods into the Russian character'; also, general education, and a reformation of Russian trade laws. Poole stressed that the Bolshevik régime did not control all Russia.

A British bank must be started in Russia, by arrangement between the ten to fifteen leading Russian joint-stock banks and private British banks; and an advisory committee formed in Petrograd of British businessmen, with a similar organization in London, formed by Steel–Maitland's new Department of Overseas Trade (DOT). ('No,' minuted Byrne here. 'A Committee under a Cabinet minister similar to the Milner Committee would be better.') There should also be a Propaganda Bureau. 'It is essential for the increase of British commercial interests in Russia that young men of good education should go out to Russia into banks, engineering works, mines, and the like; and the commercial section in Russia would keep the DOT advised of good openings as frequently as possible. Every facility should be given for Russians to obtain knowledge on similar lines in English banks and works for a few years in England before they take up permanent appointment in Russia.'[3]

Poole also enclosed his supply mission's paper of February 1 on British banking policy (detailed in the previous volume), urging the formation of three distinct banking groups, and warning against the outright purchase of any particular Russian bank — advice which had since been ignored.

The ambitious policy outlined by Poole took no account of Allied resources, or lack of them. In fact on March 23 — the day of Poole's return to London — the military representatives of the Supreme War Council decisively rejected all idea of an Allied expedition to Archangel, whether to secure the Allied stores or for any other purpose. To maintain an Allied base at Archangel, 'which would act as a nucleus for the assembly of the Russian disaffected and repentent elements', as a French admiral put it, would require two to three infantry brigades and artillery groups, stated General Weygand; and the Allies could not find such a force. The only course of action at Archangel was to ensure the destruction of the Allied stores.[4] The Allied warships and marines already at Murmansk should remain in order to try to retain the port for as long as possible.

On March 26, Major Macalpine wired from Moscow to inform General Poole of events since his departure for England. With regard to the evacuation of British subjects from Petrograd, he commented: 'I should like to add that Chicherin, Petrov and other Bolshevik leaders who had been in

England showed the Mission, in what were often the most trying circumstances, every kindness and help', explaining that 'All this hurry of evacuation before March 18 led to confirmation of the rumour that the peace terms included German occupation of Petrograd. The Russians generally seem inclined to welcome German control and occupation. They will begin, it is said, as controllers and advisers, and as soon as a suitable pretext can be found, military control will succeed civil control. There is no hope of effective Russian opposition, whatever they do.... The people, apart from the Bolshevik government circle, are apathetic.' Macalpine strongly urged the retention of a British mission at Archangel, the main port of entry into Russia: 'I certainly think that this summer we can do a great deal to prevent supplies from Russia being drawn by Germany. That is a sound, practicable and immediate aim ...'.

For the moment, Macalpine believed in full cooperation with the Bolsheviks in denying Russian supplies to the Germans: our 'policy [should be] to deal through official circles with everything so far as is possible, and to buy only in last resort', he wired via Archangel on the 28th; 'Without Russian government's goodwill and cooperation, purchase is in any case useless.' In answer to a wire from General Poole in London, he confirmed next day that he was sticking to Poole's policy: 'I agree thoroughly that indiscriminate purchasing is wasteful, and before receiving your cable I had already given instructions to that effect.... Lockhart should be reminded to work with the [Allied] committee in Moscow, and to encourage the [Bolshevik] government in their policy of evacuation [of stores]. The government is definitely, and still, the strongest force in the country.' This, of course, assumed that all the stores were to be used by the new Red Army. On the 30th, 'Pollyglot' (probably Poliakov wearing a different hat) wired in more alarmed terms to Poole: 'The Germans are making an inventory of stock,' and he listed copper, aluminium, and large quantities of rubber, steel, zinc and nickel. 'This must be a great incentive to [German] occupation. The press is influenced throughout by the Germans, but if a strong directing centre existed with British interests in view and without a sentimental management, much could be done for Britain.[5] Small shows are inefficient and noxious.' It was such communication that alarmed London.

On March 29, Colonel Keyes, who had returned to London with Poole, wrote a report on the bank schemes, for either the Foreign Office or the Treasury, and another undated report, probably for the Russia Committee. In his longer first paper, after detailing the background to the whole project, which had the double purpose of financing anti-Bolshevik elements in South Russia and the Ukraine by the formation of a Cossack bank, and of acquiring control of large sectors of the Russian economy for the British government, Keyes admitted that, with the collapse of the

Ukraine, the Don Cossacks and the Volunteer Army, the 'immediate
political advantages of the scheme are thus considerably curtailed, and we
are left, for the present, with little more than the economic and financial
possibilities, except in Siberia.... It must be noted that the Germans were
making strong efforts to capture certain banks, and that we forestalled
them by one day only with the Siberian Bank, as the contract for the sale of
the 'controlling packet' of the bank was presented for signature in Christia-
nia [Oslo] the day after the chief director [Denisov] had heard that his
agent had sold us the same shares in Petrograd.' But in the long run Keyes
was optimistic: 'I venture to say that Russia, with her enormous untapped
natural resources, given order and a fair chance of development, is the one
European country that will be able to pay her share in the War within a
reasonable time — even further, that it is the development of Russia's
natural wealth that will play a large part in helping Europe to recover. In
Russia, more than any other country in the world, the banks are based on
real wealth, and are undisputed arbiters in all commercial and industrial
undertakings.' The 'universal opinion' of all the financial and economic
authorities whom Keyes had been able to consult, not only those who had
remained in Russia, but also those who had taken refuge in Norway and
Sweden, was that the 'Bolshevik régime, though it may ruin individual
bankers, cannot, even if the war continues for another year, and they have
during that time undisputed control in Moscow and Petrograd, ruin the
banks themselves. ... [for] whatever the new form of government in Russia,
the banks must play a leading part in her reconstruction'.[6]

Keyes then detailed the holdings of the various banks in which the
British government now had a controlling interest. As well as control over
the grain trade on the Volga and in southern Russia, they controlled the
whole sugar trade in the Ukraine, 1.25 million acres of 'easily accessible'
forest, 300,000 acres of irrigated cotton land in central Asia, nearly all the
Russian insurance business, besides large coal, oil, cement and other
concerns. Although the foundation of a Cossack bank was, he admitted,
'in abeyance,' the Siberian Bank (which was 'acquired under different
conditions from the others, and is virtually under our sole control'), 'exer-
cises great influence over the most extensive, but only partially-developed
grain tracts of Russia', and had a concession for the establishment of a
Mongolian Bank, which should give it almost a monopoly in Mongolia.
'This [Siberian] bank, being more thoroughly under our control than any
other, should prove the most useful instrument of policy.'

Keyes continued: 'We have the right to nominate our own directors to
all these banks, and to all the companies controlled by them, and Yarosh-
inski [sic] undertakes to place at least 100 young Englishmen in his banks
and companies.' With their 300 or so branches, and their interests in
numerous commercial and industrial concerns, they could mount 'an
unrivalled commercial intelligence system for investigating old and new

undertakings', and could re-establish 'such of our concerns as have suffered during the disorders'; and, in particular, they could handle 'our loans and other financial interests'.

To make full use of the whole scheme, the following conditions were required: a commercial and financial policy; a British Bank, founded by the large British banks, with London and Russian branches, to which 'the Russian banks of our group', and their 300-odd branches, would themselves virtually act as branches; and suitable personnel for the Board of Control, bank directors, directors of companies controlled by the banks, and young men for service in the banks and companies, who were likely to develop into capable directors.[6]

In his undated report, probably for the Russia Committee, Keyes pursued in greater detail the setting up of the Bank Scheme, citing telegrams and their numbers. The shares in the companies, which Jaroszynski had offered as collateral for the British loan, stood in Keyes' name with the Commercial and Industrial Bank. Of the Siberian Bank share transfers, those deposited in Russian banks were held by Poliakov, with duplicates held by Keyes; and those deposited in British and French banks were held by Keyes, with duplicates held by Poliakov. After seeing Denisov in Oslo, and receiving wires from Poliakov, he warned: 'They are all very anxious and puzzled as to why payments have not been made, and Poliakov has made very strong observations as to the damage that delay in payment will cause to British credit.' In Oslo, Denisov had asked him to alter his payment to 1.5 million francs to be placed to his credit with the Société Française de Banque et de Credit, with the balance remitted to the London City and Midland Bank in London. In Oslo, Keyes had deposited 1,018 Siberian Bank shares, which were handed over on signature of the contract, with the British Legation.

He now enclosed copies of various documents: letters from the Commercial and Industrial Bank acknowledging the loan of £500,000, and placing to his order shares to the value of 35 million roubles as security; letters from Jaroszynski, taking over the loan; and letters from the Commercial and Industrial Bank, asking him to make payments of £162,500 with regard to the loan. Keyes also enclosed various documents concerning the purchase of the Siberian Bank: the sale contract; its acceptance by Jaroszynski; several share transfers; and a power of attorney, apparently given by Denisov to Keyes. (All these Siberian Bank documents are missing.)

The next day (March 30), the Foreign Office at last requested the Treasury to put through payment both for the British government's purchase of the Siberian bank, and for the British loan of £500,000 to Jaroszynski. Under the contract with Keyes, £308,000 was due as a first instalment to Denisov, and £120,000 to his assistant, Nicholas Ass, for the

Siberian bank shares. A further £162,500 should be paid to the various Russians at London banks (as alreay detailed in the previous volume); and £337,500 (being the balance of the loan to Jaroszynski) to Hugh Leech's account at the London branch of the London City and Midland Bank. This was later to give great power to the drunken young British propaganda agent, who had acted as intermediary with Jaroszynski, and who was now buying up metals and other scarce commodities in Petrograd for Macalpine. (Leech later explained that 'Jaroszynski asked Colonel Keyes to have the money due to him transferred to my account with the London City and Midland Bank in London, but this Colonel Keyes preferred at first [i.e. presumably some time in February] not to do, making the payments himself. After some days experience of this arrangement, he changed his decision and telegraphed to London to have the balance due to Jaroszynski transferred to my account.')[6]

Shortly after, Major Thornton, of the War Cabinet Secretariat, wrote urgently to Colonel Byrne about the Russian Commercial and Industrial Bank, which was the main holding bank for Jaroszynski's banking empire. This may have had some connection with the arrival in London of a French representative as soon as the French government heard of British acquisition of control of the Siberian Bank in an attempt 'to try and get on even terms with us', records Keyes. (Thornton's letter is not available; there is only an entry in Byrne's diary.) Byrne would not be drawn; the only person in England who knew anything about this matter, he replied, was Keyes, and his address was 'care of Colonel Peel', at the Foreign Office. But Keyes was strictly instructed to give this French representative no information whatever about the Siberian Bank.[6]

In Petrograd, the situation was viewed slightly differently: 'Conditions of Brest peace could be altered by international action', wired Woodhouse, the British consul, somewhat cryptically, to Poole and Keyes in London on April 2. Specialists were engaged to give a 'full account' of the financial and economic situation that had now arisen. This presumably referred to the Allied Committee in Moscow; and he asked for approval for the expenditure of 50,000 roubles, which he had advanced to them. 'I am now practically financial controller for Siberia and the banks [?of the southeast] union groups', continued Woodhouse; 'I request authority to associate Teddy with my work: I am keeping close touch with Macalpine. Scheme of importing young British [?businessmen] for the establishment of an industrial [and] commercial colony should be supported', he stated, echoing Poole's recommendations.[7]

Bolshevik power was increasing in Vladivostok, the only major Siberian town not in Bolshevik control (which Poole assigned to Japan), despite the presence of the Allied warships in the harbour. Business firms were being harassed, especially foreign firms. On March 23, a British officer wired that he and the British consul had been in touch with the local assistant manager of the Siberian Bank with a view to consolidating British financial control in Siberia. Their help was welcomed, but 'owing to lack of ready cash, bank is closed', he stated. This was due to the State Bank, now in Bolshevik hands, refusing to supply it with money or to honour its cheques, in the hope of forcing it to accept Bolshevik control. As the bank had resisted, the Bolsheviks were trying to arrest the manager and his assistant. 'The Bank Manager is raising money in Japan and Harbin, and it is expected that in a fortnight a sufficient sum to recommence operations will be available.' Confidence and proper work, however, could only be restored if the Bolsheviks were prevented from interfering. If the Siberian Bank board proposed to send funds, the assistant manager wanted them remitted to the British consul. But on the 24th, everything came to a stand-still when the Bolsheviks seized the main telegraph office and the post and telegraph workers struck. Vladivostok was cut off. On the 27th and 29th, there were telegrams (somewhat garbled) from Archangel hinting that progress was being made towards having the bank board forward funds to Vladivostok, and strongly urging that Denisov (the former managing director) should be paid in Paris the amount due to him under the contract negotiated by Keyes.[7]

On April 5th, the Treasury sanctioned the payment of the two amounts constituting the loan to Jaroszynski, but (because of further developments in the worsening Siberian situation) abruptly refused funds for the Siberian bank shares. The War Cabinet thus had full technical control of the Russian grain trade and much of the Russian economy, if the Bolsheviks could be ousted. This made successful Allied intervention all the more pressing, and desirable, for the War Cabinet — little did the other Allies know.

By late March, Vladivostok was virtually in Bolshevik hands, all immediate hopes of consolidating British financial control in Siberia seemed to have been dashed, and considerable quantities of Allied war stores were daily being sent westward by rail. Were they destined for the new Red Army, or German troops in European Russia, or German prisoners, whom the Bolsheviks were thought to be arming in Siberia? No one in London knew, and everyone expected the worst.

A Bolshevik invitation for intervention could, thus, it seemed, only apply to European Russia; but it was the possible German seizure of Siberian supplies, and possibly their control of Siberia itself, which most concerned the War Cabinet. In Moscow, Lockhart believed, optimistically, Trotsky would accept Allied military support, initially in the form of Allied instructors; there was a large French military mission then in Moscow, which had come up from Roumania. On March 28, the Russia Committee in London discussed the proposal for the despatch of a British military mission to Russia, 'in the event of cooperation with Trotsky proving feasible'. It was agreed that Lockhart should then simply become political adviser to the British commander. However, that day Lockhart wired from Moscow that Trotsky would not only welcome Allied military help, but would not object to Japanese participation, provided other Allied troops came with them, and Allied guarantees were given.[8]

But little progress was made in breaking the virtual deadlock over Japanese intervention. On March 26, Balfour sent Colonel House, via Wiseman, a draft telegram to the British ambassador in Tokyo (which would only be despatched with American approval) stating that the American view that Japanese intervention might turn Russian sentiment against the Allies was appreciated in London; but it was nevertheless felt that the advantages of intervention outweighed the dangers. The difficulty of making Russia understand that intervention was the only instrument of their salvation from Germany was admitted; but the task of making Japan understand that the Allies did not ask for joint intervention due to mistrust had still to be overcome.[9]

Wiseman forwarded a reply from Colonel House on the 29th. The German offensive of March 21 had certainly modified his views on this and other subjects; but he remained unconvinced of the value of the proposed expedition, which might be of more value to the Germans than ourselves. The forces that Japan could produce, the amount of financial and material assistance they would require, were still unknown quantities. Could any information be given on these points? And could they obtain, perhaps through Lockhart, any unofficial expression of Russian assent to Japanese and American intervention? Later on the 29th, a further message came from House stating that the President hoped that nothing would be done for the moment; the situation was so uncertain and there was no need for immediate action.[9]

Meanwhile, Lord Reading had wired a few days previously that the President was opposed to intervention on the grounds that the military authorities had not made out a sufficient case for it. The Japanese Foreign Minister, who got to hear of this, told the British ambassador in Tokyo that the views of the Allied general staffs, and of the Japanese, should be sent to the president. Balfour was told of this on the 26th, and the views of the War Office were wired to Lord Reading on the 29th. (This wire has not been traced.) The key to the problem now seemed to a direct Bolshevik invitation for intervention.

On March 30, the War Cabinet was told of the latest exchange of telegrams between London and Washington, as well as the telegram from Tokyo, urging that the Allied general staffs should put their views on Siberian intervention before President Wilson; and Lockhart's recent telegrams, 'indicating the possibility that the Bolsheviks might yet be persuaded themselves to invite the assistance of Japan'. The view was expressed that it would be 'fatal if, now that M. Trotsky and the American govern-ment were coming round to a view less hostile to Japanese intervention, the Japanese government should decide not to intervene'. It was decided that, if this had not already been done, the Foreign Office should inform the British ambassador in Tokyo of Lockhart's latest telegrams, 'indicating that the Bolsheviks were regarding Japanese intervention in a more favourable light'. This message probably had a far greater effect than the War Cabinet can have foreseen.[10]

At about midday on April 4, several armed men in Russian military uniform entered a Japanese shop in Vladivostok and demanded money; on being refused, they shot dead three Japanese clerks. (The identity of these men has never been established, but the presumption must be that they were acting either for the Japanese security services, or for the French, who were already guilty of various acts of deliberate provocation in the Far East designed to hasten intervention.) Next morning, the Japanese admiral, acting on his standing orders, landed a party of 500 marines from warships in the harbour to protect Japanese interests in the city. The Captain of *Suf-folk* followed suit and landed 50 men to guard the British Consulate. The American admiral took no action, even though asked by a member of the so-called 'Siberian provisional government' if he would protect it, if this body established itself at Vladivostok; later, Admiral Knight's stand received Washington's approval. In London, the Admiralty wired their approval to the Captain of *Suffolk*.[11] At Vladivostok, all remained calm, as the local Bolsheviks bided their time.

This local incident brought matters to a head between the British and Bolshevik governments. On the 5th (the Treasury having refused funds for the Siberian bank shares), Lockhart wired that he had been told by both Trotsky and Chicherin that these events in Vladivostok virtually destroyed all chance of Bolshevik cooperation with the Allies. The highly-alarmed Bolsheviks issued a statement condemning the Japanese landing, which was taken to be the start of intervention. Japan had been responsible for the false rumours about the German danger in Siberia and the arming of German prisoners,* and had now used a local incident to land troops. What was Allied policy, and particularly British policy, in view of the Japanese landing? Both an explanation and the withdrawal of the troops were requested. But the Bolsheviks feared the worst; further Japanese landings were certain, Lenin wired the Vladivostok Soviet on the 7th, and

---

* John Bradley, in *Allied Intervention in Russia* (London, 1968), p. 52, states that 'on landing, the marines captured a German commercial mission; its agents were all over Siberia trying to negotiate large scale purchases of Siberian grain'. He does not cite a source for this interesting piece of information — the presumption is that it came from French official documents which Bradley has seen. This is just the sort of thing that would have vitally interested the War Cabinet in London and they would have certainly discussed the matter, had they known of it. There is no mention of this in any British document that I have seen and it may have been an invention by the French or Japanese security services.

they must consider the 'best way out, the best retreat, the carrying off of stores and railroad material'. That day, Francis, the American ambassador, issued an ill-advised statement from Vologda reproaching the Bolshevik government for attaching undue weight to the Japanese landing, but claiming that there was complete understanding between the Allies on intervention, namely that there would be no invasion or seizure of Russian territory; and the Japanese ambassador emphasized that the Japanese admiral had acted without the knowledge of the Japanese government. All this appeared in the local press as a resolution against Allied intervention. In Washington, the State Department was startled to be told that there was complete Allied agreement on intervention — since the very reverse was the case — and Francis was reproved. In Tokyo, the affair led to a government crisis involving the resignation of the Foreign Minister, Motono, and his replacement by the more moderate Baron Goto.[12]

In London, Balfour had replied to Lockhart, blaming the Bolsheviks for the disorders in Vladivostok which had led to the landings, the sole aim of which was to protect lives and property in the port; this was a local incident and Trotsky should bear in mind that the Allies ardently wished to give him the fullest military support possible. On the 8th, the War Cabinet was briefly informed of the Japanese and British landing and of the ambassadorial statements at Vologda. Next day, the Deputy First Sea Lord read out a further wire from *Suffolk* (dated the 8th) emphasizing not only that no American force had been landed, but that the American admiral's plea for the use of force to prevent any removal of the Allied stores had been rejected in Washington. The Japanese government, however, had stated that they would support the Japanese admiral if he met with Bolshevik opposition; and he appeared to have proposed to Tokyo that it was desirable to disarm the Red Guards and encourage the local authorities to form a strong militia to police the town properly. (This seems to have been initially correct.) The Captain of *Suffolk*, however, considered it impracticable to disarm the Red Guards without occupation, which would itself entail military intervention; and there might possibly be active Bolshevik opposition if they were reinforced from Siberia: this would create an entirely new situation. The Deputy First Sea Lord reported that, at present, there appeared to have been no disturbances at Vladivostok since the Japanese and British parties had landed.

Balfour summed up by saying that there were 'divergent views' between America and ourselves over this incident, and America had not supported us. Our present action had been entirely local, simply to protect British subjects in Vladivostok; and both we and the Japanese had landed only very small parties.[12] Lord Derby pointed out that we had a battalion at Hong Kong earmarked for service in Vladivostok, if necessary. Afterwards, Balfour made further efforts, both in Tokyo and Moscow, to play down and close the incident.

In France, the great battle for Amiens continued. 'We stand this way', wrote the CIGS on March 31. 'From March 21 to 29 we have lost 114,000 infantry. We have sent out, or will have sent out by April 4, a further 101,000 men. They had some 20,000 out there [?in depots], but we have sent all boys of 18 and a half who are trained.... We shall have nobody for the defence of England except untrained boys of under 18 and a half....'. On April 4, Ludendorff launched a further assault on Amiens, but was again repulsed, and rather than be drawn into a battle of attrition, he broke off the attack. But it was obvious that another major attack would soon be launched against another sector of the Allied line. This was the background to an appraisal of the situation in the eastern theatre, drawn up by the military representatives at Versailles on April 8, and submitted as Joint Note 20 to the Supreme War Council. It opened in very definite terms:[13]

1. 'The military representatives, after a careful consideration of all the factors involved, are of opinion that no serious military resistance to Germany can be expected from Russia unless there is an immediate Allied intervention in that country.' (A phrase in the original British draft here, to the effect that 'any resistance to ... [Germany] must be preceded by the elimination of the Bolsheviks', was taken out on the suggestion of the French delegate.)
2. The German objectives were:
   (a) to obtain the West Siberian wheat, butter and fats (since the Ukrainian supplies were inadequate);
   (b) to obtain the Caucasus oil and minerals, and Turkestan cotton;
   (c) to create a friendly Russian state, so that most of the 47 German divisions in the East could be transferred to the West;
   (d) to use small German and Turkish forces to control the Caucasus, and north and central Persia, so as to threaten the British flank in Mesopotamia, and incite the Afghans to attack India; ('The gravity of this menace to the whole British position in the East would, they [the Germans] assume, compel the British government to divert large forces from other fronts or even frighten it into concluding peace', stated the British draft — in panic-stricken terms.)
   (e) to send German and Turkish agents into Turkestan (either by rail from Samara, or by boat from Baku to Krasnovodsk) to stir up Moslem propaganda, and secure a new sphere of control, 'which might even embrace Chinese Turkestan and the Moslem population of southern China. From Turkestan, as well as from Persia, they might hope to work up an anti-British agitation in Afghanistan'.
3. The Allied objectives were:
   (a) to limit the area from which Germany could withdraw supplies, raw materials and food and labour;
   (b) to check German military penetration generally;

   (c) to prevent the Germans withdrawing their remaining divisions to the West.

4.   These objectives could be achieved by giving 'effective military support' to every element of the Russian or non-Russian people in the Russian Empire, or in Persia, which was prepared 'actively' to oppose the enemy advance or reject his intrigues.

5.   In Siberia, that support could only be 'effectively' given by the Japanese, with the eventual help of the Czech force [then allegedly on its way out of Russia, via Siberia], and other elements that could be organized on the spot. The extent to which political problems posed by a Japanese advance into Siberia could be solved either by an invitation from 'some provisional nucleus of government in Siberia', by Allied missions at Japanese GHQ, by proclamations to the Russian people explaining the object of the operations, or by a 'definite statement' by Japan of the rewards she expected, must be left to the Allied governments. But the military representatives 'would wish, however, to point out that their conception of the Japanese advance is not that of an army of invasion, but that of a mobile base or nucleus of regular armed force affording moral, material, and (if necessary) military support to mobile Russian detachments and emissaries moving in advance and on both flanks ... such intervention should have an international character'.[13]

6.   'To be of any substantial service, the advance, of which the Japanese forces will form the nucleus, should extend as far west as possible, at least to Omsk or Chelyabinsk, but preferably as far as Samara, where it would control not only all Siberia, but also the railway to Turkestan, and the waterway of the river Volga, and afford a line of access to elements of resistance in the Caucasus, and, if the command of the Caspian be secured, also to northern Persia.'

7.   If the movement of reorganization in Siberia, of which Japan was to form the nucleus, was successful, it might encourage resistance to the Germans in European Russia, 'whether originally started by the Bolsheviks, or in any other way. In that case, the knowledge that the improvised armies of the Russian national uprising will be stiffened by the regular forces of Japan, will compel the Germans to retain a large Army in the East'.

8.   In Persia and the Caucasus, the ultimate effect of enemy success 'may be of the very gravest character and involve a most serious drain upon the military resources of the British Empire', they warned. The forces immediately engaged on either side would, however, be quite small, and could easily be supplied by British forces in Mesopotamia and India; but they insisted on the 'supreme importance of rapidity of action in this region'.

9.   There was a great need for better communications in this whole area.

All routes should be developed, 'and the railway from India through Mushki [?Kushk] pushed ahead to enable British troops to secure eastern Persia and, from Meshed, exercise an influence over Turkestan'.[13]

This paper illustrates the desperation caused by the German attack of March 21 — a fact very easy to forget. The whole paper is a military absurdity. All strategic considerations and tactical possibilities seem forgotten — let alone the lessons of the Napoleonic Wars. It would have been impossible for the Japanese, loathed by all Russians, to advance some 5,000 miles across Siberia to the Volga in a matter of a few months. Japan had clearly stated to the Allies her limited ambitions in Siberia, or at any rate to the Americans. How could any responsible military man at Versailles have imagined that Japan could be involved in, let alone instigate, a 'Russian national uprising'? General Tasker Bliss, the American military representative, refused to sign this appraisal on the grounds that the whole theme — of intervention — was the 'subject of diplomatic correspondence' by the American government.

Next day, April 9, Ludendorff launched his 'St George 1' attack in the Lys sector against the British army, whose 'astonishing early success', as Liddell Hart puts it, induced him to turn it into a major effort, and the British were almost pushed back to the sea. 'The Tiger [Clemenceau] said we should swing on our right and come back to the Somme, but I was very soon able to dispose of that', wrote the CIGS in France on April 10, 'saying that it was death to uncover the (Channel) ports, and so our right must fall back; and if the French would hold the left bank of the Somme, we would never lose touch with them'. In London the next day, 'A War Committee at 6 p.m., where I frightened them properly about this attack of the Boches, and I am frightened myself, as I am afraid it will end in the loss of Dunkirk. At 9.30 p.m. Lloyd George telephoned that he wanted me, and I went to Winston's, where he was. I told him I was anxious, and that it looked as though we might lose Hazebrouck ...' But the British army just managed to hold this crucial railway junction.[14]

Meanwhile, the Black Sea Fleet became increasingly threatened by the German advance into the Ukraine. On April 5, German troops took Kharkov; by the 12th, they were very near Odessa and the naval base of Nicolaiev, where several Russian warships were in dock. The fleet itself lay in Sebastopol. On March 21 and 22, the War Cabinet had been told that the Germans would have great difficulty in manning the Russian warships, even if they did seize them; secondly, and quite wrongly, that the Bolsheviks had given orders for the destruction of the Black Sea Fleet. This somehow led the Cabinet to believe that what the Bolsheviks actually did with the Black Sea Fleet would be a test of the sincerity of Bolshevik policy generally. No greater mistake could have been made — Trotsky in Moscow had very little control over events in Sebastopol.

However, two separate British policies were under way. The first, official, one was summarized by Balfour's wire to Lockhart stating that we considered that the Black Sea Fleet, if properly handled, should be able to command the Black Sea, and Trotsky was to be so informed. The second policy, known to the Foreign Office, War Office and Admiralty — but not to the War Cabinet — had led to Colonel Boyle's journey to Sebastopol, and his flamboyant arrangements for the Black Sea Fleet to be scuttled.[15]

The War Cabinet had been alarmed when told by the First Sea Lord on April 2 that a report had been received through the French naval attaché in Roumania that the Ukrainian government at Kiev, whose territory the Germans were rapidly over-running, had given orders for the demobilization of the Black Sea Fleet with a view to handing the warships over to the Germans; and that certain forts in Sebastopol had already been seized by armed bands of German prisoners. The First Sea Lord did not attach too much reliance to this report; there were enough forces available to counter any such movement. But he did feel that the Allied Naval Council should discuss the matter at its next meeting to concert action by the Allied fleets as necessary. In fact, Admiral Sablin (Commander-in-Chief, Black Sea Fleet) had hoisted the Ukrainian flag at Sebastopol. Trotsky, it appeared, had already lost control in the Black Sea.[16]

On April 12, the First Lord told the War Cabinet that he had been trying to arrange closer cooperation between the Allied fleets in the Mediterranean 'to meet the contingency of the Germans capturing the Russian Fleet in the Black Sea'. He inferred that he had not been altogether successful. The Admiralty proposed that the Allied Naval Council should examine the matter, with a mandate from the Supreme War Council. The French already agreed with British ideas, and there was a chance that the Italians might also. A letter from the Prime Minister to the French and Italian Premiers was thereupon approved; it stated that there was 'some probability' that the Black Sea Fleet might be handed over by Russia to Germany. This matter had, it seems, already been discussed by the Allied Naval Council, who considered it 'practicable' for Germany to man at least all the modern Russian warships and in due time render them 'efficient fighting units', so that together with German and Turkish warships at present within the Dardanelles they could operate in the open Mediterranean. 'This possibility creates an entirely new situation in the eastern Mediterranean, since the Allied naval forces are not at present organized or distributed with a view to this contingency. Moreover, in such an event, an attempt to combine with the Austrian Fleet in the Adriatic must also be regarded as a possibility.'[17] The naval situation in the Mediterranean should thus be discussed at the next meeting of the Supreme War Council, wrote Lloyd George.

The Germans advanced not only into the Ukraine and southern Russia, but also into Finland to support the Finnish White Guards against the Finnish Red Guards; and thus directly threatened the Russian Baltic Fleet at Helsinki. On April 1, the Germans seized Ekenas, a small port in south-western Finland. 'No definite action has been taken by Russian Fleet', wired Captain Cromie the British naval attaché, 'but it is hoped to get ships placed at entrance [of Helsinki harbour] ready to sink'. On the 3rd, a German squadron approached Hango [below Ekenas] and began to land German troops. 'Red Staff inform me that they cannot withstand an organized force', wired Cromie. 'Serious disorders are expected in Helsingfors [Helsinki] very shortly, as the local White Guards will undoubtedly rise when Germans commence to advance.' The Russians had blown up four of their submarines and Cromie had started to destroy the British submarines. The Baltic Fleet had no icebreaker to take the large ships back to Kronstadt, as the *Irmak*, on returning to Helsinki, had been driven back by gunfire from the icebreaker *Tarmo*, which had deserted. So far, the Russian sailors had refused to destroy the Russian warships, 'as they have much valuable loot on board', explained Cromie. 'In the event of being unable to procure destruction, the Reds have promised me every assistance if I will take charge of operations for blocking the Port ...'. This telegram was read out to the War Cabinet on April 8.[18]

Meanwhile, Cromie had sent a further wire, saying that the Germans had demanded that the Baltic fleet be removed from Finnish waters or disarmed by April 12, when the German squadron would arrive by sea at Helsinki. Captain Chastny (Commander-in-Chief, Baltic fleet) had somehow managed to remove most of the Russian warships on the 6th. What was to happen to the remainder? 'Destruction of British submarines created tremendous impression in [Baltic] fleet and in the press', Cromie added. 'Have since received assurances from several ships that they are ready to follow our example.' But in his next wire, he reported that he was having great difficulty with some Russian crews, who 'threaten to punish those who destroy their ships, and offering reward to those who hand them over in good condition.' On the 10th, Cromie stated that he had sunk two more British ships, but he much feared that in the general panic several ships would sink, through lack of icebreakers, in the Kronstadt channel and block it.[18] 'Germans demand strict neutrality of [Baltic] Fleet and disarmament of all ships and reduction of crews', he reported. 'There is no doubt Germans intend to arrive [at Helsinki] by sea on April 12th'.

The German descent on Finland caused great anxiety for the safety of Murmansk, the only northern Russian port open to British ships during the winter months, which the Supreme War Council had decided on March 23 could not be reinforced. Relations there in early April were not good. On April 1, the War Cabinet were informed of a telegram from Admiral Kemp, asking the British government to give a 'categorical undertaking' to the

Bolshevik government that we had no intention of annexing or occupying the Murmansk region, 'provided that the political status of the region remained unchanged'. The reason given was that the local Russians were suspicious of Allied intentions, 'and such suspicions make cooperation extremely difficult'.[19] But on April 12, as the Germans arrived at Helsinki, Lockhart wired that Chicherin was willing for the Allies to do all they could to help to defend Murmansk and its railway, and asked them to combine their action with the Murmansk soviet and keep him informed.

This wire, however, had not reached London by the time that the War Cabinet discussed the northern Russian situation on the 12th. It was an anxious meeting. 'The news this morning is bad', wrote the CIGS: 'The danger is Hazebrouck, for if we lose that we must retire our whole left, and we shall lose Dunkirk later. I warned the Cabinet. The other danger is that we cannot any longer make good our losses, and so we are a fast dwindling army. This is desperately serious.' At the request of the First Lord, the Murmansk position was dealt with first. The Admiralty, he stated, proposed to despatch another small cruiser there, and an American cruiser was about to sail; but what further action should be taken was for the War Cabinet to decide. Lord Robert Cecil explained that the Finns apparently wanted the port and adjoining coast, and the pro-German Finnish White Guards might move against the Murmansk railway; which would create a serious situation, against which provision must be made. 'Should troops under German influence seize Kem, this would have disagreeable results for us in the White Sea.' (It would, in fact, cut the Murmansk railway half-way to Petrograd and the overland route from Murmansk to Archangel.) A wire from Admiral Kemp was then read out, recounting the defensive measures at present possible with the available forces at Murmansk, but advising that if the thaw continued it would interrupt the Finnish operations. So far, his only definite information was of skirmishes between Finnish Red and White Guards west of Kandalaksha, the small port between Murmansk and Kem, on the southern shore of the Kola peninsula.[20]

Murmansk, it was pointed out to the War Cabinet, was (assuming that Odessa was lost to Russia) the last ice-free port on Russian territory with access to the open sea. If we tried to save it from the Finnish White Guards, we could reasonably expect the goodwill of both the Murmansk soviet and the Bolshevik government. Such action, therefore, could not be construed in the same way as the recent Japanese interference at Vladivostok. The case, in fact, could be treated in isolation from Allied military policy in the Far East. Sudden action, however, was to be deprecated; and Lord Robert Cecil undertook to send Lockhart beforehand a full explanation of any action that we might decide on. The defence of the Murmansk approaches offered no great military difficulties, and General Poole's paper indicated all that was required. (This was based on his previous paper of

March 15, written while on board ship, which was shown to Colonel Byrne on the 25th and approved by the Russia Committee on April 4, when he agreed to head a British military mission to Russia; the Russia Committee 'unanimously' agreeing that Lockhart, 'should he remain in Russia', become subordinate to Poole and simply his political adviser). However, Poole (the War Cabinet minutes state) recommended an immediate landing, and this was more than could at present be agreed.

The War Cabinet decided that the Admiralty should make all preparations for the action recommended by Poole, so that Admiral Kemp could cope with the emergency when it arose; and that the Foreign Office meanwhile should make every effort to obtain Bolshevik consent beforehand.[20]

The Assistant Cabinet Secretary, Thomas Jones, gives a more interesting account of this discussion on Russian policy — such discussions always being 'of a most inconclusive character', he remarks, because Lord Milner and Lord Robert Cecil 'utterly disbelieve' in Trotsky, whilst the Prime Minister 'holds that there is something to hope from Trotsky and the Bolsheviks'.

Lord Milner: At Vladivostok, you were threatening to take something from Russia. At Murmansk, you are saving a port for the Russians, and the local Soviet will welcome your help.
Prime Minister: I fear that we are treating the Bolshevik government as though it were no government. Under the old régime, you would not have gone to Murmansk and Vladivostok without the Tsar's permission. You are out for the same policy as during the French Revolution: seizing Toulon, and one place after another.
General Smuts: Should we not get the consent of the Russian government?
Lord Robert Cecil: I agree, but ought we to delay so long as to allow time for the Germans and Finns to get there?
Lord Milner: You want the force there to act if wanted.

(Here there is evidently some gap in the account.)

Lord Milner: Can we test Trotsky? We want to hold the [Murmansk] railway for Russia. If he says no, then we can wash our hands of him.
Prime Minister: You cannot put a proposition in that way to any country. Our first and proper attitude is that laid down by the Foreign Secretary: 'Deal with the *de facto* government, whether it is Tsarist or Bolshevik.'
Lord Milner: I have not put it in diplomatic language, as I am not a diplomatic agent to Trotsky. Is it not reasonable to tell Trotsky: there is a danger of this port being taken by his enemies and ours, and as we are going to cooperate, would he object to our holding the port? If he says 'No, I would rather you did not interfere,' then I should draw my own conclusions.

Prime Minister: Why not have our ships there with troops, and in case of danger we could land our troops?[20]

This, claims Thomas Jones, was — with some modification — the agreement reached.

When the War Cabinet considered the Archangel situation, their attention was at once drawn both to Joint Note 20 by the military representatives at Versailles, dated April 8, and the minutes of their meeting on March 23 to discuss a military expedition to Archangel, whose 'conclusion was that the minimum requisite force was not available'. The CIGS emphasized that this was part of the general military problem in the eastern theatre, which must be regarded as a whole. The main thing was to get the Japanese to move. This, Lord Robert Cecil remarked, could not be done without American consent, which did not appear to be forthcoming, save on one condition, namely by Russian invitation. As the *de facto* Russian government was Bolshevik, all Britain could at present do was to urge Trotsky by every means in our power to see the problem as we saw it and help us solve it. 'Though there might not be a great hope of success, no other course was open to us.'

Attention was then drawn to the unsatisfactory state of Allied representation in Russia. The despatch of a British high commissioner, to coordinate the various consulates, missions and political agents, was stated to be receiving the Foreign Office's consideration. It was further agreed that a full review of the whole case had not as yet been placed before the American and Bolshevik governments. The War Cabinet agreed that Balfour and the CIGS should draft a despatch for the War Cabinet's consideration, which would be sent to President Wilson, 'grouping all the isolated propositions and presenting a general scheme of policy for dealing with the eastern situation', with a view to its subsequent presentation to Trotsky via Lockhart.

Once again, a more pertinent account of this discussion is given by Thomas Jones. It began by the First Lord requesting to be told definitely what British policy was towards Archangel. The CIGS stated that Archangel was part of the Russian problem, and that problem was one problem: namely, how to prevent the Germans transferring more divisions from Russia to the western front.

CIGS: This place [Archangel] will belong to us or to the Boche. There is no more chance that Russia will have a military force that will bother the Germans in this war. I think the Japs should come to the Urals, and we should take energetic action. Unless we do that, we shall see division after division going to the West, to Hazebrouck, to Calais.
Prime Minister: What more can we do with America hostile?
Lord Robert Cecil: I fear America is hostile. Having definitely made up our

minds that we cannot act without America, the only way to do it is to try via Trotsky, but I am a heretic, for I don't believe in Trotsky.

Prime Minister: No, I am the only heretic in this room.

CIGS: I don't believe or disbelieve.

Lord Robert Cecil: I would press the questions of Murmansk, Armenia, Caucasus, the Poles, and ask Trotsky, why are you always on the side of Germany? I would push Trotsky to the utmost.

Lord Curzon: Lockhart is with Trotsky; we have Wardrop at Moscow; Woodhouse at Petrograd; we have other ambassadors at Vologda.... Our representation in Russia is chaotic.

Prime Minister: I am impressed that the men on the spot are all on one side.

Lord Milner: Poole thinks the Bolsheviks can be led.

Prime Minister: Could the Japs march to the Urals? Semenov has turned up with 300 'coolie brigands': these have to go on to Lake [Baikal], where he will then have 50 more! That is how you are going to prevent twenty German divisions going to Hazebrouck! America is sending divisions to the western front. I shall be surprised if we don't get 300,000 [American] infantry. Better a certain American support than a doubtful Japanese support.

The Prime Minister then instructed the CIGS to gather all these propositions together for presentation to President Wilson; and then, with his support, to Trotsky.

Lord Milner: Lockhart does not keep our end up with Trotsky.

Lord Robert Cecil: He is a very young man where everybody is a little mad.[20]

The gist of the Prime Minister's thinking was clear: 'Better a certain American support than a doubtful Japanese support.' Lloyd George was not going to jeopardise the despatch of American troops to France by trying to force President Wilson to agree to something that he knew he disliked, namely the unleashing of Japanese troops into Siberia. The Prime Minister, it would seem from Jones's account, had a more realistic view of the possibilities in Siberia than did his military advisers.

On April 13, a wire from Macalpine reached London via Archangel — which had taken six days in transit; by now, in fact, delays in communications were seriously affecting the despatch of orders and reports between London and Moscow. 'Movement of metals has begun', stated Macalpine, 'and an increasing number of trucks are daily being despatched. [This probably referred to Archangel.] ... It is now quite certain that pressure must be brought to bear through the central government on the metal committee.' He was going next day to Petrograd to see Lessing about it.

Colonel Byrne replied on Poole's behalf the same day: 'Communicate with Lockhart and request him to assist in every possible way. See the metal committee with Lessing and try to arrange to stop the despatch of metals.'

Two days later (the 15th), there arrived an important telegram from Poliakov, the financial adviser to the British mission, who had negotiated the Russian and Siberian bank deals for the War Cabinet, who was completely trusted and who had wide-ranging contacts. This was a message from 'influential friends in Russia' and deserves to be quoted in full.[21]

> We have nailed up our flag to the mast and will do more than our duty, but where is England! England as a great power does not exist here at the present moment. We see only small disconnected shows working without a general directing policy against each other. The present rulers, by whom an infamous peace has been concluded and who continue to execute all Germany's boundless enactions, still continue to find favour with you. They are approaching political extinction, but you continue to count with their real or imaginary susceptibilities. The military situation is hopeless because no nation is backing the central government which is working in a vacuum. Whilst the German victor gets all the desired financial, economical and political rights from the present rulers, the Allies are graciously permitted to prop up a party despotism, already dead as mutton, for a few months longer. And this for the mirage of a new army formation which at best is smoke, and more probably of German provocation! The northern route is the only loophole left; it is as yet not organised, no mobile police have been provided, nor has the consular staff been strengthened. Nothing in reason has been done to enlighten public opinion. We earnestly advise the immediate creation of a central directing representative with a clear, absolutely national and openly avowed policy, and ceasing all considerations of susceptibilities real or imaginary. In short, an embassy to the Russian nation and not to a lifeless corpse. Men's lives have paid in France for mistakes already committed here. The beginning of the great battle for the Russian raw stuff will last for years and England must not let herself be beaten from the beginning.[21]

There was a good deal of truth in all this, despite the exaggeration and rodomontade; and it was above all what many people in London wanted to believe. A contrary view, however, came from Lockhart. He noted in a wire on April 11 that the Bolsheviks were the only real power in Russia, whether a great number of Russians liked it or not. They were not pro-German; but as opportunists, they would certainly deal with Germany, or anyone else, if the Allies forced them to. But Allied intervention was opposed by every class of Russian, as the outcry over the recent Japanese landing showed. If intervention was vital, Bolshevik consent was crucial, and might still be obtained if the Japanese marines were promptly withdrawn. But Allied support of Ataman Semenov had also greatly annoyed the Bolsheviks; and Allied exaggeration of the danger from armed enemy prisoners in Siberia had been self-deceptive. Japan could not guarantee to get her troops to European Russia, without which it was difficult to see what advantage would result from a Japanese occupation of Siberia.[22]

This telegram was presumably in Balfour's possession when he wired to Lockhart on the 13th to acknowledge Trotsky's various requests for information about possible Allied military support (requests which were always much more tentative than the War Cabinet ever imagined). In what Balfour considered an important despatch (no. 65), he stated emphatically that there must first be agreement on general policy between Trotsky and the British government before any detailed scheme of military assistance could be advantageously discussed. This policy, which should guarantee that Russia would wage war against Germany by land, by sea and by economic means, must include an invitation for Allied intervention in Siberia, under firm Allied guarantees for the future protection of Russian independence. Such an invitation might be accepted, and might save Russia, if Trotsky could be relied on to play his part. As the great German attack continued in France, Balfour, in fact, took a much harder line with Trotsky.

News reached London of Lenin's order of April 7 to the Vladivostok soviet, instructing them to remove military stores and metals. This, coupled with Macalpine's wire, which had arrived (after six days) telling of the removal of metals (presumably from Archangel) caused — or perhaps was the excuse for — Balfour to send an even stronger wire (no. 68) to Lockhart on the 15th. Such action, stated the Foreign Secretary, compelled us to believe that the Bolsheviks wished to quarrel with the Allies. Trotsky was therefore to be informed that unless he accepted the general policy outlined in Balfour's wire no. 65 within fourteen days (i.e. by May 1) the British government would be forced to reconsider their attitude towards the Bolshevik government.[22]

Some of the reasons behind this ultimatum are to be found in a despatch sent by Balfour that evening to Lord Reading in Washington, which the Foreign Secretary and the CIGS had been instructed to draw up for the War Cabinet on April 12 in the form of a note for President Wilson's approval, and subsequent presentation to Trotsky — presumably before May 1. In a comprehensive survey of all the arguments making for immediate intervention in the Far East, the despatch detailed the following points:

1. British military anxiety at the uninterrupted transfer of German troops from Russia to France, which could only be checked by the creation of an important and pro-Allied force in Russia.

2. The great risk that the Germans would obtain every sort of supply from Siberia, to say nothing of the vast accumulation of military stores at Vladivostok, Archangel, Petrograd and Moscow.
3. The threat to India through Persia and Turkestan (which argument can habe been of little interest to President Wilson, but shows the extent to which this despatch was based on Joint Note 20).
4. The danger lest continued chaos in Russia should drive its victims into German arms.

Balfour continued: 'Our military advisers are unanimous in thinking that we cannot hope to set up at the present moment any military force in Russia which would be really effective, at any rate by Russian effort alone, and unless such a force exists, it is impossible to carry out any of the main purposes of our policy.' Even if the Bolshevik government could, by its own efforts, create a new army, it was highly unlikely to be used against the Germans. Their objective was a world-wide social revolution, not a national military victory, and they might well think that this objective could more easily be obtained by encouraging peaceful German penetration than by resisting German arms.

Small Allied forces landing at Archangel and Murmansk might do something, but very little, to ease a situation which could only be saved by Allied intervention from the Far East — and there were large sections of the Russian people, claimed Balfour (relying on messages from Russia like those of Poliakov), who were passionately anxious for such Allied intervention to save them from Germany. Lord Reading was to invite the American government to try, through Colonel Raymond Robins, to induce the Bolshevik government to assent to such intervention, and to say that Lockhart had similar instructions.[22]

Balfour had set May 1 as the date for his ultimatum to Trotsky to expire, as he had learnt through secret channels that an anti-Bolshevik coup in Petrograd and Moscow was timed for May Day.

3

The Russian opposition and the Czechs

Early in 1918, the main non-Bolshevik political groupings in Moscow were led by the SR President, Victor Chernov (former chairman of the constituent assembly, in which the SRs had had a large majority), who had remained in Moscow with his SR central committee; and by Krivoshein (the former Minister of Agriculture, and a right cadet), who had organized all the Cadets and other moderate elements, into the 'Moscow Centre'. But after Brest–Litovsk, and the great German attack in France, which seemed to herald a possible German victory, these groupings split up. The 'Moscow Centre' fragmented into three separate new groups. The right Cadets favoured the German 'orientation', founded the 'Right Centre', and the Cadet leader, Milyukov, travelled to Kiev to try to negotiate with the Germans. The main body of the Cadets remained pro-Ally, and formed the 'National Centre', linking themselves to General Alexeiev in southern Russia. The left Cadets managed to attract the right SRs, and formed the 'Left Centre'. While Chernov and his central committee still remained in Moscow, the main body of SRs assembled in the Volga–Urals area, where they had strong local support, to raise an armed force to attack the Bolsheviks. The left SRs were already carrying on brisk guerilla warfare against the Germans in the Ukraine, where they enjoyed strong local support from the peasantry, in an attempt to re-open the war; they were being helped by a British agent, Captain George Hill, who was also giving covert support to the Bolsheviks.

These new groups were just forming when Savinkov (former War Minister under Kerensky, and an experienced revolutionary), returned to Moscow from the Don, where Kornilov had had enough of him, and had sent him north to recruit officers and send them down to southern Russia. Moscow at this time was flooded with former officers. But there was no capable military leader to consolidate either them or the various political groups, some of which were trying to form a military force to overthrow the Bolsheviks in Moscow, while others were trying to send officers to the Urals to re-open the eastern front and attack the Bolsheviks from that quarter, and others trying to send officers down to the Don. Then there was the question of Allied or German 'orientation'. Savinkov, amidst this *mêlée*, decided to form his own secret society, which he called the 'Union for the Defence of the Fatherland and Freedom', and began to organize all available officers and cadets into army units to prepare for an armed rising, involving plans to assassinate Lenin and Trotsky. Initially, he considered allying his group with the 'Left Centre'. By mid-April, Savinkov's group seemed to observers in Moscow the most likely to make good. But the problem remained of bringing the various political groups together and of properly organizing all the officers in Moscow; Savinkov's group only comprised a relatively small number.

It seems (according to a German report of a fortnight later and an official Cheka statement published six weeks later), that both the SR leader, Chernov, and Krivoshein had been induced to give some sort of support to Savinkov's group in Moscow, and to the military commander in Petrograd, in planning a coup to overthrow the Bolsheviks on May 1, and then to attack the Germans in Finland or Estonia. These conspirators were understood to have the support of Allied agents, and Savinkov was preparing to bribe the Latvian commanders in Moscow, on whose regiments Trotsky still mainly relied while hastily forming a Red Army, to seize the Bolshevik leaders.[1] (The Latvians were doubtless told that Latvia was to be freed from the hated Germans as well.)

But for this operation, especially the latter part, these conspirators would need further substantial support; in fact the whole operation needed additional military bolstering.

On April 17, the First Sea Lord presented a paper to the War Cabinet on the Murmansk position, with special reference to Finnish designs on the Murman coast. The First Lord urged that Admiral Kemp should be informed of Allied policy towards Murmansk for guidance in any action he might have to take, and should be authorized to give the assurances outlined in his wire of the 15th, namely that the Allies had no intention of annexing the Murmansk region and would provide the local people with food and supplies. Balfour agreed. The First Lord went on to say that no military operations, other than guerilla warfare, would be possible in the area of the Kola inlet (which it was feared that the Germans might use as a submarine base) until the end of the thaw. He urged that a military expert be sent out to Murmansk to report, jointly with Admiral Kemp, on the general situation, in the event of it being possible to despatch a military force at a later date to cooperate with the Allied naval forces at present there.[2] Reference was then made to Lockhart's wire of the 12th (which stated that Chicherin was willing for the Allies to help defend Murmansk and the Murmansk railway, only asking them to combine their action with the Murmansk soviet, and keep him informed). This, the War Cabinet agreed, 'indicated that M. Trotsky was now in favour of our cooperation'. The Cabinet decided that Balfour and the First Lord should wire to Lockhart 'agreeing on broad lines' to Admiral Kemp's requests, and that the Admiralty should give similar instructions to Kemp himself. Thus, the local Murmansk people were to be assured that the Allies would provide them with food and supplies and would not annex their territory. The Cabinet also agreed that the War Office should send an officer as soon as possible to report on the situation, with special reference to the possibility of holding the Kola inlet and the force necessary to do this; and that his report should, in due course, come before the Cabinet. Now, these moves were all very well, but did little, in practical terms, to prepare resistance to a possible large-scale guerilla attack by German or Finnish forces.[2]

The War Cabinet then turned their attention to Archangel. The First Lord stated that two British supply ships, together with an armed icebreaker, had been sent there to barter stores and generally get on good terms with the local inhabitants, 'who were at present indifferent to political affairs and only wished to be fed and left to pursue peaceful avocations'. This was indeed misleading the Cabinet. The supply ships were indeed to barter the food on board, but in return for the local inhabitants handing back the Allied military stores to the British, preventing the Bolsheviks transporting them (by rail) into the interior. Of course, the unarmed locals could not prevent armed Bolshevik detachments from doing this, and the supply ships, which reached Archangel in mid-April, never discharged their food, but anchored downstream from the town and waited.

Balfour stressed that the Archangel position differed from that at Murmansk, because Archangel was involved in the general Russian situation, and in Allied intervention through Siberia. (This point had been made earlier by the CIGS in the War Cabinet on April 12, in relation to Joint Note 20, which concluded that there were no troops available for a military expedition to Archangel.) Pending a settlement of the Russian situation, 'it was felt that it might be possible' (state the Cabinet minutes) to persuade Trotsky to agree to the Czech force (now at Kursk and on its way out of Russia via the Far East) being used in the Archangel or Murmansk districts to prevent German or Finnish forces making encroachments into Russian territory. (There is no indication of who made this crucial suggestion, though it may have been Balfour.) Such approval by Trotsky, it was pointed out, 'would go some way to establish his honesty of purpose' towards the Allies — a subject which had already received favourable comment during the previous discussion on Murmansk. At this, Balfour drew the War Cabinet's attention to his wire of April 13 to Lockhart (no. 65), which set out British policy towards Russia (and to which Trotsky had to agree before any detailed scheme of British military support for the Bolsheviks could be discussed, but this is not mentioned in the Cabinet minutes

51

either). Balfour, however, made no mention to the Cabinet of his subsequent wire (no. 68) to Lockhart, giving Trotsky an ultimatum — that he must accept this British proposal within fourteen days, or British policy towards the Bolshevik government would be radically reconsidered.

The War Cabinet then requested the War Office to give particulars of the Czech force to Balfour to enable him to wire to Lockhart, directing him to urge Trotsky to authorize the use of the Czech force in the Archangel and Murmansk districts 'for the protection of Russian as well as Allied interests'. This body of élite troops, certainly the best of the small forces in Russia that had kept their cohesion during the revolutionary upheavals, would of course prove invaluable, like the Latvians, for the success of the May 1 *coup*, and the subsequent attack on the Germans in Finland or Estonia.[2]

The War Cabinet next considered the Black Sea Fleet. The previous day, the DMI had shown the Cabinet on a map the extent of the German advance into the Ukraine, and pointed out that they were now some seventeen miles east of Kharkov and were drawing near to the Donetz basin. There were now 37 German divisions in Russia, he stated (Joint note No. 20 has stated that there were 47 divisions.) The First Lord informed the War Cabinet that Captain Cromie, the British naval attaché, had reported that the Bolshevik government had made a request for British help in reorganizing the Black Sea Fleet, 'which pointed to the likelihood of the Bolsheviks asking generally for Allied assistance'. This, coupled with Trotsky's apparently favourable attitude to British action at Murmansk, seemed to augur well for a favourable response in the matter of the Czechs. As it was known that Ataman Semenov's attacks on the local Bolsheviks on the Russian–Chinese border had been causing acute irritation in Moscow (where Semenov was known to have some British support), the question was now raised in the War Cabinet whether Lockhart was aware 'that we had given instructions that General Semenov was — for the time being, at all events — to cease his activities in eastern Siberia'. Balfour undertook to look into the matter, and inform Lockhart as necessary, if this had not already been done. British plans were maturing either for imminent cooperation with the Bolsheviks, or for an imminent *coup* to oust them from power.[3]

Before proceeding further, it is necessary to consider several interrelated issues: the position of the Czech force in Russia, that of Ataman Semenov, and that of the armed enemy prisoners in Siberia.

The Czechoslovak force in Russia comprised the various Czechs and Slovaks who had been living there since before the war, together with the many Czech and Slovak soldiers in the Austro–Hungarian army, who had either been taken prisoner or had deserted to Russia — sometimes whole regiments had come over — refusing to fight their brother Slavs. The Tsarist High Command had used this efficient, and constantly expanding, little force mainly for reconnaissance work. In May 1917, Professor Thomas

Masaryk, the future president of Czechoslovakia, had come to Russia to arrange for their transfer to the western front. The final disintegration of the old Russian army and the Bolshevik *coup* made Masaryk redouble his efforts to get the Czech Corps (or Legion), which now comprised two full divisions, out of Russia. But the situation was so uncertain that he could not conclude any final agreement with the Bolsheviks before the Treaty of Brest–Litovsk.

In Paris, Dr Eduard Benes ran the Czechoslovak National Council for Masaryk. It was Benes, Czechoslovakia's future Foreign Minister, who negotiated an agreement with the French Government on December 16, 1917, whereby the Czechs, both in Russia and Italy, were recognized as an autonomous Allied army under the direction of the French High Command, with the understanding that the Czech Legion in Russia would be evacuated to France as quickly as possible; the details were to be left to Benes, Masaryk and the French military mission in Russia.[4]

As already mentioned, the first British report on the Czech Corps was made by Major Fitzwilliams on December 12, 1917, when he was sent to make an initial investigation for the War Cabinet on the prospects of the Don Cossacks at their capital of Novocherkask. Of all the little organiz-ations then milling around in southern Russia, he reported, 'I consider the Czech organization the best and the most likely to lead to the possible formation of a strong government. Reasons as follows: The Czechs know that they sink or swim with Russia; therefore they are more likely to take an unbiased view of the situation, and not to be prejudiced by the claims of any one party. They are also the possessors of two well-equipped and well-disciplined divisions, which is more than any other party can [lay] claim to. Lastly, their organization is the best and their leaders are cleverer and more hardworking than the Russians.'[5] This good report, which mainly concen-trated on the inefficiency of the Don Cossacks, probably did not reach London until about January 18. Both Fitzwilliams and Picton Bagge (the British consul-general in Kiev) now began to give financial support to the Czechs. General Alexeiev (Commander of the volunteer army) had sent the Czech Colonel Kral to try to get the two Czech divisions, then in the Ukraine, sent to the Don; but this was unlikely to be done, Major Fitzwil-liams reported to the CIGS early in January: 'After consultation with [the French General] Tabouis, I have arranged to finance Kral with 10,000 roubles a week for passing selected officers to the Don to join Alexeiev.' Picton Bagge at this time also gave the Czechs 20,000 roubles by way of a political donation; and at the request of the French mission, handed £80,000 to Professor Masaryk.

The War Cabinet did not consider the position of the Czech Legion until February 8, when the CIGS read out a draft wire to General Foch, urging that all available Polish troops, together with the two Czech divisions, should be brought up to protect Roumania from a German out-flanking move. On the 11th, the Cabinet were told that Foch had had to turn this proposal down.[6] Although the Czech National Council had given General Berthelot, head of the French military mission in Roumania, freedom of action to make such use as he thought best of the Czech Legion, he had so far been unable to move them to the Roumanian front, as the Ukrainian Rada wanted to retain this disciplined force.

By February, the Czechs were in a very awkward position. The Ukrainian Rada had just made peace with the common enemy, and their capital, Kiev, was just falling to invading Bolshevik forces from Russia. When the Germans resumed their advance into the Ukraine, they moved very quickly, and the Czechs, in their hasty retreat, were nearly cut off. They found themselves fighting alongside local Bolshevik troops. On February 10, the Czechs concluded a local armistice with the Bolshevik commander in the Ukraine. On the 16th, he agreed to the evacuation of the Czech Legion to France via the Far East.[7]

But Czech morale, already poor, was worsening. Though they remained a compact, disciplined and democratic force amongst the general disintegration and chaos, and felt a deep sense of gratitude to Russia, heightened by the achievements of the Russian Revolution, their desire to get out of Russia to help found a democratic Czechoslovak state was being undermined by the Bolshevik revolutionary 'virus' and the demoralization felt by those who had spent long years in the prisoner-of-war camps in Siberia and elsewhere. Their senior officers, as decreed by the Tsarist authorities, remained Russian. It was they who told Masaryk on February 17 of the general moral decay and increasing influence of the left wing in the Legion. He did not have much time to do anything about it. The next day, he concluded an agreement with the French military mission about the evacuation; the Czechs were to leave for France via Vladivostok and avoid all interference in Russian affairs while *en route*; in fact, they were to remain strictly neutral. They were only to oppose those forces which had openly allied themselves with Germany or Austria. On the 20th, however, when orders were issued for the Czech Legion to leave, Masaryk modified his instructions by adding that the Czechs were to defend themselves energetically, if attacked by any Russian or Slav force while crossing Russia or Siberia. Early in March, Masaryk himself went on ahead to Vladivostok (in a train commandeered for him by Major Fitzwilliams), and thence to America and Europe, to arrange for the necessary shipping to take the Czechs to Europe. (As Masaryk remained for some while in America, he virtually passes out of the picture at this point.)

By the first half of March, the Czech Legion was having to fight sharp little battles around Kiev and at Bakhmach (to the north-east) to prevent themselves being cut off by the rapidly advancing Germans, to whom they also sent emissaries to parley — and from the arrogant attitude shown them by the local German command, the Czechs quickly saw that they could expect no mercy from them. But they managed to jump clear. These minor engagements, which did much to raise Czech morale and confidence in their officers, also showed them how futile the Red Guards were when faced by regular troops. Though often heavily armed, they only retaliated once when attacked, and then fled; 'boy-scouts', the Czechs called them, 'a sort of burglars' army'.[7]

Masaryk had left political affairs in the hands of two young Czechs: Klecanda, a young Russian-speaking secretary, and Maxa, an ex-schoolmaster, who had just emerged from a prisoner-of-war camp in Turkestan. They were both unsuited to cope with the difficulties which a long journey through revolutionary Russia and Siberia entailed — and made the fatal error of trying to negotiate the details of the evacuation, in a fast-moving situation with bad communications, at one and the same time, with two widely separated bodies. While Klecanda went up to Petrograd and then to Moscow (thus cutting himself off from the Legion) to negotiate with the Bolshevik government, Maxa was at Kursk, where the Czechs were now arriving, conducting local negotiations with the Bolshevik commander of their southern front, Antonov-Ovseenko. In Moscow, where the Brest Treaty was about to be ratified, Klecanda was successful. On March 15, the Bolsheviks, in the person of Stalin, gave permission for the Czech Legion to move off into Siberia: they evidently feared such a well-disciplined body of men too near Moscow, and too near the pro-Allied forces in European Russia, who might tamper with its loyalty at this crucial moment. But in Kursk on the 16th, Maxa — out of touch with his colleague in Moscow — came to a different arrangement with the local Bolsheviks, who reproached the Czechs for abandoning the German front and leaving them, badly armed, to cope with the common enemy on their own. Maxa, under the terms of a local and vaguely worded agreement, handed over much of their artillery, armoured cars and machine guns to the Bolsheviks, who publicly thanked the Czechs for their 'brotherly gifts'.

The Czech trains rolled eastwards. But on March 22 at Penza (west of Samara on the Volga), the head of the local soviet ordered all Czech trains to be stopped and the Czechs to be disarmed. The reason given was that Antonov-Ovseenko had wired from Kursk that the Czechs had violated their local agreement with him by hiding some of their arms, and the Czechs had also been behaving provocatively towards local Russians and Bolsheviks at Penza. When Klecanda heard of this in Moscow, he at once went to Trotsky, now Commissar for War, who was openly suspicious of Czech intentions in the Far East — they might join Ataman Semenov, who was causing much trouble by blocking the Chinese Eastern Railway, and forcing the Bolsheviks to use the much longer Amur line to Vladivostok. Klecanda lost his temper, but this cut no ice with Trotsky. On the 24th, at Penza, the Russian general commanding the second Czech division marched into the office of the head of the local soviet with an armed escort and threatened to hang him if he would not release the Czech trains. Maxa strongly disagreed with this approach. Next day, he proposed, with another Russian general's backing, to hand over most of the remainder of the Czech arms in return for a free passage to the Far East. This proposal (which caused considerable dissension amongst the Czechs at Penza) was wired to Moscow, where Klecanda was threatening Trotsky even without an armed escort. Stalin replied accepting most of Maxa's proposals, but imposing conditions of his own; the 'reactionary' Russian officers were to be dismissed from the Czech Legion, which was to be disarmed (retaining only a few rifles and a machine-gun on each train) and to proceed to Vladivostok as a group of free citizens. Trotsky then showed Maxa's proposals to Klecanda, who abruptly left Moscow on hearing such extraordinary news; he died soon afterwards of pneumonia. At Penza, the Czechs handed over more of their arms (though still concealing a good number) and some of their Russian officers; and then continued their journey east. Thus, by late March, there was already considerable suspicion and mistrust between Bolsheviks and Czechs; despite the difficulties inherent in a rapidly-changing situation, the initial mistake seems to have been the Czechs' — for conducting simultaneous negotiations both in Moscow and on the spot through two different people, who failed to inform each other of the results.

The Bolshevik attitude, and especially Trotsky's, to the Czechs during late March was perhaps conditioned by parallel French negotiations with both parties. On March 18, General Lavergne (the French military attaché in Moscow) wired to the French War Ministry in Paris saying that the Czechs were now on their way to Vladivostok and urged that French Consuls along the route should be warned and shipping be provided. Foch replied on the 21st, the day of the great German attack — which suggests that Lavergne's nws was considered vital. Foch, anxious to take up a possible Bolshevik request for Allied support against the Germans, first answered an earlier telegram from Lavergne stating that the Bolsheviks were apparently impressed with Czech efforts at the battle of Bakhmach in the Ukraine and were thinking of retaining them in Russia for use as the nucleus of a new Russian army. Foch now supported this Bolshevik proposal; as the Czechs could be used on the spot, shipping was not so urgent. In fact, there was no shipping available. If the Czech Legion could not be used in Russia, Foch's staff wrote to French GHQ on the 22nd, it should be sent by rail to Vladivostok. France was at present negotiating with Japan for Japanese ships to remove the unreliable and mutinous Russian troops at Salonika, and if these negotiations were successful, the ships could transport the Czechs from Vladivostok to Europe before proceeding to Salonika. But as these negotiations would take some while to conclude, it was not yet time to concentrate all the Czechs in the Far East.[8]

In Moscow, Trotsky asked Lavergne (via Jacques Sadoul, France's unofficial agent to the Bolshevik government) whether, in the event of a further German offensive on the Russian front, he could stop the Czech exodus. Lavergne went to see Čermak, another Czech representative in Moscow, reporting the result of his meeting to Clemenceau on the 23rd, i.e. before news that local Bolsheviks had halted the Czechs at Penza reached Moscow. The First Czech Corps, reported Lavergne, was definitely going to France and any rerouting back to the West through Siberia would undermine Czech morale. But the Second Czech Corps, which was still under formation at Omsk in Siberia, could be used on the Russian front. Lavergne urged that the First Czech Corps be evacuated, as arranged. 'It would be very difficult to reroute the First Corps to Vologda to defend there the Allied embassies against the [Bolshevik] Russians alongside whom it has just fought [i.e. in the Ukraine].' The Second Corps, Lavergne added, could be used in Russia, provided it was not asked to engage in too much fighting against the Bolsheviks. The presumption must be that Clemenceau had suggested that the Czechs should be used to defend the Allied embassies at Vologda against the Bolsheviks. Evidently Lavergne did not tell all this to Trotsky, who asked whether the Czechs would support the Bolsheviks if Germany made a further attack. News must then have reached Moscow that the local soviet had stopped the Czechs at Penza.[8]

Clemenceau, who very much wanted the Czech troops on the western front, was also envisaging the possible failure of the negotiations to obtain Japanese shipping at Vladivostok. On March 24, however, the head of the French military mission at Murmansk, in answer to a query from Clemenceau, wired that he was against rerouting the Czechs and shipping them from Archangel or Murmansk. Even if the Bolsheviks permitted them to be rerouted, which was unlikely, the Czechs would be unable to hold the two northern ports, if attacked by the Germans in any force. Unless the Czechs were removed via the Far East, the Bolsheviks would certainly undermine their morale; the Czech Legion, in fact, was not considered entirely reliable. Thus, two reports reached Paris in fairly swift succession, indicating that the Czech Legion was not such a reliable force as was generally imagined. About this time, the French consul in Moscow received orders from Paris to start financing the Czechs in Russian roubles — up till now they had existed wholly on Russian money and supplies; but it remains unclear when and if the Czechs ever received any of this French money.[8]

By now the British also had become interested in the Czech Legion. On March 21, presumably under the influence of Lockhart's wires urging Allied support for the Bolsheviks (and possibly of Major Fitzwilliams's report of mid-December), the Foreign Office sent the War Office a paper on the possible use of the Czechs in Russia. The War Office did not reply until April 1 (evidently seeing no urgency about the matter). It was doubtful if there were as many as 70,000 men in the Czech Legion, stated the

War Ofice; there had only been some 42,000 when the Bolsheviks seized Kiev. They presumed (correctly) that the men were now on the Kursk-Samara railway line, probably without artillery or ammunition, on their way to France via Vladivostok. Trotsky had already asked them to become the nucleus of a new Russian army, but they had refused. (This appears to have been known in London before it was known in Paris.) But as there was no shipping available in the Far East and Czech morale was not good, they would have to remain in Russia for some while. During this time, the DMO suggested, they could either be concentrated near Omsk, where other Czech units were in formation (it is uncertain whether the War Office knew this at this time), or be rerouted to Archangel; or be concentrated in the Trans-Baikal region, for possible support for Ataman Semenov. The DMO favoured the first proposal, as they could then block any hostile action by enemy prisoners-of-war in Siberia; but before deciding what to do, he wished to know what their real military value was. This War Office reply was handed to the French military attaché in London, who forwarded it on April 2 to Clemenceau in Paris.

It is necessary to consider at this point British relations with Ataman Semenov, who was sitting with a small force roughly at the junction of the Siberian and Chinese Eastern Railways. It took the War Cabinet some time to realise that Semenov was little more than a petty war-lord; his anti-Bolshevism lay in this, and nothing else. On February 23, Balfour had wired to the British ambassador in Peking saying that the War Cabinet had decided to finance Semenov by £10,000 per month, and that he was to be given an advance of £20,000 forthwith. On March 4, a wire came from Peking saying that Semenov needed arms as well; permission was requested to give him two howitzers from the Legation guard. This was approved. Meanwhile, Japan (unknown at first to the other Allies) had more or less gained control of Semenov. He received Japanese arms and ammunition; and in mid-March, a party of Japanese gunners and a Japanese captain arrived, with whose 'requests' he was soon complying. At the War Cabinet on March 23, Semenov was still being referred to as a 'moderate'. The Bolsheviks, who knew exactly what Semenov was, were furious at his forays over the frontier and his disruption of the crucial railway traffic and had to bring up more troops to drive him back. They were also genuinely amazed at Britain's continuing support for him while Balfour was assuring Trotsky that she had no counter-revolutionary designs, and indeed wished to support the Bolsheviks as well. Early in April, when the Japanese were again urging Semenov to make further attacks over the border, Lockhart wired to Balfour to underline the Bolsheviks' resentment of Britain's support, which might well jeopardise much more crucial British aims in Moscow.[9]

When the War Office paper of April 1 arrived in Paris, the French at once showed it to Benes, who ran the Czech National Council, which had to have his agreement before making any change in their plans for the Czech Legion. Whatever view may be taken of Benes's subsequent role in this affair — and there are more than one — he was no fool. It is surprising to read in his memoirs that the War Office paper stated that the British favoured the concentration of the Czech Legion in the Trans-Baikal region, for possible support for Ataman Semenov. The War Office paper stated nothing of the sort: it favoured their concentration around Omsk. It is difficult to imagine that both the French and Benes misunderstood the paper, so the possibility remains that the French deliberately altered it before showing it to Benes. Whatever really happened, he and General Alby, the French Chief of Staff, agreed with what he imagined the British choice to be. 'I was against the use of our troops in western Siberia [which was what the War Office actually proposed]. I would only have allowed them to be sent to Archangel if it would have hastened their arrival in France. As regards the possibility of their staying in eastern Siberia [i.e. to support Semenov], I agreed, provided it was only temporary, while they waited for ships.'* Benes writes that this War Office paper has 'historical interest'. It has indeed. It marked, he claims, the start of the military negotiations which later led to political recognition from England and France. It also marked the start of the confusion and misunderstanding between England and France over the Czech Legion, which Benes was happy to exploit, exaggerate and generally confound in order to obtain that political recognition. Not for nothing did Lloyd George later refer to Benes as 'that little French jackal'.[10]

On April 4, the Japanese and British landed at Vladivostok. At this, the Bolshevik government themselves ordered the Czech trains to be halted once more. Both sides became more suspicious of each other. But the recent fighting in the Ukraine, and the realisation that their safe departure from Russia would depend entirely on their own efforts, had done much to increase Czech morale and efficiency, as well as trust in their own officers, some of whom were Russian and very anti-Bolshevik. Somehow news of this upsurge in Czech morale soon reached Paris.

On April 7, General Alby instructed all French officers in Russia to screen the Czechs carefully before embarkation and notify him of any untrustworthy elements. Simultaneously, Clemenceau replied to the War Office paper of the 1st. The French now definitely wanted the Czechs in France, since they obviously could not now be used in Russia. But as negotiations for Japanese shipping had broken down and no French shipping was available, the French would have to rely on British ships.

---

* It should be emphasised that this quotation and those that follow are from E. Benes, *Souvenirs de Guerre et de Revolution* (Paris, 1929). Eng. trans. P. Selver as *My War Memoirs* (London, 1928) is a concise abbreviation of the original text. Whether or not this was deliberately tailored for the English market, it is interesting that in the title the word 'revolution' is omitted. The English translation is also significantly different from the original on various important points concerning the Czech Legion.

Clemenceau argued that the Czechs must be brought to France, but while waiting for the British ships they might be used to support Ataman Semenov; but the final decision could not be taken until the Czechs reached Vladivostok. The British, of course, had never suggested that they be used to support Semenov; and on the 7th, Balfour wired Peking that Semenov was now to be restrained. His force, however, could join in later when Allied intervention in Siberia finally materialized. In Paris the following day, under the terms of Joint Note 20, the French even agreed that the future Japanese force of intervention in Siberia could enjoy the 'eventual assistance of Czech and other elements which can be organized on the spot'. But the French were not sincere; they only wished to humour the British in order to be sure of British ships for 'their' Czechs. It is thus not only Benes who was guilty of confusion. The British believed the French.[11]

On the 9th, Lavergne made matters worse by wiring from Moscow that as the Bolsheviks had again stopped the Czechs moving to the east again because of the Japanese landing at Vladivostok, they should not be rerouted to Archangel. On the 11th, he wired again more fully. Clashes had broken out between the Czech Legion and the Bolshevik authorities and there were continual discussions about their disarmament. Trotsky had given orders that they were to be stopped. But the Czechs realised the danger for them in disarming, and had refused to give up their weapons; and in spite of Trotsky's order, they were continuing their journey eastwards. But it was difficult to know whether, under these conditions, they could actually reach Vladivostok. Lavergne, however, stressed that the Czech Legion definitely wanted to come to France, whatever happened and that their morale was excellent. He again suggested that they be rerouted to Archangel.

It was just now that the intensive Bolshevik recruitment campaigns amongst the prisoner-of-war camps began to show some success. This was especially noticeable in Turkestan and along the Volga (at Saratov, Penza, Samara and Ufa); in the Urals (at Ekaterinburg and Chelyabinsk); and in western Siberia (at Omsk and Tomsk). The Allies, of course, feared that prisoners would be recruited much further east in Siberia, and Captains Hicks and Webster were now in Irkutsk investigating matters.[12]

These recruitment campaigns had a strong effect on the Czechs. When some Bolshevik agitators arrived at Penza, where the Czech trains had been delayed early in April, they set to work to undermine the Czech Legion, set up a party branch in the town, and founded the First Czech International Regiment there. At the railway station, they were given a special coach for propaganda and recruitment and organized meetings from which the Russian and Czech officers were excluded. They also delayed the Czech trains still further. The result was a small handful of Bolshevik recruits, and ever-increasing general antipathy throughout the Czech Legion towards the Bolsheviks. But when the Czechs realised that the Bolsheviks were having success among their bitter enemies, the German and Hungarian prisoners, they became convinced that this was part of a German–Bolshevik conspiracy against them. In fact, they were quite wrong; both the German and Austrian governments strongly protested at this forced recruitment of their men, but the Czechs were very cut off, and mild paranoia — the 'we are surrounded' complex — was very natural. They were indeed surrounded. The Czech troops became convinced, as they sat out the endless delays, that they could only survive the long journey through Siberia if they kept as many of their arms as possible, since many of the Siberian camps ahead of them, they knew, contained many of their bitter enemies — whom the Bolsheviks were now enrolling and arming. The young Czech officers began to make plans. On April 14, the officers of the First Czech Division, which had been delayed longest, passed a unanimous resolution at Kirsanov, west of Penza, not only to refuse to surrender any more arms, but calling for more arms and equipment from the Czech National Council — which of course had none, and urging negotiations with the Bolsheviks. The situation was getting out of hand. But so bad were all communications within Russia that few people in Moscow, let alone in Paris, realized how quickly Czech feelings against the Bolsheviks were hardening.

Lavergne, who was strongly against Allied intervention, presumably knew little of this when he had wired to the French War Ministry on April 11, urging that the Czechs should be rerouted to Archangel, in view of the difficulties they were likely to encounter in Siberia, and the diminishing chance of their actually reaching Vladivostok. But Lavergne's proposal was the occasion, or the pretext, for the French War Ministryu's proposal to the War Office in London on April 16 that, if the British could provide the necessary shipping, the Czechs should be brought to France via Archangel and Murmansk: a much quicker route than via the Far East. While awaiting passage, the Czechs might protect the two northern Russian ports. This was just what the British were looking for: a force, which they themselves could not provide, to protect Archangel and Murmansk after the German descent on Finland; and a force that could provide some real force in the proposed *coup* on May 1 to oust the Bolsheviks from power.[13]

This, then, was the background to the proposal, made during the War Cabinet on April 17 (presumably by Balfour) that, pending a settlement of the Russian problem as a whole (which was taken to include Allied intervention via Siberia), the Czechs might be used in the Archangel or Murmansk districts to prevent German or Finnish forces making encroachments into Russian territory; nothing was said of any French request to ship them to France.[14]

At 3.30 p.m. on the 19th, the War Cabinet had a further discussion on the Russian situation. By now, there had been an addition to the Cabinet. The previous day, Lord Derby had left the War Office and gone as British ambassador to Paris; he was replaced by Lord Milner as Secretary of State for War, and Austen Chamberlain joined the War Cabinet. (Austen was the son of the great Joseph Chamberlain, and half-brother of Neville Chamberlain. He was a firm Tory and had been Chancellor of the Exchequer from 1903 to 1906 and a contender for the leadership of the Tory Party on the resignation of Balfour in 1911; but Bonar Law, the compromise candidate, had won. Chamberlain was a man of great qualities and high principles, 'a fine type: patriotic, unselfish, courageous and indifferent to attacks', records Lord Riddell. He was also totally lacking in inspiration, wooden, irritable and even downright rude to ordinary MPs when they came to consult him. In the higher reaches of politics, his integrity in fact failed him: 'Austen always played the game', said F. E. Smith, 'and he always lost it.'[15])

On the 19th, the First Sea Lord told the War Cabinet that a Chinese cruiser had arrived at Vladivostok on the 17th. *Suffolk* had reported that the Allied Consuls had sent a joint note to the local authorities and the local press stating that the recent landing by Japanese and British marines was purely a police measure and not to be considered hostile to any section of the population, and that the marines would be withdrawn as soon as satisfactory measures had been taken to safeguard Allied property. (In fact, the British marines were soon withdrawn; and the Japanese marines followed suit on April 25.)

The Cabinet then considered a further paper by the First Sea Lord on Archangel. Balfour drew attention to his wire of the 18th to Lockhart about the removal of the Allied stores from Archangel to Vologda, adding that, since the despatch of that telegram, he had been informed by the Russia Supply Committee that this was not true; in fact, articles like flax were being sent towards Archangel. A true grasp of the real situation at Archangel was impossible until accurate information was received. (I have not found such a message; but it illustrates the general muddle about the question of the Allied stores.) The War Cabinet thereupon approved an Admiralty request for the despatch of a cruiser to Archangel to protect Allied interests. The Captain should have wide discretionary powers to deal with any situation that might arise, without previous reference to the Admiralty, if there was not sufficient time; but he could not be authorized to use force to prevent the Bolsheviks transporting any of the Allied stores from the port.[16]

The Prime Minister then raised the question of intervention. He produced Lockhart's wire of April 13 (which had reached London on the 18th), which stated that Trotsky wished the Allied governments to submit to him, at the earliest opportunity, a full and proper statement of the help which they could provide to enable Russia to carry on the war against Germany, and of the guarantees which the Allies would be prepared to give. Trotsky had added that if the conditions were friendly, he considered that the conclusion of such an agreement was both necessary and desirable. (This wire, of course, had crossed Balfour's two crucial wires of April 13 and 15, the first insisting on general agreement between the British and Bolshevik governments on Bolshevik military action against Germany — including a Bolshevik invitation for Allied intervention via the Far East — as a precondition; the second issuing an ultimatum.) Trotsky replied to neither of Balfour's wires. Trotsky's present telegram, it must be stressed, committed the Bolsheviks to absolutely nothing; and said nothing whatever about intervention. It threw the whole onus onto the Allies, whom he knew were in a disagreement on Russian policy and intervention in particular. In fact, it was a clever tactical manoeuvre, designed to delay any such intervention still further, and to give the Bolsheviks, poised between Britain and Germany, a slightly longer breathing space.

Trotsky's request, the Prime Minister continued, indicated a change in his views, and taken in conjunction with other Bolshevik requests, such as for help in reorganizing the Black Sea Fleet, 'pointed to his desire for Allied support'. The Prime Minister stated that our past appeals to the American government could be construed as a desire to impose British assistance on the Bolsheviks. Now we had an opportunity to make a new appeal to President Wilson, based on Trotsky's invitation. Lloyd George had prepared a draft containing definite proposals and summarizing the past suggestions made about Allied intervention. He urged that this should be brought up to date by the inclusion of any further points made by Trotsky in Lockhart's recent telegram, and it should then, after due consideration by Balfour, be despatched to President Wilson. If he agreed to their proposals and guarantees, they should then be forwarded to Trotsky for his consideration. (Hankey thought this move astute: 'The PM has very stubbornly and adroitly resisted the pressure from the Foreign Office and War Office to rush the Japs to "down" the Bolsheviks.')[16]

Balfour (who was 'very "sniffy" about it', records Hankey, no doubt because it would interrupt arrangements for the May 1 coup) felt that if the President did approve, we should also have to consult Japan to see if she would carry out her share of the proposals for intervention. But to save time, we should act before a reply from the French and Italian governments, 'as he was sure that they would heartily welcome any form of Allied intervention which aimed at an advance against Germany and German influence in western Siberia'. It was also suggested that, as telegrams now took five days to reach Russia, Lockhart should be sent a copy of the telegram to President Wilson, so that, if the president did approve, no time would be lost in making representations to Trotsky. Balfour stated that this would be done automatically. The War Cabinet thereupon approved the Prime Minister's proposal.[16]

That evening, therefore, Balfour wired to Lord Reading in Washington, making a further appeal to President Wilson, based on Trotsky's invitation, and backed by fresh military, economic and political arguments. Reading was instructed to enquire if the President would agree to (*a*) a joint Anglo–American proposal to the Bolshevik government for Allied military intervention by a predominantly American and Japanese force; and (*b*) to the despatch of an American technical contingent to the Far East, together with a complete American division. (Balfour, records Hankey, 'eventually sent it beginning: "I am asked by the War Cabinet to send the following" instead of treating it as though it were sent from the whole Government, including FO'.)[17]

On the 20th, Balfour took action on the War Cabinet's decision of the 17th to have the Czech Legion used in the Archangel and Murmansk districts 'for the protection of Russian as well as Allied interests', as the Cabinet minutes stated. The French government took (almost) similar action the same day: there had obviously been consultation between London and Paris. Clemenceau summoned Benes, to whom 'he clearly explained his intentions ... and spoke in flattering terms of our troops in Siberia'. Clemenceau then wired to ask the American government to send ships to Vladivostok; and the British government and French Ministry of Marine to be prepared in due course to send ships to Archangel. He next wired Lavergne in Moscow that the Czech Legion was to be rerouted to Archangel and Murmansk, whence they would be shipped to France. In a note that day to the Quai d'Orsay, Clemenceau underlined that he understood from Lavergne's reports that the Czechs were in very good fighting spirit, and it was vital to bring them to France at once. (Benes, when describing the official French attitude to him at this time, makes clear that he was entirely dependent on the French: 'The French government loyally kept me informed of all news and ideas which came from Russia, and took no important decisions [about the Czech Legion] without discussing the matter with me'; he was also moved to admit that he 'was often in a serious dilemma. ... I had very little direct contact with our army in Russia; we had no telegraph service, and no code.' Benes also makes clear what the general French attitude at this time was towards the Russian situation.[18] Even after the German attack of March 21, he wrote that 'it was firmly believed [in Paris] that a new revolution was imminent [in Russia]. ... No one believed that the Soviet régime would last.') Did the French suspect that the British had ulterior motives in wanting the Czech Legion rerouted?

In London, Balfour wired to Lockhart on the 20th saying that the War Cabinet saw the Czech Legion as the only force in Russia willing to fight the Germans. They were to be rerouted from Siberia to Archangel and Murmansk, and then shipped to France. But neither Balfour nor anyone else took action to provide any ships. In Moscow, things seemed to move with speed. On the 21st, Chicherin wired to the local soviets in Siberia that the Czech trains were again to be stopped. But this order was simply due to Bolshevik fears that the Czechs might link up with Ataman Semenov, who was once again advancing into Russian territory near the junction of the

Siberian and Chinese Eastern Railways, despite recent British orders that he was to be restrained.[18]

This was hardly appreciated in Paris when Wickham Steed, editor of *The Times,* brought Dr Benes along to the British military section of the Supreme War Council on April 22. (This, it seems, was Benes' first official contact with the British.) There were 45,000 Czechs west of the Urals, at Tambov and Samara, some of whom were unarmed, and 20,000 just east of the Urals, at Chelyabinsk, stated Benes. A further six trains, each with about 1,000 men on board, had left Omsk for the Far East on April 14; while an advance guard of two regiments, of some 2,500 men each, were now in the Far East and due at Vladivostok about April 24. This gave a total of some 75,000 Czechs, of whom about 50,000 were armed. 'As soon as prisoners heard that the Czechs were in the neighbourhood, they were leaving their prisoner camps and joining the Czechs. The numbers therefore were likely to increase', Lieutenant-Colonel Stanhope was told. Benes admitted that 75,000 might be a 'somewhat liberal' estimate of the present numbers.[19]

The Russian officers, under whom they had previously fought, had been withdrawn (this was not entirely true), and there were now no Czech officers above the rank of captain. Stanhope reported that 'they would however be quite willing to serve under French or British officers and are well disciplined, reliable and good fighters. The Czechs were not prepared to take any part whatever in the conflicts raging between one section and another of the Russian nation, by whom they had been fed, clothed and armed, and were adamant on this point, but they would fight bitterly against anything that had a tinge of Germanism.'

Such sentiments, of course, admirably suited British designs for the Czechs in northern Russia and Moscow; the Czechs were rapidly realizing that the Bolsheviks had more than a tinge of Germanism themselves. 'Both the French and British governments had wobbled as to whether the Czechs should be asked to continue fighting in Russia', he asserted, 'or whether they should be brought to one of the European battlefields, and if so by which route they should travel.' He concluded: 'Mr Stead proposed, and Dr Benes warmly supported him, that orders should be sent to the Czechs west of the Urals, i.e. 45,000 men, to move north to Archangel, and that the Allies should send food to meet them there and ships to bring them to Europe. Any attempt by Finns or Germans to interfere with the Czechs at Archangel would be bitterly resisted. Orders should be sent promptly, as the prisoners are dribbling east every day.' Colonel Stanhope supported this, and added a rider that Britain should promise to send ships 'within a reasonable period' to fetch the Czechs away from Archangel. It is clear from this document — which was not forwarded for some days to London — that both Colonel Stanhope and Wickham Stead had a very good idea of what the War Cabinet had in mind, but did not know that both the British and French governments had already sent such orders.[19]

At noon on April 22, the War Cabinet met to consider a wire from Lockhart, together with Balfour's draft reply. Lockhart's wire, sent from Moscow on the 15th, and received in London on the 20th, contained a message from Captain Garstin (one of Colonel Byrne's young officers, formerly with Poole's supply mission, and now attached to Lockhart), which stated that, in view of Trotsky's request for a 'definite statement' of the terms on which Allied intervention might be invited by the Bolshevik government, the Allied military representatives had held a meeting on the 14th and decided that the following measures would be desirable:[20]

1. renewal of alliance with Russia;
2. guarantee not to interfere with Russian internal affairs;
3. loyal collaboration with government of soviets;
4. guarantee of integrity of Russian territory;
5. allies shall declare that operating forces will cross Siberia solely in order to reach war zone;
6. troops shall be Allied and not only Japanese;
7. Russia shall be helped on Murman and Archangel railways;
8. cooperation shall be given to Armenia against Turks if desirable.

Kennan points out that Trotsky himself had more or less laid down these conditions — with the exception of nos. 1 and 3 — in late March; adding no. 3 ('loyal collaboration' with the Bolsheviks) on April 7, during a 'long and violent discussion' he had with the Allied military representatives immediately after receiving news of the Japanese landing in the Far East. The Allied officers themselves now appear to have added no. 1 and the final two.

In his draft reply, Balfour cautiously accepted these conditions 'as a basis for discussion'. As far as the British government were concerned, nos. 2, 4 and 6 could be accepted as they stood; so could no. 1, but 'reaffirmation' should be substituted for 'renewal', since we had 'always considered Russia as our Ally'. (But, one may ask, which Russia? The Russia which had died on the Don, or the Russia which had made peace with the Gemans?) Balfour's draft reply went on significantly: 'As no. 3 stands at present, it might in certain conceivable circumstances conflict with no. 2. I therefore prefer "Loyal cooperation with Russian authorities against common enemy". If one assumes that "certain conceivable circumstances" refers to the coming anti-Bolshevik *coup* on May 1 (which was to have some local Allied support), one can easily appreciate that even Balfour might jib at being asked to guarantee both not to interfere in Russia's internal affairs, and to collaborate loyally with the Bolsheviks. He also added: 'In order to give requisite military latitude, no. 5 should be amended as follows: "Allies shall declare that operating forces will cross Siberia solely for the purpose of carrying out military operations against the enemy".' This, perhaps, also has some significance, if the Bolsheviks were considered to be the enemy, or the agents of the enemy. The draft concluded that if no. 7 meant support by Allied warships and marines on board, this was acceptable, but use of troops must be subject to military exigencies. So must acceptance of no. 8. 'We are, however, most anxious to help in both cases.'[20]

The War Cabinet approved the draft reply, subject to Balfour possibly altering no. 4, so as not to imply that we would undertake to recover all the territory which Russia had lost. It then went into closed session to consider a further telegram from Lockhart (which must have been sent on April 15 or 16*) 'in regard to the proposed meeting between M. Trotsky and a representative of the British government in the near future at Murmansk'. Since no such proposal had ever been discussed by the War Cabinet, one may assume that it came from Moscow — but whether directly from Trotsky, or on Lockhart's suggestion, is not clear; however, one must also remember that both Lockhart and the War Cabinet were always more willing to believe that Trotsky wanted Allied support and intervention than was really the case.[21]

The War Cabinet decided that it was desirable that an emissary should go out to discuss the 'reorganization of Russia for military purposes' with Trotsky, and asked General Smuts to do so, and to let them have his reply next day; if he accepted, Balfour was to wire to Moscow to ask if Trotsky would arrange 'to meet a member of the War Cabinet at Murmansk'. It thus appears that the official proposal was to come from London.

The War Cabinet were indeed set on riding two horses. The War Office's view of this decision may be judged by an entry in the diary of Sir Henry Wilson (the CIGS) who attended this War Cabinet. He writes that after lunch on the 22nd, General Niessel (former head of the French military mission in Russia) came to see him: 'He was very interesting. He says Trotsky is a pure revolutionary who cares nothing for any country, including Russia, but a great deal for himself. Absolutely unreliable and without any principles of any sort, and therefore a man to be measured. I sent him to Smuts.' In view of the coming anti-Bolshevik coup, one may well ask if the decision to send out Smuts (probably to counteract the imminent arrival of a German ambassador in Moscow) reflects very well on the War Cabinet, who were, admittedly, now having to face the problem of whether to give up Calais and Boulogne, or break contact with the French army to cover the two Channel Ports — so critical had the situation in France now become.[22]

Smuts did not, in fact, answer the War Cabinet's request the next day, as hoped. There may have been various reasons for this. Probably the main one was that the Germans were in the process of launching another tremendous attack in France, and if the British line were to buckle, all would be lost; hence all minds were concentrated on France.

---

*This wire is Lockhart's no. 99. The previous wire quoted was his no. 96. The communications traffic was fairly heavy at this time; his no. 115, sent on the 21st, arrived on the 25th.

Meanwhile, conflicting advice had been coming from the British supply mission in Russia, now engaged on the crucial task of denying both Allied stores and Russian supplies to the Germans. On April 17, a wire reached London for General Poole which 'influential Russians' wished to have placed before the War Cabinet. This said that the Germans now had a stranglehold on the Bolsheviks, who could offer no resistance and had lost control of the situation. 'All German ultimatums are complied with immediately, whilst the Allies are fed with eloquent promises.' Now the Germans were about to sign a disastrous, dictated, peace with the Ukrainian Rada, which would deprive Russia of all her sugar, her best grain lands, and all the iron and coal in southern Russia. 'The late Allies should adopt distinct policy', the wire went on somewhat sarcastically. 'Russia depends at present solely on Siberian produce. ... We advise you to control and use it for enforcing stringent compliance. ... In an Oriental country the only way to be successful is to act swiftly, to be strong and to strike hard. The great war for the Russian raw stuffs has begun. Do not spoil it from the beginning. These views are vehemently endorsed by Poliakov.' (It had been despatched on the 15th.)[23]

On the 18th, there arrived another wire in the same vein from Major Macalpine (sent on the 13th). This said that Lockhart had given them little help, but the French mission had been of considerable assistance, working jointly with the British, through the Allied Committee (*Tovaro Obmien*). 'This joint Committee has thoroughly worked out the question of stopping supplies to Germany, and valuable results should ensue if a new appointment of a commissar for the evacuation [of Allied stores] can be brought off. Present commissar's actions are capable of pro-German interpretation, and I suspect that in certain cases the evacuation has been conducted in such a way that useless stores have been evacuated and really important stores left behind. This matter is being investigated.' Macalpine then gave details of the stores being evacuated, the most important of which now awaited Trotsky's sanction: 'He [Trotsky] must agree to this, which will be invaluable for munition supplies, if he is sincere in his desire to create new army. ... Since I disagree with Lockhart's policy of blindly backing present [Bolshevik] government, question of cooperation with him is difficult. I can only repeat my conviction [?formed] in the first talk about Holy War [i.e. just before the Brest–Litovsk treaty], that [Bolshevik] cooperation with Allies against Germany and formation of new army is political eyewash. Trotsky and Lenin are clearly determined to use us for their own ends. For you [i.e. General Poole] to come out here with full powers of control over all British government agents and missions is the only way out. Five British officials in Petrograd at the present moment represent three different British missions. There must be a single directing head with a corresponding head in London. Later I will report about the activity of German agents here. Please discount all reports in the meantime by one hundred per cent.'[23] All this, of course, represented the other end of the political spectrum as seen, and vehemently backed by Lockhart; but it contained a good deal of truth.

More wires from the British supply mission reached London on April 19. A British officer at Archangel had wired on the 12th with details of the supplies recently evacuated inland by the Bolsheviks. Trotsky, he added, had sent a circular to all soviets ordering them to make immediate inventories of all the stores and heavy artillery that they held. 'This is either associated with reformation of army or else this information is required by the Germans.' Secondly, there was a further wire for Poole sent by Macalpine on the 14th on the British acquisition of the Russian banks: 'Please answer the repeated requests for a decision on the question of payments on our bank dealings. Daily I am asked on this subject to send two or three telegrams.' This crossed a wire from Colonel Keyes, emphasizing that action was being taken to put through payment to Denisov at a Paris bank for the first instalment of the purchase price of the Siberian Bank. Francs had been transferred some time before to Paris (presumably by the Treasury), but a new French law regarding the bank accounts of people living outside France had delayed the transaction. 'Matter should be settled in two or three days, as energetic steps are being taken in Denisov's interests', stated Keyes.

Then came a demand, via Lockhart, for more finance for the Allied Committee. Since the Russian banks were closed, General Lavergne had wired to Paris for permission for *Tovaro Obmien* to advance 100 million roubles to finance the Russian cooperative societies (which were, as yet, untouched by the Bolsheviks) to buy up fats and sunflower oil in the Caucasus and Kuban and transfer them to Russian soap works, which were inaccessible to the enemy; only this would prevent the Germans purchasing them and thus gaining control of them — though another member of the supply mission thought that the chaos on the Russian railways and the civil war would make such an operation impossible: 'Please cable whether this financial scheme can be participated in by us.'

General Poole replied to Macalpine on the 19th, with that curious inversion of phrase that was peculiar to him: 'Although I do not wish to damp Polly's enthusiasm, you must realise that to advance any money in Russia, the authorities here are very antagonistic. The purchase of the banking interests as probably being valueless when law and order is re-established is viewed with greatest suspicion. In effecting decision on definite policy for Russia I am experiencing greatest difficulty, but hope to be able to do so.' He hoped to return with a British financial expert to review the Russian situation, which was the only way to convince the authorities in London. 'Collect all data you can in the meantime, but do not expect to get any assistance in the shape of money.' The message was certainly clear.[23]

In London on the 22nd, as the War Cabinet appeared to come closer to cooperation with the Bolsheviks, a further powerful warning against any such thing arrived from Poliakov in Moscow. A 'prominent statesman', who had been present at a recent conference attended by Lenin, wired Poliakov to General Poole on the 17th, had reported Lenin as stating that the Scandinavians and Germans would regenerate Russian industry. (It was not stated who the 'statesman' was.) Another 'reliable informant' reported that on being asked if a new war with Germany were possible, the commissar for railways had replied: 'Naturally not, but we will perhaps be obliged to pretend that the loss of Petrograd had been foreseen in the [Bolshevik] government programme.' This, said Poliakov, was during an 'authoritative' conference of economic, technical and financial experts, 'who, after exhaustive discussion, unanimously declared that with present conditions, military resistance was absolutely hopeless'. They further declared that in the struggle for the possession of Russian raw materials that was now beginning, 'the key of success lies in the control of Siberia, since Germany has or soon will have practical control of all producing areas in European Russia'. This meeting also produced 'indisputable facts', claimed Poliakov, without stating what they were, that the Bolshevik government had lost control of the situation, and was 'simply following events and acting probably under German instructions'. Careful investigation showed (again it was not stated what this entailed) that the Allied representatives in Russia had apparently no influence over the Bolshevik government's decisions. 'This summary of the proceedings', Poliakov concluded, 'is corroborated by Lessing, who was present at this conference.'[23]

A further telegram from the British supply mission reached London on the 22nd for Poole and Keyes on the subject of the Russian bank deals. This stated that an indirect source reported that the British Treasury had at last made part payment for the Russian bank shares which they had purchased, and Poliakov asked for confirmation. 'According to Leech, some payees have not been satisfied yet, and they complain bitterly.' He asked Poole or Keyes to let him know by wire if the shares had been properly transferred: 'I urgently recommend that the management of these shares be concentrated, say, in the [London] City and Midland Bank, where the shares could be registered and deposited.' He was now the sole British financial controller in Russia; Teddy Lessing was helping him, 'and I earnestly beg co-operation'.[23]

On the 23rd, Count Mirbach, the new German ambassador to the Bolshevik government, arrived in Moscow, underlining the official relationship between Bolshevik Russia and Germany; all British relations were quite unofficial. Kurt Riezler, Mirbach's Counsellor, noted with satisfaction: 'Reception at the station. Crowds of people — never before has such a victor been received with such joy. We are here in one house with all the commissions, like a monastery, horrible situation — confusion of the first days — but things are already running not too badly. Partly occupied house, partly German embassy, everywhere cigarette ends, rush of petitioners. The devil could not have caused more confusion amongst the capitalists than the Bolsheviks.'

Riezler, the German expert on the Bolshevik movement, then went to pay his first official call on Chicherin and Karakhan at the Foreign Ministry. 'Bad moral position, because our advance has already crossed the border of the Ukraine', he noted. 'We are at Briansk. It looks like a proper predatory war after a peace treaty. Without any accusation, Chicherin and Karakhan pointed out the situation on a map. This was a silent but effective accusation. I can only have the situation explained, and can express doubts about the certainty of their news. Chicherin gives me a lecture on economic policy — peculiar people. Idealism and deep corruption all around us.' At once, Riezler noticed the general and ungovernable opposition to Bolshevik economic policy, and the Brest–Litovsk treaty.

At the same time as the new German ambassador arrived, Joseph Noulens, the French ambassador to Russia, who was then at Vologda, had an interview published in the local press. Noulens was violently anti-Bolshevik (and as strongly opposed to British negotiations with the Bolsheviks). The Japanese 'question', he stated, 'in so far as it is purely Japanese', could be localized in the Far East, provided the Japanese government was 'given the satisfaction which it has the right to demand'. But he openly warned the Bolshevik government that armed Allied intervention (of a 'distinctly friendly character') was coming through Siberia — though he had 'no data of any kind' about it — because the Germans had advanced much further into Russia than was allowed them under the Brest–Litovsk treaty, thus openly hinting at German–Bolshevik collusion.[24]

The result of this interview was to make the Bolsheviks intensely suspicious of all Allied intentions and to kill stone dead the British negotiations towards a Bolshevik request for intervention. 'Noulens' interview', wrote Jacques Sadoul, the unofficial French political agent to the Bolshevik government, who loathed his own ambassador, 'has given to Trotsky and Lenin the impression of a return to the old hostility, of a clear desire to compromise the English negotiations, and in any case to put France in official opposition to England.' Count Mirbach at once protested against Noulens' statement, and the Bolsheviks demanded his recall — a demand which was ignored.

On the 25th, two more wires reached London from Lockhart, clearly influenced by the impending arrival of Count Mirbach. The first, sent on the 19th, stated that both Trotsky and Chicherin agreed with nearly all the British proposals; the only remaining difficulty was Japanese participation in the Allied force of intervention. Would the British government, Lockhart asked Balfour — well knowing that a German ambassador was about to arrive in Moscow — 'play the card of recognition'? Lockhart's second wire, sent on the 21st, stated however, that there would be more difficulties.

The Bolsheviks fully realized that if they reopened the war, the Germans could crush them well before any Allied support could arrive via the Far East. But all other Russians and Russian parties would welcome such Allied intervention, provided it was not confined to occupying Siberia; and Lockhart stressed that a strong Allied political mission must be sent out too, led by someone like Sir George Buchanan, who was very popular with the Russians. (This would also offset the presence of Mirbach.) Lockhart agreed that the Allies should give the Bolsheviks a further short period in which to invite Allied intervention, and then issue an ultimatum; that they would intervene even without a Bolshevik invitation. Lockhart, in fact, had swung round and was now backing Balfour's policy — no doubt knowing what was planned for May 1.[25]

On the morning of April 26, General Smuts answered the proposal that he should go to Murmansk to see Trotsky. His decline took the form of a paper to the War Cabinet. He had just seen a telegram from Lockhart, he added, which made the same point as he did, namely that before any action could be taken in Russia, 'some common plan must be agreed upon between the Allies'. Balfour pointed out that Britain, France and Italy had always favoured intervention in Siberia, but the Americans had not yet come to a definite decision. The difficulty was that it was impossible to approach the Japanese with any definite proposals until the Americans had answered; and the fact that the new Japanese Foreign Minister was alleged to be pro-German increased this difficulty. Smuts urged that a 'definite plan of action' be drawn up and submitted to the American government. He supported Lockhart's proposal for an Allied mission to go to Siberia (this was in his latest wire); but if it was agreed that an Allied army should intervene in Russia, he felt that the Russians, for their part, must put all their railways at its disposal and clearly understand that the Allied intention was to carry on 'active operations' against the enemy in Russia, and not just to occupy Siberia.[26]

Balfour stated that he had had a visit the day before from the American ambassador, who told him that an American secret service officer, who had been sent to Russia by the American government, had obtained many secret documents, 'which he had brought back to England'. (This was Edgar Sisson and his notorious forged documents.) 'These documents had been photographed', said Balfour, 'and the originals had now gone to America.' From the photographs, 'there was apparently ample proof that M. Trotsky had, even up to February last, been in league with the Germans, and had been obeying instructions which the German government had sent him'. In view of the fact that the provenance of these documents was well known to the SIS, it is surprising that 'C' (the head of the SIS) somehow forgot to tell Balfour that they were forgeries.

But it was felt that this did not necessarily mean that Trotsky was not now ready to cooperate with the Allies. (The Cabinet minutes do not state who made this point.) From all recent evidence, 'it could be assumed that he was prepared now to quarrel with the Germans'. Red Guards, and British and French troops, were now all working harmoniously together at Murmansk.[26]

The War Cabinet decided that Balfour should wire to Lord Reading, asking him to urge the American government to reply as soon as possible to the Foreign Office's wire of April 19, which requested American agreement to a joint Anglo–American proposal to the Bolshevik government for intervention by an American and Japanese force, and the despatch of an American technical contingent, together with a complete American division, to the Far East. The War Cabinet, in closed session, then decided that the question of the despatch of an emissary to Murmansk to meet Trotsky should wait until a reply had been received from Reading on the American attitude towards this British proposal for Allied action in Russia.[27]

The War Cabinet next had to consider the position of the Russian fleets. On the 23rd, the DNI, Admiral Hall, had explained the position in detail to the Admiralty Operations Committee, which agreed that the War Cabinet should be 'generally' informed, i.e. not in any detail; and the Deputy First Sea Lord promised to ask the Foreign Office to make every effort to obtain an early reply from Trotsky to the Admiralty proposals for the destruction of the Baltic Fleet and the employment of the Black Sea Fleet. The next day, two wires arrived from Captain Cromie. The first quoted an undated order from Trotsky to the Black Sea Fleet: 'Expect [to be] informed by radio in three day's time [of] plan for removing ships of Black Sea Fleet out of commission and unable to proceed [by] own power from Sebastopol to Novorossisk as ordered. ... Particulars are most necessary to decide finally concerning transfer of ships from S. to N.'. This appears to be the first intimation received at the Admiralty that Trotsky had issued an order for the Black Sea Fleet to put out from Sebastopol, which the Germans were now just entering, and sail east to Novorossisk, on the eastern shore of the Black Sea. Cromie's second wire stated that a total of 167 warships of various types and sizes belonging to the Baltic Fleet, which had had to put out with only one icebreaker to prevent German seizure at Helsinki, had now reached the naval base of Kronstadt, virtually undamaged.[28] Thus nearly the whole Baltic Fleet had reached home waters through the thick winter ice — a feat of seamanship which reflected highly on Captain Chastny and made him a hero to his crews.

On the 26th, however, the First Lord informed the War Cabinet that the only way to secure the destruction of the Baltic Fleet, and the destruction or removal to Novorossisk of the Black Sea Fleet, was to bring as much pressure as possible to bear on Trotsky through Lockhart, although it was realized at the Admiralty that the chance of Trotsky being induced to take such definite action was 'not very great'.²⁹ It seemed that whatever the Admiralty told the War Cabinet, they would in fact have to take action themselves, without reference to Trotsky.

In Paris, Clemenceau was now making further efforts to get the Czech Legion to France; though American troops were at last beginning to arrive, they were virtually untrained, and the Czechs were a highly disciplined force with a fine morale — just the sort of troops for which Clemenceau was desperate. But there were no ships for them, and his wire of April 20th instructing General Lavergne to reroute them to Archangel and Murmansk seemed to have been too late. The French ambassador in Tokyo had reported that the Czechs were still moving on to Vladivostok, though there had been no reply to the French request for American ships to remove them from the Far East; Lavergne meanwhile had wired for further instructions about rerouting them to northern Russia, and the shipping needed, but there had been no reply to the request for British ships to take them off from Archangel. On the 26th, therefore, Clemenceau wired to both Lavergne in Moscow and to the French military attaché in Tokyo that French officers were to be sent to both Archangel and Vladivostok to take charge of the Czech contingents on arrival, to make sure that all Bolshevik elements were excluded, and to report on them generally. Lavergne was assured that part of the Czech Legion was indeed to be rerouted to northern Russia; but even when Bolshevik assent was obtained, there would still be no British ships to meet them. The British, who obviously wished to delay the operation, also wished those Czechs who were being rerouted to be officered by the French (as Benes had agreed when with the British military section at Versailles on the 22nd). The same day (the 26th), Clemenceau informed the Quai d'Orsay of these instructions and requested them to instruct the French ambassador in Tokyo to try, once again, to obtain the necessary Japanese shipping.³⁰

At Penza, where the Czech trains were still halted, Czech communist agitators were making a determined effort to undermine their morale and the situation was becoming more and more tense. The communists felt sure that the continual delays suffered by the Czechs would unnerve the whole Legion, cause it to revolt against its leaders, abandon the idea of going to France, and finally join the Bolsheviks. There was shortly to be a congress attended by delegates from all the Czech contingents, and this, it was felt, would start the revolt. The Czech communists could not have been more wrong. The continual delays were simply hardening Czech sentiment against the Bolsheviks. On the 26th, a Czech officer, whose regiment had been held up before Penza for some time, marched on the town with a strong escort to have it out with the local Bolsheviks and the Czech communists. In Moscow, the local Czech National Council delegates had to make great efforts to prevent a clash and calm the regiment. The local Czech communists countered this by spreading rumours that they were now the only recognized Czech representatives in Russia, not the Czech National Council, whose papers were invalid; other rumours, of unknown origin, claimed that the Czech Legion was about to be completely disarmed and repatriated to Austria–Hungary: the worst possible fate for any free Czech. The Czech National Council retaliated by spreading other rumours (no doubt originating from Allied agents and reinforced by the recent arrival of Count Mirbach) that the Bolsheviks were simply German puppets. Tension was rising. While some Czechs felt they must accept any and all Bolshevik conditions to ensure a peaceful journey through Siberia, young Czech officers began to make plans to shoot their way through to Vladivostok, if necessary.[31]

But which Czechs were to leave Russia via Vladivostok, and which to go via Archangel? General Sackville-West (the British military representative at Versailles) was instructed to take the initiative and propose that the Urals should be the dividing line, i.e. those Czechs to the West should go to Archangel, and those to the East should continue to Vladivostok, as agreed with Benes on the 22nd. When the Allied military representatives at Versailles considered the matter on April 27, Sackville-West said the main concern was the large body of Czech troops near Samara; should these men be shipped to France via northern Russia? The matter was one chiefly for the French, since General Lavergne had been instructed to send the necessary orders to the Czech troops. The French general, Belin, agreed with the British proposals. These troops were of high quality and should be used as soon as possible. The French War Office thought they should go to Archangel. The only question was whether or not this decision should apply to the three Czech trainloads, which were reported on April 11 to be on the Siberian railway east of Omsk (well east of the Urals). There would undoubtedly be great difficulties in trying to ship all the Czechs via Vladivostok, but this did not apply to the small Czech force which had got as far as Omsk. (It will be recalled that there was in fact a large Czech force under formation at Omsk.) At this point, Belin produced a slightly modified draft proposal.

Sackville-West then asked bluntly what should be the 'exact dividing line' between those that should go to Vladivostok, and those that should go to Archangel. Belin replied obliquely that the 5,000 to 6,000 Czech troops which would go to Vladivostok were reported on April 11 to be east of Omsk. The main body, however, were still near Samara, that is to say, nearer Archangel. 'As agreed', he added, 'until these troops were embarked, they could be employed both at Archangel and Murmansk, and at Vladivostok, for the protection of those places.' Belin, in fact, who seems to have had no up to date knowledge of the exact whereabouts of the Czech Legion, had made considerable concessions in order to obtain British ships at Archangel — which the British had taken no steps to provide — perhaps because they intended to use the Czechs in northern Russia, and for an anti-Bolshevik *coup en route.*

The Allied military representatives thereupon submitted the following resolution on the removal of the Czech troops from Russia, as Joint Note 25, to the Supreme War Council:

1. That there is everything to be gained by securing their transportation [i.e. to Europe] at the earliest possible date.
2. That as the greatest possible rapidity can be ensured by using Archangel and Murmansk, all Czech troops which have not yet passed east of Omsk on the Siberian railway should be despatched to these two ports.[32]

Furthermore, while these troops are waiting to be embarked, they could be profitably employed in defending Archangel and Murmansk and in guarding and protecting the Murman railway. Similarly, Czech troops which have already proceeded east of Omsk, could eventually be used, as recommended in Joint Note 20, to cooperate with the Allies in Siberia.'

Thus, the dividing line was to be not the Urals, but Omsk — well to the east. But General Belin made no actual request even now for British ships to collect the Czechs from northern Russia.

But on the 30th, the calculated confusion between London and Paris over the Czech Legion was worsened when Chicherin wired to the local soviets in Russia and Siberia that those Czech trains east of Omsk could now proceed to Valdivostok, but those west of Omsk should be turned back to Archangel and Murmansk. This new order, in line with Joint Note 25, but apparently with no explanation whatever to the Czechs themselves, surprised everyone in the Czech Legion. But as Chicherin's wire was signed by a Russian officer with a German name, it could only mean one thing; it was a German–Bolshevik trap to split up the Legion and thus the more easily destroy it — such now was the state of tension and suspicion aboard the Czech trains.[33]

April 30 marked something of a watershed in British policy towards Russia. It saw various aspects of the Russian problem resolved, but none in ways that favoured the War Cabinet's views.

First, British negotiations for a large-scale Japanese intervention as far as the Urals finally broke down. On the 24th, Balfour and Wiseman (who had just arrived in London for a short visit) had first sent an optimistic wire to Lord Reading in Washington: 'Please explain to Colonel House that in my view situation is entirely altered by apparent willingness of Trotsky to invite Allied assistance against German aggression,' stated Balfour, relying on the eight conditions drawn up by the Allied military representatives. In Washington, Lord Reading went on the same day (the 24th) to see Colonel

House, who was now enthusiastic, and passed on his enthusiasm to the President.

The full British proposal, sent by Balfour to Reading on April 25, was in fact a revamped version of the wire which Balfour had been instructed by the War Cabinet on April 19 to send to Reading. The transfer of German divisions from Russia to the western front was still continuing, Balfour stated, and, 'under present conditions, can be further continued, and it is imperative to stop this movement if it can possibly be done'. (The new German attack on the western front had begun that morning.) Germany could now draw on Siberian food and supplies, 'and in these conditions, even if our defensive [in France] is successful, there is little chance that we could make a successful offensive. It thus becomes of the greatest urgency to re-establish an Allied front in Russia.' There must be joint Allied inter-vention to bring about a Russian national revival, as in the time of Napoleon, to free Russia from foreign [i.e. German] control. If the Bolsheviks would cooperate, the Allies must act with them as the *de facto* Russian government (i.e. recognize them). Trotsky had asked for a state-ment of possible Allied support and guarantees, and considered agreement desirable. The War Cabinet thought this opportunity should be seized. (In fact, it was now passed.) 'If such an offer was accepted [by the Bolsheviks], the whole position might be transformed, and if it was refused, the position of the Bolshevik government would at least be defined.' (This was as far as Balfour was prepared to go in informing the American government of what would happen if Trotsky refused his ultimatum.) Contrary to earlier British propo-sals, Balfour continued, it was now realized that it was impractical to ask Japan to act as Allied mandatory, since this would throw most Russians into German arms. The War Cabinet wished to know if President Wilson would agree to a joint Anglo–American proposal to the Bolshevik government for Allied intervention, as outlined, with an undertaking that all Allied troops would be withdrawn at the end of the war; and to the despatch of an American technical contingent, together with one complete American division, to the Far East.[34] Only American participation would make joint intervention, together with larger Japanese forces, acceptable to the Russians; and without American consent, Japan would not move. It is not clear whether Balfour informed his colleagues in the War Cabinet of this despatch.

A final variation on this theme had been despatched to Washington on April 26, when American approval was requested for a joint Anglo–American proposal to the Bolshevik government for intervention by a joint American and Japanese force. (This wire, of course, was merely a chaser to the longer Foreign Office wire of the 25th.) President Wilson saw Lord Reading on the 26th. The President declared that he would reconsider the whole problem, in view of the new light thrown upon it, but he was anxious that the situation should be closely watched in order not to be led into a trap by Trotsky; he was expecting the arrival of documents purporting to prove that Trotsky and Lenin were in the pay of the German government (the 'Sisson documents'). But because of the lack of shipping, the President turned down the British proposal for the despatch of an American force, though a regiment might be sent. He considered, however, that the recent arrival in Washington of the new Japanese ambassador, Viscount Ishii, afforded a favourable opportunity for discovering Japan's views; and he suggested that a conference be held between Ishii, Secretary of State Lansing, Secretary of War Baker, and Lord Reading. The President added that he was doubtful whether Japan would intervene at all, particularly if she was to be accompanied by American and Allied contingents.[35]

As soon as Reading's wire reached London, the Foreign Office sent back a paper prepared by the Japanese General Staff stating that they would waive any objections to joint intervention (such as they had been raising for two months) if this would remove American opposition to intervention; further, they added, they were ready to try to secure the agreement of the Japanese government to this change of view. (This military démarche, a nice sidelight on how things were then arranged in Tokyo, was clearly designed to influence, and probably disconcert, the new Japanese ambassador in Washington.)[35]

But when the British and Japanese ambassadors met the American Secretary of State and the Secretary of War on April 28, and the proposal for a joint American and Japanese intervention was discussed, Ishii made it clear that he agreed with the American view that the present moment was inopportune; the danger of uniting all the Russians to resist foreign intervention and throwing them into German arms did not compensate for the possible military advantages to be gained. Intervention, in fact, might increase rather than decrease German control over Russia.[35]

When Ishii saw President Wilson on the 30th, he made the same points, adding that Japanese troops would go no further than Irkutsk, stated Lord Reading in a report to the Foreign Office that evening. The Japanese General Staff, added Ishii, did not consider that the Japanese army of 250,000 men, with 200,000 reserves, was strong enough even to attempt to advance as far as Chelyabinsk, unless they could be assured that they were advancing through a friendly country and could count on the assistance and not the hostility of the local population. Thus, by the end of April — and long before Secretary Lansing officially informed Lord Reading on May 7 — it was clear that the President had rejected the British proposal as inopportune; the Japanese had now clearly stated that they would never advance to Chelyabinsk unless assured of virtually impossible conditions. This, as Lloyd George was later to inform the War Cabinet, marked the rejection of the first British proposal for Allied intervention in Russia; put forward on January 24, proposed again on February 25, and rejected on April 30: consistently thwarted by the American government.[36]

It was thus doubly infuriating for the War Office to be informed in late

April that there was virtually no danger from armed enemy prisoners-of-war in Siberia. The British and American officers who had been sent, with Trotsky's full approval, to Irkutsk to investigate, reported from Moscow on April 26 that they had only found one party of just over 900 Hungarian prisoners who had been armed at Irkutsk, and they were assured that this figure would not rise above 1,500. At Omsk, there was another Hungarian force, formed from prisoners who had chosen to become Soviet citizens; but this figure would not rise above 1,000. In both cases, the prisoners had been armed to ward off Ataman Semenov, and if Allied support for him ceased, it was inferred that there would be no need to arm any more. There were, of course, many more armed prisoners in Russia proper — about which the German and Austrian governments were shortly to complain in angry tones to the Bolsheviks. Captains Hicks and Webster blamed the Allied consuls in Irkutsk for much of the exaggeration about armed enemy prisoners and suggestions that the Germans might use them to take over Siberia; but their joint report affected both the Czechs in Russia and the War Office in London. The Czechs, now deeply suspicious, were convinced that Bolshevik attempts to enlist and make Soviet citizens of even a small body of Hungarian prisoners were just another sign of the German–Bolshevik conspiracy against them. The War Office was furious that their own pre-conceived ideas, carefully stoked by false Japanese and French reports, were contradicted by junior officers, even though they had been on the spot. It seemed natural that the Germans should try and take over Siberia, if there were large masses of their prisoners there; the reappearance of the 'Sisson documents' in London in April had added fuel to these false flames. The War Office demanded the immediate recall of Captain Hicks, which only strong protests from Lockhart prevented.[37]

But the War Cabinet recovered quite quickly from the failure of their first proposal for Allied intervention. On April 30, no doubt already aware of events in Washington, they considered Joint Note 25 (which laid down that those Czechs west of Omsk should proceed to northern Russia, and those to the east to Vladivostok). Balfour drew attention to Lockhart's wire no. 114 (sent from Moscow on the 20th or 21st), 'which stated that these troops were being sent to Murmansk', while Milner said that he had just received a later telegram saying that 6,000 Czech troops had already reached Vladivostok and the remainder were *en route*. According to French military sources, Milner added, there were altogether 45,000 Czech troops available, forming two good divisions, 'who were anxious to come and fight in France'. They had been assembled near Omsk and it had not then been decided whether they should go to Murmansk or Vladivostok; but as they were now apparently arriving at Vladivostok, it was a question of who should ship them to France.

'It was pointed out', state the Cabinet minutes (though it names no one) 'that the original arrangement with M. Trotsky was that these troops should be used to defend the Russian ports [i.e. Archangel and Murmansk], and that a very different situation arose if it was intended to make use of Czech troops to fight in France against the Germans.' This was a blunt, but necessary remark. The real intention of the British, it seems, was not even to use the Czechs initially to guard the northern Russian ports — let alone ship them away from northern Russia — but to oust the Bolsheviks from power; hence the stress on the 'very different' situation produced by any intention to use them in France. It was then suggested (again the Cabinet minutes do not indicate by whom) 'that it would be advisable that these troops should be used for an Allied enterprise from Siberia', but it was felt that the Czechs themselves must be consulted about where they wished to fight. There is no mention of shipping them away.

The War Cabinet decided that the matter should be discussed at the next meeting of the Supreme War Council in early May, and that Balfour and Milner should prepare a paper, based on the telegrams received on the subject to assist those Cabinet Ministers who were to attend the meetings.[38]

The last days of April saw a consolidation of the German position in southern Russia and the Ukraine. As the Germans rapidly overran the Crimea, there was great anxiety both in London and Moscow for the safety of the Black Sea Fleet at Sebastopol. Trotsky had ordered Admiral Sablin to proceed to Novorossisk and Colonel Boyle had long since bribed a sufficient number of Bolshevik sailors to take the warships there. But bad communications between Moscow and the Crimea, and reports that Admiral Sablin had hoisted the Ukrainian flag (which appear to have started rumours that he was about to confer with, and probably hand over his ships to, the German commander in the Crimea), caused extreme apprehension; Sablin, in fact, seems to have hoisted the Ukrainian flag to escape the Germans.[39]

A project was soon afoot for the despatch of a small 'British mission' from Moscow to the Crimea to take drastic steps; but it was too late. 'Lockhart writes that it is impossible to get to Black Sea even if desirable to leave Petrograd,' wired Cromie to the Admiralty on April 23. Le Page [Cromie's assistant] telegraphs from Moscow: 'Am arranging interview with T. tomorrow morning 22nd. Stated Germans intend to establish line between Petrograd, Moscow, Kursk and Rostov.' On the 25th, Cromie wired again: 'Le Page at Moscow suggested to Altfater [Commander-in-Chief, Red Navy] that ammunition at Sebastopol and Kertsch [on the eastern tip of the Crimea] be placed in Allied ships ready for destruction.' The intention appears to have been to sink Allied blockships at the mouth of Sebastopol harbour. 'Replying [to] offers of assistance, Altfater states no mission of whatever nationality was any use [?at present] as [?illness of] Black Sea Fleet must take its natural course.' With this fatalistic answer, the matter was abandoned.[39]

But on April 27 and 28, Admiral Sablin put out from Sebastopol with two battleships, five cruisers, twelve destroyer-minelayers and four transport vessels, bound for Novorossisk; only a few ships refused to leave and fell into German hands. This rather miraculous escape was not known in either Moscow or London for some time, however. (On April 30, Cromie did pass on a message from a former member of the British embassy, just back from southern Russia via Tsaritsin, and then up along the Volga, stating that the Black Sea Fleet was now at Novorossisk and German submarines were patrolling outside and blockading the port. 1,500 bluejackets had been discharged, as they refused to fight, but 4,500 agreed to obey their officers. Admiral Sablin had declared, however, that the position was hopeless and that the fleet must be destroyed. At this, the sailors decided that if such an order were issued, they would first kill all the officers, and then sink the ships themselves — for which, of course, Colonel Boyle had already promised them handsome payment. But this message, from a typically bad source — but which in fact proved to be accurate — was simply not believed in London.)

The Germans also pushed straight on east through the lower Donetz to Taganrog, and then seized Rostov, on the lower Don, from the Bolsheviks — who were simultaneously driven out from the Don Cossack capital of Novocherkask (further east), by Don Cossack forces. This completed the German advance into southern Russia. By late April, the Germans had installed a puppet government in the Ukraine under the pro-German Russian General, Skoropadsky, and were only opposed by a weak Don Cossack force on their south-eastern border; the Bolsheviks were out of the Don.

So was the forgotten, wretched little volunteer army, on whom high Allied hopes had been placed early in 1918. In late March, Kornilov, Alexeiev and the other White Russian generals had brought their little force to the Kuban, where the Bolsheviks were increasing their hold, as it declined on the Don; and when they met the Kuban leaders, the Kuban Cossacks had been driven out of their capital of Ekaterinodar by Bolshevik forces from Novorossisk on the coast. Despite the suspicions of the Kuban leaders, a loose agreement was reached for combined action against the Bolsheviks; the Germans were nowhere near. But, in early April, Kornilov was killed by a stray shell. Morale was badly shaken. Alexeiev and his colleagues decided they must break away and move off again into the steppe to reorganize.[39]

The only success in the Ukraine was the relatively modest one of Colonel Boyle's saboteurs, hastily engaged in late March. After three months, the total output of the Don and Donetz mines was cut by half, two big coal mines were full of water; there were complaints in all the workshops, and the main ammunition dump at Odessa was blown up, causing 80 million roubles worth of damage (for which his men claimed eight million roubles, but eventually accepted two million, or £80,000).

There were various strikes and explosions at Kiev and two other towns (for which a cheque for £100,000 on Holt's Bank in Pall Mall changed hands). Boyle finally sent 200 of his men off with another cheque for £10,000 to join Alexeiev in the steppe.

Finally, April 30 saw the failure of British hopes for an anti-Bolshevik *coup* in the Russian capital. In late April, since the arrival of the new German ambassador, wires from Moscow had suggested an increase in German control and influence. On the 25th a wire reached London from Macalpine, strongly condemning his colleague's suggestion that the Allied Committee (*Tovaro Obmien*) should advance funds to buy up oil and fats to prevent their acquisition by the Germans. 'It is an attempt, owing to the fact that the Russian banks are closed, to use the Allies as bankers', he stated. 'We should be at the mercy both of the Germans and the central [Bolshevik] government ... should the former [?extend their] control further in the south-east, and I doubt whether we should get back either the money or the goods.' Since the despatch of this wire, German control in south-eastern Russia had indeed been extended.[40]

On the 29th, General Poole had a wire from Teddy Lessing, warning him that the various British missions in Petrograd, through lack of cooperation, general overlapping and confusion, were failing 'to uphold either British prestige or enforce any consistent policy as would benefit us or appeal to our friends in Russia'. In Moscow, it was even worse: 'for six different authorities, five of which are hopelessly understaffed, are working independently of each other'. There must, he urged, be a single directing chief.[40] Only this could cope with centralized German control.

Much more worrying was another wire that Poole and Major Banting received on the 29th — presumably from Macalpine, in oddly laconic terms. 'The following news, which is always as startling but not often so definite, comes daily from P[oliakov]. ... You will be sorry to see that he has now finally [?ruin]ed for you both the Finnish route.' (It is uncertain how Poliakov had destroyed the Finnish route into Russia.) Macalpine then came to the core of his message: 'The ex-Belgian vice-consul at Riga, who is now [the] German financial representative here [i.e. in Petrograd], has declared to local Germans that as a guarantee for the payment of the contribution [due from the Bolsheviks under the Brest–Litovsk treaty], the occupation of Petrograd is definitely agreed to, and will take place as soon as the navigation of Gulf [of Finland] is possible. That is to say, in about twenty days Viborg will be used as a base of operations and Finnish help employed. The area occupied is to extend to the river Volkhov.'[40] There were indeed further German plans at this time for the seizure of Petrograd, when navigation was open; this was just what the Admiralty feared, and explains their fixed resolve to destroy the Baltic Fleet. The informant in this telegram, of course, was Poliakov's opposite number in the German camp.

Funds for the British supply mission were now rapidly drying up. Hugh Leech, Poliakov's other colleague, was the man in the British camp who had to produce funds and turn assets into cash. But due to long delays in the transfer of sterling sums to bank accounts in London, the Russians were no longer inclined to believe his promises; and as the exchange rate fell, they no longer wished to exchange rouble notes or shares for sterling in London, but to raise money themselves to finance anti-Bolshevik activities by selling Leech's sterling notes on the spot. As a result, Leech soon found himself in danger of arrest by the Cheka; so he started to grow a beard; and after hiding in a villa at Tsarskoe Selo, he fled to Murmansk.[41]

Then came news, first through German military sources in Petrograd, that the *coup* timed for May 1, whereby Savinkov's group, the Latvian commanders in Moscow, and the military commander of Petrograd were to have Allied support for the overthrow of the Bolsheviks, had been postponed. The Bolsheviks had discovered the plan — and May Day instead saw an impressive parade of the new Red Army on Red Square in Moscow, at which Trotsky took the salute in the presence of all the foreign diplomatic representatives.

Four weeks later, on May 30, *Izvestia* carried an official Cheka statement admitting that up to early May Savinkov's group had tried but failed to bribe the Latvian commanders. It may well have been the Germans who tipped off the Bolsheviks. On April 30, Count Mirbach reported to the Foreign Ministry in Berlin that it was still the Latvian regiments which mainly kept the Bolsheviks in power in Moscow. General Schwarz, the military commander of Petrograd, was awarded a (very clandestine) British Military Cross for his part in the abortive *coup*, and Savinkov (who admits that the Czechs had given him financial support for the first time in April) lived to fight another day.

Mirbach's sombre report, and the Kaiser's liberal comments in the margin, indicate that the contest between Germany and Britain in Russia was now intensifying. 'The despair of the old governing classes is boundless', wrote Mirbach, 'but they can no longer raise sufficient strength to put an end to the organized looting which is now prevalent. ['This will have to come from the outside,' noted the Kaiser.] The cry for organized conditions reaches down to the lowest strata of the people, and the feeling of their impotence makes them hope for salvation from Germany. ['Either England and America or we (indirectly through Russian generals)', wrote the Kaiser.] The very circles who were inveighing loudest against us before, now see us, if not as the Angel, then at least as the police constable of salvation.'[42]

The Russian pendulum had swung heavily against the British.

4

The Czechs and the Baltic Fleet

By May 1, the Germans were in fairly comfortable occupation of the Ukraine and much of southern Russia and were sending westwards by rail all the Russian grain, produce and varied metals and supplies that they could seize — sufficient to threaten the whole Allied blockade. The War Cabinet now had no Russian policy at all; both British policies of mid to late April had foundered. (The first, for intervention by a Japanese and American force through Siberia, with Bolshevik consent, had been vetoed in Washington. The second, for a secret coup to oust the Bolsheviks from power, had been discovered in Moscow.) With the war thought likely to go on until 1919 or longer, it had become even more vital to deny the Siberian grain and produce to the Germans; and with the Germans in southern Russia and able to purchase what they could not seize, the only means of doing so was by Allied occupation of Siberia up to the Urals, some 5,000 miles from the Far Eastern port of entry, Vladivostok.

The Germans were also pressing on into northern Russia through Finland, following the German landing in mid-April, which had enabled the White Finns to crush the Red Finns in the Finnish civil war. This presented a double threat to the British. If the German-backed White Finns could seize Murmansk, which the Allies (because of the desperate shortage of manpower in France) were unable to reinforce, the Germans, it was feared, could set up a submarine base there. This would effectively close the two northern Russian ports to the British, thus cutting the Allies off from all contact with central Russia. Simultaneously, the White Finns were advancing east along the northern shore of the Gulf of Finland; and by April 24, had surrounded Fort Ino, which, with Fort Krasnaya Gorka on the southern shore, effectively protected the naval base of Kronstadt and Petrograd itself.[1] If Fort Ino fell, the Germans could push on into Petrograd in a matter of hours, and seize the Russian Baltic Fleet. If the Germans seized the Russian warships — especially the 70 Russian destroyers — the situation would become 'very serious', warned the Admiralty.

84

Of the immediate British problems — the control of Siberia, the reten-tion of the northern Russian ports, and the destruction of the Baltic Fleet — the first two could only be remedied by the Czech Legion, the only pro-Allied force actually on the spot. On April 30, Chicherin, in accordance with the Allies' wishes, had wired to the local soviets in Russia and Siberia that part of the Czech Legion, now *en route* for Vladivostok, could turn back to Archangel and Murmansk. Thus both the future of the Baltic Fleet and the Czech Legion came up for active discussion in London on May 1.

'At the end of March', minuted the DNI that morning at the Admiralty, 'the Commander-in-Chief Baltic Fleet [Admiral Chastny] informed the naval attaché [Captain Cromie] that any attempt on the part of [Russian] officers to prepare the ships for destruction would meet with general opposition from the counter-revolutionaries. At the same time, Captain Behrens [Chief of Staff, Russian Admiralty] stated that it would never be agreed to surrender the fleet; he himself would give no order for its destruction. It would thus appear that no definite arrangements have yet been made to destroy the ships, and unless we can obtain the cooperation of the Bolsheviks, it will be difficult to arrange for its destruction. Mr Lockhart was asked to ascertain from Trotsky what action he proposed to take as regards the Baltic Fleet, and in informing Mr Lockhart of its withdrawal to Kronstadt, Trotsky replied that the fleet would be destroyed in case of need. Beyond this vague statement of policy, no other infor-mation has been received as to the furthering of this scheme and N[aval] A[ttaché] has not been advised of any proposed plans for carrying out destruction as an extreme measure, though he has been at Petrograd for some time. ... The Germans may quite well have allowed the Russian ships to go to Kronstadt in order to avoid trouble between the Finns and the Russians had they seized them in Finnish waters.[2] The Germans know quite well that they can seize the ships at Kronstadt just as easily,' he added.

Without informing the War Cabinet, the Admiralty directed Cromie to submit immediate plans of his own for the destruction of the Baltic Fleet; for the new British secret service agent, who was just arriving in Russia to take over all British secret operations after the abortive *coup* of May 1, could give invaluable advice and support to the politically inexperienced Cromie, since he knew more about the Baltic Fleet than any man living, having been closely involved in its construction.

The man in question was Lieutenant Sidney Reilly, of the Royal Flying Corps, then known to his employers as STI (i.e. the chief British Secret Service agent in Russia, who operated out of Stockholm, the main base for all SIS operations within Russia itself). Born Sigmund Georgievich Rosen-blum in 1874, he was the only son of Pauline and Grigory Jakovlevich Rosenblum, a rich Polish-Jewish landowner near Grodno on the River Niemen. Soon after 1890, he appears to have left home suddenly. By 1897, he had joined the British Secret Intelligence Service. It is not known why or how, but he may have been living in the east end of London (the principal haven of Polish and Russian political refugees), and been deliberately compromised by Tsarist agents with the Metroplitan Police with a view to his explusion. Possibly at this point he was recruited by the SIS who were anxious to enlist such refugees as British agents to keep a watch on the developing Russian oil industry and on Russian designs in India. This happened frequently in the 1890s. (See R. Deacon: *A History of the British Secret Service* (London, 1969), pp. 125–33.) Reilly was always secretive about his origins, and all his life told conflicting stories about himself. He had good reason to do this, for as a Polish Jew in the British service operating in Russia, he had to be particularly careful to protect his family, since the Jews were always under suspicion in Tsarist Russia (and Tsarist Poland), especially when they had won the right of representation. (The Rosenblums were active in the Jewish emancipation movement; and a close relative, Leonty M. Bramson, was a local deputy in the first Duma in 1906.) But if one reads the main account he gave of his early background, two main themes emerge: that he had gone abroad to study, was tricked and caught by Tsarist agents; and that he had been spotted as a likely recruit by British officers in another far distant land. In fact, he appears to have carried out his first job for the SIS in 1897. He married in London in 1898 as Sigmund Rosenblum and took the name Reilly from his wife's father. By this means the SIS concocted an elaborate alibi for him as an Anglo-Indian railway engineer.

In September 1904, under the name of Stanislaus George Reilly, he entered the Royal School of Mines in South Kensington to study electrical engineering. On his entry form, against the names of his parents, whose occupation is left blank, he wrote: 'I am independent of both.' He also stated that he had 'Indian experience in railway open-line work, construction and survey, in waterworks buildings roads, etc.' It is also claimed that a certificate had been obtained from Roorkee University in India showing that he was born on April 24, 1877. Research in the India Office records in London shows that a Stanislaus George Reilly, born in Calcutta on that date, and educated at a Catholic missionary school called St Fidelis at the hill station of Mussourie, graduated from Thomason Civil Engineering College at Roorkee in 1897; and that from 1899 to 1903, he was a railway engineer on small Indian railways. It was this alibi which Reilly gave in 1925 when he joined the Institute of Civil Engineers in London (from which he allegedly resigned in 1948). That same year (1925), he produced the same alibi when captured by the Bolsheviks in Moscow.

Enquiries in India show this whole alibi to have been false. Roorkee University has no trace of him; nor has the Bombay branch of the State Bank of India (formerly the Imperial Bank of India), where Reilly claimed to have banked for many years. Messrs Forbes, Forbes, Campbell and

Company, for whom Reilly claimed to have worked as assistant manager from 1920-2, have no records of him as a former employee; nor did the Bombay Water Board (for whom Reilly claimed to have been the chief engineer from 1922-5) have any trace of him in their records. Yet this was the background that he revealed in 1925 both to the Institute of Civil Engineers in London and the Cheka in Moscow; and the Institute had him on their books until his 'resignation' in 1948 — though it is generally thought that he was executed in Moscow in 1927.

In July 1905, Reilly graduated from the Royal School of Mines with the highest marks (and was the only student not to study, in fact not to need to study, a foreign language). He then went to Trinity College, Cambridge, to do research in civil engineering. In the college's records, he wrote that he was born in Calcutta, that his father's name was George (in fact, his real father was known in the family as 'Georgi'); and of his previous education he wrote, 'schools in India'. Little is known of the results of his research. He lived at 8 Jesus Lane. During this period he claimed to hold a PhD of Heidelberg University, where all knowledge of him is denied. An expert examiner of questioned documents has compared the handwriting on both the Royal School of Mines and the Trinity College entry forms with a letter known to be by Reilly, and reported that all three documents are in the same handwriting. In 1908, Reilly joined the Institute of Structural Engineers in London. (Why he called himself Stanislaus, another well-known Polish name, under this alibi remains obscure.)

This was the background to Reilly's various espionage missions in the Far East, Europe and the Middle East, where he allegedly obtained the Persian oil concessions for England from under the noses of the French. He then went to St Petersburg, where he became the Russian agent for Blohm & Voss, the German shipbuilding firm which was reconstructing the Russian Navy after the Russo-Japanese war; and was thus able to advise the British Admiralty of the latest German naval designs. While in Russia *en mission*, he scrupulously avoided his family. He remained solely in contact with his first cousin, F., an old childhood friend, then living in Warsaw; and there still exists a beautiful Leipzig edition of *The Rubáiyát* of Omar Khayyám, which he sent her from St Petersburg in March 1913, inside which there is a plaintive German inscription in Reilly's hand of part of the 29th stanza. When the war broke out, he became a commission agent for the Russian government for the purchase of war material in Japan, and later moved to New York, where he had an office on Broadway. He was then sent on various missions behind the German lines (he had fluent German, among many other languages). In spring 1918, he was sent back into Russia to organize a plot to oust the Bolsheviks.

On May 1, the War Cabinet considered the Siberian situation, as seen by the Captain of *Suffolk* at Vladivostok. Good order prevailed in the city, he reported, but this appeared merely to indicate a lull after the Japanese and British landings early in April. The Red Guards, organized by the local soviet, were said to be mainly criminals, and those who were given any authority tended to abscond with any funds. Bolshevik tyranny aroused general resentment. All this was fairly commonplace. But, he added, there was good information about the self-styled Siberian government (originally the Siberian regional Duma, elected at the university town of Tomsk during the time of the provisional government). Despite being broken up by the Bolsheviks, and its members having fled to Harbin, it was making marked progress among the local Siberian population, especially in the country districts. Since the few active members of this institution were confined to a single railway carriage on Harbin station, this only underlined the strong support which the SRs invariably enjoyed among the Russian and Siberian peasantry. It was added that representatives of this small band, who wanted independence for Siberia, were now in Peking trying to obtain Allied support.[3]

The War Cabinet also had before them an account of the interview on April 22 between Dr Benes, Wickham Steed, and a colonel of the British Military Section at Versailles. At this interview, Benes had stated that the Czechs would be willing to serve under French or British officers, were reliable and good fighters, and did not wish to take part in Russian internal conflicts, but would 'fight bitterly against anything that had a tinge of Germanism'. Benes also 'warmly' approved the rerouting of all Czechs west of the Urals to Archangel, adding that 'any attempt by Finns or Germans to interfere with the Czechs at Archangel would be bitterly resisted'. There was clearly nothing inconsistent here with retaining the Czechs in Russia and Siberia, provided that their very reasonable demands were met.[4]

The Deputy First Sea Lord now informed the War Cabinet that *Suffolk* reported that 4,000 Czech troops had now arrived at Vladivostok and were awaiting shipment to France; further, it was understood that 50,000 Czechs all told were coming to the Far East. The DMI stated that this confirmed what he had heard the day before from French sources, namely that some 6,000 Czechs had reached Vladivostok and that a similar number were expected every two days until 50,000 had arrived. These troops refused to fight in Russia and were awaiting shipment, the DMI said, 'It was presumed that the whole of the First Czech Corps, which, according to the latest inform- ation last week, were then in European Russia, had now moved east of Omsk, and were therefore in Siberia.' These troops, the DMI explained, claimed to have been so badly treated in Russia that they refused to fight there anymore, but a Second Czech Corps was being formed near Omsk, in which some 20,000 men had already been enrolled, and it was 'probable that arrangements could be made for this [Second] Corps to remain in Russia and be stationed, as was originally proposed, on the Murmansk and Archangel railways'.

In fact, the First Czech Corps was still strung out along the railway between Penza and Omsk and had just been told, by Chicherin in Moscow, that it could proceed to Archangel. It was dumbfounded at this order, which it took to be of German provenance. The DMI could not have known this. But the discussion at Versailles on April 27, which had resulted in Joint Note 25, had been before the Cabinet on April 30th, and had clearly stated that the First Corps would be rerouted to northern Russia, while the presumably better disciplined Second Corps would proceed to Vladivostok. In short, the DMI's report was not only inaccurate, it was totally at odds with the agreement reached at Versailles. Perhaps one reason that this appears to have passed unremarked is that the senior members of the War Cabinet were absent.

The Prime Minister, the War Minister and the CIGS were at Abbeville attending a meeting of the Supreme War Council, whose main concern was to repair the damage sustained during the great German attack, which in effect meant hurrying over American troops and deciding how many could be shipped per month. Tactically, the CIGS, and perhaps the others, felt that they must regain the initiative over the French in the Alliance. ('I am sure we must assert ourselves more [over the French]', wrote Sir Henry Wilson in his diary on April 27. 'We must take over high policy everywhere.')[5] He gives this brief account of events at Abbeville on May 1: 'Clemenceau led off about the agreement come to on April 24 by Milner and Pershing for May, and wanted it extended to June. Much argument. At 5 o'clock, still arguing, we formed a small committee in another room of Milner and self, Pershing and Foch; presently Clemenceau and Lloyd George joined, and in the end Pershing agreed to extend May agreement if Lloyd George would guarantee tonnage for 130,000 men in British bottoms ...'. Thus British shipping was to be fully occupied.

On the 2nd, notes the CIGS, 'I at once raised the questions of the Channel Ports and the Somme. Foch said if retirement was necessary he would conduct all along the line. I said that this was no answer to my question, and I asked my question again. Haig said that it was vital to hold on to the French. In his opinion to get separated from the French meant absolute disaster, as both army and ports would be lost. Foch said that such a retirement as we were considering would never occur, but, if it did, he would fall back to the south and base himself on France. Wemyss [First Sea Lord] and the French Admiral both seemed to think that if we lost the ports we lost everything. Foch asked for more labour. Pétain underlined my question and Foch's final answer, and that it had now been decided that for the British to hold on to the French came first, and the ports second. *This was unanimously agreed to.*'[5]

The British, having regained the initiative over the French, were determined to keep it in the discussion that followed on the Czechs. Lord Milner wished the Supreme War Council simply to accept Joint Notes 20 and 25 by the military representatives. (The first, of April 8, advocated immediate Allied intervention in Russia, mainly by the Japanese, with the help of Czech and other elements already on the spot. The second, of April 27, urged that the Czechs be shipped to France both via northern Russia and the Far East; while waiting for ships, however, they could be 'profitably employed' in defending the northern Russian ports and the Murmansk railway, and in cooperating with the Allies in Siberia, as recommended in Joint Note 20). Clemenceau emphasized that shipping the Czechs was above all a question of tonnage. They were excellent troops, who should be brought to France as soon as possible; 2,000 were arriving at Vladivostok every day. He wondered if the Japanese could ship them. Lloyd George agreed; he had heard that they were the best fighting men of all the Slav countries. If they could be assembled at Vladivostok, they might be brought away in American or Japanese ships. There were no British or Canadian ships available, and American shipping was already heavily committed. 'We are therefore faced', stated Lloyd George, 'with two alternatives:

1. The Allies should insist on the Japanese providing sufficient tonnage to ship these Czechs;
2. The Allied governments should obtain from Trotsky permission for these troops to proceed by rail to Archangel and Murmansk, from where they would be embarked for the western front.[6]

From the point of view of gaining time, the last alternative presents great advantages.'*

Milner: As regards the second alternative, I would draw your attention to the fact that on April 14, Trotsky, for reasons that we do not know, gave orders that these troops were to be halted. The Czechs refused to allow themselves to be disarmed, and on April 15, we were advised that they were proceeding on their journey.

Lloyd George: In this case, I think it is preferable to abandon the second alternative.

Clemenceau: If we ask for anything from Trotsky, he will then ask for something in return. What he now wants is an army, munitions and money. I cannot give them to him.

Lloyd George: We are all agreed that these are excellent troops, and we must use them. The question is: how to bring them to the western front? If we plunge into lengthy discussions on the subject, we will lose precious time. I feel that one country should be nominated by the Supreme War Council to find a solution to this question. The one nominated will have to

---

*These minutes are translated from the official French minutes of the Supreme War Council meeting. The English minutes are admitted by Hankey to be a somewhat rushed job intended to give Cabinet Ministers in London an immediate idea of what Hankey thought were the important points. In fact they contain distortions and errors in translation.

find the tonnage.

Clemenceau: France could not then be nominated.

The CIGS: Up to now, France has always been in charge of the Czech troops in Russia. I do not see why England should not take the matter in hand in her turn.

Lloyd George: I am against handing this question over to a committee or body of any sort. A government should take the matter in hand. Perhaps America could provide the tonnage.

General Pershing: All the ships that we have must be used to ship American troops.

Milner: I believe, as General Wilson suggests, that England is in as good a position as anyone to find spare tonnage.

Clemenceau: I am quite ready to hand this whole business over to England.

Lloyd George: We gladly accept this proposal; however, I do ask for the support of your representatives in Russia, and I insist that we organize this matter direct with them, and not through Paris, in order to gain time.

Clemenceau: That is easy to arrange. ... There will be no difficulty provided England finds the tonnage.

Milner: We will do all we pcssibly can.

Lloyd George: If we find some ships, the French authorities could see to the transport of the Czechs up to the ports of embarkation.

Clemenceau: That is agreed.

Orlando (the Italian Premier): Are we to understand from this agreement that we are abandoning the alternative of Archangel and Murmansk?

Clemenceau: No, we are not abandoning it, if we can find a way to send the Czechs to these ports.

Milner: I think we should be quite clear about Archangel and Murmansk. The troops at present *en route* towards Vladivostok are the First Czech Corps, which is 40,000 to 50,000 strong. That is quite clear. Trotsky has tried, without success, to stop them. If it is at all possible, this First Corps must be brought to Europe. But other volunteers are assembling, other groups are forming. We must see to their shipment also. Because of the difficulties of finding tonnage, they should not be made to take the same route to Vladivostok, where there is a risk of congesting the port. I think they should provisionally be grouped together near Omsk or Chelyabinsk. At the present moment, 40,000 men are the most that can be shipped from Vladivostok. I ask the Council to be quite clear about this.

This was generally agreed. But when Milner then urged the Supreme War Council to accept Joint Note 25, which, he claimed, already anticipated this alternative, Clemenceau declined; he felt they should use more precise terms. At the end of the meeting therefore, the following resolution was approved:

'The Supreme War Council approve Joint Note 25 of the military representatives, and agree on the following action:

(a) The British government undertake to do their best to arrange the transportation of those Czech troops who are at Vladivostok or on their way to that Port.
(b) The French Government undertake the responsibility of those troops until they are embarked.
(c) The British government undertake to approach M. Trotsky with a view to the concentration at Murmansk and Archangel of those Czech troops not belonging to the Army Corps which has left Omsk for Vladivostok.'[6]

But this new resolution was not more precise, as Clemenceau claimed. It was totally at variance with Joint Note 25, which also laid down Omsk as the dividing line for the Czechs that were to go to northern Russia or Vladivostok. Like the DMI in London on May 1, the Supreme War Council in Abbeville on May 2 had confused the two Czech Corps, and had assumed that the First Corps, in fact still delayed at Penza, was now well into Siberia on its way to the Far East. But since the minutes of this meeting make it clear that Clemenceau was handing the Czech Legion over to the British, in return for the necessary shipping, and the final resolution says nothing about shipping any Czechs from the northern Russian ports, the British assumed that they could use those Czechs who came to northern Russia for whatever purpose suited them best. Milner also imagined that he had pulled off quite a *coup* in returning to the original War Office proposal of April 1, i.e. the concentration of all the remaining Czechs round Omsk or Chelyabinsk, from where they could seize these two vital cities on the Siberian railway. Once the French saw what these Czechs could do to protect Siberia and northern Russia from German encroachments, and thus restore the eastern front, nothing more would be heard of shipping them to France. The British thus came away well satisfied from the Abbeville conference; but the 'imprecision' of the final resolution was not appreciated by either side.

The British and French afterwards wired to their respective representatives in Moscow, Lockhart and Lavergne, to arrange with Trotsky for part of the Czech Legion to proceed to northern Russia — it was still not known in London or Paris that Chicherin had already sent such an order, with no explanation whatever, to the local soviets; nor that the Czechs, when they got to hear of it, thought it must be a Bolshevik–German plot to split up the Czech Legion. These Allied instructions to Moscow appear to have crossed with a telegram from the French consul at Irkutsk, sent on May 3, containing a message from Colonel Paris, the French liaison officer with the Czech vanguard, in which he urged the French War Ministry to have ships ready at Vladivostok for a whole Czech division by May 15, and confirmed that another Czech division then in Siberia could proceed to France via Vologda and Archangel. Thus some French liaison officers with the Legion were already aware of Allied plans, first sent to Moscow in late April; but it does not appear that Major Guinet and Captain Pascal (the French liaison officers with Czech troops in the Volga-Urals area) knew of them.[7]

On May 5, Lavergne and Lockhart wired to Paris and London respectively that Trotsky not only agreed in principle to part of the Czech Legion being rerouted to Archangel, but also to hand over some of the Allied war supplies there to them on arrival. Lavergne added, however, that he doubted whether the rerouting project would in fact work; he also urged the French government to keep these negotiations secret, as it would undoubtedly embarrass the Bolsheviks if it was revealed that the Czechs were to be re-armed at Archangel. Confirmation of Trotsky's offer is to be found in a letter that Lockhart wrote that day to Colonel Robins, under-lining various instances of Trotsky's helpfulness to the Allies:

5. He [Trotsky] has agreed to send the Czech Corps to Murmansk and Archangel.
6. Finally, he has today [May 5] come to a full agreement with us regarding the Allied stores at Archangel whereby we shall be allowed to retain those stores which we require for ourselves.

This also appears to confirm that Trotsky did not wish it to be broadcast that he would allow the Czechs to have some of the Allied war supplies at Archangel. The French government, however, at once informed Benes of this 'great concession' by the Bolsheviks. Benes was highly pleased. 'Our military position amongst the Allies was from now on assured', he writes. 'Politically, I had Clemenceau's promise [of eventual recognition]. ... I considered the moment had come for me to settle all these questions directly with the British government.' Therefore, after a talk with Lord Derby (the British ambassador to Paris), Benes left for London.[7]

On May 6, the War Cabinet were informed of the resolution taken at Abbeville, and of a further wire from *Suffolk* at Vladivostok stating that 3,000 more Czech troops had now arrived, making 7,000 in all. It was agreed that the next step was for the British to do their best to carry out the decisions reached. The War Office was instructed to take the matter up with the Ministry of Shipping, and Balfour was asked to approach Trotsky (which, of course, he had already done).

The War Cabinet were informed that Admiral Kemp had telegraphed from Murmansk that a party of armed White Finns were advancing on

Petchenga, the Russian port east of Murmansk, and at the request of the Murmansk soviet, he had sent the cruiser *Cochrane*, with a small party of British marines and Red Guards on board, to protect Petchenga and disperse or capture any White Finns they encountered. This news undoubtedly increased the War Cabinet's fear of the eventual loss of Murmansk, so it may be useful at this point to summarize the movements of the White Finns.

In March, a fairly large detachment of Red Finns had arrived in the area of Kandalaksha, the port at the north-eastern tip of the White Sea; according to Kennan, they mainly sought food and hoped to find some near the Murmansk railway. As Admiral Kemp had very few troops at his disposal, he was glad to accept any men opposed to the pro-German White Finns; thus the presence of the Red Finns was easily tolerated by both Admiral Kemp and the Murmansk soviet to the south. But in early April, a small White Finn detachment appeared to hem in the Red Finns until the approaching thaw prevented any further movement by anyone.[8] Skirmishes took place, after which more White Finns appeared to the south at Ukhta and sent an armed party due west to the port of Kem, on the eastern shore of the White Sea. Kemp, at the request of the Murmansk soviet, hastily improvised an armoured train, fitted it with naval guns, and a crew of British marines and a few French artillerymen, and sent it down, under a French colonel, to protect Kandalaksha. Quite independently, the Archangel soviet, which was openly hostile to the Allies — and thus to the Murmansk soviet also — sent a small party on an icebreaker to protect Kem. This White Finn activity was clearly seen, both by the War Cabinet and Admiral Kemp at Murmansk, as the beginning of a general attack by pro-German forces on Murmansk, and it was for this reason that the British were anxious to have part of the Czech Legion sent by rail to northern Russia, as they were unable to reinforce Murmansk themselves.[8]

This Allied and pro-Allied activity led to a considerable exaggeration of the real northern Russian situation in Berlin. On April 22, the Bolshevik government received a German protest alleging that, according to Norwegian press reports, 6,000 British and French troops had arrived at Murmansk. On the 27th, while still investigating the matter, Chicherin sent a protest to Berlin against various German infringements of the Brest-Litovsk treaty, and asked if the German government still considered the treaty to be in force; if it did not, he asked what new demands the German government had in Finland and the Ukraine. On May 2, Chicherin replied that the reported arrival of 6,000 Allied troops at Murmansk was false and that the Bolsheviks had arrested the Russian editors who publicized it. But the White Finnish encroachments continued.

A small force now appeared near the junction of the Norwegian, Finnish and Russian frontiers, drove back the Russian frontier guards, and moved on the port of Petchenga. It was this move that led Admiral Kemp to despatch the *Cochrane.*[9] This was the position in northern Finland when on May 6 the War Cabinet were informed of the latest developments. Two days later, when the German government presented its new demands at Chicherin's request, matters came to a head in both northern and southern Finland.

When the last warships of the Baltic Fleet arrived at Kronstadt from Helsinki in mid to late April, the Bolshevik government were faced with an acute problem. The Baltic Fleet had helped to put the Bolsheviks in power and might just as easily unseat them. Many of the Russian officers were avowed counter-revolutionaries; many of the original Bolshevik sailors had deserted in Helsinki and had had to be replaced hurriedly by local Finns, who were largely under German influence. Only small groups of sailors remained entirely loyal to the Bolsheviks. The chief commissar, Blokhin, had been elected by the Centrobalt, which was in turn elected by the ships' committees. But Blokhin, it was known, was Admiral Chastny's man; and although the Bolshevik government had already abolished the Centrobalt, Blokhin was still chief commissar. Further, explosives had been positioned aboard some of the warships (allegedly aboard all) at Helsinki. But if the Bolshevik government gave orders for the Fleet to be scuttled at anchor, it would be said that the Bolsheviks were simply carrying out German orders. Admiral Chastny was now a hero to his crews for his feat of seamanship in bringing nearly all the warships safely back through the thick winter ice, with only two icebreakers, to its home port of Kronstadt; only a few vessels had been let behind at Helsinki under a Russian naval officer.

Chastny, like the good naval officer he seems to have been, was most anxious for the welfare of his fleet, and not, initially, as anti-Bolshevik as some of his brother officers would have liked. They decided to work him up against the Bolsheviks. Soon after his return to Kronstadt, he received a letter containing four documents. The first, dated March 30, was allegedly from the Intelligence section of the German General staff to Lenin, criticizing the appointment of Blokhin as chief commissar of the Baltic Fleet, since he opposed Germany's views and was hindering her plans. (Thus if the Bolshevik government succeeded in getting rid of Blokhin, as indeed they wished to do, it would be said in the fleet that they were acting on German orders.) Another document, allegedly from Russian counter-espionage to the Bolshevik government, stated that they had on many occasions reported that there were German spies in the Baltic Fleet, but no action had been taken against them. (Many of the Finns, who had been taken on as sailors at Helsinki, were undoubtedly acting for Germany.) Another document, dated April 19, again allegedly from the intelligence section of the German General Staff to the head of the Petrograd soviet, stated that they had definite information that a group of anarchist sailors at Kronstadt had decided to hand over part of the Baltic Fleet to the Finnish Red

Guards to help them defend Viborg and Biorko against the White Finns, and that such action had the approval of the Petrograd soviet. The document warned that the German High Command would consider such action to be sufficient reason to occupy Petrograd and to insist on the complete disarmament of Kronstadt and of the warships in the naval harbour. (It was probably true that the intention was either to try and hand over the remaining vessels at Helsinki, or some of the ships back at Kronstadt, to the Red Finns to hinder a possible German advance on Petrograd. Thus any move in that direction could be shown to be German-inspired.) These documents were soon going round the Baltic Fleet. (They are, of course, very similar to many of the 'Sisson documents', and were almost certainly manufactured by the Russian officers' 'wire group', which did produce some genuine material.[10])

It is probable also that Chastny had already received these documents by April 25, when he was summoned to appear before the Higher Military Council (the forerunner to the Military Revolutionary Council of the Republic). Trotsky later claimed that he and the other Bolsheviks attending the council were very favourably inclined towards Chastny when the meeting opened, because of his skill in bringing the Baltic Fleet back to Kronstadt through the thick winter ice. But they were dismayed when he began to read out a report in which he described the Baltic Fleet as being in a hopeless state; technically it was still in good condition (Trotsky reports him as saying), but the prevailing indiscipline made it quite unfit for operations; it was just 'scrap-iron'. Chastny was instructed to propose talks with the German Command at Helsinki to establish a demarcation line in the Gulf of Finland and to defend it with floating mines. He was also told that Russian warships were not to intervene against the White Finns besieging Fort Ino. But the Baltic Fleet was to defend itself if attacked, and in extreme circumstances (that is to say if there was no other way out), it was to be sabotaged. Chastny, however, had full powers and full responsibility. In due course, he instructed the Russian naval officer, left at Helsinki, to open talks with the Germans, as Trotsky had directed, though Chastny told Trotsky that he felt such action was premature. To fix a demarcation line now would simply hand over to the Germans all that had been left behind at Helsinki, and Fort Ino.

On May 1, Chastny, back in Petrograd, received a message from Helsinki saying that his representative considered it impossible to get the Germans to agree to a demarcation line at that time. Trotsky thereupon instructed Chastny to open talks with the Germans at once; Chastny wired to Helsinki again. On May 3, Trotsky contacted Chastny again, *en clair*, that if the Baltic Fleet was endangered by the Germans, even in Kronstadt, it should be blown up, and all preparatory measures were to be taken at once. (This presumably was to warn the Germans, who would be expected to intercept the wire, that it would not be worth their while to advance on

Kronstadt and Petrograd.) The Russian naval officers and the Finnish crews declined to sabotage the warships, and rumours were soon spread round the Fleet that the Bolshevik government had agreed with the Germans, in a secret clause in the Brest–Litovsk treaty, to destroy the Baltic Fleet. These rumours seem to have had a considerable effect and set many of the crews against the Bolshevik government. Trotsky's advisers now warned him that as the Bolshevik government evidently had very little control over the Baltic Fleet, which was in a state of indiscipline, it would be impossible to ensure the complete destruction of all the warships if the Germans now made a sudden attack. Trotsky then decided to organize a shock group of sailors on board each ship, who could be trusted and were devoted to the Bolshevik cause, and who would destroy the warships when ordered. To guarantee their devotion to the cause, Trotsky decided that they were to be paid handsomely as well. On May 7, the Russian officer at Helsinki wired to report that the Germans refused to answer his demand for the establishment of a demarcation line; consequently Trotsky sent Admiral Altfater, Commander-in-Chief, Red Navy, to Petrograd to make an investigation, and to report on whether the Baltic Fleet was ready to be blown up. Altfater reported to Trotsky that everything was now ready, save for the cash deposits in the bank, as the Centrobalt (still hanging on, despite its official repudiation) was opposed to paying the Baltic sailors for what it was their duty to perform.[10] The result was that the sailors grew even more suspicious of the Bolsheviks and more inclined to believe that they had already come to some secret understanding with the Germans to destroy the Baltic Fleet.

This was the position on May 8, when the German government replied to Chicherin's request of April 27 to be informed of any new German demands in Finland. In a note 'which almost has the character of an ultimatum', as Lenin described it later, the Germans demanded that the Bolsheviks expel the British from Murmansk, hand Fort Ino over to Finland (i.e. to the pro-German White Finns), and disarm and repatriate the Latvian regiments (whose bayonets were effectively maintaining the Bolsheviks in power)[11] Latvia then being under German control. Unless these demands were met, there would be 'most grave' consequences; Germany would have to undertake further military operations and occupy more Russian territory. This note was considered in Moscow to be very serious and the Bolshevik government met that same day to discuss it.

The British reaction to these German demands was both open and secret. Reilly, on arrival in Moscow on May 7, tried a direct approach. In the uniform of a British officer, he went straight to the Kremlin, banged on the gate and demanded to see Lenin. He must have produced some credentials, for he was taken straight in to see one of Lenin's close colleagues. He had been sent out specially by Lloyd George, Reilly said, to obtain first-hand information on the real aims of the Bolsheviks, as the British government were not satisfied with Lockhart's reports (so the assistant commissar for Foreign Affairs that evening told Lockhart, who records that he 'knew instinctively' that his informant was speaking the truth). It was a warning as much to the Bolsheviks as to Lockhart. But Reilly seems to have been rebuffed.

At 6.40 p.m. on May 8, the Admiralty received a wire (no. 125) from Captain Cromie saying that he had a scheme in progress for blocking Kronstadt harbour with three British steamers, which would be sunk at the entrance, and for blowing up four Russian battleships and fourteen destroyers within the naval harbour, at a total cost of about £300,000.

The scheme was considered by the War Cabinet in closed session at 11.30 a.m. on May 10. The First Lord stated that Cromie had reported that the 'chief organizer concerned is reliable, and is assisted by well-known Secret Service Officers and that all arrangements are practically completed.' (It may be taken as certain that Sidney Reilly was closely connected with this operation.)[12]

Payments for 'services rendered', stated the First Lord, were to be as follows:

For blocking of Kronstadt harbour		
1 million roubles	£32,258	
Sum for organization		
varying from £1,000 to	15,000	(according to number of ships blocked in)
	1,500	(payable in England)
		£48,758
For destruction of four dreadnoughts		
600,000 r. each	£77,420	
£7,500 each (£500 for organiz-ation and £7,000 for destruction)	30,000	£107,420
For destruction of fourteen destroyers		
250,000 r. each	£112,903	
£1,500 each (£200 for organiz-ation and £1,300 for destruction)	21,000	£133,903
For agitation propaganda		
to complete scheme: 300,000 r.		£9,677
Total		£299,758

This was based on a rate of 31 roubles to one pound sterling. Of the above sums, 5% was to be paid on engaging the necessary personnel, a further 10% on the attempt being made, and the remaining 85% if the attempt proved successful. In addition to these sums, said the First Lord, explosives were being purchased. Cromie reported that one dreadnought was now ready for demolition, two were in progress of being prepared, and one was doubtful; five destroyers were ready, five were in progress and four were doubtful. Facilities for leaving Russia, and a sum payable in pounds sterling in England had been offered to the officers concerned; this amount had not been specified by Cromie, but the War Cabinet were assured that it probably would not be considerable.

Cromie warned, however, that if the scheme was carried out it might lead to 'international complications', and certainly to the withdrawal from Russia of himself and his staff. He asked to be told immediately whether to proceed with the scheme and whether to extend it, on similar lines, to the older warships and to the ships under construction. The First Lord asked the War Cabinet for their decision.

The Chancellor asked whether the Admiralty was satisfied that the money would be 'well invested'. The First Lord assured him that the money was well worth spending. Balfour sounded a note of warning. From the Foreign Office's point of view, there would certainly be a 'strong remonstrance' against the sinking of Russian ships and the blowing up of Russian sailors, were the proposed operation to be successful. But the issue was for the Cabinet to decide. General Smuts was even more concerned about the scheme; it was a 'most grave' step to take, 'and ought to be very carefully considered in all its bearings'.

At this point, the Prime Minister decided that a special Cabinet meeting should be held to review the 'whole of our Russian policy: whether we should try to reorganize Russia with military force, in order that German divisions might be absorbed, or whether we must abandon altogether any attempt in that direction'. Such a decision must of necessity be taken before deciding whether or not to destroy the Baltic Fleet. It was agreed to hold a special discussion on Russian policy the following morning.[12]

It may be useful at this juncture to summarize events in the various Russian theatres. In northern Russia, the recent German note (unknown, of course, to the Cabinet) seemed to herald a major German attack to be mounted after the thaw in order to seize Murmansk, and a probable German occupation of Petrograd and seizure of the Baltic Fleet.

From Petrograd, a series of wires from the British supply mission reached London on May 9. The first, a personal wire to General Poole from either Macalpine cr Poliakov, outlined four possible Allied policies in Russia:

1. Allied instigation of 'immediate armed resistance' in European Russia to restore the eastern front;
2. Allied intervention to follow after several months;
3. A 'definite and energetic' Allied commercial policy to ensure that the

Bolshevik government did not resume hostilities, and to restrict Germany to a commercial and economic invasion of Russia;
4. In addition, Allied occupation of Vladivostok and the northern Russian ports, on the pretext of assisting with shipping and transport.

The first was 'doomed to failure'. If the Germans were as well informed about the Russian internal situation as was presumed, they would not need to bring up many reinforcements to counter such an attempt; and if it was put down, it would mean the 'absolute exclusion' of the Allies from Russia and its 'absolute dominion' by Germany. There seemed so little Allied organization and cooperation over Russian policy that the second proposal appeared to be ruled out too. The third policy seemed a possibility, since 'it is hard to conceive its complete failure'. But its success would depend on the pursuit of an energetic Allied commerical policy. The writer recommended the fourth, since the Allies could then 'advance' towards the second policy, or 'retire' on the third. The fourth policy would rally the pro-Allied Russian elements, 'which are rapidly losing hope of any Allied intervention against both Bolshevism and Germanism', even though the Bolsheviks were growing weaker.[13]

The thinking here was somewhat muddled; but the emphasis on the growing despair of the pro-Allied Russian elements found many echoes in other reports. A further wire from Macalpine, sent on the 8th, in answer to Poole's instructions that the British supply mission was not to spend any money, was in jollier tones: 'We are pushing on with the collection of data', he stated, 'and should be ready with heaps of powder and shot for the financial expert who is brave enough to face the dangers here, which have sent out of Russia so many of our bravest and best. Whatever you say, Polly's enthusiasm cannot be damped or even dammed, and he looks forward with the greatest satisfaction to the arrival of the expert.' Macalpine added a final message from Poliakov about the bank schemes: 'He [Poliakov] wishes again to emphasize necessity of transferring assets to some large bank which will hold them on trust for the Treasury.'[13]

On the afternoon of May 10, the Foreign Office produced a short paper for the War Cabinet on President Wilson's views on Allied intervention in Siberia. This outlined the recent negotiations between London, Washington and Tokyo; and stated in conclusion that Secretary Lansing had confirmed to Lord Reading on May 7 that the President was convinced that the present moment was inopportune, nor could a sufficient military advantage be gained. Therefore he could not concur at present in the recent British proposals for intervention. 'Lord Reading is sure that he remains unconvinced that the balance of advantage and disadvantage is in favour of action at present.'[14]

Then there were the Czechs. Not until May 8 did the Czech commanders along the Siberian railway realize that Chicherin's laconic order of April 30, given without any explanation, that part of the Czech Legion was to be rerouted to northern Russia, had been issued in agreement with the Allied representatives in Moscow. This caused total confusion. Why should the Allies agree to split up and thus weaken the Legion? On the 9th, Maxa and Markovic (members of the Czech national council) left Omsk for Moscow to clarify matters.[15]

Benes (in London) knew nothing of all this. He knew that he had no control over the Czech Legion, but was determined to make the maximum use of the Legion in extracting political concessions, *ie*, eventual recognition, from the British. On the afternoon of the 10th, Wickham Steed took Benes to the Foreign Office to see Balfour. Benes tried to play the British off against the French. He harped on all that the French had done for them, and asked for the immediate recognition of the Czech national council and the Czech Legion, 'which would show that the British Government approved our war aims in the same way that the French government did'. He reminded Balfour that the British had already made some concessions to the Poles, and claimed the right to the same treatment. Benes states that Balfour later paid 'full tribute' to their military efforts, 'and acknowledged that in Russia we were the only group which had resisted the Bolshevik chaos and for as long as possible had kept an eastern front going against the Germans'. Benes further reports Balfour as saying that the Allies had just taken the 'necessary decisions' about the Czech Legion at Abbeville. Benes himself said that the French had intimated their willingness to make an official declaration in their favour before long. Nothing was said about splitting up the Legion. It appears that Balfour realized Benes knew very little of the situation.[16] Benes does not mention that Balfour stated cautiously (as the Foreign Secretary informed the Cabinet next day) that it might well be impossible to find sufficient shipping to bring the Czech Legion to France, and asked if they would be prepared to fight in Russia. Benes replied that the Czechs had no wish to be used as gendarmes. They wished to fight the Germans; but they would not object to being used in Russia, if commanded by British and French officers. On this understanding, the meeting seems to have ended.

Balfour appears to have been aware that the Ministry of Shipping had complained strongly to the War Office on the 9th that shipping the Czechs from Vladivostok to France via North America would seriously dislocate the shipping arrangements for bringing American troops to Europe and would entail lengthy delays. And if they were brought via the Suez canal, it would mean using troop-ships that already could not cope with the requirements of India and operations in Mesopotamia.[17]

Sir Henry Wilson certainly was aware of the Ministry of Shipping's complaint when he received a wire from Clemenceau on the morning of the 11th, saying that General Lavergne had received a wire in Moscow on May

4 stating that there were still 20,000 Czechs and 3,000 Serbs west of Omsk, who were due to proceed to the northern Russian ports. (This message was presumably from one of the French liaison officers with the Legion.) The Bolsheviks, added Clemenceau, seemed prepared to allow them to be rerouted. He was evidently surprised that there were still *so* many Czechs in European Russia, and unwilling to lose such a large number to the British, as tacitly agreed at Abbeville, now stated that it was agreed in Joint Note 25 (approved at Abbeville) that these Czechs should go to northern Russia, and thence to France, leaving behind only those troops 'strictly necessary' for the defence of the northern Russian ports. The Abbeville resolution, he went on, laid down that the British representatives in Russia would negotiate with the Bolshevik government in regard to the concentration of the Czechs in North Russia. 'But it does not state explicitly how the available [Czech] elements would be brought to the western front.' By analogy with the arrangements agreed for the removal of the Czech contingents *en route* for Vladivostok, it seemed that France should be responsible for getting them to Archangel and Murmansk, and Britain for shipping them to France. He asked if Sir Henry Wilson agreed on this 'interpretation' of the Supreme War Council's resolution at Abbeville.[18] Clemenceau was in no position to complain of any imprecision in this resolution, since he had pointedly refused Milner's suggestion on May 2 that they should simply approve Joint Note 25, and had personally insisted on drawing up a resolution himself in 'more precise terms' on action to be taken — which said nothing whatever about shipping the Czechs from northern Russia, since it was tacitly agreed that in return for the British shipping the Czechs from Vladivostok, the French would allow the British to make whatever use they wished of those Czechs that got up to northern Russia; and the French presumed that very few Czechs would arrive there. It was now apparent that no less than 20,000 Czechs were going to northern Russia.

It was with this French duplicity in mind that Lord Milner and the CIGS entered the Cabinet room at 11 a.m. on May 11 for the major review of Russian policy. The First Sea Lord stated that Captain Cromie had further reported that German cavalry and motor-cars had arrived at Helsinki on April 12, simultaneously with the German warships; and the Finnish White Guards had seized the Russian trawler flotilla, which the Russians had used to sweep mines. 'The Germans and White Guards talked openly of taking Petrograd.' With that, the War Cabinet went into closed session to discuss Cromie's plan to destroy the Baltic Fleet, and Russian policy generally.[19]

The Prime Minister stated that the proposals for the destruction of the Baltic Fleet meant that the War Cabinet had to take an important decision on future policy in Russia. 'The question which had to be decided was whether there was hope of any material assistance from Russia in the future, or whether anything was to be gained by not driving Russia into the arms of Germany.' If the fleet was destroyed, it would inevitably be found out who was responsible; or it would at any rate be said that it had been carried out at the instigation of the British government. The First Sea Lord agreed that such action 'might [written over 'would probably', which is crossed out] antagonize Russia', and set Trotsky against Britain.

Balfour stated that he regarded with dismay the prospect of driving Russia into the arms of Germany. 'While we were all talking, Germany was acting.' She already had the Crimea, and part of the Black Sea Fleet (it was still not known in London that the bulk of the fleet had escaped to Novorossisk); she had Finland and was threatening Murmansk; she not only had the whole of the Ukraine, but was extending its frontiers to suit her own purposes. Moreover, Germany was gaining 'complete control' of what was left of Russian industry and finance. It would be impossible for the Russian people ever to resist, if Allied action threw them into the arms of Germany. The question he would ask was whether the destruction of the Baltic Fleet would have this effect; he felt it certainly would, if Trotsky wanted to quarrel with us — at any rate, there was some danger of it happening. Lord Milner felt that the crucial question was 'whether the Russians preferred the Germans to us: if they did not, he did not see why they should object to the destruction of the fleet'.

In Balfour's view, it was impossible to define the situation in this way. Lockhart, in a recent telegram (of about May 8), reported that Kerensky's former Minister of Trade had told him that 'nothing could now save Russia except foreign help'; many classes in Russia, who hated the Bolsheviks, looked to foreign intervention; but 'he would be the first to range himself against Japanese intervention'. Balfour emphasized that the present proposal to blow up the Baltic Fleet raised 'much larger issues', and these issues must be discussed. Lord Curzon asked what Trotsky had stated about the Baltic Fleet; he had understood that it had been arranged for the Russians to blow it up. Could not Trotsky be told that as he had done nothing, and as the danger to the Black Sea Fleet of which we had warned him had proved true, it was essential for Britain to take action over the Baltic Fleet?

Major-General Poole remarked that he was strongly opposed to blowing up the Baltic Fleet, if it meant a 'definite break' with Russia; more good could be done by 'working in Russia'. The present proposal would entail some loss of life, and this must have a bad effect. The First Lord said that everything would be done to avoid loss of life; the Baltic Fleet could be destroyed without such loss — though of course it was impossible to guarantee it.

General Smuts stressed that it was vital not to antagonize the Russians. He felt strongly that the Russian government must be consulted, 'for, to perform what was undoubtedly an act of war before consultation with the Russian government, would be, in his opinion, most reprehensible, and after such an act we must be prepared for any consequences'. The Baltic Fleet consisted of five dreadnoughts, nine cruisers, seventy destroyers and twenty-six submarines, and for such a number to fall into enemy hands would be a very serious matter. It was, therefore, essential that measures be taken to destroy this fleet in the event of imminent danger, and Britain should urge Trotsky to take the necessary measures. The Russians, in fact, should be urged to take action themselves, but at the same time the Admiralty should complete their preparations to carry out Cromie's scheme, if necessary. The First Lord suggested that Cromie be instructed to make the necessary arrangements, but not to act until so ordered. It was vital though that these warships should be disabled, particularly the destroyers.[19]

At this point, the War Cabinet adjourned to watch a march past of the American troops on their way to the western front. This evidently gave Lloyd George some ideas.

On returning to the Cabinet Room, the PM asked the CIGS whether it would be possible to transfer some Allied troops to help Trotsky, if the next German attack on the western front failed, not only to prevent more German troops being moved from the Russian front, 'but possibly, and even probably, to make the Germans transfer some divisions from west to east'. Could not the French and British governments propose to Trotsky that, if he was prepared to fight, they would give him some troops, 'and that he could also have the use of the 70,000 Czechoslovak troops now in Russia and Siberia?' If so, the Japanese would find it very difficult to refuse to join in. General Poole, reported the Prime Minister, considered the best place to land Allied troops would be Archangel, as the Murmansk situation was unclear (and the Murmansk railway was always in bad condition in summer). It was impossible to disregard Lockhart's latest telegrams about Trotsky's attitude: 'There was no doubt that up to a certain point M. Trotsky had played into German hands, but that his view had considerably changed, and that it could be assumed that it did not [now] suit M. Trotsky to be under German domination.' (This, of course, ignores the ardent desire of the Bolsheviks, and of Trotsky, to play the Allies off against the Germans, balancing the two opposing forces). Could we help Trotsky in this way? the Prime Minister asked the CIGS. Some American troops might be diverted to Vladivostok; it would be unnecessary to use highly-trained troops, but it was very desirable to send a 'nucleus' of Allied troops to Russia, 'so that M. Trotsky might feel that he had some force behind him'. Milner agreed; immediate action was necessary and time was all-important. But the Prime Minister was not so sure; reports indicated that the Germans were undoubtedly using brutal methods in Russia, especially in the Ukraine, which were arousing fierce anti-German feelings. He did not suggest a long delay, as he assumed that the next two or three weeks would show whether the German onslaught in France had been stopped.

In answer to all this, the CIGS asked for time for consideration: it would be impossible to divert any troops at present, 'and probably it would not be known for some time — at any rate for many weeks ['many' written over 'six', which is crossed out] — who was to be the master in the western theatre of operation'. General Poole suggested that it would make a start if even 5,000 troops could be sent straightaway; they could be sent to Archangel and Vologda, and if attacked at Vologda, they could blow up the Vologda railway bridge (thus cutting the Archangel–Moscow railway) and await further reinforcements at Archangel. 'The presence of 5,000 Allied troops would ensure the accumulation of 100,000 Russian troops behind them', stated Poole. (This rash remark was to have dire consequences.)

Balfour felt bound to draw attention to the arrangements being made by the French to bring the 50,000 Czechs from Vladivostok to France, for which we, as agreed at Abbeville, had to try to find shipping. Yesterday, he had seen the three Czech representatives in London and had pointed out that it seemed impossible that there would be enough ships available to bring these troops to France, and he asked if they would be prepared to fight in Russia. He had understood the answer to be that the Czechs were afraid of only being used as gendarmes in Russia, but they were very eager to fight the Germans, and if commanded by British and French officers, they would not object. Balfour emphasized that these troops would be 'invaluable' in Russia, 'particularly as they were Slavs'. Austen Chamberlain supported Balfour; the Allied Naval Council's latest report showed that there was such a shortage of shipping that all army supplies and imports would have to be reviewed. Therefore the Cabinet agreed that there was 'no possibility, at any rate at the present, of transport being available to ship the Czech divisions to France'.

The Cabinet discussed next what Trotsky's attitude would be were he to be informed that some 50,000 Czechs, and some 20,000 fully equipped American, British and French troops were ready to support him. Balfour drew attention to his recent wire to Lord Reading, stressing the 'gradual but most important change' in Trotsky's attitude, as reported by Lockhart. Balfour had said in his wire that Trotsky's present embarrassment arose from his belief, 'only too well-founded', that while the Germans could attack the Bolsheviks at once, the Allies, even if invited, would not be ready to support the Bolsheviks for a long time. The Prime Minister said that Trotsky 'could go no further than he had done. It was obvious that M. Trotsky could not trust M. Lenin, who was a disciple of Tolstoy, and that if he [Trotsky] were to make open overtures to the Allies, the Germans would know of this at once.' (It is not clear who had suggested to Lloyd George that the influence of Tolstoy was dividing Lenin and Trotsky.) The Prime Minister suggested that a special Cabinet committee should consider the best way of organizing help for Trotsky. A mission should also be sent to Russia, the importance of which Trotsky must recognize, to agree on some definite policy; the Allies however must obviously be prepared to act without waiting for an invitation from Trotsky.

Lord Curzon suggested that this Cabinet committee should also consider the proposed destruction of the Baltic Fleet; he feared that while we were discussing plans, the Baltic Fleet would be seized by the Germans. The First Lord felt that the best course was to instruct Cromie to continue his preparations. If someone could then go to Trotsky, he could be made to understand that we intended to destroy the Baltic Fleet, with or without his acquiescence, rather than run the risk of letting it fall into German hands, as had happened to the Black Sea Fleet. Balfour suggested that he should wire Lockhart, point out to him the fate of the Black Sea Fleet, and that, as it was vital that the Germans should not gain control of the Baltic Fleet, and as Trotsky had agreed to its destruction in principle, 'we considered that we [Britain] were entitled to destroy it'. He would ask Lockhart to wire at once if he had any objections, but not to speak to Trotsky about the matter; Balfour emphasized that such a telegram would enable Lockhart to reply either (*a*) that what we were about to do was something with which he could not possibly agree, or (*b*) that he did not think that the Russians would take so serious a view of our action as to be antagonized by it. Austen Chamberlain remarked that Cromie's wire stated that some ships were ready for destruction; and if this meant that explosive was already on board, interception of such a telegram might lead to the ships being searched. The First Lord said that this pointed to the need for someone who knew the mind of the Cabinet seeing Trotsky; meanwhile, preparations for the destruction of the Baltic Fleet should be continued. All that Cromie wanted was authority to spend money to complete his preparations. It was pointed out that the Germans were only 150 kilometres (90 miles), or three to four days' march from Petrograd, and Cromie would have to take immediate action, were they to advance any further.

The War Cabinet decided that Milner should summon a Cabinet committee, comprising General Smuts, the First Sea Lord, the CIGS and himself, to consider the best way of organizing help for Trotsky, and to put a definite proposal on the matter before the Cabinet. The First Lord was directed to instruct Cromie to continue his preparations for the destruction of the Baltic Fleet, and if he had reason to believe that the Germans were advancing on Petrograd and that the Fleet was in imminent danger, 'he was to take action'. Cromie was also to be informed that he had authority for all necessary expenditure, 'but care should be taken not to alienate unnecessarily the Russian government'.

May 11 was thus a major turning point in the War Cabinet's Russian policy. It was assumed, incorrectly, that Trotsky was now much more pro-Allied than before, and that only an overwhelming German presence prevented him from making a request for Allied intervention. It was concluded that Britain could safely and rightly intervene without such a request by landing a small Allied force in northern Russia, which would act in conjunction with the Czech Legion, and precipitate first Japanese and then American intervention. It was agreed both not to transport the Czechs from any Russian port (in defiance of the Abbeville resolution), but not to tell the French of this; in fact to double-cross the French, as Clemenceau had that morning tried to double-cross the War Office. It was further agreed that a British mission should go to Russia to agree on a policy with Trotsky (Lloyd George almost certainly had Smuts in mind): but whether the mission or the Allied troops were to arrive first was not stated, though it is clear that this Cabinet fell in with General Poole's dangerous assumption that the mere presence of a small Allied force would 'ensure' the instant assembly of a large pro-Allied Russian host behind them.

Finally, this War Cabinet gave full authority to Captain Cromie to blow up the Baltic Fleet if the Germans advanced on Petrograd, and they were already very close. This action would certainly have hurled all Russians, and not only the Bolsheviks, into German arms, and thus completely nullified all attempts to support the Bolsheviks against the Germans. The Cabinet, though aware of this risk, underrated it.[19] From now on, the Cabinet, when further considering Russian affairs, had to keep one ear perpetually cocked to catch the possible unwelcome echo of a mighty explosion in the Kronstadt dockyards.

5

New British Policy: Czech intervention

On the afternoon of May 11, General Smuts assembled the Cabinet committee (himself, Milner, the CIGS and the First Sea Lord) to consider what immediate steps could be taken to organize military resistance to the Germans in Russia 'while the correspondence with America and Japan in reference to intervention was proceeding'. The following conclusions were reached:

1. The Cabinet committee found much 'confusion and cross-correspondence' due to the lack of any definition of Allied spheres of military responsibility in Russia. They also found it strange that the Czechs should be removed from Russia to the western front, at a time when great efforts were being made to secure Japanese intervention in Russia; the shipping controller had reported that the shipment of Czech troops would deprive the same number of American troops of shipping, and it seemed inadvisable to ask for Japanese ships, all of which would be absorbed, when we were pressing Japan to intervene. The Cabinet committee decided that those Czechs now at, or *en route* for Vladivostok should be organized there into 'efficient units' by the French, to whom these shipping difficulties should be explained, and who should be asked to agree to such units being used, pending their eventual shipment to France, 'to stiffen the Japanese as part of an Allied force of intervention in Russia'. It was also decided that the remaining Czechs should be organized at Murmansk and Archangel, preferably the latter, by the British, and that pending their shipment to France, they should be used both to hold the northern Russian ports, 'and to take part in any Allied intervention in Russia'. Milner undertook to send a wire to Clemenceau (who had asked him about shipping the Czechs from Vladivostok under the Abbeville agreement). It was felt that the mere organization of large bodies of troops at these various Russian ports 'would in itself be a warning to Germany against the removal of further divisions to the western front'.[1]

2. The Cabinet committee decided that General Poole should proceed at once to northern Russia to advise the War Office generally about 'our intervention'; his London office would meanwhile assemble the officers and NCOs necessary to assist him in 'organizing the Czechoslovaks and other forces of intervention from Archangel and Murmansk'. The First Sea Lord undertook to send some 200 marines to defend Archangel, and the War Office to send the necessary munitions and supplies. General Poole, while holding Murmansk and Archangel, was meanwhile to consider 'how far he could work up from Archangel towards Vologda with the forces at his disposal'.

3. The Cabinet committee considered it inadvisable at present to move either American or other Allied troops from France to Russia, though the matter should be reconsidered at a later stage of the present German offensive.

4. At the War Cabinet that morning, the Prime Minister emphasized 'how difficult and indeed impossible' it was for Trotsky to invite Allied intervention, however much he might desire it, before an Allied force was on the spot to protect him against Germany. The Cabinet committee agreed that, in recent correspondence, 'undue weight' had been placed on the desirability of a Bolshevik invitation. It was, therefore, decided to recommend to the Foreign Office that the difficulties over such an invitation should be pointed out to America and Japan, 'and that they should be pressed to be satisfied with the very strong expressions which had already fallen from M. Trotsky and the Bolshevik Foreign Minister [Chicherin] without waiting for a formal invitation, which the Bolshevik government could not be expected to make in their present helpless situation'.

At 6.10 p.m. that evening, the CIGS, without waiting for Cabinet approval, put the Cabinet committee's main proposal to Clemenceau, in answer to the Premier's wire received that morning. The War Office had been 'hard at work', stated Sir Henry Wilson, trying to find shipping for the Czechs, as agreed at Abbeville, but all British and American ships were being used to bring American troops to France, and he hesitated to ask for Japanese ships, while pressing the Japanese to intervene. Meanwhile, it was vital to keep together, 'and if possible increase' the Czech troops. This he agreed required 'greater precision' in the definition of Allied responsibility for the Czechs.[2] He therefore proposed that:

1. All Czechs now at or *en route* for Vladivostok should be organized into 'efficient units' by French officers, who should keep them in good discipline and good training pending their shipment to France. 'It is a matter for future consideration whether, if it takes a long time to

collect the necessary transports', said Wilson (knowing full well that the War Cabinet had decided that morning not to provide the ships they had undertaken to provide ten days earlier), 'it may not be desirable for the time being to use these troops, or a part of them, in conjunction with the Japanese advance into Siberia. This would help to give it more of an international character,' he suggested.

2. All Czechs not at or *en route* for Vladivostok, as well as the 3,000 Serbs whom Clemenceau had mentioned, should be sent to Murmansk and Archangel (preferably the latter, as the Murmansk railway was unreliable in summer) where they would be taken in hand by British officers. 'When the local defence of the [northern Russian] ports and adjoining country [by which Wilson meant the Russian interior down to Vologda] is assured, as many of them as can be spared will be transported to France as soon as shipping can be collected.'

As might have been expected, Wilson's telegram did not produce 'greater precision', but greater confusion and suspicion. The Anglo-French game of cat-and-mouse over the Czechs continued. (Something of Wilson's real motivation is hinted at in a diary comment later that evening, after speaking with two senior British staff officers from Versailles: 'A long talk about the way in which the French are trying to take over from us militarily and economically', he wrote.)

At noon on May 13, the War Cabinet was informed that Admiral Kemp had wired from Murmansk to say that a French colonel had arrived from Moscow, 'with orders to go to Archangel to superintend the arrival there of Czechs and Serbians'. As the War Cabinet intended that the British were to take matters in hand in northern Russia, this no doubt encouraged them to approve all the Cabinet committee's proposals at once. There followed some discussion about whether a senior British diplomat should accompany General Poole when he left for northern Russia to take charge of 'British military interests' there, in order to coordinate the operations of the various British missions and consulates scattered throughout Russia: an urgent task indeed. But it was generally agreed that, for the moment, military questions were of far greater urgency, and the appointment of a diplomat was held over; ultimately, it was agreed, commerical matters would be highly important, and Balfour mentioned that he had arranged to see Sir Arthur Steel-Maitland, head of the Department of Overseas Trade. Balfour consented to Milner's request that Poole should be allowed to communicate direct with the War Office, but pending the appointment of a diplomatic official, Poole should also communicate with Lockhart, 'and should be careful not to intervene in diplomatic affairs without previously consulting him'. As Poole was to be in northern Russia while Lockhart was in Moscow, this was an open invitation to misunderstanding — and indeed disaster.

This meant that two of the Cabinet committee's proposals had been put into effect; Wilson had already approached the French over the use of the Czechs in the Far East, while General Poole was to take charge of affairs in northern Russia, including the Czechs on arrival there, and to advise the War Cabinet 'how far he could work up from Archangel towards Vologda with the forces at his disposal'.[3]

That same day (May 13), Maxa and Markovic (of the Czech national council) reached Moscow from Omsk to clear up the perplexing matter of rerouting part of the Czech Legion to northern Russia. The Czech troops still west of Omsk (the First Corps) were already grumbling about this change of direction; they feared further clashes with the Germans on their way to Archangel, and with German submarines on the passage from Archangel to France; they were apprehensive that the Germans would see that the Bolsheviks gave them no food for their journey; perhaps above all, they began to distrust their own leaders. Sensing this, the Czech national council's representatives in Moscow had already convoked a 'military congress' of Czech officers, which was to meet at Chelyabinsk on May 20, to resolve any difficulties that had arisen over the Czech Legion's exodus from Russia, and to see it was conducted in accordance with Bolshevik wishes — there had already been various incidents and minor clashes between Czechs and local soviets all along the Siberian railway. The Czech national council, in fact, wanted to reassert its authority. In defiance of this, the Czech communists called their party conference in Moscow on May 20. But on arrival in Moscow on the 13th, Maxa and Markovic were told by General Lavergne that the rerouting order had been issued in accordance with Allied wishes, and Trotsky promised to help them in their move to Archangel; Trotsky had already promised to hand over some of the Allied war supplies there to them on arrival. Maxa and Markovic therefore prepared to return to Omsk to carry out these new arrangements.[4]

Meanwhile, as the War Office waited for a reply from Paris to their suggestion that the French should organize the Czechs in the Far East for action in Siberia, and not ship them to France, they sounded out Benes, who was still in London. On the 14th, the Deputy First Sea Lord informed the War Cabinet that *Suffolk* reported that there were now 10,000 Czech troops at Vladivostok. Colonel L.S. Amery, Lord Milner's Parliamentary Private Secretary, then saw Benes, who agreed that the Czech Legion could take part in large-scale Allied intervention in European Russia against the Germans, provided they were not asked to interfere in Russian internal affairs, and that at least half of the 70,000 Czechs were brought to France.

Benes must have harboured a vague hope that this would satisfy the British, the French, and the Czech Legion itself.

But no one outside Russia — and that of course included Benes — knew that the Legion had already been involved in various incidents and minor clashes with local soviets all along the Siberian railway; and on May 14, there occurred another at that crucial town, Chelyabinsk, where the 'military congress' of Czech officers was to meet on the 20th. At Chelyabinsk station, a Czech train travelling east had been drawn up alongside a train filled with Hungarian prisoners (recently released from camps in Siberia) travelling west to Austria-Hungary. The Hungarians regarded the Czechs as contemptible traitors to their native land. The Czechs regarded the Hungarians as hated overlords. But now the roles were reversed. The Czechs were armed, the Hungarians not. As the Hungarians' train drew out, one of them hurled a piece of scrap-iron at the Czech soldiers below. One of the Czechs fell mortally wounded. The armed Czechs stopped the train, made his comrades hand over the guilty man, and promptly lynched him. The Hungarians' train rumbled off west. But the local soviet then arrived to investigate the incident, and imprisoned several Czech witnesses. A Czech delegation sent to demand their release was also arrested. The Czechs were spurred into action. They seized a local supply of arms and freed their comrades. The matter was soon settled, fairly amicably, with the local soviet. No one outside Chelyabinsk even knew of the incident.[5]

On May 15, Benes was summoned to see Lord Robert Cecil, who held out the hope of British recognition of the Czechs as Allies before the end of the war, if the Czechs in Russia would cooperate. Benes made his usual remarks; they had agreed with the French that at least 30,000 Czechs should come to the western front; they would stand by this, though agree to fight the common enemy on the eastern front, if restored. But some of the troops must be shipped at once, and Britain must help with this; the Czech Legion was in a miserable position in Siberia. But it gradually dawned on Benes during this conversation that there was a 'certain difference of opinion' between Britain and France over the Czech Legion. France, as he knew, badly needed reinforcements and was holding firm to the Abbeville agreement, and wanted the Czech troops brought as soon as possible to the west. 'As far as I could judge', he writes, 'the British, who feared a Bolshevik advance towards the East, were inclined to keep our troops in eastern Siberia to check the Bolshevik and German military advance, and the spread of Bolshevik propaganda in the Far East. [This, of course, was quite incorrect.] ... 'Lord Robert Cecil asked me without hesitation if we would not prefer to leave our troops in Siberia to play this role. ... I replied that at least 30,000 of our troops must be brought to France, in accordance with the former agreement; but this was without prejudice to helping the

Allies to restore the eastern front against Germany, if we could count on joint action for the purpose.'[6] There matters were left, and the meeting ended with no definite decision having been taken. But Benes realized that there was capital to be made out of exploiting this Anglo-French difference over the Czech Legion. He decided to bide his time.

The last of the Cabinet committee's proposals, approved by the War Cabinet on May 13, was for the Foreign Office to urge both America and Japan that though they could not expect a Bolshevik invitation for intervention, they should be satisfied with the 'very strong expressions' by Trotsky in favour of Allied intervention.

On April 30, it will be recalled, President Wilson and the new Japanese ambassador in Washington, Ishii, had discussed the latest British proposal for intervention by an American and Japanese force, with Bolshevik consent, through Siberia. Ishii had said that Japan was ready to intervene, if that would help the common cause, but the danger was that intervention might drive the Russian people, through their hostility to Japan, into German arms. The Japanese did not contemplate going beyond Irkutsk. They wished to be satisfied that the risk entailed would result in definite military advantage (i.e. divert a significant number of German troops from France to Russia). This statement was certainly designed to appeal to President Wilson's apprehensions about the matter; and it succeeded. On May 7, Secretary of State Lansing had informed Lord Reading that the President was convinced that the moment was not yet opportune for intervention, or that an adequate military advantage would be gained. He could not at present concur in the British proposals. The quasi-alliance between Japan and America, or rather the ardent Japanese desire only to intervene in Siberia with America's consent, had once again saved Russia from Japanese invasion.[7]

On May 11, Lord Reading presented Secretary Lansing with a further telegram from Balfour on intervention (sent, of course, before the War Cabinet's decision, or realization of the 11th that no Bolshevik invitation could now be expected). Lansing pointed out that the problem had really become two problems, as intervention in northern Russia involved no racial difficulties as it did in Siberia (i.e. because of Russian and Japanese mutual racial hostility). 'I further told him', Lansing reported to the President, 'that intervention at Murmansk and Archangel would receive far more favourable consideration on our part than intervention in Siberia, for the reason that we could understand the military advantage of the former but had been unable, thus far, to find any advantage in sending troops into Siberia.' Trotsky's allegedly favourable attitude towards intervention might only apply to northern Russia, and not to the Far East, Lansing continued. (This, as far as it went, was quite correct.) Lansing also doubted how far a Bolshevik invitation would go, even if it was really made. Thus by May 11, the American government admitted that racial difficulties were a strong bar to any action in the Far East — it was not only the lack of any foreseeable military advantage; and as they could see military advantage in action in northern Russia, they regarded that as a separate problem which could enjoy American support. This, as far as it went, must have been welcomed in London.[8]

On May 15, Balfour sent a summary of Lockhart's recent wires to Lord Reading, the tenor of which was that though the Bolsheviks could not issue a formal invitation for Allied intervention, they were however prepared to accept intervention. This certainly carried out the War Cabinet's instructions, but appears to have led Reading, when he again saw Lansing that same day, to press for a joint Allied effort to secure acceptance from Trotsky for intervention in Siberia. Lansing replied that he had no objection to securing acceptance for action in northern Russia, but did not see how anything could be gained by trying to obtain acceptance for Japanese action in Siberia, since they would go no further than Irkutsk. There, for the moment, matters rested.[8]

The Cabinet committee's proposals were thus all implemented. Meanwhile, at 6.50 p.m. on May 11, the First Sea Lord, on the express instructions of the War Cabinet, had sent a precise wire (no. 478) to Captain Cromie: 'You may carry on with preparations for both schemes [referring to Cromie's proposal to block Kronstadt harbour and destroy the naval vessels there; and, secondly, to his suggestion to extend this operation to include the older warships and ships under construction], but in order to prevent antagonizing Bolsheviks unnecessarily, they are not to be carried out unless it is certain that Germans are advancing on Petrograd, and that [Baltic] Fleet will fall into their hands, or you receive instructions from us. Second scheme may be extended as proposed to ships under construction. Greater importance is attached to second scheme than to the first.' Cromie would consequently have to expend much more than the £300,000 he proposed.[9]

On May 7, it will be recalled, Trotsky had sent Admiral Altfater to Petrograd in pursuit of his own plans for the destruction of the Baltic Fleet. Altfater informed Trotsky that everything was now ready, save for the cash deposits in the bank for the shock-groups of sailors on board each ship. The result of Altfater's visit was that the sailors were now even more suspicious of the Bolsheviks, and even more inclined to believe that they had already come to some secret understanding with the Germans to destroy the Baltic Fleet.

Late on the 11th, a wire reached the Admiralty from Cromie saying that the Bolshevik naval staff in Petrograd had informed him that Captain Behrens, the Bolshevik naval chief of staff, had seen Trotsky in Moscow on the 9th and that they had discussed a wire from Petrograd, presumably

Altfater's, about steps to be taken for the destruction of the warships if necessary. Trotsky had emphasized that it was vital to be 'assured and convinced' that plans had been thoroughly worked out, and would, if necessary, be implemented. (Nothing was said at this point about any cash payments.) Trotsky ordered lists to be made of the shock-groups and that the great importance of their task should be explained to them; they were to sign an undertaking to take action, when so ordered, 'in spite of any hindrance which may occur'. Behrens's wire to the naval staff in Petrograd ended thus: 'Similar incidents to those in Black Sea must not be repeated.'[9] In Moscow, as well as in London, it was still not known that the Black Sea Fleet had escaped.

On the morning of the 13th, another wire arrived from Cromie (who had not yet received the First Sea Lord's authorization to go ahead with his schemes) commenting on Trotsky's instructions. 'I put no confidence in this order, and regard it as a mere collection of words', said Cromie. 'Meanwhile am proceeding with arrangements mentioned in my [wire] 125. Progress is being made, but owing to Baltic province subjects on board [i.e. pro-German White Finns], many difficulties are being encountered.' Ships would be considered destroyed if the main turbines were completely disabled; he would also attempt to destroy the turbines in new ships and those under construction. 'It is hoped to have everything ready by May 17.' For the destruction of the four dreadnoughts and fourteen destroyers, it would be necessary to pay out about one million roubles (some £32,000) 'on trust' before any attempt was made; the rest would be paid on completion, 'after as accurate a verification as possible. Much will have to be accepted on trust', he warned, 'but everything possible will be done to safeguard British interests. Difficulties of placing out large sums of money are [*sic*] many private persons not wishing to accept responsibility these times keeping so much money at home.'[9] This expenditure was in addition to that for sinking three British transports to block Kronstadt harbour. 'Everything points to German occupation [of Petrograd] inside next two weeks, but present very acute position [of] supply question in Petrograd may retard operation. German prisoners here have all had new uniforms served out.' Cromie concluded by saying that two dreadnoughts and seven destroyers had been prepared for destruction. At noon on May 13, the Deputy First Sea Lord read out these two wires to the War Cabinet.

Cromie thus urgently needed additional finance. On May 14, the Foreign Office sent an urgent and secret wire to Consul Woodhouse at Petrograd: 'Please hold at immediate disposal of Captain Cromie 1,500,000 roubles from embassy or any other available accounts.' [This sentence originally read 'ten million', but this was crossed out by Cecil.] 'Lockhart has been asked to facilitate in any way possible.... If you have any difficulty in satisfying Cromie's needs in full, advise us immediately.' (This last sentence originally read: 'If you cannot satisfy in full Cromie's needs within above limit out of embassy accounts, you are authorized as a last resort to purchase actual rouble notes for him by sale of sterling at best rates possible.' But this too was altered.) The same day, the necessary wire was also sent to Lockhart. Woodhouse was successful: 'Am cooperating with Captain C.', he replied on the 15th. 'Have made arrangements to procure any sum required without drawing from banks.'[9]

Meanwhile, there were further disorders in the Baltic Fleet. On about May 11, the Bolsheviks convened a 'general assembly' of the various elements in the Baltic Fleet to reassert their authority, and to appoint a new chief commissar to replace Blokhin. The main nucleus of anti-Bolshevik agitation was the destroyer flotilla. Chastny had received Trotsky's permission to send the fourteen destroyers (which Cromie had been instructed to sabotage) up through the canals and locks to lake Ladoga, as a further protection against their German seizure. But the destroyer flotilla, led by two young officers, Lissanevitch and Zaseneuk, had already begun to agitate openly within the Baltic Fleet for the overthrow of the Bolshevik government and seizure of power in Petrograd by the Baltic Fleet, under the dictatorship of Chastny, to prevent the Bolsheviks handing the Fleet over to the Germans; and strong rumours that the Bolsheviks had already secretly agreed in the Brest–Litovsk treaty to do just this had been spread by these two officers. These rumours had increased as a result of Trotsky's abortive attempt to bribe shock-groups of sailors to blow up their ships. The destroyer flotilla had sent emissaries to the cruiser and battleship flotillas to obtain support, but these emissaries had been coolly received.[10]

It is not known whether the Admiralty had instructed Cromie, or a British secret agent like Reilly, to back the destroyer officers in these moves, but something of the turbulent atmosphere in Petrograd and Kronstadt can be judged from a wire sent by Cromie's assistant on May 13: 'Your 478 received.' (This was the First Sea Lord's authorization to Cromie to go ahead with his plans). 'S.N.O. [Senior Naval Officer] Baltic Fleet complains to Higher War Council that it is impossible to move destroyers to Lake Ladoga unless he be given control over tugs and Petrograd port. Shepelevski lighthouse reports enemy warship at sea. Labour disorders here probable. Large general meetings at all works today, 13th. [?Rumours of] German occupation more persistent. Probable cause non-payment by Russia of first gold installment of indemnity due May 1.' Other sources stated that the Germans said they had no troops available, that the Red Army was to be disbanded, and compulsory service reintroduced.[10]

Meanwhile, Chastny had been in touch with Trotsky about the danger to Fort Ino, the 'bulwark of Petrograd', as Lenin rightly called it, which had been surrounded by White Finn troops since April 24, and which neither the Bolsheviks nor any other power could relieve by land. Chastny reported that German warships had appeared unexpectedly off Fort Ino

116

and that it was in great danger. Trotsky replied that if the situation was considered hopeless, the fort must be destroyed. Accordingly a Russian vessel (possibly the cruiser *Oleg*) was sent out from Kronstadt and managed to remove the breeches of the heavy naval guns in the fort, and most of the material; and on May 14, Fort Ino was blown up by remote control from Fort Krasnaya Gorka, across Petrograd bay to the south. This was at once exploited by the destroyers' officers as an act of treachery by Trotsky. 'Throughout the [Baltic] Fleet and in Petrograd', he later wrote, 'people spoke of my order. Obscure forces spread the rumour in the town that the soviet authorities had agreed with the Germans to blow up the fort.'[11]

This was the background to a turbulent 'general assembly' of the Baltic Fleet, held later on the 14th. Chastny had prepared a report, which the Bolshevik naval authorities, who appear to have chaired the meeting, asked him not to read out. But Chastny had his way. (There is no exact record of this report. Trotsky later claimed — in an emotional harangue delivered at Chastny's trial — that it was of 'purely political character and a clear counter-revolutionary trend [which spoke] of the decision of the soviet authorities to destroy the fleet in such a way that one imagines it is a case of treason by the soviet authorities, and not a measure dictated by the tragic necessity of certain circumstances.' The whole document, Trotsky claimed, 'in spite of its outward reserve, is an undoubted document of a counter-revolutionary plot'.) The destroyers' officers then put forward their motion for the overthrow of the Bolshevik government and the seizure of power in Petrograd by the Baltic Fleet under a naval dictator: Chastny does not appear to have been mentioned by name. This was rejected, and it was resolved to expel Lissanevitch and Zaseneuk from the fleet, and to appoint a certain Flerovsky as chief commissar in place of Blokhin, who was to be dismissed. (The dismissal of Blokhin could, of course, be seen as a pro-German act, if the false 'Sission'-type documents, which Chastny received on return from Helsinki, were taken to be true.) But Chastny disregarded all this. He continued to deal with Blokhin, and the two destroyer officers were not dismissed. But later that day, twelve of the destroyers left for Lake Ladoga, and the remaining two on the following day.[11]

Captain Cromie, meanwhile, was in Moscow. 'The General Staff at Moscow openly agree it is very doubtful [if] their orders for the destruction of Baltic Fleet will be carried out. I suggested Allies would be willing [to] pay a certain sum for each ship destroyed as an inducement to the crews', he wired to the Admiralty. 'The idea was well received by Altfater and Behrens, who laid the matter before Trotsky. On 15th, Mr Lockhart and self visited "T.", who assured us that money was already placed in [the] State Bank for this purpose, which statement proved to be false, so I renewed offer privately to "A.",' reported Cromie, who unfortunately says no more about this crucial matter.

Trotsky, however, has this to say: 'More than once the representatives of the British Admiralty came to see me personally to ask me if we had taken the necessary measures to destroy the Baltic Fleet if the situation became hopeless. These same British officers many times contacted the Admirals in the Soviet service, Behrens and Altfater. Thus, from our point of view and from the British, the danger at that moment [early to mid-May] lay in the possibility which the Germans had of seizing our vessels by surprise, and removing them. When the organization of the shock-groups was still at a preparatory stage, one of the members of the Naval College received a visit from a well known officer of the British Navy [Cromie] who declared that England was so anxious to prevent the ships falling into German hands that she was ready to make heavy payments to the sailors whose duty it was at the fateful moment to blow up the ships. I immediately ordered that all talks with this gentleman should be broken off. But I must admit that this proposal obliged us to think of a question to which, in the bustle and rush of events, we had not yet given thought: to assure the security of the families of those sailors who were going to expose themselves to a terrible danger.'

In this statement, Trotsky is obviously protecting himself. He claims that Cromie approached only a staff officer, not Trotsky himself (as Cromie states), and that he (Trotsky) at once broke off talks with Cromie, on hearing of the matter. In fact, Trotsky told Cromie that the money required for the plan was already in the bank, and claimed that it was Cromie who gave him the idea of paying the sailors, that he himself had first put forward the idea early in May; and he now claimed that the object was to protect the sailors' families. In fact, it was to bribe the sailors themselves, who were known to be extremely mercenary. ('In the Baltic Fleet, the sailors [during the Revolution] thought first and foremost about money', comments Graf.)[12]

In the same wire, Cromie also reported that the Bolshevik naval staff had told him that the greater part of the Black Sea Fleet was now safely at Novorossisk. He was also shown a wire of the 13th from the German commander in the Ukraine to Admiral Sablin stating that the Black Sea Fleet must return to Sebastopol, or the Germans would continue their advance and seize Novorossisk. Sablin asked for instructions from Trotsky.

'My general impression of my four days in Moscow', commented Cromie, 'was that present government realize that its end is near and is willing to accept help from any quarter, even to forming a coalition.' After consultation with the Allied representatives, he agreed with them on the political value of intervention in northern Russia, but had a poor opinion of the military value of such a move, 'unless undertaken on a very large scale with utmost despatch'. He recognized the importance of holding Murmansk and Petchenga to prevent the formation there of German submarine bases ('a fact at which present government is prepared to look through their fingers'), but felt, together with many of the Allied envoys, that if Allied intervention through Siberia was impossible, it would be more in Allied interests to send out instructors for the new Red Army; otherwise it appeared 'doomed to failure'. This would bring the Red Army directly under Allied influence, and provoke Germany to advance and occupy more Russian territory, which would in turn provoke a national uprising against Germany.

There were also developments at Murmansk. On May 10, the small party of British marines and Red Guards, which had been sent aboard the cruiser *Cochrane* to meet the threat to Petchenga, fought a small engagement with the White Finns; but the thaw put an end to further threats of pro-German forces getting too near Murmansk, and in fact to all further local activity. But on the 14th, the Murmansk Soviet expressed apprehensions to Admiral Kemp that the Bolshevik government, under German pressure, would take a much harder line over the Allied presence at Murmansk, and that this possibility was already affecting local opinion. They urged the Allies to take counter-measures. Admiral Kemp wired to the Admiralty the same day saying that he expected the Bolshevik government to replace the Murmansk Soviet with hard-line Bolsheviks, and that an ultimatum would be issued demanding that the Allies withdraw.[13]

On returning to Petrograd, Cromie again became absorbed in the problem of the Baltic Fleet, but now there were additional complications: 'There is now in Petrograd an organization of Russian White Guards led by General Yudenitch, formerly Commander-in-Chief Caucasus. ... They have asked assistance from Germans, who said they would not be ready until about 23rd. ... Some members have approached our agents to form [a] liaison between White Guards and Navy.' These were probably monarchists and might well be even more harmful than the socialists. Between Dvinsk and Reval, there were now said to be 162 German battalions and 96 cavalry squadrons. At Helsinki, there were 12,000 German troops of 'exemplary' discipline. In his next wire, probably sent on the 16th, Cromie reported progress in preparing the Baltic Fleet for sabotage: four dreadnoughts and nine destroyers were now 'practically ready', and two destroyers were doubtful. 'Hoped complete arrangements by 18th. Propose carry out scheme about 21st or 22nd. Impossible decide when Germans will come in, but expected about 23rd.' There were now 25,000 German troops on the Finnish frontier, 'and with motor-cars can be in Pet[rograd] in two hours, where it is certain they will meet with no resistance. ... If scheme delayed beyond next week, I fear whole thing will fall through, rendering expenditure already paid out useless. Men at present time cannot be held too long, they vary too much.' This crucial decision to destroy the Russian warships on a fixed date was, of course, in complete violation of the War Cabinet's instructions, and was unknown in London until May 23, when all Cromie's recent wires arrived in a batch.[14]

The abrupt change in the War Cabinet's policy towards the Bolsheviks coincided with an equally abrupt change in German–Bolshevik relations. Not until May 6 did the German High Command inform the Foreign Ministry in Berlin of the discovery of the abortive anti-Bolshevik *coup* of May 1. German policy, clearly under military pressure, veered sharply. On the 8th, as the Germans' quasi-ultimatum was delivered in Moscow — insisting on the British explusion from Murmansk, Bolshevik evacuation of Fort Ino, and the disarmament of those Bolshevik praetorian guards, the Latvian regiments — German troops seized Rostov to protect the Ukraine from Bolshevik infiltration from the south-east. That same day, General Ludendorff asked the Foreign Ministry for information about the Russian internal political situation as reported by Ambassador Mirbach. 'The General thinks that it is not impossible that a government hostile to us might take over the helm', it was explained, 'and considers it advisable to prepare for this possibility by helping circles acceptable to us to take over the reins of government.'

Immediate enquiries were made of the German embassy in Moscow. Mirbach's reply, which was received late on the 10th, appears to indicate that he had succumbed to a Bolshevik *agent provocateur*, who wished to counteract the effect of the German ultimatum of May 8. The Allied envoys in Russia had that day presented an ultimatum to the Bolshevik government, in which the Allies 'solemnly' offered to continue 'even now' to support Russia with food, arms and raw materials, if the Bolsheviks would resume hostilities against Germany. If there was a general mobilization, there were hopes of Allied recognition of the Bolshevik government. 'Karakhan and Radek did not tell me of this event, perhaps because the official reacion was not to be discussed until this evening', he admitted. (This appears to have been quite untrue, though it may conceivably have been an echo of what Reilly had said at the Kremlin on the 7th). Mirbach, however, warned of 'surprises' to come, in view of the 'enormous worries' of the Bolshevik government, and its 'perplexity' about the 'restoration' in the Ukraine, and the German advance in southern Russia.[15]

Counsellor Riezler expanded on the German position in a diary entry of May 11. He noted 'busy goings-on between agents and Bolshevik women, Jews, bribes, etc. Our totally illegal actions in the south, which were most poorly explained, are possibly economically necessary,' he admitted, 'but they have taken away our basis, frightened the Bolsheviks and weakened them tremendously, they have given the *Entente* and the other socialist parties reason for large-scale action, which will hopefully be rebuffed this time. Added to this, the restoration in favour of the monarchists in the Ukraine. Even the greatest idiot would not suspect them of a movement for a separate Ukraine', he wrote. 'There are not any politics conducted any more, only war measures. If we go on like this, we will clear the way politically for the *Entente*, and give up future possibilities too — probably never before was a situation more confused. . . . The occupied areas are not safe, at home [there are] no plans, or, what is even worse, a lot of them, everything is uncertain; and on top of it, stupid uneducated officers who, with glorious lack of knowledge, believe they are able to send grand exposés on the politics in Russia to the Supreme Command of the Army, after they have spent eight days in Moscow.'[15]

On the 13th, Mirbach wired again, more explicitly and more accurately. As far as he could judge, German interests 'still demand the continuation in power of the Bolshevik government'. Despite what all other parties said, 'there is, in most cases, only the wish to be rid of the Bolsheviks', he emphasized. 'Any further advance on our part might drive the Bolsheviks into the arms of the *Entente* or, in the event of their fall, bring successors favourable to the *Entente* into power. In the event of relations with us being broken off, an event which in that case could hardly be avoided, the leadership in Russian political and economic development would fall to the *Entente*.' The Brest–Litovsk treaty would then be revised, and the border states, especially the Ukraine, reunited with Russia. German interests would best be served by providing the Bolsheviks with a minimum of essential goods and thus maintaining them in power. In spite of their decrees, something could still probably be done, 'for they are now all of a sudden much more cooperative again in economic affairs, and at least some preparations can be made for future economic infiltration'.[15]

Whether this telegram had reached the Foreign Ministry in time to be relayed to Spa for a high-level meeting that day is unclear; but State Secretary von Kühlmann took the same line. The Allies, he explained, had apparently recently approached the Bolsheviks with promises, if they would resume hostilities against Germany. He did not consider this alarming from the military view-point; but it would be very much in German interests if it could be announced, 'once and for all', that German military operations in Russia were 'definitely finished'. Ludendorff confirmed that 'this was now the case . . .'.[15]

In Moscow, Lenin had realized that the threat of a further German advance into Russia, and the increase of Allied pressure on the Bolsheviks, called for an immediate shift in Bolshevik foreign policy to maintain their precarious balance between the various imperialist powers, above all between Britain and Germany. In his 'Theses on the Present Political Situation', drafted on May 12 and 13, Lenin saw the only salvation of the soviet state in the continuation, come what may, of the 'breathing-space' obtained at Brest–Litovsk in March, until a general social revolution broke out in Western Europe to assure Bolshevik Russia of permanent survival.[16] This meant that the great imperialist powers must exhaust their aggression against each other (i.e. that the war must go on), but not against little Bolshevik Russia. But as the imperialist alliances were highly unstable, the Bolsheviks must exercise the greatest vigilance; their only policy, in fact, was 'to manoeuvre, to retreat, to bide one's time'. A Bolshevik invitation for Allied intervention was out of the question. On this, Lenin was quite explicit. Though not ruling out the idea of a military agreement with one imperialist coalition against the other, where it would not endanger the soviet state, but strengthen its position and paralyze the pressure of some other imperialist power, 'we at the given moment cannot enter on a military agreement with the Anglo-French coalition. Because what is really important for the members of that coalition is the removal of German forces from the West, which means the advance of many Japanese units into the interior of European Russia, and this condition is not acceptable, as it would mean the complete destruction of Soviet power. If an ultimatum of this nature were to be given to us by the Anglo-French coalition, we would reply with a refusal, because the danger of a Japanese move could be countered with less difficulty [or could be delayed for a longer time], than the danger of the occupation by the Germans of Petrograd and Moscow, and the greater part of European Russia.' This put things in a nut-shell; but at least it showed that the War Cabinet was not entirely wrong in thinking that there was some divergence of view between Lenin and Trotsky on the matter; at any rate, in what Trotsky was prepared to say to the Allied envoys in Russia.[16]

On May 14, Lenin took action. Chicherin (who made no important move without Lenin's direct sanction) wired — via the German embassy in Moscow — to the Bolshevik representative Joffe in Berlin saying that the Bolshevik government wished to discuss with the German government all outstanding political and commerical questions in Moscow. The initiative was welcomed. An affirmative reply reached Moscow the same day that the Germans agreed, but the discussions must be held in Berlin. (The most immediate issue for both sides was undoubtedly that of grain supplies; the Germans hoped to get Russian grain quicker; the Russians hoped to induce the Germans to let them have some of the Ukrainian grain.)

That evening, Lenin made an important statement on foreign policy to a joint meeting of the Central Executive Committee, the Moscow soviet, and representatives of the trade unions and factory shop committees, which summarized the international situation far better than Lloyd George had done in his recent summary to the War Cabinet. In view of recent attempts to restore the 'Kornilov régime', which had resulted from their increasingly difficult position, the Bolsheviks were now at a turning-point, said Lenin. Soviet Russia was 'an oasis in the midst of a raging ocean of imperialist plundering', but, he assured his audience, a 'union between the imperialists of all countries is impossible. We witness a situation where the raging waves of imperialist reaction are battering the little island of the Socialist Soviet

Republic, ready, as it were, to submerge it, but destined in the end to break on each other'.

But the international position of Bolshevik Russia was at present governed by 'two fundamental contradictions'. First, the struggle between the two greatest imperialist powers, Germany and Britain, whose ferocity made any joint action against Bolshevik Russia almost impossible. Secondly, the long-standing economic rivalry between Japan and America for mastery of the Pacific Ocean and its shores, which had stored up a 'great mass of inflammable material', and which made conflict between them inevitable; though at present, it was restrained by their alliance against Germany, which in turn restrained Japanese intervention in Russia. 'The campaign which was begun against the Soviet Republic [the landing at Vladivostok, the support of Semenov's band] is being held back,' he explained, 'because it threatens to turn the concealed conflict between Japan and America into an open war.' But it was quite possible that these imperialist alliances, however solid they might appear, might quickly break up, if the 'sacred interests' of private property and concessions should so demand. Then the present imperialist conflicts would no longer protect Bolshevik Russia. The America bourgeoisie, now at odds with Japan, might tomorrow come to terms with Japan, because the Japanese bourgeoisie might otherwise come to terms with Germany. 'That is why the situation in the Far East is so unstable.'

Lenin then turned to Germany. Most of the German imperialist classes were in favour of carrying out the Brest–Litovsk treaty, so as to have a free hand in the West. But the extreme military party, which urged the use of immediate force, irrespective of the consequences, might gain the upper hand. 'This makes clear how unstable the international situation is ... what circumspection, tact, and self-possession are required from the soviet government. ... We must manoeuvre and retreat until reinforcements come to our aid. A change to these tactics is inevitable ...'. If the extreme war party overcame one imperialist coalition to form another directed against Bolshevik Russia, Bolshevik diplomacy would do everything possible to prolong the 'brief and unstable breathing-spell' obtained at Brest–Litovsk in March. 'Since November 7, 1917, we have become defensists', he admitted.[16]

Next he considered the recent events, which had aroused 'so much alarm and panic', and enabled the counter-revolutionaries to resume their undermining of the Bolshevik government. The Brest–Litovsk treaty also implied peace with the Ukraine and Finland, where the situation was now critical; their temporary breathing-spell was ending and the stark question of war and peace had merely been postponed, though the final solutions in these two areas again depended on the American-Japanese conflict in the Far East, and the Anglo-German struggle in Western Europe. In the Ukraine, the extreme German military party thought that after setting up a puppet government, they could withdraw their troops and extract large-scale grain supplies. But they found they had to fight for every sack of grain, without which Germany could not exist, and thus retain large bodies of troops in the Ukraine, which inspired Russian counter-revolutionary hopes. Continued peace with Finland depended upon the highly delicate situation at both Fort Ino and Murmansk. Fort Ino, the 'bulwark of Petrograd', was being claimed by the White Finns. But Murmansk was a source 'of even greater friction'. The British and French both made claims to it, because they had spent millions of roubles there in constructing a port during the war with Germany. The British then landed at Murmansk, 'and we had no way of preventing the landing by force. The result was that we were presented [by the Germans] with a demand, which almost has the character of an ultimatum, [to the effect] that if we cannot defend our neutrality, [the Germans] will fight on our territory', Lenin explained. This, in fact, was the real reason for the turning-point in Bolshevik foreign policy; for the natural counter-action to the German ultimatum would have been an invitation to the Allies to intervene openly at Murmansk, and this Lenin absolutely declined.

Lenin was bitterly attacked. 'I agree that this island has become very, very small because of the policies inaugurated after the November Revolution', a right SR speaker stated, 'but it is ridiculous to talk about a breathing-spell when German armies are advancing on every front. ... We are helpless even before the reactionary bourgeoisie of little Finland. How can we utilize the clash of two imperialisms? ... It would be better to accept the aid of the Allies, of Anglo-Franco-Japanese imperialism. ... German imperialism which is penetrating into Russia ... forces us to join the Allies ... and to take the road that, thanks to your November counter-revolution, was abandoned ...'. The right SRs urged that the Brest–Litovsk treaty be declared void; that relations be re-established with the Allies; and that the constituent assembly be recalled.

The left SRs also agreed that Lenin's breathing-spell would not save the revolution. 'The essence of our policy is that we repudiate any influence. We believe that the revolution is sufficiently strong to have its own orientation. ... At this critical moment all the forces of the soviet republic should be mobilized for struggle. There are only two ways open to us. One is the revolutionary way; the other is the way of shameful retreat, of shameful concession and manoeuvring, the way of death. The fight is inevitable.'

The Mensheviks declared that the German imperialists had openly joined the Russian counter-revolutionary landlords and capitalists in order 'to destroy the conquests of the democracy'. The restoration in the Ukraine was only the prelude to the restoration in Russia of the dictatorship of the propertied classes with the aid of German bayonets. 'The [Bolshevik] government, as now organized, ... is absolutely incapable of handling the difficult task of defending the very foundation of the democratic revolution against ... reaction and ... German imperialism.' They demanded the recall of the constitutent assembly which alone could unite 'the whole proletariat and the entire democracy in the struggle against Russian and German reaction'.

But the central executive committee approved Lenin's policy — and he alone knew that the Germans had already agreed to open trade talks and settle all other matters by discussion.[16]

Two days later, Lenin gave an interview to Mirbach. 'In general, Lenin trusts his lucky star with the utmost conviction and repeatedly expresses the most boundless optimism in an almost overpowering way', Mirbach stated in a report to the German Chancellor, to which the Kaiser again added his comments. But Lenin did admit that though the soviet system was still standing firm, his opponents had increased in number, and the situation 'demands intenser vigilance than it did a month ago'. Lenin's faith was principally based on the fact that only the Bolsheviks had any organized force and the other Russian groups, though opposing the present system, 'diverge in all directions and have no power behind them to equal that of the Bolsheviks'. ('The Japanese, the Chinese, the English!?' wrote the Kaiser. 'He will have the whole Cossack army against him!') 'In some respects this is certainly true, but ... he nevertheless somewhat under-estimates them.'[17]

But Lenin freely admitted that his opponents were now no longer only to his right; there were some now in his own camp, 'where a kind of left wing has formed'. Their main complaint was that the Brest–Litovsk treaty, 'which he is still determined to defend with the utmost tenacity', was a mistake. More and more Russian territory was being occupied by German troops; no peace had been concluded with Finland or the Ukraine; famine was actually on the increase; in fact, there was no real peace at all, and certain recent events did seem to justify his opponents' attacks. He was directing 'all his desires and efforts towards a speedy clarification of matters in the north and south ['The Cossack Army will settle that soon', wrote the Kaiser], and particularly towards achieving a peace settlement with Helsinki and Kiev, with the help of our cooperation and influence ['He will be as unable to put these conditions into practice as those of Brest. He has neither government nor executive personnel', wrote the Kaiser]. Not that Lenin spoke plaintively or querulously, nor did he insinuate in any way that, if the present state of affirs were to last, he might be forced to turn back towards the other (i.e. Allied) powers. However, he was apparently concerned to describe the awkwardness of his position as graphically as possible.' ('He is finished', wrote the Kaiser.)[17]

The Kaiser's reference to the Cossack army was justified. On May 6, the Don Cossacks had finally expelled the Bolsheviks from the Don, when they reoccupied their capital of Novocherkask, only to find themselves face to face with German troops at Rostov. Neither side had any intention of moving against the other. On May 11, the first action of the Don Cossack krug (or council), which met to elect a new Ataman, was to send emissaries to the Germans at Rostov. On the 16th, General Krasnov, the senior Don Cossack officer, was elected Ataman; and his first action was to ask the Kaiser for German recognition of the Don as a separate state, for German arms and supplies, and for resumption of trade with the Ukraine. Ludendorff saw that a Cossack union under Krasnov could not only provide an alternative Russian government in Moscow if the Bolsheviks fell (as had the Allies the previous winter), but could counter the little pro-Allied volunteer army (then resting near Novocherkask), and prevent effective Allied restoration of the eastern front. Therefore Krasnov was given German military help to reconstitute the Don Cossack army. Thus in mid-May, the Germans inaugurated a double Russian policy; trade talks with the Bolshevik government in central Russia, and military support for the Don Cossacks in southern Russia.[18]

Meanwhile, some of Cromie's arrangements for naval sabotage came vaguely to the attention of the German embassy in Moscow. The situation in Petrograd was 'once again precarious', Count Mirbach reported to Berlin on the 16th. The Allies were said to be spending 'enormous sums' to put the right SRs into power and reopen the war, and were also bribing a certain Russian regiment, and the sailors on board two battleships and on the cruiser *Oleg*, which had left for Fort Ino. There were further reports that an armament works was in SR hands. Agitation had increased in Moscow as well. 'I am still trying to counter efforts of the *Entente* and support the Bolsheviks', stated Mirbach; but he asked whether the 'overall situation justifies use of larger sums in our interests if necessary, and as to what trend to support in event of Bolsheviks being incapable of holding out'. If the Bolsheviks did fall, their successors would certainly be pro-Allied.[19]

State Secretary Kühlmann replied at once: 'Please use larger sums, as it is greatly in our interests that Bolsheviks should survive.' If he required more money, Mirbach was to telegraph, saying how much. 'It is very difficult to say from here which trend to support if Bolsheviks fall. If really hard pressed, left-wing social revolutionaries would fall with Bolsheviks. These parties seem to be the only ones who base their position on peace treaty of Brest–Litovsk. As a party, Cadets are anti-German; monarchists would also work for revision of Brest peace treaty. We have no interest in supporting monarchists' ideas, which would reunite Russia. On the contrary, we must try to prevent Russian consolidation as far as possible and, from this point of view, we must therefore support the parties furthest to the left.'[19]

Kühlmann was also probably responsible for seeing that the situation at Murmansk, which had resulted in a German ultimatum, was played down and smoothed over. For after the exchanges between Moscow and Berlin on the 14th, the Germans limited their action to a severe practical warning; a German submarine began operating off Petchenga and sank some ten Russian and Norwegian local steamers and fishing boats. The Bolsheviks limited their action to strong protests to ·Count Mirbach, who merely replied that such attacks would continue unless the Bolsheviks themselves protected their own territory from Allied incursions. But the incident was over.

As can be seen from these exchanges between Mirbach and Kühlmann, undercover German financial support for the Bolsheviks had by no means stopped. In fact, as Professor Katkov makes clear, 'it went on crescendo' for some months yet. Doctor Kurt Riezler, the German expert in subversion in Russia, formerly at the German Legation in Stockholm, was Mirbach's counsellor; and working closely with him was Karl Moor, who (since 1914) had been keeping an eye on Lenin in Switzerland for the German General Staff, and in 1917 had been one of the channels for German financial support for the Bolshevik movement in Stockholm. There is little doubt that he was now engaged in the same work in Moscow, though Riezler makes no comment in his diary.[19]

This, then, was the position when the War Cabinet again considered the overall Russian situation on May 17, by which time, as Cromie had told them, the Baltic Fleet would be prepared by his agents for destruction. (In fact, Cromie had now decided that the Germans were likely to enter Petrograd on May 23, and that he would blow up the Fleet on the 21st or 22nd; but his wires were now being delayed.[20] Nor could the Cabinet know that he was getting into deep water; his agents were becoming involved not only with anti-Bolshevik elements in the Baltic Fleet, but also with pro-German Russian groups.)

On the morning of the 17th, a wire from Clemenceau to Lloyd George was handed to Lord Milner. This stated that a further meeting of the Supreme War Council must be held at a very early date (he suggested June 1) since more American troops were needed in France as soon as possible. Clemenceau went on to say that he had just seen the message from the CIGS (sent on the 11th) about the Czechs at Vladivostok, which much concerned him ('qui m'a causé le plus vif désappointement'), 'because it seems that the British General Staff intend to delay indefinitely the project for the coming shipment of this very important contingent, in spite of the decisions taken at Abbeville'. The French Premier had, that morning, received a wire from the French military attaché in Tokyo (sent on the 10th), which stated that this Czech Corps comprised 45,000 men, and 5,000 recent recruits, all of whom were well-organized, well-trained, and well thought of (by which he too presumably meant the First Czech Corps, presumed at Abbeville to be then in Siberia, *en route* for Vladivostok, but in fact — save for a small vanguard — still delayed in European Russia). He continued to report that 8,000 had reached Vladivostok by May 9, and the rest were expected to reach the Far East in six weeks' time. 'They can be embarked from now on. This seems to me a matter of the first importance', stated Clemenceau. But he still gave no indication of why he wished these troops, good as they were, to be dragged half-way round the world to France, holding up badly needed shipping for the Americans. (This French estimate of 50,000 Czechs, wrongly alleged to be at or on their way to Vladivostok, tallies with British information of this time; the Czech Legion was thought to number 70,000 men, of whom it was believed that 20,000 were coming to northern Russia.)[21]

At the early morning discussion between the Prime Minister, Lord Milner and the CIGS, the latter read out a wire from a trustworthy agent of the DMO, who reported that the central powers were now getting 'very substantial' supplies from the Ukraine: six hundred railway wagons of food were leaving every day for Austria, which was now receiving over half the total, the rest going to Germany. Food was plentiful in Austria, the cost of living had gone down considerably, and crop prospects were good in Austria-Hungary, though fats and soap were still very scarce. Germany was busy re-organizing the Ukraine and sending in large quantities of agricultural machinery. The agent also reported that he had seen 5,000 Austrian prisoners returning every day from Russia, though most of the Russian prisoners on release were staying on in Germany and Austria, where they could earn good wages. The report concluded that half the Roumanian oil wells were now in working order. (The information about the Germans and Austrians resupplying themselves from the Ukraine was correct, though probably rather exaggerated.)[22]

The Prime Minister stated that he had had a talk the day before with Leslie Urquhart, chairman of the Russo-Asiatic Corporation, which had vast mining interests in the Urals and Altai district, whom Sir Arthur Steel-Maitland, head of the Department of Overseas Trade, had brought to see him. 'Mr Urquhart was positive that any force could go straight through Russia like a hot knife through butter', stated the Prime Minister.

Urquhart's view was that the Germans were trying to get across to the Caspian Sea, and use the Volga Fleet to bring down Siberian food and produce, as well as copper, zinc, etc., from the Urals. (It is not clear where Urquhart got this information from. It may have come from French sources, as the Russo-Asiatic Corporation had connections with French banks. But it evidently much impressed Lloyd George, and coming after the report on German depredations in the Ukraine, it had maximum effect.) Lloyd George suggested that, as America did not seem disposed to take any action, Canada might send some engineers to Vladivostok; and these, together with the Czech troops, a few Japanese battalions, and such

French officers as were on the spot, 'might make a sufficient international force to take action'.

At this, Colonel Amery stated that he had recently seen Benes, who had said that the Czech troops at Vladivostok 'might be induced' to take part in 'international operations' in Russia, but only if they were assured that this would bring them into direct contact with the Austrians or Germans, and did not involve their taking part in civil war in Russia. Amery suggested that Australia might also send some engineers. The CIGS mentioned that General Poole was just starting for Russia, 'and was determined to do what he could to bring about active military operations there'. Poole was 'quite sanguine as to raising a large army'. The Prime Minister said that Lindley was also going out, 'and apparently had no belief that anything could be done at all in Russia'. It was agreed to raise the question of whether Lindley should go back to Russia at the War Cabinet immediately afterwards.[22]

At noon, after the Deputy First Sea Lord had informed the War Cabinet of the action at Petchenga, the Cabinet discussed at some length the question of using the Czech troops, now at Vladivostok, 'as a nucleus of a force on which to base Allied intervention'. The Prime Minister said that if Britain were unable to obtain American and Japanese assent to intervention, 'the question arose as to whether we should not proceed without them'. The matter should be considered from the military angle. German troops were being withdrawn from the Russian front, the British army was bearing the brunt, and no material American support had yet arrived to assist us. We thus had every reason for not allowing America and Japan to block any of our attempts to stultify these German withdrawals. If the Czech force was as good as it was reported to be, and if it was properly officered, it could possibly be used in Siberia — not, of course, alone; Allied contingents would have to be added, but these, including Canadian railwaymen, need not be very strong.

Balfour, however, did not think that the Japanese would consent to an enterprise in Siberia, unless they took a leading part. But if Britain proposed to act without them, it would force their hand, and they would at once wish to join in. Once the Japanese had agreed, American cooperation would not be long withheld. Lord Curzon reported that during the previous day he had seen the Japanese ambassador, who said that Japanese public opinion was very much divided on this question; and in any case, American consent was vital, in view of the finance and materials involved. Balfour suggested sending a telegram to Lord Reading, 'saying that we had a large force of 70,000 Czechoslovaks', who would fight well if properly led, and asking whether the American government saw any objection to their use against the Germans, with Japanese support.[23]

But Milner doubted whether this scheme would work. First, the French were 'very keen' for the Czech force to be brought to France — he had had a wire from Clemenceau on the matter that morning. Secondly, all our information indicated that the Czechs themselves were unwilling to become involved in Russian internal strife: 'Their desire was to fight Germans, and not Bolsheviks.' Bonar Law, Chancellor of the Exchequer, thought that if the Czechs formed part of the Allied force, 'thus making it clear to them that they were not fighting the Russians but the Germans', they were unlikely to object to cooperate on Russian soil.

In the discussion that followed, it was pointed out that it would be difficult to find the necessary tonnage to bring the Czechs to France. We had told the French that we could not find enough ships at present, and had suggested that it would be better to use the Czechs 'in an Allied expedition into Siberia'. The rest of the Czech force which had not yet reached Vladivostok, and which, it now appeared, amounted to some 50,000 out of a total of 70,000 men, might go to Archangel; and those Czechs not required for the protection of Archangel and Murmansk could be shipped to France. (These figures were wrong. The intention was for 50,000 to go to Vladivostok, and 20,000 to northern Russia.) Milner pointed out that Clemenceau disliked this suggestion, as only very limited numbers could be shipped from Archangel.

Lord Robert Cecil said he was 'much impressed' by the Prime Minister's suggestion. Once we had taken definite steps regarding Siberian intervention, the other Allies would soon conform. The French government had always been pressing for intervention in Siberia, and if they realized we meant business, they would allow the Czechs to be used. But Milner pointed out that as the Czech force was entirely a French creation, it was imperative that we obtain their cooperation before using the force. As far as American feeling was concerned, and its effect on reinforcements for the western-front, he would rather have 10,000 Americans in Siberia than in France.

The War Cabinet decided that the War Office should ascertain whether 'anything effective' could be done in Siberia without American cooperation, using the Czech force as a nucleus, reinforced perhaps with Canadian railwaymen, British troops from Hong Kong, and a French contingent, 'and with or without Japanese cooperation'. Lord Robert Cecil should see Benes, and 'ascertain definitely' whether the Czechs were willing to be used for this purpose, 'if it was explained to them that the object of the expedition was to fight Germans'. Lastly, if, after the above action had been taken, there was any promise of a scheme being put into operation, the Foreign Office should take such action as might be desirable with America, Japan and France.

Balfour then informed his colleagues that he had appointed Lindley as British representative in Russia.[23] General Poole, who would henceforward have only military command in northern Russia, had been instructed to report direct to the War Office and to send a copy of each report to Lindley. Thus seventeen days after the 'defeat' in Washington of the first British proposal for intervention, Lloyd George had another on the wing.

6

The Czech revolt and the French embargo

On May 18, Lloyd George wired to Clemenceau agreeing to June 1 for the next Supreme War Council's meeting to discuss the despatch of more American troops to France. Lord Robert Cecil wrote a delicately phrased letter to Clemenceau, as instructed by the War Cabinet the day before, about using the 'French' Czechs, presumed to be in the Far East, as a nucleus for Allied intervention in Siberia. (Cecil, as further instructed, had had another interview with Benes and had again asked him if the Czechs would take part in intervention in Russia against the Germans. Benes presumably agreed, subject to the conditions he had already made; but he does not say so, he merely states that Cecil was 'even more precise' than at their first meeting, and now spoke 'unreservedly' in favour of Czech independence. But Benes repeats that he again saw that the British attached 'considerable importance' to Czech political and military action; he was determined to make the most of it.[1] It is not clear whether Cecil realized this.)

The main reason for delayed intervention in Siberia, Cecil wrote to Clemenceau, was that America, because of 'tenderness' towards revolutionary Russia, and suspicion of Japan, would not approve Japanese intervention. Could nothing be done to break the deadlock and stop Germany over-running Russia with low-class troops, while her best troops were sent to the western front? 'Is there no way of creating a diversion in the East if the Japanese and Americans combine to delay matters?' There was one possibility, to use the Czechs now arriving at Vladivostok; he was satisfied that they could be used to 'start' operations in Siberia, and once they started, Japan would move and America would be unable to hold back. The British and French, who were bearing the whole weight of the German offensive, could not wait 'indefinitely' for Japan and America to reconcile themselves to intervention. To ship the Czechs from Vladivostok to France via North America would involve long delays and tie up the ships needed to bring American troops to Europe (this was doubtless thought to be a strong argument with Clemenceau). Further, stated Cecil, Benes had

131

approved his plan, provided there was an Allied declaration of recognition of the Czechs as Allies, and supporting their claims to independence; and that at least 20,000 of the 70,000 men in the Czech Legion should be shipped to France via Archangel.[2] (Now this, if true, represented a concession by Benes, and probably some sharp dealing by Cecil. Benes had reduced the number that had wished to come to France from 30,000 to 20,000 — which in fact was the alleged total, so Clemenceau had told the CIGS on the 11th, of all Czechs still west of Omsk, whom the British intended to use in northern Russia, shipping only the minimum to France. It is unlikely that Cecil ever told Benes of this.) Cecil ended his letter to Clemenceau by saying that it would be vital to make clear to the Bolshevik government that the Allies wished to retain the Czechs in Siberia to act against the Germans, and not interfere in Russian internal affairs; but the Allies need not insist upon Bolshevik approval — Bolshevik acquiescence would do.

On May 20, Benes returned to Paris, accompanied by a British general who had Cecil's letter to Clemenceau in his pocket. 'Public opinion in France and most of the political figures were coming round to the view that there was nothing further to hope for from Russia and the eastern front', recalls Benes. 'Hardly anyone believed that it was possible to restore this front; efforts to do so gave the impression of a plan which could at the very most be of some interest to the British Empire. Everyone was greatly irritated with the Russians [and not only with the Bolsheviks]', he added. This anti-British attitude may well have been true of certain circles in Paris and would correspond with the anti-French attitude gaining ground among certain circles in London, especially at the War Office.

On the 21st, Benes was summoned to the Quai d'Orsay to see Pichon, the French Foreign Minister, and his Secretary-General, Philippe Berthelot. As soon as he had explained what had passed between himself and Balfour and Cecil in London, Benes realized that there was a much greater divergence of views between London and Paris over the Czechs than he had imagined. 'The seriousness with which these questions were discussed with me at the Quai d'Orsay, the interest disclosed in my conversations in London, showed me once more that we had become a political and military factor of greater and greater importance.' The decisive moment was approaching. Pichon made it clear that France would stick to her previous agreement with the Czech national council and there would be a public Allied demonstration in favour of the Czech cause to encourage the Czech Legion, which would be brought to France as rapidly and in as large numbers as possible. 'M. Pichon assured me in very clear terms that France was resolved to fight the Hapsburg Empire to the bitter end, and would not abandon us. A reply would be sent in this sense to Lord Robert Cecil.'

It was clear that Benes now had to choose between the British and the French. He summed the situation up like this: 'Paris wanted our army in

France as soon as possible, London would have preferred to hold eastern Siberia with the aid of our legions, or at any rate wait, before transporting them to Europe, to discover what was going to happen in the East. Our troops would probably have had to guard some of the positions which they occupied.' (It is clear from this that Benes had no idea that the Czech Legion would probably be required to hold the line of the Volga, as well as positions in northern Russia.) 'As for me', Benes concludes with sudden candour, 'I naturally wanted them [the Czech Legion] used to the best advantage, that is to say for them to be sent where they were most needed, where they could be most profitable to us politically. As I expected the most from France, I therefore sided with her policy.'[3]

On the 22nd, Benes was summoned by Clemenceau, who asked him about the Czechs in Russia, and his recent talks in London. Benes asked Clemenceau directly to honour his recent promise to meet their political demands. 'He repeated them to me in precise terms,' writes Benes. 'Clemenceau told me, amongst other things, "I want all your troops in France. We think them first class soldiers. You will have a declaration from us, and we will recognize your independence. You must be independent. You deserve it. You can count on me. I will back you all the way".' These matters, Benes was told, would be settled at an Allied conference to be held in London shortly before the next Supreme War Council meeting on June 1.[3]

Clemenceau replied to Lord Robert Cecil's letter of May 18, and then wired to General Lavergne in Moscow that he was to start rerouting immediately those Czechs destined for Archangel, even against Bolshevik wishes; negotiations with them were useless and there was no need for any written authorization from Trotsky. The British and French governments were actively studying the protection of the northern Russian ports, Clemenceau went on, and Lavergne was authorized to make credits available as necessary to Czechs *en route* for Archangel; the French military attaché in Tokyo had reported that the Czechs in Vladivostok had enough funds for their pay and provisions for two months. In this wire, Clemenceau was clearly handing over the Czechs bound for northern Russia to the British for the protection of Archangel and Murmansk, or for intervention — even against Bolshevik wishes.[4]

When the War Cabinet again considered the Russian situation on May 23, they discussed intervention in northern Russia only. There was still no word from Clemenceau about using the 'French' Czechs in Siberia to start intervention. But the 'British' Czechs west of Omsk were now presumably *en route* for Archangel; and President Wilson had made it clear that though he was totally opposed to Siberian intervention, he was not averse to action in northern Russia. On May 20, the President had replied to Secretary Lansing, approving the sharp distinction between intervention in northern

Russia and Siberia, which Lansing had made to Lord Reading. 'The two parts of this question (as you properly discriminate them) must not and cannot be confused and discussed together', wrote the President. 'Semenov is changing the situation in Siberia very rapidly, apparently,' but the American Chief of Staff, General March, was 'clear and decided' in his opinion that there was no sufficient military force, 'in Japan or elsewhere,' to take any effective action in Siberia. General March was equally 'clear and decided' that no force strong enough to take effective action could be sent to Murmansk without withdrawing the same amount of shipping and manpower from the western front, and that this would be most unwise during the present German offensive in France.[5]

The American view had already reached London. On May 18, the CIGS prepared a paper for the War Cabinet on northern Russia, emphasizing that a brigade must be sent out to reinforce Murmansk; the party of 350 Royal Marines, which the Admiralty were sending on the 20th, was not enough. 'Unless we can re-establish a front in Russia, it is not clear how we can ever obtain a decision in our favour [i.e. against Germany], and the seizure of the northern [Russian] ports is a necessary preliminary,' wrote the CIGS. But as this 'small expedition' would need further reinforcement, it was 'strongly recommended' that the Americans be asked to take part, 'with a view to their eventually assuming its chief burden'. The small additional number of British troops could be sent out, 'and I recommend that this be done, but only on the understanding that it will be followed by a composite American brigade to be obtained from troops going to France'.[6] This small diversion of British troops would not affect the situation on the western front, since they needed further training before they could be put into the line in France. The CIGS thus countered the view of the American Chief of Staff.

Sir Henry Wilson's paper was before the War Cabinet when they met on May 23. But Lord Milner thought it undesirable at present to discuss with the American government the proposed despatch of an American brigade to Murmansk; meanwhile, more marines were being sent out and more troops would follow shortly. Milner urged the War Cabinet to approve the policy 'under which we used any force that can be got together' in northern Russia. There were a few Serbs in the region who might be used, and he had heard from Clemenceau that he 'agreed to the use of Czechoslovak troops at Murmansk and Archangel, except such as had already arrived at Vladivostok'. The First Lord drew attention to two telegrams from Admiral Kemp at Murmansk, one of which stated that Chicherin had informed the Murmansk soviet that more Allied troops were expected to arrive; and that unless they had received visas from Russian representatives abroad they were not to be allowed to land. But the Cabinet felt that such instructions might be only 'camouflage', reflecting German pressure on the Bolsheviks, and that no notice could be taken of such 'restrictions'. The second wire from Admiral Kemp recommended that General Poole should be in command of all forces landed in Russia, including all naval ratings landed, and that he should also be given political control. The First Lord approved of all the naval ratings landed being placed under Poole's orders, and the War Cabinet approved Sir Henry Wilson's paper, but decided that the question of American participation in the 'expedition' should be held over until Milner and Balfour thought it desirable.[7]

The War Cabinet then had to consider a strong wire from the British minister in Stockholm about the use of Finnish Red Guards to support Allied troops at Murmansk — a wire which clearly reflected Swedish apprehension at Britain's dabbling with Bolshevism, and probably Scandinavian opinion as well. Milner thought it essential that it be left to Poole 'to do the best he can with any force that he might be able to obtain'. He was not averse to Poole being informed of these objections to the use of the Finnish Red Guards, but it must be left to him to decide whether or not he would use them. The War Cabinet asked Lord Robert Cecil to draft a wire about the Finnish Red Guards and to forward it to Milner for his consideration and transmission to General Poole.[7]

The next day, General Poole reached Murmansk and the War Cabinet had to deal with both the Baltic Fleet and Japan's renewed interest in intervention in Siberia.

The turbulent and involved situation in the Baltic Fleet was rapidly moving to a climax. On the 15th, it will be recalled, Lockhart and Cromie had visited Trotsky, who assured them that there was an official project on hand for the destruction of the Baltic Fleet; and, in answer to Cromie's offer to pay a certain sum for each ship destroyed as an inducement to the crews, stated that money for this purpose had already been lodged in the state bank. When Cromie discovered that this was not so, he took another tack. When Trotsky heard of Cromie's offer, he decided to put it into effect openly; it could of course be said to be a British plan, and Trotsky must have known (as Cromie reported) that the Bolshevik General Staff openly agreed that it was very doubtful if their own orders for the destruction of the warships would be carried out. Thus British and Bolshevik plans went forward, more or less hand in hand.

On May 19, Cromie reported again what his agents were doing. 'Further meeting 18th shows progress', he wired. The scheme was being extended, so as to disable the main turbines of the warships under construction, as the Admiralty had requested. 'Occupation rumours appear to be less, so that preparations will be completed and everything in readiness,' he reported. His agents told him that there was danger of rapid occupation only from the Finnish border; there would be sufficient warning if the Germans made an advance from the Narva side (i.e. along the southern shore of the Gulf of Finland). 'Our agents are told that our scheme is merely a guarantee to signal success of official destruction scheme.'[8] Nothing would be done unless the warships were in imminent danger, so as to avoid all complication, 'but [I] consider scheme will not stand delay of more than one month', he warned.[8]

On the 21st, Captain Behrens, Russian naval chief of staff, forwarded a personal wire from Trotsky to Admiral Chastny at Kronstadt, stating that it was very probable that the departure of German officers from Finland, and the transfer to Finland of all outstanding matters to do with the Baltic Fleet, constituted 'a threat of an attack on our fleet, ostensibly in the name of Finland'. All proper measures of precaution must therefore be taken. 'Have all necessary preparatory measures been taken to destroy the vessels in case of acute emergency?' asked Trotsky. 'Have the money deposits been made in the bank in the name of those sailors who have been charged with the destruction of the vessels?' All this must be verified. Captain Behrens added that lists were to be made of the sailors who were to disable the warships. 'The lists are necessary, as it is the intention to give money rewards for successful fulfillment', he stressed. Chastny was to advise the higher military council how the destruction of the vessels was to be organized. Behrens sent this message *en clair* (which others, certainly the Germans, and possibly the British, would be expected to intercept).

Trotsky has this to say: 'I had Chastny instructed by telegram that these sailors would receive a certain sum of money from the government. This decision, in my view, in no way contradicted either naval or human morale. Anyhow, in these very difficult circumstances, it was one more chance of safeguarding the true interests of the revolution.' But this wire, which clearly showed that Trotsky, ad virtually become an Allied agent as regards the Baltic Fleet, had immediate repercussions. The sailors became restless, as there was now no immediate danger to the Baltic Fleet; they felt that Trotsky wished to destroy the warships purposely, or rather on behalf of the Germans: so said the anti-Bolshevik elements. The naval commissars were opposed to handing out several million roubles to sailors for work which it was their duty to perform. 'Our sailors never will agree to sell themselves for money', stated the chief commissar defiantly. For these various reasons, it was decided to send a delegation to Trotsky to demand an explanation.

Trotsky blamed Chastny for publicizing this wire within the fleet, and for declaring the plan 'immoral', and arguing that the plan was in accordance with a secret article of the Brest–Litovsk treaty. He, Chastny, said that the soviet authorities wished to 'bribe' the sailors to destroy the country's fleet. After this, there were rumours throughout the Baltic Fleet that the Soviet authorities had proposed to pay their debt to Germany by the destruction of the Russian warships, whilst, in reality, the exact opposite was true; it was the British who proposed offering the money, since it was a question of not handing the fleet over to the Germans, writes Trotsky. 'But the situation was very complicated', he admits, 'and thus very favourable for the diabolical propaganda of the White Guard elements. And at the head of this propaganda stood Admiral Chastny. He fostered it just as much by his actions and by his words as by his silence.'[9]

Cromie wired again to the Admiralty: 'Our Agent approached us today, 22nd, and said if scheme delayed too long, money already expended might be lost, several men having said danger no longer existed and desired return to their villages.' Cromie warned that if the Allies did take action in northern Russia, this would be used as strong anti-Allied propaganda, as had happened over the Japanese landing at Vladivostok in early April. But 'our people' recognized the good intentions of the Allies, and openly stated that they preferred Russia to be under Allied rather than German influence, until Russia could again stand alone. 'They therefore propose now obtaining sure men and preparing scheme on a certain date to be fixed when new arrangements become [?operative], although present scheme still exists in case emergencies.' Cromie wished to know whether he should accept this greater responsibility. He had just received an urgent request from the Bolshevik general staff to come to Moscow to discuss the question of Murmansk. Cromie asked to be advised of Allied intentions in northern Russia, so that he could answer any questions, to help him decide what was the 'right moment' to blow up the Baltic Fleet. If one thing is clear from these various wires, it is that the situation, involving heavy bribes and false propaganda, was ripe for explosion; but what or who was to be the casualty? The Russian warships, Chastny, Trotsky or Cromie?[10]

Late on the 23rd, the Admiralty received three wires from Cromie that were some six days late. In them Cromie stated that as the Germans were expected to enter Petrograd on the 23rd, he proposed to blow up the Baltic Fleet on the 21st or 22nd. The First Sea Lord seems to have delayed informing the Cabinet of this until he could verify what had actually happened. Enquiries showed that the Russian warships were still intact, that the Germans were not in Petrograd. On the 24th, the First Sea Lord contented himself with telling the Cabinet that Cromie had reported that the Germans 'might be expected to enter Petrograd on May 23', and that the Bolshevik government 'appeared to realize that its end was near, and that it was now willing to accept help from anyone'. No more was said; the First Sea Lord kept to himself the fact that Cromie's agents were becoming involved not only with anti-Bolshevik elements in the Baltic Fleet, but also with pro-German Russian groups.[11]

Meanwhile, Japan had expressed renewed interest in intervention in Siberia, which was due to the success of their puppet, Ataman Semenov, in advancing once again across the Chinese border into Russian territory. The British ambassador in Tokyo had warned of this in a wire of May 15. On the 18th, the Japanese Foreign Minister had instructed the Japanese ambassador in London to reopen negotiations with the Foreign Office, to whom he was to put four questions. The first three concerned British attempts to secure a Bolshevik invitation for intervention: a matter of considerable distaste to the Japanese. What prospect was there of Lockhart securing such a Bolshevik invitation? If such an invitation were to be secured, would it not entail collaboration with the Bolsheviks, which would strengthen their régime and consolidate its control of Siberia? Provided that the German advance did not extend into Siberia, were not the Bolsheviks unlikely to issue an invitation for intervention? Lastly, there was Semenov, whom the British had refused to support any longer, and whom the Japanese now claimed, untruly, they had been unable to stop making his latest advance. If the Allies now abandoned him, asked the Japanese Foreign Minister, would they not lose prestige in Russian eyes and so drive the Russians into German arms?[12]

When the Japanese ambassador came to the Foreign Office on May 22, Lord Robert Cecil told him that Lockhart had advised that the Allies should now intervene, whether they were invited to do so or not. As for Semenov, Cecil himself was willing for him to be supported, if the Japanese military authorities so wished. In like manner, the British wished to use the Czechs at Vladivostok; and Semenov and the Czechs could only take really effective action if supported by Japan. If Japan took such action, Cecil was willing to let Japan take control of the intervention operations, provided they made clear they were not hoping to seize Russian territory, but wished to help Russia and the Allied cause (the usual conditions), and that they would advance to Chelyabinsk. But the ambassador did not care for the mention of Chelyabinsk, 5,000 miles from Vladivostok. However, Cecil pressed Japan, as England's ally, to come to her aid; Siberian intervention might really affect the outcome of the German war.[13]

Lord Robert Cecil brought the matter before the Cabinet on May 24. It was obvious from the first three questions put by the Japanese Foreign Minister that Japan did not wish Britain to continue negotiating with the Bolsheviks, or to wait until the Bolsheviks asked for Allied intervention in Siberia. The Japanese were supporting Semenov, but we had told the Bolshevik government that we were not doing so and that he was advancing at his own risk. Japan wished to know what the British attitude was towards Semenov. Cecil thought we should deal 'perfectly frankly' with the Bolsheviks. He himself was prepared to back Semenov, 'provided that his activities were part and parcel of an Allied movement, otherwise we should have nothing to do with him'. It was felt in the Cabinet that we might leave Semenov entirely to the Japanese and say nothing to Trotsky unless he raised the matter. But others felt that this would not be dealing 'frankly' with the Bolsheviks; for if intervention in Siberia ever materialized, and Semenov became part of the Allied movement, we should naturally support him. On the other hand, to recognize Semenov now would be to recognise an 'avowed enemy' of Bolshevism. After further discussion, it was decided that the question involved decisions 'too momentous' to be resolved without the presence of the Prime Minister and the Foreign Secretary, and Hankey was instructed to put the matter on the agenda on the earliest possible date at which both Lloyd George and Balfour could be present.[14]

The British plan for Allied intervention was thus proceeding fairly well. President Wilson was still adamantly refusing to take action in Siberia, but Semenov's renewed advance had renewed Japanese interest in intervention, and the 'French' Czechs, it was hoped, could now spark it off. In northern Russia, President Wilson was ready to approve action, the 'British' Czechs were *en route*, and General Poole was on the spot to take matters in hand. At long last, matters seemed to be on the move.

But May 25 saw all these hopes dashed to the ground; it was a day of reckoning in the long saga of careful British attempts to find a workable Russian policy. First, Lord Robert Cecil received a vitriolic reply from Clemenceau to his proposal to use the 'French' Czechs to start the intervention in Siberia. The British proposal, wrote Clemenceau, was a 'formal contradiction' of the Abbeville agreement. Nor was this the moment, with British manpower in France declining, and when France was making the final sacrifice to maintain French manpower, for Britain to try to deprive France of courageous and well-trained troops, whose main aim was to fight for their independence in France. The British had obviously misunderstood Benes, who had assured Clemenceau that he had never contemplated allowing the Czechs to be used to initiate Allied intervention. Clemenceau forbad it. 'I insist absolutely upon the execution pure and simple of the engagements taken at Abbeville.' These stated that the British would ship the Czechs to the western front, and he had assumed that this operation was already in progress. This was a rude reply, and meant to be; it caused great offence to Lord Robert Cecil, who now saw plainly that he had been double-crossed by Benes.[15]

May 25 also saw the loss of the 'British' Czechs as well — though this was not to be known for some time, nor properly appreciated when it was known. On May 18, news reached Moscow of the incident on the 14th at Chelyabinsk between the Czechs and Hungarians, which had led to the momentary arrest of the local soviet by Czech troops. The French military mission sensed trouble for the Czech Legion and immediately despatched a courier to Major Guinet, the French liaison officer with the First Czech Corps, with instructions that the Czechs should comply with the Bolsheviks' requirements to disarm; only this, the French mission felt, would ensure continued Bolshevik approval of the Czech evacuation — and Trotsky had already agreed that the Czechs going to northern Russia should be rearmed from the Allied war supplies stored at Archangel.

The French mission were right to be alarmed. Trotsky took a grave view of the incident at Chelyabinsk. He could see the strategic importance of Chelyabinsk just as well as the British general staff. It might well link up several disconnected centres of anti-Bolshevik activity. May 16 had not only seen the establishment, with German support, of the strongly anti-Bolshevik General Krasnov, as Ataman of the Don Cossacks, but also a serious revolt amongst Red Army troops at Saratov on the Volga. Then there was Ataman Semenov, again pushing into Russian territory from over the Chinese border. He had Japanese support, and his continued success might well foreshadow the long-feared Japanese descent on Siberia, narrowly averted early in April. If the Czechs managed to seize control of the Siberian railway from the crucial railhead of Chelyabinsk, where the Czech congress was about to open, matters might escalate quickly; the Czechs were in contact with the right SRs, who were calling openly for Allied intervention. How were the Allies really intending to use the Czechs? There were no ships at either Murmansk or Vladivostok to take them to France, and it would be impossible to allow the open formation of Allied troops on Russian soil without incurring severe German displeasure; a ringing call from the coming Czech congress at Chelyabinsk might do this.

These were some of the reasons impelling Trotsky to action. On May 20, the Czech congress opened at Chelyabinsk, and the rival Czech communist congress opened in Moscow. Trotsky had orders sent to all Siberian soviets that the Czechs were to be detrained, organized into labour units or drafted into the Red Army. The next day, he had the two Czech representatives in Moscow, who were about to return to Omsk, arrested and forced to sign an order stating that in view of recent 'unfortunate misunderstandings', all Czechs travelling through Russia by train were to hand over their arms to the local soviets.

But it is now clear that Trotsky was still willing, even for a few days longer, to allow the Czechs to go to Archangel, provided they were not armed. In a statement of May 31, he claimed that his wire of May 20 meant only that they were to be disbanded, if the absence of British and French ships made their continued journey impossible. And on May 24, Lockhart wired (as will be seen from the discussions at the War Cabinet of May 27) that Trotsky had no objection to the Czechs being sent to Archangel *en route* for France, provided they were disarmed while in transit through Russia; and he was holding the Czech representatives in Moscow as hostages to see that they did disarm.

At Chelyabinsk, the Czech congress was preoccupied at its opening session with the rerouting order (which was disbelieved), and with whether or not Czech troops should continue in one body to Vladivostok, even against Bolshevik wishes. The French liaison officers strongly urged the

Czechs to comply with the Allied and Bolshevik requests. But on the 22nd, the congress decided that the troops should proceed in one body to Vladivostok and not surrender their arms. A resolution stated that the congress was 'convinced that the soviet government is powerless to guarantee our troops free and safe passage to Vladivostok, and therefore has unanimously decided not to surrender its arms until it receives assurance that the [Czech] Corps will be allowed to depart.' Then various orders from Moscow began to arrive at Chelyabinsk, including a further wire from Trotsky's staff, instructing the local Siberian soviets to begin disarming and disbanding the First Czech Corps. This wire was sent on the 23rd and intercepted the same day at Chelyabinsk; whereupon the congress passed a resolution disowning the Czech national council and set up a Czech executive committee from among its own delegates (mostly young Czech officers on the spot) and unanimously resolved to proceed 'To Vladivostok armed and even against the will of the Soviets'. These decisions were wired that day to the Bolshevik government in direct and threatening terms. The Czech executive committee, it was stated, trusted that the Bolsheviks would 'place no obstacles in the way of the departing Czechoslovak revolutionary troops ... since every conflict would only prejudice the position of the local soviet organs in Siberia.'[16] This was not just a statement of intent, but a challenge. Trotsky could not possibly ignore it.

On May 25, Trotsky was seriously compromised by Allies over the Baltic Fleet. The day before, a decision in Moscow to blow up the Black Sea Fleet had coincided with a further disorderly 'general assembly' of the Baltic Fleet at Kronstadt, at which it was decided to dismiss all sailors who refused to sign a service contract; only those who signed would be paid. The evident intention was to try and rid the fleet of anti-Bolshevik elements. Some sailors were reported to have drifted away from Kronstadt after this, back to their homes. On the 25th, Cromie reported from Moscow on the Bolshevik decision to destroy the Black Sea Fleet immediately, and his assistant, Commander Le Page, sent a significant wire to the Admiralty from Petrograd, emphasizing that the Baltic Fleet was 'absolutely no further use' as a possible Allied force, while Russia herself would be unable to use it for many years. It was therefore vital to make sure that if it did fall into German hands, the larger warships could not be used for at least twelve months. (The Admiralty, of course, were insisting on complete disablement of the Russian warships.)[17] Le Page continued: 'Rumours of occupation grow less, and men lulled into false idea of security ... one or two have begun to talk about what they had been prepared to do ... a fatal Russian fault. Now absolutely necessary to extend organization to bring in strong pro-Ally adherents, and carry out scheme on a fixed pre-arranged date and take consequences. Unless this is done, really believe everything will fail. Moreover, the longer the delay, the more is there danger of

141

leakage, especially in Russia, and exposure of organizing body to arrest [or] assassination. Germany has agents out on watch.'[17]

The wire went on to say that there were now very few Finnish troops on the frontier, and 'no German troops whatever'. The Finnish troops were mainly on the farms, preparing the land for sowing. Reports from good sources stated that the Germans were 'very disappointed' with the Russians; as everything had to be got by force, and no German troops could be withdrawn from the western front, they had decided that the best plan was to buy in the open market and pay whatever price was demanded. Le Page concluded by saying that as soon after the attempt to blow up the Baltic Fleet as possible, some fifteen Russian naval officers wished to come to England: 'Chief organizer asks permission to take his wife, to which naval attaché provisionally agreed.'[17]

The news of the Bolsheviks' decision to blow up the Black Sea Fleet and the information contained in Le Page's wire impelled both Chastny and Trotsky to action. Chastny, now certain that the Bolsheviks were acting in Germany's interests, and equally certain that he had strong support in the Baltic Fleet, resigned his command. Trotsky, discovering from Cromie's talkative agents that he had become involved in an Allied plot, which was now being supported by 'strong pro-Ally adherents' (i.e. strongly anti-Bolshevik elements), summoned Chastny to Moscow on the 25th and had him arrested as a counter-revolutionary and an organizer of an anti-Bolshevik movement in the Baltic Fleet; Chastny now knew much too much, and either he or Trotsky would have had to go. But attempts to arrest Lissanevitch, the young destroyer officer at Kronstadt, failed.

Trotsky also took immediate action that day over the Czechs at Chelyabinsk: he obviously could not temporize with these pro-Ally troops a moment longer. 'All soviets are hereby ordered to disarm the Czecho-slovaks immediately,' was the instruction given to all soviets between Penza and Omsk on the 25th. 'Every armed Czechoslovak found on the railway is to be shot on the spot; every troop train in which even one armed man is found shall be unloaded, and its soldiers shall be interned in a war prisoners' camp. Local war commissars must proceed at once to carry out this order; every delay will be considered treason.' When a small soviet near Omsk tried to carry out this peremptory order, the local Czech commander, Rudolph Gajda, led an armed revolt against the Bolsheviks, which set off a chain reaction all down the Siberian railway. On May 26, the right SRs called for the Bolsheviks to be overthrown and appealed for Allied intervention. At the same time, fighting between Czechs and Bolsheviks was taking place at nearly every station between Penza and Irkutsk. Intervention, not against the Germans, but against the Bolsheviks, had begun; and by the 28th, nearly all the important towns between Chelyabinsk and Irkutsk had been seized by only 20,000 Czechs. Leslie Urquhart had been right.[18]

By the 27th, the War Cabinet were aware only that Clemenceau had forbidden the use of the 'French' Czechs; the fact that the 'British' Czechs had done a *volte-face* and were in process of seizing the Siberian railway from Penza through Chelyabinsk to Irkutsk was unknown in London. The Deputy First Sea Lord first informed the War Cabinet of events at Vladivostok: *Suffolk* had reported that there had been a big demonstration there on May 22, at which over 10,000 people, including public bodies and workmen, had protested at Bolshevik control of the town; there had been speeches against Bolshevik tyranny and in favour of universal suffrage and an atmosphere of great enthusiasm prevailed; there had been no disorder. The captain of *Suffolk* added that the present moment appeared most favourable for the declaration of some firm Allied policy.[19]

Suffolk had also wired that the Czechs were not willing to interfere in Russian affairs. They wished to fight on the western front, but great efforts were being made by 'enemy agents' (presumably Bolshevik agitators) to dissuade them from going. The captain reported that they were men 'of splendid physique,' good discipline, and with some years experience of war and should prove a valuable force; there were 10,000 Czechs at Vladivostok and another 13,000 were expected shortly.

This must have been all the more galling for Lord Robert Cecil, who informed the Cabinet that the French Foreign Minister, Pichon, was due to arrive in London that evening, the principal object of his visit probably being to discuss Russian policy (i.e. to reinforce Clemenceau's veto on the use of these same Czechs). The War Cabinet decided that Pichon should be invited to confer with the Prime Minister, Balfour and Cecil at 11 a.m. next day in the Cabinet room, prior to a War Cabinet at noon. Cecil undertook to invite Pichon. The CIGS was asked to attend. To add insult to injury, Cecil then had to show the Cabinet the letter drafted to Benes, in return for Czech cooperation in Russia — a promise on which Benes had ratted. Cecil stated that the Czech national council had asked the British government to accord it the same recognition as the French and Italian governments had done, and he proposed to send Benes the draft letter which would accord them the 'measure of recognition' asked for, but not commit the British government to any increased war obligations.[19]

The War Cabinet then went into closed session for a further discussion on Cromie's plans for the destruction of the Baltic Fleet. The Deputy First Sea Lord reported that a wire of May 22nd had been received, stating that Cromie's agents had told him that if the scheme was delayed too long, the money already spent might be lost, since several of the men who were to carry out the plan said that the danger no longer existed, and that they wished to return to their villages. The agents proposed to procure other men who could be relied on to prepare another scheme and to fix a definite date for the fleet's destruction. The existing scheme could still be used in a case of emergency.

It was pointed out in the Cabinet that Lockhart had stated that Trotsky had agreed to the destruction of the Russian fleets in case of need, 'and it was understood that M. Trotsky was making his own arrangements for this'. The Deputy First Sea Lord mentioned that the Admiralty's scheme, to be carried out by Cromie, would entail damaging the turbines of the Russian warships beyond repair. But the War Cabinet felt that the warships must be sunk, even though this might mean blowing up some of the Russian sailors on board, which 'would involve a final break with Russia ... the question resolved itself into this', state the Cabinet minutes, 'whether, by sinking the [Baltic] Fleet, we should gain or lose more'. It was also noted that blowing up the Russian warships might result in our 'losing the services' of the Czech force now in Russia; and attention was drawn to Lockhart's wire of May 24, which stated that 'although [Trotsky] had no objection to the Czechoslovak forces being sent to Archangel *en route* to France, [he] demanded that they should be disarmed while in transit through Russia, and was holding the vice-president of the Czechoslovak national council as a hostage for such disarmament'. (This, of course, is a vital piece of evidence of Trotsky's attitude towards the Czechs as late as the 24th, after he had arrested the Czech representatives, and presumably before he received the threatening wire of the 23rd from the Czech congress at Chelyabinsk. Both in London and Moscow, the Baltic Fleet and the Czech Legion were closely linked together.)[20] But other members of the Cabinet stressed that there was a grave risk of the Russian warships falling into German hands.

The Cabinet decided that this was the essential thing to be avoided, and authorized the First Lord to send a wire to Cromie saying that he was to take whatever steps he thought necessary, deferring his action for as long as possible, subject to the above essential requirement; and so far as possible, to keep in touch with Lockhart. At four minutes past two o'clock that afternoon, the Deputy First Sea Lord wired in these terms to Captain Cromie.[21]

All that day, there was great anxiety in London about the sudden new German offensive, the 'Blücher' attack, in Champagne. The Germans had attacked, on a 50 km front, both the British 9th Corps at Berry-au-Bac and the French along the Chemin des Dames, 'and have thrown the whole line over the Aisne', records Sir Henry Wilson in his diary. 'This is really rather an amazing business, as all that country is so naturally strong. I don't like this sort of thing at all. The King sent for me at 7 o'clock and was much upset.'[22]

Benes in Paris was the first to hear of Trotsky's order of the 25th, which had led to a breach between the Bolsheviks and the Czechs. The British and French ministers, meeting in the Cabinet room on May 28, were aware of the news, but uninterested. 'The events at the end of May were considered as local events', emphasised Benes, 'and as such interpreted, rightly in fact, as expressing the wish of our troops to reach Europe. The French authorities regretted that there had been a dispute. ... As for the incident [of May 14] at Chelyabinsk, no one, either in Paris or London, attached any importance to it,' he writes.[23]

In the Cabinet room, the French Foreign Minister, Pichon, accompanied only by the aged French ambassador, Paul Cambon, saw these events as an argument in his favour as he faced Lloyd George, Balfour and Cecil. He had come to London, Pichon stated, at the express wish of Clemenceau to discuss the removal of the Czech troops from Russia and Siberia, and Allied policy generally towards the Czechs and Poles. Clemenceau had been 'greatly preoccupied' by Cecil's recent letter suggesting that the Czechs should be left in Siberia to form the nucleus of an Allied force, since he thought it 'of the first importance' that the Czechs should be sent to France, as agreed at Abbeville. Pichon had been sent to London to see that the Abbeville agreement was maintained. From all the telegrams Pichon had received from French representatives in Siberia, Japan and America, it was clear that there would be 'great inconveniences' if the Czechs were left at Vladivostok; Czech morale would suffer 'gravely' from even the briefest delay. Pichon then read out a wire from the French ambassador in Tokyo, warning of the danger of Bolshevik 'contamination' of the Czechs; he backed this up with other reports he had received.[24]

Benes had told him, Pichon continued, that all his information showed that the Czechs did not wish to be embroiled in Russian affairs, or to remain in Siberia. Benes admitted that he had told Cecil that 'if appealed to as Allies, and recognized as an independent force, they would be prepared, as a great sacrifice, to remain'. But Benes had also told Pichon that the Czech national council did not wish their troops to remain in Siberia. (This appears to indicate that Pichon was not prepared entirely to cover Benes.) The Japanese ambassador in Paris had told Pichon that his country could not agree to Czech intervention in Siberia. Balfour asked if the ambassador had given his reasons. Pichon replied cagily that Japanese diplomats never spoke freely. Cecil said that he had always realized that the Japanese would not like intervention solely by the Czechs. This was obviously a danger to Japan; but if they did intervene, it would induce the Japanese to join them, as they did not want anyone else intervening in Siberia.

At this point, the CIGS entered the Cabinet room to give the latest news of the German attack on the Chemin des Dames. He evidently spoke in depressing tones. This British and French retreat was 'very disquieting', he recorded in his diary that evening. 'The Boches are increasing their attack on the Aisne up to 35 divisions and quite possibly may turn it into their main attack. ... Milner just back from GHQ and Versailles. He cannot account for this retirement on the Aisne, and from all he heard he thought badly of it.'[25]

When the discussion was resumed, Pichon stressed how vital it was to bring all possible reinforcements to the western front. All reports agreed that the Czechs were very good troops, who would fight 'admirably'. It was worth bringing them across America, even if it delayed a few American divisions, since the Czechs were better trained than the Americans, and thus more ready for immediate action. Apart from the danger of leaving them in Siberia, there would be another political advantage in bringing them to the western front as soon as possible; namely their influence on Austria, where (according to reports) the situation was serious. Since the Allies had given real attention to the Czech movement, the Austrians had had to withdraw all Slav troops from the Italian front. Pichon read out wires from Berne and elsewhere, that indicated grave unrest in Austria, as shown by the demonstrations at Prague and throughout Bohemia (an exclusively Czech province). All this showed that Britain and her Allies would cause trouble for Austria, if we could stimulate the Czech movement. (If this was, in fact, the reason for Clemenceau's insistence on bringing these troops half-way round the world to fight in France, why had he never mentioned it before? Apparently because the British, who had been conducting abortive peace negotiations with Austria, which were now fast losing momentum, still wanted to 'go easy on' the Austrians, with a view to weaning them out of the war.) Thus, concluded Pichon, he 'demanded' that the Abbeville agreement, reached in the presence of General Foch, and the British and French commanders-in-chief in France, should be kept; and that the British government should do their best to find ships.

Lloyd George therefore sent for the shipping controller. Lord Robert Cecil said that if the French government did not accept the British plan for intervention in Siberia, as detailed in his letter, what was their plan? It was agreed that Allied intervention in Siberia was now necessary, but negotiations in Washington had failed, so what could the French suggest? At this, Pichon hedged. There had been no stronger advocate of Siberian intervention than himself, he claimed, but the French government were 'absolutely certain' that Czech intervention would achieve nothing; thus the question did not arise. But Lloyd George pressed him; what was the French government's plan? Pichon said the 'only possible plan' was to use every effort to induce President Wilson to agree to Allied action. This naturally irritated Cecil. Both British and French governments had made 'continuous representations' to Washington about the urgency of the matter, he retorted, but their proposals had always been rejected; only within the last two days, President Wilson had reaffirmed that he was unwilling to cooperate. Pichon retorted that the Czech national council all agreed that they could not intervene effectively in Siberia. (Ironically, the Czech Legion, at this moment, held nearly all the towns along the Siberian railway in western Siberia.)

Balfour pointed out that Pichon had laid stress on the good fighting qualities of the Czechs. Why then, if we could count on them to fight well in northern Russia, could it be assumed that they would not fight in Siberia? 'Their only object was to fight Germans, but that was all we asked of them in Siberia.' Pichon said the conditions were entirely different in the two regions. 'At Archangel and Murmansk, the Czechoslovaks would be asked to fight against the Germans, but in Siberia there were no Germans, and their principal role would be to maintain the railway and keep the communications clear.' Pichon again insisted on the immediate and vital urgency of bringing the Czechs to fight on the western front, 'where they would be really useful'. Balfour said the question resolved itself into this: were they to be used at some future date in France, or much sooner in Siberia? The CIGS, in answer to the Prime Minister, stated that the Czechs would probably fight better at the moment than the Americans, since they were more prepared. 'General Knox had told him that they formed the best fighting material in Russia.'

Cambon, the French ambassador, asked what a force of 25,000 men could do in Russia, even supposing that they were willing to fight there? Balfour agreed that they could do very little without Japanese intervention. Lloyd George was not so sure; according to some reports (i.e. from Leslie Urquhart), '5,000 determined men could go right through Siberia'. The French ambassador changed the subject. He was, he said, much impressed by the political effect of the appearance of the Czechs on the western front; it might tilt the balance in Austria. Pichon developed this theme. The Allies might soon be able to make an appeal to the Bohemians and Czechs, whose representatives were shortly to hold a very important conference in Paris, at which he would like to be able to state that the Czechs would join the Poles in France; this might produce important political results. Cambon then asked Lord Robert Cecil whether he would not prefer to bring the Czechs to the western front, if shipping were actually available at Vladivostok. Cecil replied sharply that he would not. The most important task at present was to restore the eastern front. In any case, some Czech troops, 'sufficient at any rate to secure the political advantages named', would be available for the western front, since half the Czech force, now being concentrated at Archangel and Murmansk, was to be brought to France. At this, the CIGS said he had received a wire that day from General Poole, stating that the French were arming and training the Serbs at Kandalaksha, but there were no Czechs there. 'They had last been heard of at Omsk.' Cecil said that there were three groups of Czechs; one at or *en route* for Vladivostok; a second at Omsk; and a third between Moscow and Archangel. (This was patently incorrect.)

Again Cambon changed the subject; the Czechs, he said, could achieve nothing in Siberia without Japanese intervention. Cecil retorted that we had tried by every means to convince President Wilson, but up to the present had failed to do so. Of course, Cecil added, he would much prefer a Japanese and American intervention, 'but failing this, it was absolutely necessary for the Allies to do something'. Cambon again said that it was useless to use the Czechs alone, if only because the Czech national council had clearly shown that the Czechs themselves did not favour this plan. He emphasized again the political importance of bringing them to the western front to influence the Austrian question. Pichon said that Czech intervention in Siberia 'would probably prove fatal to American intervention'. To promote Czech intervention alone would merely lose valuable time, and achieve no result. (This was probably the most regrettable remark of this long discussion.)

After further discussion, Balfour summarized the reasons why the British government wanted the Abbeville agreement reconsidered. Lord Robert Cecil was right in stating that if the French did not agree to the present British proposals, the Abbeville agreement should stand; there was no question of the British government trying to force the French government to abandon it. The real problem was how to make the best possible use of our limited and insufficient manpower. He agreed that the Allies were short of manpower on the western front. 'They had, however, still less manpower in Russia.' Only a foreign force could help Russia. At present, there was a tiny force near the White Sea; and only two forces in the Far East. First, there was a well-equipped Japanese army of 400,000 men, which was 'lost to the Allies' at present; secondly, there were the Czechs, 'which were actually in Russia'. Owing to the great shortage of shipping, it was a question whether the Czechs should be shipped 'half-way round the world', or left for operations in Russia. If they were brought to France, a similar number of Americans would be delayed. 'The difference, therefore, was between trained Czechoslovak troops and untrained United States troops.' The difference was only of quality, and only temporary, since the Americans would be properly trained in a few months. This was the reason why the British government suggested retaining the Czechs in Siberia, where they would form a valuable addition to an American and Japanese force, 'if the Americans and Japanese could be induced to move'. If some operations could be kept going in Russia, then some German divisions would have to be kept there. Otherwise, not only would Germany bring all her troops to the western front, but use Russian manpower as an internal labour force, and possibly even 'for recruiting soldiers'. As for the political argument, Balfour pointed out that there were already Czechs in Italy, and some were coming to France from Archangel. Thus the shipment of Czechs from Vladivostok would introduce no new political factor.

At this point, the shipping controller entered, and said that 5,000 Czechs could be shipped from Vladivostok to America between now and July; another 5,000 might be loaded by the end of July for shipment through the Suez Canal. Lloyd George asked the controller to calculate how long it would take to ship the 25,000 Czechs from Vladivostok. The conference adjourned.

When the conference resumed at 4 p.m., the shipping controller told the Prime Minister that from 4,500 to 5,000 Czechs could be shipped from Vladivostok to Vancouver between June 15 and July 15; and they would begin to come into the field in France in about mid-August. It would also be possible to bring some 9,000 Czechs through the Red Sea in about the same time; but it would mean the loss of some 30,000 tons of rice, sugar, etc. from the Far East. To ship any more Czechs than this would be a 'very serious matter indeed', he said. Pichon stated adamantly that there were two parts to the question: the principle of shipping the Czechs from Vladivostok, and the numbers that could be shipped. He had come to London to insist upon the principle agreed at Abbeville; the present conference could not discuss available shipping. Both Balfour and Lord Robert Cecil pointed out that the shipping controller had just said that he could ship about half the Czechs, exclusive of those at Archangel. Cecil added that the important thing to settle was what we could really do. Balfour retorted that Pichon wanted the principle settled.

At this, the Prime Minister remarked that past experience showed the danger of pressing for a principle unless it could be put into practice. Was it not possible, now that Trotsky seemed disposed to allow the Czechs to go to Archangel — even though he insisted on their being unarmed — to send them up to Archangel from Vladivostok? The shipping controller remarked that the Japanese could ship some of the Czechs from Vladivostok; but Cecil said that it would be difficult to ask Japan to send her troops into Siberia and to ship Czech troops away at the same time. Pichon underlined the difficulty of sending the Czechs from Vladivostok to Archangel. The question had been examined by the Supreme War Council, with the result that it was decided at Abbeville to send all the Czechs at Omsk to Archangel, not Vladivostok; there was a double interest here; to remove the Czechs as rapidly as possible from Bolshevik influence, and to send those Czechs that could not be shipped away 'flowing back to the Russian front'. Balfour pointed out that at most only 14,000 Czechs could be shipped from Vladivostok. He asked the shipping controller if the same ships could come back for more and was told that they could only do so after 'very great delay', which would have a very serious effect on cargoes from the Far East. The CIGS remarked that it was practically impossible to take troops through the Red Sea in July and August. The Prime Minister suggested that the British government should undertake to ship 4,500 Czechs from mid-June, and the Foreign Office should try to induce the Japanese to remove the remainder. But Cecil thought that this would discourage Japanese intervention still further; he would agree to approach them if this was part of a comprehensive arrangement, but it was 'most dangerous' to do anything to discourage the Japanese, who were generally inclined to be suspicious of Allied motives.

The Prime Minister asked Pichon what he had in mind in the way of Allied intervention. How was it to be brought about, how was Germany to be prevented from bringing all her forces to the western front? Pichon hedged. He had always been eager for Allied intervention in Siberia, he replied. First, he had thought of Japanese action; then the Americans' attitude made it clear that Japan could not act alone, and Japan was ready to accept Allied participation. For this American consent was necessary, 'the point to which the question always came back'. As soon as it was given, intervention could begin. The French government, from the start, had had a few troops available; they were doing all they could to influence President Wilson and sending representatives to urge him on personally. But both England and France could only act in accord with America. 'It seemed to him that Japan was now thinking of intervention without the United States' consent, which he considered would be a very serious matter.' One reason why he was against keeping the Czechs at Vladivostok and using them as a 'nucleus' for intervention was that it 'would have the air of forcing the hand of the United States, which he [Pichon] thought would be very dangerous'.

The Prime Minister said this meant that Pichon had given up all idea of persuading the American government to accept a purely Japanese intervention, but hoped they would agree to Allied intervention. But if the Czechs were shipped away, what Allied troops would be available except the Japanese? Lord Robert Cecil said that he had gathered from the reports of General Bridges, the British military representative in Washington, that American military opinion was now more favourable towards intervention. The Prime Minister said that the President was more moved by the politicians, who (so Lord Reading reported) were more and more against Japanese intervention. It seemed that until the coming American elections were over, there would be no chance of obtaining American agreement to Japanese action. How could Allied intervention, which was not mainly Japanese, be arranged except by the use of Czech troops? Again Pichon hedged. It was true that very few troops were available, but America was insisting on the principle involved, not equal numbers in the force that intervened. 'It would be enough to show the flag.' The Japanese had ample troops for safety, and Allied troops were only needed 'as a façade'. (Once again, the French were pressing for a principle.) Cecil asked Pichon how far he thought the Japanese were ready to intervene. Did it merely mean in eastern Siberia, or would they advance to Chelyabinsk and European Russia? Pichon said that once the principle of intervention was agreed, the Allies must push the Japanese as far as possible, 'to the Urals if they could'. The Prime Minister asked if Pichon had any reason for thinking that the Japanese would go as far as the Urals, or was it only a hope? Pichon stated that French sources in Tokyo reported that the Japanese were anxious to meet the danger of German penetration into Siberia. He did not think it would be difficult to convince them that they would have to go further than eastern Siberia. (A pious hope.) Cecil remarked that there were 'indications' that the Japanese Foreign Minister was prepared to go further.* Balfour added that if the Japanese intervened alone, they would probably not go beyond eastern Siberia, but if they intervened as part of an Allied force, they would be influenced by Allied opinion. Japan wanted to play a great part in the Alliance. 'As always this brought the question back to America.'

The French ambassador remarked that the question before them was the shipment of Czech troops from Vladivostok to the western front, but they were now discussing Japanese intervention, which depended upon American agreement. The Prime Minister replied that the two questions could not be treated separately. The British objection to removal of the Czechs was largely due to their reluctance to remove troops who might be of possible use in intervention. 'Intervention was a necessity. The Allied cause depended on giving help to Russia. Great Britain could not provide troops; France could not; Japan would not; therefore the Czechs might be of real use.' Pichon stated that the French government 'would not accept the principle of using the Czechs to force Japanese intervention, and later American consent'. Balfour replied that he had never thought of using them in this way, only as an addition to a Japanese force. (This is untrue. On May 17, Balfour had approved the Prime Minister's proposal to use the Czechs for precisely that purpose.)

Balfour added that one of the American objections to intervention was that since the Japanese did not have enough troops to guard the whole Siberian railway line, the Czechs could thus greatly assist. Pichon again said that it was 'materially impossible' to use the Czechs in Siberia. The Czech national council refused to allow it, while he himself saw 'great risk in appearing to be trying to force the hand of the United States.' He asked that the Abbeville agreement should be maintained in principle and that further questions should be considered by the Supreme War Council. The Prime Minister said that the British government had never undertaken at Abbeville to ship these Czechs to France, only to do their best to do so. Pichon said he quite understood; the Supreme War Council would discuss what to do with those Czechs which could not be shipped away. There appeared to be no disagreement about Murmansk. It had been decided to bring to Murmansk and Archangel all Czech troops west of Omsk, to maintain there those that could be used 'for the purposes of the Allies', and

---

*This evidently refers to a private visit which the Japanese Foreign Minister paid to the British ambassador in Tokyo on May 20, during which the former stated that he envisaged an expedition right to the Urals, provided the Allies could come to terms on military matters.[26] These were evidently the Foreign Minister's personal views; he did not even inform his office if this conversation.

to send the remainder to France. (This, of course, was a concession by Clemenceau, who had previously insisted that all Czechs sent to northern Russia should be sent to France, except a small number to defend the northern Russian ports. Now the position was reversed.)

The Prime Minister trusted that Pichon realized that the British government could not send more than 4,500 Czechs to France before the end of August. The Supreme War Council must discuss, in the presence of the Allied generals, what to do with the rest. Lloyd George again asked Pichon 'if he could suggest any other means of organizing intervention'. Pichon hedged yet again. This raised the whole question of Allied policy towards the Bolsheviks, he said. It was a matter that should be reserved for the Supreme War Council. 'It was really the old question of persuading the United States to agree.' He told Lloyd George confidentially that the French philosopher, Henri Bergson, was sailing to America on June 1 to make a personal appeal to President Wilson. This rather naturally angered all the British ministers. Lloyd George said that what he wanted to know was what France and Britain would do in the way of intervention 'even if the United States held aloof'; while Balfour — something of a philosopher himself — said that he hoped that Bergson's visit might prove effective, but stressed that President Wilson 'sheltered himself behind his American military advisers'. Did not Pichon perhaps think that the view of the Supreme War Council's military advisers, or the 'deliberate military opinion' of General Foch, with or without the support of the Allied Generals, would be most likely to have 'real weight' with the President? Pichon dodged the question. The question of command at Murmansk would also be raised at the Supreme War Council, he said. The French government thought it 'only natural' that the command at sea should be British, but he himself thought the French government would wish to have command on land. The Prime Minister remarked that this point must be settled with the generals at Versailles.

Pichon then raised the question of recognizing the independence of Bohemia (i.e. Czechoslovakia) and Poland. The Allies had agreed in principle to their independence, and he thought the time appropriate to ask the Czech and Polish national councils to give the Allies a 'formula' which would satisfy their aspirations. Lord Robert Cecil pointed out that the Allies must be careful 'only to make a declaration, not to give a guarantee'. Pichon said that self-determination was not a new war aim. All speeches by Allied statesmen had been in this sense. Cecil again stressed that it was very difficult, at any rate for the British government, to state publicly that they had added to their burdens that of securing an independent Czechoslovak state. Nor did the Czechs want us to do so. They only wanted us to recognize them as Allies, 'and to admit that their aspirations were legitimate'. The Prime Minister asked Pichon directly if the French government wished to recognize an independent Poland and Bohemia. Pichon replied

152

that all thought of a separate peace with Austria was over. 'We need trouble no more to *menager* [go easy on] the Austrians, and President Wilson had apparently come to the same conclusion.' The Allies should use every means to make difficulties for Austria, and support the Slavs and other non-Austrian or non-Magyar elements in the Austro-Hungarian Empire. Cecil said that Benes had asked for no promise or engagement, but the French ambassador said that Benes had told him that the Czech national council had asked for Allied recognition as a Czech government. Both Pichon and Cecil said they were ready to agree to this, but the Prime Minister warned against giving pledges that the Allies could not realize. 'To raise hopes that could not be fulfilled was to turn these small nations into our deadly enemies. ... We must be very careful not to make use of these peoples and expose them to all the horrors of retribution, and yet fail to carry out what they wanted.'

On this, the Anglo-French conference came to an end. Pichon had continually pressed for a principle, but had continually hedged when faced with concrete proposals, or whenever presented with uncomfortable facts. All other decisions, he stated, except for the evacuation to France of the 'French' Czechs in the Far East, were to be left to the Supreme War Council meeting on June 1.

But in Russia, French plans for intervention were going ahead. As early as May 17, Lockhart had reported that the French were actively encouraging the movement led by Boris Savinkov (the 'Union for the Defence of the Fatherland and Freedom', composed of former Russian officers, whose abortive *coup* of May 1 had been discovered and had failed, and which was now linked with the 'National Centre' party, based on the upper Volga, i.e. fairly near the 'British' Czechs). Savinkov informed Lockhart that unless supported by Allied intervention, he was as yet too weak to take action. But the French had been in close contact with him, and had told him that Allied intervention had already been decided upon and would shortly take place. A further wire to this effect had been despatched by Lockhart on May 26; Pichon had warned on the 28th that the French would want command in northern Russia. Furthermore, at some point between May 20 and 25, the French ambassador, Noulens, had overruled the orders of the French military mission, which had already sent a courier to advise the Czechs to accept the Bolsheviks' conditions for their safe evacuation (i.e. to disarm), and sent a further communication advising them to retain their arms. (But Kennan makes it clear that this second courier could not have arrived before the Czech congress's own decision of May 25 to retain their arms.) As late as May 31, however, Major Guinet, the French liaison officer with the First Czech Corps, was actively discouraging them from meddling in Russian affairs near Omsk, where the young Czech commander, Rudolph Gajda, was overthrowing the local soviets (with some support from the Russian officers' organizations). Gajda was particularly brutal, raiding trains of German prisoners on their way home, purging prisoner-of-war camps, suppressing Hungarian as well as Bolshevik groups — and taking no prisoners; these people were the same as the Germans, he told his men. Further west, the Czech groups under Lieutenant Čeček, in the Urals, were behaving with equal brutality, but becoming more involved with the local Russian officers' groups, and with Czech communists. Thus little civil wars, with all their attendant horrors, for a time raged between Penza and Chelyabinsk especially. But, more important, the fighting also brought the Czechs into contact with the SRs, whose strongest support lay in the Volga-Urals region.[27]

7

Cecil's resignation and the Czech success

At the Prime Minister's mid-morning discussion on May 29, Lord Milner, who had not been present at the Anglo-French conference the day before, reported that Clemenceau was 'quite willing' for us to have complete control over the Czechs in northern Russia, 'and generally to our settling the policy with regard to the extent to which they should be used there or sent to Europe'. (The inference is that Milner had received a further letter from Clemenceau, or had been so informed by Pichon, to appease the War Office.) But Clemenceau was determined to have the Czechs at Vladivostok brought to France. He did not think they would want to fight in Russia, or care to fight alongside the Japanese. The Prime Minister explained that it had been agreed the day before with Pichon to bring 4,500 Czechs per month to Vancouver, of whom the first 4,500 would be in France by September, but the matter would definitely be settled at Versailles. It had, throughout, been assumed that the Czechs could only be brought over at the expense of American troops. Milner pointed out that the American contingent would probably be nearly exhausted in two months' time, so there would be plenty of room to ship the Czechs eastwards from America in the ships now bringing American troops. (This had not been mentioned the day before.)[1] In any case, Milner was not sure that trained Czechs would not be more useful in France than untrained Americans; but he thought it necessary to ask the Japanese to help ship them to Vancouver, and did not think the Japanese would take this to mean that we had abandoned all idea of Siberian intervention. (Milner's *post facto* declaration on this subject, which had been exhaustively discussed the day before, may well have irritated the Prime Minister.)

When at noon the War Cabinet discussed Siberian intervention, they were faced with a note fron Lord Robert Cecil written earlier that morning. This stated that when the subject had been discussed on the 24th, the War Cabinet had directed that the matter of the reply to be sent in answer to the Japanese Foreign Minister's four recent questions should be on the agenda as soon as both the Prime Minister and the Foreign Secretary could be present. It had accordingly appeared the day before (i.e. at the Cabinet held between the two sessions with Pichon) as the first business after statements; but it was never reached, 'and I observe that it is not on the agenda at all today', he wrote acidly. Japan had put some 'very important' questions to us, 'on the answer to which her future action in Siberia probably depends. Delay will convey to her again, as it has in the past, an impression of hesitation and uncertainty. She will be more than ever convinced that we are not in earnest in our interventionist policy, that impression will spread as it did before to Washington and the President will become more immovable than ever. Procedure of this kind has already lost us four months and as I think has seriously if not fatally compromised our position in Russia. If the Cabinet are against intervention, let them say so. If they are in favour of it, let them take the necessary measures to give that policy a chance of success. To do neither one thing nor the other is in any case fatal.'[2] Cecil asked Hankey to bring this note to the attention of the Cabinet at once.

The Prime Minister replied that Cecil's note implied that the delay of four months was the British government's fault. The War Cabinet had decided on intervention on January 24, Lloyd George recalled. 'That might be called the first proposal of the British government, and it had been thwarted by the United States government.' The second proposal, made on May 17, was for 20,000 Czechoslovaks to be used as a nucleus for an expeditionary force, 'but this proposal had been negatived by M. Pichon. It did not appear clear, therefore, what more we could have done, or, what was more important, what we ought to do now.'[3]

Lord Robert Cecil pointed out that though the decision was taken on January 24, no effective step to induce the Americans to move was made until February 25; at first, the Americans were not unwilling to act, but later they had gone back on this; somehow the impression had been gained in Japan that we were not determined on action and accordingly the Japanese had complained. The American government had let it be known that they thought the British were not particularly interested, and had been driven forward by the French. (It is clear that this Cabinet meeting was acrimonious.) But Cecil ended by saying that he agreed entirely with the Prime Minister that the main thing now was future action, not criticism of the past.

Balfour supported the Prime Minister. He agreed that we had tried every possible means to induce the President to cooperate in intervention, but he had sheltered himself behind his military advisers. We had made British policy perfectly plain; that we did not propose to interfere in Russian internal affairs; that our action was directed entirely against the Germans. We had always worked with the *de facto* Russian government; first with the Tsar, then with Kerensky and his Socialists, and later with the Bolsheviks; and we would be ready to work with whatever successors they might have. We had originally backed up Semenov, and had only told him not to move further forward, as our man on the spot had 'warned us against him'; but we should support Semenov again if his force formed part of a big movement.

Lord Milner said the question now was whether we were going to allow the American attitude towards Japanese intervention to continue to paralyse us as it had done during the past few months. It would be preferable, of course, if all the Allies cooperated in Siberian intervention, but American hesitation should not be allowed to block the whole policy and leave the field clear for German influence to dominate all northern Asia. We should continue to press for Japanese intervention, 'even without the cooperation of the United States'. Cecil had found in Milner a powerful ally.

But it was pointed out (though the Cabinet minutes do not say by whom) that such a policy, if not carefully handled, might lead to a snub from Japan and a quarrel with America. On the other hand, it was argued that it was not proposed to say to America: 'If you do not come in, we shall go ahead without you.' It was simply proposed to urge General Foch at the next Supreme War Council, to point out, for the President's benefit, the 'supreme military necessity' of Siberian intervention and the need for the provision of a substantial American force; and that if the American government felt unable to cooperate, Japanese intervention would still be desirable, 'and it was hoped that the United States government would agree to such intervention being made'. Here was the nub of the whole situation, the crucial point to which all recent discussion had been leading: was Japanese intervention possible without American support, but with American acquiescence? Balfour had at first believed it was, but had subsequently changed his mind. Lord Robert Cecil now argued with increasing strength in favour of such a possibility and was supported by Lord Milner. But was American acquiescence — seemingly wedged uneasily between approval and refusal — even a possibility?

The Prime Minister said in reply that the question was to be raised at the forthcoming Supreme War Council and it was essential that he and his colleagues who were to accompany him should go into the council chamber with a 'clearly formulated plan'. The War Cabinet thereupon decided to discuss the matter again the next day.[3]

This meeting ended in considerable tension. On returning to the Foreign Office, both Lord Robert Cecil and Balfour retired to draft papers embodying their widely differing views. 'It is common ground', wrote Cecil, 'that the greater part of the force for intervention in Siberia must be provided by the Japanese.' He proceeded to summarize the Japanese view. 'In their earlier attitude, they appeared to require the approval and support of America before they would intervene except for their own protection. There seems ground for thinking that that attitude has been modified, but to what extent is not clear.' (In fact, on the 28th, the British ambassador in

Tokyo had wired to say that the Japanese deputy Foreign Minister had noticed a change in the American attitude towards intervention, and personally thought that the Japanese government might stir up the American government, since Secretary Lansing had described Lenin and Trotsky as 'nothing better than paid agents of Germany'. (This was one of the results of the arrival in Washington of the 'Sisson' documents.)[3]

Cecil then sketched out the American attitude, namely that President Wilson was against intervention in Siberia on its merits — the President's strongest reason probably being his fear of becoming involved in what the American people would think of as an 'imperialist enterprise to destroy a sister republic'. In these circumstances, 'one essential thing for intervention is to get the Japanese to move, but it is equally essential, for other reasons, not to take any action which would cause a quarrel or even a coolness between us and the United States'. It had been hoped that if the British could have induced the Czechs 'to lead the movement in Siberia', the Americans would have agreed to that much more easily than to a Japanese 'initiative'; whilst such a Czech move 'would have almost certainly induced the Japanese government to take immediate action'. But the French had rejected this plan, 'and it only remains for us to take such means as we can to secure the approval, or at least the acquiescence, of the President in Japanese intervention'. This was where Cecil parted from Balfour.[4]

Cecil urged that the Supreme War Council should express a strong view in favour of intervention and that this should be strongly endorsed by General Foch; also that we should obtain from Japan a definite statement that they were 'prepared to intervene in support of Allied interests generally. I believe they [the Japanese] would do this even if the Americans did not join in the appeal, provided the Japanese were assured of American acquiescence', Cecil said. He urged that an approach be made to the Japanese ambassador in London. He also thought it desirable that General Knox (now the chief adviser on Russian affairs at the War Office) should be sent to America to persuade President Wilson of the military need for immediate intervention. 'It is true that he is vehemently anti-Bolshevik, but he need not make that aspect of his opinions prominent', remarked Cecil. 'He understands the military situation with regard to intervention in Russia as well as any man living, and is a strong believer in its necessity. Certainly he would be more likely to produce an effect than the envoy [the philosopher Henri Bergson] whom it is understood the French government are sending.' Here then was the challenge: the War Cabinet should press for Japanese intervention — with American acquiescence.

In the Foreign Secretary's room, Balfour meanwhile was drafting 'some observations' suggested by the Cabinet's discussion that morning, which was in fact one of the most luminous of Balfour's great war-time state papers and deserves quotation in full:

'We are all agreed that the next step to be taken with regard to Allied intervention in Russia is to lay before the President the reasoned views of the Supreme Allied War Council, and to support these by an expression of General Foch's considered opinion on the subject.'[4]

We have no reason to doubt that these authorities will throw their whole weight on the side of intervention. But they may fail to persuade the President, as all the other attempts of the same kind have failed already. If they fail, the question arises as to what should be the next step. Here there appears to be a good deal of difference of opinion among those who took part in this morning's discussion. Some thought that though it was most desirable that all the great co-belligerents should act together, it was not absolutely necessary; and that intervention by the *Entente* powers and Japan would be better than no intervention at all.

On this I must observe, in the first place, that the policy is foredoomed to failure; for in my belief without America, Japan will not consent to undertake any important expedition; and, if it be replied that, after all, we can but make the attempt, I would point out that the attempt itself will not only fail, but that the mere making of it will be productive of much evil. For it cannot be made without suggesting to the President that he should stand aside and let others attempt a policy which he regards as inexpedient. This is to divide the Allies, and it is to divide the public in America. I find it impossible to believe that it will not alienate the President and cool the enthusiasm of important sections of American opinion. I should in any case regard such results with the deepest misgiving; but, holding as I do that, while the proposed policy would deeply hurt the Americans, it would not give us Japanese assistance, it seems to me that there is little or nothing to be said for it.

But, supposing that Japan were ready to go in without America, and that America, while refusing for her own part to take any share in the policy, were prepared to regard it with benevolent acquiescence, should we in these (as I think, impossibly favourable) circumstances, be justified in pressing on with the scheme?

To me it seems a most hazardous experiment. It has to be recognized that there is an element of risk in the policy of intervention, howsoever the intervening force be organized. But, if America stands aloof, the odds against success are enormously increased. All those who regard Japan with fear, suspicion, or dislike would have their hands greatly strengthened. The Allied force would no longer represent the co-belligerent powers. It would necessarily be known, not merely that America abstained from taking any share in the expedition, but that she had refused to take any share because she disapproved of it; and the refusal would be even more injurious to the moral aspect of the enterprise than it would be to the material.

I must add that these views are strengthened by the telegrams received today from Mr Lockhart. According to his report, German policy has altered in Russia, and the Berlin authorities are ceasing to bully and are beginning to bribe. Evidently Mr Lockhart has abandoned the hope he once entertained of extracting an invitation to the Allies from the Soviet government. Germans and Bolsheviks are flirting. The course steered by the latter has indeed (apart from cash) always been determined by the comparative strength of their hatred of the central powers and their hatred of the Allies. But, if their hatred of German intervention be diminished by the new German policy, while their hatred of Allied intervention is increased by the abstention of America, there is a real danger that, in attempting to rescue Russia from the grip of the central powers, we shall be treated by her as enemies and not as friends.[4]

On the morning of May 30, the military situation in France was becoming graver by the hour — the Germans were almost back on the Marne. British public opinion, tense almost to breaking point, was being undermined by allegations that were coming to light in the sensational Pemberton Billing libel case at the Old Bailey. The accusations of widespread unnatural vice, coupled with pervasive German influence, in high places in London amounted to a McCarthy-like witch-hunt against the old Liberal Party. This was the background to a crucial War Cabinet meeting on Siberian intervention.

The Prime Minister opened the Cabinet meeting saying that it was essential that he had some definite proposals on the matter to lay before the Supreme War Council. Both Cecil's and Balfour's papers then came under consideration. Cecil spoke first, stressing the three positive steps he proposed: a statement in favour of intervention from the Supreme War Council, endorsed by Foch; a Japanese commitment; and the despatch of General Knox to America.[5]

Balfour then drew attention to the conclusion he had reached in his paper: that if America refused to cooperate with the Allies, their assistance to Russia would have to be confined to action at Archangel and Murmansk, to diplomacy, and to promises of material and financial support. (Balfour had already taken action over American support in northern Russia. Late on the 28th, he had wired to Lord Reading asking him to make sure of the despatch of the American brigade to Murmansk, as agreed during the War Cabinet of May 23; nothing was said about Siberia. The Murmansk position was 'seriously endangered', and American help was 'essential', wired Balfour. The danger, in fact, was 'so extreme' that small British reinforcements were being sent out, even during the present crisis in France. But as they would obviously not be sufficient, an American brigade must be despatched, even if it were not fully trained. The President must agree, stated Balfour in some desperation, as 'great use' had been made in the past of the difference in opinion among the Allies on the Russian question.)[5]

Balfour continued that in his paper he had also posed the question whether we should be justified in pressing on with plans for intervention if Japan was ready to come in without America, and America, while refusing to be associated with our policy, was prepared to regard such intervention with 'benevolent acquiescence'.

The Prime Minister asked whether it was quite clear that America would refuse to cooperate, even if strong representations were made by the Supreme War Council, and especially if they were based on military grounds. He drew attention to Lord Reading's telegram of May 24, which stated that he found President Wilson 'quite decided' that the present moment was inopportune for intervention, and that the President had the support of his military advisers, who agreed with the views he had previously expressed, namely, that no military advantage would be gained by Siberian intervention.

Lord Robert Cecil, drawing attention to recent telegrams from Lockhart in Moscow, stated that Lockhart had become 'genuinely terrified' of the German advance into Russia, and thought that unless the Allies took some action, the whole of Russia would go over to Germany. Cecil also pointed to Lockhart's wire of the 25th, in which he stated that it was becoming increasingly clear that intervention would be 'extremely problematical' in view of the change in German policy towards the Bolsheviks; it was thus 'extremely important' that intervention should be hurried on as quickly as possible.

Austen Chamberlain observed that what might be called the two extreme contingencies had been considered, namely, that President Wilson should be pressed by General Foch and the Supreme War Council to cooperate whole-heartedly and send American troops; or, if he turned down this proposal, that the Japanese should be encouraged to intervene, assisted by the French and British, in spite of the President's opposition. But there was a third contingency that had not been fully considered, namely, that President Wilson, whilst unwilling to send American troops, or to take an active part in intervention, might be induced to regard intervention by Japan and the other Allies with good will. The Cabinet had now reached the nub of the matter.

Lord Robert Cecil pointed out that there were an unlimited number of variations between protest and support; even the President's acquiescence might mean veiled hostility. (Cecil now appeared to be shifting his ground.) But the President might, in view of his difficulties in putting American troops under the Japanese flag, issue his own proclamation on intervention, instead of joining in a joint Allied proclamation, and give technical support, though unable to send American troops. Cecil went on to express the view that because of the 'desperate' state of affairs in Russia, he was now very doubtful whether the Allies would win the war, unless there was a revolution in Austria or Germany. He suggested that Balfour should see the Japanese ambassador and ask him whether the Japanese would intervene with American approval. Balfour replied that he had sent a wire to Colonel House, enclosing one which he intended to send to the British ambassador in Tokyo, and asking if Colonel House saw any objection to his making an appeal to the Japanese on these lines. Colonel House had objected and Balfour had consequently not sent the telegram.

There was clearly no other course but to make yet another appeal to President Wilson. The War Cabinet thereupon decided, first, that the CIGS and Philip Kerr (Lloyd George's private secretary) should draft a paper, to be laid before the Supreme War Council, 'putting foward the arguments in full in favour of Allied intervention in Siberia'; and secondly, that Balfour should ask Lord Reading if it was desirable to send General Knox to America.[5]

After the War Cabinet meeting, however, Balfour called the Japanese ambassador to the Foreign Office and told him that the Siberian question was certain to be raised at the forthcoming Supreme War Council, and he would like to be able to assure the Allied delegates that Japan would agree to intervene up to the Urals; it would be most unfortunate if, American approval having been obtained, it was then discovered that Japan would not go so far. Balfour answered the crucial questions put by the Japanese Foreign Minister. The British government, he stated, had now given up all hope of a Bolshevik invitation to intervene, but he felt sure that the Allied intervention forces would be welcomed even by those people who did not now dare to invite them. As for Semenov, he had no proper claim to Allied support: the Allies had not asked him to make his recent advance. The British government, however, would support him provided that he acted in accordance with British policy; if he did not, he could expect nothing from the British. The ball was thus firmly back in the Japanese court. The ambassador promised to report all this to Tokyo. But the crucial question — whether Japan would now definitely intervene with American approval — was not put. And so matters thus remained substantially unchanged.[6]

That night, Sir Henry Wilson made the following entry in his diary: 'News today is bad, the Boches have taken Soissons and Rheims [this was factually incorrect] and tonight I hear Château-Thierry. This is serious. And as far as I can see, not a single division from Rupprecht's Army has been used, and so we are still liable to attack on the Arras-Amiens line. This is rather anxious,' he concluded with considerable understatement.[7]

On May 31, the Prime Minister and the British delegation left for the Supreme War Council's meeting. 'During the voyage', wrote the CIGS, 'I had much talk with Lloyd George, Milner, Geddes [the First Lord] and Wemyss [the First Sea Lord]. I said that Foch was trying to hold too long a line with the troops at his disposal, and that either he must shorten or he would crack; that the only place to shorten was in the north ... Dunkirk or no Dunkirk, we must shorten our line.'[7] Johnnie Du Cane, up from Foch's head-quarters, was here [Versailles] when I arrived. The news is bad, there is no question of that. The French have lost Château-Thierry and Villers-Cotterêts. This last must mean that they are not fighting. If this is so, we are done. Du Cane told me that when Douglas Haig was discussing matters this morning at Sarcus, Foch got a message from Pétain to say that he must see him at once, so Foch bundled straight off, and Weygand coming back into the rooms, before starting, said that things were 'très graves' and 'les troupes étaient très fatigués'. We know what that means. Tomorrow will be a critical day. If Rupprecht now attacks south from Montdidier to Noyon, and takes Compiègne, the French are beaten.'

While the Prime Minister was in Paris, somewhat alarming news reached the War Cabinet, under the *de facto* control of Lord Robert Cecil, about the various Russian fleets and the position in northern Russia. On May 31, the Cabinet were informed that Admiral Chastny had been arrested 'as a counter-revolutionary and organizer of an anti-Bolshevik movement in the [Baltic] fleet', and a wire reached London from Lockhart stating that general discontent with the Bolsheviks, whose power was sensibly declining, had now reached its climax. Now was the time for the Allies to agree upon intervention; they would never have a more favourable opportunity. This view was supported by a wire from Cromie, sent on the 30th and received on June 1, about his plan for the destruction of the Baltic Fleet: 'Held meeting yesterday evening May 29 and decided start scheme proposed for destruction when ready. Our agents appeared very depressed and viewed the difficulty of the position with much apprehension. They stated that Allies must adopt quickly a definite policy if advantage was to be taken of general position. The counter-revolutionary movement is growing not only amongst the sailors but also amongst the workmen and position has put the people at present in power on the alert. Steps are being now taken to suppress the movements and searches, etc. are being carried out in the streets, arms of all descriptions being confiscated. With the lessening of the threat of German occupation many officers have decided to retire leaving only young officers of little seniority in charge. It is extremely doubtful whether these can be safely approached and were it not for the fact that some organization must be kept in hand against possible emergencies, one was seriously thinking of dropping the scheme altogether.'[8]

But in the monthly disposition of Russian active fleets, compiled by the Admiralty on June 3, in which four dreadnought battleships, three predreadnoughts and fifty destroyers were listed at Kronstadt, it was clearly stated that 'Arrangements are being made to destroy the dreadnought battleships, and the oil-burning destroyers. All ships are only partly manned.' Of the warships being built, it was noted that four battle-cruisers had been launched at Petrograd. 'Arrangements are being made for their destruction', it was stated. All further warship construction was now presumed to be at a standstill.

Cecil had been alarmed about contradictory statements about the Black Sea Fleet, while the Prime Minister was still in London. At the War Cabinet at noon on the 29th, the First Sea Lord said that the Bolshevik government had signed orders for the destruction of the Black Sea Fleet, and the orders were to have been sent from Moscow to Novorossisk, where the Russian warships lay, on the 27th. But on the 30th, Cecil wrote confidentially to Lloyd George:

My dear Prime Minister
I venture to send you the enclosed telegram in case it may not reach you otherwise. It seems the first clear and unmistakeable proof we have of the treachery of the Soviet govt. and as such may be useful to you at Paris.

He enclosed a wire, sent by the British ambassador in Berne on the 29th, which stated: 'I learn that when Bolshevik mission was received by [Swiss] President, [the] head of mission, Berzine, told him Bolsheviks had agreed to disarm Black Sea Fleet in return for support which Germany would give Bolshevik missions in neutral countries. (President confirms fact that representations on behalf of Bolshevik mission have been made to him by Germans) ...'. On this wire, Cecil had scribbled in pencil: 'Meanwhile Trotsky is assuring Lockhart that he has taken measures to destroy the fleet.'[9] This, however, was probably part of Lenin's stratagem, whereby he informed the Russian admiral in the Black Sea, openly, that he was to return the Black Sea Fleet to Sebastopol, and hand it over to the Germans; but ordered him, secretly, to sink his ships at once. It would be presumed that any statement made to the Swiss President would be passed on to the Germans.

At noon on June 3, when the War Cabinet considered the situation at Murmansk, there was now no difficulty with the Americans over intervention in northern Russia. Balfour's wire of May 28, urging the immediate despatch of an American brigade to Murmansk, in fact crossed with a message from the American War Department to General Bliss stating that President Wilson was 'heartily in sympathy' with any practical military effort that could be made in northern Russia. Then on June 1, disquieting news came from Poole, the American consul in Moscow. In a wire sent on the 28th, he warned that Chicherin had told him that the Bolshevik government had decided, under German pressure, to hand over Petchenga to Finland, i.e. to the White Finns, in return for Bolshevik retention of Fort Ino, the bulwark of Petrograd. On the 1st, therefore, the President summoned Secretary Lansing, who was instructed to tell Lord Reading that the American government was 'entirely willing' to send troops to Murmansk, provided Foch approved this diversion of troops from the western front.[10]

In Russia, things were quieter. On May 24, the day after General Poole reached Murmansk, a tough Bolshevik Commissar, the Lithuanian Natsarenus, arrived from Moscow with orders to reach a balance between Allied demands in the area and German protests. On June 1, General Poole and Natsarenus had a long talk. The commissar declared unofficially that the Bolsheviks did intend to fight the Germans; they were sending two divisions up to Murmansk, and the Czechs were also on their way; he could not speak officially as long as the Allies refused to recognize the Bolshevik government. General Poole and Admiral Kemp, who was also present, replied, also unofficially, that the Bolsheviks were more likely to obtain recognition if they gave clear proof that they really meant to support the Allies against Germany. General Poole promised to arm and feed the Czechs on arrival, as well as all other troops the Bolsheviks might provide. On this note, the meeting seems to have ended. General Poole sent a wire to the War Office that before any proper arrangement could be made with the Bolsheviks, the British government would have to recognize them as the *de facto* Russian government, 'which policy I have always advocated'. This, incidentally, was quite true.[11]

But in London, events in northern Russia were viewed very differently. By June 3, the War Cabinet had also presumably heard from Lockhart that the Bolsheviks had decided to cede Petchenga, under German pressure, to the White Finns. This was the worst possible news, and justified everyone's worst fears. The First Sea Lord reported that Admiral Kemp had sent a wire relating that in reply to Lenin's protest to the German government about the sinking of Russian fishing boats off Petchenga by a German submarine, Germany had stated that such sinkings would only cease when the British withdrew from Murmansk. Lord Robert Cecil, when asked for his opinion of the Murmansk situation, replied that the matter was a military one; but if the Germans did succeed in assembling a Finnish force of some 40,000 men, the British position would become 'very hazardous' at Murmansk. 'There could no longer be any doubt that the Soviet government had gone over, lock, stock and barrel to the Germans', he added, 'and it must therefore be expected that they would assist the Germans to turn us out of Murmansk.' (Yet again, Cecil failed to discern that the Bolsheviks were above all anxious to play the British off against the Germans, to balance the two opposing imperialist powers.) In view of the possibility of Murmansk becoming untenable, the War Cabinet decided that the CIGS should ask General Poole for an appreciation of the situation there.[12]

June 1 was a grim day in Paris: 'I find it difficult to realize that there is a possibility, perhaps a probability, of the French army being beaten. What would this mean? The destruction of our army in France?' Sir Henry Wilson questioned. 'During the day there was little information, but on the whole we seem to be giving ground, but much slower.' At Versailles, where the German guns could be heard in the distance, 'Foch insisted on necessity of Haig to keep up his total of divisions, and said bluntly that, if he did not, we should lose the war. In all this I agree, and backed Foch. Lloyd George offered to allow the Tiger [i.e. Clemenceau] to send a man over, to go through Auckland Geddes' arrangements and see if he could find any men. I think this is wise, as if there is a crash, it will be well to have shown transparent *bona fides*.' Sir Henry added succinctly: 'The President, USA, has now ordered Bliss [American military representative on the Supreme War Council] not to back Japanese intervention.'[13]

This was either the result of, or the occasion for, Lloyd George voicing fears that the Germans were about to ascend the Volga and invade the grain districts of western and central Siberia (a considerable enlargement on Leslie Urquhart's fears), and telling General Bliss in agitated terms that Japan must now intervene with every man she could, even up to $2^1/_2$ million men (some five times the size of her army, including reserves), to overcome resistance *en route*, and reach the Germans in the west as quickly as possible, and then be strong enough to repel them. This fantasy demonstrates the desperation felt at Versailles on June 1. General Bliss made it clear that not even the military representatives could discuss Siberian intervention — if they did, he would disassociate himself from his colleagues — let alone the Supreme War Council, so it was decided to remit the question to the Council of Foreign Ministers and to ask General Foch to write a short paper on the matter.[14]

In Paris on the 3rd, Foch was called away, and so was unable to advise the Supreme War Council on Siberian intervention. The Council of Foreign Ministers considered the matter that morning. At 3 p.m., when the Supreme War Council came to discuss the Russian situation, 'and means of coping with it' (as the minutes state), Clemenceau asked Pichon what agreement had been reached that morning. Pichon said they had agreed on two points:

1. The necessity for Allied intervention in Russia to protect the Murman coast and Archangel;
2. The Allies, with the exception of America, consider Japanese intervention desirable.

On the second point, Pichon stated, they had recognized, as recent speeches by the Japanese Premier and Foreign Minister showed, that the Allies had 'never put a precise and official proposal to Japan'. They had decided to recommend that the Allied governments should ask Japan if she would accept certain conditions for her intervention. These were: to respect Russian territorial integrity; not to back any Russian political party; and to 'push their intervention as far west as is necessary to meet the Germans'. The Foreign Ministers thought these conditions 'indispensable', stated Pichon, and wished to submit them to the Supreme War Council before proposals were put to the Japanese government. For when the Japanese reply was received, they could then tell President Wilson precisely what their conditions were; they would then have more chance of overcoming his aversion towards Japanese intervention.[15]

Mr Balfour: We are all three agreed on these conditions. The only question in dispute is acceptance by the United States. We should not push Japan to intervene if she does not accept these conditions. If she does not accept, then we have nothing to propose to President Wilson; if however she does accept, then we shall be in a strong position with President Wilson. I think that Japan will refuse to intervene without the agreement of the United States. This is the crux of the problem.

(It was agreed to make the necessary *démarche* to Japan. M. Pichon then spoke about Allied intervention to protect the ports of Murmansk and Archangel from German seizure.)

M. Pichon: At Abbeville, it was decided to send to these ports the Serbian and Czech detachments stationed west of Omsk. But that was not a complete solution; the Allies must provide personnel to organize these detachments.

Mr Balfour: We cannot hope for Japanese help in this quarter. ... Some Czechs are expected.

Lord Milner: There are no Czechs there yet.

Sig. Sonnino (The Italian Foreign Minister): According to my information, the Czech troops have taken a fancy to Bolshevism.

M. Pichon: General Belin [the French military representative] would like to explain the military view of the question to us.

General Belin then read a French general staff paper on the importance of the retention of the Russian northern ports, because 'of the possibility of the Germans increasing submarine warfare in the Arctic Ocean, and thus linking up with their own [*sic*] military expedition in Siberia'. The Bolshevik government had done little to organize their defence. 'On the other hand, public opinion in Russia seems disposed to favour Allied intervention, which has been insistently demanded by many [Russian] parties. Action in the northern ports should be inter-Allied, and linked with the [Allied] operation in Siberia.' He then listed the small Allied forces and naval vessels already in the northern ports. 'Further, the Russian government has promised to transfer to Archangel the Czech units (about 25,000 men) which are still west of Omsk. Because of the presence of Serbian and Czech units, a French general should command the land forces. Naval defence should be under a British admiral, as at present.' General Lavergne had suggested that only four or five Allied battalions would have to be sent out.

Lord Milner asked General Belin whether this draft had been accepted by the military representatives. He was told that General Bliss had insisted that it should not be discussed because of its 'political complications'.

At this point, it was agreed to adjourn the meeting to allow the military representatives to reconsider the matter, 'after hearing the views of the British War Office'. Lord Milner, angry at French attempts to seize command in northern Russia, left with them.

When the military representatives resumed their discussion at 3.50 p.m., Lord Milner was determined to retain command in northern Russia for the British. The British War Office, he said, had received requisitions for all food, ships, equipment, uniforms; in fact, for everything in the northern Russian ports, both from the French and from their own officers. He had heard that the Czechs were arriving, and had nothing, 'and the British were expected to furnish all these things'. It was to be hoped that the Czechs were coming, and would eventually be available for duty in France, 'but one thing was certain — a chief is necessary to coordinate all efforts'. The British government had sent out a General [Poole], who was now collecting recruits, 'and the British government is paying all the bills'. They would be glad to have a French commander, 'were he prepared or able to do what they were doing. He [Milner] recognized that the Czechoslavs are French in their affiliations and that the French had a right to command them and bring them to France; but he considered that the White Sea was a British job', and having two chiefs would surely entail failure.

General Belin replied that in his draft joint note he had recognized that the command was two-fold, and that the British should have command at sea. But Milner was not to be stopped; General Poole had been specially selected to take charge of both naval and land operations. General Bliss tried to calm them both down. At first, it had seemed that the occupation of these ports would require more men than were available; but now it seemed that some 15 Czech battalions were coming, and only four or six Allied battalions would be needed. The only object Bliss could see for the occupation of these ports was to use them as bases to help 'any other pro-Ally efforts' that might be made in Russia. 'From the outset it would be necessary for the force at Archangel to push up the railroad.' It ought not to be difficult to settle the question of command.

But Milner went on and on. 'So far, everything had been done by the British with their ships, their supplies, their money, and their everything. The British government was constantly called on to furnish food to keep people alive and Archangel was full of supplies which they wanted to keep from falling into enemy hands. ... Their Admiral had done all that a naval man could do, but it had recently been represented to them that unless more was done on land, it might be impossible to hold even the naval base. ... To give their General [Poole] a start, they had sent him some marines and a few hundred soldiers and money to raise local levies, which they were told could be got. ... It was impossible at present to foresee how the situation might develop; but he did ask that the British General there who was doing all that was being done, should not be interfered with.'

Belin said that there were already some French forces there, including 2,000 Serbians, all under a French colonel, and 'that General Niessel had charge of all the activities in the interior'. The battalions to be sent out were to be Allied battalions to show that the intervention was inter-Allied. This should be made evident to everyone. But Milner insisted that 'practical considerations' demanded that all operations at present should be in the hands of one man 'particularly fitted for the duties', and the British had thus subordinated their admiral to General Poole. 'The French General [Niessel] was in the interior with other work to do and not available; while in the district in question, 95% of the effort was now being made by the British.' In answer to Bliss, Milner insisted that General Poole should command both at Murmansk and Archangel. With that, General Belin's draft was amended, and passed as Joint Note 31.

This discussion makes clear that it had previously been agreed between the British and French that General Niessel (former head of the French military mission in Russia), who was strongly anti-Bolshevik, and convinced of the need for early intervention, as Kennan points out, had already been assigned to take charge 'of all the activities in the [Russian] interior', and that Milner was determined not to allow the forces in the northern Russian ports to come under his command as well. It was thus Milner who was really insisting on a split command. It is also interesting to note that late that night, Balfour wired to Lockhart, in answer to his wire of mid-May stating that Savinkov had told him that he had been informed by the French that intervention had already been decided on, and would shortly take place. 'You should have nothing whatever to do with Savinkov's plans,' wired Balfour to Lockhart, 'and avoid enquiring further into them.' It thus seemed that the Russian interior was to be a French task.[16]

Joint Note 31 began by stating that the general situation in Russia, and especially in the northern Russian ports, had 'completely changed' since March 23 when the military representatives had decided that it was impossible to send out an Allied military expedition to northern Russia. In fact:

1. 'The German threat to Murmansk and Archangel has become more definite, and is imminent. Finland has completely fallen under German domination, and is now openly hostile to the *Entente*, and makes no

concealment of its claim to Karelia, the Kola peninsula and the Murmansk railway. Germany is actively preparing for an advance on Petrograd.

2. We are urgently requested to occupy these ports not only by the Allied representatives in Russia, but also by the majority of the Russian parties. Such occupation would be an indispensable complement to Allied intervention in Siberia.

3. The occupation by Germany of Murmansk alone, which she could make an excellent base for submarines, would make the sea-route to Archangel impossible for the *Entente*.

4. On the other hand, the occupation of Murmansk and Archangel by the *Entente* would protect the flanks of the Allied Armies, which may eventually operate in Siberia, and allow contact to be maintained with them more rapidly and more easily.

5. It will be impossible to obtain the agreement of the Czechoslovaks to keep part of their forces in these [northern Russian] regions, unless the Allies give them the material and moral support of a few Allied units on the spot, beside which they can fight the Germans.'

The military representatives urged that a military effort be made to maintain possession of Murmansk, and (if possible simultaneously) Archangel; that, to reduce the number of Allied troops required, the Czech national council be asked to agree to maintain in northern Russia, for as long as necessary, some Czech units, on the understanding that only the minimum would be needed, while the remainder, as previously agreed, would be shipped to France; that, in this case, only four to six Allied battalions would have to be sent out, together with some specialist officers, and such material and supplies as could not be obtained locally. Finally, there should be a single command to direct both sea and land defences, including 'important points' on the railways terminating at each port; and that this command should be entrusted to a Commander-in-Chief appointed by the British government, 'until such time as the Supreme War Council decides otherwise'.

The Supreme War Council approved Joint Note 31, and then considered how to ship the Czechs at Vladivostok to France (a discussion which clearly showed why Clemenceau attached so much importance to this.) Pichon stated that the Foreign Ministers were all agreed that this was highly desirable. But Lloyd George had made clear that because of shortage of tonnage, the British could only ship 4,500 to 5,000 Czechs before July 1.

Pichon: Although it was not specifically stated, it was understood at Abbeville that the British government would ask for Japanese tonnage. This has not been done. [There was another subject which they also had to discuss — the deportation of some Germans living in China, where they were allegedly creating mischief for the Allied cause.] On June 15, there will be one British ship and two Japanese ships at Shanghai, specially detailed to take the Germans now in China to Australia. In view of the urgency of shipping the Czechs, I propose that these ships be used.

Balfour (protesting that Pichon was making an entirely new proposal): It is extremely complex. When it was put before us, we did not know what trouble it would cause to the shipping programme. In London last week, we carefully examined this question. We decided to stick to the Abbeville decision, and do all that we could with the limited means at our disposal.

Lloyd George: The two questions must not be mixed up. If the Japanese do not intervene [in Siberia], they will have spare tonnage. If, on the contrary, they do intervene, all their tonnage will be used for military purposes.

Clemenceau: At present, the principal Allied interest is to push the Germans out of France. At Abbeville, England promised to approach the Japanese. She has not done so through fear, I believe, that this will impede their intervention in Siberia. ... If M. Pichon's proposal is turned down, we will lose 50,000 good troops on our front, of which we have the greatest need. At a time when the American contribution has let us down, when the British have so much difficulty in putting their fighting machine back in order, I beg this Council to let the Chinese [i.e. presumably the Germans in China] sleep in peace, and give us, within a reasonable time (two or three months) these 50,000 men.

Lloyd George: The best way to relieve the German pressure on our front is to push the Japanese to intervene, rather than ship 50,000 Czechs. ... Either Japan intervenes, or we ask her to ship the Czechs.

Clemenceau: Why should not the Japanese government intervene? I am rather inclined to believe that she will intervene alone. While we are consulting President Wilson, plunged in obstinate refusal, as we know, the question will remain unresolved. During this time, we will have the help of neither the Japanese nor the Czechs. ... The Czech national council has told us that on the day when there are 50,000 Czechs on the western front, there will be a rising in Prague, much more important than the last one. Do we have to wait for weeks for President Wilson to decide?

Balfour: If we ask the Japanese to help ship the Czechs, we must give up the idea of Japanese intervention in Siberia ... and not approach either the Japanese or American governments; we must abandon our policy in Russia, as long as there are any Czechs to ship. ... This is the problem.

Clemenceau: My conscience as an Ally forces me to state that shipping these Czechs is more urgent.

Sig. Sonnino: Does Mr Balfour give priority to the Czechs or the [German] deportees? We cannot ship both at the same time.

Balfour: Still less in the same ships.

Clemenceau: I would make the following proposal: we should decide to bring away the Czechs [30,000 or 40,000], of which 4,000 to 5,000 will sail in British ships: we should ask Mr Balfour to agree to delay the shipping of the Germans to Australia for two or three months, and ask Japan to provide the extra tonnage needed.

Balfour: Yes, but Mr Wilson and Japan must be told that it is impossible to contemplate intervention for two or three months.

Clemenceau: Not at all. I do not ask for one large operation. You ship 5,000 Czechs with your tonnage: we use the three ships earmarked for the deportees: and Japan provides a little more for the remainder of the Czechs.

Pichon: There are only 10,000 to 15,000 at Vladivostok. The others are *en route*. It is vital to remove the first lot to make room for the others.

Clemenceau: I only want 15,000 of them to begin with. That will be enough to start an uprising in Prague.

The Supreme War Council thereupon approved a resolution stating that the British government should ask Japan to help with tonnage in shipping the Czechs, 'unless and until it is required for an expedition to Vladivostok', and that the tonnage at present allotted to ship the Germans in China to Australia should be diverted to ship the Czechs, if this did not dislocate essential military shipping programmes.

Clemenceau had finally admitted that he did not want the Czechs as reinforcements on the western front, but as political symbols to influence the Austrian question. This undoubtedly influenced the British ministers against shipping any Czechs from Russia.

On May 30, martial law was declared in Moscow and the Cheka published a long statement in *Izvestia* claiming that the Cadet party was responsible for both General Krasnov's advance northwards with his Don Cossacks and for the Czech revolt; some Cadets had been seeking German support in Kiev, others, who were pro-Ally, had been bringing former Russian officers down from northern and central Russia to the northern Caucasus and Volga provinces; and this, it was alleged, had sparked off the Czech revolt. This fanned suspicions in many Russian minds that they were victims of a conspiracy that was 'widespread and international in character', and it caused a 'great sensation' in Moscow. This paranoid interpretation of international events, which was of course untrue, concentrated Russian suspicion and hatred on the 'treacherous' Cadets, and away from the Bolsheviks themselves. 'Moscow in state of siege', records Lockhart in his diary on the 31st: 'Counter-revolutionary plot discovered and five hundred arrests. Request from Chicherin to use all influence in settling Czech incident.' Lockhart then departed for Petrograd. 'Feeling in Petrograd quite different from Moscow', he records on June 2: 'Altogether quieter and further removed from the struggle. Anti-Bolshevism very strong and hardly concealed. At the cabaret jokes were made at Bolshevik expense which would not be tolerated in Moscow. Famine pretty severe and grave discontent among the workmen and sailors. Counter-revolution here possible any day.'[17]

It seems, however, that Reilly was not planning any immediate *coup*. Through old acquaintances, he had soon after his arrival got in touch with Russian officers, one of whom was the Bolshevik Chief of Staff in Moscow, one Colonel Friede, who hated his new masters and passed on Bolshevik military plans and orders to Reilly, who got them through to London. With Friede's help, Reilly also entered the Cheka under the alias of Relinsky. Now Friede was a Latvian, and Reilly quickly realized that, while Trotsky was forming the Red Army, the Bolsheviks still relied entirely on the three small forces already detailed: the Red Guards; the few thousand Chinese; and the Latvian regiments. Reilly saw that these Latvian mercenaries, who were much the most capable, could still be out-bribed to seize their present masters in Moscow, whereupon the numerous Russian officers (if only they could unite) could easily take over, and then reopen the war against Germany.[17] But any further *coup* would have to be very carefully prepared. So, for the moment, Reilly bided his time.

On June 4, the Allied envoys in Moscow protested to Chicherin about the Czechs. Lockhart's protest was by far the strongest. Balfour instructed him to state that any Bolshevik attempt to disarm the Czechs, or indeed to interfere with them in any way, would be regarded by the British government as an act hostile to the Allies, and inspired by Germany. Chicherin in reply asked if this was an ultimatum, heralding a declaration of war. But Lockhart's protest was designed only to secure a free exodus from Russia for the Czechs.[18]

Both Britain and Germany were now protesting to the Bolsheviks about the Czechs. Ludendorff's striking early success with his 'Blücher' attack had led him to consider the adoption of draconian measures in Russia. On May 26, a German Foreign Ministry paper indicated that for the time being at any rate, German interests 'can be served only by achieving friendly and trustworthy relations with the current Russian régime, and by helping to prolong and secure it, to the extent we can do this without direct interference in Russia's internal affairs'. Germany, in fact, had no choice but to support the Bolsheviks, since any other Russian régime, of whatever political colour, 'would denounce the Brest[–Litovsk] treaty, and, most probably, move closer to the *Entente*'. This policy was anathema to Ludendorff. It did not matter what party ruled in Russia, he declared on the 28th, for the Russians 'will never be our friends'. The Russian economy must be bound to Germany and bled; any Russian grain surplus to German needs must go to neutral countries and the Russian border states to make them dependent on Germany, and wean them from Allied influence. 'Help for Russia herself if the last concern', stated Ludendorff firmly.[19]

After getting a further angry note from Ludendorff of May 28 complaining of the Allied presence at Murmansk and on the Murmansk railway, and other reports, the Foreign Secretary Kühlmann sent a wire to Mirbach in Moscow on June 1 informing him that the German command in Finland reported that Polish and Czech troops were being moved to the Murmansk railway in transit for the western front (this was wrong); while a 'reliable source' stated that five trainloads of fully-equipped Serbians had been spotted on the Vologda-Perm line (this seems to have been true). 'It must be made clear to the [Bolshevik] government in Moscow that we cannot stand by and watch such undertakings on the part of the *Entente*', stated Kühlmann. If the Bolsheviks could not stop this sort of thing, then they would have to give the Germans 'more extensive guarantees' to prevent the Allies receiving support via the Murmansk coast. The German High Command was considering what action would be suitable; meanwhile, Mirbach was to discuss the matter with Chicherin at once 'in whatever way you think best, to point out to him the gravity of the matter, and to tell him that this state of affairs cannot possibly be allowed to continue'. Finally, there were other reports that a Czech corps had passed through Khabarovsk, north of Vladivostok, on the Amur river. (This report was mainly true.) 'We insist that it be prevented from travelling on to Vladivostok, should such a move be intended.'[20]

Mirbach protested; Chicherin more or less dismissed it. Miribach's reaction was to wire to Kühlmann on June 3: 'Due to strong *Entente* competition, 3,000,000 marks per month necessary. In event of early need for change in our political line, a higher sum must be reckoned with.'[21]

On June 4, Counsellor Riezler, the German expert on Bolshevism at the German embassy in Moscow, sent a private letter to the Foreign Ministry in Berlin. 'In the last two weeks, the situation has very rapidly come to a head. ... The pressure exerted by the Bolsheviks' mailed first is enormous ... but there can no longer be any doubt that the physical means with which the Bolsheviks are maintaining their power are running out ... and even the Latvian soldiers sitting in the vehicles are no longer absolutely reliable — not to mention the peasants and the workers.' This, of course, tallied with what Captain Cromie had stated on May 20. But he warned that the Foreign Ministry must reckon with one serious possibility, namely the 'resurrection of a reasonably ordered bourgeois Russia with the help of the *Entente*. ... There are Czechoslovak troops here; there are English and French in Archangel and Murmansk; and there are officers' associations and party organizations.' Joy at liberation from Bolshevik terror and the reopening of the banks and the resumption of normal commerce might help matters a lot.[21]

If that did happen, the Ukraine would reunite itself with Russia, and Germany would either have to face an 'irresistible' movement with a few divisions, or just accept matters. They must anticipate this. 'In concrete terms, that means we must spin a thread reaching to Orenburg and Siberia over General Krasnov's head, hold cavalry (directed at Moscow but concealed) ready for any eventuality, prepare a future government here with which we could agree, dipping as deep as possible into the ranks of the Cadets for it (in order, if necessary, to compromise them too), and finally revise those terms of the treaty of Brest[–Litovsk] directed against economic hegemony within Russia as a whole, i.e. reunite the Ukraine with Russia and make something out of Estonia and Livonia which we could later sell back to Russia.' This, it must be underlined, was the view of the German expert on Bolshevism, who had never considered that it would last long.

To help to restore Imperial Russia was 'not a pleasant perspective,' admitted Riezler, but this might be inevitable, since lasting Ukrainian independence was a fantasy, and the 'vitality of the united Russian soul is enormous'. The Ukraine would anyhow fall with the Bolsheviks. 'As far as my work here is concerned,' he added, 'the apparatus of our united rivals, who are working in a variety of roles, is extremely powerful, and our devalued roubles disappear at a rapid rate.'[21] He added a PS: 'Things look a little better today [June 4]. The terror seems to be having its effect and appears seriously to have disturbed the conspiracy which had been prepared. ... We might nevertheless have another six or eight weeks ...'.

On the following day, the Foreign Ministry in Berlin sent a paper to the German Treasury, asking for more funds for Mirbach in Moscow, and gave their view of the Czech role. As a result of recent Allied efforts to persuade the Bolshevik government to accept Allied demands, which would have resulted in Russian 'orientation' towards the Allies, Mirbach had been forced to spend considerable sums. The Bolsheviks had been successfully restrained, 'but every day may bring new surprises. The social revolutionaries have completely sold themselves to the *Entente* which, with the help of the Czechoslovak battalions, is trying to undermine the supremacy of the Bolsheviks. It appears that the Bolsheviks have, for the moment, succeeded in overcoming the attack of the Czechoslovak troops. Nevertheless, the next few months will be taken up with internal political strife. This may possibly even lead to the fall of the Bolsheviks.' As long as they remained in power, every means would have to be applied to make them maintain their present policy, despite severe German political demands in the Baltic, the Caucasus and the Crimea. 'This will cost money; probably a great deal of money', warned the Foreign Ministry. But the possibility of their overthrow also had to be anticipated. Relations thus had to be maintained with other political parties to assure a smooth transition of power, if they fell. 'This too will cost money.' The Foreign Ministry asked for another 40 million marks.[21]

On June 5, the War Cabinet took official note of the Supreme War

Council's resolutions. At noon on the 6th, the storm broke over the Prime Minister's head, when Balfour informed the War Cabinet that the question of Allied intervention was 'never properly discussed' by the Supreme War Council, and that consequently the War Cabinet's decision of May 30 had not been carried out.[22]

The Prime Minister explained that he had received 'very definite and precise' information about President Wilson's opposition to intervention in Siberia; it was decided that it was impossible to discuss the question fully in the Supreme War Council, but that the three Foreign Ministers should consider it instead. He had intended to ask General Foch to write a paper on the subject, but unfortunately Foch had been called away on the morning of June 3, when the matter came up for discussion. Milner however was asking Foch for this paper. Balfour retorted with uncharacteristic anger by quoting a private telegram from Wiseman in New York, which stated that President Wilson's views 'were not so emphatic against intervention in Siberia as those which had been expressed to Mr Lloyd George', as the Cabinet minutes gently put it. In this wire, it stated that the President agreed on the need for the re-creation of the Russian front, and for help to be given to the Russian people, but said that no military authority had convinced him that any scheme was likely to succeed. The President had proposed that an Allied commission should be sent both to Vladivostok and Murmansk to organize supplies, and added that if 'any recognized body' in Russia invited Allied intervention, then we should intervene.

Lord Robert Cecil, who had been so opposed to Balfour before the Supreme War Council, now supported him, and stated 'very strongly' that it was 'most unfortunate' that the Supreme War Council had not been asked to deal with this question, since it was essential that the President should receive a strong recommendation in favour of intervention from the Supreme War Council. The Prime Minister replied rather feebly (to what Hankey calls Cecil's 'outburst') that the Supreme War Council had taken note of the agreement reached by the three Foreign Ministers. Cecil retorted that the Supreme War Council had not expressed any military opinion, nor recommended any approach to the President until Japanese assent had been obtained. The way this whole question had been dealt with was 'most unsatisfactory'.

The Prime Minister tried to explain President Wilson's difficulties. The main American opposition to Japanese intervention in Siberia came from the West Coast, where the President had 'strong political interests'. It was firmly believed by these people that once the Japanese went into Russia, Siberia would practically become a Japanese province. Cecil replied more sombrely that unless there was intervention in Russia, he did not think we could win the war. Next year, unless we intervened, the Germans would certainly be able to get the Russians not only to work for them, but perhaps also to fight for them; and this would be a very significant addition to

German manpower and supplies. Nor could any force operating from northern Russia have a serious effect, 'unless it was backed up by a large expedition from Vladivostok. ... He [Cecil] did not think that the War Cabinet had ever been quite certain of what it really wanted; that it had never been sure that intervention was right; and that, consequently, this feeling of uncertainty had also been felt by our agents abroad. In his opinion, opportunities had been lost in the past, for though at first President Wilson was not unfavourable, later, political interests began to operate. Since then, we have been told that there has been a great change in public feeling in America, and he [Cecil] considered that, if strong pressure of a military character supported by a decision from the Supreme War Council could be brought to the notice of President Wilson, he might agree, although perhaps reluctantly.'

This argument found support in the Cabinet. The First Lord agreed that it had always been difficult to obtain the War Cabinet's considered view on intervention. But in view of the grave difficulties in transport and communications that an expedition from Vladivostok must encounter, the effect of an Allied effort from Murmansk should be compared to the effect of an Allied effort, even with Japanese help, west of Chelyabinsk. The First Lord felt strongly that to develop a proper railway system from Vladivostok, capable of carrying stores and supplies, under modern conditions, 'was too colossal an undertaking for the Japanese to consider, ... He [the First Lord] had never seen a considered and exhaustive study or report on the two possible efforts, and he thought the indefinite policy which Lord Robert Cecil complained of, and of which he was also very conscious, was due to the absence of such a report. This was all too true. The Prime Minister agreed that the Siberian railway could not possibly be resuscitated without whole-hearted American cooperation, and underlined the transport difficulties already existing in Siberia. Lloyd George also stressed that Clemenceau demanded that the Czechs at Vladivostok should have first claim on Japanese shipping to bring them to France.

Balfour agreed with the First Lord. The War Office had never prepared a considered statement on the possibilities of intervention, or of the size of the force that would be required. On this point, he had wired some time ago to Lord Reading, giving the reasons why the British government considered intervention necessary and saying that this wire would be followed by a detailed military argument. The telegram had been sent to the War Office, but they had declined to write any paper, saying that the matter was not entirely military. Balfour insisted that the principal factor to consider was the reception which any force might receive from the local inhabitants.

The First Lord developed this theme. The War Office should consider the possibilities of intervention from three points of view: with the Siberian inhabitants (*a*) friendly; (*b*) actively friendly; or (*c*) inert. Before this question could be effectively discussed, there must be some considered opinion on the size of the force necessary to produce useful results; and the prospect of such results must be put before President Wilson. The First Lord felt that the problem should be considered on the basis of the best results obtainable if the local inhabitants showed passive inertia. A decision must also be reached on the size of the force that could be maintained at Chelyabinsk, or beyond. He still felt, however, that a much smaller effort via Murmansk would give better results in diverting German forces from the western front. But in the absence of an exhaustive study of the possibilities of intervention in Siberia and at Murmansk, he did not see how the War Cabinet or President Wilson could adopt the definite policy for which Lord Robert Cecil asked. Balfour pointed out that the objections to any effort from Murmansk were shipping and men, and that the merit of intervention via Vladivostok was that 500,000 first-class fighting troops could be used; efforts from Murmansk would entail the removal of troops already fighting in other theatres.

The Prime Minister then suggested that, in view of Lord Reading's possible return from America for a visit, Lord Robert Cecil should himself go out to Washington to put his views on the subject to the President personally; the War Cabinet would equip him with all the necessary military arguments, and also obtain Foch's views. This led to considerable discussion, in which the point was made that even if it were impossible to develop a campaign in Russia against the German army, it was most desirable to prevent the Germans withdrawing supplies from Russia. It was also agreed that if a considerable Allied force could be concentrated at Vologda, there would be a considerable rally to it there.

The War Cabinet thereupon decided that the CIGS should prepare a paper stating the following:
(*a*) a 'detailed military argument' on Allied intervention in Siberia;
(*b*) how large an Allied army could be maintained as far west as Chelyabinsk;
(*c*) whether or not a force strong enough to prevent Russian supplies being withdrawn to Germany could be maintained at Chelyabinsk;
(*d*) how large an Allied army would be necessary to carry out active operations from Murmansk or Archangel, with or without intervention through Siberia;
(*e*) the size of the force and amount of supplies necessary for these operations if the local inhabitants were: (*i*) friendly; (*ii*) indifferent; (*iii*) hostile; (*iv*) partly hostile and partly friendly.[22]

The very fact that a proper military appreciation had never been made of the real prospects of Allied intervention in Siberia until now, when all thoughts of 'proper' intervention and opportunities for it were receding, demonstrates perhaps not so much stupidity, as extreme war-weariness. But it does show that President Wilson, 'sheltering himself behind his military advisers (as his Allied critics put it)', was right; no proper military argument, demonstrating that Siberian intervention far into European Russia was a practical military proposition, had ever been drawn up.

That evening, Lockhart wired to Balfour in exasperation. All Russians, the Bolsheviks included, expected Allied intervention at any moment; the Czech revolt had created just the right situation. Unless the Allies took full advantage of it, the hard line which he and the other Allied envoys had taken with Chicherin would endanger Czech lives. The anti-Bolshevik groups were losing hope; soon they would turn to the Germans. The Allies would never have so favourable an opportunity again. If there was any further delay in intervention, Lockhart said, he would resign.[23]

The next day, as Bolshevik trade delegates arrived in Berlin, Lord Robert Cecil resigned as Minister of Blockade. In a long letter to Lloyd George, he criticized him for not carrying out the War Cabinet's decision to obtain a strong resolution in support of Allied intervention from the Supreme War Council. General Bliss, he understood, had shown the British delegates, on arrival, instructions which precluded him from assenting to such a resolution. 'As, however, he [Bliss] is not a member of the Supreme War Council, this did not in itself prevent the [British] delegates from carrying out the policy of the War Cabinet. Still less can the reasons given to General Bliss be regarded as of importance. So far as they were of value, they were well known to us, and those that were novel were not convincing.' But this was not the most important aspect of the matter. 'For months past, as you know, I have been impressed with the extreme urgency of this question [of intervention]. Every day, and from every side, accumulates evidence of the progress made by our enemies in Russia.' He listed the way in which the Germans were breaking the Allied blockade in the Ukraine, Finland, the Baltic, the Caucasus, the Black Sea littoral, the Donetz — and soon Baku and the Caspian, from where they could ascend the Volga and obtain Siberian produce and supplies.[24]

'It has been therefore a matter of very great regret to realize that, though doubtless my colleagues fully appreciated all that was at stake, some of them, *including yourself* [presumably Lloyd George's marking], did not agree with me that the only possible remedy for this state of things was Allied intervention in Siberia, and that every effort should be made and every risk run to secure it. Of course I know that the Cabinet formally adopted this as their policy last January. But it has been treated, if I may say so, as a counsel of perfection — a policy logically unassailable, but not very attractive, which it was some consolation to know would probably not materialize.' There was the failure in early March to take advantage of the, then, relatively favourable attitude of President Wilson. There was the fact that the Japanese ambassador in London could say, only the other day, quite plausibly, that the idea of Japanese intervention on behalf of the

Allies was new to him and the Japanese government; then there was this recent incident at Versailles.

'But apart from all this, the whole tone of the discussions in Cabinet, and the telegrams sent in consequence, has been lukewarm, so that for long the President believed that we were not really in favour of the policy, but were merely acting as the mouth-piece of France, and the Japanese government complained of our indecision. The very fact that you are not conscious of all this, as you explained the other day, confirms my feeling that we do not approach the question from the same point of view. If, for instance, you attached the same importance to Allied intervention in Siberia that you do to the increase of American troops in France, I feel confident the whole treatment of the question would have been very different.

I have not forgotten the proposal you made that I should proceed to America on a special mission to President Wilson. While grateful for the confidence in me which the offer showed, I cannot think it was seriously meant. I have never questioned the ability of Reading and Wiseman to present our case, and to think that I, or anyone else with no first-hand knowledge of the Washington atmosphere and the President's personality, should succeed where they have failed would be as foolish as to believe with the French, that the President's request for military authority will be satisfied by the mission of M. Bergson.'

As he was really in disagreement with the Prime Minister on a vital question of war policy, he felt that he had better resign: 'It is clear that I cannot explain all this in public, and I should propose therefore to confine myself to a brief statement that, finding myself out of *accord with my colleagues on the methods necessary for the vigorous execution of our policy in Russia* I have felt unable to continue to be responsible for it.'[24]

Nothing in Lord Robert Cecil's letter perturbed Lloyd George more than the last sentence; any such statement might grievously harm the Prime Minister. In reply that same day, Lloyd George deeply regretted that Cecil should find it necessary to deprive the British government of his services at so grave a moment: 'That a statesman of your standing and ability should quit an important office at such a time adds greatly to the difficulties which, heaven knows, are already great enough.' If there had been fundamental differences of opinion with his colleagues on the conduct of the war, he might have understood, 'but I fail even now to discover the existence of any such difference. ... I have had all the records of the Cabinet examined carefully. ... There is no record of any suggestion of yours being turned down or of any failure on the part of the Foreign Office to carry it out.'

Cecil could not possibly make the statement he proposed. There would at once be suggestions that the British government had refused to agree to Allied intervention in Siberia. They would have to deny this, saying that Japan refused to intervene without American assent; and that the President, in spite of continuous Allied pressure, had refused to give his assent. 'Your only answer could be that President Wilson might have assented had he been more vigorously pressed. Surely he could not accept that view, and it might lead to an unpleasant conflict which might injure the good relations between the Allied governments', Lloyd George pointed out. 'If any mistake has been made at all by the government in its approach to President Wilson, I think it has been in starting with the proposal for a Japanese instead of an Allied intervention. ... But if that was a mistake, you will I am sure admit that it was just as much yours as that of your colleagues — as a matter of fact, the proposal emanated from you. We assented to it and therefore I am just as responsible as you are .... I cannot help thinking that you are attributing somewhat unfairly to your colleagues a failure which is attributable entirely to the essential difficulties of the case.' The Prime Minister once again described the history of the matter, and the two British proposals. Finally, he urged on Lord Robert Cecil the importance at this grave moment of national unity and solidarity. 'Any resignation of an important member of an Allied government must necessarily have a depressing effect on public opinion in Allied countries, very much tried as they already are with the terrible events of the war.'[25]

But Cecil was not to be deterred. He resigned — though his resignation was kept secret for several weeks.

These two letters are in fact both an obituary and a valediction to British attempts to organize intervention in Russia against the Germans. In the Foreign Office that afternoon, Balfour went through the motions of summoning the Japanese ambassador, and, in accordance with the decision of the Supreme War Council, handed him a note on behalf of the British, French and Italian governments, which formally asked if Japan would agree to intervene in Siberia, subject to the agreed conditions. When the Japanese ambassador asked how far the Allies wished Japan to go into Siberia, Balfour replied: at least to Omsk, but more preferably to Chelyabinsk.[26]

But Allied intervention, in the shape of the Czech revolt fourteen days earlier against the Bolsheviks, was already a fact in both Russia and Siberia. On June 7 (the day of the exchange of letters between the Prime Minister and Cecil), Czech troops, aided by Russian officer groups, attacked both Omsk, the capital of Siberia, and Samara, on the Volga. Both towns fell with little resistance. At Omsk, a Siberian provisional government was set up, drawing its authority from the Siberian regional duma, elected under the Russian provisional government of 1917. At Samara, the many local SRs formed the 'Committee of Members of the Constituent Assembly', under the SR leader Victor Chernov, President of the constituent assembly (which had been dissolved by the Bolsheviks). Here then was both a Siberian, and a strictly 'legal' Russian government, both strongly anti-Bolshevik.

The second British proposal for intervention — namely that the Czech Legion should start up intervention against the Germans — put forward on May 17, and turned down by the French government on May 28 — had taken place of its own accord, but against the Bolsheviks; the Czechs were one step ahead. What the War Cabinet had wished to engineer had happened of itself, quite spontaneously, just as the Cabinet were bidding it *adieu*. It was one of the more remarkable episodes of modern history, and reflects extremely well on the War Cabinet in London; their intuition, their timing, were correct. But no one in London realized that it had happened in this way. The tragedy was that the Allies were never to know that the Czech Legion had decided against sending any of their troops to the northern Russian ports. If the Czech decision to remain united had only been known, something might have been made of it.

Plate 1 The Fox: A rare early Soviet cartoon of Lloyd George, who, during the intervention period, was regarded as the leader of the Western Alliance.

Ллойд-Джордж (по Врему).

Plate 2 The 'agitational literature' issued in the form of leaflets by command of the Bolshevik Central Committee to the Allied troops advancing from Archangel.

Russian Socialist Federa' Soviet Republics

Allied invasion of Russia to suppress Workmens Revolution, and re-establish Tsarism.

Sensational plot discovered to overthrow Soviet government.

Allied complicity in counter-revolutionary plot proved

British diplomat in Moscow discovered at conspirative meeting.—Lavishly distributing bribes. Fabricating forged documents.

The following is a summary of a statement issued by the Soviet government, which discloses a widespread plot instigated by the Allied governments to overthrow the Russian revolution.

On August 14 th. at twelve o'clock, at the private room of Mr. Lockhart, the representative of the British government in Russia, an interview took place between him and a commander of one of the Soviet detatchments in Moscow.

At this meeting it was proposed to organise a rebellion against the Soviet government in connection with the British landing on the Mourman. In order to maintain close relation between the British diplomatic agents and this commander of the Soviet troops, an English lieutenant, Sydney Reiley was delegated to act under the alias of «Reis». It was proposed that certain parts of the Moscow garrison should be sent to Vologda to open the road for the English, while the rest of the garrison should arrest the Council of the Peoples Commissioners in Moscow, and establish a military dictatorship.

For this purpose on Aug. 14 th. Mr .Lockhart handed 700,000 roubles to his agents. On Aug. 22nd another meeting took place at which 200,000 roubles were assigned for the purpose of arresting Lenin and Trotsky, and members of the Council of Public Economy, seizing banks, posts and telegraphs. On Aug. 28th 300,000roubles was paid over to this commander of Soviet troops who was to go to Petrograd to establish connection with the English military group working there together with a group of Russian counter-revolutionaries.

At the same time in Moscow, meetings under the auspices of the agents of the Allied Powers were held with the object of intensifying the famine. It was proposed to blow up certain bridges on the railways, and wreck food trains, in order that the population of Moscow and Petrograd should become so maddened by hunger as to rise in revolt against the Soviet government.

Letters have been discovered with Mr. Lockhart's signature on official British government paper, delegating this commander of Soviet troops to act on behalf of the British government.

The plot was discovered by the commander disclosing the whole scheme to the Soviet authorities.

Acting on this information the Soviet authorities on the night of Aug. 31st surprised a conspirative meeting at which Mr. Lockhart was present. Although Lockhart was arrested, some of the conspirators escaped and are now at large. They have carried out a portion of the ir plans. Trainloads of food were blown up by them at Voronezh. Documents were seized at this meeting which shows that the intention of the Allies as soon as they had established their dictatorship in Moscow was to declare war on Germany and force Russia to fight again. In order to find a pretext for this, a fictitious treaty between Russia and Germany was concocted which presented the Soviet government as selling the independance of Russia to Germany. This forged treaty was to have been printed and scattered broadcast.

FELLOW WORKERS!

Here is positive evidence of the real purpose for which you have been brought to Russia.

You are being used as the tools of your capitalists who are working here in close unity with the agents of bloodstained Tzarism, for the overthrow of the first Socialist Republic, and the re-establishment of the former reign of oppression.

YOU ARE NOT FIGHTING FOR LIBERTY. YOU ARE FIGHTING TO CRUSH IT.

FELLOW WORKERS !

Be honourable men. Remain loyal to your class, refuse to be the accomplices of a great crime, Refuse to do the dirty work of your masters.

G. TCHITCHERINE,
Peoples Commissary for Foreign Affairs.

Plate 3 The band and British sailors from H.M.S. *Suffolk* lead British troops past Czech headquarters into Vladivostok.

Source: Imperial War Museum

Plate 4 Lt Sidney Reilly.

Plate 5 Colonel Joe Boyle.

Plate 6 A British sentry in North Russia.

Plate 7 Two British soldiers in North Russia.

Source: Imperial War Museum

Plate 8 Two British soldiers photographed with a group of Russian women, somewhere in Russia, during the intervention period. (negative damaged.)

Plate 9 The first International Battalion of Red Guards formed from German and Austrian prisoners in Russia, 1918.

Plate 10 British sailors from H.M.S. *Suffolk* land at Vladivostok, 1918.

Source: Imperial War Museum

Plate 11 A camouflaged Czech armoured train, 1918.

Source: Imperial War Museum

Plate 12 Czech troops, with Japanese, French and British sailors, and American Marines, at Vladivostok, 1919.

Plate 14 British troops in North Russia.

Plate 15 Russian cavalry in Siberia moving to the front, 1918.

Plate 13 In a village near Archangel, 1918.

8

The coming Intervention: the Czechs and the Russian Fleets

June and July were the dog-days of the Bolshevik regime — and of British policy towards Russia. Early June had seen the containment of Ludendorff's 'Blücher' attack between Soissons and Rheims, which had brought the Germans back to the Marne and created panic in Paris. But on June 9, as Ludendorff tried to link up the German salients at Amiens and on the Marne by the seizure of Compiègne (a move which the CIGS had feared on May 30 would finally smash the French army, but was now too late and failed), Ludendorff informed the Foreign Secretary, Kühlmann, that Germany could break the Allied blockade by the seizure of raw materials in the Ukraine and the Caucasus. With the war thought likely to go on at least until 1919, there was overwhelming feeling among the Allies that they would now have to intervene in Russia to prevent Germany breaking their blockade. The Bolsheviks were coming to realize this too, and that it would spell the end of their short rule.[1]

Now, however, intervention would probably happen simply through the pressure of events. The British plan of mid-May, strangely prophetic, for the Czech Legion to initiate Allied intervention in Russia, had been turned down in late May by the French. The French Foreign Minister had told the War Cabinet clearly on May 28 that the French government 'would not accept the principle of using the Czechs to force Japanese intervention, and later American consent'. To attempt to influence President Wilson in this way 'would be very dangerous'. In fact, stated the French Foreign Minister, Czech intervention 'would probably prove fatal to American intervention'.

Meanwhile, news of the full extent and significance of the Czech revolt had not yet reached London, where the War Cabinet had lapsed into apathy over intervention, after the crisis leading to Lord Robert Cecil's resignation. Nor of course had it reached Washington, where the key to intervention lay. Early in June, as Kennan makes clear, the American War Department had approved in principle the despatch of American forces to northern Russia to ensure Allied retention of Murmansk, but were against Siberian intervention on military grounds. President Wilson agreed with his military advisers on the 'military absurdity' of the Anglo–French proposals for large-scale intervention in Siberia; and when news reached Washington of the new Allied approach to Japan, resulting from the Supreme War Council's meeting of June 3 (at which it had been asked if Japanese forces could be sent far enough into Siberia to meet the Germans, provided President Wilson approved), it was received 'with a scepticism bordering on contempt'. But the matter had now become the dominant problem in American foreign policy. Colonel House, Secretary Lansing and the top officials at the State Department, all felt that 'something should be done' in Siberia in answer to the overwhelming flood of Allied requests for intervention; so did the President. A proposal had thus gained ground for the despatch of an allied commission to Russia.[2]

The proposal had initially been broached by President Wilson to Wiseman on May 30. The President suggested that America, Britain and France send out to Russia a civil commission to help to reorganize the Russian railways and food supplies, and organize a system of trade by barter; all of which would help to put Russia back on her feet without the risk inherent in Japanese intervention. In a further interview on June 6, Wiseman restated to the President the familiar arguments for Japanese intervention, one being the probable re-creation of an eastern front. The President would not admit that this was practical, or had any chance of success. The Japanese doubted whether they could even get to Omsk, he said, and he believed that they were anxious for an invitation to intervene solely as an excuse for occupying the maritime province. If, he added, a large Anglo–American force could have been landed in Siberia, and had advanced along the Siberian railway, the Russians might have rallied; but if we had to rely on Japanese military support, the Russians would rally to Germany. This was his reply to the observation that 'things could not be worse than they are now'. The President thought they would be much worse, if the Germans seized such an opportunity of organizing Russia against Japan. It might end in Russian soldiers fighting against us on the western front. The President said that he realized that the American government held the key to the situation. He was prepared to send a joint civil commission to both Murmansk and Vladivostok to help reorganize Russian internal affairs; and added that if an invitation to intervene reached us from any responsible and representative Russian body, we ought to accept it.[3]

Such proposals were regarded with contempt by the War Office in London. On June 9, Ludendorff's new attack went in at Compiègne, and General Knox wrote a strong paper for the War Cabinet criticizing the President's suggestion. Economic help for Russia (which Knox clearly saw simply as an attempt to further British trade interests) should not take the place of military action in Russia against the Germans. Knox, ever a practical man, suggested obtaining the minimum Japanese terms for intervention, and then satisfying them.[4]

On June 10, however, *The Times* main news summary contained the following item, based on a report from Peking, dated June 3: 'German and Austrian prisoners in Siberia are now organized under their officers, and they have driven back Colonel Semenov's Cossack force, directed against the Bolsheviks, 120 miles from Karimskaya (the junction of the Chinese eastern and Amur railway lines).' Now this news, clearly implying that the German and Austrian governments were allowing their prisoners to be reformed on Russian territory to fight in Bolshevik interests, was absolutely untrue. Some Magyar prisoners and a very few Germans had joined the communist internationalist regiments, but were in no sense reformed enemy units, and the German and Austrian governments were very angry about Bolshevik recruitment of their prisoners. But in a fluid situation, the existence of organized enemy prisoners in Siberia came to be accepted both in London and Washington. Then on the 13th, *The Times* contained the first news that the departing Czechs were in disagreement with the Bolsheviks; but it only appeared in two very small items. The first, dated June 11, was a report from Amsterdam, quoting the *Norddeutsche Allgemeine Zeitung*, which warned the Bolshevik government not to allow the Czechs, with their arms, to join the Allies; and then stated that the Bolshevik government had refused to allow them to leave Russia. The second was a Reuters report from Moscow, dated June 5, in which Trotsky confirmed his order to the Bolshevik troops to shoot any Czechs on the spot.

At the Prime Minister's mid-morning discussion on the 13th with the CIGS and Milner, the CIGS reported that when he and Milner were in France the week before, Clemenceau had stated that he hoped to get an answer from President Wilson about Japanese intervention within 48 hours, 'through an American channel'. Failing such an answer, he would agree to Foch's name being used in a telegram to the President in favour of intervention, or to Foch sending a message himself. Apparently no such answer had come from Washington, and the CIGS now gathered that Clemenceau did not wish Foch to send the message. Milner explained that Clemenceau was very reluctant, in view of the great influence that Foch's name carried with President Wilson, to make too free use of it. 'He [Clemenceau] was afraid that we had really lost the tide in connection with intervention, owing to the fighting that was going on between the Czechoslovaks and the organized prisoners of war in Siberia.' The Prime Minister remarked that Clemenceau 'was not really very eager' about Japanese intervention at the moment, both because he doubted whether President Wilson really would take any action, 'and because he was more anxious to get his Czechoslovaks away'. What is clear from this brief exchange is that the Prime Minister and his colleagues did not even yet appreciate the full significance of the Czech revolt, but did believe the story that there were 'organized' enemy prisoners in Siberia, who were engaged in fighting both the Czechs and Semenov.[5]

On the 7th, a wire from Cromie had reached the Admiralty stating that 'last week' (probably in the last days of May) there had been an outbreak of fire on board the Russian dreadnought *Sebastopol*, resulting in damage to two turrets and one boiler room, six boilers and one engine room now being out of action. Cromie implied that this was due to sabotage: 'On board ships, Russian party very small but state necessary fight to last and then destroy ships. German party very strong and growing. Conversations with many parties point that PETD [Petrograd] will certainly be occupied sooner or later.'

Then there was the Black Sea Fleet, part of which had escaped German seizure at Sebastopol, and had sailed eastwards to Novorossisk. The Bolsheviks had finally acceded to British requests to blow up the fleet there, and defy German demands that it be returned to Sebastopol. On June 10, as Cromie wired to the Admiralty again, and a Bolshevik commissar was on his way with secret orders from Lenin to blow up the remaining warships (a task which Colonel Joe Boyle, unbeknown to all other parties, had already bribed the Bolshevik sailors to do), Trotsky sent a wire *en clair* (which the Germans would be expected to intercept) stating that the warships were to be back in Sebastopol by the 19th. But the Germans issued an ultimatum: if the warships were not back by the 15th, and certain border incidents rectified, German troops would seize Novorossisk. Thus, there was to be a race for the remainder of the Black Sea Fleet.[6]

In his wire of the 10th, Cromie only commented briefly on these warships. 'German Admiral Hopman in *Goeben* now recognizes grave mistake committed in hoisting German war flag in Russian ships in Sebastopol. Everyone is against Germans.' Most of his telegram was devoted to support of his assistant, Commander Le Page, recently returned from Moscow, who argued strongly that if it had been decided to intervene, the time was ripe. 'Czechoslavs hold a large part of Siberian line and are being joined by anti-Bolsheviks; parties of officers in [? Petrograd] and Moscow are only waiting for some sign from Allies to [? join]. Financial help is needed and Germans are spending money like water and gaining ground, at their instigation pro-Ally officers are being arrested and thus it is hoped to force others over to German side. There is talk of a German plot for a turnover against Bolsheviks which may take place in two or three weeks, prisoners of war are being collected, German notes are in stronger terms and less conciliating.' Cromie added that two train loads of German soldiers, disguised as Russians, had been sent against the Czechs (there is no support for this). The German idea was to restore the monarchy; and most Russians were so tired of the present situation that at least 75% would at once support such a plan.

Cromie urged immediate intervention in northern Russia. 'The moment has arrived, further delay means failure and a strengthening of German influence and once a stable [Russian] government is formed, backed by

Germany, difficulties to turn it pro-Ally again will be unlimitable. The [Allied] Expeditionary Force must consist of a [?sufficient] number of troops, say not less than two divisions, to send a small force say as [?nucleus] and depend on concentration of friendly Russians is [?absolutely] useless, as it would indicate operations were not being taken seriously. Determined action in the East is also most essential. ... Any such movement this side [i.e. in northern Russia] will at once bring Germans across and relieve pressure on western front.' Cromie warned that the views of people who had spent practically the whole time in Petrograd should not be accepted as final. His wire concluded: 'If this enterprise is not undertaken seriously, then it is quite certain any hopes for successful destruction of [Baltic] Fleet must be abandoned. Necessity for an immediate start is also absolutely essential. Assistance of Russian forces cannot be relied upon unless stiffened by a very strong force of Allied troops.' Cromie was thus linking destruction of the Baltic Fleet to Allied intervention in northern Russia. When this wire reached the Admiralty on June 14, it was not shown to the Cabinet.[6] The Deputy First Sea Lord merely replied to Cromie thus: 'Act according to your own discretion essential point being that the ships should not fall intact into German hands.'

At the Prime Minister's mid-morning discussion on the 14th, the full significance of the Czech revolt had still not been appreciated in London. The CIGS reported that one and a half German divisions were said to be on their way to Petchenga, and that the Germans were said to be constructing three railways, one to Kem, the second to Kandalaksha, the third towards Petchenga. Unless President Wilson agreed to effective Japanese intervention in Siberia quickly, the CIGS feared that the British government would probably have to withdraw General Poole's force from Murmansk. Meanwhile, the Americans had not yet answered our 'specific' request for a brigade 'and certain other items' for the defence of Murmansk. Sir Henry Wilson's report was incorrect in every aspect. The Germans were not sending divisions to Petchenga, nor were they — nor could they be — constructing three railways to these three small ports, each of which was linked by the Murmansk railway.[7] Where were these new little railways to start from? There is no indication. Their construction through this difficult country would take some little time. But these inaccuracies would have the effect of encouraging the despatch of sufficient Allied troops to repel these German troops and obstruct these German efforts — though whether the CIGS gave this 'information' for this reason is not clear. More glaring was his misstatement that the Americans had been asked for a brigade 'and certain other items' to help defend Murmansk.

In Washington, the vague idea for the despatch of an Allied commission to Russia had received considerable impetus in early June, when the Republican opposition began to press for immediate action in Russia, in agreement with the Allies. The Democratic administration was spurred to action. It was generally agreed by Colonel House, the State Department, Reading and Wiseman that Herbert Hoover, who had been so successful in organizing the Belgian Relief Commission, was the man to head the commission to Russia. On June 13, Secretary Lansing wrote to the President urging the setting up of such a commission, to be headed by Hoover; this, he considered, 'would, for the time being, dispose of the proposal for armed intervention'. Wiseman, however, described the plan in rather different terms to the Foreign Office on the 14th. Hoover would leave at once for Vladivostok with an Allied commission to give the Russians food and supplies and to help to reorganize the Russian economy. The commission would be protected by a military force, and reinforcements would be standing by if Hoover decided to call them in. Once the commission was actually in Russia, Wiseman thought the President would be guided by Hoover's advice; and if Hoover advised large-scale intervention, even if it were mainly Japanese, the President would almost certainly accept it. There would thus be a gradual approach towards British and French policy.[8] It now seems that this was just what the President feared might happen — that he would lose control of the intervention issue. The President did not respond to Lansing's proposal.

But the commission was certainly designed to counter the proposal for immediate armed intervention; and when, on June 11, Milner sent a wire to the President asking for three American infantry battalions, two artillery batteries and three engineer companies to be sent to Murmansk (Foch, he made clear, had approved in principle the diversion of American troops from France to northern Russia), the request was badly received. The President had, of course, just before the Supreme War Council's meeting of June 3, agreed to send American troops to northern Russia if Foch agreed. But on the 14th, when Lansing discussed Milner's request with the Secretary of War and the American Chief of Staff, they were surprised, and angered, to find they were being asked for a relatively large force (the Supreme War Council had stated that no more than four to six Allied battalions in all would be needed), to be placed under British command. The matter was referred back to Paris, where General Bliss was instructed to see Foch about it. Thus Sir Henry Wilson's statement to the Prime Minister on the 14th that the Americans had not yet replied to a 'specific' request for a brigade 'and certain other items' to be sent to Murmansk was glaringly inaccurate, whether mischievous or not is impossible to tell.[9]

The following day, the indignation of the War Office and above all of the CIGS at President Wilson's delay in approving large-scale intervention in northern Russia and Siberia received a rude shock, long over-due, when the British military section at Versailles produced a comprehensive paper in answer to the five detailed questions on intervention which the War Cabinet had put to the CIGS on June 6. In view of the importance of this paper, the first and indeed only one of its kind, it is necessary to study it at some length.

I. A detailed military argument with regard to Allied intervention in Siberia.
Conclusion. Russia's present neutrality was 'not likely to continue long', and unless the present trend of events was checked by Allied military action, 'her domination and exploitation by Germany as a military asset of the central powers appears certain in the near future'. German influence was now being rapidly extended to the Caucasus and Siberia, supplies and labour were already being provided for the German army, and there were many signs that Russian recruitment had already begun, and would soon be 'of serious military importance'. Time was vital, 'and should Allied intervention be long deferred, there is little doubt but that German control of the Siberian railway will be firmly established and great difficulties presented to an Allied advance from Vladivostok'.

Though Japanese cooperation was unavoidable, we should try, at any rate at first, to play down Japan's role, and give an European 'complexion' to the expedition. When the Allies first landed, the Japanese contingent should be no larger than any other Allied contingent. The Allied force should move along the Siberian railway, 'gathering and organizing adherents in its progress'. The main Japanese force should follow 'at a considerable distance' behind, consolidating the communications. The extent of the Allied advance across Siberia could not be predetermined. 'But should the Russian attitude towards intervention prove, as it may, to be cordial and even enthusiastic, it might well prove practicable to occupy the important junctions of Samara and Penza, from the former of which railway communications run to Turkestan, and from the latter to the Caucasus, to Moscow and northern Persia.' Operations, in fact, should be 'pushed well beyond Chelyabinsk, which should not be regarded in any sense as a final objective'. (This last sentence shows the scope of the operations envisaged by the British planners at Versailles; the War Cabinet had considered Chelyabinsk as their furthest possible objective.)[10]

Japan should be in charge of the lines of communication and rear services, while the other Allies should organize the 'friendly Russian elements' into armed forces. The paper drew special attention to the 'important power afforded by the control of the large corn supplies and rich wheat-growing districts of western Siberia. All reports concur in foretelling severe famine in European Russia during the coming winter. The possession of almost the only large food reserve in Russia should provide the Allies with a powerful lever for conciliating, attracting and utilizing large sections of the Russian population', it was stressed. (And through British control, via Jaroszynski, of the Siberian Bank, which controlled the Siberian grain trade, this food reserve 'belonged' to Britain.)

189

To summarize, non-intervention involves:
1. The eventual control of Russia by Germany;
2. The acquirement of a source of manpower and material, which may go far to counterbalance the arrival of the American army;
3. Increased pressure by Germany on the western front;
4. A threat to British possessions and interests in the East which may involve the weakening of British forces on the western front.

Intervention will serve:
1. To bring against Germany a reserve of manpower, which otherwise cannot be employed against her: the Japanese army;
2. To bring against Germany a reserve of manpower and material which may otherwise be employed in her interests: the Russian population and resources;
3. To oblige Germany to detach to a distant theatre in difficult circumstances important forces, which would otherwise be used on the western front;
4. To avert, or at least mitigate, the Turko–German menace to India and British interests in the East.

II. The size of the Allied Army which could be maintained as far westward as Chelyabinsk.
Conclusion. 25 divisions — provided that
1. There were enough supply and railway troops to work and maintain the Siberian railway;
2. There were enough railway engines and rolling stock;
3. There was adequate protection for the Siberian railway.

III. Whether it would be possible to maintain an army at Chelyabinsk of sufficient strength to prevent supplies being withdrawn from Siberia to Germany.
Conclusion. It was merely a question of holding the (double-line) railway Chelyabinsk–Ufa–Samara; and the (single-line) railway Tiumen–Ekaterinburg–Perm–Vologda. This could be done by 25 Allied divisions. The Germans would need 40 divisions to drive them back, and would have to occupy all European Russia, including Petrograd and Moscow; an 'almost prohibitive' task for the Germans to undertake.

IV. The necessary force of Allied troops which would be required to carry out active operations from Murmansk or Archangel, either with or without intervention through Siberia.
Conclusion. The connection of operations in this theatre with those resultant on intervention in Siberia is at present remote, and the interaction of the two campaigns will be for a long time inconsiderable. In the future,

however, supposing that intervention in Siberia is successfully conducted and that a new line of battle is established in Russia, the utilization of the northern ports as supply bases will become one of the greatest importance. The future value of these ports is, therefore, a very high one.

But with regard to 'active operations' in northern Russia, it must be recalled that:

1. Allied troops would have to be provided at the expense of our operations in France; such operations could not, as in the case of the 'Siberian expedition', be conducted mainly by Japanese troops. 'In other words, it would involve a partition and not an increase of our total fighting power.'
2. There would be less chance of rallying anti-German Russians, as there were so few people in northern Russia; and there would be much greater difficulty in organizing and supplying them once formed. There was also no food in northern Russia, as in Siberia; and the enemy was much nearer.
3. Communications with Europe lay through submarine-infested seas, and we would also have to use British shipping, instead of Japanese shipping, as at Vladivostok.
4. Thus, until results of intervention through Siberia developed, 'we should reduce our military effort in the North Russian theatre to the minimum necessary to deny the northern ports to the enemy. Our general attitude should be defensive, though that defence should be of as active a nature as possible.

Thus for Archangel: Provided we held the White Sea, we would only need to deny the Archangel–Vologda–Zvanka–Petrograd railway to the enemy. For this, six battalions, three field batteries, three mountain batteries, three heavy batteries, and four armoured trains would be sufficient, plus railway troops, engineers, etc.

Thus for Murmansk: One and a half to two divisions and four armoured trains could defend both Murmansk port and the Murmansk railway down to Kandalaksha. 'South of this point, its successful protection is highly problematical.' Kem was of 'considerable importance' as a possible German submarine base; and if the Germans advanced against it, 'special measures' would have to be taken — to be decided by the British general on the spot, and as local condition allowed — to ensure its protection to the last possible moment. Otherwise, demolition of crucial bridges would deny other parts of the railway to the enemy for a considerable time.

Thus the total figures for consolidation of the northern ports were: one and a half to two divisions, six heavy batteries, six mountain batteries, four armoured trains, plus railway troops, engineers, etc.

V. With regard to the proposed operations, the difference in the number of men and the amount of material and supplies which would be necessary if the local inhabitants were: (*a*) friendly, (*b*) indifferent, (*c*) hostile, (*d*) partly hostile and partly friendly.

Conclusion. In northern Russia, the local people would probably actively cooperate, if we provided food. If they were hostile, they would be too few in number to cause us any trouble. In Siberia, 200,000 men (10 divisions) would be needed to protect and maintain the Siberian railway from Vladivostok to Chelyabinsk. The size of the force that could be maintained at Chelyabinsk would depend on the attitude of the local inhabitants, as follows:

(*a*) *Friendly:* 25 divisions	500,000
Allied railway and supply troops	100,000
Local labour — military	100,000
(*b*) *Indifferent or partly hostile and*	
partly friendly: 20 divisions	400,000
Allied railway and supply troops	200,000
Local labour — civil, highly paid	100,000

(*c*) *Hostile:* In this case, 'it is doubtful whether an expedition as far as Chelyabinsk would be possible, as the safety of communications would be too precarious.'

This was a devastating paper for both the CIGS and the War Office to read, since it showed that President Wilson was right in complaining of the 'military absurdity' of the proposals for large-scale intervention in Siberia. The Japanese General Staff felt that no less than 150,000 troops would be needed, even if operations were confined east of Irkutsk, which was some 2,500 miles from Vladivostok. The British planners were here considering operations west of the Volga — which was some 1,000 miles from Chelyabinsk, itself some 5,000 miles from Vladivostok. The Japanese, who knew something of the state of the Siberian railway, considered that it would take some three years for a real Allied expeditionary force to get to Chelyabinsk. Further, as the British planners intended to keep the Japanese troops in the background, guarding the Siberian line, it is clear that the Allies would have to provide the 20 to 25 divisions, which were to operate west of Chelyabinsk. But they did not have one-tenth of this number of men available. This mythical host was then to 'swan on' to Samara and Penza in the south, and to Vologda in the north; the assumption being that these railways were in good working order: of course, they were not. It must have been a further blow for the CIGS to read that the interaction of northern Russia and Siberian operations was 'at present remote', and 'will be for a long time inconsiderable'. Archangel and Murmansk, in fact, were simply future supply bases for the Siberian expedition; and until there were some real developments in Siberia, the British military effort in northern Russia should be reduced to the minimum necessary to deny the two northern ports to the enemy. On June 14, the CIGS had been telling the Prime Minister that northern Russian and Siberian intervention were closely connected. But the British planners considered that the defence of Archangel entailed occupation of Vologda, the furthest point of the Allied advance from Siberia, and the meeting place of the northern Russian and Siberian forces; and the War Cabinet on June 6, when putting these detailed questions to the CIGS, which the British planners were now answering, had agreed that there would be a 'considerable rally' by local Russians to the Allied forces at Vologda (where the Allied ambassadors were residing), if a 'considerable' Allied force could be concentrated there. Vologda was thus to be the key point. The only point at issue for the CIGS and the War Office was the number of troops needed to deny Murmansk and Archangel to the enemy. The British planners here stated that one and a half to two divisions would be needed at Murmansk, and six battalions at Archangel. But the CIGS claimed to have knowledge that the Germans were already on their way to Petchenga in strength, and were even constructing three light railways. Would these Allied forces be sufficient? This paper, however, could obviously not be shown to President Wilson; it would support his theory of the 'military absurdity' of large-scale intervention in Siberia all too well. It was not even shown to the War Cabinet. The War Office kept it strictly private.

The paper naturally contained no reference to the Czechs. But the same day that it was written (June 15), *The Times* printed the first report of the Czech revolt, and of the arrival of some Czech detachments at Vladivostok, sent from Peking, on June 10. 'The advent of large contingents of Czecho-slovaks in the Far East has brought a new factor into the situation', stated *The Times*. It was added that two Czech divisions were still scattered along the Siberian railway from Chelyabinsk eastwards, *en route* for Vladivostok. 'They have come into conflict with the Bolsheviks over the question of disarmament, and appear to have occupied the section of the railway from Irkutsk westwards. Some 14,000 have arrived at Vladivostok ...'.

The Czech revolt and the Czechs' seizure of large sections of the Siberian railway was now public knowledge. But *The Times* report was not wholly accurate, and it is necessary to look at the Czechs' true position in Russia and Siberia in mid-June. They were, in fact, split into three groups, the first, a sizeable body of troops, which, as stated in *The Times*, had got through to Vladivostok.

Owing to what Ullman calls the 'well-intentioned but disastrous mediation' of the local American Consul-General, the second group had been prevented from seizing Irkutsk, on the shores of Lake Baikal, which was the main Bolshevik military base in Siberia, and which the Bolsheviks rapidly fortified with local reinforcements and enemy prisoners whom they had been able to enlist. As Lake Baikal was a strong natural barrier, and demolition of the many tunnels through which the Siberian railway ran along the lake's southern shore would block the route to Vladivostok possibly for months, the Czechs west of Irkutsk were faced with a formidable problem. But they were led by an impetuous commander, the young Rudolph Gajda. After seizing Krasnoyarsk, which was roughly midway between Omsk and Irkutsk, and which had also briefly held out, on June 16, he prepared for an assault on Irkutsk.

The third group, consisting of most of the First Corps, was to the west of Gajda's force. Some of this group held the line from Chelyabinsk to Omsk, but most of them, at the time of the Czech revolt, were in the Penza area, on the wrong side of the Volga. They were considered by their colleagues further up the line to be in the greatest danger of being cut off from the rest of the Legion, but under their capable commander Čeček, they were fighting their way steadily eastwards; and on June 8, assisted by Russian officers and local SRs, they took Samara, where the 'Committee of Members of the Constituent Assembly' formed a Russian government. To this new regime, the Czechs, most of them ardent socialists themselves, felt a bond of sympathy. They were impressed with the welcome which their brother Slavs had given them as liberators from the Bolsheviks, whom they had overcome, as elsewhere, with surprising ease, and behind whom, they were now convinced, stood the hated Germans. All this encouraged them — rather belatedly — to consider 'exchanging an eastward withdrawal for a westward crusade', as Peter Fleming puts it. (This was, of course, precisely what the War Cabinet's proposal of mid-May had envisaged, but it had been turned down in late May by the French.) The day after the capture of Samara, therefore, Čeček called on the local American Consul and handed him some papers which he asked to be forwarded to the American ambassador, Francis; Čeček wished to explain the Czech revolt and receive instructions on the next step to take.[11]

The first full report of the Czech revolt reached Washington at the same time that it reached London: on about June 15, and caused great excitement. On June 17, after the President had read a telegram from the American minister in Peking, urging that the Czechs be left in Siberia to 'control' that region against the Germans, he at once wrote to Secretary Lansing to say that he now thought he saw the 'shadow of a plan' that might work with Japanese and other Allied support; the Czechs, after all, he reminded Lansing, were cousins of the Russians. This, it must be recorded, was exactly one calendar month after the War Cabinet had seen precisely the same thing — and before they had the example of the Czech revolt to encourage them.[11] But in Russia, American officials were being drawn into action over the Czech revolt by the simple pressure of events, and far ahead of their cautious President. This was largely due to the effect that the Czech revolt had had on the Russian opposition parties.

At the time of the failure of Savinkov's *coup* in early May, the 'Moscow

Centre', as already detailed, had split into three separate groups. The right wing, claiming to be guided solely by Russian interests (and arguing, like Lord Palmerston, that their country had permanent interests, but no permanent allies), now saw the Bolsheviks as Russia's real enemy, and were convinced that they could be overthrown with German help, or at any rate given German neutrality. The Allies, they argued, and especially England, were ready to support the Bolsheviks, if they would resume hostilities against Germany. The right wing, including the Cadet leader, Milyukov, and some right Cadets, after breaking away and forming the 'Right Centre', had begun negotiating with the Germans in Kiev. The other Cadets remained loyal to the Allies and linked themselves with the volunteer army in southern Russia; these were known as the 'National Centre'.

But the left Cadets, the right SRs, together with members of the 'co-operative movement', had formed the 'Left Centre', or 'Union for the Regeneration of Russia'. Their aims were twofold: to fight both Bolsheviks and Germans, which required the formation of a Russian army, and the co-operation of Allied troops; and to restore democratic principles in Russia and call a new constituent assembly. The new Russian government, they insisted, would not be a dictatorship (as would undoubtedly be the case if the volunteer army overcame the Bolsheviks), but a directorate of between three and five people, belonging to different parties but agreeing on a joint programme. This, of course, was a highly attractive idea to Allied officials and agents of various kinds looking for some group to support against the Bolsheviks; but it presumed the existence of democratic principles in Russia (which did not exist) and the ability of the different parties to unite, despite all evidence to date indicating that this would be very difficult to achieve. The French, however, decided to support the 'Left Centre'.[12]

At first, the 'Union for Regeneration' devoted itself to consolidation of all the anti-Bolshevik forces it could attract. A military centre was formed, which assumed leadership of the different officer organizations in Moscow, recruiting some for the proposed Russian army, sending others to the Russian provinces. 'According to the plans of the Union,' wrote a member in Paris in 1919, 'the sporadic armed clashes with the Bolsheviks, which at this time [late spring 1918] were occurring ... here and there, and being easily crushed by the Bolsheviks with the aid of the Germans [*sic*], were to give way at the most opportune moment to concentrated action on a large scale in a number of large cities simultaneously. The arrival of the Allies in more or less sufficient numbers was considered to be such a moment.'

But the Union lacked a proper military leader. An approach had been made to Boris Savinkov, which he had rejected (perhaps seeing through their democratic pretensions) probably just after his abortive *coup* of early May. Savinkov was now linked with the 'National Centre', and was preparing a better organized rising outside Moscow. The French decided to support him also. As early as mid-May, Lockhart had reported that

Savinkov's representatives had told him their organization was still too weak to act unless supported by Allied intervention; but the French had been in close contact with them and had told them that intervention had already been decided upon and would shortly take place. This was, of course, quite untrue.

The French were equally reckless in their support of the Union. From the outset, the Union maintained what it called 'regular relations and frequent contacts' with Allied officials in Moscow, Petrograd and Vologda, 'mainly through the French ambassador, Noulens'. Allied officials (and one should probably take this to mean French officials) were fully informed of the aims and membership of the Union, 'and quite frequently expressed their readiness to help in every way'. At one such meeting, Allied officials asked what the Russian people's attitude would be if Allied troops were landed on Russian soil to fight the Germans. Union representatives replied that they felt the Russian people would welcome an Allied landing, provided the Allied governments promised that Russian territory and sovereignty would not be impaired; that no new burdens, except actual fighting, would be imposed on Russia; and that after landing, the Allies would not interfere in Russian internal affairs, and would cooperate with the all-Russian government which would emerge from the anti-Bolshevik movement. The Allied officials, of course, found these conditions fully acceptable, 'and an agreement with the Allies was thus considered feasible'.

The most important question to be considered by the various Russian groups, except the pro-German 'Right Centre', was the reformation of the eastern front, with Allied support, as a base from which to attack the Germans; this was assumed to mean attacking the Bolsheviks too. Some sort of initial proposal seems to have been made in mid-May, very like the British proposal for a Japanese landing at Vladivostok and an advance through Siberia so as to form an anti-German front in the Urals, together with the Czechs and the volunteer army. (This seems to have occurred before the Czech revolt.) The Union approved this idea and worked out a plan, according to which, 'at a previously fixed time, all available forces were to be transferred to the neighbourhood of the region where the Allies proposed to land their troops, an insurrection was to be started, a new [Russian] government proclaimed, and a new [Russian] army mobilized to act in conjunction with the Allies'.

The Czech revolt speeded everything up. Early in June (it having been agreed at the Supreme War Council that the French should have 'charge of all activities in the [Russian] interior', and Balfour having instructed Lockhart to have nothing to do with Savinkov's plans), Noulens, the French ambassador, informed the leaders of the various Russian opposition groups that large-scale Allied intervention would take place before the end of June, and he promised to back this operation with substantial financial support. The time had come for action. His uprising, wrote Savinkov in Warsaw in

1920, 'could not take place in Moscow, since the Germans threatened to occupy the capital if the Bolsheviks were overthrown'. His aim was to cut off Moscow from Archangel, where the Allies proposed to land. He thus decided to seize Rybinsk and Yaroslavl (between Moscow and Vologda), Vladimir and Murom (where the Bolshevik *Stavka*, or GHQ, was located) to the east, and Kaluga, to the south. The Russian capital would then be isolated.

The effect of the Czech revolt on the Union is described by Union members in even more dramatic terms. 'The result was that, in addition to the volunteer army operating against the Bolsheviks in the South, there now appeared in the north-east a new force threatening the entire Volga line. ... Since the Allied missions [*sic*] assured us that we could expect in a short time the landing of a considerable Allied force in the North, it seemed to us that the eastern front had become a reality ...'. The Union decided to transfer its military organizations and forces out of Moscow, to the south and east. Of course, Noulens had no right to make such statements; there had been no Allied agreement on large-scale intervention.[12]

Noulens passed some of his information from Paris — in slightly more judicious and less inaccurate terms — to Francis, the American ambassador, at Vologda. This seems to have been on June 11 or 12. Francis had heard nothing from Washington. On the 13th, therefore, he wrote to Poole, the American consul in Moscow, saying that the French embassy in Vologda had heard from Paris 'that the Allied military conference in Paris [i.e. the Supreme War Council held on June 3] had agreed upon Russian intervention, but of course this is very secret; it contemplated landing of several battalions each of American, British, French and Italian troops at Archangel'.[13]

By June 15, Francis had more news from Noulens. Apparently as a result of a further wire from Paris, Francis learnt that on June 3 the Supreme War Council had decided to land Allied troops in northern Russia and had agreed, with the approval of the Czech national council, that the Czechs should remain in Russia for the present. In wiring this news to Consul Poole that same day, Francis underlined that the Allied military conference mentioned in his previous letter 'made specific mention of the Czechoslovak troops in Russia, and provided for their retention here for the present'. As Kennan points out, much of this information was inaccurate, the probable reason being that Francis misunderstood what Noulens was trying to tell him through an interpreter. There had been no agreement about intervention in northern Russia; it had simply been decided to deny the northern ports to the enemy. It was also known only to Allied officials in Russia that the Czech Legion had refused to allow part of their force to split off and go to the northern ports; a fact not known in London and Paris on June 3. The Czech national council in Paris had not approved the Supreme War Council's edict; it had merely been put to them as a recommendation. But Consul Poole naturally took the Supreme War Council's recommendation for part of the Czech Legion (allegedly *en route* for northern Russia, and to be retained there) to refer to the whole Czech Legion, now strung out along the Siberian railway and in possession of many important towns in Russia and Siberia.[13]

Noulens left for Moscow to give instructions (more or less openly) to the various groups opposed to the Bolsheviks. In a 'semi-official note' to the different Russian political organizations, he set out what he claimed were the Allied views on the Russian problem. 'The note', states a member of the Union (and this appears to be the only account we have of it), 'almost repeated the entire political programme of the Union and confirmed ... the readiness of the Allies to send an army ... to fight the Germans and the Bolsheviks. ... As a private opinion ... the note suggested a series of measures for the internal reorganization of Russia. Rejecting the possibility of an agreement with the Bolsheviks, the Allies urged ... the formation of an all-Russian coalition government in the form of a directory of three acting dictatorially until the constituent assembly should meet'. At a dinner party at General Lavergne's residence, Noulens met a French officer, Captain Bordes, just back from Samara, who gave a glowing account of events flowing from the Czech revolt: the enthusiasm of the local people towards the Czechs, the formation of the Samara government by SR members of the constituent assembly, the easy defeats over the Bolshevik Red Guards, etc. Noulens was highly impressed. He wired to Major Guinet (the senior French liaison officer with the western Czech group, then at Chelyabinsk), telling him to thank the Czechs, in the name of all the Allies, for their revolt. The Allies, Noulens said decisively, had decided to intervene in late June, 'and the Czech Army and French Mission form the advance guard of the Allied Army'. Technical and detailed orders would follow.[14]

On June 17, Poole received the message from Čeček, the Czech commander at Samara, which the American consul at Samara had had to forward to Moscow, since he was out of touch with Ambassador Francis at Vologda. (In this message, it will be recalled, Čeček explained the reasons for the Czech revolt, and asked for instructions on the next step to take.) In a covering note, the American consul at Samara said that it was 'indifferent to Czechs where they are to fight and that if the Allies so direct they will gladly remain in present position establishing new anti-German front along Volga. However, in the absence of other instructions, they will resume movement east as soon as railroad repaired which should be in a few days.' This wire was already a week old. Because of a local intelligence report that the Germans intended to counter the Czech revolt by seizing Moscow on the 21st (this report was quite wrong), Consul Poole decided that he had not enough time to consult his ambassador, let alone Washington. After discussing the matter with the French consul, Poole wired back to his colleague at Samara on the 18th, saying that he was to inform the Czech leaders that they could be assured of Allied political approval in retaining their present positions, and taking such action as the military situation might require. 'It is desirable first of all that they should secure control of the Trans-Siberian railroad, and second, if this is assumed at the same time possible, retain control over the territory where they now dominate.' Poole's colleague at Samara was to inform the French representative that the French consul joined in issuing these instructions. Thus the day after President Wilson thought he saw the 'shadow of a plan' when reading the wire from the American minister in Peking, urging that the Czechs be left in Siberia to control Siberia against the Germans, the Czech commanders received explicit political and military approval for such action from the American consul in Moscow — without a shred of authority. Neither Poole nor Francis (when he got to hear of it) reported the matter to the State Department. Kennan, surprisingly, devotes several pages to defending Poole's action, making great allowances for his 'youth, wartime enthusiasm, eagerness to make a contribution, and a willingness to risk the displeasure of [his] superiors if only the war effort could be thereby promoted'. The point is that this unauthorized initiative deeply affected the course of events which led up to President Wilson's final decision on intervention. Zeal, as Talleyrand makes clear, has little to do with diplomacy. One wonders if Kennan would have been quite as tender towards a young British consul acting as Poole did.[14]

The Bolsheviks, meanwhile, were taking decided action to counter the feverish activity of the opposition parties unleashed by the Czech revolt. On June 14, the Mensheviks and right SRs were formally expelled from all soviets. The next day, Chicherin wired to the Murmansk and Archangel soviets demanding that all Allied warships should leave the northern Russian ports immediately, in view of possible hostile action which the British and their Allies might take in support of the Czech revolt. The Murmansk soviet refused to comply with this demand, on the grounds that they were too weak to force the Allies to take action, that the Allies were defending the region from the Germans and Finns, and that the local population supported the Allies. The more disciplined Archangel soviet instructed the British armed icebreaker, which had escorted the two food ships that had been lying unloaded for two months in Archangel harbour, to sail forthwith.[14]

The Bolsheviks also took action against Noulens himself, their most powerful enemy, whom they proceeded to turn into their best ally. Probably knowing that Noulens was exaggerating the imminence of Allied intervention, and certainly having their own agents in the opposition parties, they began, at about this time, to use *agents provocateurs* to spring the internal plots, timed to coincide with the Allies' intervention, before they landed. This might seem a highly risky business, but was sanctified by

Russian tradition and had long been practised under the Tsars. It is thus well to examine with care what Noulens is alleged, from now on, to have told the opposition parties. The Bolsheviks also occasionally managed to plant agents among Allied officials, for instance, on both the politically inexperienced Captain Cromie, and on Noulens himself (his interpreter during his mid-June visit to Moscow was Réné Marchand, Moscow correspondent of *Le Figaro*, who a few months later openly went over to the Bolshevik party).

On June 7, Bolshevik trade delegates arrived in Berlin in an attempt to settle by negotiation matters outstanding between the Bolshevik and German governments. (Of chief concern to both sides was the destination of the Russian and Ukrainian harvests and grain supplies.) Their coming arrival in Berlin was known in London. It had accordingly been decided by Lord Robert Cecil, while still Minister of Blockade, to counter this by sending out to Russia a British commercial mission, ostensibly to advise the British government on the 'best means of restoring and developing British trade relations with and interests in Russia and of countering enemy schemes of commercial penetration', since Cecil had privately admitted that we had 'very scanty knowledge of the real economic situation and prospects in Russia'.

In fact, this mission, under the impression that England had acquired legal control of the Russian and Siberian grain trade, and hence of these same harvests and grain supplies (for which both Germans and Bolsheviks were negotiating), sailed for Russia the same day (June 7) to subvert these German–Bolshevik negotiations by offering to supply the Russian market with certain essential goods at reasonable prices — until Allied intervention overthrew the Bolshevik regime. Thereupon the bank schemes could be implemented, and British control of the Russian grain trade, and hence of much of the economy, would ensure overwhelming British influence over any new regime. The Bolsheviks, in fact, would soon fall, and it was essential to be ready to move in before the French.

Heading the British mission was Sir William H. Clark, comptroller-general of the Department of Overseas Trade (described by Thomas Jones as a 'biggish' man, 'once LG's Secretary at the Treasury, then jumped to a high post in India (which he failed in) then came back here to the Board of Trade. ... He is not a "great" man but he understands LG and knows the ropes ...'). Clark was to be assisted by Leslie Urquhart, who had recently alarmed Lloyd George with the idea that the Germans were trying to get across to the Caspian and use the Volga Fleet to bring down the Siberian food and produce, as well as copper and zinc from the Urals; he had also told the Prime Minister that a small force like the Czechs 'could go straight through Russia like a hot knife through butter'. It was Urquhart who had effectively initiated the second British proposal for intervention, made by the War Cabinet on May 17. Other members of this mission were H. A. Armistead (of the Hudson Bay Company, who had dealt in Russian trade throughout his life), and F. Lambert (of Messrs James Whishaw, a firm long established in Russia). Attached to the mission, with special responsibility for looking into the Russian bank schemes on behalf of the Treasury, was Dominick Spring-Rice, the assistant city editor of the (right-wing) *Morning Post.* Spring-Rice, then aged 29, was almost certainly an emissary of Dudley Ward, the Treasury's representative on the powerful Russia committee, under Lord Robert Cecil's chairmanship; he had contributed various articles on banking and economic matters to the *Economist* while Dudley Ward was assistant editor.[15]

The Treasury were still baffled by the ramifications of the bank deals. In early May, 'Pollyglot' (one of Poliakov's code-names) had, for instance, wired this explanation of 'Tindal' (possibly the code-name for the project for sending roubles down to the Don Cossacks early in 1918, which had become thoroughly confused, through cross-payments, with the purchase of the Russian banks). 'In this case Leech declares being only cover for transaction between Keyes and LW [i.e. 'live-wire', the code-name for Jaroszynski], the latter, having in December put roubles at Leech's disposal for Keyes, is entitled to receive pounds promised independently of the fact if transfer effected or not by bank. LW asked for these pounds to be put in Leech's name, but this is their own private business and concerns only themselves. I find however that immediate steps must be taken to secure possibility for Keyes of reclaiming transfer of fifteen million, which owing to conditions in the South will undoubtedly not now be paid out. Leech declares for this he will do everything possible to get Coates with transfer back, and in this case to pass transfer with his blanco endorsement to mission. The above statement has been countersigned by Leech who thereby admits your right to dispose of this fund. Leech states that pounds in question already sold here.' (This, of course, referred to the second draft for 15 million roubles which had been sent down to southern Russia to prop up the south-eastern union — now restored under Krasnov and the Germans; Coates was the former British embassy cashier, the messenger with the draft.)

But without a great deal of background knowledge, such a telegram was baffling and the disappearance of all this money in highly irregular fashion greatly disquieted the Treasury. They were sending the man from the *Morning Post* to sort things out. The mission had also been bidden by Lord Robert Cecil to consider 'as a matter of urgency the practical steps to be taken to supply the Russian market with limited quantities of certain necessary goods at reasonable prices, as a method of propaganda'.[16]

Shortly before the British commercial mission sailed, together with Lindley — now returning to Russia as British high commissioner — yet more money had to be paid into the London bank account of Hugh Leech, the contact man and British propaganda agent, who was already beginning to look like a convenient scapegoat for anything that had gone wrong with the bank schemes. On June 1, the Treasury — with a good deal of reluctance, one imagines, but almost certainly prompted by Lord Robert Cecil — paid no less than £428,000 into Leech's account with the London City and Midland Bank, this being the first instalment on the purchase price of the Siberian bank, which money was destined for the Russian banker Denisov, who had had a majority holding in the Siberian bank. The possibilities of the Germans somehow obtaining produce and minerals from Siberia undoubtedly influenced this decision.[16]

What was Germany's exact position in Russia at this moment? Counsellor Riezler gives a good account in a diary entry for June 8: 'Terror is increasing. Famine. The Bolsheviks are trying to drown the famine with violent measures against the peasants. There is an Allied plot with the St Petersburg mine [-sweeping] divisions [i.e. the destroyers], the right-wing SRs, the Mensheviks. Detours and evasions by Trotsky. The Bolsheviks have once again overcome the critical moment by numerous executions and increasing, quiet terror. In the provinces, however, the situation is bad: between Penza and Tomsk, the whole of the [Siberian] railway is in the hands of the Czechs, who consider themselves as being under the protection of the *Entente*. We consider this an intolerable situation. Therefore the Bolsheviks are like a football, which is kicked about between the two powers with menacing notes. The economic situation is becoming more and more desperate; the country can bear very much: a slow mass of people used to endurance and confusion.'

Riezler considered the future: 'The question is now: should we allow the Bolsheviks to crumble away into a state of chaos leading towards the *Entente*; should we risk the (probably not very stable) rebirth of a better order, without us or against us; or should we take the rebirth of Russia, which we have just destroyed, into our hands; should we be paid for the reunion of the Ukraine with Russia, which will take place anyway one day, and with elementary power, with a [trade] treaty and with economic hegemony? And if so, when will the time be ripe? If politics have ever sailed into unknown waters. ... Since the installation of Skoropadsky, the line we entered on with the peace of Brest has been undoubtedly bent. Only Russia's eventual restoration, or jumping from one position to the next, remains possible. But one can break one's neck at this any moment.'

Reizler concluded with a vignette of life in Moscow: 'Last night, we attended a very strange dinner with Ivan Sergeievich Chukin. When we arrived, all the guests were gathered downstairs in the cloakroom, watched over by a rough looking soldier, a police raid by the Commission on Speculation. In the end, we went upstairs, but the old man was waiting and watching what the soldiers were going to do, the whole family was frightened, and they kept apologizing to their guests. The soldiers very slowly made off ... and it took them so long that we started dining in the end. After all that, we had an excellent dinner with lovely wine. In the end, the soldiers go away, the atmosphere improves, speeches, everybody assures us with submissiveness and exuberance that they have always loved Germany, and will continue with the [trade] treaty etc. It was all very embarrassing and typically Russian. It is too frightening to imagine that we could have spoken in a similar fashion if the British had won and had cut us to pieces.'[17]

Ludendorff was bitterly opposed to negotiating with the Bolsheviks. Any Russian supplies or raw materials required by Germany should be seized by Germany, or acquired from pro-German Russians, he felt. On June 9, therefore, as he launched a further attack in France to link up the German salients at Amiens and on the Marne (and as the German Treasury was considering a Foreign Ministry request for a further 40 million marks to maintain the Bolsheviks in power), Ludendorff wrote a long and detailed paper to Kühlmann (it was little short of a diktat) on how he thought Germany should break the Allied blockade by obtaining the necessary supplies and raw materials from the former Russian empire.[17]

Because of the shortage of manpower, he began, he had had to withdraw even more German divisions from Russia. Those remaining were sufficient for occupation duties only; they would be unable to cope if the Russian situation deteriorated. Germany must, in any case, find new allies in the former eastern theatre, because of the 'obscure policy of the weak soviet government'. In the North, Finland had strengthened its military position as a result of German intervention. 'We may hope that we shall find strong military support there whatever happens', wrote Ludendorff. But the Ukraine, which was 'essential to our survival and to our supply of raw materials', had not succeeded in building up its own army. German troops must therefore be used in the Ukraine. He then turned to the Caucasus, and particularly to Georgia, a Christian state, whose hopes Germany had long been raising. Georgia must be recognized and protected and a Georgian army organized. 'If Georgia is our advanced base, it is to be hoped that the Caucasian territory will be gradually pacified and that we should be able to draw from there the raw materials we so urgently need.' But the Turks were also active in the Caucasus, where raw materials meant the Baku oil. Georgia must therefore be protected from the 'greedy Turks', who must also be denied the Tiflis–Baku railway and Baku itself. The railway from Batoum via Tiflis to Djulfa in the south was, however, vital for Turkish operations on the Mesopotamian front, and this must be made secure for Turkey. 'The guiding principle should be that Turkey should not hinder the development of the Georgian army and the provision of raw materials from the Caucasus', stated Ludendorff firmly. Germany should also make contact with the Caucasus Cossacks, and investigate the situation in Armenia and her bitterly hostile neighbour, Muslim Azerbaijan.[18]

Ludendorff then spoke of the Bolshevik government itself, whose 'dishonourable endeavours' he regarded with the 'gravest distrust'. He listed the Bolsheviks' use of German prisoners in Russia, their support of the Finnish Red Guards in Finland, their 'preferential treatment' of the Allies on the Murmansk railway, and the presence of the Russian warships in Novorossisk, all coupled with their desire to restore economic relations with Germany. 'Especially annoying' was their attitude towards the Czechs, claimed Ludendorff; instead of disarming them 'as agreed', they either armed them or allowed them to proceed to both the Murmansk and the Siberian railways, both of which the Allies wished them to occupy in order to 'dominate Russia'. (This had been the original British intention in mid-May.) Then, he claimed, the Bolsheviks 'went through a *volte-face* and suddenly declared that the Czechoslovak troops wanted to disarm. Their mendacity thus came into the open.' (This is inaccurate, and merely demonstrates that under war-time stress, people are more prone than ever to believe what they wish.)[18]

Recently, Bolshevik claims had only increased when they discovered that German troops would not cross the demarcation line. They were in fact adopting the same tactics as at the start of the Brest–Litovsk negotiations, that is, delaying decisions that were important for Germany, and working against Germany as often as they could. 'We can expect nothing from this government,' went on Ludendorff, 'although it lives by our mercy. It is a lasting danger to us which will diminish only when it recognizes us unconditionally as the Supreme Power and becomes pliable through its fear of Germany and concern for its own existence. Therefore a strong and ruthless treatment of this government appears to me still to be indicated.' Basic German demands must be unconditionally and swiftly complied with so as to avoid 'unpleasant surprises' in the East.

So far, the Bolshevik government had not proved that it could rule its own territory; and there were 'powerful trends' working against it, of which Germany had to take note, and with which it must entertain relations, 'in order not to find ourselves suddenly high and dry'. They must in fact acquire contacts with the right-wing monarchist groups that (Ludendorff wrongly claimed) the Allies were also supporting.

In view of the importance of Ludendorff's comments, it is necessary to consider the points he raises individually. (Finland, his first point, will be dealt with later.) First, the Caucasus. After the Bolshevik revolution and Russian armistice, two new powers had emerged in the Caucasus: the Transcaucasian commissariat (mainly Menshevik) at Tiflis in Georgia, with delegates from all three Caucasus states — Georgia, Armenia and

Azerbaijan; and the (mainly Armenian) Bolshevik soviet at the oil centre of Baku. The Transcaucasian commissariat had arranged an armistice with Turkey on December 5, but the Turks kept pushing on into the Caucasus. The British government thereupon decided to support loyal Russian forces in the area, who would agree to fight on against Germany and Turkey, and to set up Georgian and Armenian states to prevent the enemy spreading a Muslim movement eastwards towards India, Major-General Dunsterville was appointed head of the British mission to the Caucasus charged with implementing this policy; but soon after setting out from Baghdad in late January, he encountered such difficulties in northern Persia that he was unable to reach the shores of the Caspian until early in June. The British government therefore fell back on the distribution of subsidies. But the strong racial antagonisms in the Caucasus defeated these efforts also. As soon as the local British mission began to hand out money to the various national groups, as well as to the local Russian command, Turkish and German agents spread the news that the British were only financing the Armenians. Thus the Russian Muslim troops, who were the Armenians' bitter enemies, were easily induced to hold up Russian troop trains on the Tiflis–Baku railway, and seize their arms to defend themselves against the Armenians. Finally, when Armenian troops massacred the inhabitants of some Kurdish villages, British financial support to all local parties had to be stopped.[19]

Early in April, when the Transcaucasian commissariat refused to recognize the Brest–Litovsk treaty (which ceded Batoum, Ardaghan and Kars, north-east of Erzerum, to Turkey) and declared that they were independent of Russia and wished to make their own peace with Turkey and Germany, the Turks, under Nuri Pasha, renounced the treaty and advanced further into the Caucasus to occupy Armenia and set up a Muslim state of Azerbaijan on the western shore of the Caspian, with its capital at Baku, then under Armenian Bolshevik control. A further massacre of Armenians seemed inevitable. The final Turkish objective was to seize the Persian coast, on the southern shore of the Caspian, rally all Muslims in the Caucasus, Transcaspia and Turkestan, and descend on India. But during a brief peace between the Transcaucasian commissariat and the Turks early in May, Georgia appealed to Germany. The Germans, eager to keep the 'greedy Turks' from Baku, whose precious oil they wanted for themselves, sent a small force, which landed in Georgia on May 25. The next day, as the Transcaucasian commissariat was dissolved, and Georgia, Armenia and Azerbaijan declared their independence, Dunsterville requested permission to land a British detachment at Baku to help to organize the local Bolshevik forces in the face of an anticipated Turkish attack. The War Cabinet's eastern committee turned this request down on May 28, on the grounds that Dunsterville's task was to maintain a barrier against a Turkish advance into Persia; any forward move to Baku would weaken the Persian barrier. On June 4, Turkey made peace with Georgia, and with that part of Armenia which they had not already seized. The Turks were now free to march, with their Azerbaijani allies, on the oil town of Baku. A clash between the Germans and Turks in the Caucasus was thus imminent; Georgia had given full transit rights on the Caucasus railway to Turkey, but control of the railway to Germany.[20]

Ludendorff's next point, namely Bolshevik recruitment of German prisoners in Russia, was only a minor irritant to the German High Command; forceful protests were made, but there was never any question of taking further action. Ludendorff's eagerness to make contact with Russian right-wing monarchist groups was much more significant — and was in fact considerably understated in his paper to Kühlmann. Conversations with the Cadet leader Milyukov and the 'Right Centre' in Kiev were certainly under way, but they had no force at their elbow. General Krasnov, Ataman of the Don Cossacks, had.

On the day of his accession as Ataman (May 18), General Krasnov wrote a letter to the Kaiser asking for German recognition of the independent Don republic. On June 5, before a reply was received, Krasnov proclaimed publicly that the Don was an independent state, until such time as Russia was once more united. This suited the Germans well. The original purpose of their advance into the Don country was to occupy the Donetz coal fields so as to ensure fuel for the Ukrainian railways. But when they saw that Krasnov was well-disposed to them, the Germans thought they could secure political as well as economic control of south-eastern Russia. On June 11, an envoy arrived from the German commander at Kiev to inform Krasnov of the Kaiser's views on the Russian situation. There was to be no restoration of united Russia. The former Russian empire was to be divided into four separate independent states: the Ukraine, the south-eastern union, central Russia and Siberia. Krasnov's task was to organize the south-eastern union, expel the pro-Allied Volunteer Army from the Don, and support Germany if the Allies managed to restore the eastern front.

Krasnov's envoy in Kiev warned him that their position was far from good, since the Don was between the hammer and the anvil; the Germans, if they wished, could give part of the Don to the Ukraine and leave the other part to be plundered by the Red Guards. But they had 'one enormous advantage, possessed by neither Moscow nor Kiev and we should use it in full measure'. The Germans were puzzled by the Don Cossacks. 'As one representative of the German command puts it, we are a "Sphinx" to them.' On the one hand, the Germans would like to help the Don Cossacks to secure their good will and material advantages; but they were afraid that the Cossacks, once strong again, might do them harm. At present, the Germans were finding it 'rather difficult' to control the Ukrainian peasant movement; as the Ukrainian government could not deliver the agreed quota of grain, German troops had to seize it in the villages and were meeting considerable opposition. So the Germans were forced to send not three, but six army corps to occupy the Ukraine, and would need still more in reinforcements. 'Naturally, under such circumstances, the Germans have no desire to arouse the hostility of the Cossacks and thus to find themselves under the necessity of sending one or two more army corps and of weakening the western front.'[21]

Krasnov's envoy in Kiev advised him to refrain from expressing any hope of seeing Russia once again united; to maintain correct relations with the 'uninvited guests' now in the Don; and to have no relations with their former allies, 'who thus far have given us nothing and in many ways have betrayed us. They can give us no aid and the Germans will see to it that their influence does not extend beyond the Urals.' In return, the Germans would supply all necessary arms and military equipment; settle the Don boundaries with Kiev and Moscow; and help organize the south-eastern union. Krasnov accepted these terms, and thus secured German recognition and support.[22]

The German request for the expulsion of the volunteer army from the Don required some diplomacy by Krasnov. He had paid a visit to their commander, General Denikin, at his headquarters, south-east of Novocherkask, on May 28. The meeting was acrimonious. Denikin strongly deprecated any contact whatsoever with the Germans. Krasnov said it was too late to change his plans. Denikin demanded a single command. Krasnov said that would depend on Denikin's plans — Krasnov, of course, was in much the stronger position. If the volunteer army would attack Tsaritsin, on the lower Volga, he would place any available Cossacks under Denikin's command. Now was the time to strike; while a move northwards would give the volunteer army a proper Russian base, far away from petty intrigues in the Kuban. But Denikin refused, on the grounds that this would involve him with the Germans. Finally, they agreed simply on their common opposition to the Bolsheviks. Denikin would proceed with his campaign to liberate the Kuban; once the capital, Ekaterinodar, had been freed, a joint attack on Tsaritsin could be reconsidered. The question of a single command would be held over; for the present, the volunteer army would be responsible for protecting the southern frontier of the Don against the Bolsheviks. For this, Krasnov undertook to supply Denikin with finance, arms, ammunition and supplies (which, of course, came from the Germans). The two men parted, and Denikin prepared to set out for the Kuban.

But later, when some Cossack officers began to complain of Krasnov's German orientation and set off to join Denikin, and while rumours spread that the Czechs were restoring the eastern front and had taken Saratov, Tsaritsin and Astrakhan on the lower Volga (these reports were untrue), the German command in Kiev became alarmed. Krasnov was required to give an undertaking that no Czechs would be allowed into the Don country, and that if German and Czech troops clashed, the Don Cossacks would remain neutral. To see that Krasnov kept to this undertaking, the German command in Kiev formed two pro-German Russian 'volunteer' forces, called the 'Southern Army' and the Astrakhan Corps, of some 7,000 officers and men. These were described as 'thoroughgoing monarchist organizations', which flew the Romanov flag, wore the Romanov colours (black, orange and white) on their sleeves, and printed millions of old Tsarist roubles. With their support, Krasnov pressed on towards Tsaritsin on the Volga, and Voronezh — half-way to Moscow.

Ludendorff thus had a well-prepared force to oust the Bolsheviks from power, or to ensure a smooth transition of power to the right-wing Russian groups, if the Bolsheviks fell. But German plans for the formation of a south-eastern union, as a separate Russian state, were to prove as illusory as they had to the British and French early in 1918. The various small groups, tribesmen and mountaineers, failed to unite; but Krasnov succeeded in concealing this fact from the Germans.[22]

Ludendorff had also complained of the presence of part of the Black Sea Fleet in Novorossisk, and of their refusal to return to Sebastopol, as agreed under the Brest–Litovsk treaty. On June 10, while a Bolshevik commissar was on his way to Novorossisk with secret orders to have the Russian warships there blown up, Trotsky sent a wire *en clair* (which the Germans would be expected to intercept) saying that they were to be back in Sebastopol by the 19th. But the Germans issued an ultimatum that if they were not back by the 15th, and certain border incidents rectified, German troops would seize Novorossisk. In Petrograd, there was much uncertainty. 'Captain Behrens [the Bolshevik naval chief of staff] lately approached a group of prominent anti-Bolshevik officers whose confidence I have,' wired Cromie to the Admiralty on the 19th, 'asking their advice and aid to destroy Black Sea Fleet as his delegation failed to get sailors' confidence. These officers in turn approached Le Page and myself as to our opinion whether B. and the party he represents were bona-fide in their desire for destruction and the best means of using this offer. B. is unaware of our support to the agent selected to whom he has promised every aid. Military Intelligence telegram Moscow to London 18th states on 17th Sablin [Commander-in-Chief, Black Sea Fleet, then in Petrograd] on his own responsibility sent wireless message to Tikhmenyeff SNO [at Novorossisk] ordering immediate destruction. Message which is known to be against [Bolshevik] government['s] wishes was acknowledged.' This wire gives some idea of the confusion in Petrograd about the fate of the Black Sea Fleet.[23]

It was the same in Novorossisk, where the Bolshevik commissar from Moscow could not get his orders for the destruction of the warships obeyed. Amidst tumultuous scenes, the acting Commander-in-Chief, Tikhmenyeff, with the support of his officers, ordered all his ships to prepare to return to Sebastopol. The crews of the two battleships and some of the destroyers decided to obey, those of the other destroyers and small vessels adamantly refused to do so. Crowds gathered round the few doubtful ships, and a howling mob swarmed aboard one of the battleships and induced her engine-room complement not to put to sea. Finally, one battleship, together with some destroyers and small vessels, sailed back to Sebastopol, while the other battleship was torpedoed by a destroyer and sunk; the other seven destroyers scuttled themselves.[23]

In Moscow, the Bolsheviks were furious at being tricked by the Russian naval officers in the Black Sea, and decided to issue a sharp warning to any of their brother officers who might have similar ideas about the Baltic Fleet. On the 20th, Admiral Chastny, former Commander, Baltic Fleet, whom Trotsky had arrested on May 25, was hurriedly brought to trial on a charge of disclosing Trotsky's secret wire of May 21 (in which he directed that the Baltic sailors were to be bribed to blow up their ships if necessary), and of distributing forged documents (similar to the 'Sisson' documents) to discredit the Bolshevik government. In an emotional harangue, Trotsky — the sole prosecution witness (none of Chastny's witnesses was allowed to testify) — did his best to extricate himself from his involvement in the Allied plot over the Baltic Fleet and heaped abuse on Chastny, 'a very dangerous counter-revolutionary, whom I think should be punished without mercy'. Trotsky's speech reads very hollowly. But the Supreme Revolutionary Tribunal condemned Chastny to death, and the sentence was carried out immediately. The Second Congress of Soviets had in fact abolished the death penalty, and two left SRs (whose party was strongly against it) were prevented from taking their seats in the tribunal, two Bolsheviks being deputed to take their places. It was a rigged trial — it was either Chastny or Trotsky. Captain Cromie reported that the death sentence was 'solely due to Trotsky's efforts. Apathy [of] general staff incredible', he added. 'Sentence reported carried out at dawn 22nd, await outbreak on part of Lyeviesers [?Lissanevitch, the destroyer commander in the Baltic] against Bolsheviks.' But nothing happened — save for the murder of Volodarsky, the Bolshevik press commissar, by persons unknown. At this, Uritsky, head of the Petrograd cheka, made what Lockhart calls a 'disgusting attack' on England. 'He accuses us of organizing Volodarsky's murder. I sent in a fairly stormy note to the Bolsheviks', he records in his diary. But whoever was responsible, it seems clear that Volodarsky was murdered in retaliation for the murder of Chastny.[24]

In July, Colonel Joe Boyle, who had previously bribed the Black Sea Fleet sailors to sabotage their ships, received a visit, while ill in hospital in Roumania, from four sailors who had come to collect their money. When they saw he was somewhat hesitant, as well he might be, they drew knives and threatened to kill him. Boyle gave them one cheque for £150,000 for the battleship they claimed to have sunk, and one for £120,000 for the seven destroyers; he would pay them the balance, he said, when he was up and about, and could make further enquiries. They said his cheques (drawn on the local military attaché's personal account with Holt's Bank, Pall Mall) would be presented in the United States, and they asked him to name a guarantor there. Boyle gave them the name of his son, who was working in the Klondyke gold mines. (It is impossible to make out how Boyle calculated these payments.)[25]

So ended the struggle for the Black Sea Fleet. The Germans got a battleship and a few destroyers. But the struggle for the much more crucial Baltic Fleet continued apace. On June 24, the Admiralty received a lengthy report from Cromie, despatched on the 15th, which outlined the position on intervention as well. 'Following from Vinogradoff our chief agent', began Cromie with appalling indiscretion. 'Businessmen in contact with Germans state latter do not intend to advance or permit the Finns to advance on Pet[rogra]d until Allies make a definite [?landing in] North, as Germans find they can gain more by political intrigue than by their open offensive which they now seem to regret. If Germans make first move, the [Russian] press will be probably pro-Ally, but it is organized by Germany ready to agitate against an intervention on the part of Allies. Germans do not now wish to seize [Baltic] Fleet by force, but hope to gradually obtain [its] possession by 'Germanizing' Russia. This is probably in progress, judging by the way in which Russian sailors are leaving while Estonians remain. If Allies do not intervene, Germany hopes to gradually obtain all she requires by intrigue, but she thinks the Czechoslav affair the first step of Allied campaign. The success of the movement appears to afford satisfaction to a large section of populace.'[26]

Cromie then gave extracts from Vinogradoff's report. If the destruction of the Baltic Fleet was to be assured, there must be 'real action' at Kronstadt. 'You hope to get Russian material to back you up; if you do not wish to lose this possibility you must go on, if not, it will be too late and all is lost. Every day Russia becomes softer and weaker and by herself is worth nothing, but with an outside impulse may be reborn. If you do not come, Russia will turn to Germany, whom she sees approaching slowly but surely. Russia's future will be decided not in years and months, but in weeks and days. If you do not come you lose, if you come later than a month, you will find only wadding and sand and will need too many of your own forces. You have our sympathies now, but lose them every day by your indecision and you lose even more, Russia's faith in England. If your strength is not a thing of the past, you must move on and move quickly. When you move you will start much agitation against England [but] you [will] awake all who are friends, if [you] come too late you lose these friends with faith in England. All your losses are German gains. ... I regret this letter, but I must say it, I feel the moment critical and possible result irremediable. You [i.e. Cromie] do not know Russia and you do not understand [not you personally] the moment.'

Cromie commented as follows: 'From personal observation and that of my staff the above is only too true. England's great prestige in Russia is falling daily and that of Germany ascending. Russia has been led to expect intervention in the North (but this idea has not been propagated from this office) and is building her hopes on it. I submit with all respect and perhaps knowledge that the present apparent indecisive policy is doing more than anything else to ruin England's present and future prestige and will undoubtedly affect future relations between the two countries. Intervention on a thorough scale is the only thing that will save the situation and Russia, and I repeat that forces raised locally cannot be relied on unless each unit is stiffened by at least 25 per cent Allied troops.' Cromie's message remained the same: only intervention on a 'thorough scale' in northern Russia would prevent the gradual Germanization of all Russia — including the Baltic Fleet.[26]

9

The coming Intervention: northern Russia and Siberia

On June 18, President Wilson told Marcel Delanney (the new French ambassador to Tokyo, then in Washington, and the bearer of a personal note from Clemenceau in favour of Siberian intervention) that he was reconsidering the question, and would make known his decision within ten days. The British and French governments, unaware that the President had seen the 'shadow of a plan' in the telegram from Peking urging that the Czechs be left to 'control' Siberia, assumed that American policy was veering towards the setting up of an Allied commission to Russia and Siberia, under the leadership of Herbert Hoover; in other words, that intervention in Russia and Siberia was to be turned down.

At the Prime Minister's mid-morning discussion on the 19th, Lord Milner reported that in spite of the efforts of Marcel Delanney and General Berthelot (who was also in Washington), the President still refused to sanction Japanese intervention in Siberia. Milner urged the need for action. The Japanese were probably now prepared to go in 'with very slight encouragement', although they would want something better than a demand for a series of pledges on their intentions, unaccompanied by any promise of support. Milner thought it urgent 'to have another try at the Americans'.[1]

The Prime Minister urged the need for weighing very carefully the danger of setting Russia against us, which would be the inevitable result of sole Japanese intervention. 'This was one of the cases where a mistake might prove fatal. If Germany once got the gigantic manpower of Russia into her hands, the Allies would be bankrupt', he warned. The right thing, he reflected, would have been to have used the Czechs 'as a nucleus of a democratic anti-Bolshevik movement in Siberia, which could have formed a government, and then invited the Japanese in to help. ... If Siberia was once in hand', the Prime Minister went on, 'it might be possible to save Russia as well, especially as Siberia controlled the food supply. What was needed was somebody who could help organize and inspire such a movement, someone like Chinese Gordon, with a streak of genius in him.'

212

The names of General Knox and Leslie Urquhart were suggested, the idea being that they, with certain other officers and plenty of money at their disposal, should make their way into Siberia as civilians, reverting to military rank if the situation developed favourably.

On June 20, the British public had more news of the Czech revolt, when *The Times* printed a report, sent from Stockholm on the 19th (which had originally come from Petrograd via Berlin), that Czech and Russian troops were seizing Ufa and Ekaterinburg in the Urals, and Omsk and Tomsk further east. (The first part of this report was wrong; Ufa and Ekaterinburg were not seized until July, but, in view of the paucity of news of the Czech revolt to date, a little exaggeration in the other direction can have done no harm.) Next day, the central Czech group, held up west of Lake Baikal, and consequently prevented from joining their comrades who had got through to Vladivostok, launched a strong attack, under their commander Rudolph Gajda, on the Bolshevik stronghold of Irkutsk. On the 22nd, Major Guinet, the French liaison officer at Chelyabinsk, received the wire from Noulens thanking the Czechs, in the name of all the Allies, for their revolt, and informing them that Allied intervention would take place in late June, and that the Czech Legion and the French mission formed the advance guard of the Allied army. This undoubtedly encouraged the Czechs enormously. They now had a definite aim, in the vanguard of the coming Allied attack. On the 24th, their local paper openly described the Czech Legion as the Allied vanguard. They were to restore the eastern front against the Germans on the Volga, and an Allied army would come to their aid, via Vologda and Viatka.[2]

The Foreign Office, meanwhile, were even more embittered than the War Office at the evident failure of their efforts to secure Japanese intervention through American consent. On June 21, Ian Malcolm, Balfour's private secretary, abruptly terminated his summary of the telegrams and correspondence since December 7, 1917, on Allied intervention in eastern Russia, as he called it, with a stinging attack on both America and Japan — which probably reflects real, as opposed to official, Foreign Office feeling on the subject. The real reasons for the failure of the negotiations to secure military action in Siberia did not appear in the exchanges quoted in the summary, he wrote; they were to be found elsewhere. 'The obstinacy of President Wilson must be attributed, not to the lack of any effort or argument on our part to secure his cooperation, but rather to his own sincere belief that his reputation as a Prince of Peace will be jeopardised if he mixes himself up with a policy which he believes will end in annexations and interference with the domestic concerns of Russia. But he also has his eye on the November elections, which already threaten to go against him, and will certainly do so if he holds out the hand of confidence to Japan. The American hatred of all yellow races is thinly, if at all, disguised; the very thought of the yellows being brought in to redress the balance of the whites is repugnant to them, especially when it may involve the consequent loss of commercial advantages in the new and lucrative market of East Russia.'[3] This was why our cogent arguments to President Wilson had fallen upon intentionally deaf ears. 'If reasons could have satisfied him, he was supplied with them in abundance; what he needs are votes and a reputation for consistency at all costs. Therefore he has hardened his heart and will not let his people go to East Russia, though he apparently consents to intervention at Murmansk where there is no 'colour' complication.'

Malcolm was equally scathing about Japan:

'She makes no secret of her power and readiness and intention to swoop down upon Siberia if and when it may suit her to do so. Like other 'young' nations (including America), she prefers playing a "lone hand". Her geographical position suits that kind of game; her working knowledge of alliances is small and not altogether satisfactory. She complains that England has suspicions of her; she rehearses our alleged exertions, at the beginning of the war, to confine her activities to the Yellow Sea; our action in connection with Tsing-tao;* our insistence on guarantees that, if she intervenes in East Russia, her occupation shall be temporary, her territorial gains nil, and the scope of her operations extended to meet our dangers in India. For these reasons, and feeling that she is of the Alliance rather than in it, she procrastinates: at one moment she is breast high for intervention as guardian of the peace of the Far Eastern world, but it must not be "mixed", for that would wound the susceptibilities of a sensitive people. At another moment, when her dignity is smoothed by the flattering invitation to act as mandatory of the Allies, she readily accepts [*sic*], ... but suddenly backs out of the engagement (remembering her ancient wounds at our hands) on the grounds that she cannot move without the assistance of American money and metals, which she knows very well that she will never get.

It is quite conceivable that the system on which she plays her war game is that, when all talk of international intervention has passed, she can enter and occupy as much or as little of Siberia as she chooses, building up for herself a position of immense political and commercial importance east of the Ural mountains, whilst Russia lies dying and the great powers of Europe are killing one another on the western front. That is quite a straightforward, oriental method of revenge against America, who dislikes her, and England, who distrusts her.'[3]

---

*In August 1914, Japan declared war on Germany; and in November, with British help, seized the German port of Tsing-tao, in the bay of Kiaochow, in northern China, violating Chinese neutrality. The Japanese, encouraged by the benevolent attitude of the Western Allies, decided to press their advantage; and in January 1915, they presented the Chinese government secretly with '21 Demands', which would have completely subordinated China to Japan. Four of the five groups of 'demands' were accepted by China; but the fifth group, which required the Chinese government to appoint Japanese political, military and financial advisers, was not enforced due to British mediation. The Japanese resented this British interference.

This was an emotional outburst; but emotion, not military arguments, had in fact formed the basis of the British appeal to President Wilson. Clemenceau, however, now played his trump card with the President. On the 23rd, he had Foch (to whose military opinions the President paid the greatest heed) despatch this telegram to President Wilson:

> J'apprends de source sûre que les Allemands ont rappelé de Russie un certain nombre de Divisions dans les dernières semaines. Cela parait être un argument militaire décisif en faveur de l'intervention des Alliés en Sibérie puisque ces divisions sont à destination du front occidental. Foch.

> I learn from a reliable source that the Germans in the last few weeks have recalled a certain number of divisions from Russia. This appears to be a decisive military argument in favour of Allied intervention in Siberia since these divisions are destined for the Western Front. Foch.

Clemenceau sent a copy of this telegram to Lloyd George.[4]

On June 24, the Japanese ambassador handed Balfour a reply to his note of the 7th, drawn up as a result of the Supreme War Council's note of June 3, which asked if Japan would agree to intervene in Siberia subject to certain conditions, and provided America gave her consent, and advance as far west as was necessary to encounter the Germans. The Japanese reply first reaffirmed the original Japanese position, as stated in their note of March 19 to the American government, namely that the Japanese government could come to no decision on intervention until America and the Western Allies were in full agreement on the matter. But if they did eventually intervene, they would agree to the first two Allied conditions, namely, guarantee to respect Russia's territorial integrity, and not to interfere in Russian internal politics; but they could not accept the third condition: to advance as far west as was necessary to meet the Germans, in view of the grave, practical difficulties entailed in such an operation. They could advance no further than eastern Siberia. Finally, Japan claimed the supreme command of all Allied forces, when they did intervene. In view of the British military section's paper of June 15, Japanese reluctance to advance beyond eastern Siberia was understandable. But Balfour interpreted their reply as meaning that the Japanese would try to advance as far west as possible, but would assume no obligation to do so, in view of the embarrassment that failure might entail. The Japanese ambassador seems to have agreed that this was so (full allowance must here be made for Japanese tact and desire to please), adding that the 'somewhat ambiguous' wording of the note was probably chosen to placate an influential section of the Japanese public, who considered that Japan's present obligations to the Allies were defined by the Anglo–Japanese Treaty of 1902, which limited Japanese military obligations to the Far East.[5]

The Japanese ambassador also saw the Prime Minister, who stated at that morning's discussion with Milner and the CIGS that the ambassador had given him some idea of the 'immense political difficulties' which confronted the Japanese government, quite apart from America's attitude, in trying to obtain a decision on intervention. They first had to convince an inter-party committee, then their elder statesmen, and finally the Emperor. Moreover, an important opposition leader had declared himself firmly against intervention, although two of his newspapers were in favour of it. These difficulties to a certain extent explained Japan's slowness in taking any initiative.[6]

At the War Cabinet at noon, the DMI reported that he had received a wire from Harbin, in Manchuria, dated June 21, from which it appeared that there had been a clash between Ataman Semenov's troops, which numbered about 2,000, and a Bolshevik force of about 10,000, which included some 8,000 German and Austrian prisoners. (This last figure was gross exaggeration.) Semenov, however, had driven the enemy away from the Siberian railway and the situation was considered satisfactory. It had at one time been feared that if Semenov's force entered Manchuria, they would be disarmed by the Chinese, but it had now been arranged with the Chinese that Semenov's men would not be disarmed, unless they retired along the Chinese eastern railway. On the 20th, the wire added, there had been a meeting at Harbin of SRs from all over Siberia, who had asked for intervention 'to help Russia to restore the eastern front and to annul the Brest–Litovsk treaty'. This, of course, pleased the Cabinet. It was pointed out that such information would help to obtain American support for intervention, and also supported statements made by the Prime Minister in his conversation with the Japanese ambassador. The War Cabinet decided that the DMI should give Balfour a paraphrase of this wire, so that he might inform the Japanese ambassador of its contents.[7]

The Cabinet next gave serious attention to the situation in the Caucasus. On June 4, the DMI had told them, somewhat belatedly, that the Germans were sending two battalions across the Black Sea, probably to Batoum, to cooperate with the Turks in the Caucasus. (In fact, a small German force had landed in Georgia on May 25.) The Germans were said to be considering making Tiflis a base from which to protect the flank of the central Asian area. On June 10, the CIGS reported that it seemed that a whole German division had been moved to the Caucasus. This, the Cabinet realized, might create rather a serious situation, but little could be done about it. (In fact, the German force actually present was much less than a division.) On the 24th, however, the DMI reported rather different news from the Caucasus. There had been 'considerable trouble' between the Germans and Turks about who should occupy Baku first. The German High Command at Constantinople had agreed with Enver Pasha that neither country's forces should advance beyond an agreed neutral zone. The Turks, however, were not keeping to this agreement and were still pushing on towards Baku; 7,000 Turkish troops were near Kjurdamir (80 miles west of Baku), and some 3,000 had been sent to turn that town from the north. The Germans were complaining that the Turks, contrary to their agreement, had advanced along the Tiflis railway, entrenched themselves, and 'fired on the Germans'. The DMO explained that the German High Command had sent instructions that an attack on Baku was to be prevented, as they feared that if the Turks and Tartars got into the town, they would loot it and burn the oil-wells.[8] German reinforcements were coming from the Ukraine and would advance on Baku, which was full of Armenians, frightened of the Turks.

The Prime Minister commented that this was a 'remarkable situation', and asked whether we could not take advantage of the Turks and Germans falling out over Baku. The Turks, he remarked, were evidently more anxious to acquire this rich country than to regain Mesopotamia or Palestine. We might thus be able to arrange some peace terms with the Turkish government, by which this Muslim territory was given to them. Lord Curzon remarked that the Baku question was being fully discussed by the Eastern Committee that afternoon. A wire had arrived that morning stating that General Bicherakhov (the pro-British Cossack officer, who was cooperating with Dunsterville and had offered his services to the Baku soviet, pretending to be pro-Bolshevik) had been to Baku and returned; a report from him was expected shortly. General Dunsterville had also wished to take a British detachment there, but had been dissuaded since all available British troops were required for the Persian cordon to the south. Lord Curzon felt that in order to satisfy Turkish pan-Muslim ambitions, they would have to be given Azerbaijan; but since we were protecting the rights of Persia, it seemed impossible to barter territory adjoining the Persian cordon. Lloyd George remarked that it would be better for us for the Turks to hold Baku, since it was improbable that they would ever endanger British interests in the East, whilst Russia might well do so, once she was restored.[8] But shortly after this Cabinet discussion, the War Office wired to Dunsterville, sending new instructions in the light of the changing military and political situation in the Caucasus. Though a permanent occupation of Baku was out of the question, British objectives would be achieved if he could secure complete control of the Caspian flottila, and other shipping on the Caspian, and destroy the oil-rigs, reservoirs and pipe-lines at Baku.

What the Prime Minister did not realize was that the future of Baku was an integral part of the German–Bolshevik trade talks in Berlin. The Bolsheviks were insistent that Baku and its oil should remain part of Russia. The Germans supported them. They wanted the oil, but they wanted it from the Bolsheviks, not from the Turks. Hence German troops were being sent to ward off the Turks.

The trade talks in Berlin were designed by the Germans to secure the eventual Germanization of Russia. When they opened in mid-June, the Bolshevik delegates stated that they were willing to work in the 'closest collaboration' with Germany on economic matters, and suggested that Germany should authorize the Ukrainian government to deliver 360,000 tons of grain to Bolshevik Russia, which should be given a free hand in the Ukraine to see that this was done. Since the Bolsheviks themselves needed only 180,000 tons, they would undertake to hand over the other 180,000 tons to the Germans. They would also make Russian textiles, copper and 'other natural resources' available to Germany. Such proposals would form the basis for the development of 'further intimate political and economic relations'. The Bolshevik government, the delegates claimed, now considered the Brest–Litovsk treaty as a *fait accompli*, which had to be accepted 'once and for all', and Trotsky as well as Lenin now sought closer relations with Germany. But Russian public opinion would not permit an open alliance at present. They should sign a treaty which would prepare the way for such an alliance; and the delivery of grain to the hungry in the Russian cities would do just this. This future alliance would be based on the Brest–Litovsk treaty, but the Bolsheviks would make concessions beyond its provisions; they would grant independence to Estonia and Lithuania on the sole condition that the Germans permitted Russian trade through the Baltic ports, when they annexed these territories. Asked if Bolshevik Russia would accept German military help in Russia against the Allied invaders, the delegates said that the Bolshevik government was quite capable of driving the British out of Murmansk and dealing with the Czechs without Finnish or German military support, if Germany would protect the Russian rear by calling off the Don Cossacks; this would also avoid the danger of a new war in the East: a phrase which touched a very sensitive nerve at this time in Berlin.[9]

Ludendorff rejected these Bolshevik proposals. The German High Command would never agree to share the Ukrainian grain with the Bolsheviks, who should prove with deeds, not words, that they really had broken with the Allies and now wished to live at peace with Germany. Such deeds should include the dismissal of Trotsky as Commissar for War, an agreement with Finland for joint action against the British at Murmansk, and use of Bolshevik troops against Czech and British forces (Ludendorff was perhaps foreseeing British intervention). If the Bolsheviks gave these proofs 'unconditionally', Ludendorff would agree to make concessions in minor matters to get their way in the most important ones, such as Bolshevik recognition of Lithuanian, Estonian and Georgian independence. The talks continued.[9]

These Bolshevik proposals were not wholly honest. While they were being made in Berlin, Chicherin (no doubt aware that a British economic mission was on its way to Russia) was telling Phillips Price, the *Manchester*

Guardian's correspondent in Moscow, that if the Allies 'seriously wish to assist Russia, they should first recognize the Soviet government'. Bolshevik policy was to keep Russia neutral; but if either the Allies or the Germans showed increased hostility, they would cooperate with the least hostile. (This showed commendable honesty.) 'The Soviet government considers its immediate task is to conclude economic agreements both with the Allies and the central powers', added Chicherin. This press report somehow got past the British censor. On June 19, Phillips Price received a wire from his editor, C. P. Scott, asking him to find out if the Bolsheviks would discuss trade relations with England; he was to discover what they could offer, and what they wanted in return. (The War Cabinet, as yet, had not even been informed that a British economic mission was on its way to Russia.)[10]

On the 20th, the British economic mission arrived at Murmansk (and the Russia Committee in London were informed by Dudley Ward, of the Treasury, of the exact position regarding the British controlling interest in the Russian banks, which had been secured via the British loan to Jaroszynski). Phillips Price again saw Chicherin, who emphasized that the Allies and the Germans were, in fact, cooperating against Bolshevik Russia. The Germans were trusting that, by cutting off their corn lands, they could starve out the Bolsheviks in Moscow and then overthrow them with Krasnov's Don Cossacks. The Bolsheviks might thus break with Berlin. If the Allies wished to counter this, they must first recognize Bolshevik Russia, and secondly provide agricultural and railway repair equipment; the Bolsheviks could offer raw materials and forestry and railway concessions in northern Russia in return. 'We have already made an offer to Germany to treat on this basis and to America through Colonel Robins [of the American Red Cross],' stated Chicherin. 'We have not yet made a similar offer to England, because we do not know whether the good words of Mr Lockhart to us represent the views of the British government or only his own ...'. There was thus to be an open contest between England and Germany over Russian trade. But did Chicherin realize the real intention of the British economic mission in coming out to Russia — to make preparations for putting the Russian bank schemes, negotiated early in 1918, into operation as soon as the coming Allied intervention had overthrown the Bolshevik regime?[10]

In the German embassy, Counsellor Riezler was going even further than Chicherin feared. In a letter of June 25 to von Bergen (who was in charge of subversion in Russia at the German Foreign Ministry), he wrote: 'We do what we can: (*a*) to induce the Bolshevik generals to fight the Czechs as hard as possible; (*b*) to delay any *coups* of the right-wing SRs and other *Entente* supporters here and in St. Petersburg. This might be possible for another few weeks, but it will fail one day. Development of [our present policy] is against us, the Bolsheviks are used up, and we have to invent something else. . . . If we succeeded in bringing under one hat the bourgeois group [Krivoshein and the Cadets], who have tried to make contact with us, with the Siberians, and one of the Don Cossack generals; and if we then succeeded in overthrowing the Bolsheviks with this combination, or if we helped them with the overthrow from the Ukraine and in St. Petersburg, we could possibly sign beforehand a workable treaty with these people. This would hand all the Russian mineral wealth over to us, and the roads to the east and the south-east.'

If there were a bourgeois regime, things would function reasonably, despite everything. The task would be difficult, but not impossible. Germany gained nothing from chaos and, despite the negotiations in Berlin, they could not get anywhere with the Bolsheviks in power in Moscow.

Riezler admitted he knew nothing about the military situation in the West, and what the prospects of peace there were; but he did not believe that Germany was strong enough to renounce possibilities in Russia, and support the peace in the East purely with bayonets. The Secretary of State should thus be authorized, in case they came to an understanding with Russia restored, to hold out the prospect of dismantling an independent Ukraine, and the survival of Russia with an independent Estonia and Caucasus. Then they could try to achieve a combination in Moscow which would overthrow the Bolsheviks (preferably on their own, and only if necessary with minimal German help), and which would join Germany in action against the *Entente*. 'Nobody can guarantee to succeed with such policies, because of the incalculable chaos, but perhaps such a development is possible, thanks to the Czechs.'

He continued: 'I do apologize for these outpourings. We have reached the parting of the ways — if we do not take this way, we will have to ensure continuing chaos, and we will have to try to oppose and to destroy a bourgeois reconstruction with the help of the *Entente*. But then we cannot expect economic advantages and successes here. These would only be possible under a bourgeois regime, but then they would be plentiful. It is extremely hot here, lack of space in the house, too many people, soldiers and salesmen of all descriptions, for whom one is supposed to act as a nanny.'[10]

June 24 was a day filled with discussions on Russia. That afternoon, Lloyd George had talks of nearly two hours with a man once of crucial importance on the Russian scene, Alexander Kerensky, who had recently fled the country on a Serbian passport given him by Bruce Lockhart. Kerensky now had very little influence in his own land. But the discussion is of interest for the light that it throws on Lloyd George's thinking on Russia at this point. He had found Kerensky a 'much more effective person' than anticipated, Lloyd George reported to the Imperial War Cabinet that evening.

Kerensky had been 'very much to the point' during their discussions, 'and had not wasted a word'. He regarded Trotsky as pro-German, while Lenin 'lived in the clouds'. Kerensky thought that Russia 'was now ripe to take up arms again against Germany. There had been quite a renaissance there; the Russian people were at last beginning to understand the meaning of the Brest–Litovsk treaty.' The Ukraine 'had got its fill of Germans', the people loathed them, a partisan war had broken out, and the Germans were in considerable difficulties.[11]

Kerensky wanted to know what we were prepared to do, but Lloyd George retorted that he wanted to know what the Russians themselves were prepared to do; Kerensky talked of intervention, but what did he mean by that? Lloyd George had stressed the 'difficulty of our intervening with a [Russian] government that did not want us'. Kerensky used the word 'support', and when asked what he meant, said 'military support', adding: 'We consider it possible to reconstruct an eastern front with the help of the Allies.' The Russian people were against Japanese intervention, but in favour of Allied intervention; if, however, Japanese intervention was merely part of an Allied plan to help Russia, they would not quarrel about the number of Japanese troops. 'On this point, he had been quite businesslike', said Lloyd George.

He emphasized that the Allies, as often stated, wished to stand by Russian democracy to the end. 'From the practical point of view, however, they were in a position of great difficulty. The *de facto* government in Russia was apparently as hostile to the Allies as it was to Germany.' Kerensky asked if this meant that the Allies could do nothing at present. The Prime Minister repeated that so long as the *de facto* government maintained its present attitude, 'the situation was extraordinarily difficult for the Allies. If there was a government in Russia which was willing to extend its hand to the Allies, they would help it with food, arms and in every possible way. But what could they do so long as the only government which existed in Russia appeared to be just as friendly to the Germans as it was to the Allies.'

At the Imperial War Cabinet that evening, when 'Willie' Hughes (the Australian premier) asked Lloyd George what evidence Kerensky had produced of the support he had in Russia, Lloyd George replied that Kerensky stated that he had 'definitely [been] authorized' to come to England to clear up relations between Russia and the Allies by all politically active Russian elements, except the reactionaries and the Bolsheviks; in fact, by what he called the executive committee of the constituent assembly, that represented most of the Russian people, which on May 18, had passed a resolution repudiating the Brest–Litovsk treaty. He added that he would have come before, 'if he had thought it desirable'. (It is curious that Kerensky makes no reference here to either of the Russian governments at Samara or Omsk.)

Kerensky went so far as to say that Bolshevik military power was 'pure sham'. They governed by means of an efficient police force, but as soon as they came up against any serious military force, like the Czechoslovaks, the police were powerless. The Russian workmen were getting 'very sick' of the Bolsheviks, and Kerensky quoted resolutions of workmen's committees and of SRs, 'practically demanding the reconstitution of the Alliance'. The Bolsheviks, he added, were stronger in Moscow than anywhere else. Lloyd George had asked him, somewhat brutally, whether the Russians had any attachment to their country. When a Russian village was lost, did they feel, like the French, that their finger had been cut off? 'This had rather appeared to stagger M. Kerensky for the moment', Lloyd George reported that evening. Kerensky replied vaguely that they realized they were being cut off from the sea, and could thus not exist as a country, and when pressed, said that the common people realized this too.

Robert Borden, the Canadian Prime Minister, observed that Kerensky's view that the Bolsheviks were failing was confirmed by recent Foreign Office telegrams. Lloyd George remarked that Kerensky had impressed him as being honest and in earnest, but 'he [Kerensky] was probably a Jew, though most likely he would not admit to this' (This was quite unfounded; he was a pure Russian). Borden added that the information obtained by the Prime Minister from Kerensky 'merely left us where we were before, namely, that we ought to have Allied intervention and not Japanese intervention'.[11] Hughes ended the discussion by suggesting that Kerensky's support for this view might go far to satisfy President Wilson.

William Massey, the New Zealand Premier, asked whether the western front would be weakened if a certain number of Allied troops accompanied the Japanese army, if it did intervene in Siberia. Lloyd George replied that it would not. It was only proposed to send a nucleus 'to give the appearance of Allied intervention', which would be taken from the garrison at Hong Kong or from northern China. In reply to Hughes, Lloyd George reminded the Imperial War Cabinet in conclusion that President Wilson had not as yet agreed to intervention.

Events in the Far East now began to assume a momentum of their own. On June 25, the Czech leaders at Vladivostok met the local Allied consuls and naval commanders and told them that they would have to go back up the Siberian railway to rescue their colleagues; alarming reports were arriving of the military situation at Irkutsk, which the central Czech group, under Gajda, had attacked on the 21st.[12] The Czech leaders made an urgent request for the immediate despatch of an Allied expeditionary force of 100,000 men to assist them, and for large quantities of arms.

This request had not reached London on the morning of the 26th, when the Prime Minister, at his mid-morning discussion, emphasized how undesirable it was to ship Czech troops away from Vladivostok just when the rest of the Czech Legion 'was forming a nucleus of a possible counter-revolution in Siberia', and when those at Vladivostok might do good work in preventing the Bolsheviks from sending away Allied stores, as at Archangel. We might have to ship 4,000 to 5,000 away to satisfy Clemenceau, but it would be better to procrastinate over the rest. News of the Czech revolt, now just a month old, was still only arriving fitfully in London, but there was now enough information, it seems, for Lloyd George to realize that the British proposal of mid-May — for the Czechs to initiate intervention — had been realized spontaneously. The War Cabinet had been right all along. This undoubtedly increased Lloyd George's confidence.[13]

When the Imperial War Cabinet met again at 6 p.m. that evening, they studied the recent Japanese note, and restudied the account of the interview between Lloyd George and Kerensky. The Prime Minister, after reading the Japanese note, said that it meant that Japan was prepared to intervene in Siberia, if America agreed and if Japan had overall command; but Japan would not commit herself to go beyond central Siberia. Lloyd George stressed that 'what mattered to us was not who was in occupation of eastern Siberia, but who was at Omsk'. (And Lloyd George now knew that the Czechs had liberated Omsk.) He had gathered in his talk with the Japanese ambassador that the Japanese considered themselves bound by an obligation of honour under their treaty with the British government; but as this treaty only applied to the Far East, they did not feel bound to press on to the west, as the Allies wished. Milner remarked that he felt it had always been 'rather a tall order' to ask the Japanese to undertake to go to any particular place.[14]

Borden stressed that our real objective was to try to induce the anti-German elements in Russia to unite in their opposition to Germany. It was quite clear that they could make no headway without Allied intervention. He argued that intervention must — nominally, at any rate — be Allied, and that Japan must not benefit territorially; but he understood that the Japanese note accepted both these conditions. If, therefore, Japan would go as far as Irkutsk, we should encourage her to do so; perhaps once she had embarked on the expedition, she could be induced to go further. Borden felt it would be a mistake to reject an offer to intervene at all.

Both Hughes and Massey strongly supported Borden. Hughes reckoned that, from an Australasian point of view, there were considerable advantages in encouraging Japan to devote her energies to Siberian intervention. However, careful consideration must be given to the effect on Russian opinion. It would be admirable if Japanese intervention enabled the Czechs to succeed and Kerensky to 'rally' Russia; so long as it enabled us to win the war, matters could be cleared up in Siberia later. But it would be disastrous if Japanese intervention made the Russians combine against Japan and say that they would rather have the Germans than the Japanese. Borden remarked that this was a point on which they could only express their opinion; it was impossible to foresee the exact results.

There was then a brief exchange on the question of the supreme command. Massey asked whether it could be given to Japan. Lloyd George said there would be no objection so far as British troops were concerned. They had already served under Japanese command in the Kaiu-Chau expedition, and the Allied contingents that would intervene in Siberia would not, individually, be larger than the British contingent at Kaiu-Chau. Lloyd George asked Borden whether Canadian railway engineers, if sent, would object to serving under Japanese command. Borden thought there would be no objection. Milner remarked that unless Japan was to be treated as an equal, it would be better not to ask her to intervene at all. She would be supplying almost the whole force that was to intervene, and it would be impossible to refuse her the supreme command. This closed the discussion.[14]

As the British were continually being baulked over Siberian intervention, which looked like being ruled permanently out of court by some presidential announcement on about June 28, they naturally redoubled their attention on intervention in northern Russia, which was nearer and more feasible, and in which the President had shown more interest. The crucial factor here was the real extent of the German presence and German influence in Finland (the only point in Ludendorff's paper of June 9 which has not yet been considered). Finland, Ludendorff wrote, had strengthened its military position as a result of German intervention. 'We may hope that we shall find strong military support there whatever happens', he had written confidently. How far was this true?

At the War Cabinet on June 19, the First Lord drew attention to a letter, dated June 15, from the Allied naval council (written as a result of Joint Note 31 on intervention in northern Russia, approved by the Supreme War Council on June 3), which recommended that there should be a single command to direct both land and sea defence of the northern Russian ports. The First Lord said that he had consulted Lord Milner and understood that Joint Note 31 did not mean that the general in command on land should control naval operations in these waters as well. This was satisfactory; but the First Lord suggested that, as it was undesirable to raise the question again at the Supreme War Council, Milner should write him a letter explaining General Poole's orders, so far as they related 'to his non-interference in naval control afloat'. The War Cabinet, in approving this proposal, which had clearly ruffled the Admiralty's feathers, clearly demonstrated that the decision of June 3 at Versailles on single command was designed simply to freeze out the French from any say in northern Russian land operations.[15]

The First Lord then drew attention to a further point raised by the Allied naval council at its meeting in London on June 11 and 12 about the situation at Murmansk and Archangel. If we allowed the Finns or Germans to secure a submarine base between the Kola inlet and the Norwegian coast, like Petchenga, or bases on the western shore of the White Sea between Kandalaksha and Onega (which latter port could be used by both submarines and patrol vessels), it would be impossible to safeguard naval traffic to Murmansk and Archangel. We had information that a Finnish force was assembling for an advance on Petchenga and an 'unknown force' further south with light railway appliances was preparing to advance on Kandalaksha. There were further reports that the enemy were building barracks in Finland for 12,000 men and that motor-boats were being assembled on Lake Ladoga. (These reports were similar to those previously given to the Cabinet by the CIGS.) It was thus a question of what the policy of the War Cabinet was on the defence of Murmansk, Archangel, and the adjoining provinces. Because of the northern Russian climate, Allied troops must be on the spot within the next two months, if these regions were to be effectively safeguarded. This would entail removing some of the anti-submarine forces (presumably from the Atlantic and the North Sea) to protect troop transports and supply ships in the Arctic. It was a question of whether the advantage in the retention of these northern Russian ports would not be outweighed by the additional losses in merchant shipping that would result from the withdrawal of the anti-submarine forces from their present duties. But if we allowed the Germans to secure a base at Petchenga, warned the First Lord, it would be very difficult to drive them out again.

The CIGS said that he was going into the matter of how many troops would be needed to secure effective control of these areas. His preliminary investigations showed that two and a half infantry divisions alone would be required. As soon as his estimates were completed, he would send them to the Admiralty for consideration of the naval questions involved. But the CIGS was inclined to the belief that unless occupation of Murmansk and Archangel was backed up by Siberian intervention, 'it might be desirable to abandon the Murman coast'. He was forgetting that the British military section at Versailles had stated in their paper of June 15 that the connection between northern Russian and Siberian intervention was 'at present remote', and that their interaction would be 'for a long time inconsiderable'. Initially, in fact, the two operations were not interdependent.

The Prime Minister took up the next point in the same paper, and hoped that the CIGS would bear in mind that although Siberian intervention might be impossible, 'it was possible that Russia might be in existence in 1919 [presumably as a restored and united state], in which case Archangel and Murmansk would be invaluable as inlets to Russia'. It was thus 'essential' to maintain our position in northern Russia, if this could be achieved without the commitment of large forces. The CIGS added that he had just had a reply from Washington to say that the despatch of an American brigade to

Murmansk was still under consideration, the reason being that the American government wished to have Foch's views on the matter. Milner noted that the Americans had already been told what Foch recommended.

The War Cabinet decided that the War Office should put the 'whole problem' to General Poole and ask him to estimate the size of the force he thought necessary to hold Petchenga, Murmansk, Archangel and the western shore of the White Sea. He should also be invited to express his views on the subject generally. The Cabinet thus removed this crucial problem from the CIGS, and placed it firmly in the hands of General Poole.

Later, the War Cabinet appear to have reconsidered this decision. For the First Lord, accompanied by Colonel Richard Steel (the DMO's staff officer with special responsibility for military operations in the Russian theatre) and Captain Bernard St G. Collard (the deputy director of the operations division at the Admiralty), left hastily for a swift and secret visit to Murmansk to investigate matters.[15]

The hurried return of the First Lord's mission from Murmansk led to a decision on British intervention in northern Russia. On June 23, shortly after the (presumed) arrival of the First Lord at Murmansk, the British expeditionary force, accompanied by a training mission, also arrived at Murmansk under the command of Major-General C.C.M. Maynard. (The proposed task of the expeditionary force was to protect the Murmansk region from White Finnish or German attacks; that of the training mission was to proceed to Archangel as soon as the ice melted and there to train and equip the Czechs, still supposedly on their way to northern Russia, as well as any Russian or other volunteers they might come across.) The training mission consisted of some 560 men, and the little expeditionary force comprised three companies: an infantry company, a machine-gun company, and a company of engineers; some 600 men in all. It was a very small affair. The American brigade had not materialized. On the 20th, when General Bliss saw Foch, on the instructions of the American War Department, Foch approved the diversion of one or two battalions to northern Russia. This led to an acrimonious exchange between the American War Department and the British War Office, who had increased the proposed size of the force, without Foch's authority, to a whole brigade, together with a demand for overall British command; but nothing materialized.[16]

On arrival, Maynard was told by General Poole, his superior officer, that no fewer than 15,000 pro-German White Finns were marching against the Murmansk railway. Maynard decided to defend the railway line at Kandalaksha and Kem; and on the 27th, he set out to survey the position to his south. From the outset, he realized that the local railway workers were actively hostile. At Kandalaksha, he found a train containing the first detachment of Red Guards, under Commissar Natsarenus, about to proceed north. Their commander was drunk, and unwilling to discuss anything. As there was nothing to stop the train going straight through to Murmansk, Maynard posted machine guns round it, and forbad it to move. He then left for Kem, which was firmly under Allied control with a British warship in its small harbour. On arrival, he discovered two more troop-trains of Red Guards, and others, followed by an armoured train: all were under orders to travel north and drive the Allies out of Murmansk. Maynard summoned up reinforcements from Murmansk, and had the Red Guards at Kandalaksha and Kem disarmed. This seems to have been surprisingly easy to do, but unfortunately it gave the British the impression that all Bolshevik troops could be dealt with in similar fashion.[16]

On the same day, Colonel Steel and Captain Collard RN, who had accompanied the First Lord on his brief visit to Murmansk, prepared a report on the position at Murmansk, probably on board a destroyer making all speed back to England. It was a very positive report:

The Petchenga area. The enemy's offensive preparations were not so advanced as anticipated, and his difficulties were greater than supposed. 'There is no confirmation of the previous report of the construction of a light railway from Rovaniemi northwards.' (Rovaniemi is north-east of Tornio, the port on the northern tip of the Gulf of Bothnia, and west of Kandalaksha.) 'The difficult nature of the country renders rapid construction for any distance improbable.' It was reported that no supplies existed in these parts, and that there was great scarcity in Finland. 'It may be assumed, therefore, that any operation undertaken by the enemy during the next few months would be in the nature of a raid limited to a few hundred men with machine guns and possibly some field artillery.' There were 400 British sailors and marines holding Petchenga with machine guns; they could easily be reinforced from Murmansk.[17]

Kola. At present, 1,950 Allied troops were available for use in the Kola inlet (including 1,200 British troops, which had just arrived, and included 500 of General Poole's mission for Archangel). 'No enemy movements in this area are reported.'

The Murmansk railway, from Kandalaksha southwards. 'Former reports of enemy activities aiming at cutting the line between Kandalaksha and Soroka were exaggerated.' Colonel Steel mentioned a small force of twelve men, with two machine guns. 'The [Rovaniemi-Kandalaksha] road between Kualajarvi and Allakurti is reported to be under repair, but no confirmation of any railway construction from Rovaniemi to Allakurti has been received.' Reconnaissance parties had found only two small outposts consisting of 20 men each. 'Boats had been requisitioned [perhaps on lakes to the south of Kandalaksha], and a raid by 300 to 400 men on the railway is considered possible, but no large construction of barracks at Ukhta [west of Kem] as previously reported is in progress.' There were some 450 to 500 Finnish White Guards at Ukhta. The position further south was then considered. 'Recent reports point to a German–Finnish concentration of about 10,000 at Sortavala [on the northern tip of Lake Ladoga] with advanced detachments of 1,500 and 1,000 at Salmi [on the north-eastern shore] and Suojarvi [further north] respectively. The object is reported to be an advance in the near future on the railway and Petrozavodsk.'

Collard and Steel then detailed the 1,350 French and Serbian troops at Kandalaksha, and the 150 British, plus an armoured train, at Kem. 'The above troops are sufficient to deal with any raids from the west which are possible in the near future. In the event however of any large movement by railway from the south based on Petrozavodsk, these small forces would gradually be forced to retire on Kandalaksha, giving up the railway and the western White Sea ports as they withdrew. Any advance by the enemy could be greatly retarded by the demolition of the numerous bridges on the railway, preparations for which are now under consideration. ... To sum up, there appears to be no danger of an immediate enemy advance in force on the Kola or Petchenga inlets, which are the important places for us to hold. The Murman railway as far south as Kem acts as an outpost to the Kola inlet and is not yet seriously threatened. We should, however, be prepared for a raid on Petchenga and for a retirement on Kandalaksha.' In both cases, some field artillery and aircraft, preferably seaplanes, in addition to the present forces, were 'considered essential'.

From this report it appeared that the enemy forces, for the defeat of which the CIGS had told the War Cabinet that two and a half Allied divisions would be needed in northern Russia, virtually did not exist. The First Lord attached this report to his memorandum on northern Russia, dated June 28, which he appears to have submitted to the Prime Minister on the same day. He drew attention to the very difficult terrain, very poor communications and few roads in the region around the White Sea, which was only open to shipping from June to late October, and from which there were two railways down to central Russia: one from Murmansk through Zvanka to Petrograd, the other from Archangel to Vologda.

'It is down one of these two lines of railway that General Poole, with such forces as are at his disposal, is to carry the "fiery Cross". General Poole has been entrusted by His Majesty's Government with this mission, and he has studied it and has faith in a reasonable possibility of success in what he himself describes as a "gamble", and therefore in such matters as have been specifically entrusted to his judgment, one cannot perhaps usefully, with very limited knowledge, criticise or urge contrary views.' Poole thought that with 3,000 more men than he now had, he could go down the Murmansk railway towards Zvanka and collect a native force of

10,000 'anti-Germans'. In this case, he would be based on an ice-free port, but would have to rely on a poor railway of 'very considerable length', with 'innumerable' bridges, which could easily be sabotaged by small parties from the Finnish border. But with 5,000 more men than he now had, Poole thought that if his landing at Archangel had naval support, he could go down the Archangel–Vologda railway, and collect some 100,000 'anti-German' Russian irregulars. Poole was 'strongly in favour' of the Archangel project, as this railway line was shorter, and safer from raiding parties, though Archangel was only open from June to late October; in this he was supported by Eric Geddes, First Lord of the Admiralty. Poole preferred the 'bigger gamble', because on arrival at Vologda, he could also 'collect' the 25,000 Czech troops west of the Urals, and obtain Siberian supplies. 'He admits that this is an off chance, but he holds the view — and I think rightly — that if you are going to gamble at all, you should stake boldly.'

There were two points to consider. First, could we deny the Murman coast as German submarine bases for attacks on our ships going to northern Russia? The country around Petchenga, stated the First Lord, was 'a continuous swampy waste intersected by a few unmetalled and very poor roads and tracks, with low-lying hills covered with scrubby birch and swamp bushes'. No successful enemy attack could be made without using a wholly disproportionate force, which would be known well in advance. Poole thought that his present forces, backed up by a ship's guns, could hold the inlet and the Murmansk peninsula. On the western shore, there were many inlets between Kandalaksha and Soroka suitable for submarines; but the impassable country, which was 'by no means wholeheartedly pro-German or pro-Finnish', and our control of the railway, made an attack impracticable for the Germans. From Soroka round the southern shore, the water was too shallow for submarines, though Poole's forces did not hold the land side. It was agreed that the present forces could deny the enemy the potential submarine bases along the Murman coast.

Secondly, what were the difficulties of using Archangel as a base, after Poole had landed there? On June 26, stated the First Lord (presumably the day on which he had left for England), Poole had received 'authoritative' information from agents in Archangel that pro-German elements there were in control; and as the local soviet had, a few days before, demanded on instructions from Moscow the departure of a British armed icebreaker, it was clear that an armed landing would not be welcomed by the Archangel populace. Poole had also heard that Mudyugski Island, off Archangel, in the River Dvina delta, was defended by 6″ batteries; that submarine observation mines were being laid; and that resistance could be expected. Poole had thus postponed the despatch of his landing force. He and Admiral Kemp would first go to Archangel, without any force, simply to parley. The First Lord agreed with Poole that it would be 'a great mistake to make the initial move an hostile one with forces which in the circumstances he [Poole] did not consider adequate if serious opposition was met with'. Admiral Kemp and Poole would go to Archangel, as soon as the ice melted, 'in an inoffensive yacht'. If they failed to obtain the 'friendly concurrence' of the Archangel authorities to a military landing, there would be a 'distinctly hostile' combined operation to seize Mudyugski Island and proceed up river to 'dominate' Archangel and to land troops; 'thereafter advancing, as circumstances may permit, down the line to Vologda, recruiting such friendly Russians as may be on the road ...'. It was 'obvious', stated Geddes, 'that with any western European nation, which had the capability of organizing resistance, the undertaking would be a serious one. It is only because of the comic opera element in the Russian situation in the North ... that such an attempt is considered at all justifiable by our naval and military commanders on the spot. There is no doubt that the whole enterprise is a gamble; it may conceivably put us in the position of being committed at a later date (but I can hardly conceive it to be before the spring of 1919) to a larger military enterprise ... but if it is decided this winter to have an additional 5,000 Allied troops operating on the lines south of Archangel, it must, I suggest, be recognized that it is a limited but essential gamble ...'. The British government would be risking 'hostile operations in a country with which we are on a semi-friendly basis, and which may resent it'. They were also risking some prestige, and some 6,000 men, 'who may be completely annihilated. ... On the other hand, if it "comes off", it is possible — and General Poole has reasonable faith in that possibility — that the diversion may have very far reaching effects. ... In adopting this view, I confess to having been largely influenced by the general total absence of organizing power which is apparent among all Russians in the North of Russia, and apparently throughout all Russia, and by the large element of "opera bouffe" [*sic*] in the present methods of government ... if my trip to the North of Russia has done nothing else, it has taught me to read official telegrams dealing with the Lenin–Trotsky government not through the spectacles of Whitehall, but through the spectacles with which one has read the history of the rise and fall of the minor South American republics, and it is because of this character in everything Russian in the Archangel–Murmansk district, that I have sufficient faith in the possible effect of a small, compact, well-organized, and determined effort such as General Poole proposes to make.' Geddes went on: 'Whether this northern operation is combined with the intervention of powerful forces from and via Vladivostok or not, if it succeeds it will be a serious check to German domination of Russia, and a great asset to our prestige and post-war commercial interests.' The 5,000 additional men and supplies, which Poole asked for, were practically covered by the decisions of the Supreme War Council on June 3, and would give this 'daring venture' the best chance. Geddes concluded: 'I would disregard the wishes of the Bolshevik government and act on the lines General Poole wishes with 5,000 more men — but at once.'[17]

When forwarding these two papers to the Prime Minister on June 28, the First Lord added a short personal note to underline the 'extraordinary element of comic opera existing, without realizing which one cannot form a correct opinion of the situation in the North of Russia'. The Bolshevik government had an English-speaking Russian general at Murmansk, formerly belonging to a 'crack cavalry regiment', who had been well-known in London society. He commanded no troops, but was said to have been sent a wire by Lenin (the reference is probably to Chicherin's wire of June 15) stating that the British were to be driven out of Murmansk. He went on board the British flagship, 'and gave a copy of the telegram to General Poole and asked him what he should do!' He then sent a reply to Moscow saying that the British were stronger. (The reference is to Major-General Nikolai I. Zvegintsev, former commander of the Tsarskoe Selo Hussar Regiment of the Guards. He and Georgi M. Vesselago, a naval officer, were the chief figures behind the Murmansk soviet. Poole referred to them openly as 'Sviggens' and 'Vessels', and treated them with easy-going condescension that the Russians may well have seen as contemptuous.)

The First Lord ended his note to the Prime Minister thus: 'There is really no Government; there is no organization; and there is no authority. Orders are issued by the central government at Moscow, but no one obeys them unless they wish, and the various committees meet and take different views. I am assured that what I saw is typical of what is going on under the Lenin–Trotsky government in all parts of Russia, *and if that is so*, it must be perfectly clear that no reliance can be placed either upon the government exercising any authority, or upon their ability to carry out any undertaking which they may come to with the Allies. Also if what I saw in northern Russia is really typical of the whole country, it simplifies very much the consideration of what should be done in the East through Vladivostok.'[17]

This paper has been quoted at considerable length because of the effect it seems to have had on the Prime Minister, who did not show it to the War Cabinet. It was a truly appalling paper, perhaps the worst ever sent in by a Cabinet Minister on returning from a crucial foreign mission. Though the First Lord chose to leave the decision to General Poole, which rather begged the question of why he had bothered to make a rush journey to Murmansk at all, he proceeded — at very considerable length — to equate some minor 'comic opera' events at Murmansk with events in the whole of the former Russian empire, on absolutely no authority at all; someone had told him so. This, then, was the result of the long-standing decision, taken by the War Cabinet in mid-April, for a Cabinet Minister to go out to northern Russia! The paper by Steel and Collard, and a very small part of the First Lord's paper, did effectively deal with the alleged danger of German submarine bases (in fact, there was no such danger), with the alleged presence of the Germans and Finns in Finland, and with their railway building activities. (Here too there was much less danger than was imagined.) Of particular interest in the First Lord's paper was the news that Poole had been planning to land at Archangel in the very near future; but nothing was said of any liaison with the French, who, it will be recalled, were 'in charge of all the activities in the Russian interior'. Had they been told that the landing had been delayed? There is no knowing. They, of course, could by now have told Poole that he would find no Czechs at Vologda. The Czechs on the Volga had been told by Noulens that Allied intervention would take place in late June; and, apparently, that an Allied army would come to their aid on the Volga via Viatka, well east of Vologda — so their local paper had claimed on June 24. But the First Lord's paper seems to have convinced the Prime Minister; Poole's gamble could proceed, and with 5,000 more troops, he could 'collect' 100,000 'anti-German' Russians. The War Office was presumably shown this paper, and acquiesced.

At noon on the 28th, the War Cabinet were briefly informed that a British economic mission had gone to Bolshevik Russia (eight days after it had actually reached Murmansk); and that General Dunsterville, who had now been ordered into Baku, had not yet reached the port of Enzeli, on the southern shore of the Caspian; but that more Turkish troops were apparently advancing north-east on Baku from Tabriz.[18] The Prime Minister urged the need for making financial arrangements to enable the Czechs to pay their way in Russia and Siberia and thus retain the friendship of the local people. It was pointed out that the French had made all arrangements to bring the Czechs to Vladivostok and that previous financial arrangements, when the Czechs were in the Ukraine, had been made between Foch and the DMI. The Cabinet decided that the DMI should contact the French War Office so that the necessary money might be made available to the Czechs, 'for use either on their way to Vladivostok, or in Russia or Siberia'.

The Prime Minister then drew the War Cabinet's attention to the impression, 'which apparently prevailed in America', that there was a division of opinion among the Allies on Russian intervention. Balfour remarked that a telegram to Lord Reading was now being prepared in the Foreign Office, and would be sent that day, asking President Wilson not to commit himself on intervention.

On June 18, President Wilson had stated that he would reach a decision on the Russian problem within ten days. The Allies, who had no means of knowing otherwise, took this to mean that he would come out against Siberian intervention, and for the despatch of an Allied commission to both Vladivostok and Murmansk, under the leadership of Hoover. All the evidence in Washington pointed this way. The Departments of Commerce, Agriculture and Labour were all obviously hard at work. The Allies were horrified. On the 19th, however, Professor Masaryk, with strong backing from the State Department, was received by the President, who for some time had been showing an aversion to receiving any lobbyist on a Russian theme. Then Secretary Lansing openly backed the Czechs. On the 23rd, the British embassy sent the State Department a copy of a wire from Lockhart, expressing extreme apprehension at the danger of the Allies not intervening and leaving the Czechs to their fate; the outcome might be German seizure of Moscow. Lansing sent this straight to the President, with an accompanying note: 'As these troops are most loyal to our cause and have been unjustly treated by the various soviets, ought we not to consider whether something cannot be done to support them? ... Is it not possible that in this body of capable and loyal troops may be found a nucleus for military occupation of the Siberian railway?' It was almost word for word what Lloyd George had been saying since May 17.[19]

The next day (June 24), a wire reached Washington from Admiral Knight at Vladivostok, describing the Czech military position, and stating that Irkutsk had been seized by German prisoners (who were now quite beyond Bolshevik control, a further wire stated); and that it was in fact the Germans and German influence that were preventing the Czechs reaching the Far East. As previously pointed out, this was quite wrong; but the message from Admiral Knight had a decisive influence on the State Department. They were now firmly in favour of American support for the Czechs. On the 25th, however, the President held a special Cabinet meeting (attended by the Secretaries of Commerce, Agriculture and Labour, as well as Lansing and the Secretary of War) at which the emphasis was on economic aid for, and the revival of, commerce with Russia. The President spurred his men on. He would, they knew, decide on his Russian policy by the 28th. Kennan suggests that this was some sort of smoke-screen to protect the President from his own men while he quietly reached his own decision.

Events then seemed to move smoothly for the President. On the 26th, a wire arrived from the American Consul at Vladivostok, relaying the request of the Czech leaders there for Allied military support. The Czech leaders had decided that the 15,000 Czechs, who had reached the Far East prior to the Czech revolt, would have to turn back up the Siberian railway to break through to Irkutsk (now, the State Department believed, under German control) in order to link up with their colleagues in the central Czech group in western Siberia. The Allied consuls agreed that this was necessary; Allied arms and supplies should be sent, together with an Allied force (whether the figure of 100,000 men was given in this wire is unclear). Also on the 26th, the Japanese ambassador in Washington informed Lansing of the recent Japanese reply to the Allies, in answer to Balfour's request of June 7 for Japanese intervention. In their reply, the Japanese government had simply stated that they could reach no decision on intervention until there was complete agreement on the subject between the American and Allied governments. The President was highly pleased. He had read the Japanese ambassador's note 'with genuine pleasure', he told Lansing. He had been freed from the need to make any personal reaction to the Allied proposal for intervention of early June. The Japanese had done it for him. He now had a completely clear field to reach his own decision, which would entail achieving a fine balance between a demonstration of American friendship for the Russian people and encouragement for the anti-German forces in Russia, without ensnaring America in large-scale, and thus foolish, Allied military adventures in Russia, and linking America with their 'ulterior political designs'.

But the field was not as clear as the President imagined, for the Japanese had lied to him. Since only the first part of the Japanese reply to the Allies had been communicated to him, the President was unaware that the Japanese had a definite Siberian policy of their own — as indicated by the parts of the Japanese reply which had been carefully concealed from the Americans, namely that they agreed to the first two Allied conditions for intervention (respect for Russian territorial integrity, and non-interference in Russian internal politics), but would not go so far into Siberia as to meet the Germans, only into eastern Siberia. This, in fact, meant that Japanese policy was to intervene in eastern Siberia, as soon as she could secure the agreement of both America and the Allies; and this was the method she used to try to secure American agreement. This the President could not, on June 26, have known.

Important pleas from the French and British now reached the President. On the 27th, Foch's message arrived, claiming that the recent withdrawal of German divisions from Russia to the western front was a 'decisive military argument' in favour of Allied intervention in Siberia. This, with his respect for Foch, President Wilson could not ignore. The British plea was more anguished. On the 28th, Lord Reading (who that day received the full text of the recent Japanese reply from the Foreign Office) personally handed to the President a message from Lloyd George and the War Cabinet, strongly urging him not to make known his decision until the views of the Supreme War Council, which was to meet again on July 2, had been made known to him.[19]

It was at this moment that both Vladivostok and Murmansk fell, like ripe plums, into Allied hands. On the 29th, the Czechs seized control of Vladivostok from the local soviet with very little difficulty and with the cordial approval of the British, American and Japanese naval commanders, who landed detachments to help the Czechs keep order, prior to the Czechs proceeding back up the Siberian railway in support of their colleagues on the wrong side of Irkutsk. On the 30th, the Murmansk soviet decided to defy the Bolshevik government's orders from Moscow, and to 'formalize' their cooperation with the Allies by a written agreement. Thus, just before the crucial Supreme War Council, intervention in both Siberia and northern Russia became an established fact.

10

The American decision

On July 2, the Supreme War Council met to discuss a lengthy British paper on Allied intervention in Russia and Siberia, drawn up by Hankey, in consultation with Lord Robert Cecil, now Assistant Secretary of State at the Foreign Office. This paper, the apotheosis of the British case, carefully designed as a final attempt to win over President Wilson, deserves to be examined with care.

Since the council's previous meeting, it began, there had been a 'complete change' in the Russian and Siberian situations, which made Allied intervention 'an urgent and imperative necessity'. First, Czech action had transformed the situation in Siberia. There were now 50,000 Slav troops in control of the railway in western Siberia, who were 'totally disinterested' in Russian internal politics, yet determined to fight Germany for the liberation of their own country. Their success proved that most of the Siberian people were no longer on the Bolsheviks' side, 'and must be friendlily disposed to the Allied cause'. It also dissolved the apprehension that Allied intervention would meet opposition serious enough to make an advance through western Siberia very difficult. Provided that intervention took place in good time, there would be a Slav army in western Siberia to which Russian patriots could rally; this also removed the risk of Russian public opinion being thrown into the arms of Germany, as might happen if the intervening force was predominantly Japanese. However, the Czech force was in grave danger of being cut off by the German and Austro–Hungarian prisoners' 'organization' at Irkutsk and an appeal for immediate military support had been made by the Czech national council to the Allied consuls at Vladivostok. The Allies had to take immediate action, if they did not want these 'brave allies' to be crushed. To fail to help these 'faithful troops', now desperately fighting for the Allied cause, would not only discredit the Allies for ever, but might have a disastrous effect on the Russian, Austro–Hungarian and Balkan Slavs, proving that the Allies were unable or unwilling to make effective efforts to save the Slav world from falling completely under German domination. On the other hand, it would probably be a simple and speedy matter to push an expeditionary force through to Irkutsk to overcome the German prisoners' 'organization', and join hands with the Czechs, if it was undertaken immediately. This was why Siberian intervention was an urgent necessity, both to save the Czechs, and to take advantage of an opportunity, which the Allies might never have again, of gaining control of Siberia.[1]

Secondly, there had been a 'great change' in the Russian internal situation. There was no doubt that the Bolsheviks' power was declining. It was daily becoming clearer to all Russian classes — including ex-soldiers, peasants and workmen — that the Bolsheviks could not fulfil their promises of a social millenium and that anarchy, disorder and famine lay ahead under the Bolshevik regime. All Allied representatives in Russia agreed on this. It was further clear that the Bolsheviks had no real power with which to support their own government. They had found it impossible to form an effective army. They remained in power only because Russia was too divided to create an alternative organization to take their place. There was, however, 'much evidence' that the best liberal and democratic elements in Russia were beginning to lift their heads and make contact with one another. They were animated partly by disgust with the autocratic methods of the Bolsheviks, partly by determination not to accept the humiliation and partition of their country under the Brest–Litovsk treaty, and partly by growing fear of German domination. In fact, all elements of the Russian population, save for the dwindling minority of the Bolsheviks, today recognised that intervention was 'necessary and inevitable', since it was the only alternative to continuing anarchy and disorder, ending in universal starvation. The only point on which opinions differed was whether this intervention should be Allied or German. The reactionaries and the German agents among the Bolsheviks naturally preferred German intervention. The liberal and democratic elements were insistently demanding Allied intervention, and despite their desire for economic aid, did not conceal the fact that their most essential need was military support. Unless they could obtain effective Allied military support for their armed struggle, and a base upon which to rally, the movement for national freedom and regeneration would surely be crushed by the reactionary forces, backed by German bayonets. But if the Allies really wished to bring effective help to liberal Russia, they must not only occupy Murmansk and Archangel, in order to hold bridgeheads from which troops could if necessary advance rapidly from northern Russia towards the centre, they must also seize control of Siberia up to the Urals without any delay. If the Germans gained control of western Siberia, and of Archangel and Murmansk at the same time, they would close the last means of contact between Russia and the outside world and obtain possession of the food supplies without which Russia would starve. The Germans had already made the Black Sea a German lake; they were also advancing as fast as possible towards the Caspian, in order to control the Volga and the water communications of western Siberia; and they were preparing to occupy the Murmansk coast before winter. If they succeeded in these objectives, German domination of Russia would be complete. They would not only control all Russian resources, but they could force the Russian population, under penalty of starvation, to serve them, not only as labour, but possibly even as recruits for their armies in the field. All hope of the regeneration of Russia on truly democratic lines thus depended on Allied seizure, without any delay, of the granary of western Siberia.

Thirdly, Allied intervention was essential to win the war. There was no doubt that, if the Germans failed to gain a decision in the West in the next few weeks, they would return to the East, and would strive, by all the means in their power, to paralyse any Russian regeneration before the end of the war. They knew as well as we did that the Allies had only the smallest chances of victory on the western front in 1919, unless Germany was forced once more to transfer a considerable part of her forces from west to east. It would thus be one of the primary objectives of German policy to prevent the reformation of an Allied front in eastern Europe during the coming autumn and winter. And she would attempt to do this, either by establishing a Russian government favourable to herself, or by destroying all possibility of organized resistance to German disorganization of Russia. If the Allies were to win in 1919, one of their primary objectives should be to arouse and support the Russian national movement in order to reform an eastern front, or at least to encourage in the occupied territory, behind the German lines, a vigorous spirit of independence, capable of forcing Germany to maintain considerable forces in eastern Europe. At present, intervention, as a practical policy, was easier than it had ever been. The Japanese had now agreed to send an expedition to Siberia, provided they were assured of American approvall and effective American support. (During the discussion of this British paper, Lloyd George said that Balfour wished 'for numerous reasons' to add here: 'And though they [the Japanese] have not engaged themselves to go beyond Irkutsk, there is no ground for thinking that this necessarily represents the limits of their effort.' This was simply wishful thinking; the Japanese had clearly stated that they would not go beyond eastern Siberia.) They had, the paper went on, also accepted the two conditions, which the Supreme War Council thought to be necessary conditions for Allied intervention, namely, to disregard Russian internal politics, and to promise to evacuate Russian territory. Czech troops were already in occupation of western Siberia. The addition of American and Allied detachments to the Japanese army would create a force which was really inter-Allied and acceptable both to Russian and Allied public opinion, especially if Russian troops, under Russian leaders, were associated with it. If the Allies acted immediately, it should be possible for them to gain control of the Siberian railway from one end of Siberia to the other, up to the Urals, in the space of a few weeks. Only

America's consent and cooperation were now required to set in motion an operation which would probably succeed, and if it did, was bound to have decisive results on the future of the war.

On the other hand, refusal to intervene immediately could not fail to have consequences which would obviously be disastrous to the Allied cause. First, it would mean abandoning the Russian people to triumphant German militarism, and the destruction of all hope for the resurrection of Russia during the war as the liberal Ally of the western democracies. Secondly, it would completely nullify the effect of the Allied blockade, for if Germany secured effective control of central Russia or Siberia, she would be freed of her chief anxiety about the supply of raw materials and food. Thirdly, it would mean an 'indefinite prolongation' of the war, and abandonment of the Allies' hope of victory in 1919. Fourthly, it would mean abandoning yet another little nation's army, the Czechs, to the mercy of Berlin, with disastrous consequences to Slav feelings in Russia, in the Balkans, and throughout the world.

But for the policy of armed intervention to be successful, an adequate military force must be employed. (During discussion of the paper, there was dispute about the frequent use of the phrase 'considerable force'. Lloyd George explained that it had been inserted in the British draft 'because an impression appeared to exist in the United States that only a very small force would do — a division and one or two battalions of specialists. That was a dangerous delusion, and he had emphasized this by mentioning a force of, say, 50,000 to 60,000 men, of which the greater part would be Japanese'. The Supreme War Council thought a considerable force should be used of at least 100,000 men. Foch had suggested the same number. The Czech leaders, too, had appealed for at least 100,000 men. Baron Sonnino suggested that the figure of 100,000 be left in the text, but the word 'adequate' should be substituted for 'considerable' and this was agreed.) The Allied representatives in Russia, the paper continued, were agreed that, while economic assistance by the Allies was important, military intervention was 'absolutely essential'. The Czech leaders had informed the Allied consuls at Vladivostok that in their view 100,000 men were needed to save the situation. It was thus clear that while the rest of the Allies should send what troops they could, the bulk of the expeditionary force must be provided by the Japanese.

For these reasons, and after careful consideration of the military situation, and of Allied prospects in all theatres of war, it was concluded that immediate Allied armed assistance to Russia was 'imperative'. Pledges should be given to the Russian people, as agreed at the previous meeting of the Supreme War Council; the Allied force in Siberia should be under a commander 'appointed by the power that provides the largest number of troops' (an over-delicate reference to Japan); the Allied force at Murmansk and Archangel should be increased 'as the Allied military advisers may recommend'; and finally, 'relief expeditions under American direction and control [should be sent out] to supply the wants and alleviate the sufferings of the Russian people'.

It was then added: 'The primary object of this Allied action being to cooperate with the Russian nation in restoring the eastern front, as a first step towards freeing Russia, the closest coordination must exist between the inter-Allied Army and the Russian people.' (During the discussion, there was disagreement on the above sentence, which had initially read 'the closest coordination must exist between the inter-Allied Army and the Russian Armies'. Baron Sonnino had said, 'Bearing in mind the number of armies, or so-called armies, existing in Russia, he [Sonnino] thought it would be better to substitute for the words "Russian armies" the expression "Russian people". President Wilson would certainly agree to this.' This was generally agreed.)

In view of all their arguments (stress being laid twice on the importance of the despatch of an 'adequate' Allied force to Siberia), the British paper concluded with an 'appeal to President Wilson to approve the policy here recommended, and thus to enable it to be carried into effect before it is too late'.[1]

The Supreme War Council now approved the paper, as modified, and it was agreed that Balfour should send it by telegraph to Lord Reading, who should consult the other Allied ambassadors in Washington on the manner of its presentation to President Wilson.

This paper, the final appeal to President Wilson, pulled out all the stops, used every possible argument in favour of intervention — and stood every anti-intervention argument on its head. First, the Czechs and their seizure of the Siberian railway: their success did not prove that the Siberian people must be friendlily disposed to the Allied cause. They had carried out swift military actions, which had nothing to do with the local population, who wished to remain neutral. Next, the overwhelming preponderance of the Japanese in the intervening force would not necessarily remove the danger of precipitating the Russians into German arms, as had all along been feared. Nor was there any German 'organization', prisoner or otherwise, at Irkutsk; and Lloyd George was simply giving easy credence to nervous local reports. To abandon the Czechs might, however, have adverse consequences on Allied relations with the Slavs elsewhere. Lastly, it might be a simple and speedy matter to push through to Irkutsk, but no further; the Japanese, incidentally, had reckoned that even this would need seven divisions, or 150,000 men.

Secondly, the Russian internal situation, the Bolsheviks, reactionaries and 'German agents', and the liberal democrats: there was no evidence that 'German agents' among the Bolsheviks desired German intervention. The Bolsheviks were equally hostile to German and Allied intervention. The liberal democrats certainly desired Allied intervention, but they were as

divided as the paper made out. What business was it of the Allies to intervene simply to unite them? (The repeated reference to 'regeneration',
incidentally, would appear to indicate that the British were pinning their
hopes mainly on the 'Union for the Regeneration of Russia'.) It should be
noted that two references to Kerensky in this paragraph were struck out on
French insistence. Lastly, as the paper by the British military section at
Versailles of June 15 made clear, the Allies only wished to seize the western
Siberian grain supplies in order to obtain a powerful lever with which to
influence the Russian people; they only wanted to do what they feared the
Germans might do. There was nothing particularly humanitarian about it.

Thirdly, Allied intervention and Allied victory: the Allies' realization, as
plainly stated in the paper, that they only had the smallest chance of victory
even in 1919 is very instructive. But there appears to be little evidence that
the Germans were really envisaging a substantial return to the east, despite
Ludendorff's recent demands to the Foreign Ministry.

Fourthly, Balfour's illusions about Allied intervention and Japan: the
Japanese reply handed to Balfour on June 24 had made it clear that they
could undertake to go no further than eastern Siberia; but he had tried to
twist its meaning to a willingness, though not a promise, to push as far west
as possible. The Japanese ambassador appears to have encouraged Balfour
in this erroneous assumption, entirely in a desire to please. The Japanese
Foreign Minister was much grieved on hearing what had transpired
between Balfour and his ambassador.[2] On July 1, he wired from Tokyo,
saying that the Japanese government's decision not to undertake to
proceed beyond eastern Siberia was guided by what was practical and feasible, and their decision was 'categorical and final'. Japanese troops would
encounter great obstacles if they tried to go further; and this, together with
ever-lengthening lines of communications, would result in failure against
the enemy, whom the Allies wished them to encounter somewhere near the
Urals. In the light of the British military section's paper of June 15, this was
an honest reply, considering the number of troops which the Japanese
could employ. On July 3, the Japanese ambassador handed the Foreign
Minister's wire to Lord Robert Cecil, who persisted in believing that
Japanese troops would try to push forward from eastern Siberia; Cecil even
contacted Balfour in Paris to the same effect. Wilful self-deception could
go no further. The statement in the Supreme War Council's paper that the
Allies could seize the Siberian railway as far as the Urals in a few weeks
does not merit further scrutiny.

Lastly, even the statement that 100,000 troops would be needed was
false. The British military section at Versailles had stated on June 15 that
30 divisions of Allied troops (600,000 men) would be needed both to
protect and maintain the Siberian railway up to the Urals, and to take
action there against the Germans. The Japanese thought they would need
150,000 men if they went only as far as Irkutsk.

In the final paragraph, due reference was made to the despatch of relief expeditions to Russia under American control (which the President was thought to be considering in lieu of intervention), but these expeditions, it is clear, were to come in the wake of intervention. The Allied force in northern Russia was to be increased. But the main emphasis was on the need for the 'closest coordination' between the inter-Allied army and the Russian armies. This clearly referred to the clandestine forces of Savinkov, of the 'Union for the Regeneration of Russia', and of the 'National Centre', and the volunteer army in southern Russia. This, as the previous Supreme War Council had stated at its meeting on June 3, was the responsibility of the French.

Thus the final appeal for Allied intervention to President Wilson, made by the Supreme War Council, the highest military authority of the Allies, was shot through with gross — and fairly easily detectable — military error, extreme exaggeration, and wilful self-deception. Hankey, the author of this paper, did not even attend this meeting, commenting somewhat oddly that it would be 'better to leave them to discuss without record'. The real reason for Hankey's absence appears to have been his foreboding about Lloyd George's behaviour during the discussions. For some days, Hankey records, the Prime Minister had been in an 'extraordinarily perverse and irritable frame of mind', which a bad channel crossing had only exacerbated. And indeed at one point during the Council's meeting, Lloyd George made such an 'extremely violent' attack on the French, and was so rude to them generally, that Milner actually had to propose a halt in the discussions.[2]

At the next meeting of the council on July 3, Clemenceau drew attention to the situation in Russia and Siberia (a discussion of which should surely have preceded the final appeal to President Wilson). Clemenceau asked Sir Eric Geddes, the First Lord, to tell them of his experiences at Murmansk. Sir Eric attempted to show that the Russian people paid no attention to orders from Moscow, a situation 'which he had been assured by competent observers' was 'typical of the whole of Russia'. The account of General Zvegintsev, Lenin's order, and his discussion with General Poole was related, and was followed by an involved anecdote about an attempted requisition of food, which showed that the local soviets were divided amongst themselves. 'If, as he was told by those who knew Russia, this was typical of what was going on everywhere, the general conclusion was that Russia must be treated as being without a government or common policy.' General Poole was hoping to use his small Allied nucleus as a rallying point for anti-German Russian elements, and was intending to advance with 5,000 men from Archangel down the railway to Vologda to collect 100,000 Russians — though he admitted the enterprise was a gamble (in the French minutes, this appeared as 'un coup de dé ').

The First Lord then drew attention to his paper, dated June 28, on the northern Russian situation, which was addressed to the Prime Minister, and was now circulated to the meeting. It will be recalled that in this there were jovial references to Poole and his 'fiery cross'; a passable description of the northern Russian countryside; a sound argument against the possibility of the Germans using any part of the Murman coast for submarine bases; a comparison of the whole Russian state (simply on the basis of what he had seen in northern Russia) to a minor South American republic; and a recommendation that Poole should be sent 5,000 more men. (In the French translation, the word 'gamble' now became *un baccarat*.) As regards Archangel, the First Lord added, till ten days ago [i.e. about June 23] General Poole had thought that the people were friendly. He had since learnt that German agents had arrived at Archangel, and that the town authorities [the Archangel soviet] had asked the British armed icebreaker to leave the port.' (There appears to be no evidence that German agents had arrived at Archangel; the local soviet simply followed the Moscow line.) The Murmansk soviet had completely broken with the Bolshevik government, and had allied itself with General Poole, who 'proposed to use it for the purpose of negotiating with Archangel. Should Archangel not join this league, it would be attacked by our naval forces.' Poole's 5,000 men would then go down the railway to Vologda to gather around them the 100,000 Russians. Most of the ships at present in the port were not of sufficiently shallow draught to go up the River Dvina to Kotlas, whence there was a railway line down to Vyatka (via which, Noulens had told the Czechs on the Volga, an Allied army would come to their aid). Several special boats would be sent out, the First Lord continued, and it was hoped to send two gun-boats. It was open to the other Allies to send out some boats as well.

The French Foreign Minister, Pichon, said he was 'very much struck' by these remarks, which coincided with those made by General Berthelot, after studying this region on his return from Russia (some little while ago, it should be remarked). All they now had to do was to stick to the Supreme War Council's previous decision, and to hurry it along. General Poole had insufficient forces.* He should intervene quickly. Baron Sonnino, too, wanted intervention to be carried out swiftly.

M. Clemenceau: We therefore maintain our previous decision, but ...

Sig. Sonnino: Let us put it into operation at once.

Orlando, the Italian Premier, said that two Italian battalions were ready. General Bliss remarked that the American troops were also ready, but the American government wanted certain points to be cleared up before sending them off. After the previous council meeting, he had sent a wire to Washington saying that six Allied battalions would have to be sent to inter-

---

*There are marked differences here between the French and British minutes. Since the French minutes constitute the official version, and the text both here and in the following passage is highly critical of British action, reliance has here been placed on the French minutes.

vene in the White Sea ports. But since then, Secretary Baker had received a telegram asking him to send 5,000 men with artillery and specialists. He had been unable to reconcile this demand with Bliss's wire.

At this, Lord Milner launched into an explanation. The previous resolution had stated that a small number of Allied troops, amounting at most to six battalions, should be sent out. Half a British battalion was already on the spot, half were *en route*, and a French battalion had been promised, when General Poole asked for three more battalions. His request appeared to be within the terms of the resolution. There seemed to be no other source but America for these further battalions. Milner had asked Clemenceau and Foch if they would object to them being withdrawn from the American contingents *en route* for the western front, and they had agreed. He had therefore sent the wire mentioned by General Bliss, which appeared to conflict with the previous resolution, but in fact did not. (This was a partial explanation by Milner.) General Bliss remarked that Secretary Baker had presumably thought that these six battalions would be split up equally between the Allies, and did not understand why America should be asked for a force practically equal to the total force recommended in the resolution.

Foch remarked that agreement must be reached on how the troops were to be split up; Mr Baker had wired him for his opinion. Milner's telegram to Mr Baker had asked for two batteries, with horses and munitions, as well as three infantry battalions, and this would represent a considerable effort. Foch was unaware that any such decision had been taken by the Supreme War Council, but he would raise no objection if no further demands were to be made on America.

It was thereupon decided that the French, British and Italian governments should expedite the despatch of the forces (six battalions) recommended in Joint Note 31, and that the American government should be asked to send three battalions, in addition to those units already asked for by the British government in their telegram of June 11; and that the British government should be asked to ship these troops to northern Russia. It was also agreed that a summary of the First Lord's statement, together with the above resolution, should be wired to Washington for President Wilson's information.

The council next discussed the situation at Vladivostok. Pichon read a telegram from the Allied consuls there with an appeal from the Czech national council for Allied military help to enable the Czechs in western Siberia to make their way to Vladivostok. In the wire, attention was drawn to the 'progressive arming' of German and Austrian prisoners at Irkutsk and Khabarovsk, north of Vladivostok, on the Amur line. It was also stated that the mining of railway tunnels by the Bolsheviks would be completed in three weeks. It seemed clear that the Czechs at Vladivostok would not embark for France until the rest of their colleagues on the Siberian line had rejoined them. It was expected that Allied intervention would induce 'several hundreds of thousands of Russians' to rally to the Allied cause.

Pichon thought that this wire, which came from the entire Allied consular body, had been sent to Washington, but a note, based on this wire, could be sent to President Wilson.

Balfour said that he had heard from Peking that Vladivostok had fallen to the Czechs as a result of the local soviet refusing to allow munitions there to be sent westwards, doubtless to the Czechs in western Siberia. He had also had another telegram giving details about the capture of the town.[3] (This second wire had been read to the War Cabinet in London at noon on the previous day, but there was no mention of Pichon's wire.) Pichon remarked that this supplied information for a further plea to President Wilson. Sonnino agreed that it should be passed on to him, but that they should not make too much of it ('il ne faut pas trop insister').

(A later telegram, unknown to the Supreme War Council on July 3, but read out to the War Cabinet in London on July 4, stated that the Czech commander at Vladivostok had reported that he had had news that Bolshevik troops and war prisoners from Nikolsk, the junction of the Amur and Chinese eastern railways, just north of Vladivostok, had been sent to blow up a tunnel some thirty miles from Vladivostok; and a Czech regiment had been despatched to frustrate this, and to push on to Grodekovo, north of Nikolsk on the Chinese eastern line, and so on to Harbin. A further wire stated that on July 2, the Czech commander had explained that he needed to send every available man to Irkutsk, and he gave details of the forces opposed to him at various places *en route*: 15,000 Red Army men, 12,000 armed prisoners, 50 guns, and a reserve of 25,000 armed Red Guards. He also asked that the Allied warships in Vladivostok harbour should guarantee a reserve of 1,000 men to be landed in support of the small Czech force left behind, in the event of an attack after the main Czech force had departed. The Allied naval commanders were asking their governments for immediate approval of such measures, as action might have to be taken very shortly. Of the 15,000 Czechs at Vladivostok, 13,000 would leave for Irkutsk by July 4. They had been given 10,000 rifles from the Allied stores at Vladivostok, but were in urgent need of guns and rifle ammunition.[4] The Czechs had now taken the tunnel referred to in the first wire, and were approaching Nikolsk. The War Cabinet thereupon approved the measures proposed.)

At this point, Clemenceau asked whether anyone knew when they would receive the President's answer. The march of the seasons took no account of such things; if we went on waiting, the ice would come and make any expedition impossible. Balfour remarked that he understood that the President would speak on the matter the next day in his speech during the Fourth of July celebrations. Clemenceau said that the President should speak the next day, but he now knew that he would not. He would prefer to receive the President's answer through a diplomatic channel, but it was vital to have an answer somehow. The Supreme War Council should, however, decide what to do if the President should not agree to intervene.

Sonnino thought that all they had said should be communicated to the President, but no decision on further action should be taken until they had his reply. Lloyd George remarked that there was one decision they could take: the Czechs, in their previous telegram, had asked for 14,000 rifles. The British had a very large stock of rifles in America, bought with British money, and once destined for the Russian army. These rifles, with 700 million rounds of ammunition, could be supplied to the Czechs, if shipping were available. This proposal was adopted by the council.

The Supreme War Council's final appeal for Allied intervention was handed to President Wilson by Lord Reading on the afternoon of July 3. Shortly afterwards, Secretary Lansing telephoned to the White House to announce that the Czechs had seized control of Vladivostok. The next day, sometime during the junketings of the Fourth of July, Lansing wrote a paper for the President on the Siberian question. Czech seizure of Vladivostok and Czech success in western Siberia, he wrote, had 'materially changed the situation by introducing a sentimental element into the question of our duty'. America now had a responsibility to help the Czechs. Lansing urged that arms be sent to those in Vladivostok, together with some troops to help them police the Siberian railway and disarm and disperse the enemy prisoners opposing them. Helping the Czechs, argued Lansing, was entirely different from intervention on other grounds. But even if some American troops were sent, Japan would have to be relied on to supply the main part of the necessary force. A proclamation of intent and of non-interference in Russian internal affairs should be made at once. The Allied commission to Russia, which had been under consideration, should also be sent and should 'proceed westward from Vladivostok following as closely as possible, with due regard to safety, the Czechoslovaks'. A decision could be made later on its final destination and duty, depending on how the commission was received by the Russian people, and on what military opposition it encountered. There are certain points to be noted here. One cannot help feeling that the phrases 'sentimental element' and 'our duty' had some connection with the date of the paper — the Fourth of July. In addition, the Allied, or rather American, commission had now definitely taken second place; it was to follow the intervening force, as trade follows the flag, not the other way round, as Lansing had argued in his paper of June 13.[5]

Lansing's paper reached the President on the morning of the 5th. That afternoon, he instructed Lansing, the Secretary of War, the Chief of Staff, the Secretary of the Navy, and the Chief of Naval Operations, to attend a special meeting at the White House the next day, July 6. At this meeting, the President said that he had studied the question of present conditions in Siberia, as influenced by the Czech seizure of Vladivostok, by the landing of American, British, French and Japanese naval parties, and by the occupation of the railway in western Siberia by other Czechs, 'with the reported taking of Irkutsk by these troops' (this point was wrong). He had also read and discussed the Supreme War Council's final appeal 'favouring an attempt to restore an eastern front', and Secretary Lansing's recent paper. As a result, he had come to the following conclusions. It was 'physically impossible' for an Allied military expedition to restore an eastern front, even east of the Urals, 'even if it was wise to employ a large Japanese force'. In fact, it was impossible even to advance west of Irkutsk. But the present position of the Czechs required the American 'and other governments' to try to help the Czechs at Vladivostok to link up with their colleagues in western Siberia; and the American government, 'on sentimental grounds and because of the effect upon the friendly Slavs everywhere', would be subject to criticism, and doubtless held responsible if the Czechs were defeated by lack of such effort. Since America, however, was unable to provide any 'considerable force' within a short time to help the Czechs, the following plan would be adopted, subject to Japanese agreement.

1. Japan should supply the Czechs at Vladivostok with arms and ammunition, the American government sharing the expense and supplementing the supplies as quickly as possible.
2. A military force of 7,000 Americans and 7,000 Japanese should assemble at Vladivostok to protect the communications of the Czechs returning to Irkutsk; and Japanese troops should be sent at once.
3. American and Allied naval vessels should land available forces to hold Vladivostok, and cooperate with the Czechs.
4. The American and Japanese governments should publicly announce that their aim was to help the Czechs against German and Austrian prisoners, not to interfere in Russian internal affairs, but to respect Russian political and territorial sovereignty.
5. They should then await further developments before taking further steps.

With the exception of the American Chief of Staff, who was convinced that Japan would not limit herself to 7,000 men, the meeting agreed with the President's conclusions, which were certainly remarkable. He had entirely rejected the argument contained in the Supreme War Council's lengthy appeal for the restoration of the eastern front — and in this military opinion he was right. But what could 15,000 Czechs and a combined American–Japanese force of 14,000 do on the line between Vladivostok and Irkutsk? The Japanese thought that at least 150,000 troops would be needed if they went no further than Irkutsk. Then there was no mention of an Allied commission to Russia; nor (more ominously) any mention of the British and French, who had been pressing the President for months on this issue. As far as can be judged, the President was banking on the very appearance of American and Japanese troops, in equal numbers of course, causing a powerful pro-Allied swing in Russian public opinion; while the Czechs, who were of course Slavs or half-Russian themselves, did the necessary at the sharp end. But this, once again, was very near to what Lloyd George and the War Cabinet had proposed on May 17 — only to have their proposal shot down a fortnight later by the French, on the grounds that it would incur the mortal hostility of the American President.[5]

On Monday morning, July 8, the Japanese ambassador was summoned to the State Department, where Secretary Lansing informed him of the American decision. No action was taken to answer the Supreme War Council, nor even to inform the British and French ambassadors of what had occurred; indeed, Lord Reading called on the President to discuss another matter later that afternoon, and the President made no mention of his decision. Only later that day did it occur to Lansing that Japan would at once inform the Allied governments, who would (quite naturally) be furious at having heard nothing directly from Washington. With the President's approval, Lansing thus summoned the British, French and Italian ambassadors in turn next morning. When Reading was told, he too was furious, mainly because of the exclusion of the other Allies from the proposed intervention. Lansing appears to have given slightly different versions of the President's decision to the French and Italian ambassadors. That afternoon, Reading brought his French and Italian colleagues with him back to the State Department to demand to know whether it was the American intention to confine the intervention to American and Japanese troops, and to exclude Allied troops even from the initial landing at Vladivostok. An acrimonious exchange followed between Lansing and Reading. Lansing said he could see no advantage in discussing the matter with the President until the Japanese had approved; and if they had failed to consult the Allies, the Americans would only be acting in a way that the Allies had often acted towards them. Reading insisted that Allied troops must take part in the initial landing. Lansing replied that this was more a question of national pride than a practical matter; it merely showed how wise the Americans had been in not consulting the Allies first, as it would only have caused delay; he was 'not disposed to consider the sentimental phase but only the expedient side of the question'.

This was a very curious episode. Lansing, in his paper to the President, had urged American support for the Czechs on 'sentimental' grounds. But five days later, he was accusing Reading of being 'sentimental' in wishing Allied troops to be included in the initial landing in the Far East. The probable explanation of the American attitude, which smells strongly of panic, is that they were faced with a *fait accompli.* On July 6, the day on which the President had made known his decision, the Murmansk soviet signed a formal agreement with the local Allied representatives for the defence of the area (at which the Bolsheviks cut the Petrograd–Murmansk telegraph wires, and blew up the bridges between Kem and Soroka, thus isolating Murmansk from the Russian interior); and in the Far East, Czech and local Allied representatives issued a proclamation declaring that Vladivostok was now under Allied protection. Thus both Russian ports of entry for an intervening force — in northern Russia and the Far East — had fallen into Allied hands — with the hearty concurrence, in both cases, of the local American representative. With the Supreme War Council's appeal in his hands, which President Wilson had condemned as military absurdity, he nevertheless had to 'do something'. This is what he did. The telegram which Lord Reading sent to the Foreign Office on the night of July 9, however, informing Balfour of the American decision, was studiously correct.[5]

During the deliberations at Versailles and Washington, two serious anti-Bolshevik revolts occurred in Russia: one in Moscow, a political revolt by the left SRs, designed to force the Bolsheviks to break with Germany; and one just outside Moscow, a military revolt led by Savinkov, and designed to coincide with Allied intervention in northern Russia. The result was that the Bolsheviks, by adroit use of *agents provocateurs*, succeeded in eliminating not only the left SRs (their last remaining political rivals), but both the nerve centre of the pro-German 'orientation' in their midst, and the most dangerous pro-Allied group among the Russian opposition. Based on a shrewd calculation that German power was on the decline, and that Allied intervention was imminent (though not nearly so soon as people imagined), this series of *coups* was a triumph for Lenin and the hard-pressed Bolshevik party.

Germany was, in fact, conducting two separate policies towards Russia. While she was engaged in trade negotiations with Bolshevik delegates in Berlin, mainly designed to secure more Russian and Ukrainian grain for herself, she was also (mainly in the person of Ludendorff) vigorously supporting General Krasnov and his Don Cossacks in south-eastern Russia, whom she could swiftly use either to take over the central Russian government, if the Bolsheviks fell, or to put the Bolsheviks down. The Foreign Ministry in Berlin wished the Bolsheviks to remain in power, and were prepared to sign a favourable trade treaty to keep them there, since the German diplomats considered that Bolshevik policy in Russia suited German interests better than any alternative policy by any other conceivable Russian government. They were consequently opposed to German support for Krasnov. But on June 25, the German ambassador, Mirbach, had written privately to the Foreign Secretary, Kühlmann, in Berlin, reviewing events in Moscow since his arrival in April. 'After two months' careful observation, I can now no longer give Bolshevism a favourable diagnosis', he stated firmly. 'We are unquestionably standing by the bedside of a dangerously ill man, who might show apparent improvement from time to time, but who is lost in the long run.' Not only would Bolshevism soon disintegrate of its own accord, but there were 'all too many elements' working tirelessly to bring it down, and to assure themselves of the succession. Germany might thus soon be faced with the 'most undesirable state of affairs possible': SRs, backed with Allied money and Czech arms, leading a new Russia back into the Allied ranks. Germany must therefore foster a new Russian regime 'favourable to our designs and interests — and this does not necessarily mean the immediate restoration of the Monarchy'.[6]

The nucleus must be composed of right-wing moderates and left Cadets, which would draw in many influential Russian industrialists and bankers, and could be further strengthened 'if we could draw the Siberians into it — though this would indeed be our hardest problem. Then, even further vistas, based on the mineral resources of Siberia, would appear ...'. Germany would not even have to apply a great deal of force to achieve a change of 'orientation' in Moscow, and could keep up appearances with the Bolsheviks to the very last moment. 'The continual mismanagement here, and the equally continual violent blows being struck against our interests, could be used as a motive for a military advance at any time we chose; and any military advance made by us on any considerable scale — and it would not even have to be directed against the two capitals — would automatically lead to the fall of Bolshevism.'

The strength within Bolshevik Russia of the pro-German 'orientation', as it was called, was enormous. Even the Cheka, as Professor Katkov shows, could not arrest certain individuals without the consent of the German embassy. But, probably from some time in early June (when Counsellor Riezler apparently first warned that the Bolsheviks would probably fall and that Germany only had six to eight weeks in which to decide whether to set up a pro-German bourgeois regime in Moscow instead), the Cheka, while still ostensibly submitting to German demands, began a fierce underground struggle to neutralize and eliminate the pro-German faction and its forces. By the time of Mirbach's letter of June 25, making it clear that the ambassador himself now supported Riezler's — and, incidentally, Ludendorff's — line, and was also playing a double game, the head of the Cheka's department dealing with German espionage and surveillance of the German embassy, a left SR called Blumkin, reported that he had a 'complete plan' of the German embassy, 'that his agents were supplying him with all the information he wanted, and that he was thus able to make contact with the whole of the German orientation'.[7]

Mirbach's letter of June 25, advocating an anti-Bolshevik *coup*, ended with a warning: 'Of course, nothing can be had absolutely free: we shall have to pay some kind of price, if not immediately.' Germany's new Russian friends would not accept blindly the Russian map as drawn by the Brest–Litovsk treaty. They might have detached themselves from Poland and most of the Baltic States. But the amputation of Estonia would arouse much bitterness, because of the loss of the port of Reval, 'while it has become a positive political axiom that the permanent separation of the Ukraine from the rest of Russia must be proclaimed as impossible'.

Now it was in the Ukraine that the left SRs, who were still in political alliance with the Bolsheviks, found their main support. While the Bolsheviks relied mainly on the urban proletariat, the left SRs were the party of the peasants, and the Ukrainian peasants were being treated with systematic brutality by German troops in their endeavours to extract grain supplies for Germany, while the Russian peasants were being harried by Bolshevik requisitioning parties also after grain to try and avert starvation in the Russian towns. The left SRs were thus more and more against the German–Bolshevik line. But though they had withdrawn from the Bolshevik government in protest at the Brest–Litovsk treaty, they had retained their positions on the central executive committee, on the various soviets, and bodies like the Cheka. Appalled at the increasing suffering of their colleagues in the Ukraine, they were now no longer willing to tolerate Lenin's 'breathing-spell', his servility to the Germans, and his attempts in Berlin to increase Russian trade with Germany. The left SRs denounced the Bolsheviks as 'Mirbach's lackeys'. The Bolsheviks now considered the left SRs as effective only when it came to words. 'The Don Quixotes of the Revolution, they are attractive in the pages of a novel, but utterly ridiculous in politics.' But on June 24, the day before Mirbach wrote privately to Kühlmann, the left SR central committee secretly decided to force Lenin to end the 'breathing-spell' by assassinating 'outstanding representatives of German imperialism', and to concentrate SR forces in Moscow if it came to a clash with the Bolsheviks. They gave public warning that their patience had run out. On the 30th, Marie Spiridonova, a leading left SR, openly castigated the Bolsheviks in the central executive committee for sending food and goods to Germany; only an armed uprising could now save the revolution, she declared. The next day, her colleague, Kamkov, warned the Moscow soviet that trouble was inevitable unless the Brest–Litovsk treaty was repudiated and Mirbach expelled from Moscow. The coming fifth congress of soviets was thus assured of some stormy sessions. But by July 4, when the congress opened, Lenin had already decided what should be done, not only about the left SRs, but also about Mirbach — and the former Tsar and the Russian Imperial Family as well.[7]

Up to now, the reader will have found no reference to the Imperial Family, since after the War Cabinet had made an offer of asylum in England to the Tsar and his family in March 1917, the offer was withdrawn at the express wish of King George V, the Tsar's cousin, early in April; and thereafter the War Cabinet appear never to have discussed the matter again; indeed, considerations for the Imperial Family seem to have played no part in the formulation of British policy. In 1917, the Imperial Family had remained under guard at Tsarskoe Selo from March 21 to August 14. To ensure their safety, the provisional government then decided that they would have to be moved. On August 19, they had arrived at Tobolsk, in Siberia, and were again placed under guard.

Just after the signature of the Brest–Litovsk treaty in mid-March 1918, the Kaiser replied to the King of Denmark (the Tsar's first cousin, who had asked for urgent German intervention on behalf of the Romanovs) that demands from Berlin might be interpreted by the Bolsheviks in Moscow as a desire to bring about a Romanov restoration; the neutral Scandinavians were better placed to make overtures. But the Kaiser promised that he would do what he could, when he could, to ensure the safety of the family. On April 30 (seven days after the arrival of Count Mirbach as German ambassador in Moscow), the Imperial Family arrived at Ekaterinburg, in the Urals, and were lodged in the house of a merchant called Ipatiev, who was given a few hours to leave; and there they remained under close guard.[7]

On about May 7, Count Benckendorff, former Marshal of the Russian Imperial Court, wrote to Count Mirbach (whom he had known personally before the war), placing responsibility for the safety of the Romanovs squarely on the Germans; Benckendorff insisted that his appeal should reach the Kaiser himself. The German view appears to have been that while the Tsar's fate was a matter for the Russian people, the safety of the 'German princesses' (the Tsarina, who was a Princess of Hesse, and her daughters) was a matter of legitimate concern to the Germans. On May 10, three days after receiving Benckendorff's appeal, Mirbach reported to the Foreign Ministry in Berlin that he had handed a note to the Bolshevik government stating that the German government expected that the 'German princesses will be treated with all possible consideration', and that threats against their lives and 'unnecessary petty annoyances' would not be allowed. At the Commissariat for Foreign Affairs, Karakhan and Radek (head of the central European department) had received this statement 'with an indication of understanding and a complete willingness to insist that such action be prevented'.

From then on, Mirbach's demands for assurances about the Romanovs persisted. There are indications that the Germans may have offered German help or support to the Tsar, and that he refused it; also that the Germans may have decided to kidnap the Tsar against his will; and further, that the Tsar may have been taken out of Ekaterinburg in mid-June — presumably to hold discussions with someone — and then been brought back to Ekaterinburg, where for some while there had been a German Red Cross Mission, based in a train. When reports of the murder of the Tsar appeared in the Moscow press in June (this may well have been Bolshevik 'kite-flying'), Mirbach's demands increased. By mid to late June, Lenin knew that the growing success of the Czech revolt would soon force him to take some final action about the Tsar and the Imperial Family at Ekaterinburg, which would obviously soon fall. In the last days of June, Goloshchokin, the regional war commissar in the Ural soviet, an old friend of Lenin, was summoned to Moscow for discussions about the Imperial Family, and a decision seems to have been taken.

On July 4, a Moscow paper printed an interview with Lenin, in which he denied rumours of the Tsar's death. Beloborodov, Chairman of the Ural soviet, wired to Sverdlov, head of the soviet state, and Goloshchokin in Moscow, stating that a Bolshevik official had just been sent to Ekaterinburg 'to organize the matter in accordance with instructions of centre. No cause for apprehension.' A new and reliable guard commander, with mainly Latvian guards, had been sent to take over at the house at Ipatiev, and the existing guard, which had become increasingly drunk and disorderly, had been removed.[7]

On that same day, the fifth Congress of Soviets opened in the Bolshoi Theatre, attended by 1,425 delegates, of which 868 were Bolsheviks and 470 left SRs; Mirbach attended as a spectator. Trotsky warned the congress that agitation was being carried on in certain Red Army units on the Ukrainian front to incite them to attack the Germans; this would seriously threaten their policy towards Germany. 'One of the commissars reports that stories are being circulated to the effect that the soviet government is selling out the Ukrainians ... buying up all the cloth for the Germans, sending bread to Germany, etc.' Trotsky could not say definitely who these agitators were, but it was 'more than likely' that they belonged to the parties opposed to the Brest–Litovsk peace, who were in favour of resuming the war, or were agents of the Anglo–French bourse. (Trotsky was careful not to name the left SRs.) The previous day, he went on, he had despatched this order: 'I hereby order that all agitators be arrested and brought to Moscow for trial by the extraordinary tribunal. All armed agents of foreign imperialism who advocate an attack [on the Germans] and are caught opposing the Soviet Government should be shot on the spot.'[7]

This caused violent protests from the left SRs. Kamkov retorted that the situation on the Ukrainian front 'cannot be explained away so simply as by blaming it on German and French provocation'. It was the result of the 'healthy revolutionary psychology of the people, who could not swallow the bait of a breathing-spell and refuse to serve German capital. ... We have most accurate information that among the army units, especially the Ukrainian, there is a healthy revolutionary movement. ... You cannot compel them to stand patiently and wait until you give orders, and you cannot give orders until Mirbach gives them to you. We declare that our party is going to support this healthy revolutionary movement.' Zinoviev then made the congress face the issues: 'We have come to a parting of the ways with the

Lefts ... if this is a challenge to battle, we accept it. ... We stand by the workers stationed at the front who are carrying out the decision of the congress of soviets.'[7]

After the left SRs had conferred privately, Marie Spiridonova announced their decision. 'Comrade Bolsheviks, we pick up the gauntlet! ... You may carry off the victory at this meeting because you have a majority here, but you do not have a majority in the country.' After Trotsky had spoken again, the Bolsheviks introduced a resolution 'on war and peace', stating that the congress resolved that the 'power of decision in matters of war and peace belongs only to the all-Russian congress of soviets ... and that all army units must submit in these questions to the orders of the central organs of the soviet government ... '. The left SRs refused to vote, and left the theatre in a body; after which the resolution was passed.

Sometime after the end of the day's session, which had seen a hostile demonstration against Mirbach (or possibly during the interval when the left SRs momentarily withdrew), the left SR Chekist Blumkin, who was responsible for countering German activities, came to see Spiridonova at the Bolshoi Theatre; and after some talk, offered to assassinate Mirbach. The offer was accepted. Whether Blumkin initiated this or was summoned is not clear. But, as Professor Katkov states, it is known that certain left SRs employed by the Cheka were at that time acting as Bolshevik agents; and if Blumkin was such an agent, he could not have made such an offer without the direct sanction of Lenin himself.

When the congress resumed on the 5th, Sverdlov, chairman of the central executive committee, on which the left SRs had retained their seats, warned them that the soviet government had recovered from the 'terrible blow' received at the conclusion of the previous congress in mid-March, when the left SRs had resigned, after the ratification of the Brest–Litovsk treaty. Until recently, the left SRs had worked with the Bolsheviks on the central executive committee. Now, they were disputing with the Bolsheviks on issue after issue. Spiridonova vigorously refuted this. Lenin then spoke. 'Our policy at Brest–Litovsk has been justified. ... The food question is the most important and all efforts are being concentrated on its solution. ... We are face to face with the most difficult period in our revolution — the time of awaiting the new crop. ... We are not waging war on the peasants, but are endeavouring to save socialism and divide the bread in Russia.' Kamkov delivered the final attack on Bolshevik policy. 'Comrade Lenin is confident that the policy pursued will save the Russian and the international revolutions. The question is whether the peasant is satisfied, and whether Bolshevik policy will not be fatal to the revolution. ... Comrade Lenin is trying to frighten us by saying that nothing will be left of the party that leaves the soviet. As it stands today, the soviet is nothing but the dictatorship of Mirbach. We are not going to leave the soviet, and you, Lenin, cannot put us out. We shall defend the cause of the peasants and workers; we shall work for real socialism and not for the make-believe socialism which now exists.' Zinoviev made the final point against the left SRs. 'You are trying to stir up the peasants against the workers.' Both parties then introduced resolutions. The left SRs condemned Bolshevik policies and called for the repudiation of the Brest–Litovsk treaty. They were defeated. The Bolshevik resolution approved the soviet government's policies and urged mass terror against the enemies of the revolution; their resolution was passed. Bruce Lockhart records that during Kamkov's speech, a French intelligence officer in the same box applauded fiercely. But throughout the left SR demagogy, a Russian observer merely noted that Lenin seemed impatient.

In Kiev that day, Count Alvensleben (a senior German diplomat, with connections at the German court) asked two prominent Russian monarchists to meet him urgently; he had vital information for them. The Kaiser, he told them, wished at all costs to rescue the Tsar; and between July 16 and 20, rumours would be spread of the Tsar's death, which should not alarm Russian monarchists. Like similar rumours current in June, these would be false, but would be necessary for the Tsar's rescue. The Russians were asked to keep this information secret and to give the impression that they believed these rumours. This would appear to indicate that the Germans and Bolsheviks had come to an agreement about the Tsar; under cover of a further rumour of his death, he would in fact be abducted by the Germans. But this agreement was weighted heavily in favour of the Bolsheviks. Lenin could either hand the Tsar over to the Germans, as apparently agreed, and deceive the Russian people, and the Allies, with reports of his death; or he could actually shoot the Tsar, deceiving everyone — Germans, Russians and the Allies — with reports of his death, and insinuations that the Bolsheviks had abducted him themselves.

The next day (July 6), Savinkov's organization suddenly seized Yaroslavl, between Moscow and Vologda, on the Moscow–Archangel line, and Blumkin and an accomplice, armed with a pass signed by Dzerzhinsky himself, called at the German embassy on some pretext, assassinated Mirbach, and escaped. As the Cheka descended on both the Bolshoi Theatre and the left SR headquarters to round up their rivals (Blumkin miraculously escaped and was not to be found for nearly a year, when he was even more miraculously pardoned), Lenin issued a statement to all soviets that Mirbach had been wounded by a bomb. 'This is obviously the act of monarchists and provocateurs who want to draw Russia into war in the interests of the Anglo–French capitalists, who have already made the Czechoslovaks their hirelings.' These criminals must be found, Lenin insisted. A further official statement issued shortly after stated that 'two scoundrels, agents of Russo–Anglo–French imperialism', had killed Mirbach. 'One of the rascals who carried out this act of provocation — which the Soviet press has for long and repeatedly connected with a plot of

Russian monarchists and counter-revolutionaries — is, according to information obtained, a member of Dzerzhinsky's Commission' (i.e. the Cheka), who had 'treacherously defected' from the service of the soviets to those who wished to draw Russia back into the war, and restore the power of the capitalists and landowners. 'Thanks to these left SR scoundrels', it continued, 'who let themselves be lured on to the path of the Savinkovs and Co, Russia is now on the brink of war. ... The left SRs responded to the first steps which the soviet authorities in Moscow took to arrest the murderer and his accomplice by starting an uprising against the soviet government.' Lenin had thus done his utmost to counter possible German reprisals and maintain the balance between the British and the Germans. He had implicated the left SRs in the murder with the Allies, but was now proceeding against Savinkov as well; there was no doubt which side he was on. It should be added that there was no left SR uprising. While a few of the wilder spirits momentarily seized the Moscow telegraph office and despatched telegrams to all and sundry asking for support — declaring that they alone had killed Mirbach — the majority resisted arrest. After the Bolsheviks had shelled their headquarters next day, the remaining left SRs were taken away by the Cheka, who then moved against the pro-German 'orientation'.[7]

This was, at first, kept quiet from the German embassy. On July 8, Riezler warned the Foreign Ministry in Berlin that the Bolsheviks seemed to know that Milyukov and Nabokov (the Cadet leaders) had spoken to the German embassy in Kiev. 'On the morning before the assassination [of Count Mirbach], I brought up again in conversation with Karakhan, for a special reason, that the commission to fight the counter-revolution is permeated with enemies of the Bolsheviks. Instead of stopping intrigues by the *Entente*, they imprison harmless monarchists, and this only because the latter call on the embassy — in vain. Karakhan then told me confidentially that he knew about our counter-revolutionary connections. He said that, not from the embassy, but from other quarters, at first in Moscow, later on in Kiev, efforts were made to orientate bourgeois circles towards Germany, particularly the Cadets, who were changing their views rapidly, and that things were being stirred up against the Bolsheviks.'

Riezler pointed out to Berlin that the latter was not true. 'The Bolsheviks had reason enough to be grateful to us if we helped them to divide the bourgeois elements, and prevented an united counter-revolutionary front, which would be dangerous only to them. They therefore should not interfere when the bourgeois circles become orientated towards Germany. Although Karakhan seemed to have calmed down about the intentions of the German government, I would recommend to be extremely careful when keeping up the connection with Milyukov.'[7]

Savinkov's premature revolt at Yaroslavl was also probably triggered off by a Bolshevik *agent provocateur*. In late June, the French Ambassador apparently wired to General Poole at Murmansk asking what his plans were. Poole replied on the 30th that he intended to land at Archangel 'soon' with a considerable force. But on June 26, as the First Lord had reported to the Prime Minister, Poole had postponed his operation, and on July 3, he warned the War Office that the success of both his landing and his further progress inland depended on the extensive use of secret agents to organize an uprising in Archangel and in other towns in the Russian interior. On July 5, the American ambassador at Vologda had passed on a wire to Poole from a British SIS agent called Maclaren asking Poole for immediate instructions on securing the Archangel–Moscow railway. Maclaren stated that he had reached agreement with the 'Union for the Regeneration of Russia' for their small local force at Vologda to seize the town in support of the Allied landing at Archangel. But unless he had immediate instructions, Maclaren warned, this little force might make a premature move on the basis of false information which Trotsky was already spreading; there were, for example, rumours that the Allies had already seized another station (presumably north of Vologda) on the Archangel line.[8]

This has considerable relevance to Savinkov's reasons for launching the revolt. 'Through Grenard [the French Consul]', Savinkov stated six years later, 'Noulens sent me a telegram from Vologda in which he definitely stated that the landing would take place between the 3rd and the 10th of July ... and insisted that we begin the insurrection on the 5th of July.' Grenard, writing in 1933 (when the former Allied envoys in Moscow all began to publish their memoirs), insists that Savinkov moved on his own initiative and 'in violation of his promise not to undertake anything without the cooperation of other Russian parties'. Though Savinkov's statement was made at his trial, when he presumably might have said anything in return for his life, both versions may be true. The truth, in fact, is sometimes useful, even at a soviet show trial. Conceivably, Grenard may have sent this wire, presumably before June 26, when Poole postponed his descent on Archangel. More probably, a Bolshevik *agent provocateur* sent a false wire. What is certain is that on the day of the revolt, Lockhart wired to Balfour saying that the French had given two and a half million roubles to the 'National Centre' (to which both Savinkov and the volunteer army in southern Russia were linked), and told them that intervention was already agreed upon, and that the Russian opposition had committed themselves on the basis of this information; and, secondly, that Savinkov, in his insurrectionary proclamation, stated that he was acting in cooperation with those who had seized other towns along the Volga, and with the Samara government, which were 'under the command of General Alexeiev'.[9]

What links were there, if any, between the left SRs and Savinkov; and were they through British agents? It is certain that the left SRs, Savinkov and the Bolsheviks all had agents within each others' organizations. Captain George Hill was at this time organizing guerilla action against the Germans in the Ukraine, and was certainly in touch with the left SRs, as well as with Savinkov, whom he did not like. 'My distrust of him was a matter of frequent contention between myself and Sidney Reilly, who had a blind belief in the man', records Hill. But if the link was Reilly, it certainly went wrong. On the afternoon of the 6th, when Lockhart was waiting at the Bolshoi Theatre for the soviet congress to resume, unaware that Mirbach had been assassinated, Reilly suddenly burst into his box with 'only the vaguest idea of what had occurred'. He only knew that 'something had gone wrong'. When a nervous sentry dropped a hand grenade, which caused a loud explosion on the floor above, Reilly and a French agent began to empty their pockets, tear up such documents as they had on them, and eat those which it was too dangerous to stuff down the lining of the sofa cushions.[10]

After the annihilation of the left SRs, the Bolsheviks could concentrate on the suppression of Savinkov's revolt, a much more serious affair. Savinkov had originally intended to surround Moscow completely, to cut it off from all contact with the surrounding area by seizing Yaroslavl and Rybinsk (between Moscow and Vologda), to the north, Vladimir and Murom, to the east, and Kaluga to the south. But no insurrections took place in Kaluga and Vladimir, and there was failure at Rybinsk. (Presumably the Bolsheviks moved first in these three towns.) But Yaroslavl was seized, with the help of local workers and peasants, on the 6th; and on the 8th, Murom fell to Savinkov. In his insurrectionary proclamation there Savinkov stated that they had been compelled to act by 'the events of the last few days', though no mention was made of the assassination of Mirbach, who was roundly abused as the controller of the Bolsheviks. Most of the proclamation was devoted to praise of the Czechs, whose western group, under their commander Čeček, was now making real progress. On the 7th, having seized Ufa (thus linking up with the central Czech group and protecting Samara, the Czech–White Russian base, from attack from the east), Čeček issued a general order that the Allies, with the support of their Czech national council, had proclaimed the Czech Legion to be the 'vanguard of the Allied forces' in the restoration of an anti-German eastern front 'in conjunction with the whole Russian nation and our Allies'. The Samara government agreed that Čeček should be in command of all Czech and Russian forces on the Volga front, where it was decided to consolidate: then advance up the Volga to Simbirsk (where there was an arms depot), and fortify and hold the town; then proceed down the Volga to Saratov, where there had been a good deal of anti-Bolshevik disaffection, to encourage a general revolt — the Orenburg Cossacks would protect their eastern flank — and possibly link up with the volunteer army, now in the Kuban. These measures, it was confidently believed, would coincide with the arrival of the long-expected Allied army.

In Moscow, Riezler now thought that the end of the Bolsheviks was at hand: 'Bolsheviks are intending to avoid the question of the execution of the SR leader [Chernov] by letting him escape. Observers of the most different views expect the fall of the Bolsheviks within a few days. A new uprising would lead to victory of the left-wing SRs. Monarchists reply to the question whether they would be strong enough to take over power from the SRs, in case of an uprising, with 'no'. Rule of the SRs would lead in the end to the rule of monarchists, because of total anarchy and pogroms against the German and Russian bourgeoisie.'

More rapid developments could not be excluded, because news from the provinces stated that the SRs were advancing along the railway lines coming from the North and the East, that Nizhni-Novgorod (between Kazan and Moscow) was in their hands, that Murom had been taken, and that the SRs and their peasants had advanced up to 130 km along the railway line from Murom. Riezler could not watch the lax Bolshevik treatment of the assassins of Mirbach, not only because of the question of dignity, but also for political reasons. He believed that Germany must wait for the SRs, and for total anarchy; in the meantime, the royalist movement had to come from the Ukraine, and had to be led to victory. Riezler therefore asked for authority to break off relations with the Bolsheviks, until Mirbach's assassination had been punished: 'Considering the strange situation here, which can only be assessed from close quarters, and because of the possibility of very fast developments, I ask you to give me full power. ... As the railway men on the eastern lines are united with the SRs, and as the same situation on the western line is cutting our embassy off, I beg to ask you to reply immediately.'

Riezler also noted that the leaders of the Latvian regiments, upon whom the Bolsheviks especially relied, and who had taken a major share in putting down the SR *coup* after the assassination of Count Mirbach, were in touch with him, because the Latvians believed that the Bolshevik regime had reached its end, and they wanted to return home.[11] They wanted the German government to allow them to return in freedom, and they asked for an amnesty. On July 10, Riezler forwarded this request to Berlin; the Foreign Ministry granted the amnesty.

Events moved quickly. Though Savinkov lost Murom again on the 8th, rioting broke out in the city of Kazan on the Volga, an area crucial to the defence of Moscow from the East, and the new Bolshevik headquarters on their eastern front. On the 10th, Muraviev, the Red Army commander on the Volga front, a left SR, arrived at Simbirsk with 1,000 men, broke up the local soviet, and issued orders declaring an armistice with the Czechs and war on the Germans. The road to Moscow from the east seemed wide open. Muraviev, however, was surrounded by loyal Bolshevik elements and shot himself. The Bolshevik government, not wishing to give the crushed left SRs credit for this short-lived revolt, announced that Muraviev had been 'bought by Anglo–French imperialists'. In this, they appear to have been correct. Professor Katkov quotes this remarkable report by Riezler at the German embassy to the German Foreign Ministry, dated July 14: 'Like many of his officers, until 14 days ago Muraviev was persuaded, by considerable financial subsidies from us, to adopt energetic measures against the Czechs. Fourteen days ago the intermediary who was used for this purpose was arrested by the *Okhrana* [as Riezler liked to call the Cheka, using the old Tsarist name] and the contact was cut off. Chicherin and Karakhan have openly admitted that Muraviev would not have defected without remuneration.' According to Bradley, Muraviev (a former French soldier), received 'financial subsidies' from a French colonel in Odessa. Thus, when the fifth Congress of Soviets closed with the formal expulsion of the left SRs, the Cheka had taken decisive action to reverse the pro-German 'orientation', but were now faced with the growing power of the pro-Allied groups: the Czechs on the Volga and Savinkov at Yaroslavl.[11]

There was little that British officials could do either in Petrograd or Vologda, in the wake of Mirbach's assassination, which seemed to presage the imminent occupation of Moscow by the Germans. In a series of telegrams to the Admiralty, Captain Cromie reported that 'all records were destroyed on outbreak of street fighting on July 7. I consider it inadvisable to keep any record whatever of important documents during present crisis except codes which are always ready for immediate destruction. Telegrams for London are not accepted.' In another wire on the 10th, he said he had had 'no communication with Moscow for last four days. Vologda declared a [?blocked] area. Messenger failed to get beyond Petrozavodsk and has returned. Since 7th, all quiet in Petrograd.' In a third wire, however, he informed the Admiralty in staccato fashion that he 'proposed to carry out scheme [for the destruction of the Baltic Fleet] early next week.' Should the scheme be successful, he would have to pay out £840,000 for the destruction of the battleships and destroyers, and more for steamers and ships still under construction. In a final wire, Cromie stated that Admiral Sablin, former Commander-in-Chief, Black Sea Fleet, was 'in extreme danger of suffering same fate as Captain Chastny'. Cromie had given him a letter to show to the British consul at Archangel, asking for Sablin to be given a passage to England. (None of these wires, however, reached London until early August.)[12]

Lockhart was also anxious to arrange for a certain party to leave Russia. He sent three wires on the subject. The first seems never to have arrived. The second, sent as 'extremely urgent' on June 21, stated: 'A very useful lady, who has worked here in extremely confidential position in a government office, desires to give up her present position. She has been of the greatest service to me and is anxious to establish herself in Stockholm, where she would be centre of information regarding underground agitation in Russia in the event of Bolsheviks being over[?thrown] by the Germans. Not only have her services to Allies been considerable, but it would be highly important for us to have inside information of future movement. Lady is not Bolshevik, but is known to all leaders of the movement. In any case, she promises to take no part in political agitation work.' Lockhart asked for permission to arrange for her to leave Russia secretly, via Murmansk.

'This is a little doubtful', minuted the Russia Department, when the wire reached the Foreign Office late in June. 'He should have done it without asking, if it is really worth it', added Lord Hardinge. The War Office, however, approved. 'There is no objection', was its reply on July 7; but Lockhart never seems to have received it. In mid-July, he sent a third and more explicit wire: 'Very secret. Trotsky's secretary, (Eugenia Schelepina), a Russian lady of great character and considerable charm, is now [?anxious to] leave Russia. She has been extremely useful to me, is thoroughly pro-Ally, and might possibly be of great service to us in giving information respecting Bolsheviks. ... She proposes to start for Sweden with Mr Ransome, who has now come to conclusion Bolsheviks have come to the end of their rule. The simplest way of getting her out of the country would be if you could authorize consul-general here to put her on Ransome's passport as wife. I feel confident we have nothing to risk either from her or from Ransome, who is now in favour of Allied intervention. They should both be useful in giving us information of underground work of Bolsheviks. ... As we may be quite sure that revenge which Russian middle classes will take on Bolsheviks will be far more violent than any excesses committed by Bolsheviks, I should like to save life of lady who has been of great use to me during time when Bolsheviks were supreme in Russia.' By the time this reached the Foreign Office in mid-August, it was too late to reply.[13]

Lockhart was also wiring in mid-July about the crucial question of the provision of funds for anti-Bolshevik groups in Moscow. On July 15, the Treasury replied to a Foreign Office letter of the 13th, 'relative to financial assistance to various pro-Ally organizations in Moscow'. As the British government was proposing to finance Allied activities at Murmansk and Archangel, the Treasury felt that it would be 'more fitting' if the French government financed pro-Ally activities in Moscow. On July 16, therefore, Balfour personally approved the following wire to Lockhart: 'We are discussing with French government the question of severally dividing with them expenses incurred in Russia, and this will include the financing of pro-Ally activities in the Moscow area. Pending an agreement, you should request your French colleague to provide in the first instance any sums considered necessary for the above purpose.'[13]

At Vologda, the little party of Allied diplomats, joined on July 7 by Lindley and the British economic mission, also found themselves entirely cut off from Moscow on the outbreak of Savinkov's revolt at Yaroslavl, just to their south. They at once despatched a joint telegram to Admiral Kemp at Murmansk, emphasizing the vital necessity of an immediate Allied landing at Archangel. On the 9th, they received a despairing plea from Savinkov's men for Allied support, and another wire went to Admiral Kemp. Nothing, of course, happened.[13]

In Berlin, trade talks continued between Bolshevik and German delegates, despite the assassination of Mirbach. On the 7th, during an important exchange, the Bolsheviks pressed for a German loan, without which they claimed they could not comply with the provisions of the Brest–Litovsk treaty. The German reply was merely to repeat their claim for six billion marks in indemnities. Though the Germans did not now raise the question of the independence of the Baltic States, a vital point for them, they reported that the Bolsheviks were unlikely to resist these demands, if they could 'be assured that, later on, the Ukraine and the Donetz basin would be returned to them', since they were Russia's 'life-lines'. The Germans did, however, repeatedly press the Bolshevik delegates to accept German military help in Russia, but this was continually rejected, since the Bolsheviks were rightly apprehensive of the use to which Ludendorff would put German troops once they were in Russia. Nevertheless, a German delegate commented at the end of this meeting on the 7th that a German–Russian understanding 'seems to be in the offing, if it is handled expertly'. The difficulty, of course, was getting the German High Command to relinquish their hold at any time on the Ukraine and the Donetz basin, which were providing the essential supplies to Germany, otherwise denied by the Allied blockade.[14]

The official German reaction to Mirbach's murder was delayed for a few days, because of a political crisis ending with the dismissal of Kühlmann from the Foreign Ministry for favouring peace talks with Britain. Finally, on the 11th, the Kaiser decided to accept Lenin's explanation and blame the whole thing on the Allies, partly to create a strong anti-Allied atmosphere, presumably to counteract the peace moves by his former Foreign Secretary, and partly because Germany had no alternative; a secure eastern frontier and Russian supplies were all important. 'We have to support the Bolsheviks under any circumstances', insisted the Kaiser. Lenin's judgment had been right, and he could now do whatever he liked with the Tsar.

When the War Cabinet met on July 10, Lord Reading's wire of the previous day, giving the dramatic news of President Wilson's decision on intervention in Siberia, had not yet reached London. How much, though, did

Lloyd George and his colleagues know of the equally dramatic events that had been taking place simultaneously in Bolshevik Russia? Presumably that the German ambassador in Moscow had been assassinated, and that Savinkov had started a serious uprising, cutting Moscow off from both Archangel and Vologda, the future junction between the intervening forces from both northern Russia and Siberia, and where the Allied ambassadors were holding out. And if the Prime Minister knew of these two events, he presumably equated them; and the only conclusion he can have drawn was that immediate Allied intervention was an imperative necessity.[15]

At the War Cabinet, the Deputy First Sea Lord described events at Vladivostok. At Nikolsk, the junction of the Chinese eastern and Amur railways, north of Vladivostok, the Czechs had captured an enemy force sent to blow up an important tunnel. In front of Nikolsk, the Czechs had found a force of 2,500 men, with six guns, 'worked by Germans'. After a two-day battle, however, the enemy force had escaped by train up the Amur line towards Khabarovsk, blowing up bridges and railway trucks in its wake. The Czechs had taken 1,000 prisoners, of which 600 were Hungarians, and brought them back to Vladivostok, where the Czech commander had explained the extreme seriousness of the situation to the Allied consuls and the naval commanders. As he had to garrison both Vladivostok and Nikolsk, and protect the railway, he would only have 8,000 men for any further move back up the railway to rescue his colleagues, who were cut off at Irkutsk. Therefore, he asked the Allies to garrison Vladivostok. All the Allied commanders thereupon agreed that an Allied expeditionary force should be despatched immediately, and that they should inform their governments accordingly. The captain of *Suffolk*, who supplied this information, added that all the Vladivostok hospitals were full and urged that the Japanese should be asked to relieve the pressure, not only at Vladivostok, but also by the provision of medical supplies for the Czechs in the firing line.

When asked what troops could be sent immediately, the CIGS said that there was a British battalion at Hong Kong and, he believed, some French colonial troops, but he would have to confirm this with the French War Office. It had not been intended to send any artillery, and as far as he knew, there was none at Vladivostok; guns could be sent most rapidly from India. The Deputy First Sea Lord remarked that the Navy could not be of much help; at most, only one or two six-inch guns could be landed from *Suffolk*. In the face of this rather negative talk, the Prime Minister stated that it was 'very important' for us to consider how we could support the Czechs, 'if President Wilson came to the conclusion that he was unable to assist us'. Balfour said he favoured the immediate despatch of troops to Vladivostok to protect supplies and preserve order; this, he felt, 'could not be considered as intervention in Russia'. (This, incidentally, was very similar to the advice which Secretary Lansing had given to the President in his decisive paper of July 4). Balfour asked what action was to be taken about obtaining Japanese medical assistance. It was agreed that the Foreign Office should contact the British ambassador in Tokyo as soon as possible.

The War Cabinet decided that the CIGS should move a British battalion to Vladivostok immediately to preserve order there and protect supplies; secondly, that he should telephone the French War Office informing them of the Cabinet's decision, since the Vladivostok situation was considered 'so serious', and should suggest that French troops should also be moved there; if this was agreed to, they should ask how many would be sent and their probable date of arrival. Thirdly, he should report the French reply to the Prime Minister. The Cabinet also decided that Balfour should inform the British ambassador in Tokyo of the Cabinet's decision and ask him to impress on the Japanese government the urgent necessity of giving medical assistance in Vladivostok and to the Czech troops in the firing line. Secondly, he should wire to Lord Reading to inform President Wilson of the Cabinet's decision and the reasons that had prompted it, and of the 'urgent' British appeal to the French to cooperate.

The War Cabinet's attention was then drawn to a wire from General Poole, asking for a further British battalion to be sent out to Murmansk. It was pointed out that there were now about 1,200 British troops there. The CIGS undertook to make enquiries about what further troops could be sent, and to report to the Cabinet.[15]

It was also agreed, it seems privately, between the Prime Minister, Milner and Balfour, that General Knox should go out to Vladivostok 'with somewhat special and extended powers'; in fact, to try and form the 'friendly elements' among the Russian troops into some sort of an army; but officially, this was simply a War Office appointment. Balfour wired to Reading saying that Knox was on his way via North America, and asked him to arrange for Knox to have interviews at both the State Department and the War Department.

Shortly after 5 p.m., Hankey went to see the Prime Minister, who had just received Lord Reading's wire with President Wilson's proposal for a force of 7,000 American and 7,000 Japanese troops only to intervene in Siberia. 'Ll.G. was furious with Wilson and most sarcastic', records Hankey, 'comparing him to Gladstone and the inadequate Gordon relief expedition.' Balfour, Milner, Smuts and the CIGS were summoned. It was agreed that both the Prime Minister and Balfour should prepare replies to President Wilson. A proposal to despatch an expedition limited to 14,000 men, and without reference to the exigencies of the military situation, was 'really preposterous', Lloyd George said to Reading, in what Hankey called a 'very direct and rather scathing' reply. Unless modified, it would be too little, and too late. As the Bolsheviks were becoming more and more pro-German, it was now simply a race between the Allies and the Germans for

the control of Siberia. If the Allies did take action, they must send sufficient troops to see that the Czechs 'will not have their throats cut by
German and Austrian prisoners', and definitely to secure control of Siberia
up to the Urals against attack by German and Bolshevik forces. The
American proposal might also be deeply injurious to Japanese pride, and
drive them into an attitude of resentful neutrality. A large Czech force,
already on the spot, would certainly counter-balance the effect of a large
Japanese force. So would British, French and Italian contingents. Lloyd
George trusted that these views might enable Reading to demonstrate to
the President the 'total inadequacy' of the American proposal, and persuade him to modify them along the lines of the Supreme War Council's
resolution. The Prime Minister, in fact, rejected the President's decision.
But being a politician, he added a bit lamely that if they could get no more
than this little force, they must accept it and get something moving without
delay. Unless it arrived in Russia before the winter — and the Russian
harbours would freeze in a few months — they would never save Russia
from becoming a German province. (In fact, only Archangel would be ice-
bound; both Murmansk and Vladivostok are ice-free ports). Balfour sent
an equally critical reply to Reading. While politely welcoming the American decision to do something, and conceding that the proposal might
please American public opinion, he warned — in very sharp terms for
Balfour — that 'from a military point of view it is indefensible, and plainly
cannot stand'. Thus both the Prime Minister and the Foreign Secretary
imagined that they could force up what they took to be President Wilson's
opening bid on intervention; and for the moment, the War Cabinet were
not informed.[16]

The next day, the CIGS reported to the War Cabinet that the British
battalion at Hong Kong had been ordered to Vladivostok, but so far he had
received no answer from Clemenceau about the number of French troops
that would be available. The Japanese, however, had given 10,000 of their
rifles and 3 million rounds to the Czechs; and the CIGS had also wired to
General Bridges, the War Office's representative in Washington, to request
him to discover how many Russian rifles and how much ammunition were
available in America.[17]

But that day, the central Czech group, under their able commander
Rudolph Gajda, occupied Irkutsk, after a battle lasting three weeks; and all
real danger of the Bolsheviks, with their illusory hordes of well-drilled
enemy prisoners, annihilating the Czechs was now over. The Czech groups
were again more or less reunited and prepared to hold fast, as instructed by
the American Consul Poole, until the Allies intervened. But their virtual
reunion destroyed the whole *raison d'être* behind the President's decision
on intervention.

11

Reactions in London and Tokyo

In Moscow, now that Lenin had seen that the Germans did not intend to retaliate for the murder of Mirbach, the Bolsheviks proceeded to play the Germans off against the British over trade talks. On June 20, the British economic mission, under Sir William Clark, had reached Murmansk, where they interviewed General Poole and Hugh Leech, who made the journey from Petrograd to see them on the 25th. Colonel Keyes, who had come out with the mission, reprimanded Leech for some of his actions taken in the British embassy's absence, but told him that the money owed to him for the attempted transfer of roubles to southern Russia earlier in the year had been paid to his account in London. Leech said that was the first he had heard of this, and was glad. 'He also dilated on his loneliness in Petrograd as a British agent since the departure of the embassy', reported Lindley.[1]

Leech described Jaroszynski's present state of mind 'as one of anxiety to know whether he enjoyed the confidence of His Majesty's Government. So great was this anxiety that he was willing to take the uncomfortable and rather dangerous journey from Petrograd to Murmansk in order to see me [Lindley] if required.' Leech said that Jaroszynski's entire hopes for future business success were based 'on what he called the certainty of a counter-revolution which would overthrow the Bolsheviks, and re-establish laws of property'. He was thus anxious about the future of the Russian banks under his control. 'They had not sufficient currency to meet the demands of their depositors for withdrawal, demands that had been mounting up since the Bolsheviks had controlled the banks in December 1917; and a moratorium seemed the only possible remedy. This Mr Yaroshinsky [sic] was anxious to avoid, as in his opinion, it would damage the credit of the banks still further.' Leech, apparently on his behalf, then made tentative enquiries about whether the British government could assist him in this difficulty; and if so, to what extent. 'When asked why the banks as a whole could not come to some arrangement with the state bank, which would then presumably be friendly, Mr Leech could only say that the state bank would be able to do nothing, whereas if His Majesty's Government took no steps in the matter, the German government would print the necessary notes, and give them only to banks that were friendly to them!' This was a reasoned answer by Leech to a stupid question, which betrayed a complete misunderstanding of the present Russian situation, as it was absurd to imagine the state bank doing any sort of a deal with the Russian banks, which the Bolsheviks regarded with such animosity.

Discussion then turned to the Board of Control over the five Russian banks, to which Jaroszynski had agreed as part consideration for the British loan of £500,000. He already held a controlling interest in these five banks, but to what extent these shares were encumbered by loans Leech did not say. However, the voting power was, according to Leech, intact, and the loans were unlikely to be disturbed, because they had been made by banks which Jaroszynski controlled; Leech reported that it was illegal in Russia for banks to lend on the security of their own shares, but control of several banks enabled this to be done legally. 'Mr Yaroshinsky is ready to place the shares [that] carry the controlling interest in these five banks at the disposal of the Board of Control of four persons, two nominated by His Majesty's Government, and two by himself', reported Lindley. 'For the sake of his own credit, however, he wishes to keep them in his own name, so far as this is compatible with the main scheme. The Board of Control would leave the management of the banks as at present, but would hold the undated but signed resignations of all directors. It would then proceed to foster the interests of His Majesty's Government and of Mr Yaroshinsky through the medium of these banks, and presumably Mr Yaroshinsky thinks that His Majesty's Government would save the banks from any mishap they might meet, owing to his speculative activities.'

This seems to have ended their discussion with Hugh Leech. Armistead, a member of the economic mission, then privately informed Lindley that Leech 'was regarded completely as a man of straw before the war', though Armistead admitted that he did not know about his activities since. 'And yet Mr Leech, during his visit to Murmansk, was negotiating for a ship repairing enterprise, to the capital of which he himself was to contribute up to £60,000', reported Lindley in some perplexity. Leslie Urquhart, who had also come out with the mission, next told Lindley that he had had occasion the previous summer to inquire into Jaroszynski's standing, and was informed that his 'real private fortune' was no more than two million roubles. Spring Rice felt there was enough evidence to justify an attitude of 'very great caution' by the British government towards both Leech and Jaroszynski, 'and care should be taken that they be not allowed to lower British credit by being too publicly associated with any financial scheme, on which His Majesty's Government may embark'.[1]

On June 27, Colonel Keyes, accompanied by Leech, left by train for Petrograd. Keyes' main purpose was to obtain an order for the delivery of 8,600 shares of the Siberian Bank from the head office of the Russo–

Asiatic Bank. This would enable the Treasury to obtain delivery of these shares from the bank's London branch.[1]

On arrival at Vologda on July 7, Clark and his colleagues began to discuss what they simply refer to as 'commercial matters' with Noulens, Stevens, of the National City Bank, and with the American ambassador, who complained to Secretary Lansing in Washington on the 11th that this British mission seemed set on doing exactly what he had warned the Russians that the Germans were trying to do — exploit the Russian economy. When this news reached Lord Reading, he sensed danger; this, coupled with Lloyd George's refusal to accept the President's decision on intervention, might cause the President to withdraw. In a flurry of telegrams between Washington and London on the 11th — the speed was unprecedented — Balfour blandly explained that this small mission had merely been sent out to advise on the best means of 'restoring and developing' British trading 'interests' in Russia, and countering German schemes of commercial penetration. Even this cannot have mollified the Americans. On the 14th, with the trade negotiations in Berlin going reasonably well, and with the evident wish to put pressure on the Germans to hurry them along, Clark received a written guarantee from the Bolsheviks that if the British economic mission visited Moscow, they would certainly be allowed to leave again when they wished. (This was just three days after the Allied envoys at Vologda had politely refused a request from Chicherin that they should come to Moscow, where they would almost certainly have been held as hostages.)[1]

On July 15, Ludendorff launched a new attack in France in the Rheims sector and a high level conference at Spa between the German High Command and the Foreign Ministry failed to reach agreement on two important items in the draft trade treaty, namely the future of the Donetz basin, and of the Baku oil centre. The Donetz was, in fact, under the effective control of the Don Cossacks, whom Ludendorff, in opposition to the Foreign Ministry, wished to continue to support. German control of Baku, however, involved a dispute with Turkey rather than with the Bolsheviks, who at present held it. The German High Command had sent instructions — presumably both to Constantinople and to the small German force in the Caucasus — that a Turkish attack on Baku was to be prevented, as the Germans feared that if the Turks and Tartars got into the town, they would loot it and set fire to the oil-wells; German troops coming from the Ukraine would occupy Baku. But the Turkish advance continued.

The British were just as concerned: if the Turks pushed on over the Caspian into Transcaspia, their agents and their influence might then penetrate into India. The whole Transcaspian area was under the control of the Bolshevik soviet at Tashkent, to the north of the crucial railway which ran from the Caspian port of Krasnovodsk to Kushk, on the Afghanistan border; and early in July, when the Tashkent soviet sent Red Guards to quell a revolt in the towns along the railway caused by a severe shortage of food, the railway workers also rose up and were joined by the Red Guards who liquidated their commissars. This led to the formation in mid-July of an SR and Menshevik committee at Ashkhabad, just over the north-eastern frontier of Persia, which also claimed control of Transcaspia, and soon established control of the railway from Krasnovodsk to Merv, the junction of the lines to Tashkent and to Kushk. Hence Major-General Malleson, who was sent from India with a small force to Meshed in north-eastern Persia, principally to watch over the Transcaspian railway, had on arrival in mid-July to deal with the Ashkhabad committee rather than with the Tashkent soviet. Both, however, were still at each other's throats — and the Tashkent soviet had in its service some 6,000 troops, many of whom were armed German and Austrian prisoners from the large prisoner of war camps in the area, and 3,000 of these were actually stationed at Kushk on the Afghan frontier. Hence Malleson was forced to intervene in the bitter skirmishes that were soon taking place.[2]

Despite the failure of the new German attack in France, Ludendorff continued to thwart the Foreign Ministry's desire for a speedy conclusion to the negotiations on the draft trade treaty in Berlin. On July 18, Foch launched a long-prepared counter-stroke, with massed tanks, against the over-exposed flank of the German salient on the Marne, which was finally to give the initiative along the whole western front to the Allies. Meanwhile, Ludendorff was planning a new military offensive on the eastern front to drive the Bolsheviks out and ensnare the new pro-German bourgeois regime with much stricter German controls. He believed his military attaché's reports from Moscow that the Bolsheviks' future was hopeless, and that only two German battalions would be needed to restore order in Moscow, overthrow the Bolsheviks and instal a new regime. (Nothing, of course, was said in these reports of the fact that the Cheka had now moved in earnest against the pro-German 'orientation' and was undermining German influence with the opposition as well). But Ludendorff was also alarmed at the growing influence of Bolshevik propaganda among his own troops. On the 21st, he urged the Foreign Ministry to agree to further support for the Don Cossacks, who should be recognized as totally independent of Russia. The Bolsheviks, he was certain, were merely stalling in the trade talks, as they had done in the Brest–Litovsk peace negotiations, until the Allies could come to their support and restore the eastern front against Germany. The new Foreign Secretary, Hintze, vigorously denied this. The trade treaty could be concluded, he told Ludendorff, as soon as the German delegates agreed not to interfere in Russian internal affairs and stopped supporting separatist movements like the Don

Cossacks. Ludendorff refused to agree and deadlock continued.

Germany's actual position in Russia at this time can be seen in more detail in a series of reports made by Counsellor Riezler from the German embassy in Moscow to the Foreign Ministry in Berlin. In a long report on July 19 to Chancellor Hertling, Riezler summarized the position from Moscow: 'Because of the uncertainty of the whole situation, in a country split by escalating civil wars, it is almost impossible to come to a conclusion about the possibilities open for our politics. But since the whole situation is forcing us to take a course which is to our advantage, on a ship that is thrown about in storms, I shall have to try. ... The Bolsheviks are dead. The corpse is alive, because the grave-diggers cannot agree who should bury him. The battle, which is going on at the moment between us and the *Entente* on Russian soil, is no longer a battle over the favour of this corpse. It has now already become the battle over the succession, over the orientation of a future Russia.'[3]

The *Entente* possessed two trump cards in this battle: first, the 'agitational' effect of a Russia severed as a result of the Brest–Litovsk treaty, particularly the cutting off of the Ukraine and the embargo on its grain. The other trump card was the important military factor created by the *Entente*, namely the Czechs. Up to now, Germany had only been able to set against this the deep desire of the ordinary Russian people, and of the middle classes, for peace. This factor, however, could be decisive. More and more people, even the bourgeoisie, were coming to the conclusion that there would be no peace without German approval; and without peace, there would be no order. The German orientation of the middle-class monarchists was based solely on this premise.

The weakness of the *Entente* position was that they wanted to restore order by war. If Germany decided to take the risk and lead the counter-revolution, it might be possible to overthrow the whole *Entente* counter-revolutionary structure by setting up a pro-German government in Moscow and in Petrograd which would speak for peace and order. In this way, it would also be possible to stretch out a hand towards the Siberian government on the far side of the Czechs, who would then be isolated. If this succeeded, the advantages for Germany were obvious. Only a bourgeois Russia, led by them to victory, could give them economic advantages, raw materials and goods. There would be better prospects for success if Germany could offer Russia the hope that an understanding with her would in future unburden the peace of Brest from those conditions, such as the Ukraine, which would always be unacceptable to any Russian; and 'if we could gradually construct a moral peace out of the formal peace — that is how the bourgeois parties express it'.

The *coup*, which would lead to the victory of a pro-German bourgeois government in Moscow and Petrograd, could succeed if the *Entente* combination did not win before Germany was ready. The monarchist officers' organization in Moscow could win if, first, the neutrality of the Latvians was assured, and, secondly, if Germany withdrew her protection from the Bolsheviks by taking some sort of action, and lent her prestige to the new order. Germany could succeed if the generals in the south were able to instruct their small armies to accomplish a counter-revolution in the provincial towns.

'It is not out of the question that we could assure the new government of the neutrality of the Latvians for the *coup*, possibly even the help of the Latvians against the Czechs, maybe by assuring them free return to their home country, maybe by a guarantee to the Latvians, who are peasants without their own land, that they would receive land from the hands of a new orderly Russian government. The Latvians might accept such a guarantee, although they very strongly distrust any sort of Russian government. If this risk is taken, we would have to start working on it immediately, and negotiations would have to start with a future new government on the political situation after the overthrow of the Bolsheviks.'[3]

On July 22, Riezler sent a wire to the Foreign Ministry informing them that he had just had a discussion with Gregory Trubetzkoi (former director of the Russian Foreign Office, now the delegate of the monarchist cadets in Moscow), who stated that his group must take action soon, because of the ever-increasing terror, and the moral effect of the assassination of the Tsar. This group relied on industry, commerce and the big landowners. In Moscow, it had about 4,000 officers; they were organised but had no weapons, although they might be able to seize weapons before the *coup*. But the group considered an increase in their strength under pro-German orientation was now more difficult, because hope in Germany was waning, and the progress of the Czechs brought new hope.

Even if an isolated *coup* in Moscow succeeded, it could not be sustained unless the Don Cossack generals and the Russian masses, which would have to be organized in the Ukraine, marched off towards the north beforehand. Moscow would have to be informed of these movements from the south about three weeks in advance, because the mounting terror meant that preparations were much more difficult and needed much more time. Military intervention from Germany was not asked for, only help from the Ukraine and Don area, and weapons, munitions, and general help in organization. But if the attitude of the Latvians was first assured, then prospects for a *coup* in Moscow could only be positive.

Trubetzkoi said that a new Russian government could unite the country under German orientation only if a link-up with Germany guaranteed a reunited Russia. Mutual concessions and guarantees would have to be agreed in advance in a secret exchange of letters, as well as the first programme of the new government. In the long run, he thought combined action would be psychologically impossible without the Baltic provinces. Formal neutrality of Russia would also have to be preserved. When Riezler asked him about neutrality towards the Czechs, and the occupation of Murman, he said there would be sufficient grounds to abandon neutrality if the Allies did not leave, after being asked to do so.[3]

Trubetzkoi asked the Germans to begin negotiations soon, and to give Moscow or Kiev, and the group in the Ukraine, more freedom of movement. Riezler had little doubt that mediators like Trubetzkoi, who had already reduced his demands during their conversation, would at first play easy to get. His German orientation, was, however, as he openly admitted, only derived from the realization that a stable order could regrettably not be achieved with the help of the *Entente*, or by war with Germany. Despite this, Riezler warned, even these circles would combine with the *Entente* as being the only way out, because of the increase in the present terror, the impossibility of sustaining the officers' organizations (who were literally being hunted down and executed daily by the dozen), and the evaporation of faith in Germany. Riezler therefore strongly recommended that negotiations should be started, and that the group should be so informed. Baron Nolde, who belonged to this group, was apparently in Berlin. He then sent a sharp warning to the Foreign Ministry: 'It is a serious disadvantage to us in our political and economic negotiations with the government that the opposite side is being informed about the progress of the negotiations in Berlin, and about any other events, while we are not. Rumours of various types, e.g. that it has been agreed in Berlin to recognize the decree on nationalization without recompense, cause considerable upheaval in circles who favour us politically, and it helps the interests of the *Entente* propaganda. Without precise information, it is impossible to act against this successfully. I therefore urge you to inform the embassy by wire about the results achieved, and about the progress of the negotiations in Berlin.'

On July 23, Riezler wired again that the Siberian government's delegate had informed him the day before that the preparations of the right-wing monarchists, who had connections with the Siberians, were almost complete. The Church played a special role. The delegate proposed a detailed plan, with many concrete and well-worked out details, which were doubtless risky. In Petrograd, there were already 4,500 officers, 28,000 employees, students, etc., 4,000 guns, 200 Brownings, 4 machine guns. The Petrograd–Vologda–Viatka–Perm–Ekaterinburg railway line was of major importance, and a group of railway employees, and a great number of the workers on those lines, were supposed to be on the movement's side. A high-ranking officer, who was a transport specialist, was head of the northern railways in the Bolshevik transport office, and he would distribute the carriages on the line so that, at the time of a *coup* in Petrograd, the transport of ten Siberian regiments could be quickly arranged. Six regiments would be distributed on the Perm–Viatka–Vologda line, and four were destined for Petrograd. The security of the line would be assured in the best manner possible in advance, and transport of flour would soon be prepared in all details.

They believed they could hold Petrograd for twelve to twenty-four hours, and they asked Germany, for the sake of the 'safety of the Germans' (the Latvians would guarantee their safety up to the arrival of the Germans), to be there with a few battalions within eighteen hours. The news of the Germans' rapid advance would split up the existing battalions of the Red Army. The Bolshevik sailors were largely used for building railway lines near Murman, and the rest were demoralized. Four weeks were still necessary for the strategic movement of the Siberians, and for the transport of bread.

Riezler reported that the Siberian delegate made 'an honest, active but passionate impression'. He replied 'yes' when asked whether they needed money. He accepted the offer only on the condition of being able to sell valuable goods to Germany at reasonable prices. This group, however, was apparently at the moment united with the Czech–*Entente* combination against the Bolsheviks.

Riezler warned that it must be realized that action against the Bolsheviks at present united everybody, because of the increasingly unbearable pressure on the bourgeoisie and the peasants, and friendship would very quickly be replaced with hostility to the Bolsheviks (as in the case of Muraviev). 'Only the Czechs want war,' stated Riezler, 'everybody else wants peace.'

All this was certainly risky but, considering the present chaos, it was not impossible to 'tear through' the middle of the *Entente* combination by agreeing to this in order to isolate the Czechs and make contact with Siberia. The rest of Russia would follow suit; soon there would be a victory in Petrograd, in particular if the Don Cossacks started marching north at the same time. Riezler therefore recommended proceeding with the Petrograd and Don plans simultaneously, as the first was too risky on its own.

The Siberians were content with vague hopes from the Brest–Litovsk peace, with which they calmed down the nationalists. *Entente* supporters were in the minority in the Siberian government, and would have to disappear completely if more false promises of the *Entente* were uncovered. The Siberians would be cheaper to Germany politically than any other combination because, starting from Petrograd, they would have to take action under German guns, while Moscow felt that she was still far away from German influence. Apart from this, Church interests and right-wing monarchists were most important. But in consideration of the mood in Siberia, the catch-words 'Constituent Assembly' would have to be used.

The Siberian delegate had left for Omsk the previous night, and would return in about three and a half weeks. Contact with the Germans would be maintained. This group wanted to know whether they would receive the necessary help for Petrograd. Riezler recommended supporting them and the other groups he had already described, together with simultaneous action from the Don, in order to concert the final action as far as possible. If they succeeded, he preferred the Petersburg combination, as it was politically more advantageous. Next day (the 24th), he wired the Foreign Ministry: 'Military attaché sent yesterday a telegram to the Supreme Command about his views of the plan.'[3] It was now up to the Foreign Ministry to commit themselves.

On July 26, Secretary of State von Hintze duly sent a wire to the Kaiser and Supreme Headquarters of the Army that Counsellor Riezler had reported it was possible that the Bolshevik regime could be removed from power. He pointed out that the last rising of the left SRs, following the murder of Count Mirbach, could only be suppressed by the Latvians while, from outside Russia, the *Entente* was doing its best to restore the eastern front against Germany on Russian soil, mainly by the use of the Czechs, who were gradually moving nearer towards Moscow, and who were, he underlined, 'in the present circumstances, the most important military factor in Russia. As opposed to that, a German intervention could mainly be based on the deep desire for peace of the whole Russian people. This could be the decisive factor, if used with circumspection. More and more people, and even the bourgeoisie, realize that there will be no peace without Germany wanting it too; and without peace, order will not prevail. The so-called German orientation of the bourgeois classes with monarchist tendencies is based purely on this recognition. The weakness of the position of the *Entente* is therefore that they want to bring war with order.'

Von Hintze proceeded to list the groups who were in line as successors to the Bolsheviks: (*a*) the Moscow Cadets; (*b*) the right-wing monarchists, based in Petrograd; (*c*) the Siberian government at Omsk; (*d*) the Don Cossacks. He outlined Riezler's arguments in support of each. 'If we decided to take the lead in the counter-revolution, Herr Riezler believes it to be possible to rely at first on all four groups. The promise, however, of a revision, though limited, of the peace of Brest would be unavoidable. It would also be important noticeably to move away from the Bolsheviks, in order to gain the already badly shaken trust of the monarchist circles. A neutral attitude of the Latvians, who would have to be won over, would be necessary for a successful *coup* in Moscow. An absolutely necessary condition for success with the Moscow *coup* would be to strike at the same time, on a day previously arranged, as carefully prepared similar action was taken in St Petersburg [*sic*], and an advance made from the Ukraine, from the Don Cossack area, and from Siberia. Such success is constantly threatened by the *Entente* troops, and the advance of the Czechs, who are paid by the *Entente*.'

The Secretary of State asked that a discussion on this matter should be reserved until he arrived at headquarters. He then apparently sent a general reply to Riezler that, in the meantime, he was to keep on supporting the Bolsheviks, and only 'get in touch' with the other parties. But Riezler knew that this would not work for long, as one could not 'get in touch' with a despairing bourgeoisie without having to say 'yes' or 'no' within a few weeks.

On the 27th, Riezler in turn replied to a wire from the Foreign Ministry that the latest news was that talks were taking place at that moment in Petrograd about a *rapprochement* between the right-wing monarchists and the Siberian group. It would be in German interests, stated Riezler, to have at the beginning as colourless a coalition as possible, with a programme of peace and order and the liberation of Russia from the Bolsheviks. Establishment of the actual form of government would have to be given initially to a 'representation of the people' (i.e. Constituent Assembly), which would have to be called after the restoration of order. If an understanding between the Petrograd groups and the Germans could be achieved on this basis, the Moscow 'right-wing centre' could join in, after a victory in Petrograd. The Cadet leaders could not officially join this combination.

If this government succeeded in improving the food situation, perhaps through Siberian help, perhaps through the lifting of the grain monopoly of the Bolsheviks and the current terror against the big landowners, it would be welcomed not only by the bourgeoisie, but also by the landowners, and by the Church, and initially also by the rest of the population. Experience showed that behind the Czech front line there was peace, the price of bread was going down, and cooperation between everybody (from the SRs to the right-wing monarchists) worked reasonably well, because they all hated the Bolsheviks.

Apart from the Czechs, Savinkov's volunteers, right-wing SRs, Mensheviks and left-wing cadets, Riezler continued next day, the *Entente* also had at their disposal a few officers' organizations with similar views, a few Siberian units, and some hired Poles. How far these organizations had been weakened because of their last failure was difficult to say. *Entente* power was also based on the equally strong hatred of the Bolsheviks amongst the starving workers, the farmers and the bourgeoisie. This grew stronger with the increase of Bolshevik terror. If the *Entente* alone remained hostile towards the Bolsheviks, then hatred and hunger would lead the *Entente* to victory. Apart from this, the Latvians urgently wanted to get away from their uncomfortable position; and, at the moment, they placed their hopes on Germany, because the Germans could guarantee their return, and they believed German promises more than those of the *Entente*.

If their hope in Germany failed, the Latvians would also be available to the *Entente*, in return for security and landownership. The *Entente* party in Russia would then have prospects for a while of reasonable order in case of a victory, in particular if the new Russia only demanded economic war against Germany. It would force Germany, however, to show its full power, and to cut off the Murman connection. If a German counter-revolution was victorious, in particular if the Siberian combination was successful, and the connection via Murman remained interrupted, the *Entente* organizations could only cause local difficulties.

On the 28th, Riezler also informed the Foreign Ministry that the military attaché, when asked how many German troops would be needed to support German politics, in case of a change of Russian government, had sent the following message to the Supreme Command:

1. If circumstances were favourable:
   (*a*) *For Moscow*: one efficient battalion, with all modern weapons. This battalion would have to have arrived in Moscow before the *coup*. Condition: neutrality of the Latvians, at first achieved by payments.
   (*b*) *For Petrograd*: neutrality of the Latvians, demonstrations at Pskov, Narva and Viborg, also Kursk and Orsha.
2. If they wanted to be safe, and did not want to use the Latvians, neither in a passive nor in an active way, a new campaign would be unavoidable, because of the length of the insecure communications in the rear. Apart from railway guards, six shock divisions would be needed. It was assumed that the enemy consisted of 30,000 Latvians, and the same number of Czechs, but that they would not act in a consistent way.

    The weakness of the military organizations of the right-wing parties lay mainly in the lack of guns, machine-guns, and in particular lorries; guns could be found quickly. 'One would also have to get over the fact that, at the moment, there is no united military organization at all, there are only circles of five to ten persons, who either know very little, or nothing at all, about each other.'[3]

The military attaché here underlined the basic weakness in Riezler's whole assessment of the anti-Bolshevik parties — that they consisted only of very small groups.

Lenin, once sure that no retaliation for Mirbach's murder was intended, proceeded to outwit the Germans over the deal he had made for the rescue of the Tsar, which it was agreed would be covered by reports of his death, to be issued between July 16 and 20. The Bolshevik military position was rapidly deteriorating. The Czechs held the middle Volga line. Further north, Simbirsk and Kazan were in a state of semi-mutiny. Savinkov held Yaroslavl, north of Moscow. Another Czech force was rapidly approaching Ekaterinburg, where the Imperial Family was under close guard. By July 14, the Regional War Commissar Goloschchokin was back in Ekaterinburg from Moscow with instructions on what was to be done. On the 17th,

Karakhan telephoned to Lockhart in Moscow with the bare news that the Tsar had been executed. The next day, the Bolshevik press bureau published a statement by the central executive committee saying that they had been informed by the Ural soviet that because of the threat posed by the Czech advance on Ekaterinburg, and because of the discovery of a new counter-revolutionary plot, aimed at rescuing the Tsar, he had been shot on July 16. 'The wife and son of Nicholas have been sent to a safe place', it was stated. It had been proposed to put the Tsar on trial, but recent events had prevented this. The central executive committee, it was added, approved the action of the Ural soviet.

On the 20th, the Czechs were in the suburbs of Ekaterinburg, which was about to fall and contradictory rumours were sweeping the city about the Tsar. The local soviet was trying to seize foreign residents as hostages, 'counter-revolutionaries' were being shot, and rival factions were fighting in the streets, when Goloshchokin was told over the telegraph from Moscow that he could publish an agreed text. At a workers' meeting in the city theatre, he made no attempt to hide the hopelessness of the situation, but said that the Czechs and Whites would never get the Tsar, as he had been shot; the Tsar's family had been taken away from Ekaterinburg. Within hours of this statement, a notice was stuck up on walls round the town, giving the news of the Tsar's execution. The last paragraph stated: 'The family of Romanov has been sent away from Ekaterinburg to another and safer place.' Shortly afterwards, Red Army soldiers were seen tearing these notices down.

In Moscow that day, Counsellor Riezler, on instructions from the Foreign Ministry in Berlin to make urgent representations on behalf of the Tsarina, saw Radek, and condemned the shooting of the Tsar, and gave 'urgent warning against further action of this nature'. Riezler reported that 'Radek thinks personally that if we show a particular interest in the women of the Imperial Family who are of German extraction, they might be permitted to leave the country.' Riezler suggested that if the Bolshevik delegates in Berlin really offered to move against the Allies in Russia, with German support, 'our acceptance might be conditional on their undertaking to grant freedom, on humanitarian grounds, to the Tsarina and the Tsarevitch (the latter on the basis that he is inseparable from his mother)'.[3] Riezler seemed to believe that the Tsar had indeed been shot, and the other members of the Imperial Family, including the Tsarevitch, had been spared; Radek was prepared to encourage the belief that the 'German princesses' were alive.

On the 23rd, Chicherin also saw Riezler, who called again on the instructions of the Foreign Ministry in Berlin and asked for particular assurances that the Imperial Family was safe. Chicherin listened in silence. The next day, on further instructions, Riezler called again. Chicherin refused to give any assurances or make any promise, but answered rather vaguely that, as far as he knew, 'the Tsarina has been taken to Perm'.[4] Riezler imagined that he was being humoured to avoid further German anger. But there is now evidence that Chicherin may have been telling the truth, that the Tsarina and the grand duchesses may in fact have been taken to Perm.

What effect the presence of the British economic mission in Bolshevik Russia had on the German Foreign Ministry's pressure on the German High Command is uncertain. On July 17, while Savinkov's revolt continued at Yaroslavl, a British officer arrived at Vologda to inform the Allied ambassadors that General Poole intended to land at Archangel in late July (frenzied efforts were now being made by Allied agents in Archangel to organize an uprising to coincide with the landing), and to request them to leave Vologda, as their continued presence there might impede Allied military operations.[5] Support for Savinkov was clearly on the way. The Allied diplomats prepared to depart, and Lindley decided that Clark and his economic mission could go on to Moscow. Because of Savinkov's revolt, this entailed travelling via Petrograd, where they remained — rather mysteriously — for some six days, discussing the 'economic situation' with certain British and Russian businessmen. (One wonders whether Clark realized the dangers run by these Russians.) Germany, Clark found, had been able to manipulate the exchange in Russia to her very considerable advantage. Previously, the British and Germans had been competing against each other in buying up roubles, mostly via Scandinavia. But the Germans had now stopped doing this, 'and when we were in Petrograd', Clark reported later, 'they had lately opened a special office where deposits could be received from Germans, and also from Russians recommended by German friends. ... As the Russian banks were closed, and this German office afforded a security not afforded elsewhere under the Bolshevik regime, the deposits were very considerable ... [and] eased Germany's position in Stockholm by making it less necessary for her to purchase roubles there, and thus tended to depreciate the rouble and to appreciate the mark in Scandinavia.'[6]

Clark therefore took a hard look at the Russian bank schemes. In view of the coming Allied intervention in Siberia, he and his colleagues first looked into the affairs of the Siberian Bank. They managed to find a rather terrified Poliakov, who had personally negotiated this deal on behalf of Colonel Keyes with the former managing director and main shareholder, Denisov. Poliakov, as far as they could see, was more or less in charge of the little that was left of the Siberian Bank. He urged that the branches in Siberia in the areas free from Bolshevik control should be reopened with funds provided by the British government. Clark protested that these branch banks would attract no deposits. Poliakov added hopefully that the

Siberian Bank held an important concession in regard to the establishment of a bank in Mongolia, though just before its nationalization by the Bolsheviks, he admitted gloomily, the former directors had taken a large block of shares in the Amur Transport Company (which owned the important Amur railway line) from the Siberian Bank's vaults, and he did not know where these shares, or these former directors, had gone.

Discussion turned to the high purchase price paid to Denisov. Clark found Poliakov 'at least evasive', though Poliakov claimed to have objected to the proposal at the time, and in this General Poole later supported him. 'He [Poole] had seen Mr Poliakov's written protests against the scheme as originally proposed', Clark later reported, but Poliakov had been overruled, 'as they would involve the negotiations breaking down, and it was essential on political grounds that this should not occur. In the General's view, Mr Poliakov had saved His Majesty's Government from a very doubtful speculation and evolved a more practical scheme with less liability and a fair possibility of great future economic advantage to this country [i.e. England].' But it was 'natural to expect that once the British Government had expended such a large sum of money in the purchase of shares, they would finance and strengthen the [Siberian] Bank', and after denationalization by some future White Russian regime, the British connection would increase the price of the shares, thus giving Jaroszynski, who had an option to purchase them at cost price, a large profit at the British government's expense. Clark was exceedingly suspicious that there had been some hanky-panky; that either Denisov or Jaroszynski, or both, had given Poliakov a large commission to engineer this arrangement. But, of course, there was no proof. 'He [Poliakov] appears to be energetic, but somewhat superficial', Clark reported, underlining 'the objections ... to placing in a highly confidential position a gentleman who is not a British subject, and of whom comparatively little is known'. Clark, unknowingly, was directly criticizing the War Cabinet who, through mistaking his identity, had personally appointed Poliakov. Clark advised that until conditions were more normal in Russia, the Treasury should make no further payments to Denisov. Meanwhile, they should obtain possession of the shares that had been bought from him, most of which were still, supposedly, lying heavily mortgaged in the vaults of other Russian and foreign banks. Clark also recommended that Poliakov should be replaced by young Dominick Spring-Rice, who had come out with the economic mission, and who made some specific observations about the Siberian Bank.

1. Jaroszynski had an option, free of cost, to purchase 44,000 shares at 1,500 roubles a share. 'Should these shares be worth so high a price when his option becomes due, I am convinced that he will be able to obtain somehow funds sufficient for the repayment of the loan of £500,000, which he obtained from His Majesty's Government.'

2. The capital of the Siberian Bank was now 120,000 shares. 44,000
   shares, the number sold by Denisov to the British government, was
   thus 16,000 shares less than the number required for complete control
   of the bank, if such control was wanted. 'I think Denisov must have
   known this when he sold, but I cannot find in the papers any evidence
   that he represented himself to be selling a clear majority of the shares.'
3. As the Siberian Bank was at the moment nationalized, like all other
   banks, it would be necessary to await not only the cancellation of the
   necessary decrees, but the actual scheme under which denationalization was to be carried out, 'before any reasonable estimate of the value
   of the bank and its shares can be formed'.[6]

Clark next looked into the matter of the British loan to Jaroszynski,
which had enabled the British government, again via Jaroszynski, to obtain
control of the other Russian banks. Again, he felt certain that the middle-
man who had negotiated the deals (Hugh Leech) had made money out of
both sides, though there was no proof of this. Clark merely commented
that 'in several directions, his activities were not in the interests of His
Majesty's Government, more particularly later on when he acted as Mr
Jaroszynski's representative'. (Spring-Rice also has some further remarks
on Leech at this stage. A senior British embassy official, who had been in
Petrograd on July 6, had there seen both Keyes and Poliakov, from whom
he was made aware that the exact relations between Leech and the British
government 'were the object of much discussion in Russian financial
circles'. This matter should be cleared up. 'If Mr Leech is really as bad as
many people suggest him to be, something should be done to prevent him
damaging British credit by posing as a British agent.') Clark was also
surprised at the security for the loan accepted from Jaroszynski (this, it
must be remarked, was not Leech's doing); though the shares of the little
railway, which ran through rich mining country in Siberia, might be worth
par value, both oil companies were 'in great financial straits', and of no
value at all.

Clark concluded thus: 'The political and military representatives of His
Majesty's government, who were directly concerned in the actions under
review, were, on some important points, badly advised by those who
assisted them in carrying through the technical details.' But Clark felt
doubtful whether there were 'adequate grounds for committing His
Majesty's Government to large liabilities in purchasing control of banks
which were defunct for the intents and purposes in view. In our opinion,
when once the original object of the scheme had disappeared, and it was
decided not to proceed with the formation of [a] south-eastern [Cossack]
bank, a serious error of judgment was committed in carrying through a
modified and altered scheme under which £500,000 was lent to Mr Jaroszynski on very insufficient security, and a large number of Siberian Bank

shares were bought by His Majesty's Government at a very high price and a free option thereon given to Mr Jaroszynski.' In other words, it was not only the agents Poliakov and Leech who were to blame, but the principals, General Poole, Lindley and Colonel Keyes, and the Russia Committee in London as well. Clark added a recommendation that Spring-Rice should be authorized by Lindley to go to Petrograd at the 'earliest opportunity' to obtain from Poliakov 'any further information which may be required and any documents bearing upon the deals'. But as they were ante-dated, they were illegal, at least under the Bolshevik regime.

There were, of course, practically no documents, save for Jaroszynski's copies of the original letters of agreement, buried 'somewhere in Petrograd' sometime in late February; while the great majority of the actual shares were all presumably still lying, heavily mortgaged, in the vaults of other banks, unless the Bolsheviks had removed them. Clark, in fact, only half understood the double purpose of the original purchase of all these bank shares, which was not only to obtain control of these Russian barks, but to pass funds through them to the volunteer army and Don Cossacks early in 1918. In the general turmoil, it had all been conveniently forgotten. Nor does Clark appear to have seen Teddy Lessing, the contact man between Lloyd George and the Russian bankers, who was related to Poliakov, who had, in fact, been appointed on May 18 by the Treasury (with the Department of Overseas Trade's agreement) as General Poole's Russian financial adviser. Poliakov later claimed that in the first half of 1918, when he was negotiating these bank deals without any official connection with the British embassy, he had saved the British government more than £4 million; and that these negotiations were 'fraught with serious danger personally to myself'.

Clark in effect decided that the Russian bank schemes could be of no use in the coming Allied intervention in northern Russia and Siberia, and that the British government should follow the German example, and also acquire roubles 'other than by purchase' (presumably in Scandinavia), by opening the 'British Bank of Russia' to obtain deposits and issue rouble notes under British guarantee. (For, as Clark's colleague Armistead pointed out, both Kerensky and the Bolsheviks had been churning out rouble notes, and 'there are now thousands of notes in circulation bearing identical numbers, letters and dates of issue, which makes it impossible to identify the genuine note'.) A temporary issue of unguaranteed rouble notes, as made to the Murmansk soviet, would not be nearly enough. Sterling sales should cease. But until a 'British Bank of Russia' opened in Moscow or Petrograd, British consuls should be authorized to accept rouble deposits and sell British war bonds. Clark next looked into the affairs of *Tovaro Obmien* (the Allied company that was buying up Russian goods of possible use to the Germans), and stopped Major Macalpine from spending some 400 million roubles on buying up cotton and flax. Just as they were about to leave for Moscow for discussions with the Bolsheviks, Clark and his colleagues were told that Jaroszynski, who was in hiding in Petrograd, would see them on their return.[6]

In Moscow, as Savinkov's revolt at Yaroslavl continued, Lockhart was now openly supporting the Russian opposition; on July 16, without any authority, he had given one million roubles to the 'National Centre'; and on about the 21st, after a secret meeting with General Alexeiev's ADC, he had sent a courier with ten million roubles to the volunteer army in the Kuban.

Colonel Keyes was engaged in similar activities. But the 'only way I could get money down to the volunteer army was by sending women agents with their skirts lined with thousand rouble notes,' he records. 'A few only of these got through.' Keyes himself was arrested twice by the Bolsheviks at this time. On the first occasion, he was stopped in the street as a suspicious character when carrying five million roubles in notes, for which the penalty was death. They were press-packed into two slim 'bricks' in his jacket pockets. (Luckily he was wearing a Burberry overcoat, which, besides pockets, had two openings through which to pass the hands to the inside. On his way to Cheka headquarters, while protesting volubly at his arrest, he managed to move the two 'bricks' into his Burberry pockets. On arrival, he took off his Burberry, cast it casually down on a chair — and it was promptly sat upon by an old peasant woman.) When taken in to see the Commissar, he was made to empty his coat pockets, which were found to contain nothing but oddments. He stated indignantly that he was an Irish revolutionary, and that they had no right to arrest him. When asked what an Irish revolutionary was doing at this time in the middle of Russia, Keyes stated that the Irish had their own revolution, and that he had come to see how the Russians were managing theirs, and he thought they were making a pretty poor job of it. A lively discussion ensued, and a bottle of vodka was produced. Eventually, he was bidden farewell, pocketed his possessions on the table, and pulled his Burberry out from under the old peasant woman as he went out. Later, Keyes was arrested a second time by the Bolsheviks (the circumstances of this arrest are unclear), 'and had much difficulty in getting out of the country'.[6]

On July 23, as the Bolsheviks finally suppressed Savinkov's revolt, the British economic mission arrived in Moscow, where they were introduced to Chicherin, Bronsky and Goukovsky (Commissars for Trade and Finance), by an acutely embarrassed Lockhart. What Clark and the Bolshevik commissars discussed is not clear. Lockhart, whom Clark seems to have misled about what he knew of British plans for intervention, simply speaks of him 'breathing peace and commercial treaties'. If Clark really did ask for permission to open a 'British Bank of Russia' in Moscow in return for some sort of British economic help, the Bolsheviks certainly turned him down. Clark merely remarks that it was 'not possible to arrive at any practicable arrangements on commercial matters with the Bolshevik government'. Clark then went to see the British consul, presumably to tell him to start accepting roubles, and to sell British war bonds; and from there, went on to the English Club, which 'entertained us at luncheon'. It was all fairly leisurely. The verdict on this episode must be that the Bolsheviks, who did not wholly understand why the British economic mission had come out to Russia, failed to use its presence in Moscow to bring pressure on the trade talks in Berlin.[6]

The Americans, and especially President Wilson, had all along been suspicious of British intentions when they urged intervention in Russia. Now the Americans had agreed to intervention of a sort. Then there had come news of the economic mission and its ulterior designs on the Russian economy. Now there were further grounds for American suspicions. When the War Cabinet met at noon on July 16, Balfour stated that he had just received the following wire from Lord Reading: 'I should deprecate General Knox coming here. He is too much identified with past regimes and there is too much suspicion given that Allies (confidential, chiefly French but also ourselves) are striving for a reactionary political regime and especially are anti-soviet in their policy. Nothing makes President more apprehensive than notion that intervention may develop by Allies taking sides in political contest. The President would not understand why you are sending General Knox. The fear here would be that he would gather around him from past acquaintance just those Russians who would symbolize reaction. Confidential. May I make suggestion that you should send General Bridges? He knows so well views here and has just that wide outlook which seems so necessary.'[7] (In a separate telegram to Lloyd George, marked 'personal and most secret', which was not disclosed to the Cabinet, Reading stated that the American government felt that Knox had even been against the March revolution, and would gather round him in Siberia a clique of former Tsarist officers, giving a reactionary aspect to a Siberian expedition. In fact, the Americans felt that any intervention would come under the control of the *ancien régime*. Reading urged that the British government should also send out a socialist delegation to Siberia. This would have a good effect in Russia, and, what was more, a 'most excellent effect' in America, and would dissipate much of the 'present doubt and criticism'. Reading warned that the President's suspicions would have to be allayed if he were ever to permit American action on a proper scale. The President, in fact, was 'still opposed to intervention and somewhat apprehensive lest the step he is now willing to take should lead him into a much more extended policy'.)[7]

Balfour, alluding to his telegram from Lord Reading about Knox, told the War Cabinet that he would be 'very loath' to override Reading's advice about persons whom we might send to America; he should have full authority in such matters. The War Office were sending General Knox to

Siberia, Balfour reminded the Cabinet, and his quickest route was via North America. At first sight, there appeared to be little objection to his taking this route, but the Americans would come to know of it and wish to know why he was going. In fact, he was not going to command any troops at Vladivostok, because we would only have some 1,000 men there and were unlikely to have more; it was not a general officer's command anyway. The War Office were proposing to send him as military attaché 'with somewhat special and extended powers', stated Balfour delicately. 'Although General Knox was not a reactionary as the term was understood by the members of the Cabinet, there was no doubt that he was anti-Bolshevik, while a man of his strength of character, knowledge and ability was bound sooner or later to play a political part. Moreover, it was practically impossible for anybody to go to Russia, whether in an official position or not, without becoming mixed up with her internal politics and her political parties, which were so closely bound up with the military situation.' Balfour feared that the Americans 'would suspect General Knox of intending to take a reactionary line and of attempting to revive the *ancien régime*'. The point was whether Knox could take another route avoiding America; whether Reading's advice should be overridden; or whether someone else 'less capable and more colourless' than Knox should be chosen. Lord Robert Cecil stated firmly that the intention was for a military officer to go to Siberia only to take charge of 'our' military interests there; but this required 'a really good man'. Everything seemed to point to Knox being the right man. He knew Russia thoroughly, and his past judgments and forecasts had, almost without exception, proved correct (as for intance on Kerensky, the Bolsheviks, the state of the Russian army, etc.). He would doubtless find it difficult to avoid politics in Siberia, but he would be a most useful liaison with the Russian troops there. Cecil then came to the point. 'What we wanted was that friendly elements among the Russian troops should be collected and formed into an army.' There was no Englishman more competent than Knox for such a task.

This was the first time that the Cabinet had been told that the British were going to organize a Russian army in Siberia, as well as in northern Russia, though the First Lord's paper of late June, explaining in some detail how General Poole intended to operate in northern Russia, had not been circulated to the Cabinet. The Cabinet's present view was that though it might be impossible for Knox to avoid crossing American territory on his way to Siberia, it was undesirable that he should go to Washington. 'General Knox was associated with the old regime', the Cabinet felt, 'such as General Alexeiev and others. President Wilson seemed inclined to believe that the Conservative elements in England were just as keen now to revive the old regime in Russia as they were early in the nineteenth century to restore it in France, and also feared that our intention in going to Russia was not so much to defeat the Germans as to crush the revolution.' But it was generally agreed that it was important that Knox should proceed to Siberia and should start at once, but that it would be difficult for him to avoid crossing American territory without him being seriously delayed.

The War Cabinet decided that Knox should go to Vladivostok at once, travelling as unostentatiously as possible, and not go to Washington, 'and in no circumstances grant any interviews while on the way'. It was also decided that the Foreign Office should send a 'carefully worded' reply to Reading, pointing out that Knox had 'very exceptional qualifications' for the post of head of a British military mission 'attached to the headquarters of the future Allied Commander-in-Chief in Siberia'. But the War Cabinet, in this discussion, had clearly recognized that there were strong differences of opinion between President Wilson and themselves on intervention and that the despatch of Knox would heighten these feelings and suspicions; nevertheless, it was decided that Knox should proceed. The rift between Washington and London was thus widened. 'The Americans think Knox is the sole antagonist in Russia', commented his future ADC, then in Tokyo, two days later. The origin of this American mistrust of Knox was probably the belief that he had master-minded Kornilov's revolt in September 1917. But he was out of the country at that time; the real culprit was General Barter. For the Americans, however, Knox was a symbol of British imperialism, of British guile and hypocrisy.[8]

When the Imperial War Cabinet briefly discussed intervention that evening, it was pointed out 'that there was no time to be lost if intervention was to take place, and that every delay was dangerous'. The CIGS stated that he had had a wire from General Bridges in Washington saying that President Wilson 'had just reached a decision' on both northern Russia and Siberia, and that it would be passed on immediately to Lord Reading. (This seems to reinforce the view that President Wilson's decision of July 6 was taken in London simply as an opening bid on intervention.) The CIGS added that the American Chief of Staff had informed him that any American troops allotted to the operations in northern Russia would be taken from General Pershing's troops, and Pershing would arrange matters. The Prime Minister stated that a British battalion was being sent from Hong Kong, a French battalion from Indochina, and American troops were being got ready in the Philippines, and Japan, America and England were sending rifles and ammunition to the Czechs at Vladivostok. Borden added that Canada had offered to send three battalions.[9]

Sir Henry Wilson's news that the President had just reached a decision on overall intervention probably startled the Prime Minister and certainly propelled him into immediate action. Without telling the Foreign Office, he decided that he, not Balfour, should answer Reading, and that he should answer his 'personal and most secret' telegram. Lloyd George began with a strong defence of Knox. 'There is no man in the British army who knows Russia as Knox does ... he is not a politician, his whole interest lies in soldiering. . . . It is an absolute mistake to think he was identified with the old regime.' Knox alone had consistently stressed the corruption and ineffi- ciency of the Tsarist regime and had thereby made himself so unpopular with the Tsarist authorities that for a time he had had to be replaced. After careful consideration of Reading's warning, the War Cabinet had decided that Knox should proceed to Siberia. 'In going out he will not be concerned with politics but solely with the conduct of efficient military operations.' (But Balfour, at the War Cabinet, had recognized that the military and political situations in Russia were inseparable.)[10]

Lloyd George strongly denied that British policy favoured Russian reaction, even going so far as to claim that the establishment of a liberal, progressive and democratic regime in Russia was virtually a British war aim. This was essential not only for world peace, but also for the security of the Indian frontier; the restoration of a reactionary regime would not only see Russia closely allied to Germany, but Russia aggressive. British relations with the Bolsheviks since early in 1918 should be sufficient proof that British policy was not to encourage Russian reaction, but to let the Russian people choose their own form of government.

The President's fears and suspicions of where intervention might lead him could only be allayed by strong Presidential action. Lloyd George said that he would back the President's policy all the way, 'always provided it is an effective policy and not a policy of drift. You can tell the President that provided he will really act in Siberia and make it primary object of his policy to establish effective Russian and Allied control over whole Siberian railway to the Urals before winter sets in, I will give him all the support of which I am capable', he stated. 'What I am frightened of, however, is that we shall drift along until it is too late to save Russia from falling under German domination.' Only immediate Allied intervention could now save Russia from this. 'I am interventionist just as much because I am a demo- crat as because I want to win the war', he added with a touch of desper- ation. He was 'much attracted' to Reading's suggestion for the despatch of a socialist delegation to Siberia as well; but there were no British labour leaders up to such a mission, and there would be little use them making speeches if their Russian audience understood no English. 'If, however, the President proposes to send powerful political delegation', Lloyd George assured Reading, 'we would certainly send liberal or labour representatives to accompany it.'[10]

It is easy to criticize, even to ridicule Lloyd George's desperate efforts to convince President Wilson that British policy was something other than what it really was; it was ridiculous to suggest that it was virtually a British war aim to secure a change of regime of any sort in a former Allied country. British relations with the Bolsheviks would hardly enable the Russian people to choose their own form of government; vicious Bolshevik suppression of the constituent assembly, the offspring of the only free elections in Russian history (save for the first Duma in 1906), was all too vivid in everyone's memory. But even Lloyd George could not disguise the basic difference between American and British policy; any policy not aimed at securing effective control of the Siberian railway from Vladivostok to the Urals before winter was a policy of drift.

But the Prime Minister's plea, despatched via Wiseman on the 17th, arrived too late. That day, President Wilson officially informed the Allied ambassadors in Washington of the American decision on intervention, apparently to counter leaks in the Japanese press. His statement, unlike his decision of July 6, also covered intervention in northern Russia. On receipt of the Supreme War Council's request for three more American battalions for northern Russia, Secretary of War Baker and General March, the American Chief of Staff, had discussed the Murmansk expedition with the President. On July 8, Secretary Baker had wired to General Bliss in Paris asking for his views. 'None of us can see the military value of the proposal', he added. Bliss (who had listened to the First Lord's paper, and had heard all about General Poole and his 'fiery cross') stuck to his view that this British proposal was too grandiose to be carried out by such Allied forces as could be made available; the small Allied force that could be provided should confine itself to holding the northern Russian ports throughout the winter, and secure such Allied stores as had not already been removed. But on this issue, the provision of three more American battalions, the President gave in; he had refused so many British and French requests, he told Secretary Baker, 'that they were beginning to feel that he was not a good associate, much less a good ally ...'.[11] Indeed, the whole tone of the President's *aide-mémoire* of July 17, typed by the President himself without consulting anybody else, is apologetic, especially in the opening paragraphs. 'The whole heart of the people of the United States is in the winning of this war', it begins, and goes on (in terms of self-justification and high-minded *naïveté*, which read very oddly today) to explain why American forces could not be diverted from the western front. It was, however, the 'clear and fixed' opinion of the American government that military intervention in Russia 'would add to the present sad confusion in Russia rather than cure it, injure her rather than help her', and would not help to win the war against Germany. 'It cannot, therefore, take part in such intervention or sanction it in principle.' Even if military intervention succeeded in restoring an eastern front against Germany, it would be 'merely a method of making use of Russia, not a method of serving her'. Such assistance would arrive too late to save the Russian people from their present distress, and their resources would have to be used to support foreign armies instead of restoring their own. 'Military action is admissible in Russia, as the government of the United States sees the circumstances, only to help the Czechoslovaks consolidate their forces and get into successful cooperation with their Slavic kinsmen, and to steady any efforts at self-government or self-defence in which the Russians themselves may be willing to accept assistance.' The 'only legitimate object' for the use of American or Allied troops in the Far East or in northern Russia was to guard military stores which might subsequently be needed by Russian forces, and to give them such aid 'as may be acceptable' to help them organize their own self-defence. 'For helping the Czechoslovaks there is immediate necessity and sufficient justification.' Recent developments had made it clear that the Russian people themselves desired it. The American government was therefore glad to contribute the 'small force' at its disposal.

It yielded also to the Supreme War Council's judgment in establishing a 'small force' at Murmansk to guard the military stores at Kola, 'and to make it safe for Russian forces to come together in organized bodies in the north', but it could go no further than 'these modest and experimental plans'. The American government could not, and would not, be able to take part in 'organized intervention' in 'adequate force' (a phrase to which the Supreme War Council had attached great significance) either in Siberia or northern Russia. It would use the few troops it could spare only for the purposes stated, and would withdraw these troops and transfer them to the western front if the plans in which it was now intended they should co-operate should develop into others 'inconsistent' with American policy.

But the American government wished to state, 'with the utmost cordiality and good will', that none of these decisions was meant in any way as a criticism of what the other Allied governments might think it wise to do. 'It wishes in no way to embarrass their choices of policy.' It merely wished to state frankly what American policy was; and in restricting its own actions, it was not trying, 'even by implication', to limit the action or define the policies of its Allies. The American government hoped to safeguard the Czech rear operating from Vladivostok in close cooperation with a small military force 'like its own' from Japan, and if necessary from the other Allies. It further proposed to ask all concerned to join in assuring the Russian people in a public declaration that neither in Siberia nor in northern Russia would there be any infringement of Russian sovereignty, any intervention in Russian internal affairs, or any impairment of Russian territorial integrity; but that each Ally wished to give 'only such aid as shall be acceptable' to the Russian people in their efforts to regain control of their own affairs, territory and destiny.[11]

Finally, the American government wished to send to Siberia as soon as possible a civil commission, consisting of merchants, agricultural experts, labour advisers, Red Cross and YMCA personnel in order to relieve the immediate economic needs of the people there in some systematic way, as opportunities might occur. But this commission would not be linked to the military support to be given in the rear of the Czech forces moving west; it would follow later.

The President's *aide-mémoire*, stripped of its high-minded and (to the Allies) naïve and half-offensive phraseology, showed that the American government was against military intervention in Russia, since it would not help to win the war against Germany. The Supreme War Council's plea was thus rejected. But military action was permissible to help the Czechs 'consolidate' and link up with their 'Slavic kinsmen', and to 'steady any efforts at self-government or self-defence in which the Russians themselves may be willing to accept assistance'. A 'small' American force could thus cooperate with a 'small' Japanese force and similar 'small' Allied forces. All this presumably referred to Siberia. It was also agreed to send a 'small' American force to Murmansk to guard the military stores at Kola (although there never had been any there or at Murmansk), 'and to make it safe for Russian forces to come together in organized bodies in the North'. But though the American government did not wish to criticize or embarrass the Russian policy of the Allied governments, 'even by implication', American forces would be withdrawn if the plans President Wilson had in mind developed into others inconsistent with American policy.

What exactly did the President mean by all this? First, with whom were the Czechs to consolidate? Were their 'Slavic kinsmen' the other Czech groups, or was this an oblique reference to those Russians who were friendlily disposed towards them? On June 17, the President had reminded Secretary Lansing that the Czechs were the cousins of the Russians. What was meant by the phrase 'to steady any efforts at self-government or self-defence' which the Russians themselves might accept? It might mean giving advice from a distance, or direct involvement in the political and military situation, which the President elsewhere appeared to rule out. Next — of extreme significance — to which Russians was he referring? There was a civil war going on in Russia and Siberia, but no mention was made of this; nor of the fact that the Bolsheviks, the *de facto* power, were certain to resist military intervention or any military action. Which Russian forces were to be enabled 'to come together in organized bodies in the North', and for what purpose? Finally, the direct threat to withdraw American forces if they became involved in a more extended Allied policy cancelled the President's assurance that he was not trying to influence the Allies in their choice of policy. And who, incidentally, was opposing the Czechs in Russia and Siberia? In his decision of July 6, the President had stated that this opposition was offered by German and Austrian prisoners. In his *aide-mémoire*, there was no mention of these enemy prisoners. Kennan suggests that President Wilson envisaged that the very arrival of American and Japanese forces in Siberia to support the Czechs would cause a violent swing in local public opinion towards the Allies, which would lead to the formation of a thoroughly democratic Siberian government; which in turn would lead to a similar change in Russian public opinion and in the

Russian government. If this is so — if in fact the President really intended to use the Czechs as an Allied spearhead — then one can only say, again, that he was adopting the same plan as the British had in mid-May, which had been turned down by the French in late May, on the grounds that it 'would probably prove fatal to American intervention'.

When the President's *aide-mémoire* reached London on July 20, it was received with resentment, but was accepted; the march of military events would soon force the President to increase the size of the absurdly small forces. While the Prime Minister's office prepared a draft reply, Balfour wired to the British ambassador in Tokyo asking him to urge the Japanese government, with all the influence he could muster, to accept the President's proposal; but the ambassador was left in no doubt by Balfour that the proposed American and Japanese forces would prove to be 'wholly insufficient', and that 'events will almost certainly compel the Allies either to increase their armies or to withdraw them'.[12]

At noon on July 22, the Prime Minister brought the *aide-mémoire*, together with a memorandum in reply, before the Imperial War Cabinet, having invited the Dominion Prime Ministers to attend. Lord Reading, it was explained, had asked for an early reply, as he was seeing President Wilson the next day. The Prime Minister stated that 'it was difficult not to take exception to the tone of the President's *aide-mémoire*, and he was inclined to believe that it was written in order that it might sooner or later be published'. It was the British government's duty to counter the President's suggestion that 'we were endeavouring to set up a reactionary government in Russia, and that President Wilson alone was protecting the liberty of the Russian people. Liberty meant that the Russian nation should have the right of setting up any government they chose. If they chose a republican government, or a Bolshevik government, or a monarchical government, it was no concern of ours.' There was also the President's suggestion that intervention in Siberia would divert Allied efforts from the western front. The whole point of asking the Japanese to intervene, stated Lloyd George, was that their forces could only be used in an eastern theatre, and so there would be no diversion of Allied efforts in the West.[13]

The Prime Minister then read out his memorandum, which set out the points which he thought should be emphasized in reply to the President. First (in answer to his statement that he attached so much importance to the western front that he was reluctant to withdraw any American troops from France for operations elsewhere), it should be stated that the Allies never contemplated the despatch of large American or Allied forces to Siberia. Their proposal was, in order to save troops which could fight on the western front, that the bulk of whatever troops were needed for the Siberian expedition should be provided by Japan. Secondly (in answer to President Wilson's evident impression that the British government had ulterior designs on the Russian constitution), it should be stated 'that we had not the slightest intention or desire' to back one form of Russian constitutional settlement or another, but were anxious for the Russian people to determine their own constitution without any outside interference. Thirdly (in regard to the President's point about the restoration of the eastern front), it should be stated that the Allies had not contemplated the immediate restoration of Russian military power. All they hoped was that Russia would recover enough strength to offer a serious threat to Germany in the East, and thus absorb large German forces which would otherwise be sent to the West; and since it was highly probable that the Germans could not spare large forces from the West, they might be driven to abandon their plans in the East. 'Russia would thus be liberated from the German yoke.'

The memorandum concluded by saying that the British government welcomed the American decision to send a 'small force' to Vladivostok to cooperate with the other Allied forces, but were not satisfied that a force of 20,000 men would be equal to rescuing the Czechs from Samara to Irkutsk, and 'deplored' the American decision to confine Japanese military aid to a force of 7,000 men.

It was suggested in the Cabinet that in the answer to the President, emphasis might be laid on the Russian economic resources that Germany would obtain, which would give her the means and moral encouragement to continue the struggle. Though it was generally agreed that this was a 'very strong part' of the case for Allied intervention, it was pointed out that this reply was not intended to be a full survey of the case, but rather an answer to the points which the President had 'misrepresented' in his *aide-mémoire*. It was asked if it was intended that Balfour's draft wire, suggesting the despatch to Siberia of an Allied political mission under American leadership should be sent to Washington. Balfour said that he had made this suggestion in order to convince American public opinion that the British government was not undertaking intervention in Siberia merely 'to serve their own ends'.[13]

The War Cabinet decided that Balfour, in answer to Lord Reading's telegram, which contained the President's *aide-mémoire*, should send a reply based on the Prime Minister's memorandum, 'with so much of his own draft telegram as he thought fit', and that it should be mentioned that the matter had been discussed by the Imperial War Cabinet. In the reply however, Balfour, besides repeating all Lloyd George's points, toned down the criticism of the size of the forces proposed (there was no mention of the word 'deplore'), and omitted all reference to an Allied political mission. In a private wire to Reading, Balfour admitted that he was evading the issue. But Reading was in no way to suggest to the President that the British government considered the proposed American or Japanese forces to be adequate. 'To us it seems almost certain that either Allied expedition will fail or it will have to be largely reinforced; we hope the latter. But these are hopes which you can hardly convey to President.'[14] Thus, as in mid-May when the British government had proposed to use the Czechs to initiate intervention, they hoped that circumstances would force the hands of the American government.

Meanwhile, all the news reaching the War Cabinet from Vladivostok underlined the need for immediate action. On July 15, the Deputy First Sea Lord had informed the Cabinet that personnel from the Allied ships in the port were now guarding all the various districts where the huge stocks of Allied supplies were stored, so as to free Czech troops urgently needed for a further advance inland, though a few Czechs would remain to protect outlying districts, so that (presumably) the Allies did not have to venture inland. There was now a combined Allied patrol in Vladivostok, which included the Czechs, formed to demonstrate united Allied action. Allied guard-boats were patrolling the harbour entrance, but as they were inadequate, a request was made that destroyers should be sent as soon as possible from Japan. On the 19th, the Cabinet was told that the Bolsheviks had seized all steamers in the river Amur and that several had arrived at Nikolaievsk, at the mouth of the river opposite Sakhalin Island, north of Japan. Though these steamers were only shallow-draft ships, the Japanese admiral at Vladivostok had wired to Tokyo for the immediate despatch of destroyers to watch the Amur estuary. Then on the 24th, the CIGS informed the Cabinet that *Suffolk* had warned that a 'very heavy' enemy attack on Vladivostok was imminent, though by whom or from which direction was not stated. The British battalion from Hong Kong was due at Vladivostok on August 2. Balfour remarked that a proposal had been made to both the British and American governments that some Chinese troops should be added to the Allied force in Siberia (again the source of the proposal is not given). The Americans had discouraged the proposal, and Balfour said he was inclined to do the same, partly because it would encourage the idea that Allied intervention in Siberia 'was taking the form of a yellow invasion'. The Cabinet supported Balfour.[15]

Meanwhile, Czech troops on the Volga, whose rescue from the clutches of the Red Guards and enemy prisoners was the purpose of Allied intervention, were in fact more in danger of over-extending their small forces in aggressive attacks against the Bolsheviks. For they had been assured that they were the 'vanguard' of the Allied forces coming to restore the eastern front along the Volga against the Germans, and they were in confident mood as they prepared to advance from their base of Samara up the Volga to Simbirsk, and down it to Saratov. By July 18, the Czechs had reached Nurlat, just east of Simbirsk, while Kazan to the north remained in a state of semi-mutiny. From Nurlat, Captain Bordes, an energetic French liaison officer with the Czechs, sent a courier to General Lavergne in Moscow with details of how to contact the local Czech command. On the 22nd, Simbirsk fell to a Russian and Czech force, and there was great rejoicing at Samara. The Allies were soon coming, via Vologda. 'All our calculations rested on this', records a Russian politician at Samara. On the 25th, another Czech force seized Ekaterinburg, on the Omsk–Vologda line, to assist the Allies in their coming link-up with friendly forces in Siberia. The Allied ambassadors now fled Vologda for Archangel. In Moscow, when Lockhart informed Clark and his British economic mission of what was happening, they asked for permission to leave (having received a guarantee from the Bolsheviks while in Vologda that should they come to Moscow, they would be free to leave again), but Chicherin would initially allow them only to go to Petrograd, where they saw Poliakov and Macalpine again; Jaroszynski would not now come anywhere near them. They subsequently took a train for Archangel.

On the Volga, the Czechs began seriously to over-extend themselves. On the 25th, Captain Bordes received news at Simbirsk that the Bolsheviks were evacuating Kazan, the crucially important city on the Volga bend, where the huge Russian state gold reserves were lying in railway trucks. Bordes sent another courier to Lavergne in Moscow, and then flew to Samara to try to persuade Čeček (commander of the Czechs and Russians on the Volga) to take Kazan, thus leaving the road open for an advance on Moscow from the east. Both sides knew this. It was probably Bordes and his aircraft which were described by a Russian politician at Simbirsk in his diary on July 26, emphasizing the confusion of those hectic days: 'A French aviator arrived. He had made his way through Kazan. He came from Lavergne with the news that the Allies were already approaching Vologda. I am sending him by aeroplane to Čeček.' This, of course, was nonsense; but was probably due more to misunderstanding in hectic circumstances than to the intervention of the usual Bolshevik *agent provocateur*. The writer goes on to say that delegates had arrived from Kazan saying that everything was ready there for an insurrection. 'The delegates implore us to come to their aid, saying that the people of Kazan will revolt in any event.' The writer claims to have secured Čeček's consent to an advance into Kazan, and to have sent the delegates back again with this news. 'We must push on and on as long as the Bolsheviks are in a state of panic.' Although the Bolsheviks were in a state of panic, Čeček saw that such a move would indeed over-extend his forces, and forbad it. But on the 27th, Captain Bordes received instructions from Lavergne in Moscow. He was to inform General Alexeiev in the Kuban that a Serb force at Tsaritsin (on the lower Volga bend) was ready to take the town when required, which would enable the Czech and Russian forces on the Volga to link up with the volunteer army in southern Russia. Bordes was also to request Czech and Russian forces to take Kazan.[16] This seems to have induced the junior leaders at Simbirsk to disregard Čeček's orders and press on to Kazan.

The long-awaited Japanese reply to the President's proposal of July 6, which had been marginally amplified in his *aide-mémoire* of the 17th, had now reached Washington. The Japanese ambassador, Viscount Ishii, informed the Assistant Secretary of State, Frank Polk, on the 24th that the Japanese government could not limit its force to 7,000 men, as the President had suggested; any foreign restriction of the Japanese force to a specified number would be unacceptable to Japanese public opinion. It was not intended to send a large force, the ambassador assured Polk, but a full division of 12,000 men would be despatched initially, though the final number would depend on what opposition they encountered from the Bolsheviks and enemy prisoners. The ambassador then produced a draft Japanese declaration to the Russian people, which stated that Japan was anxious both to satisfy American wishes, and 'act in harmony' with their Allies, the British and the French, but with due regard to Japan's 'special position' in the Far East. Japan now, in fact, saw that she could at last get the best of all possible worlds. The declaration confirmed that the first Japanese contingent would go to Vladivostok and a further contingent, if necessary, would be sent to guard and operate the Siberian railway. The day before, the Japanese Foreign Minister had told the American ambassador in Tokyo what this meant. Japanese troops would proceed along the Chinese eastern and Amur lines as far as their junction at Karymskaya. (This, incidentally, was a few hundred miles short of Irkutsk; and the Japanese General Staff had calculated that a force of seven divisions (150,000 men) would be needed even if operations were carried only this far into Siberia.)[17]

President Wilson was horrified, his first reaction being to withdraw immediately from the whole adventure, and Polk was instructed to tell the Japanese ambassador this.

At the Prime Minister's mid-morning meeting with his ministers on July 27, Lloyd George drew attention to the latest wires from Lockhart in Moscow, stressing the danger of further delay in intervention, and suggested that they be sent to the President; in view of all the arguments 'from the other side' which were forwarded to him, it was important 'to keep on pouring the right stuff into President Wilson'. Lord Robert Cecil explained that these telegrams were sent to Lord Reading in any case, and he no doubt used his discretion in communicating them to the President. At this, Balfour personally undertook to see that the substance of these particular telegrams was immediately conveyed to the President.[18]

Cecil then recounted a talk he had had with the Japanese ambassador, who had told him of the Japanese reply to the American proposal, which was accepted, though Japan reserved the right to increase their contingent. It also stated that it was a military impossibility to lay down beforehand exactly how many troops would be required for a military operation. (Balfour, it will be recalled, had strongly encouraged such a reply.) The ambassador had explained that a Japanese division of 12,000 men would be sent to Vladivostok at once, and another division a little later to guard the railway. The Japanese government, he added, would shortly put forward a declaration of their 'disinterestedness' in Russian internal affairs.

During the discussion, a further wire arrived from Lord Reading stating that the American government considered the Japanese reply not as an acceptance of their proposal, but as a counter-proposal. Reading did not consider the Japanese point about the restriction of the size of the Japanese force as very serious, and it might be met by the despatch of more American troops. But President Wilson took a more serious view of their demand for greater freedom from the detailed restrictions 'imposed' in the American proposal. (This seems to refer to the draft Japanese proclamation, which spoke of Japan's 'special position' in the Far East and her wish to 'act in harmony' with the British and French, as well as with the Americans.) Reading did not think the President would give way on this point, and that eventually Japan would accept the American formula — though this, which implied that the Japanese should merely hold territory or railheads behind the Czechs, could not be carried out in practice as a military operation, 'as the President himself was beginning to realize'.

The Prime Minister stressed that whether or not this American attitude would involve delay in reaching an agreement, it was essential to send whatever forces were available to help the Czechs at once. He drew attention to a wire from Tokyo, showing that Bolshevik forces were 'considerably superior' to the Czechs in eastern Siberia. He asked what was being done to ship Canadian troops to Vladivostok, as already agreed. Borden, the Canadian Premier, agreed that Canada was to send three battalions, and some artillery and engineers, but shipping had not yet been arranged. A Ministry of Shipping official confirmed that there was shipping for 10,000 men in the Pacific, which could be assembled at Vancouver, though some might take a month or more to arrive there. But there should, at any one moment, be at least two ships near Vancouver, which could get three battalions away in a few days for the 16-day journey to Vladivostok. As the matter was of great urgency, the Prime Minister asked Borden to take the business in hand on behalf of the Imperial War Cabinet, and give such orders as he thought fit. This was agreed.[18]

Borden asked if there would be any 'awkwardness' if Canadian troops reached Vladivostok before the discussions between the Americans and Japanese were concluded, and before any proclamation was issued. It was pointed out that the British battalion would already have arrived by then, and that the Japanese 'independent proclamation of disinterestedness' would probably also have been published. A short discussion followed about the draft Allied proclamation ('Allied' here presumably meaning Anglo–French), which had been drawn up by Sir George Buchanan, the journalist Harold Williams, and a Russian 'in language appropriate to the Russian taste'.

Lloyd George's real view on Siberian intervention was summarized in staccato fashion when, according to Thomas Jones, he made this remark to his Cabinet colleagues on the 30th: 'We are trying to press Wilson to go a little further; Japs have taken the line we expected they would take — they felt it an insult to be asked to send 7,000 men. Now the Japs are taking the bit between their teeth.'[18]

Thus, with Allied intervention in Siberia now imminent, there was still no agreement on Allied policy. Hectic negotiations took place between the Americans and Japanese to try to paper over their differences (negotiations in which, as Kennan rightly makes clear, the Japanese finally had President Wilson 'cornered'). Simultaneously, various powers on the brink of intervention were drafting proclamations of 'disinterestedness' in Russian affairs. The sole Japanese interest was to seize the maritime provinces for themselves; the main British interest was to seize control of the Siberian railway up to the Urals (a project as preposterous as it was unattainable), and to organize a Russian army to fight the Germans and their Bolshevik supporters; in Washington, the chief interest was in keeping a close watch on Japan and avoiding all involvement in the devious imperialist schemes of the British. These were the real interests of the various Allies in intervention; their 'disinterestedness' in Russian affairs can be judged accordingly.[19]

A British force under General Dunsterville, now assembled at the port of Enzeli, on the southern shore of the Caspian, had also been ordered to intervene in Russia: to secure control of the pro-Bolshevik Caspian flotilla and to move into Baku to destroy the oil-rigs, reservoirs and pipe-lines there before the Turks and Tartars, in defiance of German demands, burst into the city. The British consul in Baku, Macdonnel, was instructed by Dunsterville from over the water to spare no expense in inducing the (largely Armenian) Baku soviet to issue an invitation for the British to intervene and to secure control of the Caspian flotilla. Macdonnel was a resourceful fellow. While on the best of terms with the chief Bolshevik commissar, an Armenian called Shaumian, to whom he developed every rational argument on the advantages of inducing the Baku soviet to issue the necessary invitation (and with whom he had long talks on the future of socialism), he was also engaged in large-scale bribery of members of the Baku soviet and the Caspian sailors through a varied army of spies and agents. Many of these were double and sometimes triple agents for other persons and bodies, all jammed together in this multi-racial oil port; but

Macdonnel seems to have retained their prime allegiance, mainly through the liberal disbursement of drink. (With bloodthirsty hordes of Turks and Tartars almost at the city gates, whose first desire on entry was to slit the throat of every Armenian they saw, the whole Baku population was drinking heavily, and drink was scarce.) Soon people were coming surreptitiously to Macdonnel to ask when the British were coming. Not a few were *agents provocateurs*, who were carefully warded off. Macdonnel maintained contact with Dunsterville in various ways. As overland couriers down into Persia, he always used girls, usually nurses and servants. His best courier was the Baku soviet's former typist, who went no less than four times to Dunsterville and back with Macdonnel's despatches concealed inside the leather buttons of her coat. Another useful agent was a local Russian priest, who was being watched by the Bolshevik secret police, and whom Macdonnel himself consequently could not meet. 'So I got my lady typist to hand him notes as she kissed the cross and received documents from him while she took the blessing,' he records. Some of Dunsterville's messages were obtained by bribing local wireless operators, for which he was arrested; he soon got off 'by frankly owning up to Shaumian', who evidently knew that Macdonnel might soon be useful.[20]

On July 16, the local SRs and Dashnaks (members of the Armenian party) in the Baku soviet proposed, with varied support from Macdonnel, that the British be invited in to Baku to protect them from the Turks and Tartars, who were slowly approaching. (On July 19, the CIGS told the War Cabinet that they were now only some 50 miles away from Baku.) The proposal was narrowly defeated, but Shaumian asked the Bolshevik government in Moscow for advice. Stalin replied in blistering fashion from Tsaritsin forbidding them to seek support from the British 'imperialists'. Lenin supported him. But by now, the sailors of the Caspian flotilla, with financial encouragement, decided that they would go over to Enzeli and bring back Dunsterville's force, even without the consent of the local soviet. This decision appears to have heavily influenced the Baku soviet, who on the 25th carried a motion in favour of inviting the British in. The Caspian sailors thereupon overthrew the moribund soviet; Macdonnel had succeeded in his difficult mission.* As he could not leave Baku openly, he bribed the Bolshevik secret police to conceal him on the post-boat and take him over to Enzeli. As he arrived at Dunsterville's tent, a British naval mission was setting out from Baghdad, hauling heavy naval guns across the barren countryside of Mesopotamia, to take and then arm the Caspian flotilla. But though Dunsterville could not cross over for a few days, the Turks held off their final assault on Baku, probably under strong German diplomatic pressure: possession of Baku was one of the still outstanding

---

*When Macdonnel's final report reached the War Office after the German armistice, the General Staff sent it straight on to the DMI, as it was 'most extraordinarily interesting and reads like a fairy tale'. The DMI agreed, and sent it on to the CIGS: 'I recommend you to read it — a modern Arabian nights.'

points holding up agreement on the trade treaty between the Germans and Bolsheviks in Berlin.[21]

The Allies were thus poised to intervene in Siberia, the Caucasus and northern Russia. On July 28, as the Allied ambassadors and diplomats from Vologda took ship at Archangel (Clark and the British economic mission arrived just as the ships were about to leave, and running briskly down the quayside, they just scrambled on board), the new German ambassador, Karl Helfferich, arrived in Moscow to replace the murdered Mirbach. Two days later, the left SRs — now banished from all soviets — struck back, in accordance with their resolution of late June, and assassinated the German Commander-in-Chief in the Ukraine, Field-Marshal Eichhorn. The day before, Lenin had made a speech declaring that war had once more returned to Bolshevik Russia, the 'socialist fatherland', whose enemy was now Anglo–French imperialism; and he denounced Eichhorn's murder as further evidence of Allied provocation to make German troops intervene in Russia. This induced the Germans not to respond. (There seems little doubt that the left SRs alone were responsible for Eichhorn's murder, and that this was no act of a Bolshevik *agent provocateur*. When Captain George Hill, the British agent who had been supporting left SR sabotage against the Germans in the Ukraine, next visited Trotsky, he tore up his passes, and ordered his arrest.) In Moscow, the little British community, now headed by Lockhart and his small staff, and the British consul Wardrop, together with Cromie, Macalpine, Lessing and a few others in Petrograd, anxiously awaited the long-expected Allied intervention, all too aware that they would probably be seized as hostages. The leading British secret agents, Hill and Reilly, went underground: Reilly had many aliases in case of trouble, and now 'entered' the Cheka under the name of Relinsky; very soon he would be ready to strike.[22]

In London, Lloyd George seemed to be seized with doubt at the last minute. On July 31, he told the Imperial War Cabinet that he had received a report (whence it came he did not say) stating that the Germans were unable to gain much advantage from the Russian situation, and that the Allies were under a 'complete misapprehension' about German power and influence there. Russia, the report claimed, was so disorganized that the Germans could do nothing there; it merely absorbed some 30 German divisions, 'but they were in despair there and did not know quite what to do'. (This was in many ways true, but it was somewhat late in the day to take such an attitude.) In reply to the Newfoundland Premier, Lloyd, the Prime Minister agreed that Germany did not appear to be able to do much in Finland either ('a most difficult country', according to the First Lord, who had recently been there). It is possible that the Prime Minister's doubts were due to the British interception of some of the German telegrams that had been passing between Moscow and Berlin.

Milner, however, countered Lloyd George's doubts. In reply to the Australian Premier, Hughes, Milner said that the Germans were indeed anxious to exploit Russian mineral and oil resources. The most important oilfields were at Baku, now threatened by the enemy. The British were trying to push a force into Baku, but while the enemy's communications were fairly good, ours ran right across an 'inhospitable and undeveloped' part of Persia. We should like to destroy the oil-wells at Baku before the enemy could reach them, but probably could not do so, (for the news of the defection of the Caspian flotilla, the fall of the Baku soviet, and the invitation to Dunsterville to enter Baku, had not yet reached London.)[23]

On August 1, the CIGS resolved the Prime Minister's doubts, when he informed the Imperial War Cabinet that General Poole had wired to say that an advance guard had already left Murmansk for the attack on Archangel. It was being followed by the main force, numbering 2,700 British, French, American, Polish and Russian troops, besides the ships' companies. There were about 8,000 enemy troops at Archangel, but it was hoped that an anti-Bolshevik rising would take place in Archangel as the Allied troops landed. The first attack, the CIGS added, would not be on Archangel itself, but on Mudyugski Island, which protected the channel through the River Dvina delta into Archangel harbour. But Poole's information was wrong in one important aspect; he was in fact launching the attack on Archangel with just 1,200 men, less than a quarter of the number that he said he would need to carry the 'fiery cross' down to Vologda to raise a Russian force to fight the Germans; and even this, he had admitted, was a gamble.[24] The tragedy here was that if rumours of large-scale German activity in Finland had been believed (and their denial was the only good thing to come out of the First Lord's ill-starred mission to Murmansk), then a proper force of two and a half divisions (50,000 men) would have probably been sent to northern Russia, as the CIGS wished.

That night, the Japanese government suddenly issued an independent proclamation, without any warning to Washington or the Allied capitals. It contained some modifications to please the Americans, but the manner of its publication indicated that Japan saw that the race for Siberia was now on. The Americans had no choice but to follow suit.

President Wilson had all along been faced with two major problems over intervention in Siberia. The first was political, and highly complex. For months he had been badgered by his British and French allies to take action to stop the enemy's steady encroachments into Russian territory, which would enable the Germans to break the Allied blockade and so defeat the Allied and American armies on the western front. The action they urged was the unleashing of the Japanese, who were hated by the Russians, distrusted by the British and French, and wished only to carve out a piece of eastern Siberia for themselves — and would only do this with American consent. The President was a true liberal democrat, but his so-called liberal democratic Allies were in fact right-wing capitalist imperialists; Japan was openly imperialist, while Russia, a former extreme right-wing Ally, was now an anti-capitalist and extreme socialist 'neutral' (so extreme socialist that it was even more autocratic than the Germans, who were themselves the President's real enemies). The second problem was a military one, and simpler. President Wilson was no strategist, but from Washington he could see further and clearer into the Siberian wastes than the generals in London and Paris; and greater distance lent no enchantment to the view. Field-Marshal Montgomery held that the first rule of war was: 'Don't march on Moscow': presumably he meant from the Niemen, from which Napoleon had set out on his 600-mile march, and failed. How much less advisable to march on Moscow from Vladivostok — some 6,000 miles away — up the longest and most precarious transcontinental railway in the world (only completed the year before).

President Wilson clearly saw the 'military absurdity' of his Allies' plans for Russian intervention, and with a Peace Conference, and a League of Nations (to be personally sponsored by the President) already on the horizon, the 'President of Peace' could not now don the mantle of an imperialist. The tragedy was that his final decision to 'do something' to placate his Allies by small-scale intervention still entailed American invasion of a neutral and indeed revolutionary state, and was to infuriate both his Allies and the Russians on both sides in the Russian civil war.

In his 'Fourteen Points' speech of January 8, the President had stated that the future Russian policy of America and the Allies would be the 'acid test of their good will, of their comprehension of her needs as distinguished from their own interests, and of their intelligent and unselfish sympathy'. But the President failed his own acid test. Indeed such action, some later felt, was so unlike him that it marked the 'beginning of the sad end'. The first casualty of Allied intervention was not an Allied soldier, but the idealism of Woodrow Wilson, whose dilemma was of classic and international proportions, and was also the first of a new age: how was a real liberal democrat to deal with the extreme socialist of the twentieth century?

But after so many delays, so many British proposals turned down in Washington, and the final, best and most far-sighted turned down by the French on the grounds that it 'would probably prove fatal to American intervention', no such niceties troubled Lloyd George.

12

August 1918:
the Allies intervene

August 1 may be taken as the day when Allied intervention in Siberia, northern Russia and the Caucasus passed from the hands of the diplomats into those of the military; when, in the words of a Bolshevik government appeal to all Allied workers, the Allied governments 'have thrown off their masks, and shout openly of a campaign against the workers and peasants of Russia'. But Allied workers were warned that 'this open attack of Anglo–French capital on the workers of Russia is merely the culmination of an eight-month underground fight against Soviet Russia'. But the eight-month underground diplomatic 'fight' had resulted in very little agreement. President Wilson was almost wholly antagonistic to what he imagined the interventionist plans of his Allies to be; and it is no doubt for this reason that there is no mention of the United States in the Bolshevik government appeal.[1]

Amongst the Allies in the Far East, there was nothing but suspicion and mistrust. On August 3, as President Wilson issued a press communiqué (simply a paraphrase of his vague, and now long distant *aide-mémoire* of July 17), and the War Department gave orders for the despatch of American forces from the Philippines to Siberia, British and Japanese forces landed at Vladivostok (the British force consisting of the Middlesex Regiment — all elderly men, of C.3 category, known as the 'Hernia Battalion', under the command of the ebullient trade union leader and MP, Colonel John Ward). So serious, however, was the local Czech situation thought to be on the Ussuri front (between Vladivostok and Khabarovsk) that on August 3, the War Office in London approved half of the Middlesex being sent speedily to support the Czechs until sufficient Japanese troops had arrived. They were not long in coming.[2]

But the Ussuri front was not the only far-eastern front where the Czechs were imagined to be in danger of annihilation from both Bolsheviks and enemy prisoners. On August 4, Lloyd George informed the War Cabinet that General Dietrichs (a Russian officer in command of the Czechs in the

Far East) reported that the Czechs faced a 'most critical' situation both at
Lake Baikal and at Khabarovsk; and the only solution was the immediate
despatch of Allied help to both fronts. Balfour said that wires had been
sent the night before to Washington and to Tokyo, urging immediate action
to save the Czechs. After some discussion, it was agreed that Dietrichs'
report should be telephoned to Clemenceau in Paris, who should be told
that the War Cabinet, who had been hastily summoned, were 'much
alarmed' at the news, and were sending wires to both President Wilson and
the Japanese, pressing them to take 'instant' action. It was hoped that the
French government would give 'immediate instructions' to both Washington and Tokyo in the same sense. It was also agreed that Balfour should see
the Japanese ambassador that afternoon, and impress upon him the
importance attached by the British government to immediate action being
taken to save the Czechs.[3]

This, of course, was simply an encouragement to the Japanese to do
what they had wished to do all along: to send many more than 7,000 troops
into Siberia, deliberately flouting the conditions imposed by President
Wilson.

Clemenceau now rapidly dropped his previous insistent demands that
the Czechs should be shipped to France. The Czech objective now, he stated
in a directive issued on August 5 to the French general Maurice Janin,
who was to command all French and Czech forces in Siberia, was to
cooperate with the Allied forces of intervention, and establish a link
between their bases in Siberia and the Allied forces in northern Russia, and
with the pro-Allied groups in southern Russia. The final Czech objective
was the restoration of the Siberian railway from end to end, and then the
creation across Russia, from the Black to the White seas, 'of a tightly knit
network of centres of resistance, capable of forming a barrage to German
expansion towards the East'. But these results, it was underlined, which
depended upon complete Allied agreement, could only be obtained
progressively.[4]

'The first objective', stated Clemenceau, 'is the occupation of the Irkutsk
region, so that the Czech forces at Vladivostok can again link up with the
Czechs, who are cut off west of Baikal. A move will then be made (again
subject to Allied agreement) towards the Urals and the Russian interior.
But the Czech forces in central and western Siberia must be sent off
without delay, so as to cooperate in linking up with the Vladivostok group;
and also in establishing communications with the bases on the Arctic
Ocean, first by Ekaterinburg, Viatka and the Dvina; and later by Samara
and Vologda. It is vital that these communications be established before
winter. As soon as effective links have been established up to the Urals, he
[Janin] will strengthen communications with the bases on the Arctic
Ocean, and with the Allied forces operating from them; and at the same

time, stretch out a hand to the anti-German groups in the Volga and Don regions as far as the Black Sea.*

On the 6th, Czech and Russian forces on the upper Volga bend finally attacked Kazan, the Bolshevik GHQ staff defected, and Bolshevik troops scattered and fled in dismay, leaving huge quantities of material and supplies behind them, and the whole huge Russian state gold reserve, stacked in railway wagons. The workers rose up east and north of Kazan — along the River Kama and around Viatka (on the Vologda–Ekaterinburg line). To the south-east, the Orenburg Cossacks launched a revolt against the Bolsheviks. For the victors of Kazan, with another Czech force — which had just taken Ekaterinburg — behind them, the way to Moscow now lay right open, and the British could reinforce them via Vologda. Both sides knew the position was crucial.[5]

When Trotsky left Moscow on the 7th to assume control, he did not know that Kazan had fallen the day before. As his train drew into Sviyazhsk station (opposite Kazan), he found demoralized troops rushing in from all directions, each little group huddled together, the only common factor being a readiness to retreat still further. 'The soil itself seemed to be infected with panic', he writes. The fresh Red detachments he had brought with him 'were immediately engulfed by the inertia of defeat'. Accompanied by some Latvian regiments, who had stood firm, Trotsky sent their commander, Vatsetis, to take over at Viatka, while he carried out a bitter purge at Sviyazhsk, and summoned fresh troops from Moscow. It was the slow arrival of promised reinforcements, which had caused a 'psychological collapse' that had led to the Kazan 'catastrophe', he wired Lenin. He called for good communist troops, gunners, engineers, NCOs, revolvers. 'Despatch one good band to Sviyazhsk', he ended.[6]

At Kazan, relations between Czechs and Russians were at their most exuberant; the local people loaded the Czech soldiers with gifts and flowers. When Colonel Kappel led a raid behind the Bolshevik lines, he captured all Trotsky's codes (in which Lenin clearly sounded desperate), and very nearly seized Trotsky himself. Captain Bordes, of the French military mission, was busy from morning to night: repairing aircraft, bombing Trotsky's train, supervising the evacuation of the gold reserve, handing out arms, arranging political deals, and keeping in touch with General Lavergne in Moscow.[7]

On the 6th, the CIGS reported to the Imperial War Cabinet that the

---

*Clemenceau sent a copy of these orders to Lloyd George on August 19. Unfortunately, General Janin was not even to reach Vladivostok until mid-November; though doubtless the terms of the directive reached the Czechs by other means.

situation at Vladivostok was 'not very satisfactory'. According to information just received from the Japanese military attaché, only one Japanese
division, and not two, was being mobilized; and only one Japanese brigade
(of 12,000 men) would be sent to Vladivostok by August 12 (5,000 more
men than the total stipulated by President Wilson). Canadian reinforcements could not arrive for some time, though it would be well before
winter. Rifles, said the CIGS, were being sent to the Czechs from America;
but the main difficulty would be to get them past the tunnels near Lake
Baikal, which were reported to have been destroyed. Attention, however,
was drawn to Lockhart's wire that 'considerable' Russian forces were rallying to the Czechs. It was generally agreed that the 'principal weakness' in
the situation was the 'considerable block' of Bolshevik forces, supported by
enemy prisoners, between Lake Baikal and the Chita region; though in
dealing with this difficulty, the Japanese would have the advantage of the
use of the Manchurian railway.

Attention was then drawn to President Wilson's communiqué, which
'came in for considerable criticism'. It implied that Allied policy was
designed to make use of rather than help Russia, and that America was
Russia's only true friend; it would let the enemy know 'exactly the limitations' of Allied action in Siberia; and it gave the impression that only
America was sending material and supplies to Russia. But it was generally
agreed that nothing must be done to estrange America, or promote
controversy.[8]

The Prime Minister asked his colleagues whether, in his statement to
Parliament the next day, he should make some reference to the subject;
and if so what. Lord Robert Cecil suggested that the Prime Minister should
ignore what President Wilson had said, and explain to Parliament 'exactly
what our desires are, and what our policy still is'. Our first object, he
should explain, was to support the Czechs, but in order to help them, 'it
was necessary to restore some sort of order [i.e. in Russia] — or, rather, as
Mr Balfour [intervening] suggested, to give the Russians a chance of
restoring order — and to get rid of tyranny'. Lloyd George should point
out, Cecil went on, that Germany was setting out to destroy Russia as an
economic competitor, and doing her utmost to make Russia dependent on
her. In Poland, Germany was destroying the means of production,
especially in the manufacturing centre of Lodz, just as she had already
done in Russia, her object being to restrain Russia's development as a
possible rival. Balford commented that Germany's aim was to make Russia a
producer of raw material under German control. He agreed that Germany
was doing her best to ruin Poland as a competitor, but doubted if she had yet
done this to Russia. Otherwise, he agreed with the general line suggested by
Cecil.

Next day (the 7th), the CIGS, in some real agitation, drew the War
Cabinet's attention to a 'rather alarming' telegram from the Czech repre-

sentative in Vladivostok to Professor Masaryk (the Czech leader) in Washington, in which he asked: first, whether the Czechs should concentrate at Vladivostok; secondly, whether they should 'clear out of Russia'. The CIGS warned that if we agreed to the latter proposal, 'we should be in a very serious position', as we should be 'absolutely unable' to restore the eastern front, which would place Allied troops at Archangel and Murmansk in an untenable position, both of which were matters of 'grave concern'. Although no immediate decision was called for from the Cabinet, it was vital to prevent any 'hasty and premature' action by President Wilson, 'whose one idea in consenting to Allied action in the Far East had been to save the Czechoslovaks'.[9]

At this, Balfour briefly outlined the events which had led up to Allied intervention in the Far East. 'Some months ago, our policy had been to get the Czechoslovaks out of Russia', he admitted. The French were then seriously alarmed about the manpower shortage in France, and had insisted that they be brought from Russia to the western front. But at an Allied conference at Versailles, it had been pointed out that there were no ships available, and that the Czechs 'were required for the general purposes of the Allies in Russia'. Clemenceau had finally agreed. Although President Wilson was strongly opposed to a 'bold' Siberian policy, he had consented to the despatch of troops to Vladivostok to save the Czechs. With this the President's 'co-belligerents' had to be satisfied, but they had always hoped that he might eventually be induced to agree to 'their larger policy'. Balfour also underlined that the Americans had never accepted the expeditions to northern Russia being linked with Allied action in the Far East. Balfour suggested the War Cabinet should act as follows. He would wire to Washington 'explaining the whole case'. He would send a similar wire to Paris, with the arguments against the removal of the Czechs from Russia, to discover if Clemenceau agreed; and if he did, he would be asked to wire to the French ambassador in Washington to consult Britain's ambassador, before either saw the President. At the same time, Lord Derby (the British ambassador in Paris) should confer with Benes.

Balfour explained that he did not quite agree with the CIGS's view of the Czech wire. He did not think they had any real intention of clearing out of Russia. They simply intended to go into winter quarters. Their view was: 'We must fight; we must win; we must organize; we must go into our winter quarters; we must prepare for future military operations; we must reassure the local populations as to our good intentions.' (Balfour, it must be admitted, was fantasizing somewhat, in the same way that he had assured both himself and his colleagues that the Japanese would go to the Urals, although they had stated quite positively that they would not.) If the Cabinet agreed with his suggested action, he went on, he would bear in mind the views of the War Office and Foreign Office when drafting the telegrams. But he could not agree to a joint telegram from the French and

British governments to the President, since the President disliked concerted pressure.

Lord Milner pointed out to the Cabinet that the French government had been able to take a much wider view since the constant American reinforcements had so extensively relieved the manpower situation on the western front. The present question of the Czechs was essentially one for the Supreme War Council, which would not normally meet for another fortnight. The War Cabinet thereupon agreed to defer a final decision until the Supreme War Council met in a week or two; but further agreed that it was 'most necessary' that the President should not commit himself 'definitely and prematurely' on the matter. The action proposed by Balfour was thus approved.

On August 2, General Poole's little armada steamed into Archangel, where he found that a Russian naval officer called Chaplin had launched a highly successful *coup* against the local Soviet; and when British officers marched into the town, carrying the traditional bread and salt, they were officially welcomed by an SR government, headed by the veteran revolutionary Nicholas Chaikovsky, a former member of the Constituent Assembly, now of the 'Union for the Regeneration of Russia'. The operation could not have gone more smoothly. Chaplin was then appointed to command such Russian troops as existed. As news came that two groups of Latvian troops had defected from the Bolsheviks just north of the crucial junction of Vologda, an American marine party commandeered a railway engine and some trucks, and pursued the retreating Bolshevik forces some 75 miles down the line in the direction of Vologda, until a blocked bridge prevented further pursuit. A party of troops followed them down the line; another was sent up the Dvina river towards Kotlas. Both parties were soon engaged in heavy fighting. The only word of warning came from General Maynard at Murmansk; in just over a month's recruiting, he had only managed to enlist 1,200 men. But Poole, who also began enlisting Russian volunteers, was relying mainly on the Czechs.[10]

At the War Cabinet on August 6, Lord Robert Cecil circulated a draft proclamation to be published in Russia about the Allied landing. It was originally drafted as a joint Allied manifesto; but the Allies had preferred to issue their own, and it had therefore been modified. It now came in for criticism 'on the ground that its promises were out of proportion to the modest size of our intervention'. It was however decided to publish it in Vladivostok, Archangel and Murmansk. It was then agreed to publish the following communiqué at Archangel: 'Allied forces, naval and military, with the active concurrence of the Russian population, landed at Archangel on August 2. Their arrival was greeted with general enthusiasm by the inhabitants.'[11]

In fact, this statement was false. The Allies had landed with the active concurrence of Chaplin and a small group of conspirators, and their arrival was completely ignored by an important sector of the population: the workers.

Next day, the CIGS reported to the Cabinet (apparently in defiance of the First Lord's report of late June) that in northern Russia, the Germans had already laid 130 km of railway line towards Petchenga, which meant there was only another 270 km to complete. This indicated very rapid progress. But it was pointed out (by whom the Cabinet minutes do not indicate) that the expeditions to both Archangel and Murmansk 'were in the nature of a gamble, but we were quite justified so long as we were still able to maintain an eastern front in Russia. If, however, that front disappeared, our forces in the north would be in a very dangerous position.'

Balfour, however, thought that our two small forces at Murmansk and Archangel, which were linked only by sea, and were liable to attack by greatly superior forces, were in a 'very precarious' situation. He referred to a telegram from Washington of August 5, in which the State Department, after consultation with the War Department, made it clear that the American government could supply food for Archangel, but could not ship it, since no ships could be diverted from supplying American troops in France. We not only had to provide for the two little expeditionary forces in northern Russia, Balfour went on, but were also proposing to feed the local population in these areas; we were even contemplating supplying the people at Vologda. In view of the shipping problems, he wondered whether Britain was pursuing the right policy.[12]

The CIGS retorted that provided America would guarantee the food, we should be able to provide the ships. He was in touch with the Ministry of Shipping, and did not at present ask for a Cabinet decision.

At Archangel, Poole appointed a French colonel as military governor of the town — in expectation of the arrival of the Czechs. On the 9th, as the Allied ambassadors arrived from Murmansk, the British consul at Helsinki wired the Foreign Office with the crucial news that German troops were rapidly leaving Finland. This, no doubt, was due to the Allied breakthrough on the western front; but it meant that Poole's rear base at Murmansk was now clear of danger.[13]

With the precarious military situation in both Siberia and northern Russia in mind, and convinced that, whatever anyone said, the two fronts were interdependent, the CIGS now set to work to restore the eastern front, whether President Wilson or Balfour liked it or not. On the 9th, Sir Henry Wilson sent a detailed memorandum to the French and Japanese general staffs (with a copy to the British military representative in Washington), in which he supported the estimate of the Czech commander at Vladivostok that eight Allied battalions were needed to support the Czechs on the Ussuri front, while three divisions (60,000 troops) were needed to force a passage through to the Czechs at Lake Baikal. As the British General Staff considered these estimates reasonable, all the troops allowed for under President Wilson's proposals (14,000) would be wanted for the Ussuri front. It was thus suggested that Japan should supply the three divisions needed to push through to Lake Baikal; to save time, they could proceed through Manchuria. This was just the support Japan needed to override the President's carefully balanced proposal for a joint American–Japanese force.[14]

Next day, the CIGS sent General Poole fresh orders for northern Russia. He was to advance and link up with the Czechs in central Russia; and, with their support, to secure control of the Archangel–Vologda–Ekaterinburg railway, and the river and rail links between Archangel and Viatka. If, however, the Czechs turned east to link up with their compatriots further into Siberia, Poole was simply to raise local Russian forces, and defend Archangel. He was warned that no further troops, beyond the 5,500 American troops he had been promised, could be sent. In general, his policy was to be aimed at 'restoring Russia' to enable it to withstand German influence and penetration; he was thus to help the Russians take the field 'side by side' with their Allies in order to regain control of their country. Like Knox, Poole in fact was to organize a Russian army. Poole at once sent an urgent message to the Czechs to move west, and seize Perm and Viatka, and thus link up with him.[15]

It was left to Balfour to break the news as gently as possible to the Americans, and try to obtain their consent. On the 9th, the British chargé d'affaires in Washington had an informal discussion with Frank Polk, Acting Secretary of State. He claimed that since the Czechs in the Far East were in an 'emergency situation', the American government should ask the Japanese government to send all the military support they felt necessary. He further told Polk that unless the Americans objected strongly, the British government would make a similar request to Japan themselves (which, via Sir Henry Wilson's memorandum, they had already more or less done). Polk reacted very strongly, expressing more than surprise that the British should make such a claim so early on; the American government would make no change in any plans, until American troops, still *en route*, had reached Vladivostok. As a result, the British chargé d'affaires warned Balfour against putting too much pressure on the President; in future, the Japanese should make their own requests to the State Department.[16]

But Balfour persisted. On the 12th, the Foreign Office, in spite of the severe rebuff which the British chargé d'affaires had received from Frank

Polk, actually had the British embassy in Washington deliver a formal note on the matter to the State Department. As the Czechs in the Far East were in an 'emergency' situation, the Americans were formally asked to request the Japanese to send all the necessary military support; and unless the State Department strongly objected, the note went on, the British would make a similar request to the Japanese as well. Small wonder that an angry note came back from Secretary Lansing that the American government would be 'gravely embarrassed' if the British did approach the Japanese.[17]

At the Imperial War Cabinet on the 12th, the DMO, in reply to the Prime Minister, admitted that the Czech position 'was probably not quite so bad as either the Japanese or ourselves were making out'. Balfour agreed, and said that President Wilson 'was suspecting this, and believed that we were trying to manoeuvre him into a big expedition into Russia by exaggerating the danger to the Czechs. It was undoubtedly our policy to try and get President Wilson to agree to action in Russia on a large scale, but it was important not to let him see that we were doing so.' Lord Robert Cecil, by way of explanation, said that he had been 'a good deal alarmed' on the 10th about the Czech position; his alarm was due to the fact that the note of danger came, not from the Japanese, but from General Dietrichs, their commander. Lord Milner stressed that their position might be serious in the East, yet much better in the West (but there was little news of Czech activities on the Volga in London). General Smuts then, unwisely, drew attention to a German article, reproduced in the evening papers, which claimed that 300,000 Russians (an absurd figure) had joined the Czechs; and Cecil stated (correctly) that it had been officially announced that the German mission had been withdrawn from Moscow.[17]

Cecil continued to say that he was concerned at the signs of 'growing difficulty' at Vladivostok between the British and American representatives. He cited: the criticism of the American proclamation; the trouble over martial law, which all the Allies, save the Americans, had wished to proclaim; the British representative's proposal that local Russian labour should be used to repair the railways; and his remark 'that it had best be done without telling the Americans'. (This was evidently the recently-appointed British high commissioner for Siberia, Sir Charles Eliot, an experienced diplomat, who had spent five years in Petrograd; and was also a noted traveller, scholar and administrator, until recently Vice-Chancellor of Hong Kong University.)

All these instances, Cecil insisted, were signs of 'growing irritation' with America. 'This was very serious, as we did not wish to have friction with the Americans.' He had had a long talk with Lord Reading (then back in London from Washington), and had discussed a proposal whereby the Americans might be asked to content themselves with holding Vladivostok, and to give the rest of the Allies a free hand in Siberia. Reading was not enthusiastic, though he did not definitely exclude the proposal. Hughes (the Australian Premier) thought the only worthwhile course would be to get Japan to send the necessary troops. Cecil remarked that the Japanese wished to remain in American favour, 'and, if possible, to divide us a little from the Americans, at any rate to prevent our having a common policy in the Pacific'. (But the recent efforts of the CIGS, abetted by Lord Robert Cecil, had been exclusively aimed at dividing the Americans from the Japanese.)

The Prime Minister then asked the DMO if any troops could be sent to Siberia from India. The DMO said none could be sent from India, but a division might be sent from Mesopotamia. At this, the discussion ended.

Balfour then expressed anxiety about Archangel. General Poole was apparently trying to reach Vologda, to try to induce the local population to rebel; and there seemed to have been some response. But Poole's position would entirely depend upon the extent to which he could feed the people. Lord Robert Cecil (mindful of the CIGS's recent orders to Poole to advance) replied strongly that Poole was trying to move up the River Dvina towards Viatka, so as to link up with western Siberia, in which case 'ample' food stocks would be available. The DMO remarked that the Czechs were at Ekaterinburg, but there was a 'big block' of Bolsheviks between them and Poole; though one of Poole's recent wires spoke of the possibility of a pro-Allied rising in between at Perm (where the Tsarina and 'German' princesses are now believed to have been at this time). At this point, Hankey reminded the meeting that at the last War Cabinet, the CIGS had said he was in touch with the Ministry of Shipping about shipping American food to Archangel, and had said he did not want a Cabinet decision. But the Prime Ministers were satisfied on hearing that the CIGS had the matter in hand.

Lloyd George then remarked that there were many signs that Germany was becoming 'very anxious' about the eastern front, 'and it seemed probable that they had some news that was lacking to us'. (It may well be that Lloyd George's puzzlement was due not only to the relative absence of telegrams from Russia, but also to the fact that he knew that the SIS were planning an anti-Bolshevik *coup* in Petrograd and Moscow, but they could give him no details of when it might occur.) Cecil said that Basil Thomson (Assistant Commissioner of Police) had sent him a copy of a speech by a Bolshevik who had just arrived from Russia, who spoke with 'great pessimism' about Bolshevik prospects; the monarchists, he said, were the only alternative to them. The Cabinet's attention was also drawn to newspaper reports that Lenin and Trotsky had fled.

Replying to the Prime Minister, Balfour said he hoped Lockhart would escape any mishap. Britain had threatened Litvinov (the Bolshevik representative in London) with reprisals. Lloyd George remarked that Lockhart had been in touch with the Bolsheviks' enemies, 'and had actually given money to General Alexeiev'; if the Bolsheviks discovered this, his position would become 'very dangerous'.[17]

In the Caucasus, British troops also pushed forward into Baku, to forestall the Turks, and set fire to the oil-wells before they could be seized. In Transcaspia, Major-General Malleson, based at Meshed (in north-eastern Persia), was endeavouring to obtain control of the Transcaspian railway, which was the subject of a bitter dispute between the Ashkhabad committee and the Tashkent soviet. On August 1, Malleson warned the War Office that the Ashkhabad committee had asked him for support against the Red Guards at Merv, the junction of the lines to both Tashkent and Kushk (on the Afghan border). He urged the War Office to let him support them, as he could thus gain control of the east Caspian port of Krasnovodsk, opposite Baku. The War Office gave him a free hand. As Malleson sent some Indian machine-gunners to support the Ashkhabad committee, General Dunsterville finally landed on August 4 at Baku, to face the encircling Turks. These two small British forces would enable the main British objective — command of the Caspian — to be secured in between them. 'To gain control of the Caspian Fleet and mount as many guns as become available is the first essential', the War Office reminded the Mesopotamian command on the 3rd — while a naval mission struggled up from Baghdad, man-handling guns across north-western Persia.[18]

In Moscow, the Bolshevik government, who now had rapidly to discover new ways of playing the British off against the Germans, knew nothing of the strength of the British force lately arrived at Archangel. What they undoubtedly did know was that Captain Cromie had in his possession at the British embassy a large sum of money in sterling, some £840,000, earmarked for the destruction of the Baltic Fleet, but which could now be used to finance a *coup*, so that General Poole could have as bloodless an entry into Petrograd as he had into Archangel.

This was the task of Sidney Reilly. Acting under his alias as the Cheka agent, Relinsky, he now took in hand the politically inexperienced Cromie and his sterling hoard. The Bolsheviks were determined to get hold of this sterling first. Something of the struggle can be seen in a wire from Cromie, sent on the 5th. During the last two days, he began, the British and French consulates had been raided, and about 7,000 Russan officers and civilians had been arrested, the majority being sent to Kronstadt. (The Danish envoy Oudendyk, who took over the protection of British interests, and was known affectionately as 'Uncle Ou', records the 'sickening sight' of watching the Russian officers being dragged from their houses, marched through the street, and forced on to a barge at the Palace Quay. 'The barge was towed across the river and then made fast under a little door in the walls of the Peter and Paul Fortress. The door opened as of itself, and one

by one the young officers stepped up and disappeared into the dark interior
... and the door swung to. It was like sheep entering the slaughter-house.')[19]
The arrests were still proceeding, Cromie continued, and wholesale assassination was probable. 'We have sent a memorandum to Lockhart [in
Moscow] suggesting an ultimatum be sent in to [Bolshevik] government
that if any harm falls on the officers, the [Allied] expeditionary force will
take the form of a punitive expedition.' (Many of these officers were
Cromie's personal friends.) 'Suggest a proclamation be issued stating if
these officers are shot, the [Bolshevik] government will be held strictly
responsible. This would bring very large section of public over to our side.'

Cromie went on to relate a remarkable offer that they had just received.
The Bolshevik government were asking for £1 million sterling. They had
replied that they were prepared to advance it on the following conditions:

1. at an exchange rate of 50 roubles to the pound and delivery at
   Archangel (the current exchange rate apparently was 40);
2. guarantees for the safety of all foreigners 'here' (presumably Petrograd);
3. guarantees for the safety of all Russian officers arrested.

Negotiations had not yet been started, he went on. He asked for more
information of future plans. They had had several offers of river gunboats,
but had refused such offers until they were sure they could be sent, and fuel
would be available. Cromie concluded: 'Great discontent here in Red
Army chiefly let [i.e. Lettish], amongst whom we are agitating. Bolsheviks
[in] general very nervous.'[20]

The transmission of this last paragraph in the normal naval code was
most unwise and undoubtedly made Cromie, if this wire was intercepted
(and there is fair reason to suppose it was), a marked man. Tampering with
the loyalty of the Lettish troops would make Cromie *persona non grata*, to
say the least — and these were not normal times. It is impossible to say
whether the alleged Bolshevik demand for the money in return for sparing
the lives of these men was in any way genuine.

As Allied officers were now forbidden to send wires abroad or within
Russia, or move from one town to another, Cromie next wired direct to
General Poole at Archangel informing him that during the past two days,
British subjects had been arrested by the Bolsheviks without any charge
being made against them; but only two had been detained. He was protesting vigorously, and expected an explanation the next day. 'If unsatisfactory', he warned Poole, 'propose informing soviet that as British officials
and subjects are threatened with arrest, and possibly bodily harm, we have
informed our government and have requested every effort be made by our
troops (at Archangel) to advance to our rescue.' The British consul and the
Danish minister (now in charge of British interests) had apparently agreed

to sign an undertaking on behalf of the French government that, if Petrograd was occupied, French troops would not carry out reprisals against Russians for the committing of any political acts by order of the soviet, provided there were no further arrests of any French subjects. But he and the British consul had refused to sign a similar document without the instructions of the British government. All British officials who were arrested at Moscow on the 5th were now released, and placed under house arrest. They had sent a warning that they would probably be evacuated, and that the British community in Petrograd should be ready to leave with them.

Cromie went on to warn Poole. 'Commissar here [Uritsky] threatens to intern all Allied subjects as soon as you occupy Vologda.' Cromie had destroyed all cyphers but the present one, and was not allowed to wire in any direction; Poole was thus asked to inform the Admiralty of this message. 'Position of Soviet power in Petrograd is becoming rapidly untenable', Cromie went on 'They are giving orders for evacuation of various units and places. It is evident they are in touch with Germans. Lenin is at Peterhof and a yacht under Swedish flag [is] ready to take him away.'[20]

This last statement was not true. But the Bolsheviks were indeed in touch with the Germans. With the size of Poole's force at Archangel unknown, there was veritable panic in the Bolshevik government in Moscow. On August 2, Chicherin went in person to the German embassy to see Ambassador Helfferich to ask for military support against the British in northern Russia (something which the Germans had long pressed on the Bolsheviks, and which the latter had hitherto always refused). Chicherin stressed that an open German–Bolshevik military alliance was still impossible, and German troops must be kept out of Petrograd; but the Bolsheviks now wanted German intervention, and parallel German action against the British to start without delay. Chicherin also asked the Germans to mount an offensive against Alexeiev, and to stop supporting Krasnov. Helfferich reported to the Foreign Ministry that this *démarche* showed the 'extremes of the dilemma' on which the Bolsheviks now found themselves. He urged his government to pretend to comply with this request for intervention, but at the last moment to make a common front with the Cossack leaders, and overthrow the Bolsheviks. Since this advice was quite contrary to Foreign Ministry directives, which he refused to carry out, the Foreign Minister Hintze ordered him to leave Moscow forthwith, and report to Berlin, leaving the German embassy in Riezler's charge.[21]

However, Helfferich's advice made good sense to Ludendorff, who believed that the Bolshevik downfall was imminent. He believed he still had enough troops in the east to drive out the British, and overthrow the Bolsheviks at the same time. He could advance 'at any time' towards Petrograd with six or seven divisions, he wired to Hintze on August 6, and, provided Krasnov guarded the German flank on the Volga, several divisions could be deployed on the Rostov–Voronezh railway. 'This represents a force with which we can, as far as I can see, support a new government in Russia, one that has the people behind it.'

Hintze quashed such dangerous ideas the same day, and at length. He first queried Ludendorff's hope for supporting a Russian government that had the people behind it. 'This is a highly restricting stipulation; for a government that has the people behind it does not need our support, at least not in its internal affairs.' It was still possible to use German troops against the British in the North, and the Czechs in the East and South, regardless of which regime was in power. The Bolshevik government had asked for such intervention against Germany's enemies; 'any other government — we have to be perfectly clear about this — is either immediately or within a short time a friend and ally of the *Entente.* We do not have any friends worth mentioning in Russia; whoever informs Your Excellency to the contrary is deceiving himself'. There were no reports of mutinies in the Red Guards. If the new Russian government did not have the people behind it, the available German divisions would not be sufficient to support it. He thus still favoured waiting for the start of the Bolshevik downfall, so that they could quickly come to terms with the victor. But they had no interest in provoking a rapid end to the Bolshevik regime. 'We have milked them for all they are worth; our quest for victory requires us to continue doing so as long as they remain in power. Whether or not we like the idea of working with them is unimportant as long as it is useful to do so.'

There were certain signs that the Bolshevik end was nigh; but that could either be tomorrow or be postponed for months. 'Instability is a characteristic of Russia. Chicherin's cry for help and the attempted expulsion of the English and French consuls are more reliable signs of the approaching collapse than rumours are.' The SRs were split; and the bourgeoisie divided into a number of different groups, whose unity 'could only be brought about by a Russian and a genius. This genius has not yet come forward. All these groups, with the exception of some individuals, have one thing in common: hatred of Germany. The Siberians, who were recommended to us as Allies, have, according to newspaper reports, declared war on us. What, after all, do we want in the East? The military paralysis of Russia. The Bolsheviks are doing a better and more thorough job of this than any other Russian party, and without our devoting a single man or one mark to the task. We cannot expect them or other Russians to love us for milking their country dry. Let us rather be content with Russia's impotence.

The Bolsheviks are the only Russian party who have taken sides against the *Entente.* That is daily becoming more evident, and it is our duty to intensify this conflict, as we have been doing of late. ... If they [the Bolsheviks] fall, we can observe the chaos which may result with calm detachment, until we think the country is weak enough for us to restore order without great loss to ourselves. If no chaos develops, but a new party takes over right away, then we have to move in under the heading: no war with

Russia nor with the Russian people, no conquests, rather order and protection for the weak against their being ill-used by our enemies.' Hintze preferred the first alternative.

He sent this detailed paper to the Chancellor and the Kaiser, who signified 'complete agreement' with Hintze's policy. Ludendorff climbed down. 'I completely agree with Your Excellency that we are aiming at Russia's military paralysis, but, on the other hand, I am of the opinion that we have to prevent Russia, in her helplessness, from falling prey to the *Entente*, a danger which is by no means out of the question, even if we reach an understanding with the Bolsheviks in Berlin. 'I am prepared to fight against the British on the Murmansk coast, if we can occupy Petrograd.' Otherwise, he completely agreed with Hintze's policy; he had no intention of attacking or subverting the Bolshevik government. But the Bolshevik request for a German attack on Alexeiev should be met with words rather than deeds; honouring such a request would entail giving 'unilateral support to the Bolsheviks, which I cannot recommend'.

Ludendorff had been somewhat restrained on the eastern front. But from July 18, the initiative had finally and definitely passed to the Allies on the western front; and all late July, the Allies had been delivering local offensives to improve railway communications, and prepare for a major counter-stroke on the Marne. It came, led by 450 tanks, and in complete surprise, on August 8, and sent the Germans reeling; it was the 'black day of the German army in the history of the war', Ludendorff wrote. And it was only one day after he had replied to Hintze about sending German troops to fight the British on the Murmansk front, and to occupy Petrograd.[21]

Reilly's task was not only to launch a *coup* to overthrow the Bolsheviks, but also to undermine any attempts at open Bolshevik collaboration with the Germans once the Allies had openly intervened on Russian soil. A successful *coup* depended upon money — a great deal of it. In mid-August, Bruce Lockhart, who was about to leave Russia, hastily began to collect financial support for the White Russians at the (still unraided) American consulate in Moscow, where the Allied consuls were holding daily surreptitious meetings. In Petrograd, Reilly and Cromie, with nearly £1 million sterling, which the Bolsheviks had failed to blackmail out of them, were busily plotting at the old British embassy, agitating among the Latvian troops (as the Germans had been doing), and trying to discern exactly what the Bolsheviks were planning with the Germans.

On about August 14, matters became clear. Ludendorff dropped his objections to the German–Bolshevik trade treaty, and this was rapidly reflected in the editorials of the Berlin newspapers. As it became known that the Bolshevik delegates Krassin and Adolf Joffe, who were back in Moscow, were returning to Berlin to sign the trade treaty, the Bolshevik mission in Berlin wired Moscow that the Germans now agreed to send German troops, via Petrograd and Vologda, to the northern Russian front, under the nominal command of Russian officers. Reilly had access to what was passing on the wires between Moscow and Berlin, and his plan was now complete. The Latvians were to arrest Lenin and Trotsky, and after distributing leaflets with details of the trade treaty in the Moscow streets, destroy them with ridicule by parading them in the streets (clad, apparently, only in their shirts). The Russian officers would then be mobilized, and a provisional military government set up, which would recall the constituent assembly. Part of the newly-assembled Russian force would march to join the Czechs on the Volga, while part would march to Petrograd, where a rising would take place. Uritsky (head of the Petrograd Cheka, and generally in charge of the old Russian capital) would also be arrested, and the bridges in Petrograd, and on the Petrograd–Vologda railway, blown up to stop the German troops getting through to Archangel. The signal for the *coup* would be news of the actual signature of the trade treaty in Berlin.[22]

The success of such a *coup* also depended upon the support of a sufficient Allied and Russian army at Archangel, and proper support from the Russians and Czechs on the upper Volga. It was known that Poole's force was limited to only 1,200 men. Could he succeed in getting through to Vologda, and down the River Dvina to Kotlas and Viatka, thus linking up with the Czechs, seize the food stocks in western Siberia, and raise more Russian troops?

By now (mid-August), the Bolsheviks at least knew that Allied officials and agents in Russia knew more than they should of their plans, even if they did not know the details of the Allied *coup*. According to precedent, the Bolsheviks decided to use *agents provocateurs* to spring the plot before it was ready. On the 15th, when the Danish Minister Oudendyk went to see Uritsky about the release of British and French hostages, Uritsky stated flatly that he knew what was going on in the old British embassy. Cromie indeed seems to have abandoned security. In a note he sent to Lockhart, via a youth called Smidchen who appears to have been an *agent provocateur*, confirming that he was making his own way out of Russia, Cromie stated that he hoped to leave with a bang. Smidchen, he added, might be of some use. Smidchen took the note straight to a Latvian Colonel Berzin, who took it to Peters (deputy head of the Cheka), also a Latvian, with a wife in England.

The Bolshevik position was desperate. The Latvians themselves were now under suspicion, on the Volga and elsewhere. Colonel Berzin, seemingly disillusioned with the Bolsheviks, was at this time in touch with Colonel de Vertement (head of the French Deuxième Bureau in Moscow), and with Xenophon Kalamatiano (of the American Secret Service). As

Reilly avoided both the French and the Americans, he had made discreet contact with Berzin through his colleague Captain Hill. Whether Berzin's recent change of heart was in any way genuine is unclear. But the Allies now had four columns outside the city, and their fifth column inside. It was evident that something was shortly going to happen. Why not go to Lockhart, and obtain a pass through the lines? If the Bolsheviks went under, even loyal Latvian comrades had a right to save themselves. If the Bolsheviks survived, they could denounce Lockhart for taking part in a plot, and become Bolshevik heroes.

By the 15th, the German embassy, under Riezler's control, had finally left Moscow, *en route* for Berlin. For the last few days before their departure, records Riezler, German negotiations with the Latvians about their return to Latvia had improved considerably. Now the Germans had left. The Latvians appear to have changed sides swiftly. That same day (as the French agreed to finance pro-Ally operations in Moscow, while the British financed operations in northern Russia), Colonel Berzin, armed with Cromie's note and with Smidchen in tow, called on Lockhart at his flat in Moscow; the Latvians, he said, were ready to go over to the British on the Archangel front. Could Lockhart give them a pass?

After conferring with his French colleagues, Lockhart duly did so the next day, and put Berzin in touch with Reilly. These two met on the 17th, and discussed the despatch of Bolshevik units to Vologda, which would be handed over to the British, and the seizure of Lenin and Trotsky at a central committee meeting in Moscow; and Reilly evidently gave Berzin a considerable amount of roubles. On the 18th, Reilly told Lockhart that his negotiations with the Latvians were going well. After Lockhart had left, he added (probably trying to obtain cover), he might perhaps be able to use them to stage a *coup* in Moscow. Lockhart, who perhaps did not wish to know, claims that he and the French told Reilly he was not to do so. (However, Lockhart's unpublished diary, which it is clear has details of his relations with Reilly at this time, remains closed until the end of the century.) Whatever was said, Reilly decided to go ahead.[22]

It will be recalled that Reilly had for some time been in touch with Colonel Friede (the Bolshevik Chief of Staff in Moscow, also a Latvian), who had been passing on military information to Reilly. On the 20th, Colonel Friede's sister told Reilly that the central committee would meet in the Bolshoi Theatre on the 28th. Would this be too soon? Would the trade treaty be signed by then? Reilly had further meetings with Berzin to discuss the seizure of certain Bolshevik offices to obtain details of the trade treaty. Reilly was now being urged to meet his Allied colleagues to arrange for cooperation. In Berlin, Foreign Secretary Hintze assured Joffe, who had been making last-minute objections to the treaty, much to German alarm, that the German government would force the Turks to stop their military expedition on Baku; and on this assurance, the Bolshevik delegates agreed

317

to sign. The date was August 23. This news was no doubt rapidly passed to Moscow. On either the 23rd or 24th, Reilly attended a meeting at the American consulate — much against his will — where he found the American Consul Poole, the French Consul Grenard, Colonel de Vertement, and Réné Marchand (the Moscow correspondent of *Le Figaro*), who surprised Reilly by suddenly asking him for his name. Reilly muttered 'Rice', and went off with Colonel de Vertement into another room. While they were in animated discussion, Reilly suddenly noticed that Marchand had come into the room and was listening.

In Moscow and other Russian towns, the people were on the verge of starvation. On the 25th, *Izvestia* reported that Allied agents had just blown up three precious food trains at Voronezh station, when the Don Cossacks, with German backing, broke into Voronezh province. Marchand, therefore, who had in fact only overheard part of the conversation between Reilly and the French Colonel, went straight off to the Bolsheviks, and told them that he had just heard this man Rice and Colonel de Vertement discussing plans for the demolition of bridges on the Petrograd–Vologda railway (along which German troops were to proceed, *en route* for the Archangel front). The Bolsheviks listened attentively to Marchand: more evidence, they told him, of the wicked imperialists trying to starve out the people of Petrograd. They must have been alarmed. How much did Reilly and Colonel de Vertement know? It was announced that the central committee meeting had been delayed until September 6.

In Berlin, the trade treaty was finally signed on the 27th, by which the Bolsheviks agreed to sell part of the Baku oil to the Germans, connive at German use of the Black Sea Fleet, and pay a very large indemnity. In return, the Germans agreed to cease supporting the Don Cossacks, to permit Bolshevik trade in grain and coal with the Ukraine, and (nominally) to send German troops via Petrograd and Vologda to drive out the British, and to grant German recognition to Georgia and Estonia, while allowing the Bolsheviks other outlets to the Baltic. This time there was really no need to intercept any wires. On the 28th, a German newspaper reported that there had been an exchange of notes between the Bolshevik and German governments. That night Reilly returned to Petrograd, accompanied by Berzin, to complete the details of the uprising.

Now that Reilly had been given the signal to launch his *coup*, what were the prospects of support from Poole at Archangel, and from the Czechs on the Volga? At Archangel, Poole had not only failed to get through to the Czechs; indeed, he could barely feed his own troops and the local inhabitants at Archangel, who depended on him. Things were no better at Murmansk. General Maynard wired on August 18 that the many local strikes were entirely caused by the absence of pay and food for the workmen. He had no pay to give them, and very little food; yet food supplies had been expressly promised by the British government. So no food could be sent to Archangel from Murmansk. On the 20th, Poole prevailed upon the Archangel government to declare conscription, but to defer the call-up until after the harvest had been gathered in. In London that day, the DMI admitted to the War Cabinet that the food situation at Archangel was 'acute', and that if Britain was to meet Poole's needs, action had to be taken within three weeks, or the ships would be unable to unload, and get away from Archangel before the ice. The DMI said that Poole needed 40,000 tons, but only 15,000 tons were being shipped in. It was decided that the War Office and Minister of Shipping should make 'definite proposals' for the Cabinet to consider. The DMI added that the food situation at Murmansk also gave rise to a 'certain amount' of anxiety, but the question was not so acute as Archangel, since Murmansk was ice-free.[23]

Proper support from the Russians and the Czechs on the Volga meant that they must, at least, hold their present positions from Samara north to Kazan; that they must properly combine; and that the Czech position in the Far East must be rectified, so that they held the entire length of the Siberian railway, up which Allied troops and especially supplies could be despatched with all speed from Vladivostok to the Volga front.

Unfortunately, the Volga front was already beginning to decline, due to disunity between the Russians on the east bank, and Trotsky's feverish activities on the west. The liberation of Siberia from the Bolsheviks had produced two main White Russian governments: one at Samara, composed largely of SRs, former members of the constituent assembly; and one at Omsk, which was much more right-wing, and thus thoroughly antagonistic to Samara. This had resulted in Omsk refusing to send any grain to Samara, and Samara in turn refusing to send iron, and other products from the Urals, to Omsk. Above all, army officers began to desert from Samara to Omsk, which soon had a small Russian army under training; which was a sufficient excuse for Omsk to refuse to send any troop reinforcements to the Volga front. 'When I arrived at Samara', wrote General Boldyrev (later Russian Army Commander at Omsk), 'Colonel Kappel, one of the most outstanding leaders of the [Samara] people's army, presented me with a virtual ultimatum: that for the sake of an army exhausted by uninterrupted marches and fighting, a general political unification was immediately imperative. Representatives of the Czechoslovaks declared the same thing.'[24]

An attempt, backed by the Czech National Council, the French Mission, and the 'Union for the Regeneration of Russia', had accordingly been made to form an all-Russian government at a conference at Chelyabinsk in mid-July. The Samara delegates maintained that they represented the nucleus of the all-Russian government, which would be formed when enough members of the constituent assembly had arrived; whereupon all regional governments, like the one at Omsk, were to surrender their authority. The Omsk delegate said his only purpose in coming was to coordinate 'practical activities', not to discuss the formation of such a government. However, it was agreed to hold a second conference in August.

In mid-August, the Czechs again urged the Russians to form a central government. Their tone had changed: 'Three months have passed since the Czechoslovak army rose against the Bolshevik usurpers. At first we had to defend our own freedom, but very soon we decided to ... come to the rescue of the Russian people. ... We hoped that the Russians themselves would make an effort to re-establish their military and political organiz-ation. ... Unfortunately, the work of reconstruction is progressing very slowly. ... All this is happening at a time when the Czechoslovak forces are gradually diminishing, while those of the Bolsheviks are steadily increasing through reinforcements. ... Three months of constant fighting have brought the Czechoslovaks to physical exhaustion ... and they naturally ask themselves the question: why is it that after three months so little has been done by the Russians to form organizations of their own? Instead of a national government being established, we witness strife among the differ-ent parts of Russia. ... The political situation imperatively calls for the formation of a central government. ... Only such a government could count on the material and moral support of the Allies.'[24] But too few delegates turned up for the second conference at Chelyabinsk. It was agreed to hold another conference at Ufa on September 7.

Across the Volga, such disunity and lethargy were not lost on Trotsky, feverishly reorganizing his troops. 'Stubborn fighting is in progress here', he wired Lenin on the 13th. He sent for the tried Second Petrograd Regiment; but, led by the military commissar Panteleev and the military commander, they seized a steamer to escape to Nizhni–Novgorod. They were caught, and Trotsky had the commissar and commander and every tenth man shot. Then the Latvians refused to go into action. But by the 15th, Trotsky was able to wire Lenin that, although their command apparatus was weak, there was now a 'great improvement'. Across the Volga went taunts and threats. 'Remember Yaroslavl, you counter-revolutionary bandits of Kazan, Simbirsk, and Samara!'[25]

From Moscow, Lenin harried Trotsky unmercifully. He was 'astonished and alarmed' that their attack on Kazan was slowing down; there must be 'merciless annihilation' of Kazan. Trotsky replied angrily that he was not 'sparing' Kazan. Now that he had enough men, he wired on the 21st, 'I hope to bring matters swiftly to a head'. But the problem of command remained unresolved. Lenin was warned urgently that both supplies and operations must be coordinated under a Bolshevik commander-in-chief, with a proper staff. 'Give the matter thought', Lenin minuted to Trotsky underneath. 'How about appointing Vatsetis Commander-in-Chief?' Trotsky initialled this.[26]

The Bolshevik position further down the Volga then deteriorated. A White Russian plot was uncovered amongst the Bolshevik staff at Saratov. Owing to 'extremely dangerous falterings' due to treason, Lenin wired, Trotsky must visit the Saratov front in person. Trotsky evidently paid a swift visit, and wired back to Lenin that the proposals for the integration of the Red Army Command were 'unquestionably right', but there were difficulties over the choice of the commander-in-chief. He had more than once suggested Vatsetis; but he could only take over 'after the first victory'. But the further proposal to replace general staff officers by military commissars was 'utterly worthless'. Vatsetis (whom Lenin suggested) and his staff were all former officers, whose employment Trotsky defended against the military commissars. This was to be a perennial bone of contention within Bolshevik ruling circles — and especially between Trotsky and Stalin.[27]

What was being done to rectify the Czech position in the Far East so that they held the entire line of the Siberian railway, up which Allied troops and especially supplies could be despatched with all speed to the hard-pressed Volga front?[28] On August 16, half of the American contingent finally arrived from the Philippines; the remainder reached Vladivostok a few days later, so there were now 14,000 more Allied troops on the spot.

On August 21 (by which date the initial Japanese contingent of 12,000 troops had been strengthened by 12,000 more, and had spread into the Chinese eastern railway zone in Manchuria), the War Cabinet again considered the Czech predicament in the Far East, and the Japanese desire to increase their forces by 6,000 to 7,000 more troops (a desire which had presumably been fulfilled). Lord Curzon said the Czech position was 'more than precarious', and President Wilson would bear a very great moral responsibility 'if the Czechoslovaks were exterminated', because he had not allowed the Japanese to increase their forces.

Austen Chamberlain said that the two telegrams about the Japanese desire to increase their strength should be passed to Foch, who should wire to President Wilson, urging that the Czechs should be relieved, and emphasizing its important bearing on the present new operations on the western front, if German anxieties on the eastern front were thus increased. But Lord Robert Cecil thought any further attempt to bring further pressure on the President might produce a reverse effect. The President was well aware of the British view, 'but his policy was not ours; he did not believe in the possibility of reconstituting the eastern front'. It was his principle not to intervene in any country unless the inhabitants so requested. Cecil, however, was wiring that day both to the Japanese and the Czechs; if the Czechs themselves appealed direct to President Wilson, it might have more effect. All the wires received at the Foreign Office on this question were passed in full to Washington for the President's information.

It was suggested to the Cabinet that this was a particularly appropriate moment for Foch to contact the President, now that the initiative in France had definitely passed to the Allies. Foch could say that unless the Czechs were relieved, his campaign on the western front would be ruined. (This was a highly stretched argument. Foch was now beating a 'tattoo' on the German army, a series of rapid blows, each broken off when the immediate object had been obtained, each paving the way for the next, each interacting; but to suggest that the Czech situation in the (very far) East would in any way influence this situation was stretching the argument to the extreme.)[29]

The War Cabinet decided that Cecil should consult Lord Reading (who was still in England) about whether to forward the two telegrams without comment to President Wilson; whether they should be accompanied by a statement 'that we did not wish to put further pressure on the President, whose views we respected even though we did not share them', but felt bound to impart this information; or whether Foch should be asked to send a separate communication, in which case the CIGS should take the necessary action. Cecil was empowered to take such action as might be agreed with Lord Reading.

The anxiety about how to deal with President Wilson was not confined to Cecil and Reading. Between August 20 and 22, a veritable flood of anxious letters and wires flowed between London, Washington, Paris and Tokyo about how to get help for the Czechs without further exacerbating the President. On the 22nd, Cecil told the War Cabinet that Reading thought it inadvisable to send the two telegrams, with the suggested comments; Foch should be asked to make a *démarche* with the President. The CIGS had thus been asked to contact Foch. The Cabinet were also told that the captain of *Suffolk* had wired that the Czech commander at Vladivostok had asked for some British twelve-pounders and six-inch naval guns to use on their trains on the Manchurian front. It was decided that the captain of *Suffolk* should consult General Knox, who was due at Vladivostok in a few days.[30]

The Japanese had by now got the message. On the 25th, as Czech and Japanese forces finally eliminated the Bolsheviks on the Ussuri front, the Japanese ambassador in London told Balfour that more Japanese reinforcements would be sent to Siberia; it was hoped the British government would approve. Balfour expressed his pleasure; the number of troops needed to achieve 'our objects' in Siberia was 'entirely a military question'. Nothing could have better underlined the great split between London and Washington on Siberian policy. England had placed herself firmly on the Japanese side. On the 27th, the CIGS told the War Cabinet that Foch was reluctant to intervene with the President — but this, of course, did not now matter. The Japanese, the CIGS went on, were reinforcing their troops 'on their own initiative', and had achieved success on the Ussuri front, but were not yet in contact with the main body of the Czech forces. The extent of the

Japanese reinforcements, however, was not made clear to the Cabinet.[31] In fact, the Japanese General Staff announced the day before that 10,000 more troops had embarked for Vladivostok, and another 20,000 were being mobilized for the Manchurian front. Soon they had no less than 72,000 troops on the mainland — which was exactly the figure which the CIGS had recommended to them on August 9.[31]

Thus Reilly had no support from Poole at Archangel nor from the Czechs on the Volga when the signal, in the form of the signature of the German–Bolshevik trade treaty in Berlin, was given to Reilly in Moscow to launch his *coup.*

On the 29th, the Cheka struck in Moscow. As a result of Marchand's disclosures, the French Deuxième Bureau office was raided, and all French agents seized, save for Colonel de Vertement, who escaped over the roof. Hill at once broke off all contact with the French, and sent an agent to warn Reilly in Petrograd; but the agent was caught on the train. The Cheka then swooped on the ballerina's flat, where Reilly was to be found when in Moscow. She managed to conceal two million roubles on her person; but, as the Cheka were about to leave empty-handed, Colonel Friede's sister walked into the flat with documents for Reilly in her music-case; that night Colonel Friede was arrested. But although the Bolsheviks had only discovered a small part of Reilly's plot, what they did discover alarmed them: perhaps Reilly was at that very moment having copies of the trade treaty duplicated for distribution as leaflets on the streets of Petrograd and Moscow? The danger was acute. Reilly must be found at all costs.

In Petrograd, Reilly had gone straight to a flat he held in the name of Massino to find that Cromie had sent over a bottle of wine, and that Berzin had called, promising to return on the 30th. He then discovered that some of his other Petrograd addresses were being raided, and that he was being followed. Risking all, he went straight to Cheka headquarters: as Relinsky, the Cheka agent, he was told by an accomplice, he was safe. He walked out, abandoning every other alias.

On the 30th, Reilly's plot was prematurely exploded, as the Bolsheviks intended. That morning, Uritsky was shot dead in front of Cheka head-quarters in Petrograd by a Russian cadet, who made off on a bicycle and disappeared into a building opposite the British military mission. That evening, after addressing a meeting at a Moscow factory, Lenin was shot at by a left SR called Dora Kaplan, and was carried off seriously wounded.[32]

The Bolsheviks began the 'Terror'. After midnight, Lockhart was dragged from his bed by the Cheka. Peters showed him the pass which Lockhart had given to Berzin. 'Where is Reilly?' he demanded. Lockhart refused to reply. On the Volga, Trotsky was drafting a wire to Lenin, when an urgent message came from Sverdlov: 'Come here without delay. Ilitch has been wounded; how dangerously is not known. All is calm.'[32]

In Petrograd, Reilly rang up Cromie on the morning of the 31st, and arranged to meet him in a cafe at noon. Cromie did not turn up. That evening, Reilly decided to risk a visit to the British embassy, but he found it already surrounded. Covered by the guns of two Bolshevik destroyers in the river, the Cheka had descended on the great house. As they battered down the front door, the British consul dashed upstairs to destroy some papers, covered by Cromie at the head of the staircase with a revolver in his hand. Most of the old embassy staff were in the chancery being paid when suddenly 'in rushed an excited man in an overcoat and a soft hat, with Browning pistols pointing towards us in each hand, while he shouted at the top of his voice '*Rooki vverkh*! [hands up].' After a few moments, shots were heard. As the Cheka had begun to come up the stairs, Cromie had fired, killing one man, wounding another. The Cheka returned the fire. Cromie fell, mortally wounded, and then pitched headlong down the great scarlet and white staircase. As the embassy staff, and Lessing and others, were marched out, they saw Cromie's body lying at the foot of the stair-case, and his blood on the second stair from the bottom, where he had struck his head. His body was then mutilated by the mob (which had surged into the great house with the Cheka) and flung out of a second floor window. Reilly, mingling with the other Cheka agents outside, vanished into the starving city.

Cromie's murder had a great moral effect in both Russia and England. It aptly signified the end of any British presence whatsoever in the old Russian capital — a presence and influence that had once been so strong. In London, it was taken by some to justify British intervention on its own; no further excuse was needed. (But in July 1924, by which time he was a Liberal MP, Teddy Lessing told the House of Commons that Cromie would never have been killed, if he had not been armed, and 'shot two of the assailants before he was shot himself. ... I was within a few yards of Captain Cromie when he was shot. ... As a matter of fact, they did not fire first.')[33]

Later that same evening, the Bolsheviks told the Dutch Minister Oudendyk, who had come to protest, that they had documents 'proving conclusively' that the British were involved in Uritsky's murder. Though Lockhart was released on September 1, the hunt for Reilly was intensified; so long as he remained at liberty, the terrible danger remained of the streets of Moscow and Petrograd being deluged with incriminating leaflets about the trade treaty. On the 2nd, as the Terror increased in violence, the central committee hastily ratified the trade treaty. But since they were alarmed at the ominous account of the Allied plot, revealed only 'to a small extent' by seized documents, they decided to denounce the treaty publicly as a forgery; there was, after all, an excellent precedent in the patently forged 'Sisson documents', which the Allies had foisted on them.[34]

That same day, an official statement was therefore issued announcing the suppression of an Allied plot, based on bribery and forged documents, to capture members of the central committee and to proclaim a military dictatorship. Reilly, it was stated, was one of Lockhart's chief agents, and had been handing out large amounts of roubles in bribes. 'Instructions were found that in the event of a successful revolt, forged secret correspondence was to be published, between the Russian and German governments, and forged treaties were to be manufactured, in order to create a suitable atmosphere for renewing the war with Germany.' It was also agreed that this statement should be issued at greater length in leaflet form as 'agitational literature' to the advancing Allied troops.[34]

On the 3rd, when this statement appeared in the Bolshevik press, with extensive revelations of a plot organized by Lockhart — for it would not do for it to be too apparent that the whole Bolshevik government was being had by the ears by a British secret agent — Lockhart was much surprised. 'Papers today full of the most fantastic accounts of an Allied conspiracy of which I am said to be at the head', he recorded in his diary that day. 'The account, which reads like a fairy-tale, includes "buying over of Lett troops", "shooting Lenin and Trotsky", "taking Petrograd and Moscow by hunger", "blowing up bridges", and "appointment of dictator" not to mention the wildest and most false account of my arrest.'[35]

Captain Hill at once sent a girl courier to the ballerina's flat, offering to take over Reilly's network. She was too late. The Cheka had returned. Though her story was believed, and she and the ballerina again escaped, another girl then walked in with documents for Reilly from the American secret agent Kalamatiano. That afternoon, he was arrested. Only Reilly and Hill remained free.[36]

On the 4th, news of Cromie's death was brought to the attention of the War Cabinet in London. Lord Robert Cecil said rumours had reached him that the former Tsarina and the 'German princesses' had been killed. What remained of the British embassy had been moved to Moscow, and no embassy documents had been left in Petrograd. Cecil felt strongly that the British government should take some action over the murder of Captain Cromie. He suggested that Litvinov should be imprisoned, or at least interned, and a strongly-worded telegram 'should be sent to the Revolutionary government threatening personal reprisals against its leaders'. There had been no information from Lockhart since August 17, when he was reported to be at Moscow. The Foreign Office had practically reached agreement with the Soviet government to repatriate the British representatives in Moscow, when the Soviet government put forward fresh terms. These 'inclined the Foreign Office to think that the British reresentatives had all been killed'. The Cabinet decided that Balfour should discover whether Litvinov could be legally interned and, if so, it should be done. Secondly, Balfour should wire to Moscow, 'threatening reprisals against M.

Trotsky, M. Lenin, and the leaders of that government, if the lives of British subjects were not safeguarded'.[37]

In Moscow the same day, as it became apparent that the Bolsheviks were in control, Peters (the deputy head of the Cheka) again arrested Lockhart (whom he proceeded to treat with some leniency, even allowing his girl friend Moura Benckendorff into his cell for regular visits), and announced that it was he himself who had organized a fictitious plot to spring the real plot within the British embassy. The same day, Réné Marchand, who had given Reilly away, was induced to write an open letter to President Poincaré. The Allies, wrote this Bolshevik dupe, could only have approved of what Reilly was doing if it was admitted that the Bolsheviks had formed a close alliance with Germany. 'Also I am aware that this is actually what is currently said, and that certain Allied agents even live for the search ... of "documents" which will establish the "alliance".' Marchand said he himself had on previous occasions suspected some complicity between the Bolsheviks and the Germans. But 'today it is difficult seriously to suppose that the Soviet government has decided to bind its fortunes with those of the central empires ... whatever should be the future development of military events, I consider it unlikely that the Soviet government would ever resolve to call Germany to its aid.' Merchand had well served the Bolsheviks.

On the 6th, as the Dutch Minister Oudendyk organized as full a state funeral as possible in Petrograd for Cromie (whose body was borne through the streets bearing one large wreath from the British Admiralty), and Balfour and Chicherin exchanged sharp telegrams, Reilly returned to Moscow, where photographs, rewards and warrants for his arrest (under every possible name, including Relinsky) were posted all over the city. Reilly suggested to Hill that he should give himself up in exchange for Lockhart, and so clear him. Hill advised him to leave. Reilly finally managed to escape from Moscow by train in a railway compartment reserved for the German embassy, and then from Petrograd on a Dutch tug.[38]

The possibility of Moura's involvement in the springing of Reilly's conspiracy has been raised in a biography of H.G. Wells by his son Anthony West (in 1984). In the 1930s, Moura (then Countess Budberg) was Wells's mistress. In 1934, he was invited by the Soviet government to pay a semi-official visit to Russia. Moura refused to accompany him: it would be too dangerous: her position *vis-à-vis* the Soviets was as it had been in 1920; she would still be in great danger. They agreed to meet again in Estonia (then independent), on Wells's return from Moscow. But in Moscow, where Wells had an interview with Stalin, he soon discovered from Russian writers that Moura had been visiting Russia regularly for years. It was clear not only that Moura had told Wells a pack of lies, but had long been a Soviet agent. When confronted with this in Estonia, Moura admitted everything. She had been controlled by someone or other since 1916, when the Germans had caught her spying for the Russians, and told her she could either spy for them too, or be shot. Since then, she had simply done what the realities of each new situation had required of her. Survival was all. This was all she apparently told Wells; she would give no details of her activities. Wells, states his son, kept all this to himself at the time.

The whole truth may never be known. Some of the evidence in the Bolshevik archives would certainly reveal a story of double-dealing and treachery, which would seriously violate the time-hallowed revolutionary myth. It may suffice to say that it is: (*a*) quite probable that the British were somehow involved in Uritsky's murder, and that it had simply become a race as to who would strike first; and (*b*) more than probable that the British had nothing whatsoever to do with the attempt on Lenin. The last thing that Reilly would have wished to do was to murder Lenin, and thus turn him into a Bolshevik martyr. The attempt on Lenin was most probably an immediate (and despairing) left SR reaction, triggered off by the earlier killing in Petrograd, to the news that Lenin had now concluded another treaty with the hated Germans.

Three diary entries in Lockhart's published diary perhaps give his view of the Moscow plot.

September 24. Today *Izvestia* published the letters to Poincaré of one of the French agents, Marchand, in which he mentions a meeting at the USA consulate where the blowing up of bridges and rails was discussed. Although I was not at this meeting and knew nothing about it, my name is still mentioned as the instigator of everything and arch-criminal. Although the meeting was said to have been presided over by (the American consul) Poole, no mention of the Americans. For political reasons of course!

September 30. Peters told me the other day before Moura that the Americans were the worst compromised in this business and that what they (the Bolsheviks) had against me was nothing. And yet not one word has been said against the Yanks!

November 18. [Back in England] Saw Rothstein [the chief Bolshevik agent in England] and had a long talk with him. He does not believe the story of the Moscow plot.[39]

Professor Kennan does not discuss this episode in *The Decision to Intervene.*

Perhaps Consul Poole knew that he was compromised. On September 30, he stopped in Oslo on his way out of Russia, where he went for a quiet talk to the British embassy. In a 'personal and most secret' telegram to the Foreign Office, the British ambassador wired that Poole had told him confidentially 'that there is strong suspicion that an agent named Reilly, whose wife appears to be living in New York, and who was officially known as ST, has either compromised Lockhart, who employed him in propaganda among Letts (two groups indec), by exceeding his instructions and endeavouring to provoke a revolt against the Bolsheviks, or has even betrayed him. ... Reilly advocated encouraging a revolt, but Lockhart, after consulting the United States consul-general [Poole] and the French consul-general [Grenard], refused to do so, and instructed Reilly to limit his efforts to propaganda with a view to deterring the Lett soldiers from resisting Allied forces. It appears that Reilly was in communication with a certain Russian strongly suspected of being an *agent provocateur*, to whom he had given an address at which he still remained some days ago. Lockhart (group indec) arrested. Neither Reilly nor the Russian has been arrested, and they are still at large. Hence suspicion.'

On October 1, R.A. Leeper (Political Intelligence Department, Foreign Office) commented thus: 'I have seen several reports from Reilly (ST) and have always found them quite satisfactory. MIIC [the former name for MI6] will know all about him. It seems to me possible that Reilly, when he found the game was up and Mr Lockhart could not be saved, hid himself because there was nothing else left to do. But whether Reilly acted falsely or merely unwisely, Mr Poole's account of the story clears Mr Lockhart from the charges made against him by the Bolsheviks which have been exploited by the Germans. This would be useful to us if we wished to publish a denial of the Bolshevik story.'

Balfour agreed. 'This may be most useful', he minuted underneath. The Russia department added that Reilly 'will be closely interrogated when possible. This telegram does not definitely state that he disregarded Mr Lockhart's instructions. He is able to pose as a Bolshevik and obtained a passport from Litvinov.'

The matter was referred to the DMI, who in turn consulted MI6. They sent the following written reply on October 10: 'Reilly is an officer who was sent to Russia as a military agent last March. In June, it became apparent that his utility as a military agent was being impaired by the fact that he was in touch with Mr Lockhart, who was using him for some political purpose. Reilly had been warned most specifically that he was not to get into any official position, or to get mixed up with politics; therefore when it became apparent that he was doing so, a wire was sent ordering him to proceed to Siberia to report on German prisoner of war camps — this with the idea of getting him away from the political atmosphere, in which he was being involved. ... He apparently never went there; perhaps he was ordered not to do so by Mr Lockhart. He certainly had no business to be doing propaganda, which he apparently was instructed to do by Mr Lockhart. ... MIIC have all the details of this man's career, and I suggest that it is advisable to wire to Sir M. Findlay [in Oslo] to advise him and Mr Poole that they should not raise a hue and cry about Reilly until we know more about the circumstances. We have had one report that it was a Lettish officer who gave the plot away; and because it has failed, it does not seem right or just that the blame should be cast on a man who should properly have never been employed on such work. Presumably the clue, to which the United States consul-general refers, is the fact that Reilly's wife is in America. MIIC have her address, and incidentally some of Reilly's valuables and his will.'[40]

It may be as well to read this SIS report on Reilly and his activities with a good deal of reserve, to say the least. The report admits that he was a military, not a political, agent; and was presumably to limit himself to military work. But with all the plots and counter-plots in Bolshevik Russia that summer, political and military matters had become inextricably mixed. As already stated, Bruce Lockhart's exact relationship with Reilly towards the end remains officially obscured for another twenty years. But on return to England, Reilly presented Bruce Lockhart with a silver cigar case, on which the inscription in part reads: 'in remembrance of events in Moscow in August and September of [1918] from his faithful Lieutenant Sidney Reilly'. There may well be more truth in that inscription than in the SIS report.

Reilly is more explicit elsewhere about the part he played. For the Dutch tug owner (who brought Reilly out of Petrograd, and discussed the whole episode with me in 1970 in The Hague) later received a remarkably frank letter of thanks from Reilly written in German on October 10, explaining exactly who he was. 'I am an English officer, Lt Sidney Reilly RFC [Royal Flying Corps], have been for about six months on a special mission in Russia, and have been accused by the Bolsheviks of being the military organizer of a great plot in Moscow. The Russian papers from September 3 and later will inform you sufficiently about me. [The tug owner agreed with me that this remarkable frankness was designed to shut his mouth.] In any case the Bolsheviks have done me a great honour: on my account they have published a special decree that foreign counter-revolutionaries will be punished exactly like Russians and they have put a great price on my poor head. I can boast of being "the most sought after man" in Russia.' He enclosed some photographs: 'Naturally, I am now clean shaven and ... look really quite respectable! Probably I will soon return to Russia — but from the other side and I hope that then for a change the Bolsheviks will run away ...'.[41]

13

November 1918:
minor intervention fails

The failure of Reilly's *coups* in Moscow and Petrograd, and the failure of the Czechs to make contact with the Archangel forces, coupled with the lack of adequate Allied troops and food, now led to a crisis in northern Russia. On August 30, the DMI brought an alarming telegram from Admiral Kemp before the War Cabinet. The military situation at both Murmansk and Archangel would become 'very serious', said the admiral, unless considerable reinforcements, in addition to the 5,500 men of the American 339th Infantry (who had sailed from Newcastle on the 25th), were sent out before the end of October. At Murmansk, the present intention was to withdraw all troops from the south of Kandalaksha (on the north-western tip of the White Sea), and also from Petchenga. Such withdrawals would be 'politically disastrous', stated the admiral. 5,000 more troops would be needed to hold on in these areas. The CIGS agreed that the news from Murmansk was not good. The First Lord said the Admiralty proposed to replace the British cruiser *Cochrane* with the Russian *Askold*. The general naval situation had developed considerably in the last two months. The North Sea barrage had proved much more efficient than anticipated, and its overall effect was increasing. Britain would lose all this if it had to abandon the Arctic ports. The First Sea Lord then stated (in defiance of the telegram from Helsinki of the 9th that the Germans were leaving Finland) that if the Germans prolonged the railway they were building, they would be able to construct new sea bases for both submarines and surface raiders.[1]

During the discussion that followed, on whether it would be better to abandon Archangel, or Murmansk and Petchenga, if such a withdrawal was inevitable, the CIGS remarked that 'our effort in that theatre was based on the assumption that we should obtain the support of about 20,000 Czechoslovaks. This project, unfortunately had not materialized.' The First Lord added that if we lost both Petchenga and Murmansk, Archangel was bound to fall as well, as the enemy could then operate with submarines against our flank. With that, the War Cabinet agreed that it was 'very important' to reinforce the White Sea ports, if this could be done without prejudice to the present offensive on the western front. The CIGS was directed to report on how many reinforcements were needed to hold the ports, and whether these troops could be found.

September 1 saw another fervent appeal to the War Office from General Maynard at Murmansk. He was expecting a German offensive in the early autumn (perhaps this information was derived from Reilly's access to the Berlin–Moscow wires, since all German troops had by now left Finland). Maynard thus also urgently appealed for reinforcements to protect the port of Murmansk, and the outlying strategic positions. By now, the strike on the Murmansk railway had made all communications with British bases to the south extremely difficult. Once again, he complained that his repeated requests for cash to pay the railway-workers had all been ignored; and had he received some cash, the position would not be so difficult.[1]

Maynard's wire was brought before the War Cabinet on September 3. If action was to be taken, stated the CIGS, it would have to be taken quickly. Men could be obtained from the 25th division, now at Aldershot, being prepared for France; from Ireland; and from Home Defence. The CIGS preferred the third alternative; with the improved naval arrangements in the North Sea, the risk of an enemy raid upon our coast was now minimal. If there was to be compulsory service in Ireland, the forces there could not be reduced. The First Lord supported the CIGS, but warned that the Admiralty could give no guarantee there would be no enemy raid on our coasts. The CIGS then read out a letter from General Poole, sent from Archangel on August 12, saying that he had advanced some 70 miles south of Archangel, and had seized great quantities of machine-guns, ammunition and general booty. He had recruited 600 Russian troops in the first week, but the Russians showed a 'general disinclination' to fight on either side. The Cabinet directed the CIGS, 'if he considered it urgently necessary', to withdraw troops from the 25th division or from Home Defence for service in northern Russia. The Cabinet further approved the action taken by the shipping controller in providing ships to send provisions to Archangel. The War Office at once informed Maynard and Poole that 5,000 more troops would be sent out to Murmansk — in line with the Rear-Admiral's request, considered by the Cabinet on August 30.[2]

At the next War Cabinet, attention was called to recent information showing 'an increased tendency of the Bolsheviks to support the Germans', apparently such as the German–Bolshevik trade treaty, and the attack on the British embassy. But Lord Robert Cecil thought it unlikely that the Germans would get any manpower out of Russia. The Bolsheviks had failed several times to enforce conscription, and the Russians clearly did not wish to fight anymore for either side. It was further encouraging to note that the Germans had been unable to obtain men from the Baltic states. Thus the Archangel government's conscription of 5,000 men might have a bad effect. Milner and the CIGS agreed. The Cabinet decided that the War Office should wire to General Poole that the British government regretted the recent conscription at Archangel; and that the Foreign Office should send a similar telegram to Lindley for his information.

Cecil then said he feared that 'if it were true that the Czechoslovaks were now in control of the whole Trans-Siberian railway, the Americans would be reluctant to allow Japanese forces to remain in Siberia, and would try to get the Czechoslovaks out of Siberia for use elsewhere'. From one of his telegrams, it seemed that Sir Charles Eliot (the British high commissioner) was thinking of travelling through from Vladivostok to Omsk.[3]

On September 4, the 5,500 men of the American 339th Infantry (mainly Poles from Michigan and Wisconsin) reached Archangel, and part were hastily sent 75 miles down the Vologda railway to join in bitter fighting with local Bolsheviks, while another part were sent 100 miles up the Dvina river in boats to try and seize Bereznik, as a winter base. This was, of course, in flagrant violation of President Wilson's aide mémoire of July 17 that American troops, either in the Far East or in northern Russia, were not to take part in 'organized intervention'.

That day, word reached Chaplin (the Russian naval officer, who had ousted the local Soviet in a *coup* on General Poole's entry into Archangel, and was now in nominal command of local Russian forces) that members of the Archangel government had been negotiating with the British and American envoys for an Allied loan and *de facto* recognition, in return for a local timber concession; and that these negotiations had reached a satisfactory conclusion. Chaplin was most displeased: the Archangel government, which he had more or less formed, was already much too left-wing, and too much under Allied influence for his or his brother officers' liking. Then at 10 p.m. that evening (according to Chaplin), General Poole told him that the Allied envoys had recommended their governments to recognize the Archangel government forthwith. Chaplin immediately decided to overthrow the Archangel government, and replace it with a strong military regime — he hoped under General Gurko.[4]

Two questions arise: first, who was General Gurko, and what was his significance in the northern Russian situation? Secondly, what truth was there in the report of the impending recognition of the Archangel government, and how did General Poole come to know of it? General Vasily Gurko had been Russian Chief of Staff under Tsar Nicholas II, during Alexeiev's illness, and was a competent officer. Now that Kornilov was dead, and Alexeiev was engaged in the Kuban, Gurko was the senior Russian officer in emigration. After the March revolution, he had been given a lesser post on promise of loyalty to the new regime. But early in

August 1917, he had been arrested, when it was discovered that he had written to the Tsar, declaring his continued devotion to the cause of the monarchy. The provisional government decided to send him abroad, and obtained a British passport for him. In mid-September (at the time of the Kornilov affair), he had left for Archangel, to be received by Admiral Kemp, who had him to stay on his yacht. On arrival in London, King George V gave General Gurko a reception at Buckingham Palace, an ill-conceived gesture which gave Gurko to think that England still supported the Russian monarchy. The General then went to Paris.[5]

On July 1, 1918, General Gurko, still in Paris, wrote to Lord Milner (the Secretary of State for War) in London. He recalled that a month before he had applied for a visa to come to England, but his request had been refused. Around June 20, he had again applied to come to London to see John Murray, his publisher; and asked Lord Milner to intercede on his behalf. He openly threatened that if he was turned down again, England would lose a good friend, which he had always been, at a time 'when you have not many of them in Russia'. He warned that he might again be close to government circles in Russia; and added that Kerensky had been allowed to come to England. A refusal for him (Gurko) would sooner or later become known in Russia.

On July 6, Lord Milner's secretary wrote to Gregory at the Foreign Office, enclosing the letter, and asking for a decision. 'I understand from our conversation this morning on the telephone that the War Cabinet are interested in this matter ...'. On July 10, the Russia Department minuted: 'General Gurko's letter reads very like a threat to HMG to initiate an anti-Ally campaign if not permitted to visit England. At the same time, it might be advisable to grant him the necessary facilities and let his visit be publicly known as showing that the British government do not restrict the grant of visas to any one political party. Notwithstanding his protestations, General Gurko's pro-English sentiments are open to doubt.' On the 11th, Sir George Clerk minuted, 'This is a very unpleasant letter and very much what I should expect from the writer. ... What happened was that in May last General Gurko wanted to come here from Paris to see the members of the War Cabinet. But we could never get the members of the War Cabinet to say if they wanted to see General Gurko, and as on general grounds there was no particular advantage in having him hanging about London and adding to Litvinov's suspicions of HMG, the visit was politely turned down.'

Clerk suggested that a reply be drafted for Lord Milner 'to the effect that it was not known here that General Gurko wished to come for personal reasons, and that there will of course be no objection to his doing so. Explain that Kerensky was allowed to come to this country from Russia in just the same way as the general himself, except that the former was not received by the King. Add that Lord Milner is sorry that General Gurko should think it necessary to threaten HMG with the loss of his friendship, of the value of which they are so well aware. And inform DMI.' Lord Hardinge added: 'I would omit the last sentence.'[5]

Balfour initialled this; and a letter was drafted and sent to that effect. The grant of a visa for General Gurko to come to London caused some unease in official circles in Paris. On July 29, the French ambassador despatched a note to the Foreign Office stating that some French newspapers had published a report from London announcing that the British government had appointed General Gurko as commander of Russian and Allied troops at Murmansk. At the same time, this Russian officer had asked while in Paris for a British passport, which had been granted to him. M. Pichon, the French Foreign Minister, did not attach any importance to the news, which contradicted the decisions of the Supreme War Council on Inter-Allied command in northern Russia; and had asked M. Cambon, the French ambassador, to let him know if the British government were considering the possibility of using the services of the General in the Archangel region.

'The French ambassador would add that General Gurko has shown himself in France to be a man of violent temperament, and to be a fervent believer in the restoration of absolutism in Russia. His unbalanced state of mind has prevented the Russian Legion, which he himself formed, from being able to keep going in France, and has contributed to the disagreements of the different Russian elements living in France. The services of the general in Russia would thus be more dangerous than useful to the Allies.'[5] The Foreign Office replied that the British government 'entirely concur in the views of the French government regarding General Gurko, and would be entirely opposed to any proposal to utilize his services at Archangel or elsewhere in Russia.'

This answer had to be repeated in public. On August 5, Mr King put down a question in the House of Commons, and asked the Foreign Secretary 'whether he is aware that General Gurko has publicly declared for a restoration of the monarchy; and whether he can assure the House that General Gurko is not in command of the Murman expedition?'

Mr Balfour: I have not seen the declaration to which the hon. Member refers. General Gurko has nothing whatever to do with the Murman expedition.

Mr King persevered. On August 8, he asked the Foreign Secretary again, 'whether he is able to give an assurance that General Gurko has nothing to do with either the Archangel or Vladivostok expeditions, which are being conducted by the Allies against the Soviet Government of Russia, and that General Gurko will not be allowed to join the Vladivostok expedition?'

Lord Robert Cecil: This question contains implications, and attributes motives, which are not in accordance with the facts. I can, however, assure the hon. Member that General Gurko has nothing to do with either the Archangel or the Vladivostok expeditions.

Mr King: Is the noble Lord aware that there was no implication, at any rate in my mind, when this question was asked?

Lord Robert Cecil: It must be perfectly evident to the hon. Member, or to any-one else reading it, that it is very offensive.

General Gurko continued his activities unabated. Late in August, there were signs that he was making his influence strongly felt in certain quarters in England. At a Russia Committee meeting on August 22, Sir George Clerk raised the question of General Gurko's monarchical activities in this country, 'reporting that the general was doing great harm by advocating the most ultra-reactionary principles and exerting influences on Russian officers about to be despatched to Murmansk and Archangel under British auspices'. It was agreed that the War Office should inform the Russian military attaché that it was impossible for them to employ any Russian officers 'who publicly identified themselves with any political faction'.[5]

Meanwhile, there was growing disaffection among the various Russian groups at Archangel, and Lindley and General Poole were at odds. On August 12, Lindley wired the Foreign Office that there had been friction with General Poole; he cited various instances, one in detail: 'While discussing, last night, with General Poole [the] position of Chaikovsky's administration, he told me many Russian officers were dissatisfied with it, and had asked him what would be his attitude if they turned him out. He himself considered it incompetent and muddling, and had replied he would remain neutral as Russian government was no concern of his. This answer was in these circumstances direct encouragement to turn it out. I pointed out to General Poole the folly of allowing a lot of Russian officers to turn out the government. ... I saw general [Poole] again today, and he told me he was on his way to tell Russian officers that he was on the side of existing government as he agreed with what I had said ...'.

Chaplin and his brother officers did not abandon their plan to overthrow the Archangel government. They wanted a Russian general at Archangel whose name would command respect. There was no suitable general at the time in Archangel, Chaplin records. So in mid-August, he talked the matter over with General Poole, and asked Poole to let him have a list of all Russian generals living in England, France and Finland. This arrived in late August, and Chaplin immediately decided on Gurko. He at once asked Poole to request the British government to allow General Gurko to leave for Archangel. This request was badly received in London (there is no reference to this in the Foreign Office files); the reply stated that Gurko was unacceptable to the Allies, as he was too right-wing. But Chaplin still appeared to hope that Gurko could somehow come out.

There was then a short lull. On September 3, Lindley wired London again. 'I learn that Mr Chaikovsky is disappointed at receiving no private messages of sympathy from London though he has done so from Paris. I would suggest that some societies or private individuals interested in Russia might send messages. Sir G. Buchanan would probably know who is interested.' When this arrived on the 4th, the Russia Department minuted: 'This might be arranged, but it would be necessary to avoid anything from anyone of official standing which might commit us to Chaikovsky.' Sir George Clerk disagreed: 'I do not think there would be any harm in a private message of sympathy from the Secretary of State', he minuted the same day. 'It could be on general lines, without committing us to M. Chaikovsky's govt.' 'Very well', wrote Lord Robert Cecil underneath, which Lord Hardinge initialled. On September 7, Balfour accordingly sent a wire to Lindley: 'I am consulting Sir G. Buchanan as to messages, but meanwhile you may express to M. Chaikovsky my personal hope that the attempt to restore and revive Russia, in which he is taking so prominent and honourable part, may be crowned with complete success.'

But this came too late. On the evening of September 5, General Poole warned Chaplin that the Allied envoys had recommended the immediate recognition of the Archangel government. Chaplin now decided to overthrow it in favour of a strong military regime under General Gurko, which would command the respect of the Allies at Archangel.

How did the Foreign Office decision to send Chaikovsky a private message from Balfour come to General Poole's knowledge, and who changed it to 'recognition'? The information undoubtedly came from Lindley, who merely recommended a 'private message of sympathy' to Chaikovsky from some private individuals in London. It was the Foreign Office decision (that cannot have reached Poole) that Balfour himself should send such a private message. General Poole is undoubtedly the culprit who deliberately misinformed Chaplin.[6]

On the morning of September 6, Chaplin published a proclamation to the people of Archangel: 'Citizens! The country has reached the limit of its suffering. ... Only a strong and well-organized military force can give us freedom from German oppression and hope of a brighter future for Russia. ... While warmly welcoming our Allies and highly valuing the aid which they are now giving us in our fight for the existence of our country, we should all remember that shame and disgrace are ahead of us if the whole burden of the struggle falls on the shoulders of the Allies. We must build the welfare of our country with our own Russian hands, and buy our resurrection with our own blood.' From the Volga to the Baikal, 'a mighty wave of reconstruction' was rising. Russia's 'political organism' and a Russian people's army were in process of formation there. 'From the North let us go to meet Russia's faithful sons coming from the East.'[7]

The military *coup* aroused widespread local opposition. The cooperative societies and *zemstva* strongly complained. The Archangel workers called a general strike. The Allied ambassadors, led by the American, Francis, had the deposed ministers returned to Archangel on a British warship. By the evening of the 8th, all was nominally as it was before; but Chaikovsky and his SR ministers had suffered a severe loss of face. General Poole then chose this moment to send a strong wire to the War Office that they should give the Czechs sufficient support to push them towards him, instead of retreating eastwards. In contrast, Lindley told the Foreign Office that the Allies at Archangel must now choose: either to cooperate with the Russian authorities, who had popular support; or to enforce Allied military occupation. No longer could they pursue both policies at the same time. Unless given more control over the use of British military forces, he asked to be allowed to resign.[8]

But it was President Wilson whose reactions bore the greatest weight. In a note of September 8 to Secretary Lansing, he first stressed that General Poole's efforts to get the Czechs to push through to Archangel were the most striking illustration of the 'utter disregard', both of this British general, and indeed 'of all the Allied governments', of the policy to which the American government had 'expressly confined' itself. It was also 'out of the question' to send Czech reinforcements from eastern Siberia: the Czechs would only receive American aid if they were brought out eastwards, not westwards. 'Is there no way — no form of expression — by which we can get this comprehended?' he asked Lansing.

The next day, the President instructed Secretary Lansing to inform the British government that unless General Poole changed his whole attitude in dealing with the Archangel government, his recently-arrived American troops would be entirely withdrawn from his command. Lansing took action both through the British chargé d'affaires in Washington, and through the American ambassador in London. The American military representative then successfully induced the permanent military representatives at Versailles to refuse to send out any more troops to northern Russia; and the War Office had to tell Poole it was now impossible to send him the reinforcements they had wanted him to have to break through to the Czechs.[8]

On September 9, the Foreign Office received a wire from Lindley about Chaplin's *coup*. 'Although General Poole certainly did not approve of *coup d'état*, I have no doubt that language of his officers led Captain Chaplin to believe it would be winked at', said Lindley. 'I should mention that I have been assured positively that late Emperor's brother [the Grand Duke Michael Alexandrovitch] is hiding in this neighbourhood, and that *coup d'état* is not unconnected with his presence. Our military authorities declare they know nothing of this, but I am not satisfied that story is untrue, and it is widely believed in the town.' (This would have given the monarchist General Gurko the necessary royal 'cover'.) In a summary of recent events for the Foreign Office, Lindley wired again a few days later recalling that Chaplin 'meditated a *coup d'état* as long ago as August 11'. Balfour closed the whole episode, so he thought, on September 18. 'The incident may be allowed to sleep', he minuted.

The Americans, however, had not forgotten the incident. On the 26th, Secretary Lansing informed his ambassadors in London, Paris, Rome and Tokyo that as it was plain to the American government that in northern Russia, 'no gathering of any effective force by the Russians is to be hoped for', the Allied governments would be advised, 'so far as our cooperation is concerned' (and the American contingent there was large) to abandon all military effort in northern Russia, save for guarding Archangel and Murmansk themselves, and the surrounding areas. 'No more American troops will be sent to the northern ports.'[9]

On October 1, Major-General Edmund Ironside arrived at Archangel as the new Chief of Staff, to be 'laughingly told' by Poole that he could not think why the War Office had sent him out; all was in 'good order', his force would soon be 'considerably strengthened', whereupon they would march with all the White Russian armies on Petrograd and Moscow, and put the Bolsheviks down. Now Ironside (a future CIGS) was not only an able military leader of the line, and an experienced staff officer, but an expert linguist (including Russian and French).[10]

Ironside observed that Poole had no local general staff, there was no accurate map kept, and orders and instructions had mainly been issued by word of mouth. Just south of Archangel, Brigadier Finlayson (Poole's present chief of staff) was trying to control all Allied troops (both those 120 miles up the Dvina river, and those 100 miles down the Vologda railway), who were trying to raise Russian recruits. Finlayson said that the local people had no desire to oust the Bolsheviks; and his men were going no further. Both decided to urge Poole to separate the two fronts, and give command of the Dvina front, the more important, to Finlayson. Poole agreed. A French officer took over on the Vologda railway. Finlayson then hurried down the Dvina, where there was trouble: since the British gunboats had suddenly been withdrawn, the Bolshevik gunboats had begun a heavy bombardment of Allied positions. During a heated argument with Poole, the naval officer in charge claimed that he was entitled to withdraw his boats after October 1, and that Poole knew this. There was clearly little liaison between Poole and his outlying commanders. However, he was still intent on advancing; and he demanded that 5,000 further reinforcements, on their way to Murmansk, be sent to Archangel instead. Maynard complained that this would prevent him even keeping open the overland route to Archangel, via Soroka and Onega.

On the 7th, having sent some of his more militant SR colleagues off south to Samara, Chaikovsky finally reformed the Archangel government with various bourgeois ministers, to please the Allies. A Russian governor-general remained in charge of military and internal affairs, and he appointed a deputy at Murmansk, who was to be in charge of all administration. The Murmansk soviet was dissolved. After these changes, Lindley warned Poole that unless 'our adventure here' was to begin and end with the occupation of Archangel, the local Russian people must have their own government, which 'must appear to have real authority'. Poole was not to interfere.[10]

The War Office then decided on future policy. In a wire of the 10th to both Maynard and Poole, it was stated that as there was now no likelihood of a German attack through the Arctic wastes, Maynard was thought to have more than enough troops to defend Murmansk and Petchenga. His force could therefore either all be withdrawn to defend the two ports, or be deployed down the Murmansk railway (which the War Office favoured) to keep open winter communications with Archangel, via Soroka and Onega, and to maintain advanced bases against the Bolsheviks. Maynard was to retain all his present force. But when he then sent the Liverpool battalion down by sea to Soroka, Poole simply 'collared' the battalion when the ship put in at Archangel. Poole then wired the War Office on the 13th with a plan for a further offensive down the Vologda railway to raise more recruits in this thickly populated area, and he asked for the reinforcements which he still imagined were on their way to Maynard; the mere presence of British troops in these areas would produce a 'revulsion of feeling' against the Bolsheviks. The very next day, Poole somewhat mysteriously left Archangel 'on leave' — to talk over northern Russian matters with the War Office. In fact, Poole had been recalled. Ironside took over. On the 16th, the War Office entirely rejected Poole's plan.[11]

Affairs at Archangel were much worse than Poole had let on. When Ironside called on the Russian commander and his chief of staff, he found them both 'very nervous and jumpy' and terrified of their men. The French battalion, he found, had been 'seriously affected' by the approaching armistice on the western front. So had the Americans, who told Ironside that they would not then take the offensive. Ironside wired this news to the War Office straightaway.[12] The CIGS brought Ironside's wire before the War Cabinet on the 18th. This news, he stated, raised the 'whole question' of future British military policy in Russia, if there was to be an armistice with Germany. Balfour agreed that if there was an armistice, 'we were faced with a serious state of things in Russia.' The 'main justification' of British intervention had been to prevent German absorption of Russia. Only recently, the Supreme War Council had forbidden any more troops to be sent to northern Russia, while President Wilson had always taken a 'very strong line' on Russia generally.[13]

Austen Chamberlain said it was most urgent, in view of the American attitude, to have a military and diplomatic discussion with France on future Russian policy if there was an armistice. If the French battalion at Archangel would not fight after an armistice, the French government must be asked to agree to a joint decision on future policy. The War Cabinet decided that the Foreign Office should send wire to Lord Derby (the British ambassador in Paris) asking him to draw Clemenceau's attention to the attitude of the French battalion at Archangel, and to request him to take steps to deal with the matter.[13]

There was also trouble with the Russian and British troops at Archangel. Since the countryside was now impassable with choking mud, the local British commander on the Dvina front, who was considering making an attack, could not contact Finlayson. But, hearing that the Bolshevik troops might desert, he decided to attack near Kuliga village on the 27th. However, on the first sight of the enemy, the White Russians bolted 'and the two platoons of Royal Scots on their right also bolted as soon as their platoon officers were knocked out'. Only some Polish troops 'behaved themselves'. Allied troops, who had lost 77 men, and a large amount of arms and equipment, retreated briskly.[14]

Finlayson arrived to sort matters out. The decision to attack, he reported to Ironside, was 'justified and well-conceived', but the 'execution was disastrous'. He strongly suspected that the attack had been given away in advance, which was 'one of the great difficulties in this country', he complained, 'where every civilian may be a Bolshevik in disguise for all we know'. But it was his report on the British troops which alarmed Ironside. 'I questioned several [of the Royal Scots Fusiliers] as to why they lost their arms and equipment, and the answer generally received was: "They prevented me from running fast enough".' Two days later, Ironside experienced 'our first Russian mutiny', when Russian troops refused to turn out for his inspection (at which the Russian officers at once left the barracks).

Ironside therefore summed up the general situation in very clear terms. Since his arrival, he reported to the War Office, he had been particularly struck by the 'poor quality' of both the Allied commanders and troops sent out to northern Russia. 'The adventure was apparently a gamble', he stated, 'and it was thought that the arrival of the Allies in this country would create a sort of revulsion of feeling ...'. Thus the recent disaster on the Dvina front 'cannot but have the worst effect upon the people of this country who look to us as war-like people who have come to assist them'. He proceeded to give his opinion of the various Allied detachments. Since the Royal Scots Fusilier officers were 'not trained in any kind of warfare', the regiment was 'certainly not fit to carry out active operations'. Many soldiers of the American 339th Infantry regiment, which was 'apparently chosen because it had a very large number of Poles and Russians ... the very worst class of material to send out to Russia', were 'imbued with the spirit of Bolshevism', while Bolshevik agents in northern Russia were able to spread Bolshevik propaganda in the regiment as a whole 'by medium of the Russian-speaking American soldiers'. The American officers were 'one and all, of the lowest value imaginable', and he had never seen an American regiment as bad as this in France. Their Colonel Stewart, 'not a man of much energy', had secret orders limiting any orders he was given in the field; and this was the 'common property of the troops themselves, and both officers and men have freely discussed this matter'. On one occasion, Ironside continued, American troops had 'behaved exceedingly badly', and he did not think that this regiment was 'fit to carry out active operations'. The French 21st Colonial Infantry Regiment had efficient officers, and had 'fought exceedingly well', but their colonel was 'weak and useless', and 'on two separate occasions, the battalion refused to undertake operations ordered'. After an armistice in Europe, Ironside was absolutely certain that American and French troops would carry out no more offensive action. Thus, he concluded, until some good officers were sent out, it would be 'quite impossible to carry out any further military operations'.

This sombre report caused some disquiet when it reached the War Office. 'We had the very greatest difficulty in raising the Royal Scots Bn', commented the general staff. The Deputy CIGS was also disturbed; the report was 'not very pleasant reading', and contained 'many lessons to avoid in future'.[14]

Lindley confirmed much of Ironside's report in a private letter to Balfour shortly after. 'The local situation is quite quiet', he wrote, 'but I confess that the spirit amongst the American and French troops is rather disquieting. The former loot our stores to a degree which far surpasses the pilfering which seems inevitable among soldiers and sailors. They come with motor lorries and remove loads at a time, in spite of the protests of the sentries. Their officers are unable or unwilling to stop this practice and I have protested time and again to the chargé d'affaires in vain. Then the Americans have fought badly and cannot be relied upon at a pinch. ... The French are the sweepings of the Lyons depot, well-known throughout France as the most insubordinate and troublesome. ... A company refused to leave for the front the other day. ... The French ambassador has visited them all, and given them a good talking to. ... As regards our own men ... the battalion of Royal Scots up the river are "B2" or something of the kind. Anyhow their physique is most defective and quite unsuited to bear the hardships they have been undergoing and will continue to undergo this winter. ... It results from all this that our position will not be secure until the troops here, more especially the Americans and French, are volunteers. With our present forces, we are exposed to very unpleasant developments any day.'[15]

Before describing the rapidly developing situation in Siberia, it is right at this point to consider the general views on Russia of an important section of the War Cabinet in early September.

Lord Robert Cecil, and certain others in the War Cabinet, were evidently as dissatisfied with the failure of Reilly's *coup* in Petrograd and

Moscow as with the failure of Chaplin's efforts on behalf of General Gurko at Archangel. It would be necessary to lead the Russians more gradually towards the desired policy. In early September, Cecil circulated to the Cabinet a short paper by Poliakov (who had managed to escape to London) on the case for moderate republicanism in Russia. To his colleagues, Cecil added a few words of his own. 'Personally, I doubt the possibility of establishing a democratic republic in Russia at present. But I agree that any identification of Allied intervention with monarchical restoration would be disastrous. That is a strong reason why the policy of President Wilson is regrettable. By disinteresting himself in intervention, he necessarily leaves the direction of the movement more and more to the Japanese, and the Japanese, like the Germans, cannot afford to be anything but monarchical.'[16]

Cecil went on: 'To re-establish order in Russia will be a herculean task. No half-baked constitutionalism could possibly succeed in it. The only possible way out seems to be a provisional military government to be followed when order has really been re-established by a constitutional assembly. Whether the military dictatorship, once in power, will be content to abdicate seems very doubtful — indeed, one may say it certainly will not unless under the influence of the Western democracies. We should therefore aim at securing military chiefs whom we can trust, supporting them financially as well as by armed force and making ourselves indispensable to them — Alexeiev and Denikin seem the best combination available for the purpose. It should be remembered that a permanent military despotism in Russia would be a very serious menace to the peace of the world', he warned in conclusion.

In this paper, Cecil had mentioned military chiefs in southern Russia. It must therefore have been with real interest that he read a wire from General Knox in Vladivostok, received in early September, that he had found a similar candidate for Siberia. 'There is no doubt', wired Knox, 'that he is the best Russian for our purpose in the Far East.' The man in question was Admiral Alexander Kolchak, late Commander of the Black Sea Fleet. When the revolution broke out, Kolchak acted with commendable firmness for as long as possible. In the summer of 1917, the provisional government sent him to the United States to attend a conference on mine-laying. Passing through London in August, he informed the First Sea Lord that in the Baltic Fleet (in which the Admiralty were much more interested) discipline was non-existent in the battleships, but conditions were more satisfactory in the destroyers and submarines. This turned out to be quite correct.[17]

On return from America, he was in Tokyo in December 1917, when he heard that Russia was likely to leave the war. He informed the British ambassador that he wished to place his services 'unconditionally and in whatever capacity' at the British government's disposal, and would even fight on land on the western front, 'and as a private soldier if so required'. The War Cabinet were informed on December 26 that the Admiralty had replied to him 'that if he and his officers could bring crews with them to this country, we would place vessels at their disposal which they could man'.

But the vessels were on the Caspian Sea. On January 9, 1918, the DMI had asked General Dunsterville, then about to set out from Baghdad across Persia to the Caucasus, if he would like Kolchak attached to his mission; he was 'highly recommended', and might be 'extremely useful' in reorganizing the Russian steamers on the Caspian. (Kolchak would have been furious if he had ever found out about this, as such duties would have been far beneath the dignity of a former commander of the Black Sea Fleet, and this was partly why he had not expressed a wish to serve in the Royal Navy). But Dunsterville was delayed in Persia.

When Kolchak arrived in Singapore on March 11, he found a wire from London asking him to return to Manchuria to join the board of the Chinese eastern railway. This was not at all what he wanted to do either; he was 'very undecided', but after an exchange of wires with the War Office, he sailed for Peking, where he was asked to control the allocation of funds to the various little Russian forces in Siberia: this would entail agreement with Ataman Semenov, who, he was told, would be greatly reinforced. After consultation with the directors of the Russo-Asiatic Bank (who controlled the Chinese eastern railway which Semenov occupied), and with the 'concurrence' of the British government, Kolchak agreed.[17]

But in early May, when he asked the Japanese for arms, he was rebuffed. He was also rebuffed by Semenov, who refused even to inform him of his plans. After struggling on for another two months, Kolchak had then retired, apparently defeated, to Japan. There, in mid-August, this capable and efficient man, neurotic, though curiously un-Russian in many ways, had met General Knox. Now, he had presented Knox with a detailed memorandum on the reorganization of a Russian army. Both agreed that this could only be undertaken with British supervisers, instructors, and material and supplies — and that they would have to start from scratch; the existing officers and N.C.O.s would all first have to be retrained.

On the last day of August, the Czech forces at Lake Baikal, unaided by any Allied troops, finally overcame local Bolshevik resistance; and the central and eastern bodies of the Czech Legion re-met near Chita. The Czech Legion was once again reunited.

It was at this moment, with the Czechs freed and in complete control of the Siberian railway from one end to another, and with Knox and Kolchak actively planning the restoration of a Russian army, that the American commander in Siberia, Major-General William S. Graves, stepped ashore at Vladivostok. It was not the case that his orders were now somewhat outdated. As military orders, they had always been completely meaningless. A former Secretary to the American General Staff, he had become a divisional commander at Palo Alto, California, in July 1918. On August 2, he had received a wire to proceed to the Baltimore Hotel at Kansas City to meet the Secretary of War, who, in somewhat hurried manner, had told him of his new posting, thrust a copy of the President's *aide-mémoire* of July 17 into his hands and said: 'This contains the policy of the United States in Russia which you are to follow. Watch your step; you will be walking on eggs loaded with dynamite. God bless you and goodbye.' Some 60 years of hindsight makes it evident that the Secretary of War's haste was due to considerable embarrassment at having to hand over such meaningless orders to a military commander. And Graves, on arrival at Vladivostok, was completely baffled; and his bafflement quickly gave way to resentment at his Allied colleagues, who had detailed orders; and then to total paranoia, that he was being persecuted on all sides. Such was the result of the injection of American military power into Siberia.[18]

On paper, everything looked good for the Czechs. On September 2, three young Czech officers were promoted for their part in the revolt, and to encourage them to face the Bolshevik counter-attack that was surely coming. Lt. Syrovy (33) was promoted general and Commander-in-Chief of all Czech and Russian forces on the Volga. Gajda (26) became general in charge of the First Division; Čeček (32) became general and took over the Second Division. There was then a slight difference of opinion between the British and French on where the Czechs on the Volga should now go. On the 4th, Clemenceau's amended orders for the Czechs (the French had just appointed their Ambassador Regnault in Tokyo as French high commissioner for Siberia) were sent along to Lloyd George. These were much the same as the orders for Janin. But on September 5, the Russia Committee in London strongly disapproved of the Czechs moving towards Tsaritsin and the Donetz basin, rather than northward to Vologda (as allowed in the French orders). It was agreed that the War Office should wire to Knox that this was not in accord with the British view; the Czechs should exert every effort towards 'establishing connection with General Poole's forces'. Thus did Cecil make his view prevail in the Russia Committee.[19]

But this was slightly academic. Across the Volga, came taunts and threats from Trotsky, who was almost ready to counter-attack, and retake Kazan. From Moscow, came dire warnings from Lenin, unused to military delays. If they now had more troops on the Volga front, he wired Trotsky on August 30, then 'special measures' must be taken against the senior commanders. 'Should you not announce to them that from now on we shall adopt the example of the French Revolution and commit for trial and even sentence to be shot *both Vatsetis and the Army Commander at Kazan and* the senior commanders in the event of the operations meeting with delay or failure?' (Since both Vatsetis and the local Commander might easily become aware of the contents of this telegram, Trotsky rather naturally drew a large red pencil line through the phrase given in parentheses).[20]

From London came expressions of unease and concern at what was happening in Siberia; the supposed success of Allied intervention was only producing more disputes between the White Russians themselves. Unless they could unite, Balfour warned Eliot, they would inevitably go down to disaster. At the same time, the British government disliked interfering in Russian internal politics, and trusted that the Russians themselves could set up a reliable administration, which would prevent the Allies having to impose one section of Russian political opinion on the others, or establish their own military occupation. Such were the British government's hopes. But it might well be, stated Balfour, now openly echoing Cecil, that the rival Russian factions could only be held together by a provisional military government. This would have to be presided over by a Russian who had won his position by the strength of his own personality; and whose strength lay on Russian, not Allied support, though the Allies would of course help him. But there seemed no such outstanding Russian in view. The 'nearest approach' seemed to be General Alexeiev, far away in the Kuban. Eliot was not to suggest Alexeiev, but should support him if there were any indications that a movement, under his leadership, seemed promising.[21]

Next day (September 10), there were indications that the policy advocated by Lord Robert Cecil was moving slowly forward. The DMI read to the War Cabinet two telegrams from Vladivostok, stating that General Dietrichs had resigned as Czech commander in the Far East on a voluntary basis, as he now felt it to be his duty to reconstruct a Russian military force in conjunction with the Allies. The telegrams stated that General Gajda had between 4,000 and 5,000 Czechs in the Oliviania district (on the north-western end of the Chinese eastern railway, just south of the junction Karymskaya). There were also units of the Siberian army. At present, however, it was impossible even to make a rough estimate of the troops available for the Siberian government. There were enough officers for five corps, of which three had been already formed; at Omsk, Tomsk, and Irkutsk. The two others were to be the Amur and the Ural. In the former three districts, the classes of 1919 and 1920 had been called up. General Semenov had been appointed Chief of the Amur district, and would try to raise one cavalry and one or two infantry divisions. But the telegram stated that Dietrichs was 'somewhat doubtful' of the new Russian formations.[22]

He thought all the 12,000 Czechs previously in Vladivostok, and all Allied troops, should be sent at once to the Volga. Enemy strength there was reported to be 80,000. They were opposed by the First Czech Division, and a Czech formation recently sent west, about 40,000 men in all. There was also a Russian national army, of some 60,000 men, largely composed of peasants.

Balfour's advice was a little premature. The day before he sent a wire to Eliot about keeping a look out for a likely Russian dictator, a Russian state conference had opened at Ufa (on the Samara–Chelyabinsk line) for the purpose of setting up an all-Russian government. There were between 150 and 170 delegates, from as far afield as Estonia and Turkestan, representing every shade of anti-Bolshevik feeling; and some, perhaps many, thought it would produce as little as such gatherings had in the past. The strongest group, of 73 members, was the committee of SR members of the constituent assembly, from the Samara government. As before, their main opponents were the Siberian government from Omsk. At the opening session, the SR chairman introduced a motion of greetings to the 'valiant and loyal' Allies, and a 'fraternal welcome' to the 'brave' Czech troops, who had come to their aid.[23]

As the opening speeches were being made, Trotsky struck across the Volga, and took Kazan. 'September 10 is a red-letter day in the history of the socialist revolution', he proclaimed. 'It is a turning-point. The advance of the enemy has at last been stopped; his spirit is broken.' Next day, he wired triumphantly to Lenin that now that the Red Army was properly organized, the fate of Simbirsk, Ekaterinburg and Samara were also sealed. Trotsky was proved right. 'I complement you on the taking of Simbirsk', Lenin wired back on the 12th. They must now make every effort to clean up Siberia. 'Do not be niggardly with monetary awards.'[24]

That day (the 12th), the Czech representative at Ufa replied to the motion of welcome with a strong warning: 'We Czechoslovaks extend to you our heartfelt wishes for success ... and trust that at this state conference you will be able to form an all-Russian government, which can actually depend on all strata of the Russian people. ... We entertain this hope especially in view ... of the gravity of the moment, which follows upon two warnings that have been given us. The first was the collapse of the front north of Ufa, a break which thus far has not been liquidated; the second was the fall of Kazan. Gentlemen, we must all unite so that we shall not need to fear a third warning.' This was greeted with applause.

After hearing speeches from other delegates, delegates from the Siberian government urged that the all-Russian government should be organized as a directorate of no more than five persons, to be selected by the state conference. Its aim should be to restore Russia, and resume the war against Germany and Austria in cooperation with the Allies and the Czechs. The state conference then passed a resolution, welcoming the landing on Russian soil of troops from England, America, France and Japan, who had come to restore the eastern front against the German invader.[25]

It is doubtful whether news of these resolutions ever percolated through to any of the Allies. But on the 16th General Knox sent one of his most powerful warnings to London. There was no doubt, he wired from Vladivostok, that the Czechs on the Volga were 'at their last gasp'. Only the Americans and Japanese had the means to save them. Unless they acted at once, there would be no further chance of restoring the eastern front in European Russia, and the opportunity finally offered by the opening of the Siberian railway would be wasted.[26]

On the 17th, the CIGS brought several of Knox's telegrams before the War Cabinet (not all of which had previously been circulated) about the 'differences of opinion' which had arisen about who was to be responsible for the formation and control of the new Russian Army in Siberia. The CIGS said that 'amongst our Allies, there seemed to be a general disinclination to entrust this task to a British officer'. The Americans and French wanted a Frenchman chosen. At this, Balfour commented that 'our relations with the United States at the moment were not of the best. The Americans had got it into their heads that we wished to push them into a policy that they did not like, and the unfortunate mistake recently committed by General Poole at Archangel had rather confirmed them in this impression.'

The CIGS said the immediate question on which he wished a Cabinet decision was whether Knox should be allowed to go ahead and raise 3,000 men, with the help of General Dietrichs. Knox also reported that there was a certain amount of confusion, since no one had been appointed to coordinate the efforts of raising a Russian Army. Knox himself was quite willing to waive his claim, as long as someone was appointed; but he stressed that some steps must be taken at once. It was suggested in the Cabinet that Knox should be authorized to go ahead and raise these 3,000 men, and the question of the ultimate command could be settled by the Supreme War Council. But it was pointed out that as the whole expedition was under a Japanese commander-in-chief, they should be consulted on who was to raise these Russian levies; but they had no representative at Versailles. There was no other body, though, which could settle a matter of this nature.

The War Cabinet decided that Balfour should consult with the CIGS, and draft a wire to Knox, authorizing him to raise the 3,000 Russians, but stating that the ultimate control of collecting Russian troops for the Siberian army would be settled by the Supreme War Council. 'The telegram should also warn General Knox to be careful in his relations with the French and American representatives in Siberia on this subject.' The Cabinet also considered it advisable that the French should be informed of the steps it was proposed to take; and Balfour and the CIGS should jointly consider how this information should be passed to them.[27]

Balfour raised the whole subject again with the War Cabinet on the 20th. British relations with the American government over raising Russian levies in Siberia were 'far from satisfactory', he complained. In fact, the lack of Allied cohesion over executive action in Siberia was of 'great anxiety' to him. He constantly received wires from Knox urging that certain action was absolutely necessary. He could not help Knox in any way, because the Allies jointly had to agree to any of Knox's proposals, before action could be taken. Balfour said that if he wired to Washington, supporting a proposal by Knox, this would have the very reverse effect. Balfour called the position one of 'extreme gravity', which was 'liable to paralyse him diplomatically'. Matters could only get worse if five different Allies had to be consulted every time some action had to be taken in Siberia. As well, Balfour had to cope with the American assumption that we were trying 'to push them into an enterprise of which they were suspicious'.[28]

To coordinate Allied action, Balfour thought something similar to the Supreme War Council was required to sit at Washington, though differently constituted. One reason for such a suggestion was that, whenever President Wilson sent someone over to represent him on an important international matter, the President at once thought his emissary 'had been "got at" by the Ally concerned', if he took a view suppporting that Ally, and not the President. Only the suggested council could remedy this. Balfour did not think such a council at Washington should be constituted like the Supreme War Council, which was a permanent military body, occasionally supplemented by a big political body, like Prime Ministers. The council at Washington should be a politico-military body, able to take decisions and give orders. Each member should have the right of appeal to his government, and we should be in constant touch with our representative; but the council should be able to act collectively and quickly. Balfour suggested it meet at Washington, but as there was a Japanese commander-in-chief and troops, the Japanese might press for Tokyo, as it was nearer the scene of operations. Washington, however, was more central and accessible for the Allies. During the discussion, Vladivostok was discussed as a meeting place; it was generally agreed that this, if possible, would be the best choice. Balfour undertook to draft a suitable telegram on this subject for circulation to the War Cabinet for their consideration.

Bonar Law then raised the matter of the previous Cabinet decision about Knox's request to raise 3,000 Russians, with the help of Dietrichs. Afterwards, he understood, Balfour and the CIGS had met, and did not entirely agree with the decision as recorded. The CIGS explained that, when he saw Balfour that afternoon, they had drafted a wire which had been sent to Knox. This wire did not give permission to Knox to raise the 3,000 men, but told him to give all possible help with our supplies and material to do so. Balfour explained that he was 'rather nervous' of giving Knox the necessary permission without first consulting France and America. The CIGS intimated that if it would help Balfour in negotiating with the French, the War Office would be willing to withdraw any claim for Knox to have ultimate control over the forces raised. Rather than quarrel with the French, the CIGS was quite prepared for Knox to serve under General Paris (head of the French military missions in Siberia).

The War Cabinet decided that before authorizing General Knox to raise 3,000 Russians, Balfour should wire to the French and American governments, informing them of the steps we proposed to take; and adding that, in view of the extreme urgency of the matter, if they had any objections, we should be glad to know of them speedily. It was further decided that this decision should govern the previous Cabinet decision on the matter.[28]

Meanwhile, there were developments at the Russian state conference at Ufa. On his arrival at Ufa, the French Colonel Paris was alarmed at the activities of Major Guinet, who had for too long been considering himself the chief French officer with the Legion; he had over-immersed himself in Russian internal politics, and had been promising the Russians and Czechs literally anything on behalf of the Allies. Guinet was strongly reprimanded, made supply officer, and forbidden to meddle in politics.[29] Then, on September 21, the Siberian government, aware that the state conference was rapidly coming to a close, and that the Samara SRs had an overall majority, decided to reduce that majority by arresting the SR members of the Siberian Regional Duma, and dissolved the Duma itself (from which incidentally the authority of the Siberian government sprang), demanding the resignation of all SRs in the government itself. The SRs appealed to the Czechs, and for a time the situation looked ugly. But the outcome was drastic removal of support for the Samara SRs.[30]

On September 23, the Ufa conference finally nominated a five-man directorate to act as an all-Russian provisional government until the constituent assembly could meet. The five men were: N. D. Avxentiev and V. M. Zenzinov (right SRs from Samara), General Boldyrev (a competent military officer), V. A. Vinogradov (a Cadet), and P. V. Vologodsky (Prime Minister of the Omsk government and a Cadet). It was agreed to continue the war against the Germans. In view of the well-known ability of the anti-Bolsheviks to engage in endless discussion without ever reaching agreement, this was a remarkable result. Little notice was taken of it in London. This was so marked that a few days later, at a Russia Committee meeting, Gregory (head of the Russia Department at the Foreign Office) said that the Allies were asking what attitude the British government intended to adopt towards the Ufa conference; the Italian government thought the moment had come for giving it support. Nabokov (chargé d'affaires at the old Russian embassy) had written on the same lines. But the chairman, Lord

Robert Cecil, stated flatly that, in the absence of much fuller information 'it was out of the question to take such action'. It was decided to reply to any enquiries that were made that the British government were considering the matter, and hoped to receive full information about the Ufa conference from Sir Charles Eliot. Meanwhile, the British government did not consider that the moment had arrived 'for supporting or formally recognizing' the Ufa conference. And it was clear that Cecil would see that it received no support until a real leader had emerged.[31]

On September 25, the War Cabinet considered Balfour's draft wire to Washington about the control of Allied forces in Siberia. Lord Reading (then in London) said he had already discussed the advisability of sending such a telegram with Balfour, to whom he had put one or two objections. Reading then outlined these objections, which were 'of a highly confidential character', to the Cabinet. Balfour emphasized that his wire did not touch the 'big question' of Allied policy in Siberia, but simply emphasized that, whatever the Allies proposed to do there, could not be done with the present machinery. Even if President Wilson had a 'very limited' policy in Siberia, some Allied organization was necessary, which could settle questions and issue orders speedily — and without constant reference to the Allied governments concerned. Balfour understood that the President would like to have some international organization, based at Washington. 'At the present moment, the United States were represented on several international organizations, which were either in this country or in France, and the President felt that he had little or no control over his representatives.' Balfour therefore thought it might be a sound diplomatic move if the suggested 'Allied Siberian Council' should be based at Washington. This would enlist the President's interest, and even to some extent involve his honour, if decisions were taken at Washington. Lord Reading added that he appreciated these points; it would be a great advantage, and please the Americans, if the council sat at Washington.[32]

Lord Curzon stressed that the Siberian situation was serious. Unless some sort of machinery was set up to deal promptly with the problems that arose in Siberia, 'there was a danger of the whole movement petering out'. Although Vladivostok was undoubtedly the best place for the proposed Council, we ought to make a *beau geste* and suggest Washington. But the proposal should be entirely separate from policy, and put forward simply as a useful piece of Allied machinery. Austen Chamberlain suggested first putting the proposal for the council to be at Washington to President Wilson only; and say that, if he approved, the other Allies could then be consulted, either on his or our initiative, whichever he preferred. Admiral Hope, on behalf of the First Lord, said that the present naval liaison at Versailles was working very well; and if the proposed council materialized, the Admiralty would like a similar liaison at Washington. The War Cabinet decided that Balfour, together with Reading, should redraft the opening of the proposed telegram, to meet Reading's objections, underlining that the proposal was merely one of machinery, and entirely independent of policy to be adopted. Subject to the Prime Minister's approval, Balfour should then send the telegram to President Wilson alone, in the first instance.

Having dealt exhaustively with machinery for control of events in Siberia, the War Cabinet then had to turn to a matter of policy in the region. The CIGS now produced a paper about the supply of essential material for the Russian forces in Siberia. Although the French and British governments were still considering who was to be responsible for their organization, immediate action must be taken to provide and despatch clothing and equipment for up to 100,000 men. The QMG said the bulk of what was needed, save for winter overcoats, about which he would have to contact the Canadians, could be ready in about ten days. It would go via Canada and America, and would need little shipping. The Cabinet thereupon approved the despatch to Siberia of clothing and equipment, as Knox had asked, for up to 100,000 men.[32]

But President Wilson rendered these elaborate discussions null and void. On the 26th, Secretary Lansing informed his ambassadors in London, Paris, Rome and Tokyo that in Siberia, the Czechs would receive no more American support unless they retired east of the Urals. As was usual in such communications, the American note then added that such limitations upon American action were not to be taken as criticism of Allied policy. But Secretary Lansing added confidentially to his ambassadors: 'The ideas and purposes of the Allies with respect to military operations in Siberia and on the "Volga front" [sic] are ideas and purposes with which we have no sympathy. We do not believe them to be practical or based upon sound reason or good military judgment.'[33] The President and Lansing were right; but they underestimated the extent to which the British were to refuse to accept defeat in Russia in the months to come, even though their strategy had long since been condemned.

By now, Foch had decided to strike for victory on the western front that autumn, instead of waiting for the campaigning season of 1919, as had all along been imagined by the Allied planners and others. Victory was in the air. On September 26 to 28, Foch's grand assaults fell on the western front, and the German line threatened to crack. Next day, Bulgaria capitulated to the Allied Armies at Salonika. At this news, the German High Command lost its nerve; on the 29th, they took the momentous decision to appeal for an armistice. Ludendorff soon recovered his nerve. But Prince Max was now appointed Chancellor to negotiate a peace move. On October 3, he appealed to President Wilson for an immediate armistice.

In London, the War Cabinet now felt they could disregard Secretary Lansing's uncompromising rejection of all their plans for Russia, delivered through his various ambassadors on September 26. On October 2, the War Cabinet considered a draft despatch by Lord Robert Cecil on Allied policy in Siberia, which it was proposed to send to Washington. Balfour called for the military view: could we do anything in European Russia, if America refused to help 'beyond the point she had indicated'? The DMO explained that the success of the Archangel 'expedition' depended upon the force of Allied intervention from the Far East; and owing to the delay in the despatch of American troops, there was 'little likelihood' of these two forces joining hands before winter.[34] (This was putting it mildly indeed.)

Lord Robert Cecil said that his only doubt was whether, in his despatch, he had stated 'too definitely' that our War Office took the view that we could hold the Volga line. The DMO now hedged; it might now be too late, but he would not say it was 'quite impossible' to hold the Volga line, as the eastern situation changed so much from day to day, and was greatly influenced by events on the western front.

Cecil reminded the Cabinet that President Wilson's position was that he would send supplies to Siberia, but would not guarantee to send them beyond the Urals. Cecil wanted to know whether the War Office thought we could supply the Czechs with everything necessary, relying on Japanese and French support only, 'or were we entirely dependent on the United States?' The DMO declined to answer this question off-hand, but personally doubted if much could be done without American supplies.

Balfour said there was 'always a possibility' that Japan might now say that since the American government had laid down the policy to be followed in Siberia, Japan could not go beyond it. Hence, if the British government proposed to support the Czechs fully, we could only count on the French and Italians. It was then suggested that the only alternative to sending this despatch was for us to continue our policy, without giving any information to President Wilson. Lord Reading (still in London) remarked that he fully agreed with Cecil's draft, and it was exactly the way in which he himself would have approached the President. It would be unwise not to inform the President of the steps we proposed to take. At this, Lord Curzon said he was not afraid of what President Wilson might say in reply to our despatch, but he did fear a 'military disaster' if we could not link up with the Czechs west of the Urals. 'We were undertaking a dangerous and precarious task', he warned. The War Cabinet decided that the draft despatch should be sent to Washington, but it should not emphasize 'too strongly' the point that the War Office thought we could hold the Volga line.

The Cabinet then had to consider a paper by the CIGS with regard to General Knox raising a force of 3,000 Russians, with the help of General

Dietrichs. As the Cabinet had already approved this proposal on September 20, they now requested Balfour to wire to Washington, informing the American government of the steps we had taken, adding that this undertaking was not considered 'inconsistent with American policy'.[34]

It was now, in fact, clear that with victory on the western front in sight, the War Cabinet, at long last, was now prepared virtually to disregard President Wilson's views on the eastern front (correct though they unfortunately were), and adopt an entirely independent policy. But the information on which this policy was based, especially about the Czechs and the Volga front, was sketchy in the extreme, to say the least. Balfour's warning, however, that Japan (seeing that Germany was defeated and America was at the head of the Western Alliance) would swing back into line with the President's original policy for Siberia, was timely. He might have added that Japan would now swing in like measure against British policy, especially a newly independent British policy.

The War Cabinet received a strong warning next day (October 3) when the First Sea Lord reported receipt of a wire from *Suffolk* at Vladivostok, stating that the Czechs there continued to receive 'alarming reports' about the position of their colleagues on the Volga. 'It was stated that they were completely exhausted by incessant fighting, and were doomed unless Allied support was received immediately.' British troops had left the Vladivostok area for the west on September 30, and it was understood that the Americans were now prepared to send troops as far west as Omsk. The total number of American troops which had reached Vladivostok on September 29 was 8,000. The Amur railway (the northern section of the last stretch of the Siberian railway) was now in Allied hands, as the Japanese had linked up with Allied forces (presumably Czech) operating from Chita (the junction of the Amur and the Chinese eastern railways).[35]

But this Allied help was too late. The Volga 'front' was cracking up. The Russian peasant troops of the Samara government were totally untrained, the Czech troops began to see that it was their generals' campaign, not theirs; there were no Germans to fight on the Volga anyhow. A rift set in between Czech officers and soldiers. On October 4, Trotsky seized Syzran, on the Volga bend below Samara. On the 8th (as General Alexeiev died in the Kuban), Trotsky took Samara itself. The Ufa directorate hastily moved to Omsk, taking the state gold reserve, where the two SR members received a chilly reception from the right-wing Omsk government.[36]

Word then reached Vladivostok that the Omsk government had called up no less than 200,000 very raw recruits. Knox was appalled. This number, he was sure, must be substantially reduced, for there were no funds available to pay them, and not enough of the many Russian officers, idling their time away in the old garrison towns, had been pressed back into service to lead them. Otherwise, Knox had visions of a vast armed rabble, the most dangerous situation to contemplate with Bolshevik propaganda rife. As he began his journey up the Siberian railway to Omsk, Admiral Kolchak had just arrived there ahead of him in an attempt to reach southern Russia to join General Alexeiev, whom he regarded as his chief. But on arrival at Omsk, Kolchak was given the news of the death of Alexeiev. He was induced by General Boldyrev to become the directorate's Minister of War. Kolchak, 'the best Russian for our purposes in the Far East', was therefore the man whom Knox was coming to meet, and now holding a crucial position.[37]

At Omsk, Kolchak found all the Russian officers saying that Avksentiev was just another Kerensky; that the directorate was a repetition of Kerensky's regime; that by following the path down which Russia had already once travelled, they would inevitably again lead her to Bolshevism. The Siberian army, in fact, had no confidence in the directorate.

As War Minister, Kolchak had to attend the daily sessions of the Council of Ministers, where he found a 'quite unmistakable atmosphere of disagreement' between the Siberian government and the directorate. The atmosphere was 'extremely tense'. The chief disagreement concerned the appointments to the cabinet of ministers, which was to be formed under the directorate, but was to a very large extent simply the old Siberian ministry. In this 'atmosphere of struggle', Kolchak found it almost impossible to conduct any work whatsoever. The struggle chiefly centered around two persons: Ivan Mikhailov, whose inclusion was insisted upon by the Siberian government; and the SR Rogovsky, whom the directorate advanced. Ivan Adrianovich Mikhailov was a native Siberian, the son of an exiled liberal, who had joined the Siberian government at its formation in February 1918 as a moderate socialist. He was then about 25 years of age. But he soon came to represent the extreme conservative wing; and from then on, the politics of the Siberian government were, generally speaking, in his hands, as he showed himself to be an extremely skillful politician and intriguer. He held the post of minister of finance throughout all the various changes of the Siberian government, 'and is said to have been a prominent participant in most of the important political plots during the time of the Siberian anti-Bolshevik governments,' according to Varneck and Fisher. Mikhailov was especially objectionable to the directorate because of his active part in the suppression of the SR members of the Siberian regional Duma, just before the formation of the directorate at Ufa.[37]

It was Mikhailov's candidacy that gave rise to yet another serious complication — the interference of the Czechs. Both Czech representatives (Kosek and Richter) called on Vologodsky, then on members of the directorate, and on several of the ministers, and declared in the name of the Czech national council that the Czechs did not agree to the candidacy of Mikhailov and several others, and that they insisted that these persons should not be included in the Siberian government. To Kolchak, as an entire newcomer, the candidacy of Mikhailov or anyone else was an entirely open question. Kolchak had not known them before, had never met Mikhailov or the other members of the government; and when this question was raised, he kept silent. But President Vologodsky reported that the Czech representatives had said that if the composition of the new Russian government was not pleasing to the Czech national council, the Czech troops would leave the front.

Before this meeting, Kolchak had conferred with General Boldyrev, who said he found it very difficult to deal with the Czechs, that the Czechs were already abandoning the front, and did not want to fight anymore. Thus the statement of the Czech delegates — that if there was any change in the council of ministers they would leave the front — showed quite clearly that they were being simply duplicitous, and would have left the front in any case. Kolchak saw their threat as an empty one.[37]

Kolchak thereupon spoke in a very deliberate manner to the council of ministers. He did not know either Mikhailov or the other members of the government, but the visit of the Czech delegates that day was an 'imperative indication' that he must support these persons. 'I insist that the government sharply and definitely, once for all, stop the interference of the Czechs in our internal affairs, which are absolutely none of their concern.' This tipped the balance. The council of ministers thereupon made a 'categorical decision' to appoint Mikhailov as Minister of Finance, and then considered the question of Rogovsky. He was an SR, whom the directorate wished to appoint as Minister of Public Order. By now, the directorate had split into two groups — one consisting of Avksentiev and Zenzinov, and the other of Vologodksy and Vinogradov; General Boldyrev stood in the middle. As a military man, and as the commander-in-chief, he did not occupy any definite political position. He tried, as it were, to be a conciliating element between the two contending groups. Rogovsky's appointment was opposed by the Siberian government; so he was appointed Assistant Minister of the Interior, in special charge of militia — his candidacy for this position even being bitterly opposed by Omsk military and conservative circles, who contended that he was creating seditious SR forces under the cloak of his militia.[37]

The Japanese, who had been eager to exploit the rift between London and Washington to get the maximum number of Japanese troops into eastern Siberia, now turned against the British. Japan was now eager to stay in line with America, now that a German defeat seemed imminent, and was especially unwilling to see a pro-British Russian restoration of any sort in Siberia, which she saw as her rightful sphere. In front of the Japanese army in Siberia, Japan wished to have a variety of puppets, whom she could manipulate at her will, according to the fluctuations of the civil war in Russia. To make their point, Japanese troops held up a train with the 25th

Middlesex Regiment on board, *en route* for garrison duty at Omsk; and then tried to arrest Knox himself on board another train. From Irkutsk, Knox sent a wire to the War Office that Semenov was entirely in the pay of the Japanese, who had offered him the command of all the Cossacks east of Lake Baikal. This would act to the serious disadvantage of what Kolchak was trying to do at Omsk, i.e. weld all the various Russian, Siberian and Cossack elements into an effective anti-Bolshevik force. From London, Balfour sent a wire to the British ambassador in Tokyo on the 16th with an urgent appeal for Japanese help for the Czechs. The Japanese reply was uncompromising. As they had stated on June 24, there would be grave military difficulties in any attempt to proceed beyond eastern Siberia. Japan, in fact, had got what she wanted out of the Western Allies, and did not propose to do anything whatever in return.

On October 18, the War Cabinet had a somewhat agitated discussion on Siberia. President Wilson, Balfour reminded his colleagues, had always taken a 'very strong line' on Russia generally. He would have nothing to do with the restoration of the eastern front, and held that Russia must work out her own salvation without interference. He had only agreed to Siberian intervention to enable the Czechs to get out of Russia through Vladivostok. 'If we now withdrew our forces from European and Asiatic Russia, we should suffer a serious loss of prestige, and should be letting down our friends.' The American military representative at Versailles had taken a 'very definite attitude' towards American involvement in Russia, and made it quite clear that America 'would have nothing to do with it'.[8]

Austen Chamberlain said it was most urgent, in view of the American attitude, to have a military and diplomatic discussion with France on our future Russian policy, if there was an armistice. 'The French took the view that their old relations with Russia, and their interests [i.e. investments] in that country gave them special rights and privileges.' General Smuts emphasized that the Allies must be clear about political and military questions in Russia, before an armistice with Germany. 'Bolshevism was a danger to the whole world, and we were already committed at Murmansk, Archangel and in Siberia.'

Lord Robert Cecil said there were 'two big Russian questions', which demanded immediate consideration. First, the Baltic States, created by Germany at Brest-Litovsk; secondly, intervention in Russia. 'He [Cecil] hated the idea of abandoning to Bolshevik fury all those who had helped us, but he quite saw that it might end badly if we tried to destroy Bolshevism by means of military interference.' Japan and France were also concerned; but there was no point in consulting France, 'until the British government had agreed upon its policy'. It was also important to know the present position of General Alexeiev's forces in the Caucasus, as a British Fleet might possibly enter the Black Sea. Bonar Law thought it would assist the Cabinet to come to a conclusion if a joint paper could be drawn up by the Foreign Office, the War Office and the Admiralty on the present position, and our future policy in Russia. Chamberlain trusted that such a paper would contain definite proposals for the Cabinet to accept or reject. The War Cabinet decided that the Foreign Office, the CIGS and the First Sea Lord should prepare a paper on present and future military policy in Russia.[38]

The SR members of the constituent assembly, led by their President Victor Chernov, who had had to leave Samara in a great hurry, wanted to go on to Omsk to back up the two SR members of the Ufa directorate. But as they heard stories of bitter hostility to them there, they went on the 19th to Ekaterinburg, where they were welcomed neither by the Czechs nor by anyone else — the First Czech Division was collapsing, regiment by regiment, into mutiny. On the 24th, as Chernov saw reactionary influence growing, he issued a manifesto in the name of the SR central committee to all SRs stating that 'all party forces must be mobilized immediately, given military training and armed, in order to be able to withstand at any moment the attacks of counter-revolutionists'.

When the Chernov manifesto became known at Omsk, there was real trouble. That day, General Knox agreed with Kolchak (Minister of War) and Boldyrev to provide all that was necessary to form a proper Russian army, provided Russian officers controlled it absolutely, and kept out of politics; and provided the Omsk government could induce Japan to give support to them, and not to the Cossack Atamans like Semenov. Thus the Chernov manifesto — which ran completely counter to this agreement, especially to giving full control to the old-time Russian officers — caused the greatest resentment. Knox strongly urged Boldyrev that the Ufa directorate must come to terms with the Omsk government. From London, Balfour supported this. On the 27th, by which time news of Alexeiev's death had reached London, Balfour sent a wire to Eliot saying that the British government considered that a strong Russian government, with a strong Russian army, must be formed at Omsk.[39]

The possibility of British recognition of the Ufa directorate (known as the all-Russian provisional government) had already generated a good deal of discussion within the Foreign Office. On October 8, Sir Charles Eliot sent a wire, which was received in the Foreign Office on the 13th: 'I had a conversation yesterday with Mr Avxentiev, head of all-Russian Government', he stated. True relations of all-Russian and Siberian governments are not quite clear. ... Mr Avxentiev spoke of Vologodsky in a perfectly friendly way but there are rumours of serious dissensions and there are certainly many difficulties in distributing offices at Omsk. Pavlu [the Czech delegate] told me Czechs have decided to give all-Russian government their whole-hearted support and intimated that they did not like Siberian government. ... Avxentiev spoke apprehensively of Americans because they seemed ready to regard Bolsheviks as a political party worthy of consideration, and not as miscreants who deserve nothing but punishment. Avxentiev is a powerful speaker and cuts a good figure here, because he is a man of European culture, which is rare in Siberia, but I doubt whether he is sufficiently distinguished to be accepted as ultimate head of the Russian state.' The Russia Department commented on the 14th: 'Previous telegrams gave the impression that the all-Russian government had been accepted by nearly all the non-Bolshevik elements on both sides of the Urals. It is clear that personal questions are still playing the principal part in the political situation.'[39]

Professor Simpson (of New College, Edinburgh), who was an authority on Russian affairs, at this point sent the Foreign Office a description of some of the men of the Ufa directorate. Avxentiev had been Minister of Internal Affairs in Kerensky's Government; Vologodsky, premier of the Omsk government, was President of a local Judicial Court in Siberia; Chaikovsky was head of the government at Archangel; while General Boldyrev had been Commander of the Fifth Army Corps under Kerensky, and was a Russian soldier of distinction. Simpson went on to point out that these men were directly representative of those to whom Allied agents, principally the French, had made promises of Allied support in the spring of 1918 in Moscow and Petrograd. 'In a recent conversation with Mr Kerensky, the latter assured [me] that the activities of the 'Union for the Regeneration of Russia' (i.e. the group of parties whom Kerensky was empowered to represent) were carried on on the understanding that assistance, financial and military, was to come from the Allies. Mr Kerensky says that these negotiations took place with Mr Grenard (the French consul in Moscow) in May, because at that time Mr Lockhart was supposed to be sympathetic with the Bolsheviks. General Boldyrev was at the head of the military committee of the union. Mr Kerensky further states that nothing was set down in writing, but that the negotiations were proceeding favourably when he left.'[39]

But Professor Simpson's paper did not make clear the dissensions within the Ufa directorate. 'We were merely representatives and champions of different groups', a member of the directorate wrote later, 'with divergent and hostile political and social ideals — a fact which made it difficult to form a definite and solid majority. ... The most vulnerable spot of the directorate was its detachment from the masses. A child of the intelligentsia, it was absorbed too much in high-sounding principles. ... It remained cut off from the real life of the peasant, the worker, and even the petty artisan; cut off from those problems ... which on the other side of the civil war front were solved so radically.' Thus did the Ufa directorate carry on its uneasy coexistence with the Siberian government at Omsk.

On October 14, the French ambassador in London wrote at some length to Balfour pointing out that Maklakov (the Russian ambassador in Paris) had passed to the French government a telegram from Ufa, in which the leaders of the Ufa directorate made clear their programme for the restoration of a provisional government for the whole of Russia, based on Allied recognition. Pichon considered the programme satisfactory in principle, but pointed out that it was drawn up by theorists, of whose means of taking action little was known, and whose authority as regards the whole of Russian territory was limited. Meanwhile, the Allies had agreed not to intervene in Russian internal politics. It was nevertheless necessary to enter into immediate contact with men of good will who had succeeded in setting up an embryo of central government, and to give them material and moral help. The request for recognition made by the Ufa directorate thus obliged the Allies to make a joint response to President Avxentiev. M. Pichon trusted that the British government would hold the same view, and proposed to send the following reply to Ufa:

The Allied governments have received the telegrams sent by the Ufa directorate to the Russian ambassadors, making known the programme of the Ufa directorate for the restoration of the Russian state. The principles on which the Ufa directorate intends to carry out its policy are the recognition of the Russian alliances and treaties, and cooperation with the Allies against Germany. The Allied governments are glad to salute the dawn of a new age for Russia, thanks to the restoration of a disciplined military force, which has enabled order to be restored. They will gladly keep in touch with the Ufa directorate through agents, who will be instructed to assist in every way with the work of the Ufa directorate, until the time when, by the success of their action, their resolution, and the free consent of the population, they may receive the 'consecration' of official recognition.

The Allies, who ardently desire to help Russia, and to work together with its leaders for the restoration of the state, will give the Ufa directorate all the moral support that it needs, as well as all material assistance in their power.[39]

On October 17, J.D. Gregory (head of the Russia Department) minuted: 'In a memorandum on Russian policy generally, sent in today, I have pleaded for the full recognition of the all-Russian government. The half measures suggested by the French will only disappoint and fail in their object. It is the sort of action which is so often tried and satisfies nobody. We are almost at a crisis as regards Russia. Intervention is, temporarily, at a standstill. The non-Bolshevik Russians are for once showing a certain cohesion. They have set up a government which embraces all parties and conflicting personalities. It seems of the first importance to give them all the external support that is possible. If we do so, and they collapse nevertheless, we have done no harm and we can but try again. We shall have demonstrated our anxiety to do all in our power to help Russia and we shall have gained the good will of all the non-Bolsheviks from one end of the country to the other.' Lord Robert Cecil ticked this. Sir Ronald Graham minuted: 'Sir C. Eliot has reported against the recognition of any Russian government so long as the various governments are, as at present, in disaccord. The whole situation in Russia deserves careful discussion and consideration by the Allies.'

On October 19, the French embassy sent a note, urging approval of their *démarche* of October 14. But on the same day, a wire arrived from Sir Charles Eliot (sent on the 17th): 'I saw Mr Vologodsky this morning at Novonicolaievsk on his way to Omsk from Vladivostok. He admitted there are serious differences of opinion between himself and Mr Avxentiev, that is between Siberian government and all-Russian government, but hoped that mutual concessions would ensure harmony. Until the two governments come to an agreement, it seems to me that there can be no question of recognizing still less of subsidizing either of them. I propose to wait two or three days at Omsk to see if any result comes of their conference, and then to return to Vladivostok. A telegram forwarded to me from Archangel leads me to suppose you can communicate with Mr Chaikovsky and I venture to suggest that he should be asked whether he really supports the all-Russian government of Omsk of which he is stated to be a member.' Sir Ronald Graham minuted underneath. 'Tel[egraphed] accordingly. Sir C. Eliot is certainly right in considering that we cannot recognize or subsidize two rival governments, or at least two which are in disagreement.'

Lindley replied: 'Government of Omsk has Mr Chaikovsky's nominal support but he knows nothing of its doings except what he is told by my colleagues and myself.' This was not very satisfactory. Sir Charles Eliot then wired from Omsk that Avxentiev and Vologodsky wished a message to be sent to Chaikovsky that as they were quite out of touch with Archangel, they had been unable, when the provisional government was formed, 'to have your opinion respecting manner in which the central government will be reconstituted in Russia and respecting its relation to government of Archangel'. They asked Chaikovsky to issue a statement on behalf of the Archangel regional government declaring its readiness to accept the all-Russian government constituted at Ufa. 'Considering your consent certain, I ask you to take necessary steps and to communicate them to our representatives abroad.' This Chaikovsky agreed to do.[39]

On October 22, Gregory minuted again that no decision appeared to have been arrived at on the French ambassador's request; but in view of Sir Charles Eliot's wire received on the 19th, stating that the principal members of the government (Vologodsky, of the Siberian government, and Avxentiev, of the all-Russian government) had already disagreed, 'the suggestion that it should be fully recognized was evidently premature. In these circumstances, we should perhaps adopt the French formula which promises recognition on fulfilment of the necessary conditions.' The same day, Sir George Clerk minuted: 'I am not familiar with what has passed on this question, but on general grounds I should hesitate to recognize, even conditionally, any Russian government without full consultation with Sir C. Eliot. I annex a draft tel[egram].' Sir Ronald Graham added: 'We shall thus ascertain whether Sir C. Eliot has modified his previous position.' The French proposal was therefore sent to Sir C. Eliot, and he was asked for his views.[39]

On October 27, Sir Charles Eliot sent a further wire from Omsk, which reached the Foreign Office on the 29th: 'Negotiations which have taken place between all-Russian and Siberian governments will probably shortly result in the formation of a single government claiming to represent all Russia. The supreme power is invested in a directorate of five persons with five substitutes. ... The five at first acting will be Avxentiev (president), Vologodsky, Boldyrev, Vinogradov and Zenzinov. Many objections have been raised to the last named who is a social revolutionary of the most advanced type, but Avxentiev assures me that he is not an internationalist. He is merely a substitute for Chaikovsky, but it is feared that the latter's age will prevent him from arriving until the railway between Archangel and here is open.' A ministry was being formed, chiefly comprising nominees of the Siberian government, 'which thus gets its reward for abdicating'. They were moderate men, not socialists, and all professed to have no party views. Kolchak would be Minister of War. They wanted to appoint a diplomat as Minister for Foreign Affairs, but had not yet found a suitable man. This ministry was not a Cabinet and had no collective responsibility. The members were responsible individually to the directorate, who would have the right to make all future appointments. 'These arrangements are to be confirmed by a meeting of the constituent assembly, to be held in February, but meanwhile there is serious difficulty and difference of opinion about the Tomsk Duma which commissioned Vologodsky to form Siberian government. It is proposed to summon it shortly for a single sitting at which it is to accept the resignation of the Siberian government and then dissolve itself.'

Both Avxentiev and Vologodsky had made a joint statement about the new government's policy, subject to the assent of the constituent assembly. In internal matters, it would favour 'moderate democracy'. Its precise attitude towards socialism was not clearly defined, but it was opposed to the nationalization of factories and banks. In foreign policy, it was 'wholeheartedly' pro-Ally and anti-German. It accepted all treaties and obligations which had been accepted by the Kerensky government. It agreed to the independence of Poland, but thought that the Ukraine, the Caucasus and Baltic States and Finland should be autonomous, and members of the Russian republic, 'but not independent'. Eliot concluded that he was leaving Omsk that night (the 27th), and hoped to reach Irkutsk on October 30.

The Russia Department minuted here [on the 30th]: 'This seems to be a step towards the formation of a proper government but not a definitive one and until something is settled one way or other we can only "wait and see".'[39]

On October 30th, the day on which the empires of Austria-Hungary and Turkey collapsed, and four days after Ludendorff had resigned, the War Cabinet in London had its usual routine meeting, during which Lord Curzon asked the DMI for information about the various Allied forces in Russia. At Archangel, said the DMI, there had been no link up between Allied forces and the Czechs on the Volga. Allied forces at Archangel would have to remain inactive during the winter due to severe weather conditions. The Czechs had had to give ground on the Volga, 'and were considering a retirement on the Urals, where they would endeavour to hold the passes'. (All news about the Czechs was thus very out of date.) The Czechs were in a 'precarious position', admitted the DMI, as the Allies were not helping them with arms, equipment or food. As the Cabinet were aware, American troops had not been allowed to leave the Vladivostok area, while the Japanese declined to move their forces west of Lake Baikal. The only force that appeared to be trying to help the Czechs was a composite French, British and Italian force, about 2,000 to 3,000 strong, which was not far east of Omsk.

Lord Robert Cecil then raised the question of the training of Russian forces, and the position of General Knox, who had been permitted to train 3,000 Russians on the understanding that he might have to hand over to the French when they arrived at Vladivostok. But the French had now issued orders that no one was to train the Russians but themselves. This would leave General Knox with little to do in Siberia, and it had been suggested that Knox and all British supplies destined for the Russians should be withdrawn. Cecil hesitated to agree with this; the French might raise no objection to our withdrawal, but it would result in a complete breakdown, involving the whole movement for reorganizing the Russian forces. He urged the War Office to send an officer with full information to Lord Milner, who was in Paris, so as to reach a working agreement. The Cabinet approved this measure. But later in the meeting, it was learnt that before the CIGS had left for France, he had studied the whole Siberian position, and would raise it with the French while in Paris. Thus, the Cabinet decided that the DMI should send a reminder to the CIGS, informing him that the Cabinet had discussed the matter that morning, and requesting him not to fail to come to some arrangement with the French government.[40]

On the 31st, the DMI assured the War Cabinet that he had sent the CIGS additional papers on the whole matter by aircraft that morning, and that

Sir Henry Wilson was now in touch with the French. The DMI added that he had a report that the Middlesex Regiment had arrived at Omsk; and that a naval detachment, with guns from *Suffolk*, had reached Ufa, and was now operating with the Czechs.[41]

But this news was already out of date. On October 28, the independence of Czechoslovakia had been proclaimed at Prague. As a result, the Czech command in Siberia had ordered a general retirement of all Czech troops along the whole eastern front. On November 3, some of Cecil's doubts were resolved. Eliot wired that he and Knox agreed it would be disastrous to stop active cooperation with the Omsk government at that moment; the arrangements at Omsk, though hardly perfect, were an honest attempt to restore order that deserved support if the Ufa directorate and Omsk government could be brought together.[42]

On November 4, the Russian chargé d'affaires in London, Constantin Nabokov, passed on the following telegram to Balfour, adding that it had also been sent to Paris, Rome and Washington. 'Owing to the brilliant successes of our Allies on the Western and other fronts, and to the evident collapse of Germany, the opening of peace negotiations in the near future appears to be certain. Russia's participation in the negotiations between the Allies respecting all questions which are of vital interest to Russia must be assured. This participation is only possible after official recognition of the [all-Russian] provisional government by the powers of the *Entente*.'[42]

The Russia Department at the Foreign Office considered this. 'We have not yet heard that the negotiations which are proceeding at Omsk have reached a successful issue', they minuted, 'but no doubt the time is approaching when the question of recognition will have to be decided one way or other.' Someone else added: 'Meanwhile a reply expressing general sympathy and an assurance that these questions are receiving our constant and careful attention.' 'Is Russia a belligerent?' queried Balfour underneath. 'As far as I can see', replied the Russia Department, 'Russia can only be described as a belligerent on the theory that as the government which declared war on Germany was recognized by us, and as we have not recognized any Russian government which has made peace with Germany, Russia must still be recognized as at war with Germany. It is quite possible, however, that it may be a very long time before we recognize any Russian government. If and when we do recognize a Russian government, it is not clear how Germany, which has already in her own estimation made peace with Russia, can be expected to make peace over again with it. It is also quite possible that by the time we recognize a government in Russia, there will be no government in Germany recognized by us for it to make peace with. This appears to be a *reductio ad absurdum* of the theory of Russia's belligerency. The suggestion that because certain German troops are taking part in a civil war in Russia between two authorities, neither of which we recognize (although we are supporting one of them to a certain extent), therefore Russia is at war with Germany, seems untenable. On this theory, Germany must have been at war with Finland at the time of the Finnish civil war, which is absurd.'

The matter was dropped; and a warm, though general, reply was sent to Nabokov. More news reached the Foreign Office about Siberia on November 6. 'No official notification has yet been made about the formation of a provisional Russian government', wired Sir Charles Eliot from Irkutsk on November 1. 'I hope it will be made very soon, but British vice-consul at Omsk telegraphs that crisis is still acute. If communication proposed by French were made now, it would seem like backing one party against the other. French high commissioner agrees with this. Strong point in proposed Russian Government, which is called the directorate, is that Siberian government is prepared to sacrifice its separate existence. This shows there is a serious desire shared I think by all educated classes in Siberia to maintain order and unity and that directorate inspires some confidence. Weak point is that serious divergence of opinion in this directorate menaces its ultimate stability when present crisis is passed. ... There is a considerable monarchical party among officers and educated classes. [?Tsarist national] anthem has several times been played at public gatherings, sometimes with and sometimes without disturbance.'

The Russia Department considered this on the 7th. 'This tel[egram] is not very encouraging on the whole. It is clear we can make no sort of declaration until the gov[ernmen]t is actually formed, and sets its own house in order.'[42] Sir George Clerk added: 'We must now reply to the French note of October 14, explaining the position.'

A note was therefore sent to the French ambassador that the British government agreed in principle with the French government about the Russian provisional government, and concurred in the terms of a proposed French declaration, which might be issued with advantage, 'if and when an united government is definitely established at Omsk', it was underlined. 'In the present conditions, however, until it becomes quite clear that a regular agreement has been reached between the so-called Siberian government and the directorate, and the composition of the government finally settled, they are advised that to make any declaration might be interpreted as an attempt to support one party against another, and they would therefore prefer to postpone the issue of any declaration until the situation becomes somewhat clearer.'

This situation did, however, clear somewhat later on the 7th, when a telegram arrived from the British vice-consul at Omsk, sent on the 2nd: 'An agreement has been arrived at between all-Russian government and Siberian government which I am given to understand was signed last night.' He was further informed that Avksentiev, the SR member of the directorate, would go to Tomsk to attend a meeting of the Siberian Duma, which would then be dissolved. 'As far as I can gather', the vice-consul added, 'the constitution of Cabinet meets with local approval.' 'This is satisfactory', minuted the Russia Department cautiously. 'It is to be hoped that the harmony will be maintained.' All concerned, including Balfour, initialled this.[42]

Next came a telegram from the British ambassador in Tokyo that a prominent Russian had refused the post of Foreign Minister in the new Russian Cabinet, as he was pessimistic about the future, 'and I gather that he has not much confidence in solidarity of new Cabinet'. 'Not very encouraging', minuted the Russia Department on November 10, 'but we have had hints of lack of unanimity in the new directorate already. Nothing will apparently prevent these Russians intriguing against one another in such a way as to destroy all chance of stable and orderly government.' 'They are hopeless', added Sir Ronald Graham — a former secretary at the British embassy in Petrograd.

Then came confirmation of the existence of the new Russian government from Sir Charles Eliot: 'The formation of all-Russian government and ministry at Omsk is [?officially] announced and well received', he wired from Irkutsk on November 6. 'Scheme seems to me a serious attempt to unite Russia. ... French high commissioner is disposed to sympathise but United States officials are critical. ... Nothing is known here about attitude of southern Russia.' This wire reached the Foreign Office just after a further request from the new government, forwarded by Nabokov, for British recognition. The Russia Department now swung round. 'Sir C. Eliot appears to be rather favourably impressed by the provisional government and in any case it is the only organized body in existence in Russia. As we are not yet in a position to show our good will by sending military assistance, would it not be well to lend it the moral support which recognition would entail. The French and US governments have doubtless received identic[al] communications? Consult them as to the answers they propose to return.'[42]

However, no real unity had yet been achieved in Siberia. On November 5, when the Ufa directorate discussed the Chernov manifesto at Omsk (which General Knox left that day), even Boldyrev suggested arresting Chernov and his SR colleagues at Ekaterinburg. But this was turned down. Kolchak stayed at Omsk only a very short time, and about November 7 or 8, left for the front to see the commanders, and to investigate the supply services, and all the needs of the Army. Just before he left, it was agreed that Boldyrev should take strong measures against anyone trying to prevent him from taking over all Russian forces raised at Samara and Ufa.

Kolchak then received an invitation from the Czech Command to come to Ekaterinburg on November 9 or 10, to be present at the ceremony of presenting colours to four Czech regiments. He attended the ceremony, accompanied by Colonel Ward, and a party of the Middlesex Regiment; and at a banquet that evening, met for the first time various Czech officers and Syrovy. Foreign representatives were also present. He also, for a second time, met Gajda, who had very different political views from his brother Czech officers. (Kolchak had previously met Gajda at Vladivostok. Even then Gajda had spoken strongly in favour of military dictatorship. 'Of course, this is a question for the future', he had told Kolchak, 'as at present everything is still in a process of construction and development. But I personally think that it is the only possible way out.')[43] Although Kolchak did not have any talks at the banquet, he visited various military units on November 11, and paid formal calls on Gajda, Syrovy, and others, and encouraged them to fight on. Gajda asked about the political situation at Omsk. Kolchak said it was 'extremely unsatisfactory', since the agreement between the Siberian government and the directorate was a 'mere compromise', from which nothing good could be expected; that future conflicts were 'almost unavoidable', as the directorate had no prestige and influence; that the Siberian government, which had united Siberia, and which had already been in power for six months, was handing that power over with a 'certain reluctance'. Conflicts would undoubtedly arise, but Kolchak could not say exactly what. Gajda replied: 'The only recourse which is still possible is dictatorship'.

Dictatorship, Kolchak retorted, could only be based on an army, and that only a person who had created an army, and could rely on it, could speak of dictatorship. Who then could undertake the task of dictator under existing conditions? Only one of the men on the front, because dictatorship could only survive if backed by an armed force. Gajda said nothing, but remarked that events would lead to it inevitably, because the directorate was undoubtedly an artificial undertaking. 'I know what is going on in Cossack circles. They are advancing their candidates; but I think that the Cossack circles are unable to cope with this task, as they look at this question too narrowly.'[43]

Kolchak travelled to the nearest front, which was not far from Ekaterinburg, and 'gained the impression that the army's attitude toward the directorate was hostile, at least on the part of those commanders with whom I came in contact. All expressed the opinion quite positively that now only military power could mend matters; that the existing combination of five directorate members yielded and would yield nothing but conflict, intrigue and political strife, and that in such a situation it was impossible to conduct a war ...'.

At Ekaterinburg, in fact, an imminent clash was now seen approaching. The SR President Chernov induced his SR colleagues, members of the constituent assembly, to let the reactionaries make the first move; then, with Czech support, they would seize Ekaterinburg and expel the Siberian troops. But, as it was felt that Knox had been influencing the Czechs against the SRs, it was decided to hold a large meeting on November 23, to which foreign consuls would be invited to make it clear that they, the SRs, members of the constituent assembly, stood for freedom and democracy.[43]

On his return to Omsk, between Petropavlovsk and Kurgan, Kolchak met General Boldyrev's train on its way to the front. Kolchak reported the results of his trip. Boldyrev was travelling to Chelyabinsk to meet the Czech Command as his relations with the Czechs had become very strained and difficult. The Czechs were leaving the front; there were threats of serious complications on the Ufa front, against which the Red Army was launching an offensive, and the Czechs were leaving the front entirely unprotected. Boldyrev said: 'At Omsk, things are not well either — undoubtedly there is ferment among the Cossacks. People talk in particular about some overturn, some move, but I do not attach serious importance to this.' He added: 'All this is artificial, but we must live through such a stage, and I hope that it will be quite possible to carry on, as the directorate consists entirely of men who have no personal aims, and are trying to do what they can; so I think nothing serious will happen from this side.' The two men parted.

Was there to be a military *coup* against the SRs, as at Archangel? For it was by now certain that the only two groups that could defeat the Bolsheviks could not combine. The SRs, who were popular with the Russian people, did not have the political weight to use the hated Russian officers as 'military specialists' as did the Bolsheviks. But nor did the officers have the sense to use the SRs as 'political specialists' to satisfy the Russian people. Violence was in the air at Omsk.

As German military power rapidly declined that autumn, Trotsky (who had recently become chairman of the Military Revolutionary Council of the Republic, with Vatsetis as his Commander-in-Chief) was much more concerned about southern Russia than about the Siberian or northern Russian fronts, since once the Dardanelles were open, Allied fleets could enter the Black Sea, and Allied supply ships the Black Sea ports to bring massive support to his opponents. Therefore, it is necessary, considering the German decline, to review operations on the southern Russian front: the Ukraine, the southern Russian front itself (of which Stalin was now in charge), the Caucasus, the Caspian, and Transcaspia.

As the Germans fell back on the eastern front, they decided to leave the buffer state of the Ukraine in disorder, even though both Germans and Ukrainians still had a common interest in Ukrainian independence. Thus while German relations with the Bolsheviks remained outwardly good, and German troops continued to 'protect' Kiev and Kharkov, the Germans now undermined their own puppet ruler Skoropadsky, and released from prison Simon Petlura (former War Minister of the Ukrainian directorate), who would also need German support against the Bolsheviks.[44] On the southern Russian front itself, Trotsky had dealt with the Czech-Russian danger on the middle Volga, and was now concerned with the activities of General Krasnov's Don Cossacks, with their waning German support, near Tsaritsin on the lower Volga. With the arrival of Allied supply ships, Krasnov might very quickly change sides; he had originally accepted help from the Germans, and might now just as readily accept help from the Allies. Stalin had become chairman of the southern front, and was walled up with his cronies at Tsaritsin. Trotsky was very dissatisfied with the way things were being managed. Having finally had enough, he wired to Lenin on October 4: 'I categorically insist on Stalin's recall.' Despite the enormous Bolshevik forces at Tsaritsin, things were undoubtedly going badly there; but the 'Tsaritsin people' had not even sent in any military reports. Unless this was done at once, Trotsky would have Stalin's henchmen arrested and tried. There was only a short time to launch a major attack on Krasnov, as the autumn weather would soon make the roads impassable; and a major attack was impossible unless the Tsaritsin front cooperated. 'There is no time for diplomatic negotiations', he wired; 'Tsaritsin must either obey orders, or get out of the way ...'. Next day, Trotsky wired again that the commander-in-chief had complained to him that 'Stalin's actions are disrupting all my plans'. Stalin was immediately recalled to Moscow.[45]

The main cause of friction was the employment of former officers, the 'military specialists'. On October 13, Trotsky sent a wire to Dzerzhinsky (head of the Cheka) saying that those former officers who were now willing (in view of 'changed circumstances') to work for them, should be sent straight to him, providing there were no serious charges against them, and that they signed a document, which stated that their families would be arrested if they deserted or sabotaged the Bolshevik cause. This would also 'lighten the load on the prisons', Trotsky pointed out. But this evidently did not itself produce the desired results. On the 23rd, Trotsky wired again saying that as their troops on the southern front were 'still lacking in steadiness', good party workers must also be sent out, and all 'military specialists' released from the staffs and sent to him, accompanied by military commissars.

However, that day Trotsky was informed that Stalin had arrived in Moscow with news of three major victories near Tsaritsin. Stalin's colleagues would obey orders. Their main grievance was the delay in delivery of ammunition. 'Stalin would very much like to work on the southern front', and was not issuing any ultimatum for the dismissal of the military commander. Trotsky was asked if he would 'talk matters over personally with Stalin', so that they could work together 'as Stalin so much desires'. They were receiving 'frantic' telegrams in Moscow that ammunition was not arriving at Tsaritsin. Therefore, Trotsky travelled to Tsaritsin himself. The ammunition shortage, he reported, was due to the 'incredible, completely rabid' firing going on. There must be economy. The Tsaritsin front had no special privileges. But Trotsky decided to proceed warily. Stalin's colleagues could remain, if they obeyed the military commander. There was a vast army at Tsaritsin, 'peculiar in its make-up,' he added sarcastically, 'together with ill-disciplined commanders'. The Trotsky–Stalin quarrel died down for the moment — but no general attack was possible on Krasnov's Don Cossacks before the autumn rains closed operations.[46]

Meanwhile, General Alexeiev and the volunteer army had been consolidating themselves in the Kuban province in the northern Caucasus. In mid-July, they had seized the crucial railway junction of Tikhoretskaya, thus cutting both the Rostov–Petrovsk and the Tsaritsin–Novorossisk railways: they now mastered the railways between the Caucasus and the rest of Russia. In mid-August, the volunteer army took the Kuban Cossack capital of Ekaterinodar. In late August, they seized the Black Sea port of Novorossisk. The volunteer army was now 40,000 men strong. They refused to join Krasnov in his march into central Russia, and decided to strike south to the Caucasus, and east to the Caspian. Unfortunately, the efforts of the local British mission to ease their path both south and east had been unsuccessful. In mid-June, the British mission had been actively financing the Terek Cossacks, based on their capital of Vladikavkaz, to launch an uprising against the local Bolsheviks. But this had led to a premature rising in late June, which the Bolsheviks had quelled, driving the Terek Cossacks out of Vladikavkaz, and killing Colonel Pike (the head of the British mission) and dispersing the remainder.

The volunteer army was, in fact, finding it a hard task as it advanced painfully down the Rostov–Grosni railway towards the Caspian. In late October (by which time General Denikin had taken over command on the death of Alexeiev), there was still confused and bitter fighting in the Caucasus, and the Bolsheviks still held the towns of Armavir and Stavropol. The Terek Cossacks now cut the railway behind them, and surrounded Stavropol; but when the Bolsheviks made a desperate fighting retreat, the Terek Cossacks collapsed. Some made a detour west to join up with the volunteer army, while others made off to join the Russian General Bicherakhov (who had now emerged as the chief British agent in the Caucasus) at his base of Petrovsk, on the west Caspian shore. With his small group of men and ships, he was now being financed by General Dunsterville in Baku; Bicherakhov in turn kept the remainder of the British mission in the Caucasus in funds.[47]

The somewhat complicated situation in and around Baku, where the British were actively cooperating with the local Bolsheviks against the Turks, was made reasonably clear to the War Cabinet on August 20, when the DMI reported that it now appeared that General Bicherakhov had never gone to Baku (as was evidently intended) but was at Derbent. It was from there that he sent a message to Dunsterville that the Turks (presumably he meant the Daghestani Tartars) had occupied a position about 80 miles north-west of Baku; that the Bolsheviks were sending troops to Baku from Astrakan; and that he himself had been attacked by the Bolsheviks at Derbent, but had defeated them. Having been now joined by half the original Bolshevik garrison at Derbent, he was proposing to occupy Petrovsk (further up the coast), where he would try to obtain reinforcements from the north Caucasus to help Baku.[48]

By mid-August, a British naval mission, under Commander Norris, had succeeded in making their way up from Baghdad across north Persia to the Caspian, hauling naval guns with them. Their task was to seize as much of the Caspian shipping as possible, and thereby command the sea. Norris first occupied the port of Enzeli (on the north Persian shore), and then seized and manned the only two vessels there, which he took to Krasno-vodsk (the east Caspian port, opposite Baku). There was other shipping on the Caspian under the command of Bicherakhov at Derbent.[49]

In London, the state of affairs in Baku was necessarily obscure. On August 27, the CIGS told the War Cabinet that Britain now had 600 men there, and it appeared a 'very defensible' place. The First Sea Lord added that the naval contingent had reached the Caspian; more men were on the way and would be ready to take over the Caspian ships as they became available. But there was hardly any general information from the Caspian, he complained; it was nearly all of a technical nature.[50]

On the 30th, the CIGS had more news of Baku for the War Cabinet, and it was 'rather disquieting'. On the 26th, about 600 Turks supported by seven guns had made a determined attack, ending in a bayonet charge, on a section of the line held by the North Staffordshire Regiment; and our men had been forced back, sustaining casualties. A wire had also been received the day before from the Commander-in-Chief, India, that he had news of a steady increase of Turkish strength in front of Baku. The Turks possibly intended to advance east from Tabriz (south-west of Baku) either immediately, or when they had collected enough supplies. (The CIGS was here hinting either at a flanking move on Baku from the south, or a Turkish move along the southern shore of the Caspian.)

The wire from India, the CIGS went on, added that a recent message from Dunsterville within Baku disclosed both the futility and risk of trying to manage or come to some arrangement with the 'discordant and suspicious' elements in the central Caspian government, which now claimed to govern Baku. It was pointed out that Dunsterville's force was 'dangerously small'. The Commander-in-Chief, India, suggested the time had now come for Dunsterville to receive definite orders to seize the Caspian flotilla and any other shipping he could collect, and do the utmost possible damage to the oilfields and the port of Baku. The CIGS pointed out that although there were plenty of troops in Mesopotamia that could be sent to Dunsterville's support, it was impossible to get them up in time, owing to lack of transport. An order for 1,300 Ford cars for Mesopotamia had been placed with the American government, but the order had been declined. There the Cabinet left the matter, without taking any decision on pulling out of Baku.[50]

For the first half of September, the Cabinet were deluged with rumour about the situation at Baku. On the 3rd, the Deputy First Sea Lord said that Norris had sent a wire saying that the fall of Baku was imminent; but his wire was undated. The CIGS said this meant that our two battalions there were probably lost. On the 6th, the CIGS admitted that the Baku situation was 'most obscure'. Of two ships that had reached Krasnovodsk, one said that Baku had fallen, the second said it had not, owing to the timely arrival of Cossack reinforcements. On the 10th, the DMI said the situation was 'still uncertain'.

Finally, having kept the Turks from the oilfields for six highly important weeks, Dunsterville evacuated all his men under cover of darkness, and brought them to Enzeli on the night of September 14. This was briefly reported to the War Cabinet on the 17th. What they were not told — indeed, in their thankfulness that the British troops were safe, they might not have cared — was that after breaking down the city's last defence, the Turks had then stood aside, while their Azerbaijani allies swarmed into the great oil port and massacred some 9,000 Armenians.[50]

When Bolshevik complaints of the occupation of Baku obtained no response from Turkey, the Bolshevik government informed the Turks that they no longer considered the Brest-Litovsk treaty in force between the two countries.[51]

British occupation of the port of Krasnovodsk (on the eastern shore of the Caspian) was a quasi-legal act; as on August 19, Major-General Malleson, from his base at Meshed (in north-east Persia), agreed terms with the Ashkhabad committee, and signed an agreement for mutual cooperation against Bolshevik, German or Turkish penetration in Transcaspia. For his part, Malleson obtained the right to garrison and protect Krasnovodsk, promised to make other troops available to help protect the Transcaspian railway, and said he would provide financial support for the Ashkhabad committee. Troops had to be provided for the defence of the railway straightaway, as the local Bolshevik forces had been reinforced; and on the 28th, Indian infantry barely managed to beat back a sharp attack just north of Meshed.[52]

This account cannot end without reference to the affair of the 26 Baku commissars. They were members of the previous government at Baku, who had been imprisoned by the central Caspian government; and then, in the disorder of the fall of Baku, had escaped, taken ship for Astrakhan and safety. But the boat had then put in to Krasnovodsk, where they were reseized by the Ashkhabad committee on September 15. Five days later, they were taken further up the railway line and all shot. (This *cause célèbre*, which has long been blamed on the British, is well described in Ullman, p.320–4, to whose account I have nothing to add.)

In London, the Eastern Committee discussed Malleson's agreement with the Ashkhabad committee on October 17, and expressed concern at his promise to provide them with financial support. Vigorous Treasury opposition was expressed. The Viceroy, however, supported Malleson. Although the Ashkhabad committee was 'thoroughly untrustworthy', it was the only body with whom the British could deal in Transcaspia, and should continue to receive British support. Next day, the Eastern Committee decided that Malleson was to remain in Transcaspia to protect the Persian frontier against Bolshevik invasion, and to keep Bolshevik influences out of Afghanistan. On November 1, the Transcaspian forces, reinforced by Malleson, showed their worth, when after a bitter battle, they retook the crucial Merv oasis.[52]

But as victory over the Germans and Turks approached, the British decided to divest themselves of Bicherakhov, the main British agent in the Caucasus since the demise of the local British mission. Above all, they wanted his ships. On October 3, General Thomson, who had brought another British force up from Persia, wrote bluntly to Bicherakhov that his subsidy would end that month. He would be paid 12 million roubles, and the armoured cars loaned to him were to be returned. Commander Norris would supply and pay six million roubles a month to the ships of the Caspian flotilla at present under his control, provided they denied the Caspian Sea to 'our enemies'. The intention, of course, was by these means to take over his ships. Bicherakhov was very angry at what he saw as British duplicity. He was known to be a British agent; and as Turkish propaganda had made the local tribesmen 'incredibly anti-British', they were about to try to drive him into the sea, and his troops would now make off if not paid. But to the fury of Norris, Bicherakhov then scored a notable naval victory over the Bolsheviks on the Caspian. On the 25th, Norris reported that Bicherakhov had just captured some 4,500 Bolshevik troops, sent from Astrakhan, and all their 18 ships. 'That the above capture of ships should have fallen to the Russians is particularly galling to the Royal Navy', he wired. Four days later, the Admiralty laid down that British policy was for the British flotilla on the Caspian to keep all hostile forces from using the sea, and to assist friendly forces; they were only to capture or sink Russian vessels if they showed active hostility. Norris thus sent four of his ships up to Petrovsk to confer with Bicherakhov, while the fifth went up to Guriev to contact the Ural Cossacks. Lenin was perturbed by what he saw as this recent British success. 'Can we achieve victory over the English on the Caspian, and how soon?' he asked Trotsky on November 7.[53]

Meanwhile, there was one small matter to be cleared up about the Black Sea — namely the sabotage of the Black Sea Fleet by Colonel Joe Boyle's private band of Bolshevik sailors. On November 8, Colonel Boyle had a further meeting in Roumania with certain Bolshevik sailors, who claimed to have sabotaged the fleet, and were constantly pestering him for more money. By now, he was apparently satisfied that they had done what they claimed. 'This programme was actually carried out', reported this normally astute man, 'and I am therefore convinced it was worked by my agents.' Under their agreement with Boyle, they claimed no less than £1,284,440. Boyle, unwilling for them to start making complaints, eventually beat them down to a round million, which he thought reasonable. Having already made them a payment on account of £270,000, he therefore made up the sum with one cheque for £230,000, and two for £250,000.

Boyle then wrote out a long, final report to General Ballard (the British military attaché in Roumania, who had engaged Boyle for this task, and on whose blank cheques these large sums were made out). When passing it on to the War Office, Ballard reported glowingly on Boyle, and recommended him for a KCB for outstanding service. Up to October 1918, strikes and sabotage masterminded by Boyle had also held down 20 German and 10 Austrian divisions in the Ukraine.[54] It is instructive to note what happens to such reports when great wars are over. For it caused consternation in Whitehall; and when the CIGS returned the file to the Foreign Office, the matter rested. Colonel Boyle, however, greatly feared for the safety of his son in the Klondike, whom he had named as guarantor for the cheques; and he wrote four times to the CIGS for a decision on the matter. He was finally told to attend the War Office on March 11, 1919.

But on March 7, Lord Hardinge (Permanent Under-Secretary) saw Boyle at the Foreign Office. Though General Ballard had given a 'rather wider interpretation' to the Foreign Office instructions than was apparently intended, Boyle was told that his method of calculating payment was an 'arrangement of an essentially amateurish nature'. But since payment had been made under duress, surely these 'enormous claims' could be reduced when presented? No, said Boyle stoutly. What, Hardinge then asked, had happened to these 'parties'? Two were dead, two were alive, reported Boyle. The cheques, he felt, would be presented in due course; and if they were not then honoured, he and his son were in great danger. In despair, Hardinge dropped the subject.

'He struck me as a rough diamond', he reported to Balfour, 'but an honourable and straightforward man.' Though there was 'little doubt' that Ballard exceeded his orders, there was at the time considerable anxiety that the Germans might seize the Black Sea Fleet. 'Had it then been suggested that the Russian Fleet could be destroyed for the sum of about £1 million sterling, it would, I imagine, have probably been welcomed at that moment, for I think I am right in saying a similar amount was placed at the disposal of Captain Cromie for the destruction of the Russian [Baltic] Fleet at Kronstadt.' How far, though, was an agent justified in issuing cheques 'according to his own sweet will'? Ballard should not have given *carte blanche* to Boyle, who promised 'vastly greater sums than would have been offered by an experienced agent'.

Hardinge then saw the Treasury, who said there was no further credit available; though Parliament might authorize payment as secret wartime operations 'which could not be divulged ... but were of a successful nature'. Still no decision was taken. On March 11, when Boyle came into the War Office in some desperation, he was received coldly, and given no answer. But the War Office were now searching for a scapegoat, and turned on Ballard. 'I suggest that the bargain seems bad to us in March 1919', he wrote in self-defence, 'but that in March 1918 it would have been considered well worthwhile.'

On September 22, Ballard informed the War Office that the cheque for £10,000, which Boyle had given to those of his men whom he had sent off to join Alexeiev in the Kuban, had finally been presented to Holt's Bank in Pall Mall. It is possible that this was the only cheque presented, and that it was paid, though there is no proof. Three days later, however, Ballard had certainly lost his job, and been reduced to the rank of colonel.[54] (Colonel Joe Boyle continued to flourish. In 1921 he was acting for Royal Dutch Shell; and with the support of Lord Curzon, the Foreign Secretary, almost secured a large oil concession in the Caucasus from Krassin. But this project was sabotaged at the Genoa Conference, and then merged into the abortive 'Europa Consortium'.)

British policy in southern Russia generally in early November is perhaps best expressed in Sir Henry Wilson's diary entry for November 5: 'Much talk with Milner this morning about our future action in Europe, in Russia, in Siberia. We are entirely agreed to keep out of Austria-Hungary, Poland, Roumania, Ukraine and north of Black Sea except in so far as is necessary to beat the Boches. But on the other hand, from the left bank of the Don to India is our interest and preserve.'[55]

The French Premier Clemenceau took a more positive view. On October 27, he instructed General Franchet d'Esperey (French commander of the Allied armies at Salonika) to 'make plans for the formation at Odessa of a military base for operations of Allied forces in southern Russia.' General Denikin, now in command of the volunteer army, at once prepared a detailed report on the needs of his force, together with a plan of campaign for an advance on Moscow, which he sent to both Franchet d'Esperey, and to General Berthelot (head of the French mission in

Roumania); and the arrival of Allied troops was eagerly awaited.[56]

After the Brest-Litovsk treaty, the British had simply marched in step with the Germans on Russian policy; though the German double policy of simultaneous support for two opposed Russian factions was generally more successful than that of the British, in spite of the — entirely fortuitous — replacement of the virtually moribund volunteer army by the vigorous and well-disciplined Czech Legion. By the German armistice, the gamble of small-scale intervention, with America hostile and Japan unpredictable, had indeed failed, and both Allied and Czech troops were becoming openly mutinous. But the Bolsheviks, at any rate, now saw their main danger in the imminent arrival of large Allied armies and navies through the Dardanelles in open support of their opponents in southern Russia. Were the Allies, after the armistice, and with America presumably even more hostile than ever, now going to play the card of medium-scale, or indeed major intervention?

Sources

Chapter 1

1. C.E. Callwell, *Field-Marshall Sir Henry Wilson: His Life and Diaries*, ii (London, 1927), p. 73
2. Cab 27/189
3. R.H. Ullman, *Intervention and the War* (London, 1961), p. 173
4. Cab 27/189
5. Foreign Office [F.O.] 95/802; War Cabinet 369
6. Cab 28/3; War Cabinet 366; Lloyd George Papers F45/9/11; Foreign Office summary
7. Ullman, pp. 131–3; War Cabinet 366
8. Foreign Office summary of correspondence, etc., concerning Allied intervention in East Russia, dated June 21, 1918, covering the period December 7, 1917, to June 13, 1918. (Davidson Papers, file 'J.C.C.D.-Russia 1918')
9. Foreign Office paper, May 10 (Davidson Papers, file 'JCCD: Russia 1918')
10. Foreign Office summary
11. F.O. 95/802; War Cabinet 369
12. War Cabinet 370; Callwell, pp. 73f
13. J. Bradley, *Allied Intervention in Russia* (London, 1968), pp. 48–64; Ullman, pp. 156f
14. War Cabinet 409a; D. Woodward, *The Russians at Sea* (London, 1965), pp. 180–93; War Cabinet 219; S. Roskill, *Hankey: Man of Secrets*, i [1877–1918], (London, 1970), Nov 23 ['Hankey']
15. War Cabinets 281a, 292, 293, 294
16. H. Graf, *La Marine Russe dans la Guerre et dans la Revolution* (Paris, 1928), pp. 307f
17. Woodward, pp. 174–8; War Cabinet 320; F.O. 95/802
18. Adm. 137/1731; War Cabinet 349
19. Graf, pp. 311f; Adm. 137/1731; War Cabinet 365
20. War Cabinet 335
21. Adm. files: China 1918
22. E. Sisson, *One Hundred Red Days* (Yale, 1931), pp. 457–88
23. G.F. Kennan, *The Journal of Modern History* (June 1956)
24. Adm. files: China 1918
25. Adm. 137/1731
26. War Office [W.O.] 0149/6333
27. War Cabinets 369, 370; Adm. 137/1731

Sources

28. W.O. 0149/6333
29. W.O. 33/924; Cab 27/189
30. G. Hill, *Go Spy the Land* (London, 1932), pp. 96–101, 104–9, 114–48
31. Graf, pp. 311–17; Adm. 137/1731; D. Fedotov-White, *The Growth of the Red Army* (Princeton, 1944), pp. 70ff; see also E. Mawdsley, *The Russian Revolution and the Baltic Fleet* (London, 1978)

Chapter 2

1. Callwell, pp. 74–80
2. Descriptions of the Russian banking scene are taken from W.O. 0149/7335; from wires, reports and minutes in F.O. 371/3964, 3977, 3979, 3988, 3994–6, 4021–4, 4029, 4038; and from certain general sources [hereinafter known as the 'Bank Schemes']. See also F.O. 371/3326
3. Cab 27/189
4. Cabinet paper G.T. 4137
5. Cab 27/189
6. Bank Schemes; Keycs Papers
7. Cab 27/189
8. F.O. 95/802; Ullman, pp. 136f
9. Foreign Office summary
10. War Cabinet 378
11. War Cabinet 386, 387
12. Bank Schemes; Ullman, pp. 147–9; G.F. Kennan, *The Decision to Intervene* (London, 1958), p. 104; War Cabinets 386, 387.
13. Callwell, pp. 81f; Cab 25/121
14. Callwell, pp. 88–90
15. War Cabinets 369, 370
16. War Cabinet 380
17. War Cabinet 390
18. Adm. 137/1731; War Cabinet 386
19. War Cabinet 379; Ullman, p. 175
20. Callwell, p. 90; War Cabinet 390; T. Jones, *Whitehall Diary* (London, 1969), pp. 59–61
21. Cab 27/189
22. Foreign Office summary; Ullman, pp. 159–61

Chapter 3

1. J. Bunyan, *Intervention, Civil War and Communism in Russia* (Baltimore, 1936), pp. 172–85; Z.A.B. Zeman, *Germany and the Revolution in Russia, 1915-1918* (London, 1958) [hereinafter referred to as Zeman], no. 121; M. Phillips Price, *My Reminiscences of the Russian Revolution* (London, 1921), pp. 287–90
2. War Cabinet 393
3. War Cabinet 392, 393
4. Kennan, pp. 136–44
5. Cab 27/189; F.O. 371/3283
6. War Cabinet 341, 342
7. Bradley, pp. 81–92; Sisson, p. 270

8. Bradley, pp. 65–80
9. Ullman, pp. 138–41
10. E. Benes, *Souvenirs de Guerre et de Revolution* (Paris, 1929), p. 184
11. Bradley, pp. 65–80; Benes, p. 186
12. Bradley, pp. 48–64, 84–92
13. Ullman, p. 154; Bradley, pp. 65–80
14. War Cabinet 393
15. Jones, *op cit*, pp. 236, 243; *Lord Riddell's Intimate Diary of the Peace Conference and After* (London, 1933), p. 369; F. Lloyd George, *The Years that are Past* (London, 1967), p. 184
16. War Cabinet 395; Hankey, April 19
17. Foreign Office summary; Hankey, April 19
18. Bradley, pp. 65–80; Benes, pp. 189–91; Bunyan, p. 85
19. Cabinet paper G.T. 4414
20. War Cabinet 396; Kennan, pp. 124–6
21. War Cabinet 396*a*
22. Callwell, p. 93
23. Cab 27/189
24. Bunyan, p. 71; Kennan, p. 211; K. Erdmann, ed., *Kurt Riezler: Diaries, Essays and Documents* (Gottingen, 1972), April 24 ['Riezler']
25. Ullman, pp. 161–4
26. War Cabinet 400
27. War Cabinet 400*a*
28. Adm. 137/1731
29. War Cabinet 400
30. Bradley, pp. 65–80
31. Bradley, pp. 84–92
32. Cab 25/121
33. Bunyan, p. 85; Bradley, pp. 84–92
34. Bunyan, p. 73f; Kennan, pp. 346f
35. Foreign Office summary; Foreign Office paper, May 10; Kennan, pp. 346–9
36. War Cabinet 420
37. Ullman, pp. 157–9
38. War Cabinet 401
39. Adm 137/1731; W.O. 0149/6333; D. Footman, *Civil War in Russia* (London, 1961), pp. 61–5, 68
40. Cab 27/189
41. Bank Schemes
42. Zeman, nos. 120, 121; Phillips Price, pp. 287–90

Chapter 4

1. War Cabinet 409*a*
2. Adm. 137/1731
3. War Cabinet 402
4. Cabinet paper G.T. 4414 in Cab. 24/50
5. Callwell, pp. 96–8
6. These Supreme War Council minutes are in Cab. 28/3
7. Bradley, pp. 65–80; Benes, pp. 194f; Kennan, pp. 200f
8. War Cabinet 405; Kennan, pp. 250f
9. Bunyan, pp. 114f; Kennan, p. 257; Ullman, pp. 174f

Sources

10. L.D. Trotsky, *Ecrits militaires*, i: *Comment la Revolution s'est armée; Les specialistes militaires et l'Armèe Rouge: la première trahison*, (Paris, 1967), trans. from the Russian by G. Belet; the American Consul Poole's report, dated June 24, 1918, quoted in Sisson, pp. 433–44
11. Bunyan, pp. 115, 121; Kennan, p. 258; Adm. 137/1731; R.H.B. Lockhart, *Memoirs of a British Agent* (London, 1932), pp. 272–80
12. War Cabinet 408*a*
13. Cab. 27/189
14. Davidson Papers, file JCCD: Russia 1918
15. Bunyan, pp. 85f; Bradley, pp. 84–92
16. Benes, pp. 207–10
17. Ullman, p. 170
18. Cabinet paper G.T. 4527 in Cab. 24/51
19. War Cabinet 409*a*

Chapter 5

1. War Cabinet 410
2. Cabinet paper G.T. 4527 in Cab. 24/51
3. War Cabinet 410
4. Bunyan, p. 86; Bradley, pp. 84–92
5. War Cabinet 411; Bunyan, p. 86; Bradley, p. 81; Ullman, p. 170
6. Benes, pp. 208–11
7. Foreign Office summary
8. Kennan, pp. 266f
9. Adm. 137/1731; F.O. 371/3329
10. Adm. 137/1731; Consul Poole's report
11. Trotsky, *op cit*
12. Adm. 137/1731; Trotsky, *op cit*; Graf, p. 335
13. Kennan, pp. 260f; Ullman, pp. 175–7
14. Adm. 137/1731; Trotsky, *op cit*; Graf, p. 335
15. Zeman, nos. 121–5; Riezler, May 11
16. Bunyan, pp. 116–25; Kennan, pp. 131–5, 220–22, 259f; G. Freund, *Unholy Alliance* (London, 1957), pp. 17f
17. Zeman, no. 127
18. Bunyan, pp. 32–5; Footman, pp. 70–77
19. Zeman, nos. 128, 129; G. Katkov, *Russia 1917* (London, 1967), pp. 112, 114; Kennan, pp. 260f; Ullman, pp. 175–7
20. Adm. 137/1731
21. Lloyd George Papers F50/2/36
22. War Cabinet x3 of May 17
23. War Cabinet 413

Chapter 6

1. Benes, p. 211
2. Lloyd George Papers. F50/2/38; Ullman, pp. 169–71
3. Benes, pp. 212–16
4. Bradley, pp. 65–80; Ullman, pp. 169–71

5. Kennan, pp. 267, 353
6. Cabinet paper G.T. 4589 in Cab. 24/51
7. War Cabinet 415
8. Adm. 137/1731
9. Consul Poole's report; Trotsky, *op cit*
10. Adm. 137/1731
11. Adm. 137/1731; War Cabinet 417
12. Foreign Office summary
13. Ullman, pp. 200f
14. War Cabinet 417
15. Ullman, pp. 169–71
16. Bunyan, pp. 86–90; Kennan, pp. 155f
17. Adm. 137/1731
18. Bunyan, pp. 91, 185–7; Bradley, pp. 84–92
19. War Cabinet 418
20. War Cabinet 418*a*
21. Adm. 137/1731
22. Callwell, p. 101
23. Benes, pp. 201–4
24. These minutes are in Cab. 28/3
25. Callwell, p. 102
26. Ullman, p. 201
27. Ullman, p. 190; Kennan, pp. 155–9; Bradley, pp. 92–8

Chapter 7

1. War Cabinet x 5 of May 29
2. Cabinet paper G.T. 4683 in Cab 24/52
3. War Cabinet 420; Kennan, pp. 268f; Foreign Office summary
4. Davidson Papers (file JCCD Russia 1918)
5. War Cabinet 421; Kennan, pp. 268f; Foreign Office summary
6. Ullman, p. 201
7. Callwell, pp. 102f
8. War Cabinet 423; Foreign Office summary; Adm. 137/1731
9. Lloyd George Papers F6/5/27
10. Kennan, pp. 268–70
11. Ullman, pp. 179–81
12. War Cabinet 424
13. Callwell, pp. 103f
14. Ullman, p. 203
15. These minutes are in F.O. 371/3434 and Cab. 25/121
16. Ullman, p. 190
17. Bunyan, p. 190; Phillips Price, pp. 287–90; K. Young, ed., *The Diaries of Sir Robert Bruce Lockhart: 1915-1938* (London, 1973), May 31 and June 2, 1918
18. Ullman, p. 189
19. Freund, pp. 13–15
20. Kennan, p. 370; Zeman, no. 130
21. Zeman, nos. 131–4
22. War Cabinet 426 and 427; Hankey, June 6
23. Ullman, p. 190
24. Lloyd George Papers F6/5/28

25. Lloyd George Papers F6/5/29
26. Ullman, p. 202

Chapter 8

1. Zeman, no. 134
2. Kennan, pp. 381–5
3. Foreign Office summary
4. Ullman, pp. 197f
5. War Cabinet x 12
6. Adm. 137/1731; Trotsky Papers nos. 22, 23
7. War Cabinet x 13
8. Kennan, pp. 385f; Ullman, p. 207
9. Kennan, p. 368; Ullman, pp. 195f
10. Cab. 25/121
11. Kennan, pp. 291, 388; Ullman, p. 212; Footman, pp. 94–7; Bradley, pp. 92–8; P. Fleming, *The Fate of Admiral Kolchak* (London, 1962), p. 82
12. Bunyan, pp. 172–92; Ullman, p. 190
13. Kennan, pp. 312f
14. Bunyan, pp. 184, 191; Bradley, pp. 98–103; Kennan, pp. 294f, 314f; Ullman, pp. 181f
15. Cab. paper G.T. 4812 in Cab. 24/55; Jones, p. 16
16. Cab. 27/189; Bank Schemes
17. Freund, p. 18; Bank Schemes; Riezler, June 8
18. Zeman, p. 134
19. This account of events in the Caucasus and at Baku is taken from the British Consul Macdonnel's final report in W.O. 0149/6409; the British military mission's final report in W.O. 0149/7232; other reports in F.O. 371/3979; Ullman, pp. 305–16; *The Journal of the Central Asian Society*, x (1923), pt 3
20. Bunyan, pp. 50–5; Ullman, pp. 305–7
21. Bunyan, pp. 32–47
22. Footman, pp. 80f; G. Stewart, *The White Armies of Russia* (New York, 1933), p. 54
23. Adm. 137/1731; *The Trotsky Papers*, i: *1917–1919* (The Hague, 1964), nos. 22, 23; Woodward, pp. 189–93
24. Trotsky, *op cit*; Adm. 137/1731; Young, June 22, 1918
25. W.O. 0149/6333
26. Adm. 137/1731

Chapter 9

1. War Cabinet x 15
2. Bradley, pp. 92–8
3. Foreign Office summary
4. Lloyd George Papers F50/3/4
5. Ullman, pp. 203–5
6. War Cabinet x 16
7. War Cabinet 435
8. War Cabinets 425, x 10, 429, 435; Ullman, pp. 307f

9. Freund, pp. 18–20
10. Phillips Price, pp. 276f, 287–9; F.O. 95/802; Riezler, doc. 16
11. Imperial War Cabinet 19*b*; Lloyd George Papers F201/3/9
12. Ullman, pp. 212f
13. War Cabinet x 17
14. Imperial War Cabinet 20*a*
15. War Cabinet 432
16. Kennan, pp. 263f, 368f, 373f; Ullman, p. 182
17. Lloyd George Papers F18/1/26
18. War Cabinet 437
19. Kennan, pp. 388–94

Chapter 10

1. These Supreme War Council minutes are in Cab. 28/4; Hankey, June 27
2. Ullman, pp. 205f; Hankey, p. 569
3. War Cabinet 439
4. War Cabinet 441*a*
5. Kennan, pp. 394–7, 405–8; Ullman, pp. 184, 213
6. Zeman, no. 136
7. G. Katkov, *The Assassination of Count Mirbach*, St Anthony's Papers, no. 12, Soviet Affairs, no. 3 (London, 1962); Bunyan, pp. 197–225; T. Mangold and A. Summers, *The File on the Tsar* (London, 1976), pp. 278f, 285f, 292f; Riezler, doc. 19
8. Kennan, pp. 436f; Ullman, p. 235
9. Bunyan, pp. 181, 193f; Ullman, p. 231
10. Lockhart, pp. 290–306; Hill, pp. 188–97
11. Bunyan, pp. 194–6, 224; Bradley, pp. 98–103; Footman, pp. 98f; Katkov, *Count Mirbach*; Riezler, doc. 20
12. Adm. 137/1731
13. F.O. 371/3334; Kennan, pp. 442f
14. Freund, pp. 20–22
15. War Cabinet 443
16. Ullman, pp. 217f; Hankey, July 10, 11
17. War Cabinet 444

Chapter 11

1. Bank Schemes; Ullman, pp. 233f; F.O. 371/3284
2. Freund, pp. 22f; Ullman, pp. 311–15
3. Freund, pp. 14f, 22f; Mangold and Summers, pp. 53–6, 297; Riezler, docs 21-31
4. Ullman, pp. 231f; Mangold and Summers, p. 298
5. Ullman, p. 234
6. Bank Schemes; Ullman, pp. 231–4; Keyes Papers; F.O. 371/3334
7. War Cabinet 446; Ullman, p. 220; F.O. 371/3334
8. Fleming, p. 95
9. Imperial War Cabinet 24*b*
10. Ullman, pp. 221–3

Sources

11. Kennan, pp. 377f, 482–5
12. Ullman, p. 226
13. War Cabinet 450
14. Ullman, pp. 226f
15. War Cabinet 445, 449, 451
16. Bradley, pp. 98–103; Footman, pp. 99–101; Bank Schemes
17. Kennan, pp. 411f; Ullman, p. 228
18. War Cabinet x 26 Jones, p. 66
19. Kennan, p. 413
20. W.O. 0149/6409
21. War Cabinet 449; Ullman, pp. 308f
22. Bunyan, pp. 128, 138f; Hill, pp. 212–30
23. Imperial War Cabinet 27*a*
24. Imperial War Cabinet 27*b*
25. Kennan, p. 412; Ullman, pp. 228f

Chapter 12

1. Bunyan, pp. 139f
2. Kennan, pp. 412–17; Ullman, pp. 258–74
3. War Cabinet 454
4. Lloyd George Papers F50/3/16; Kennan, pp. 412–17
5. Bunyan, pp. 299f; Bradley, pp. 98–103
6. Trotsky Papers nos. 32, 35, 37, 83; Footman, pp. 145f
7. Bradley, pp. 98–103
8. Imperial War Cabinet 27*c*
9. War Cabinet 455
10. Ullman, pp. 236–54; Kennan, pp. 425–7; Footman, pp. 172–6
11. Imperial War Cabinet 27*c*
12. War Cabinet 455
13. Ullman, pp. 236–54
14. Ullman, pp. 258f
15. Kennan, pp. 418; Ullman, pp. 240f
16. Ullman, p. 259
17. Imperial War Cabinet 29*b*; Ullman, pp. 259f
18. Ullman, pp. 315–26
19. W.J. Oudendyk, *Ways and Byways in Diplomacy* (London, 1939), p. 277
20. Adm. 137/1731
21. Freund, pp. 23–26, 251–3
22. This account of Reilly's conspiracy is taken from: S.G. Reilly, *The Adventures of Sidney Reilly* (London, 1931), pp. 6–99; Hill, pp. 205–61; Lockhart, pp. 308–25; R. Marchand, *Allied Agents in Soviet Russia* (London, 1918); Oudendyk, pp. 276–86, 292–300; Degras, pp. 96f; Bunyan, pp. 146–8; M.Y. Latsis, *Two Years of Struggle on the Internal Front* (Moscow, 1920), pp. 19–22; Freund, pp. 23–31; Ullman, pp. 285–93; Trotsky papers no. 62; G. Bailey, *The Conspirators* (London, 1961), pp. 3–33; Command Paper no. 8 no. 1 (1919): 'Bolshevism in Russia'; *Pravda*, September 5, 1918; *The Times*, October 24, 1918; Riezler, August 17, 28; F.O. 371/3334 [hereinafter referred to as 'The Reilly Conspiracy']
23. War Cabinet 461; Ullman, pp. 236–54
24. Bunyan, pp. 333–7
25. Trotsky Papers nos. 32, 35, 37, 83; Footman, pp. 145f; Bunyan, p. 300

26. Trotsky Papers nos. 39, 40, 42–4, 48
27. Trotsky Papers nos. 50, 53
28. Kennan, pp. 412–17
29. War Cabinet 462; Ullman, pp. 258–74
30. War Cabinet 463; Ullman, p. 260
31. War Cabinet 464; Ullman, p. 261; Kennan, p. 415
32. The Reilly Conspiracy
33. Hansard, July 7, 1924 (H.C. Deb 5s vol. 175, cols. 1847–9)
34. The Reilly Conspiracy
35. Young, September 3, 1918
36. The Reilly Conspiracy
37. War Cabinet 469
38. The Reilly Conspiracy
39. Young, September 24, September 30 and November 18, 1918
40. F.O. 371/3319
41. Reilly to H. van den Bosch: letter dated Reval, October 10, 1918

Chapter 13

1. War Cabinet 466; Kennan, pp. 425–7; Ullman, pp. 236–54
2. War Cabinet 468; Ullman, p. 243
3. War Cabinet 470
4. Lord Ironside, *Archangel 1918–1919* (London, 1953), pp. 24–40; C. Maynard, *The Murmansk Venture* (London, 1928), pp. 123–51; Footman, p. 182; Kennan, pp. 425–7; G.E. Chaplin, *Beloe Delo* [*White Affairs*], iv (Berlin, 1928), pp. 27–9
5. R.D. Warth, *The Allies and the Russian Revolution* (Duke U., N. Carolina, 1954), p. 132; F.O. 371/3334 and F.O. 95/802
6. F.O. 371/3319, 3339; Chaplin, p. 27
7. Bunyan, p. 309f
8. F.O. 371/3339; Ullman, pp. 236–54, 264
9. Ullman, p. 251
10. Ironside, pp. 24–40; Maynard, pp. 123–52; Ullman, pp. 239–57; Footman, p. 182
11. Ullman, pp. 236–54
12. W.O. 0149/5900
13. War Cabinet 489
14. W.O. 0149/5900
15. Lloyd George Papers F59/1/27
16. Davidson Papers: file JCCD: Russia 1918
17. Fleming, pp. 54f, 73; Caucasus States, box 3 (BMMC 8); War Cabinets 219, 306; Ullman, p. 271–9
18. Kennan, pp. 413–15; Ullman, p. 261
19. Bradley, pp. 103–5; Lloyd George Papers; F50/3/16; F.O. 95/802
20. Trotsky Papers nos. 61–3
21. Ullman, pp. 258–74
22. War Cabinet 471
23. Bunyan, p. 340
24. Footman, pp. 104–26; Trotsky Papers nos. 67, 69, 77; Bunyan, p. 303
25. Bunyan, pp. 342f, 350f
26. Ullman, pp. 258–74

27. War Cabinet 473
28. War Cabinet 475
29. Bradley, pp. 98–103
30. Bunyan, pp. 338f
31. F.O. 95/802; Bunyan, pp. 352–6
32. War Cabinet 477
33. Ullman, p. 264
34. War Cabinet 481
35. War Cabinet 482
36. Bunyan, pp. 356–8, 361f
37. E. Varneck and H.H. Fisher, *The Testimony of Kolchak and Other Siberian Materials* (Stanford University, 1935), pp. 157–64, 246; W.H. Chamberlin, *The Russian Revolution*, ii (London, 1935), p. 175; Ullman, pp. 258–74
38. War Cabinet 489
39. Bunyan, pp. 356–8, 361–6; Ullman, pp. 258–94; F.O. 371/3341
40. War Cabinet 493
41. War Cabinet 494
42. F.O. 371/3341; Ullman, pp. 258–74
43. Varneck and Fisher, pp. 148, 165–9; Ullman, pp. 271–9
44. Report by Prince Ouroussov in F.O. 371/3963
45. Trotsky Papers nos. 73, 76, 80
46. Trotsky Papers nos. 83, 86–9
47. W.O. 0149/6074, 7232; Chamberlin, pp. 139–42
48. War Cabinet 461
49. W.O. 0149/6074
50. War Cabinets 464, 466, 468, 470–1, 473
51. Bunyan, p. 130
52. Ullman, pp. 315–26
53. W.O. 0149/6074; Ullman, pp. 315–26; Trotsky Papers no. 98; War Cabinet 500
54. W.O. 0149/6333
55. Callwell, p. 148
56. W.O. 0149/5859

Select Bibliography

Primary material

War Cabinet papers
Foreign Office papers
War Office papers
Admirality papers

Secondary material

Bailey, Geoffrey *The Conspirators* (London, 1961)
Benes, Eduard *Souvenirs de Guerre et de Revolution* (Paris, 1929)
Bradley, John *Allied Intervention in Russia* (London, 1968)
Bunyan, James *Intervention, Civil War & Communism in Russia* (Baltimore, 1936)
Callwell, Major-General Sir C.E. *Field Marshal Sir Henry Wilson: His Life & Diaries*, volume 2 (London, 1927)
Command Paper no 8, no 1 (1919)
Chamberlin, W.H. *The Russian Revolution*, volume 1 (New York, 1935)
Chaplin, G.E. *Two Coup d'Etats in the North*, Beloe Delo, volume IV (Berlin, 1928) p. 12–31
Davidson Papers (House of Lords)
Degras, Jane *Soviet Documents on Foreign Policy*, volume 1 (London, 1951)
Fedotov-White, D. *The Growth of the Red Army* (Princeton University, 1944)
Fleming, Peter *The Fate of Admiral Kolchak* (London, 1963)
Footman, David *Civil War in Russia* (London, 1961)
Freund, Gerald *Unholy Alliance* (London, 1957)
Graf, H. *La Marine Russe dans la Guerre et dans la Revolution* (Paris, 1928)
Hansard (Parliamentary Proceedings)
Hill, George *Go Spy the Land* (London, 1932)
Ironside, Field Marshal Lord, *Archangel 1918-1919* (London, 1953)
Jones, Thomas *Whitehall Diary*, volume 1, ed. Keith Middlemass (London, 1969)
Kennan, George *The Journal of Modern History*, June 1956
—— *The Decision to Intervene* (London, 1958)
Katkov, George *The Assassination of Count Mirbach* (St Anthony's Papers, no 12, Soviet Affairs, no 3: London, 1962)
—— *Russia 1917* (London, 1967)

Journal of the Central Asian Society, volume 10, 1923, part 3
Kettle, Michael *The Allies & the Russian Collapse* (London, 1981)
Keyes Papers (India Office)
Latsis, M.Y. *Two Years of Struggle on the Internal Front* (Moscow, 1920)
Lloyd George, Frances *The Years that are Past* (London, 1967)
Lloyd George Papers (House of Lords)
Lockhart, Robert Bruce *Memoirs of a British Agent* (London, 1932)
Mangold, Tom, and Summers, Anthony *The File on the Tsar* (London, 1976)
Marchand, Réné *Allied Agents in Soviet Russia* (London, 1918)
Mawdsley, Ewan *The Russian Revolution and the Baltic Fleet* (London, 1978)
Maynard, Major-General Sir C. *The Murmansk Venture* (London, 1928)
Oudendyk, W.J. *Ways and Byways in Diplomacy* (London, 1939)
Price, M. Phillips *My Reminiscences of the Russian Revolution* (London, 1921)
Reilly, Sidney *The Adventures of Sidney Reilly* (London, 1931)
Riddell, Lord *An Intimate Diary of the Peace Conference* (London, 1933)
Riezler, Kurt *Diaries, Essays, Documents*, ed. Karl D. Erdmann (Gottingen, 1972)
Roskill, Stephen *Hankey, Man of Secrets*, volume 1 (London, 1970)
Sisson, Edgar *One Hundred Red Days* (Yale University, 1931)
Stevenson, Frances *Lloyd George, a diary*, ed. A.J.P. Taylor (London, 1971)
Stewart, George *The White Armies of Russia* (New York, 1933)
Trotsky, Leon *Ecrits Militaires*, volume 1. *Comment la Revolution s'est armée; Les specialistes militaires et l'Armée Rouge: la premiere trahison*, translated from the Russian by Georges Belet et al. (Paris, 1967)
Trotsky Papers, volume 1, ed. Jan M. Meijer (The Hague, 1964)
Ullman, Richard *Intervention and the War* (London, 1961)
Varneck, Elena, and Fisher, H.H. *The Testimony of Kolchak and other Siberian Materials* (Stanford University, 1935)
Warth, Robert *The Allies and the Russian Revolution* (Duke University, 1954)
Woodward, David *The Russians at Sea* (London, 1965)
Young, Kenneth *The Diaries of Sir Robert Bruce Lockhart, 1915-1918* (London, 1973)
Zeman, Z.A.B. *Germany and the Revolution in Russia, 1915-1918* (London, 1958)

Index

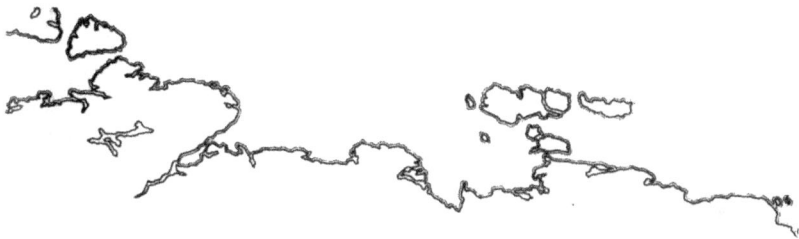

S I A

Amur Line

Lake Baikal

Trans-Siberian
Railway

Irkutsk

Karymskaya

MANCHURIA

Chinese Eastern
Railway

Khabarovsk

Altay Mountains

MONGOLIA

Harbin

Vladivostok

Peking

Tokyo

JAPAN

CHINA

INDIA

For Product Safety Concerns and Information please contact our EU
representative GPSR@taylorandfrancis.com
Taylor & Francis Verlag GmbH, Kaufingerstraße 24, 80331 München, Germany

www.ingramcontent.com/pod-product-compliance
Lightning Source LLC
Chambersburg PA
CBHW050559270326
41926CB00012B/2109

*9 7 8 1 0 3 2 6 7 6 1 9 7 *